PRINCIPLES OF EVERYDAY BEHAVIOR ANALYSIS

Second Edition

PRINCIPLES OF EVERYDAY BEHAVIOR ANALYSIS
Second Edition

L. Keith Miller
UNIVERSITY OF KANSAS

BROOKS/COLE PUBLISHING COMPANY
MONTEREY, CALIFORNIA
A DIVISION OF WADSWORTH, INC.

Printed in the United States of America

10 9 8 7 6 5 4 3 2

Library of Congress Cataloging in Publication Data

Miller, L Keith.
Principles of everyday behavior analysis.

Bibliography: p. 273
1. Behavior modification—Programmed instruction. I. Title.
BF637.B4M53 1980 153.8'5 79-27797
ISBN 0-8185-0373-4

Acquisition Editor: *Todd Lueders*
Manuscript Editor: *Derek Gallagher*
Production Editor: *Sally Schuman*
Interior and Cover Design: *Ruth Scott*
Illustrations: *John Foster*
Typesetting: *Instant Type, Monterey, California*

Preface

This thoroughly revised second edition of *Principles of Everyday Behavior Analysis* is designed to teach the basic principles of behavior analysis to the beginning student. It differs from other introductory books in five major ways: it covers a broad range of material; it uses both everyday and professional examples of behavioral principles; it uses a new method of exposition called "concept programming"; it contains extensive provision for review; and it has been extensively field tested and revised.

The book teaches 67 different behavioral concepts, including concepts that are frequently not covered in introductory books, such as generalization programming and conditioned punishment. Everyday examples are extensively used to help students see how the principles apply to their own lives. Unlike many introductory texts, the book also provides the student with a firm grounding in research methods in the first quarter of the book. These ideas are illustrated through the use of over 1200 brief examples involving everyday situations such as dormitory living, friendships, and campus activities. In addition, 35 longer examples of how these ideas have been applied to solving actual behavioral problems are presented along with graphs showing the outcome. Thus the student who completes the book will be thoroughly familiar with the way behavioral principles influence his or her everyday life as well as how behavioral procedures can be applied to a wide variety of problem situations.

The book uses "concept programming" to teach basic behavioral principles. Each of the 21 nonreview lessons is divided into parts. First, a concept or related set of concepts is introduced, defined, illustrated, and discussed. Second, a reading quiz is included that permits the student to test his or her understanding of these concepts (with answers included in the book for self-checking). Third, a set of 20 brief examples of everyday situations is presented. Some of the examples illustrate the concepts just introduced, some review prior concepts, and still others illustrate nonconcepts that must be carefully discriminated from the concepts. Through a series of programmed questions, the student is taught to identify the concepts that are involved in each situation (with answers to all questions included for self-checking). Fourth, three forms of a quiz using entirely new questions and examples are included in the back of the book (without answers) for use in testing the student.

The book contains four lessons devoted exclusively to review. Each of these lessons provides an overview of a major section of the book. Each concept introduced in that section is defined. And an extensive practice review is provided, containing new questions and examples, that permits the student to review his or her understanding of the entire book up to that point. By using these lessons in conjunction with the Review Exams (provided in the Instructor's Manual), which also contain new questions and examples, the instructor can ensure long-term conceptual mastery of the material.

The book differs from many introductory textbooks in that it has been revised based on extensive field testing *until it actually teaches.* The first edition was revised six times based on the errors made by over 400 University of Kansas students as well as students from several other colleges and universities. The second edition represents another extensive revision based on experience with hundreds of additional students at several universities. The error rate for all exams is well below 10% for University of Kansas students.

This edition has been thoroughly revised and updated. Many additional current examples of behavioral research have been added. Thirty-five of these have been presented at considerable length in order to provide the student with a greater knowledge of how behavioral concepts and procedures are actually applied by professional psychologists. In addition, the number of everyday examples that the student is called upon to analyze have been more than doubled. This addition has made it possible to use entirely new questions in the lesson quizzes, thus permitting a better test of generalization for the student. I have also added "helpful hints" before many of the reading

Every instructor considering adopting the book will find it useful to request an *Instructor's Manual* from Brooks/Cole, Monterey, California. This manual explains the book's structure in greater detail, reports extensive experimental research on the effectiveness of various components of the method, and presents numerous alternative procedures for using it most effectively. The manual also includes sample administrative forms, answer keys to the lesson quizzes, four forms of review exam for each review lesson, answer keys for the review exams, and a training manual for student instructors.

quizzes. These hints alert the student to terms and concepts that are frequently confused, explain special features of the book, and illustrate important points for the student to keep in mind as he or she proceeds to the reading quiz. Finally, experience with using the book in a wide variety of settings has permitted me to weed out the explanatory material and questions that were ambiguous to the student. The instructors using this edition will find that the answers to all questions are much more definitive than in the first edition.

I owe a great debt to my friends and colleagues for their support and encouragement while I was working on this book. Steve Fawcett, Mike Kelly, Rich Feallock, Ron Mann, Don Baer, Mont Wolf, and particularly Hal Weaver provided a great deal of help designing the first edition of the book.

The second edition owes a great debt to Richard O'Connell, who provided data on student errors at California State University at Northridge, detailed explanations of conceptual problems his students were having with excellent suggestions on how to overcome them, and many useful suggestions for improving the book. I am also grateful to my other second-edition reviewers, Alan Glaros of Wayne State University and Jack Hartje of University of North Florida.

The second edition also benefitted from the excellent suggestions of Tom Welsh.

Finally, thanks go to innumerable people who contributed pieces of themselves to me: To Nate Azrin for those countless late-night and early-morning discussions about operant conditioning with a young assistant professor of sociology, to Jim Sherman for being a friend I could count on, and to Dave Born for his helpful reading of the first edition as it neared completion.

I would also like to thank Meredith Mullins for her tender loving care in helping me express myself effectively. But, above all, thanks must go to Don Bushell for luring me into the nicest and most productive colleagues that I will ever experience, and to my wife, Ocooee, for teaching me how to keep my head together.

L. Keith Miller

To the Student

This book is designed to teach you the basic principles of behavior analysis. Although you will be required to memorize little material, after working through a series of 25 lessons you will have advanced significantly toward the goal of thinking like a behavior analyst. Each lesson focuses on a basic element of behavior analysis. A lesson begins with a brief section that defines and explains a basic area or concept. You will then be presented with a Reading Quiz to permit you to see whether you got the most important points in the definition and explanation of the concepts. The answers appear at the end of the questions. *You should check your answers!* If you make errors, you should reread the beginning of the lesson.

The lesson then presents a series of 20 examples drawn from everyday situations. You will analyze each specific situation in terms of the behavioral concepts that you have learned up to that point. Specifically, you will decide whether the basic element of that lesson can be used to analyze the situation, whether an idea from an earlier lesson applies, or whether no ideas learned up to that point apply. Thus you are required to practice using these basic skills and to distinguish among them. This analysis of situational examples is important because it teaches you how to use behavior analysis correctly.

The first few situational examples in each lesson are "programmed"—that is, you are given a series of hints for the first few examples that will draw your attention to the most important parts of the examples. Answers to all questions are listed at the end of the questions so that you can check your answers. After the first few examples, the amount of hinting decreases until you get no hints at all for the last ten examples. By this programming of hints, you will be helped to use the basic ideas at first, and then, as you learn them, you will be gradually put on your own to use what you have learned.

In addition to the regular lessons, there are four review lessons. The review includes questions drawn from everything that you have learned up to that point. Situational examples based on concepts from past lessons are also provided so that you can review everything that you have learned.

If you have trouble passing the class quizzes assigned to you by your instructor, consider changing your study methods. First, be sure to write out your answers to the "Reading Quiz" before attempting to answer the questions in the example section. These questions provide a review of the basic principles taught in that lesson. Second, be sure to write out your answer to each question about the examples. It has been found that making an active, written response to programmed questions assists most people to learn the material. Third, always check the correctness of your responses to the first ten questions by looking them up. This feedback can help you correct misunderstandings of the material that may have developed. This is the best possible preparation for any quizzes administered by your teacher. Note, also, that some of the questions on the self-quiz are similar to those in the example section but have been changed enough to make a different answer correct, so read the self-quiz questions closely.

Contents

PRINCIPLES OF EVERYDAY BEHAVIOR ANALYSIS

Second Edition

UNIT ONE
Behavioral Research Methods

Lesson 1

Introduction to Everyday Behavior Analysis

You may have heard about the new and remarkably successful approach to human problems called "behavior modification" or "behavior therapy." This approach has been found to be more effective in the area of psychiatry than traditional "talking therapy" (Levitt, 1963; Eysenck, 1960)[1]; more effective in university instruction than the traditional lecture-and-discussion approach (Kulik, Kulik, & Carmichael, 1974); and more effective in teaching disadvantaged children than traditional educational approaches (Bereiter & Midian, 1978; Bushell, 1978). Similar findings exist for such diverse problems as treating mental patients, teaching assertiveness and other social skills to young adults, and even creating workable alternative institutions such as communes and buying cooperatives.

Behavior modification is a very young discipline that did not begin large-scale publication of its results until about 1970. Figure 1-1 shows the growth of scientific publications relating to behavior modification since 1960. As you can see, there were virtually no publications in 1960 and few even by 1965, but by 1970 a very strong growth had begun. By 1977 over 1000 scientific publications per year were appearing. This figure well illustrates the growth of the field itself. It is a very new field that has rapidly earned a reputation for effectiveness in helping alleviate a wide range of human problems.

Behavior modification has also come under sharp attack from a number of skeptics who feel that it is either too good to be true or a dangerous interference with people's freedom. One such skeptic, former Vice President Spiro Agnew, branded it as antithetical to his view of democracy (Agnew, 1972). Some psychologists have expressed concern about what they view as the "manipulation" inherent in behavior modification (for example, Jourard, 1959). Still others have confused it with surgical approaches such as lobotomy, drug approaches such as Anectine (which temporarily produces total paralysis), and even the psychological torture of prisoners through long-term isolation.

The term *behavior modification* can easily be misunderstood. It seems to point to any method

[1]All references are contained in the reference section at the end of the book. Many of the references are also listed at the end of each lesson, with a brief description of their content.

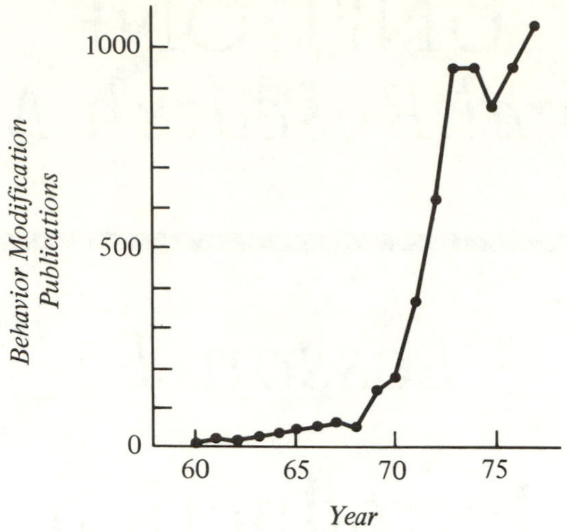

Figure 1-1. The number of behavior modification publications per year. Data 1960 to 1972 taken from "A Comparison of Behavior Therapy and Traditional Therapy Publication Activity," by P. W. Hoon and O. R. Lindsley, *American Psychologist*, 1974, *29*, 694–697. Copyright 1974 by the American Psychological Association. Reprinted by permission. Data after 1972 are taken from counts of behavior modification and related articles listed in *Psychological Abstracts*.

by which behavior is modified or changed—including surgical, drug, and coercive methods. This has led to at least one writer suggesting that the term (but not the field) was dead and should be buried (Krasner, 1974). Similar considerations led the founders of one of the major scientific journals in the field to title it *Journal of Applied Behavior Analysis* rather than *Journal of Behavior Modification*. The emphasis, they thought, should be on the analysis, the understanding of behavior for applied or practical ends. This book will follow their lead and refer to the field as "applied behavior analysis," or often simply behavior analysis.

Behavior analysis is a behavioral science that develops and experimentally analyzes practical procedures for producing changes in socially significant behaviors (Baer, Wolf, & Risley, 1968). It experimentally analyzes such procedures through the use of single-subject experimental designs in which reliability of the observations has been verified (Kazdin, 1975). Thus it is a behavioral science that attempts to produce procedures of relevance to the practical problems of the world that have been developed and tested through the use of rigorous scientific methods.

Behavior analysis has three main characteristics. First, it focuses on behavior, on what people actually do and say, rather than on such private events as thoughts, feelings, and attitudes. Second, it studies the environmental influences on people's behavior, the antecedents and consequences of their behavior. Third, it uses single-subject designs to experiment with different environmental arrangements to determine which are most effective.

One of the major historical influences on behavior analysis was the work of B. F. Skinner in "operant psychology" from 1930 to 1960. Thus, he is often considered to be the founder. While many practitioners of behavior analysis have been psychologists, some sociologists have argued that it has special relevance to their field and have coined the term *behavioral sociology* (Burgess & Bushell, 1969). At least one economist has argued for a "behavioral economics" based on behavior analysis (Kagel & Winkler, 1972). The principles of behavior analysis have been applied to problems in political science, social welfare, architecture, education, and medicine, to name only a few. Thus it is impossible to pigeonhole behavior analysis solely as a branch of psychology (Kazdin, 1975).

The emphasis on behavior will be ever present throughout the book. The first quarter of the book will introduce you to the idea of single-subject experiments. The remainder of the book will introduce you to the idea of antecedent and consequent influences on behavior. Throughout the book these ideas will be illustrated in two ways: by brief digests of published behavior analysis experiments and by brief fictional stories. Both types of illustrations have been selected so as to be relevant to common everyday situations. In addition, references to more specialized publications dealing with more severe behavioral problems are provided throughout the book. The emphasis of the book is to demonstrate the relevance of behavior analysis concepts to understanding and improving everyday life.

Figure 1–2. B. F. Skinner, the major contributor to the development of operant psychology. Many of the methodological principles and concepts of behavior analysis grew out of operant psychology. Photograph courtesy of B. F. Skinner.

ADDITIONAL READINGS

Bandura, A. *Principles of behavior modification.* New York: Holt, Rinehart & Winston, 1969. A comprehensive review of behavior modification. This book may serve as a valuable reference for the broader meaning of the term *behavior modification* as it is used by psychologists.

Goodall, K. Shapers at work. *Psychology Today,* November 1972, p. 6. This is an extremely well-written, popular introduction to the psychologists who started the field of behavior analysis.

Ullman, L. P., & Krasner, L. *Case studies in behavior modification.* New York: Holt, Rinehart & Winston, 1965. An early compendium of research on specific behavioral problems.

Willis, J., & Giles, D. *Great experiments in behavior modification.* Indianapolis: Hackett Publishing, 1976. Brief accounts of 100 great experiments in behavior analysis. This is an excellent book for obtaining an overview of the research that characterizes the field.

The following is a list of journals that publish most of the behavior modification literature:

Behavior Modification. A journal started in 1977 that contains a wide array of behavioral articles.

Behavior Research and Therapy. This journal was founded to publish the early applications of behavioral psychology to therapeutic problems. Many of the studies published in this journal are innovative and thought provoking.

Behavior Therapy. This journal was founded in 1970. It publishes case studies and experiments primarily with "clinical" problems.

Cognitive Therapy and Research. Another recent (1977) journal. This journal is devoted to reporting experiments that deal with cognitive behavior and its analysis. This reflects a recent trend in which behaviorists have become increasingly interested in examining and analyzing behavior that has heretofore been considered to reflect "mental" processes.

Journal of Applied Behavior Analysis. This journal was founded in 1968 by those behavior analysts who were strongly influenced by "operant-conditioning" principles and the works of B. F. Skinner. In general, the research published in this journal is marked by sophisticated and carefully executed experiments.

Journal of Behavior Therapy and Experimental Psychiatry. A journal devoted to well-designed studies primarily in psychiatric settings.

Journal of the Experimental Analysis of Behavior. This journal was founded in 1958 by operant conditioners. It contains primarily basic research on animal subjects, but some of the early behavior analysis research that was influenced by "operant-conditioning" principles was published here.

Journal of Personalized Instruction. This journal reports studies that experimentally analyze academic behavior in colleges and universities.

Helpful hint: Words in **boldface** type in the text are basic concepts that you should be very familiar with as you will meet them throughout the book. The underlined words are key words that you should carefully attend to; they are often the answers to questions in the exercise portion of the lessons.

LESSON 1 READING QUIZ

Note: The questions presented below give you the opportunity to see if you understand the major ideas presented in the material that you just read. It is strongly recommended that you write your answers rather than just think them, as educational research has clearly shown that test performance is much higher if you write them (see the article by J. G. Holland, 1965, for the details of that research). It is also strongly recommended that you check your answers. Otherwise, you might practice the wrong answer without knowing it. You may check the answer to the first question, labeled "4," by looking at the answer section following the quiz and finding "4." The order of the labels has been scrambled so that you won't accidentally see the answer to the second question when checking the answer to the first one. Some of these questions will also appear on your lesson quiz and review exam.

(4) Behavior modification has been found to be more effective in the area of psychiatry than traditional "____________________ therapy."

(10) Behavior modification is a very young discipline that did not begin large-scale publication of its results until about __________.

(11) Behavior modification has come under ____________________ from a number of sources, because it seems to point to *any* method for modifying behavior.

(6) The term *behavior modification* can easily be ____________________.

(1) This book will not use the term *behavior modification;* rather, it will use the term ____________________.

(8) Who is often considered to be the founder of behavior analysis? ____________________

(9) Behavior analysis is a behavioral science that develops and experimentally analyzes practical procedures for producing changes in socially significant ____________________.

(2) The first characteristic of behavior analysis is that it focuses on ____________________.

(13) The second characteristic of behavior analysis is that it studies ____________________ influences on people's behavior.

(14) The third characteristic of behavior analysis is that it uses single-subject designs to ____________________ with different environmental arrangements.

(3) The first quarter of the book will introduce the idea of single-subject ____________________.

(12) The last three quarters of the book will introduce the idea of antecedent and consequent influences on ____________________.

(7) The emphasis of the book is to demonstrate the relevance of behavior analysis concepts to understanding and improving everyday ____________________.

(5) The name of the behavioral science that develops and experimentally analyzes practical procedures for producing change in socially significant behaviors is ____________________.

(15) You should pay particular attention to words that appear in **boldface** print and to words that are ____________________.

READING QUIZ ANSWERS

(1) *behavior analysis* (2) behavior (3) experiments (4) talking (5) behavior analysis (6) misunderstood (7) life (or behavior) (8) Skinner (9) behavior (10) 1970 (11) attack (12) behavior (13) environmental (14) experiment (15) underlined

Lesson 2

Definitions of Everyday Behaviors

The focus of behavior analysis is behavior. This focus means that behavior analysis is interested in analyzing, understanding, and modifying all aspects of human behavior, including anything that a person does that can be observed by another person. Thus, obvious body movements—such as grasping, hitting, walking, and moving the head—are relevant to behavior analysis, as well as less obvious body movements—such as talking, looking, and reading. Talking involves moving the vocal muscles and the mouth and tongue. Looking and reading involve orienting the head and moving and focusing the eyes. But our attention is not restricted only to large-scale and small-scale muscular movements that are visible outside the body. We also investigate internal changes that can be physically detected. These would include biological functions that are now being controlled by biofeedback, such as hand temperature, stomach acidity, spasticity of the stomach, and even brainwave activity (Karlins & Andrews, 1972). In short, the subject matter of behavior modification includes all observable aspects of human conduct.

However, the emphasis of behavior analysis is on modifying the behavior, not just observing it. The behavior an analyst selects to be modified is one that is in some way problematic. Thus a parent may wish to decrease a child's crying or nagging; a teacher may wish to increase the amount of time that a student spends studying; a university student may want to increase the "consideration" that his or her roommate shows to him or her; or a middle-aged person may wish to decrease his or her intake of food so that he or she loses weight.

Once a behavior has been identified as problematic, the next step is to specify it in a way that allows clear and precise observation. Generally, such a specification is called a "behavioral definition."[1] A **behavioral definition** is a statement that specifies exactly what behavior is to be observed.

Behavioral definitions are frequently easy to formulate. For example, a father complains that his child cries too much when put to bed at night. A behavior analyst would formulate a statement that specifies exactly what behavior concerns the father. The behavior analyst might arrive at a definition that includes obnoxious, loud crying, while excluding talking and other soft noises made by the child. Thus, the father and the behavior analyst might agree that a cry is any vocal noise made by the child that is loud enough to be heard outside the child's room and that does not involve recognizable words. The underlined words would constitute a behavioral definition, because they tell the behavior analyst what should be observed as a cry. It might be added that this definition could include singing without words. If the parent wasn't upset by singing, the definition would have to be changed to refer only to nonmusical noises. This definition of crying eliminates soft cries that cannot be heard outside the child's room, talking that can be heard outside the child's room, and loud singing (if the addition to the definition were used). Thus the behavior analyst knows exactly what to consider as crying.

The formulation of a behavioral definition for crying is quite simple because the word itself refers to a well-understood behavior. Thus, the purpose of the definition is to clarify exactly what is to be considered a cry and what is not. However, there are many words that refer to human conduct that are not as clear as this. For example, a teacher may complain of the bad attitude that

[1]A behavioral definition is also referred to as an "operational definition," although this is used primarily in other branches of psychology.

one of his or her fourth-grade students exhibits. While most of us would agree that the child must be doing something that annoys the teacher, it is almost impossible to guess what it is. In fact, it may be more than one thing. The term *bad attitude* doesn't begin to specify the behaviors that might be involved.

A behavior analyst faced with a complaint about a child's bad attitude would have to question the teacher to obtain a more specific idea of his or her complaint. He or she might find that the teacher doesn't like the fact that the child isn't studying very often, is whispering to friends, and is often rude. The analyst would not attempt to formulate a behavioral definition of the general term *bad attitude.* Rather, he or she might formulate a definition of each behavior (studying, whispering, and rudeness), or he or she might focus on only one of the behaviors, such as studying, with the idea that if the one behavior can be modified, the other behaviors will no longer occur. In any event, a vague term such as *bad attitude* should be broken down into more exact behavioral words defined as specifically as possible.

There are several reasons why it is desirable to deal with specifically defined behaviors. First, it makes communication among everyone much clearer. The teacher concerned with the child's bad attitude might really be concerned with the child's lack of studying. A behavior analyst might assume, on the other hand, that the teacher was concerned with the child's rudeness. If the people involved do not break the vague term down into more specific behavioral words, they might not be working on the same behavioral problems.

A second reason for specifying behavioral terms is to maintain a consistency of observation. People frequently let their hopes influence their observations if what they are observing is only vaguely specified. For instance, if a teacher is trying to change a child's poor attitude by being more loving and accepting of that child, he or she might start ignoring some of the signs of the attitude that originally upset him or her. The teacher might have initially been upset by nonstudying, impertinence, running around, and whispering, but, with a commitment to a method for change and with hope for a change, he or she might unconsciously ignore the lesser aspects of the bad attitude, such as the child's running around and whispering. In this way, the teacher might conclude that the child's attitude had changed for the better when, in fact, it may have remained exactly the same. Only the teacher's definition of what constituted a bad attitude may have changed. Thus, maintaining consistency of observations is an important benefit of using specific behavioral definitions.

When a specific behavioral definition has been developed, behavior analysts then attempt to find ways of "directly observing" the behavior. In order for an observation to be considered a direct observation the observer must personally see (or hear) the behavior and must record it (usually by writing) immediately after seeing it. (There is one exception to the requirement that the observer personally see the behavior. If the observer personally sees a physical result of the behavior, such as a floor that has been swept, the situation is considered a direct observation. See the method of outcome recording in Lesson 3 for more information.)

Behavior analysts have almost always insisted on working only with directly observed behavior. There are many reasons for this requirement. If an observation is not recorded immediately, the observer must rely on memory when communicating his or her observations. Numerous social psychology studies have shown this dependence on memory to result in highly inaccurate reports (for example, Allport & Postman, 1945).

One implication of the practice of relying on direct observation is the strong bias against using questionnaries or interviews in which people are asked to describe observations of their behavior or someone else's behavior at some earlier time. For example, questions like "How often did you watch TV last week?" and "How many times per week do your wife and child argue?" would not be used. Behavior analysts frequently do use self-reported direct observations, however, as long as the observations are recorded at the time and place that they occur. For example, keeping a diary of each time that TV is viewed, the times, date, and what program, might very well be used by behavior analysts. Normally this type of data would be supplemented by a second person verifying at least some small portion of the diary (see Lesson 3).

The practice of relying on direct observation does not mean that written or spoken behaviors by people are not of interest. The performance of students on written exams, speaking in public, responding to a job interview, and writing a creative essay are all behaviors of interest to behavior analysts. Behavior analysts have also been interested in how people describe behavioral procedures. For example, students exposed to a college course in which behavioral procedures were used to improve learning were asked how they liked the course compared to their usual courses

(McMichael & Corey, 1969). The fact that they liked it more implied that they would recommend to friends to enroll in it, that they would not drop it, and that what they learned would be in a positive spirit. Had they indicated that they liked it less, then this would suggest that the procedure would not be acceptable even if it did create more learning. In all of these examples in which a behavior analyst might be interested in spoken or written behavior, the behavior itself is of direct interest. The interest is in the written exam, the public speaking, the interview behavior, or the ratings on the college course. These behaviors are not interpreted to provide information about some other behavior that has not been directly observed.

A recent development in applied behavior analysis is the attempt to observe very complex, subtle and even subjective aspects of human behavior. Very often this has resulted in behavioral definitions that are not intuitively obvious to the average person. Wolf (1978) has suggested that in such cases the behavior analyst measure the "social validity" of his or her definitions. An early example of this approach involved a behavioral approach to public speaking behavior. Fawcett and Miller (1975) defined "good public speaking" in terms of eye contact with the audience, animated gestures, position on stage, greeting the audience, and several other behaviors. To validate their definition a speaker who was initially very low in these behaviors spoke before an audience who rated his "overall performance"; after training designed to increase the frequency of these behaviors he again spoke to an audience and was rated on overall performance. There was a high correlation between the amount of the defined behaviors and the rating given by the audience, thus providing evidence that the behavioral definition was reasonably consistent with the audience's more subjective and unspecified definition of good public speaking. The use of social validity data to support the appropriateness of behavioral definitions will undoubtedly increase in the future as behavior analysts approach more and more complex and subtle behavior. It provides scientific evidence that the analyst's translation was reasonable.

In summary, behavior analysts are concerned with the modification of a problematic behavior. The first step in deciding how to help someone modify problematic behavior is to develop a behavioral definition that focuses on some specific aspect of behavior. Most behavioral definitions are stated in a way that will make it easy to directly observe that behavior.

EXAMPLES OF BEHAVIORAL DEFINITIONS USED BY BEHAVIOR ANALYSTS

Four examples of behavioral definitions developed by applied behavior analysts are outlined below. They are offered as illustrations of how human phenomena that may appear to be complex, subtle, or subjective may be profitably approached as human behavior. Needless to say, these are only a tiny sample of the behavioral translations that appear in the behavioral literature.

Tension. Budzynski and Stoyva (1969) defined tension as a high level of electrical activity in the forehead muscles (frontalis) measured with an electromyograph (EMG). Tension in these muscles is often accompanied by general tension in other parts of the body. Without intervention from the psychologists, most subjects were not very good at controlling their level of tension. Similar definitions have appeared for other stress-related problems, such as migraine headaches and ulcers. The field of biofeedback has treated these problems as behavioral, rather than mental, and treated individuals by providing feedback concerning their immediate behavior. Many individuals can voluntarily eliminate the problems with such feedback.

Creativity. Goetz and Baer (1973) studied the creativity of 4-year-old preschool children while they built structures out of blocks. They developed a list of 20 categories that classified all possible blockforms and carefully defined each category. For example, one category was called a "story," which was defined as "any two or more blocks placed one atop another, the upper block(s) resting solely upon the lower," another as the "balance," which was defined as "any story in which the upper block is at least four times as wide as the lower," and an "elaborated balance," which was defined as "any balance in which both ends of the upper block contain additional blocks".
These investigators then defined "creative block building" as the building of a form that had not appeared in any previous construction by that child. Incidentally, the children built almost no creative forms until reinforced by the teacher for doing so.

Learning. Skinner (1954) defined "learning" as the production of overt behaviors that correctly respond to a series of progressively more difficult educational questions. This approach permitted Skinner to depart from traditional educational practice in which learning was thought of as an unobservable mental process that could only be approached indirectly by testing.

It led to the development of material in which small units of information are presented and frequent questions asked to determine student mastery. The emphasis in this approach is on the educator improving the materials and method of administration until the average student can master it—that is, on teaching! Students are not regarded as dumb; rather, teachers and material as inadequate. This book is based on this definition of learning.

Conversational skills. Minkin and his colleagues (1976) studied the conversational behavior of a group of delinquent 12- to 14-year-old girls. They examined three components of skilled conversational behavior: asking many conversational questions, providing a lot of positive conversational feedback, and talking a reasonable amount. Each of these components was carefully defined. For example, "providing positive conversational feedback" was defined as a brief utterance of no more than three words that indicated that the person either (a) approves, (b) concurs with, or (c) understands what the other conversant is saying. To determine whether this behavioral definition (all three components) captures what most people regard as skilled conversation, the investigators videotaped a number of conversations in which some of the conversants displayed a great deal of the three behaviors while others displayed little of it. They showed these videotapes to a cross section of adults and asked them to rate the conversational skills of the conversants. They found a very high correlation between a composite score of the three behaviors and the adult ratings of skilled conversation, thus indicating the social validity of the behavioral definition.

ADDITIONAL READINGS

Mager, Robert F. *Preparing instructional objectives.* Belmont, Calif.: Fearon, 1962. This book is helpful in explaining how to prepare sound behavioral definitions, particularly in educational settings.

LESSON 2 READING QUIZ

Note: Answer the following questions before going on to the examples, which apply these ideas to practical situations. If you cannot answer some of these questions, reread the introduction to this lesson.

(21) The focus of behavior analysis is on ____________________ .

(22) The subject matter of behavior analysis includes all ____________________ aspects of human conduct.

(6) Behavior analysis is not restricted simply to observing behavior; it is also concerned with developing ways to ____________________ behavior.

(15) A behavioral definition is a statement that specifies exactly what behavior is to be ____________________ .

(12) Suppose that we agree that "crying" is any vocal noise made by the child that is loud enough to be heard outside of the child's room and that does not involve recognizable words or singing. What is the name for the underlined statement? ____________________

(8) The purpose of a behavioral definition is to clarify ____________________ what behavior is to be observed.

(20) Behavior analysts would take a vague term such as "bad attitude" and try to break it down into more specific ____________________ words.

(10) The first reason for specifically defining behaviors is that it makes ____________________ among everyone involved much clearer.

(1) The second reason for specifically defining behaviors is that it helps to maintain a(n) ____________________ of observation.

(11) Direct observation requires that an observer must personally ____________________

_____________ the behavior and must _____________ it immediately.

(13) The one exception to the requirement that the observer see the behavior is when he or she personally sees a physical _____________ of that behavior.

(3) If an observer personally sees and immediately records a behavior (or a physical result of a behavior), then this procedure is called a(n) _____________ observation.

(14) Behavior analysts rely on direct observation because observations that involve memory, such as questionnaire or interview data, result in highly _____________ reports.

(23) Behavior analysts do not use questionnaires in which people are asked to describe observations of their behavior that occurred at some _____________ time.

(7) Behavior analysis may use self-reported data as long as the observations are recorded at the _____________ and place that they occur.

(25) Behavior analysts often analyze spoken or written behavior because they are interested in that _____________ itself.

(19) To determine whether the behavioral definition of good public speaking singled out the same behaviors that most people attended to (perhaps without knowing it), the investigators asked the audience to rate several instances of public speaking. This would be an example of measuring the _____________ validity of a behavioral definition.

(17) Budzynski and Stoyva (1969) defined "tension" as a high level of electrical activity in the _____________ muscles.

(4) The statement by Budzynski and Stoyva (1969) that tension is "a high level of electrical activity in the forehead muscles" would be called a(n) _____________.

(9) Goetz and Baer (1973) define creative blockbuilding as the building of a form that has not appeared in any _____________ construction by that child.

(24) The observers in the Goetz and Baer study recorded each form that they saw a child build as soon as they saw it. The procedure that they used would be an example of _____________ _____________.

(2) Skinner (1954) defined learning as the production of overt _____________ that correctly respond to a series of progressively more difficult educational questions.

(16) Minkin and his colleagues (1976) define "providing positive conversational feedback" as any brief utterance that indicated that the person approves of, concurs with, or _____________ what the other conversant is saying.

(5) Minkin and his colleagues (1976) asked a cross section of adults to rate the conversational skills of conversants on videotape. They found a very high correlation between their behavioral definition of skilled conversation and the adult ratings—thus indicating the _____________ of their definition.

READING QUIZ ANSWERS

(1) consistency (2) behaviors (3) direct (4) behavioral definition (5) social validity (6) modify (7) time (8) exactly (9) previous (past, former, and so on) (10) communication (11) see (or hear); record (12) behavioral definition (13) result (14) inaccurate (15) observed (16) understands (17) forehead (or frontalis) (19) social (20) behavioral (21) behavior (22) observable (23) other (24) direct observation (25) behavior

LESSON 2 EXAMPLES

Note: The following examples illustrate the concepts in this lesson as they apply to everyday situations. It will help you learn these concepts if you will carefully read the examples and write out your answers to the questions. It has been shown that just thinking your answer is not nearly as effective in learning (Holland, 1965). Also, you should look up the answers to any questions that you are in doubt about. The answer to the first question can be found by looking after the number 16 in the listing of answers. The number 16 was randomly selected to prevent you from accidentally seeing the answer to the second question when looking up the first. Similar examples appear on the lesson quiz so answering these questions and checking your answers will be excellent preparation for the quiz.

Example #1

Ms. James is unhappy with the amount that Fred spends studying in her fourth-grade class. If a behavior analyst were to help her to change Fred's study behavior, the first step would be to decide exactly what constituted study behavior. If you were in the classroom, you would probably assume that Fred was studying when he had a book in front of him and was looking at it.

(16) A behavioral definition is a statement that specifies exactly what ______________ ______________ is to be observed.

(20) In this example, the statement "He had a book in front of him and was looking at it" would be a behavioral definition of ______________________________ .

(8) Direct observation is said to occur when the observer can personally see (or hear) the behavior and records the observation at that ______________ .

(18) If you were to sit in Ms. James' class and record those times that you saw Fred looking at the book, then your observations of Fred's studying would be an example of ______________ ______________ observation.

Example #2

Many members of the commune felt that Sarah didn't do a good job of cleaning the common areas when it was her turn. Bob Behaviorist felt that they were wrong about Sarah, so he decided he would make a behavioral definition of "cleaning" that he could use to compare Sarah's performance with everyone else's. He made a checklist of aspects of the job that included such items as (1) floor cleared of particles, (2) furniture placed right, (3) flat surfaces dusted, (4) rugs vacuumed, (5) ash-trays emptied, (6) room cleared of objects that do not belong there, and (7) wastebaskets emptied. He showed the list to the two people doing the most griping to see if it covered what they would mean by a good cleaning job. They suggested adding that the floor be cleared of stains. Using the revised checklist, Bob wrote down his inspections for two weeks and found that Sarah completed 85% of the items on the checklist. Several members scored as low as 45%, making it clear that Sarah was not the worst member in cleaning the common areas, nor was her score of 85% unacceptable.

(17) Direct observation usually involves the observer's actually seeing a person doing something. However, there is one exception to this: you may observe a physical ______________ ______________ of the behavior.

(7) In this example, a clean floor, furniture placed right, and so on are part of a(n) ______________ ______________ of cleaning behavior.

(22) Since an observer can see the physical result of Sarah's behavior (assuming that she is the one who did the cleaning), and since the observer wrote down his observations immediately on a checklist, this situation would involve the ______________________________ observation of cleaning.

(14) The statement "Cleaning will mean floor cleared of particles, furniture placed right, flat surfaces dusted, rug vacuumed, ashtrays emptied, room cleared of objects that don't belong there, and wastebaskets emptied" specifies exactly what behaviors (or their results) are to be observed. Therefore, this statement would be called a(n) ________________ definition.

Example #3

Bill had a son in fifth grade. His son had often been "aggressive" in the past and had gotten into a lot of trouble. Bill decided to visit his son's class and to observe him to see if he was being aggressive. However, Bill knew that the word "aggressive" is vague and could actually refer to many different behaviors. He decided to limit the term "aggressive" to times when his son hit or pushed another child. He specifically ruled out yelling or talking in an angry way at another child as being "aggressive."

(1) The statement "aggression will refer only to hitting or pushing another child" would be called a(n) ________________, because it specifies what Bill was to observe.

(15) If Bill immediately wrote down any instances of aggression that he saw, then this would be an example of ________________.

(13) If Bill phoned the teacher and asked her, "Has my son been aggressive this year?" would this be an example of direct observation by Bill? ________ Would it be an example of direct observation by the teacher (assuming that she didn't write her observations down)? ________

Example #4

Ms. Thompson read a book on how to act assertively. One aspect of acting assertively, according to the book, was to openly accept praise. She decided to count each time people praised her in some way and she looked them in the eye and thanked them. She used a wrist counter to immediately record her successes.

(6) Ms. Thompson's use of the wrist counter would be an example of ________________ because she could hear her own thank-you and record it immediately.

(12) "'Accepting praise' means looking the person in the eye and saying thank you" would be called a(n) ________________.

Example #5

Frank had a terrible habit of saying "no" to any request by his son for a favor. He wouldn't let his son have extra ice cream, he wouldn't give him a ride to the movies, and he wouldn't play games with him. Frank decided to find out just how often he said "yes" and how often he said "no." He bought two golf-score counters that he could wear on his wrists. Every time he said "no," he pushed the button on one counter, and every time he said "yes," he pushed the button on the other counter. By using the counters, Frank was able to record his observations when they occurred, without having to stop to write them down. He found that he said "no" 17 times and "yes" 3 times the first day.

(21) "A 'no' will be counted every time Frank's son makes a request and Frank says 'no.'" This statement is called a(n) ________________.

(2) In this example, Frank was recording what he heard himself saying, and he was recording it when it happened. Therefore he was using ________________.

Example #6

Professor Barton was having trouble with a student by the name of Elbert who was being "rude." Professor Barton's meaning of "rude" was that Elbert had several times asked to talk over the grading of an essay exam.

(5) The statement "rude means making a request to discuss the grading of an essay exam" would be called a(n) ____________________________________ .

(11) If Elbert asked five other professors whether his request to discuss the grading of an exam was rude, he would be questioning the ____________________________________ of Professor Barton's definition.

Example #7

Dave decided that Vince was "mad at him" because he had been told that Vince thought he was a mean guy.

(3) Is the conclusion based on Dave's direct observation? ____________

Example #8

Ann decided that Vince was mad at her: she had heard him say to a friend "Ann is a mean lady," and she had immediately recorded the comment.

(10) Is Ann's conclusion based on direct observation? ____________

Example #9

Marge insisted that she was liberated from the usual female passivity in her relationships with men. When she said she was "liberated from passivity" she meant that she went up to men at a party and was the first to speak. John disagreed with this definition. He selected ten strangers and asked them to rate her "liberation from passivity" at several parties. At the first party Marge did not initiate any conversations. At the second one she initiated conversations often.

(4) The underlined phrase would be called a(n) ____________________________________ of "liberated from passivity."

(19) John's use of ten strangers to rate Marge's behavior at two parties was a method for determining the ____________________________________ of Marge's definition.

Example #10

John wanted to measure the littering behavior of his family on a picnic. He decided to observe this behavior by measuring its outcome—namely, the amount of litter. He carefully picked up all litter as his family was leaving the area, weighed it, and wrote the weight down. He also was careful to completely clean the area before the picnic started. He defined litter as human-made objects bigger than a quarter inch across that were not permanent parts of the picnic area.

(9) The procedure that John used to measure litter would be called ____________________ ____________ .

EXAMPLE ANSWERS

(1) behavioral definition (2) direct observation (3) no (4) behavioral definition (5) behavioral definition (6) direct observation (7) behavioral definition (8) time (9) direct observation (10) yes (11) social validity (12) behavioral definition (13) no; no (14) behavioral definition (15) direct observation (16) behavior (17) result (18) direct (19) social validity (20) studying (21) behavioral definition (22) direct

Lesson 3

Methods for the Observation of Everyday Behaviors

The observation of behavior plays a crucial role in behavior analysis in two major ways. First, procedures designed to modify a behavior can be evaluated by behavior analysts using observational data to determine their success. Do the observations reveal that the procedure has produced more of some desired behavior (or less of an undesired behavior)? Second, these procedures may be evaluated by potential consumers to determine their effectiveness. A wife may ask "Has this procedure produced observable changes in the behavior that I desire to increase in my spouse?" A major characteristic of applied behavior analysis—and one that most distinguishes it from other behavioral sciences—is that it insists on the use of observational data gathered within a single-subject experimental design to document the effectiveness of procedures claimed to be effective in changing behavior.

An illustration of the first role of behavioral observation might arise if a behavior analyst wished to teach young children to be more "creative" in their use of building blocks. The behavior analyst would first have to develop a behavioral definition of "creative" (perhaps one based on the actual arrangement of blocks after the child has created a design). This process of creating a definition would involve a direct observation based on a result of behavior.

The behavior analyst would then observe the creativity of the child before using the teaching method and again afterwards to see whether the method was indeed successful. By these observations the analyst can evaluate his or her success and adopt the method if it really works or change the technique until he or she finds a method that does work. Thus, the direct observation of creative behavior gives the behavior analyst a tool with which to improve and perhaps perfect his or her teaching method.

The second role of observation is illustrated by permitting anyone who is interested in the teaching method to evaluate its success. By using the method and observing whether children's creative behavior is indeed modified, the interested person can evaluate the behavior analyst's claims. The possibility of such clear-cut evaluations of behavioral procedures is a major strength of behavior analysis.

The remainder of this lesson explains the four basic methods commonly used by behavior analysts to observe behavior.

Outcome recording. A behavior is recorded if a specified result of that behavior has been observed. Thus the observer does not watch the behavior itself but rather some result of the behavior. Because of this, the observation usually takes place after the behavior has been performed.

An example of outcome recording might involve the observation of a child's dishwashing behavior. Rather than watch the child wash each dish, the observer might simply check to see if the dishes are clean. If they are clean, then the observer would conclude that the dishwashing behavior had occurred and would record it. Notice that the observation is of a result of dishwashing behavior—clean dishes—and not of the behavior itself. The observation can therefore be made only after the behavior has been performed.

Other examples of outcome recording might include: observing table-building behavior by seeing whether a finished table exists; observing studying behavior by seeing whether the student can answer questions about the material on a test; observing littering behavior by counting the number of pieces of litter. All of these observations focus on the result of performing a behavior rather than on the behavior itself.

Outcome recording may involve the observation of a series of behavioral results. For instance, if you wished to observe whether a person washed all the dishes, you might make up a list of all types of items to be washed: dishes, glasses, silverware, pots, and serving spoons. Then you would check each category if all such items were found to be clean. Such an approach permits a much more detailed observation of dishwashing behavior. It would, of course, still be an example of outcome recording even though a cluster of behavioral results is being observed.

If you think that a method of observing should be classified as "outcome recording," be sure to analyze carefully whether a result of the behavior is being observed (rather than the behavior itself) after the behavior has been performed.

Event recording. A behavior is recorded if the observer sees (or hears) the complete behavioral episode. Usually the behavior is of brief duration and has a definite beginning and end. In event recording, unlike outcome recording, the behavior itself is observed.

An example of event recording might involve counting each time that a student raises his or her hand to answer a question in class. The observer would record a hand-raising behavior when he or she sees the behavior performed. Since hand raising is extremely simple, the observer would be recording a complete behavioral episode consisting of moving the hand up and holding it in raised position.

Event recording can also be used to record such simple behaviors as: a person interrupting his or her partner, a public speaker uttering a swear word, or even a shopper entering a store. The emphasis in this type of recording is usually on how many times the behavior occurs—how many times the person interrupted, how many swear words were spoken, or how many customers entered the store.

Event recording can also be used to observe the actual performance of such behaviors as dishwashing and table building. In contrast to outcome recording, the observer must watch the actual performance of washing dishes or building the table. These acts would be recorded only when the entire activity is complete. While they are complex activities, they of course have a definite beginning and end.

If you think that a method of observation should be classified as event recording, be sure to analyze whether a complete behavioral episode is being recorded based on watching the behavior at the time it is being performed.

Interval recording. A behavior is recorded if some part of one or more behavioral episodes is observed to occur within one of a series of continuous time intervals.[1] This method of observation is usually used to observe long, ongoing behavioral episodes that may not have a definite beginning and end. Usually the overall observational period is divided into intervals of a convenient length and the observer determines whether or not the behavior occurs during some portion of each of these intervals. Note that the record indicates only whether or not the behavior occurred in each interval—not the number of occurrences.

For example, interval recording would be an ideal method for observing the TV viewing behavior of a child. If the observer were to watch the child for the afternoon, he or she would divide it into a series of continuous time intervals of a convenient length, perhaps 15 seconds. The observer would then record for each of those 15-second intervals whether or not the child had watched TV for at least a portion of that interval. For the purposes of interval recording it does not matter whether the behavior occurs for the whole interval or only a portion of it. The objective is to discover what percentage of all the intervals contain at least some TV viewing.

TV viewing is a good example to clarify the difference between event recording and interval recording. TV viewing usually does not have a definite beginning and end. A child may frequently glance away from the set or may remain glued to it for a period of time. The intent of interval recording would be to determine during what percentage of the intervals the child is viewing the TV. Event recording would not work well to answer this question because it might count many

[1]Continuous means that the beginning of each time interval starts at the end of the prior time interval with no interruption.

times that the child looked at the TV, but each time might be of different length. Thus saying that the child looked at the screen 112 times would have little meaning. Did those 112 times cover five minutes or five hours?

Interval recording might be used to observe how much studying behavior a child is engaging in; how much a person speaks in an informal conversation; what percentage of the time a person has his or her hand raised; or how much of the evening is taken up by someone washing dishes.

If you think that a method of observation should be classified as interval recording, be sure to determine whether a behavioral occurrence is recorded if any portion of a behavioral episode occurs within an arbitrarily defined interval that is one of a series of continuous intervals. Remember that no more than one occurrence is recorded for one interval.

Time-sample recording. A behavior is recorded if some part of one or more behavioral episodes is observed to occur within one of a series of discontinuous intervals. This method is identical to interval recording except that the intervals do not follow one another continuously. It gets its name because the observer is obtaining the measure of the behavior during a sample of the time period rather than during all of it. It is most often used where an observer must cover a fairly long period of time or where he or she must alternate between observing several different individuals.

For example, time-sample recording might be used to observe a child watching TV. The observer might watch the child for 5 seconds every 5 minutes to see if he or she is watching TV. During the other 4 minutes and 55 seconds between observations the observer would be doing something else. The time intervals are discontinuous because of that period of nonobservation. The ultimate data would involve a statement of what percentage of the intervals the child was observed to be watching TV.

If you think that an observational method is time-sample recording, be sure to determine whether a behavioral occurrence is recorded if any portion of a behavioral episode occurs within an arbitrarily defined time interval that is one of a series of discontinuous intervals.

One variation of this method involves observing several individuals sequentially. For example, suppose that a teacher checks for 30 seconds to see if Tom is studying, then shifts to observe Diane for 30 seconds and then returns to observe Tom again. The teacher would be using time sampling because she is observing each of them for discontinuous 30-second intervals.

Another variation on the method involves making observations during randomly selected observational periods. For example, if a professor checked for 5 seconds to see whether a particular student was awake after he or she had been lecturing for 5 minutes, 9 minutes, 17 minutes and 25 minutes, the professor would be using time sampling.

In summary, there are four widely used methods of observation. Outcome recording involves observing the result of a behavior (unlike the three other methods, which observe the actual behavior). Event recording involves observing complete behavioral episodes as they are occurring. Interval recording involves observing whether or not a behavior occurs during continuous intervals. And time-sample recording involves observing whether or not a behavior occurs during discontinuous intervals.

Should you ever examine an observational method that might be confused between outcome recording and any other method, it will always be labeled as outcome recording if a result of the behavior is being recorded rather than the behavior itself.

BEHAVIOR ANALYSIS EXAMPLES

Three examples of the use by behavior analysts of the observational procedures outlined in this lesson are provided in this section. The intent of the section is to illustrate how the procedures are actually used.

Study behavior. Walker and Buckley (1968) analyzed the study behavior of Phillip, a bright fourth grader who did very little work in school and was therefore not getting good grades or learning. They defined study behavior as "looking at the assigned page, working problems, and recording responses." They divided their 10-minute observational period into 10-second intervals and made a check mark on the interval if Phillip engaged in study behavior during it. Figure 3–1 shows a sample of their observation form. By using contingencies linked to these observations, the authors were able to increase the occurrence of Phillip's study behavior from about 40% to over 90% of the intervals.

1	2	3	4	5	6	7	8	9	10	11	12	13	14	15	16	17	18	19	20	21	22	23	24	25	26	27	28	29	30
	✓	✓	✓	✓	✓										✓	✓	✓							✓	✓	✓	✓	✓	✓

Figure 3-1. Recording sheet for observations on the study behavior of Phillip, a fourth grader with a studying problem. Adapted from "The Use of Positive Reinforcement in Conditioning Attending Behavior," by H. M. Walker and N. K. Buckley, *Journal of Applied Behavior Analysis*, 1968, *1*, 245–250. Copyright 1968 by the Society for the Experimental Analysis of Behavior, Inc. Used by permission.

Self-recording. Lindsley (1968) recommended that behavior analysts use the kind of wrist counters often used by golfers to record their scores (see Figure 3-2). They have been used in a variety of ways to record discrete behaviors, most often in teaching people to record their own behaviors—such as smoking, smiling, and making positive comments to others.

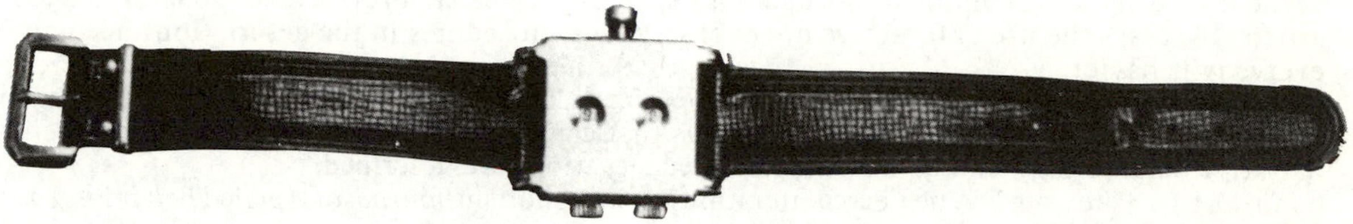

Figure 3-2. A wrist counter that can be used for recording such behaviors as smoking, smiling, and complaining. Adapted from "A Reliable Wrist Counter for Recording Behavior Rates," by O. R. Lindsley, *Journal of Applied Behavior Analysis*, 1968, *1*, 77. Copyright 1968 by the Society for the Experimental Analysis of Behavior, Inc. Used by permission.

Behavioral commune. Feallock and Miller (1976) used the checklist shown in Figure 3-3 to help the 30 members of a commune to systematically observe the results of the lounge-cleaning behavior of their members. The checklist was used by a specially appointed member after the lounge was supposed to have been cleaned. Similar checklists were used to specify the results of all basic housework throughout the commune. Each of the entries, such as "pick up trash," was provided with a careful behavioral definition so that the members would know exactly what behavioral results to record. The observations clearly revealed that very little cleaning was undertaken in the absence of a behavioral intervention. By giving their members a rent reduction contingent on these observed cleaning results, the members were able to maintain a clean and well-run house. (Can you determine what method of observation was used in this example?)

Lounge

☐ a. Pick up trash
☐ b. Sweep up dirt
☐ c. Vacuum and shake out rugs
☐ d. Empty out and clean ashtrays
☐ e. Empty trashbasket, replace liner
☐ f. Mop tile
☐ g. Return items to proper place
☐ h. Pick up trash in telephone room
☐ i. Sweep up dirt in telephone room
☐ j. Mop floor in telephone room
☐ k. Provide clean paper and pen at phone
☐ l. Return items to proper place from phone room
☐ m. Replace burned-out bulbs

Figure 3-3. Inspection checklist for lounge-cleaning behavior in a behavioral commune. Adapted from "The Design and Evaluation of a Worksharing System for Experimental Group Living," by R. A. Feallock and L. K. Miller, *Journal of Applied Behavior Analysis*, 1976, *9*, 277–288. Copyright 1976 by the Society for the Experimental Analysis of Behavior, Inc. Used by permission.

Note #1: In the remainder of the book, I will make a distinction between behavior and response. When referring to a type of activity, I will use the word *behavior*; a single instance of a behavior will be called a "response."

Note #2: This lesson provides an introduction to the most commonly used methods of observation. For example, Kelly (1977) reported that each method was used in the following percentage of cases in the *Journal of Applied Behavior Analysis* from 1968 to 1975: outcome recording, 8%; event recording, 50% (including trial-by-trial); interval recording, 15%; time-sample recording, 15%. These methods together account for 88% of the data collection procedures using human observers reported in the *Journal of Applied Behavior Analysis.* For information on other observational procedures, consult Bijou, Peterson, and Ault (1968), Hartmann and Peterson (1975), and the other added readings at the end of this lesson.

Note #3: Repp, Roberts, Slack, Repp, and Berkler (1976) found that when the frequency of behaviors is high, interval recording and time sampling underestimate them.

ADDITIONAL READINGS

Bijou, S. W., Peterson, R. F., & Ault, M. H. A method to integrate descriptive and experimental field studies at the level of data and empirical concepts. *Journal of Applied Behavior Analysis,* 1968, *1,* 175–191. This article discusses the use of objective direct observation procedures in the description and analysis of everyday behavior.

Brandt, R. *Studying behavior in natural settings.* New York: Holt, Rinehart & Winston, 1972. This book describes a variety of observational procedures that can be used in the study of everyday behavior: narrative data, ratings, and data from simulated situations are described.

Hartmann, D. P., & Peterson, L. A neglected literature and an aphorism. *Journal of Applied Behavior Analysis,* 1975, 8, 231–232. This article cites 12 references to discussions of observational technology in social psychology, education, and child psychology.

Rosenthal, R., & Rosnow, R. L. *Artifact in behavioral research.* New York: Academic Press, 1969. This book discusses the effect that being observed has on people's behavior. Because people may act differently when they know they are being observed, the resulting data can be misleading. This phenomenon is known as "reactivity" and is an important issue in behavior analysis.

Wright, H. Observational child study. In P. Mussen (Ed.), *Handbook of research methods in child development.* New York: Wiley, 1960, pp. 71–139. This chapter describes the application of "ecological" psychology to direct observation. It contains explanations of methods that have been adopted by behavior analysts, many of which are documented in this reading as early as the 1920s.

Helpful hint #1: It may be helpful to ask a series of questions to determine what method of observation is being used in a specific example. You might begin your analysis of a specific example by asking: "Does this method involve time intervals?" If not, then it is either outcome or event recording. To distinguish between them, ask: "Does this (non-time interval) method involve the result of a behavior?" If so it is outcome, if not it is event. If the method involves time intervals, then you should ask: "Are the time intervals continuous?" to decide whether interval or time-sample recording is involved.

Helpful hint #2: Some students have incorrectly labeled interval recording as time sampling by making a simple mistake. Suppose that an observer is recording whether or not a behavior has occurred in consecutive 15-second intervals and that the behavior does not occur during each interval. These students have reasoned that the behavior did not occur during consecutive intervals, therefore it occurred during discontinuous intervals—making the observational method time sampling. This is incorrect. The definition requires only that the person be observed during a series of continuous intervals to determine whether or not a behavior occurs. It does not require that the behavior actually occur during each of those intervals.

Helpful hint #3: When responding to questions in this lesson be sure to use the terms designating specific methods of direct observation where possible. If you are asked what method of observation is involved in some example where all complete behavioral episodes are recorded immediately, do not answer "direct observation." Use the more specific term "event recording." Your answer will be considered incorrect if you do not use the more specific answer.

Helpful hint #4: Key words in the definition of each method of observation are underlined to call your attention to a major idea. Be careful not to look only for those words, however, as they may occur in an example of another method. So to answer a question, you must understand the concept rather than just memorize a key word.

LESSON 3 READING QUIZ

(19) By observing behavior, the behavior analyst can ____________________ the success of a procedure designed to modify a behavior.

(9) The second role of behavioral observation is to provide potential ____________________ with a means to evaluate any claims for a particular modification technique.

(18) Outcome recording is based on observing a(n) ____________________ of behavior, rather than the behavior itself.

(27) An observational method is termed ____________________ recording if the result of a behavior is observed after the behavior has occurred.

(17) Event recording is based on recording a response only when the ____________________ behavioral episode has occurred.

(26) Usually event recording is used when the behavioral episode has a definite beginning and end and is of ____________________ duration.

(7) Interval recording involves recording a response occurrence if any part of a behavioral episode occurs within one of a series of ____________________ time intervals.

(16) When using interval recording, an occurrence is scored if some ____________________ of a behavioral episode occurs within the interval.

(25) Interval recording is usually used for rather long ____________________ behaviors.

(6) Which of the following behavioral events would be scored as an occurrence in interval recording? (a) The person starts the behavior within the interval; (b) the person doesn't start the behavior within the interval but does finish it within the interval; (c) the person starts the behavior prior to the interval and continues it past the end of the interval; (d) the person makes the complete response during the interval; (e) all of the above. ____________

(15) Time-sample recording is similar to interval recording except that the intervals are ____________________.

(24) If John is observed for one interval, then not observed for four intervals while other individuals are observed, and then he is observed again, this is an example of ____________________ recording.

(5) If John is observed during a series of randomly selected intervals, the method of observation is ____________________ recording.

(14) Suppose that the result of some behavior is being observed once every hour. What method of observation is being used? ____________________ recording (Check the answer to this one!)

(4) If a response occurrence is scored only when a complete unit of behavior has been observed, what method is being used? ____________________ recording

(13) If a response occurrence is scored only when a result of some behavior is complete, what method is being used? ____________________ recording

(23) The behavior itself is observed for which of the methods? ____________________ recording

(3) If continuous intervals are used to observe one person, what method is being used? ____________________ recording

(12) Behavior is recorded during arbitrary intervals for what methods? ____________________ recording

(22) If one individual is observed for brief intervals separated by a considerable amount of time, what method is being used? ____________________

(2) Walker and Buckley (1968) analyzed the study behavior of a fourth grader by recording when he was "looking at the assigned page, working problems, and recording responses." This statement would be called a(n) ______________________________ .

(11) Walker and Buckley (1968) recorded the occurrence of study behavior in Phillip in a series of 10-second intervals that followed one another immediately. They were using ______________________ recording.

(21) Lindsley (1968) recommended the use of a simple wrist counter so that people could count the number of cigarettes they smoked as they smoked them, the number of times they smiled, and so on. These would be examples of ______________________________ recording.

(1) Lindsley's suggestion that people use wrist counters to record their own behavior immediately after they see or hear (or feel) it would involve those people in the ______________________ observation of their own behavior.

(10) The checklist of cleaning results used by Feallock and Miller (1976) would constitute an example of ______________________________ recording.

(20) If Feallock and Miller (1976) had asked the members to rate the cleanliness of the commune at various times to see if there was a correlation between the behavioral definition of cleanliness and the members' definition, then they would be investigating the ______________________ of their definition.

(8) A single instance of a behavior will be referred to by the word ______________________ .

(28) To analyze an example, begin by asking: "Does this method involve ______________________?" If it doesn't, ask: "Does this method involve the ______________________ of a behavior?" Otherwise ask: "Does this method involve ______________________ time intervals?"

READING QUIZ ANSWERS

(1) direct (2) behavioral definition (3) interval (4) event (5) time-sample (6) (e) all of the above (7) continuous (8) response (9) consumers (10) outcome (11) interval (12) interval and time-sample (13) outcome (14) outcome (15) discontinuous (16) part (17) complete (18) result (19) evaluate (20) social validity (21) event (22) time sampling (23) event, interval, and time-sample (24) time-sample (25) ongoing (26) brief (27) outcome (28) time intervals; results; continuous

LESSON 3 EXAMPLES

Note: You should practice your mastery of the concepts in the lesson by answering the questions accompanying the following examples. You should also check your answers.

Example #1

David was taking English 159 from Professor McNault. He had expected a discussion course but he found that the professor talked so much that there was little time left for discussion. David divided the class period into 100 30-second intervals and recorded all of those intervals during which the professor talked without interruption. He found that 65% of the intervals contained uninterrupted talking by Professor McNault. David was very disappointed with his course.

(31) David's method of observation is called "interval recording" because he observed the professor's talking during a series of ______________________________ intervals.

(20) His method would be an example of time-sample recording if he observed for 5 seconds every 5 minutes (leaving himself the rest of the time to take notes on the class), because he would be observing the professor's talking during a series of ______________________________ intervals.

(30) If David counted the number of words spoken by the professor, he would be using event recording because he would be recording the occurrence of behavioral episodes—each word being an ________________ behavioral episode.

(10) David collected all of the written tests given out by Professor McNault and counted them at the end of the semester (there were 17). David was using what method of observation? ________________ recording

Example #2

Four behavioral observers were observing John, a particularly poor fourth-grade student. John was doing very poorly in spelling. Observer #1 divided his or her observational time into 15-second intervals and noted whether John was studying his spelling during each interval. Observer #2 went to John's desk at the end of the spelling period and counted the number of answers written in John's book. Observer #3 counted every time that John got out of his seat. Observer #4 watched John's studying for a 15-second interval every 5 minutes.

(19) Observer #1 recorded John's studying during a series of continuous 15-second intervals. What method was he or she using? ________________ recording

(29) Observer #2 recorded the number of written answers by consulting a result of John's studying. He or she was using ________________ recording.

(9) Observer #3 counted complete behaviors of John getting up from his seat and was therefore using ________________ recording.

(18) Observer #4 recorded John's behavior for 15 seconds and then did something else for the rest of the 5 minutes before observing John for another 15 seconds. Therefore, he or she was using ________________ recording.

(28) Observers #1 and #4 both used 15-second intervals. The difference was that Observer #1 used intervals that were ________________ while Observer #4 used intervals that were ________________.

(8) In a sense, Observers #2 and #3 both counted complete units. The difference is that Observer #2 observed the ________________ of behavior while Observer #3 recorded ________________ units of behavior as they occurred.

Example #3

Most of the members of the commune wanted to buy a new couch for their living room. Ted opposed this, however, saying that nobody ever used the living room. The commune appointed Ted to conduct a study to see how often people were in the living room. Because Ted was a student and had to spend a lot of time studying, he couldn't afford to sit in the living room all day and record the behavior of the other housemembers. So, he set up a schedule to visit the living room for a brief time every 15 minutes and observe whether anyone was sitting there.

(17) What type of behavioral measurement was he using? ________________ recording

(27) Ted's method differed from event recording because he was not observing the occurrence of each ________________ unit of behavior.

Example #4

John had just gotten his essay paper back from the professor. He had spent weeks doing research on *The Whole Earth Catalog* and was very proud of his work; however, the professor had given him a B. John couldn't see anything wrong with the paper except that he had used a split infinitive. The professor told him that the essay was excellent but that his incorrect English had cost him an A. So John decided to count the number of times the professor used a split infinitive during his lectures. He found that, after five classes, the professor had split his infinitives seven times. John gave him a B–.

(7) What kind of measurement technique was John using? ______________________ recording

(16) John's method of observing differs from time sampling because he was not observing behavior during a series of ______________________ intervals.

(33) John's method of observing is not an example of outcome recording because the observation was not made of the ______________________ of the behavior after it was completed.

Example #5

The Bales wanted to teach their 5-year-old daughter to make her bed and clean her room every day. She was supposed to do this right after school. To find out if she cleaned her room, the Bales checked her room every day to see whether the bed was made, the floor swept, the trash taken out, and all toys put away.

(6) In this example, cleaning behavior is checked for a brief time every day. Someone might guess that this was time-sample recording because the behavior was observed during discontinuous intervals. However, it should be classified as outcome recording because the Bales are observing the ______________________ of cleaning behavior.

Example #6

Heddy was interested in ecology. She decided to investigate the behavior of picnickers in a local park by stationing herself where she could view the families sitting at the picnic tables. Her first method of investigation was to wait until a family was gone and then collect and weigh all the trash that they had left behind. She found that each family left behind an average of 17 ounces of trash.

She then decided to observe the families as they were picnicking so that she could discover their pattern of littering the area. She watched families and counted the number of objects that they dropped on the ground. She found that they dropped an average of 12 pieces of trash during their picnics.

As the next step, she decided to determine the pattern of dropping trash as a function of time. She watched individual families during 15-second intervals while they were having their picnics. She found that they dropped trash during only 5% of the early intervals but during 55% of the intervals of their last 10 minutes in the park; they were dropping trash every 30 seconds toward the end of the picnics.

Finally, she wanted to observe all the families in the park at the same time, instead of only one family at a time. She observed family #1 the first 15 seconds to see whether they were littering the park. Then she switched to family #2 and noted whether they dropped trash during the second interval. Because there were four families, it took her one minute to watch all of them once. After she watched each family once, she started over again—that is, sampling each family's behavior once a minute.

(15) When Heddy collected the junk and weighed it, she was using what method? ______________________ recording

(26) When she watched the families and counted how many times they dropped objects on the ground, she was using what method? ______________________ recording

(5) When she observed families to find out the pattern of dropping trash as a function of time, she was using what method? ______________________ recording

(14) When she watched all the families at the same time, watching each family for only a part of an interval, she was using what method? ______________________ recording

Example #7

Mary and Rex decided that a small group of people had come to dominate the meetings of their committee. They decided to measure this domination and report their results at a future meeting of the committee. They recorded the name of the person doing the most talking during each 15-second interval of the meeting and found that 3 of the 20 people present at that meeting were speaking during 76% of the intervals.

(25) What method of observation was used in this example? ______________________ recording

Example #8

Dee felt that public schools were ruining her children's interest in education, so she started investigating the local "free schools." She was impressed with the freedom of these schools but worried about the bigger children bullying the smaller ones. She decided to compare the different schools by observing how often the bigger children bullied the littler ones. She recorded whether any bullying was going on in the classroom during a series of 15-second intervals covering the first 2 hours of the school day. She found that bullying occurred about four times more often in the free school.

(4) Dee was using ______________________ recording.

Example #9

The Behavior Research Commune had successfully set up programs for keeping the house clean, but they hadn't been very successful in keeping the house repaired. They decided to pay cash for each repair job completed and determine the amount of pay for each job by inspecting to see how well the damaged area had been repaired.

(13) What method of observation was used in determining payment? ______________________ ____________ recording

Example #10

Fran observed Professor Young to see how arrogant he was. She decided that she would record every time that the professor said to a student "No, you're wrong" or the equivalent.

(21) Her decision as to what to record would be called a(n) ______________________. ____________.

Example #11

Mary was concerned about the rampant sexism appearing in TV "jiggle" shows. She wanted to write a paper about it containing specific numbers as to how much sexism was occurring. Since she did not have time to watch every show all the way through, she arranged to observe for ten randomly scheduled intervals of 10 seconds each during each program.

(3) She was using ______________________ recording.

Example #12

If Al wanted to find out how much of the day his child spent studying in school, he might go to the school and observe whether his child was studying during each 20-second period of the day.

(12) He would be using what method of observation? ______________________
recording

Example #13

Mr. Kabe was the principal of the Pickney grade school. He decided over Thanksgiving vacation that good teaching for a kindergarten teacher could be measured by measuring the percentage of the time that the teacher spent talking directly with one child. So he explained this to his teachers and asked them to spend more time in that manner. He then asked all 13 parents who had visited their children's classes both before and after the change in teaching style to rate the amount of good teaching that they had seen. He found that they rated the new style to be somewhat better teaching.

(23) Mr. Kabe was attempting to determine the ______________________
of his behavioral definition.

Example #14

Fred was interested in the extent to which people were positive and supportive of one another in casual interactions. His sociology professor suggested that he use a questionnaire approach and ask people how often they were positive toward other people. Fred wanted better information than that, however, so he recorded only what he personally heard and saw at the time of the observation.

(2) Fred was using ______________________.

Example #15

Being a bit of a gossip, you want to know how often John has his girlfriend in his room; so you make a note every time she visits.

(32) You would be using what method of observation? ______________________
recording

Example #16

To decide whether the public areas of a dorm are clean enough, you might make a checklist of things that should be clean (such as floors, ashtrays, trash baskets, and so on) and check once a day to see whether they are clean.

(22) You would be using what method of observing? ______________________
recording

Example #17

If a living group is having trouble with people griping during the dinner hour, an observer might sit at the table and note whether anyone is griping during each 30-second interval.

(1) He would be using what method of observing? ______________________
recording

Example #18

Martha wants to determine the actual amount of violence on prime time TV. She decides to record every scene in which there is a weapon (gun, knife, and so on) present, every scene that involves physical assault on a person, and all scenes in which one person is yelling in anger at another as "constituting violence."

(11) Her decision as to what to record would be called a(n) ______________________________ ________________.

Example #19

Barb was a new student senator. She was very concerned that parliamentary procedure was not being followed when the chairperson's friends wanted to get something done. She counted the number of times that a motion was passed without fully observing correct procedure. She noted an average of about three per meeting.

(24) What method of observation was Barb using? ______________________________ recording

EXAMPLE ANSWERS

(1) interval (2) direct observation (3) time-sample (4) interval (5) interval (6) result (7) event (8) result; complete (9) event (10) outcome (11) behavioral definition (12) interval (13) outcome (14) time-sample (15) outcome (16) discontinuous (17) time-sample (18) time-sample (19) interval (20) discontinuous (21) behavioral definition (22) outcome (23) social validity (24) event (25) interval (26) event (27) complete (28) continuous; discontinuous (29) outcome (30) complete (31) continuous (32) event (33) result

Lesson 4

Reliability of Everyday Observations

RELIABILITY

A major concern in any attempt to measure behavior scientifically is whether the observations are accurate. Unfortunately, there is usually no way to directly measure accuracy. Suppose that we want to find out how often Don says "ain't" in a small-group conversation. We might observe Don for an hour and count 23 "ain'ts," but how can we be sure that Don actually said "ain't" 23 times? We could have tape-recorded the discussion and had someone else count the "ain'ts," but if the new answer is 27 times, who is right? We could have another person count from the tape recording, but if she counts 25 times, who is right? There is no absolute way to measure accuracy.

However, if two observers independently count the "ain'ts," the more closely they agree, the more accurate the count is likely to be. In other words, agreement between two independent observers is indirect evidence of accuracy. Behavior analysts call the extent to which two independent observers agree in their observations **reliability.**

The following discussion concerns the descriptive approach to reliability, which is frequently used by behavior analysts. This approach is distinct from the statistical approach, which is widely used by traditional psychologists (for example, Cronbach, 1960).

COMPUTING RELIABILITY

Reliability is measured most accurately and most easily when each observation of the two observers can be directly compared. For example, if two observers are using a time-sampling method of observation, their records may be compared interval-by-interval. To calculate reliability, the percentage of agreements between the two observers is used. This is computed as the agreements (A) divided by the agreements plus the disagreements (A+D). Thus, the formula for reliability is A/(A+D).

To measure reliability, it is necessary for two people to observe the same behavior at the same time using the same definition of the behavior. If Carl and Priscilla observe Johnny reading from 9:00 to 9:30 each morning, but Carl defines reading as Johnny sitting in front of an open book while Priscilla defines it as Johnny orienting his eyes toward the book and making eye sweeps from one side of the page to the other, their agreement would not constitute an example of reliability. Likewise, if Carl came in late and observed from 9:30 to 10:00 while Priscilla observed at the regular time, their agreement would not be a valid measure of reliability.

Suppose that Carl and Priscilla start observing at the same time and observe Johnny's reading according to the definition used by Priscilla. Their first five observations might be recorded as follows, with "R" representing a reading response and "N" a nonreading response.

	1	2	3	4	5
Carl:	R	R	R	R	N
Priscilla:	R	N	R	R	N

In this example, both observers recorded a reading response in the first, third, and fourth intervals and a nonreading response in the fifth interval. Thus, their observations agree in four intervals. The observers, however, did not agree on whether reading was occurring in the second interval. Carl recorded that it was occurring, and Priscilla recorded that it was not occurring. Therefore, the second interval is an example of disagreement. Notice that the observations that disagree are circled to help prevent counting disagreements as agreements.

Reliability, in this example, would equal the number of agreements (4) divided by the number of agreements plus the number of disagreements (5). Thus, A/(A+D) = 4/5 or 80%.

When two observers use interval recording and start each interval at the same time, an interval-by-interval count of agreements and disagreements is possible.

Any method of observing that produces a detailed record of each observation can be compared in the same way. For example, if outcome recording is used to observe a series of jobs, then the record for each job can be compared. Suppose that the members of the behavioral commune observe how well the job of setting the table is done. They might observe whether a knife, fork, spoon, plate, glass, and napkin are placed at each position on the table. Two observers recording their observations might produce a record as follows, with "yes" indicating that all place settings have been given the item and "no" indicating that one or more places have not been given the item:

		Annie	*Bob*
1.	Knives	yes	no
2.	Forks	yes	yes
3.	Spoons	no	no
4.	Plates	yes	yes
5.	Glasses	yes	yes
6.	Napkins	no	yes

To compute reliability, circle the pairs of observations that do not agree. Then use the formula for reliability, A/(A+D), which in this case would be 4(4+2) = 4/6 or 67%.

Reliability can be computed in a similar way for event-recording data if the record of an event by one observer can be directly compared with the record of the other observer. This is frequently not the case since a simple total is usually obtained, rather than records of "happening" and "nonhappening" events. However, sometimes a series of different events may be recorded, event by event.

For example, two observers might record whether a tutor greeted students, smiled, asked them if they had any questions, praised their correct answers, and tested them. Each observation is an event that either occurred or did not occur. The record for the two observers might look like this:

		Mark	*Joan*
1.	Greeting	yes	yes
2.	Smile	yes	no
3.	Questions	yes	yes
4.	Praise	no	yes
5.	Test	yes	yes

Analyze this case yourself by circling and then counting disagreements. Use the formula A/(A+D) to compute reliability. Did you get 60%?

Thus, what might be called the "observation-by-observation" method of computing reliability can be applied to all methods of observation if the results include instances when the behavior occurs and instances when it does not occur. This method of computing reliability is the most desirable and informative method.

Two methods of observation frequently do not result in observation-by-observation records. When outcome recording and event recording are used, the most frequent outcome is a simple count of the number of times that the behavior was observed, with no records of nonoccurrences. Thus, we might find that the fat lady at the circus left 753 candy bar wrappers in her dressing room on Wednesday morning. This report means the observer counted wrappers and found a total of 753. But there is no record of noninstances of wrappers. Thus, if someone else reports 753 wrappers, we have no way of knowing whether he counted the same wrappers. We don't really know for sure if there is agreement.

Similarly, if one observer reports that Harry smiled 50 times on Saturday afternoon, we know the total instances of smiling reported, but we don't know how many nonsmiles occurred. Thus, if a second observer reports 40 smiles, we don't know whether they both observed the same 40 smiles (with the second observer missing 10 smiles), or whether there were really 90 smiles, and the two observers recorded entirely different instances of smiling.

Thus, in those methods of observation in which only a total count is reported, the exact agreement between the observers cannot be determined. However, it is generally assumed that the overlap in the two counts represents agreement and the nonoverlap represents disagreement. Thus, in the case of the fat-lady observations, agreement would be 753/(753+0) or 100%. And in the case of the observers of Harry, we assume that the overlapping 40 observations of smiling represent agreements and the 10 added smiles reported by the first observer represent disagreements. Thus, we would compute their reliability as 40/(40+10) or 80%.

Notice that the formula for reliability stays the same, A/(A+D). A simplification of the formula is obtained by simply dividing the larger number into the smaller number.

This method of computing reliability is called *counting reliability* and is applied in any situation in which observation-by-observation reliability cannot be used. It does not use specific comparisons, and, therefore, it is less desirable.

In general, most researchers shoot for a total reliability of 90% or more. However, with a new behavior definition, a figure of 80% or more is acceptable. Examples used in this text deal with an "old" behavior definition unless otherwise specified.

Note #1: This lesson provides only a brief introduction to the issues involved in determining the reliability of observational data. That this is a critical issue in behavior analysis is attested to by Kelly's (1977) finding that 94% of all research articles published in the *Journal of Applied Behavior Analysis* report reliability and the widespread belief that it is one of the most important characteristics defining behavior analysis (for example, Kazdin, 1975). Part of the spring 1977 issue of *Journal of Applied Behavior Analysis* was devoted to detailed consideration of many aspects of reliability not discussed in this lesson.

Note #2: Increasingly, additional information is being required to determine whether a reliability figure indicates sufficient reliability. Sometimes the level of reliability that would be attained by the chance agreement of two observers is used to determine if the observed level is sufficiently greater than that to warrant confidence. Sometimes *occurrence reliability,* the reliability of just those intervals in which at least one observer records an occurrence of the behavior, is used (for example, Hopkins & Hermann, 1977). Also, computing the correlation between the event totals counted by two observers on several occasions is sometimes used instead of the percentages described in the lesson.

ADDITIONAL READINGS

Baer, D. M. Reviewer's comments: Just because it's reliable doesn't mean that you can use it. *Journal of Applied Behavior Analysis,* 1977, *10,* 117–119. This article argues that statistical estimates of reliability are not functional for behavior analysis.

Hartmann, D. P. Considerations in the choice of interobserver reliability estimates. *Journal of Applied Behavior Analysis,* 1977, *10,* 103–116. Hartmann presents an argument for using statistical estimates of reliability. See the rejoinder by Baer.

Hopkins, B. L., & Hermann, J. A. Evaluating interobserver reliability of interval data. *Journal of Applied Behavior Analysis,* 1977, *10,* 121–126. The authors describe how to compute the probability that two observers will agree by chance. They recommend that all observation-by-observation reliability figures be accompanied by a statement of what chance agreement would be. They also recommend the use of two more refined measures of agreement when the behavioral rates are extreme.

Kazdin, A. E. Artifact, bias, and complexity of assessment: The ABC's of reliability. *Journal of Applied Behavior Analysis,* 1977, *10,* 141–150. An excellent discussion of the many factors that can affect the value of observational data.

Kelly, M. B. A review of the observational data-collecting and reliability procedures reported in *The Journal of Applied Behavior Analysis. Journal of Applied Behavior Analysis,* 1977, *10,* 97–101. This article summarizes the type of reliability procedures used in some 200 *JABA* research reports. An excellent statistical summary of current usage.

LESSON 4 READING QUIZ

(5) The accuracy of behavioral observations is indirectly measured by what behavior modifiers call ______________________.

(13) Reliability is the extent to which two independent observers ______________________ in their observations.

(10) Reliability can be determined only when two people observe the same ______________________ at the same ______________________.

(12) The formula for computing reliability is ______________________.

(4) Two observers using interval recording make the following report:

Observer A:	X 0 X 0 0
Observer B:	X X 0 0 0

Circle disagreements, and then compute the percentage of agreement: __________

(9) Can observation-by-observation reliability always be computed with interval recording? __________ Can it always be computed with outcome recording? __________

(3) The most desirable and informative method of computing reliability is called the ______________________ by ______________________ method.

(8) Two methods of observation that frequently do not permit observation-by-observation computation of reliability are ______________________ and ______________________.

(7) If one observer counts 13 events and another observer counts 16 events, we can apply the reliability formula by assuming that the observers agree on how many observations? __________

(2) The percentage of agreement between two sets of observations is called the ______________________ of those observations.

(11) What is considered an acceptable reliability figure by most researchers? __________

(6) A lower figure is accepted in the case of ______________________ behavioral definitions. The lower figure is __________.

(1) If a behavior is observed at two different times, with one observer counting 20 instances and the other observer counting 19 instances, can you conclude that the observers are reliable? __________

READING QUIZ ANSWERS

(1) no (2) reliability (3) observation; observation (4) 60% (5) reliability (6) new; 80% (7) 13 (8) outcome recording; event recording (9) yes; no (10) behavior; time (11) 90% (12) A/(A+D) (13) agree

LESSON 4 EXAMPLES

Example #1

Fred and Charlie counted the number of times that their roommate Murray cracked his books to study one Saturday. Fred counted 10 times while Charlie counted only 9 times.

(37) To determine if Fred's and Charlie's counts are reliable, you must first determine whether they were counting the same behavior at the same time. Were they? __________

(26) If they were, then you must count their agreements, which in this case you should assume would be __________, and their disagreements, which would be __________.

(13) Then you should use the formula (A/A+D), which in this case equals ______________________.

(36) Next, determine whether this is an old or new definition. Unless otherwise specified you should assume that it is a(n) ______________________ definition.

(25) Finally, you must determine whether it meets the criterion of 80% for new or 90% for old. Does it? __________

(12) In this case you have determined that their observations are ______________________ __________.

Example #2

Sam and Marge checked every half hour to see if their new baby was sleeping. Their first ten observations were (S = sleep; N = nonsleep):

Sam:	S S N S N S S N S N
Marge:	S N N S N S N N S N

Their definition of sleep was a new and complicated one.

(35) Were they observing the same behavior at the same time? __________

(24) They agreed __________ times and disagreed __________ times.

(11) Their reliability is __________.

(34) What figure is needed for their observational reliability to be acceptable? __________

(23) Are their observations reliable? __________ (Check this answer.)

Example #3

Roger counted the number of times that Terry threw his clothes down rather than putting them away. He counted 17 times. Bunny, his friend, counted 20 times during the same period of time.

(10) Were they counting the same behavior at the same time? __________

(33) Their reliability is __________.

(22) Is this an acceptable level of reliability? __________

Example #4

Frank and Marsha are the cleaning inspectors for their living group.

		Marsha	Frank
1.	Floor clear of objects	X	X
2.	Rug free of objects	0	0
3.	Tables clear of dust	X	C
4.	Trash basket emptied	0	0
5.	Ashtrays	X	0

If they mark down an "X," it means the job is passable; if they mark down an "O," it means that it isn't. Frank and Marsha use a written manual describing how to determine whether each of the jobs has been done properly. They both inspect at 8:00 in the evening. Their definitions are new.

(9) Frank and Marsha agree on their scoring of __________, __________, and __________. (List numbers of jobs.)

(32) The reliability is computed by the formula A/(A+D), which in this case equals __________.

(21) To decide whether their observations are reliable, you must ask two questions: First, does the computed reliability attain the criterion? __________

(8) Second, is this a situation in which reliability may be validly computed (that is, the same behavior is observed at the same time using the same definition)? __________

(31) Which of the following conclusions is warranted? (a) No conclusion is possible because reliability can't validly be computed; (b) the observations are reliable; or (c) they are unreliable. ____________

Example #5

Owen was appointed to obtain an objective measure of the number of gripes made during dinner at the Behavior Research Commune. Mary was appointed to record gripes once a week so that there could be some measure of Owen's reliability. On Thursday, when they were both observing, Owen counted 19 gripes, and Mary counted 20 gripes.

(20) Is this evidence that their observations are reliable enough? ____________

Example #6

Joan and Nel feel that Professor Brainbuster says "uhh" too often during lectures. Joan counted 48 "uhhs" during Monday's lecture. To make sure Joan was unbiased in her counting, Nel counted "uhhs" during the next lecture and found 50. They decided that their counts were so close that Joan's count must have been correct.

(7) Is this evidence of acceptable reliability? ____________

Example #7

You and a friend often watch the *Tonight Show*. You both feel that Johnny Carson treats good-looking women guests in a way different from the way he treats "plain" women guests. You decide that he tends to keep the conversation limited to the careers of the plainer women. To check this, you use an interval-measuring procedure to score the percentage of intervals in which the conversation is about the women guests' careers.

(19) One way to check your accuracy would be for you and your friend to simultaneously observe Johnny's treatment of women and compare your scores. Your agreement is a measure of ________________________.

Example #8

The church members were considering whether to continue using some of their space for private worship. There were differing opinions on how often the private worship room was used, so the members appointed Sue to measure its use. She asked Dick to test her reliability. They both observed at ten specified times during the day. She noted that the room was used during only one of those times. Dick noted two uses of the room. Their records were as follows (an "X" means that a use of the room occurred):

Sue:	0 0 0 X 0 0 0 0 0 0
Dick:	0 0 0 X X 0 0 0 0 0

(30) The reliability in this case equals ____________.

(6) Does the reliability meet the criterion? ____________

(18) Can you conclude that the reliability of these observations is acceptable? ____________

Example #9

The dorm members wanted to decide whether to buy new games for use in the lounge. First, they wanted to know how much of the time the existing games were being used. Fran and Willie agreed to spend two hours a day in the room and observe how much of that time a game was being played. Their data for the first ten periods of observation (60 seconds each) were as follows ("X" stands for occurrence):

Fran: X X X X 0 X 0 X X X
Willie: X X X X X X 0 0 X X

(39) What method of observation was being used? ______________________

(5) What is the reliability of these observations? ____________

(38) Are their observations acceptable? ____________

Example #10

Marie was using behavioral methods to teach a group of women how to be more assertive. She had a behavioral definition of assertiveness. Some of her students questioned her definition, so she took videotapes of her students' performance before and after training and showed them to a cross section of adults, asking them to rate how assertive the taped individuals were acting. They rated the students as more assertive after training than before, just as the behavioral definition did.

(17) Marie was attempting to establish the ______________________ of her definition.

Example #11

Two students observed Professor Brainbuster to find out whether he was looking at the students when he lectured. They did this in 15-second intervals. The first ten observations were:

Student 1: 0 0 0 0 X 0 0 X 0 0
Student 2: 0 X 0 0 0 0 0 X 0 0

(4) Compute the reliability. ____________ Is this an acceptable level? ____________

Example #12

Marc sometimes thought of himself as a Sultan. He made up a checklist of 15 services that he expected of Anna every day: serve him breakfast in bed, bring him his clothes, pour his bath, and so on. During the first day of his system, he asked Anna to bring him breakfast in bed; she looked at him kind of funny but did it. He then marked it down on his checklist. He then asked her to pour his bath and to be sure to put cologne in it. She looked real funny this time, went into the kitchen, and then threw a pot of water on the Sultan.

(29) What method of observation was the Sultan using? ______________________ recording

Example #13

Dave observed the study behavior of each of 16 pupils in the fifth grade for 10 seconds before moving on to the next. Every 4 minutes he started over again with the first pupil.

(16) He was using ______________________ recording.

Example #14

Dom observed each story on the evening news for a week. He found that 50 of the news items were biased toward the status quo. John wanted to see if Dom was correct, so he watched the evening news the next week and found that 46 of the items were biased toward the status quo. He decided that Dom's observations were accurate.

(3) If you translate "accurate" as "reliable," do you agree with his conclusion? ____________

Example #15

The coach carefully diagrammed the football play on the blackboard. The diagram showed exactly what each player should do. He and the assistant coaches then used this diagram during the game to determine whether each player had carried out his assigned duties.

(28) The diagram constitutes a(n) ______________________ of "assigned duty."

Example #16

Barb inspected the cleaning jobs according to a 50-item checklist at 8:00 Thursday night. She found that 40 of them had been done. Jan inspected them Friday night and found 39 done.

(15) Is this evidence of reliability? __________

Example #17

Two members of the radical organization NEW checked the number of shoppers going into Discriminating Nick's store just before NEW started a boycott. One member counted 180 shoppers, and the other member counted 200 shoppers.

(2) Compute the reliability. __________ Is it acceptable? __________

Example #18

Three members of the ecology committee were worried that they talked too much, so they asked two other members to observe the number of 10-second intervals during which they did most of the talking. The first ten observations were (with "T" indicating the trio and "O" indicating others):

(1)	T T T O T O T O T T
(2)	T T T T T O T O T T

(27) Does this evidence permit you to conclude that the observations are reliable? __________

Example #19

Alice and Jane watched ten commercials shown on late-night TV to determine how many of them were advertising products that were ecologically harmful. Their results were (where "H" stands for the occurrence of harmful product):

Alice:	H H N H N H H H N H
Jane:	H H H H N H H H H H

(14) Compute the reliability. __________ Is it acceptable? __________

Example #20

Bob and Gary wanted to find out how much time the children at the Yellow Brick Road Free School were spending learning to read, write, and do arithmetic. They observed in 30-second blocks of time using a new behavioral definition. Their first 20 intervals were (S = studying; N = not studying):

Bob:	S S N N N N N N N N N N S S N N N N N S
Gary:	S S S N N N N N N S N N S N N N N N N S

(1) Compute the reliability. __________ Are their observations reliable enough? __________

EXAMPLE ANSWERS

(1) 85%; yes (2) 90%; yes (3) no (4) 80%; no (5) 80% (6) yes (7) no (8) yes (9) 1, 2, 4 (10) yes (11) 80% (12) reliable (13) 90% (14) 80%; no (15) no (16) time-sample (17) social validity (18) yes (19) reliability (20) yes (21) no (22) no (23) yes (24) 8; 2 (25) yes (26) 9; 1 (27) yes (28) behavioral definition (29) event (30) 90% (31) (c) (unreliable) (32) 60% (33) 85% (34) 80% (35) yes (36) old (37) yes (38) no (39) interval recording

Lesson 5

Experimental Design for Studying Everyday Behavior

The purpose of a behavioral experiment is to find out whether the behavior of a single individual (subject) can be modified by a particular "treatment." For example, if we are interested in increasing the amount of cleaning a roommate does, we might experiment with the effects of constant complaining. In this case, the behavior to be modified would be cleaning behavior, and the treatment would be complaining. The purpose of an experiment would be to find out if complaining does increase the cleaning above its original or "baseline" level.

Before describing how such an experiment might be conducted, two words should be defined: baseline and treatment. The **baseline** is a record of the rate of a behavior prior to the treatment. The **treatment** is the method introduced to modify the rate of a behavior.

To find out whether the complaining increased the amount of cleaning, we might compare the rate of cleaning with and without complaining. In other words, we might first measure the cleaning behavior during a baseline period in which there are no complaints. Then, we might measure the cleaning behavior during the treatment period in which there are complaints when the cleaning rate is low. If we found that the roommate did about 25% of his or her cleaning during the baseline period and 75% during the treatment period, we would have evidence that complaining works. This procedure is a simple **comparison design,** which involves comparing the effect of the baseline condition with the effect of the treatment condition. Figure 5-1 illustrates the baseline condition of such a design with Sarge's "rational leadership" behavior, using training as the treatment.

Figure 5-1. If Sarge is later trained in "rational leadership," observing him "before" and "after" would be an example of a *comparison design.* Cartoon copyright © 1973 King Features Syndicate. Reproduced by permission.

Unfortunately, a simple comparison design still leaves many doubts about what actually caused the increase in cleaning.[1] For example, Jack's roommate may have just started dating a girl whom he wishes to invite over to the room; he may be cleaning it for her, not because Jack is complaining. There are usually too many alternative reasons to determine which reason is the most direct cause of the behavior. Jack's roommate may be cleaning more now because his schoolwork, job, or other duties have eased off or because he has seen how unhappy his previous cleaning habits made Jack. Therefore, it is hard to say that the increase in cleaning behavior proves that the treatment works; the rate change may have simply been a coincidence.

Behaviorists have invented two experimental designs that can prove whether or not a treatment works. In the first design, called the **reversal design,** the experimenter begins with a comparison between baseline conditions and treatment conditions; then he or she goes one step further and reverses to the original baseline conditions. In our example, the behaviorist would find the rate of cleaning without complaints, then find the rate of cleaning with complaints, and finally reverse to the original condition to find again the rate of cleaning without complaints. Assume that results showed 25% cleaning in baseline and 75% during treatment. If cleaning returned to 25% during the reversal, the behaviorist could assume that the complaints had directly influrnced the change. If cleaning stayed at 75% during the reversal, the experimenter could not be sure whether the treatment was effective. By stopping the treatment, he or she can find out whether the behavioral change also stops. If it does, then there is sufficient evidence to conclude that the treatment is responsible for the change.

When using a reversal design, it is unlikely that there will be alternative reasons for any new change in behavior. The first change could have been caused by some other event that happened to coincide with the beginning of the treatment, but a second change that happens when the treatment is discontinued is too coincidental. However, if the researcher feels that the behavioral changes might have been a coincidence, he or she can introduce a second reversal, restarting the treatment. If cleaning increases to 75% again, few people will doubt that it was the treatment that caused the change. Usually, however, only one reversal is necessary as proof.

A second experimental design is called the "multiple-baseline" design. A **multiple-baseline** design is a design in which a treatment is introduced at different times to determine its effects on two or more classes of behavioral observations. For example, suppose that the roommate in our example also interrupted Jack during study time. We might also obtain a baseline on interruptions while obtaining the baseline on cleaning. The researcher does not introduce the treatment condition on this second behavior until the basic comparison design has been found effective with the cleaning. So we might take a baseline for a week's cleaning and then record the results of a week of treatment (complaining). During this time, we would also be getting a two-week baseline on interruptions. If complaining worked to increase the amount of cleaning, then at the end of the two-week baseline period we might try complaining to reduce the rate of interruptions. If complaining also reduced the rate of interruptions, these coinciding results would be good evidence that the treatment was effective, rather than some alternative events. If complaining did not reduce the rate of interruptions, however, then we could not conclude that the change in cleaning was a result of the complaining; it may have been just a coincidence. For those people not convinced by two separate examples of the treatment's working, a third behavior could be studied, a procedure similar to the second reversal in the reversal design.

There are many different kinds of multiple-baseline designs. The example here involves two behaviors of only one person (the roommate). However, the same behavior in two people could have been studied—that is, a baseline of cleaning established for two people. The first person is subjected to the treatment of complaining, and, if it works with him or her, it is tried on the second person. If it is effective for both subjects, the chances are slim that an unknown alternative cause was responsible for the change. A similar situation exists when the same behavior of the same person is studied, but in two different situations. These three types of multiple baselines are called (a) multiple baseline across behaviors, (b) multiple baseline across persons, and (c) multiple baseline across situations.

In summary, the simplest design involves just a comparison between baseline and treatment. This procedure can be criticized because it does not rule out alternative causes of any change. Two experimental designs, reversal and multiple-baseline designs, can rule out such coincidences convincingly.

A reversal design involves using the sequence of baseline, treatment, and reversal to baseline.

[1]The excellent book by Campbell and Stanley (1963) describes more complex designs, which are capable of eliminating some alternative explanations that plague simple comparisons.

A multiple-baseline design involves using the same treatment on two classes of behavior observations at different times.

BEHAVIOR ANALYSIS EXAMPLES

Energy conservation. Palmer, Lloyd, and Lloyd (1977) conducted an experiment designed to evaluate several methods for reducing the usage of electricity in a single middle-class family. They observed the family's daily usage of electricity for 16 days, then provided daily feedback on the cost of electricity used by the family for ten days, and then simply observed usage again for an additional 30 days. This design is illustrated in Figure 5-2. They found that providing cost information reduced usage more than 10%. To establish the generality of their finding they studied three other families and found similar results. This study suggests that one way to encourage energy conservation may be to install meters that provide families with information on the cost of their daily usage of electricity—although this would not be too popular with the electric company!

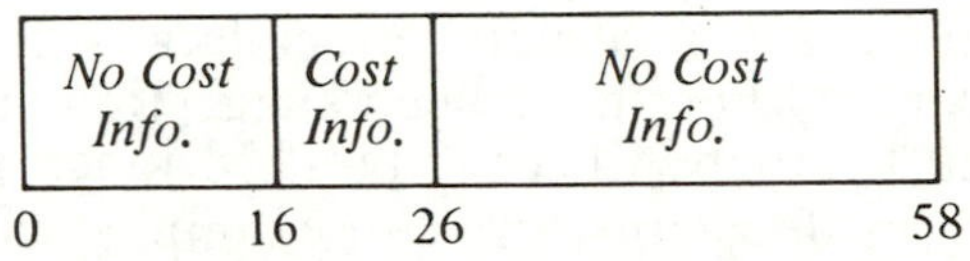

Figure 5-2. Design of an experiment on reducing electrical usage

Coaching football. Komaki and Barnett (1977) developed a method for improving the coaching of football to 9- and 10-year-old boys in a Pop Warner League. Their method involved specifying the player duties carefully to each boy, rehearsing the play, carefully recording whether the boys did what they were supposed to do during practice scrimmages and games, and providing immediate feedback and praise for correct performance. The coaches used a checklist to record the plays as they occurred. The experimental design involved observing correct completion of the quarterback option play during ten sessions without feedback, then providing feedback for the option play for the rest of the 26 sessions. The power sweep and counter plays were kept in the nonfeedback condition longer: 14 sessions for the power sweep and 18 for the counter play; only then was feedback provided to the players. This design is illustrated in Figure 5-3. Correct performance was about 60% for all plays before feedback and over 80% after its consistent use.

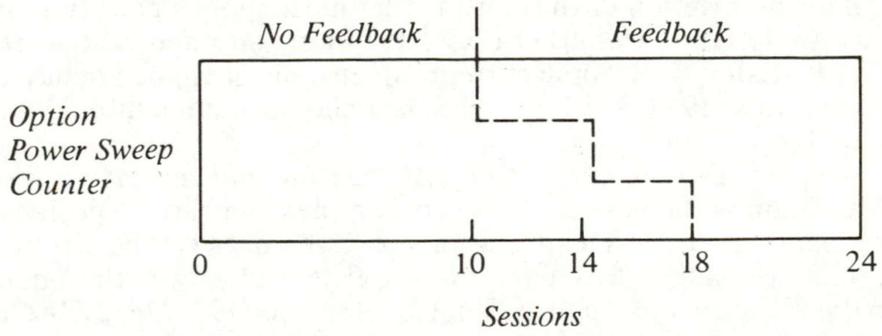

Figure 5-3. Design of an experiment on the effect of reinforcement on the execution of three football plays

Test anxiety. Meichenbaum (1972) examined the effect of a behavioral approach to the anxiety of college students over taking tests. Meichenbaum determined their GPA (along with several other measures) before and after helping them. He taught them to identify anxiety-producing thoughts that they emitted before and during tests. He then taught them to relax and to develop the habit of thinking more constructive thoughts before and during tests. Figure 5-4 illustrates this design. He found a small increase in GPA after his training.

Note #1: The basic designs outlined in this lesson are single-subject designs, used to establish the effectiveness of a treatment for one individual. If the researcher wishes to establish that the

Before Training	After Training

Figure 5-4. Design of an experiment to reduce test anxiety among college students

treatment has generality for many individuals, as most do, then he or she must replicate the experiment by repeating it with a number of individuals. There is no universally accepted criterion for determining how many individuals it must be repeated with, but the question may be thought about in a way similar to reversals. If the procedure works with several similar individuals, this suggests some generality for that type of individual. More generality might be established by trying it with different types of individuals. Usually an experiment will be restricted to similar types of individuals with replications on different types of individuals left to subsequent research. The question of generality is analyzed extensively by Sidman (1961).

Note #2: Applied behavior analysis has usually sought effects that are powerful enough to be obvious when looking at a graph of the data. This has involved the visual inspection of the graphed data to determine whether there is a treatment effect large enough to be socially important (Parsonson & Baer, 1978). Recently, there have been suggestions that such data be subjected to statistical analysis (for example, Kratochwill & Brody, 1978; Jones, Vaught, & Weinrott, 1977), but powerful arguments have been made against this (for example, Michael, 1974; Baer, 1977a). The use of social validation techniques to determine the importance of experimental data may represent the most direct solution to this difficult methodological problem (Kazdin, 1977).

Note #3: Another experimental design that is sometimes useful is called the "multi-element" design. It involves alternating the experimental conditions frequently, often every day. If the behavior occurs in the two conditions at a different rate, then this is taken as evidence that the treatment is effective. This design also rules out alternative explanations. An example is given by Loos, Williams, and Bailey (1977), who compared the rate of completing language arts units by third grade students with and without the presence of a teacher's aide. To determine if an aide was helpful they alternated randomly between having an aide and not having an aide. When the aide was present the students completed 28% more units.

ADDITIONAL READINGS

Baer, D. Maybe it would be better not to know everything. *Journal of Applied Behavior Analysis*, 1977, *10*, 167–172. An excellent description of the reasons that most applied behavior analysts do not rely on statistical inference to determine whether they have found an important treatment effect.

Baer, D. M., Wolf, M. M., & Risley, T. R. Some current dimensions of applied behavior analysis. *Journal of Applied Behavior Analysis*, 1968, *1*, 91–97. This is a classic statement of the methods and goals of applied behavior analysis.

Campbell, D. T., & Stanley, J. C. *Experimental and quasi-experimental designs for research.* Chicago: Rand McNally, 1963. This book is the best exposition of complex comparison designs available. It outlines methods by which many alternative explanations of differences can be eliminated.

Jones, R. R., Weinrott, M. R., & Vaught, R. S. Effects of serial dependency on the agreement between visual and statistical analysis. *Journal of Applied Behavior Analysis*, 1978, *11*, 277–283. Jones suggests that visual interpretation of data is unreliable.

Kazdin, A. E. Assessing the clinical or applied importance of behavior change through social validation. *Behavior Modification*, 1977, *1*, 427–452. Kazdin provides a thorough overview of social validation techniques for assessing the importance of behavior change.

Kratochwill, T. R., & Brody, G. H. Single subject designs: A perspective on the controversy over employing statistical inference and implications for research and training in behavior modification. *Behavior Modification*, 1978, *2*, 291–307. A discussion of recent trends in the use of statistical inference in behavior modification. The authors argue that statistical inference is used even in *Journal of Applied Behavior Analysis* (but by less than 20% of the articles) and that it should be used more often.

Michael, J. Statistical inference for single-subject research: Mixed blessing or curse? *Journal of Applied Behavior Analysis*, 1974, *7*, 647–653. A discussion of the implications of using statistical inference in conjunction with single-subject designs.

Risley, T. R., & Wolf, M. M. Strategies for analyzing behavior change over time. In J. Nesselroade & H. Reese (Eds.), *Life-span developmental psychology: Methodological issues.* New York: Academic Press, 1972.

This is an advanced statement of the methodological ideas underlying the two designs taught in this chapter.

Sidman, M. *Tactics of scientific research.* New York: Basic Books, 1961. This book is the classical statement of the logic underlying single-subject research designs. It was written prior to the widespread use of such designs with applied human research, and so it focuses on basic research.

Wolf, M. M., & Risley, T. R. Reinforcement: Applied research. In R. Glaser (Ed.), *The nature of reinforcement.* New York: Academic Press, 1971. This article includes an excellent description of the experimental designs used in behavior analysis research and a discussion of comparison designs.

LESSON 5 READING QUIZ

(11) The purpose of a behavioral experiment is to find out whether the rate of a behavior can be modified by a particular ____________________ .

(10) The record of the rate of a behavior prior to treatment is called a(n) ____________________ .

(19) A method designed to modify the rate of a behavior is called a(n) ____________________ .

(9) If experimenters compare a baseline condition with the treatment condition they are using what type of design? ____________________

(8) A simple comparison design is limited because it does not rule out ____________________ explanations of an observed change in the behavior under study.

(18) A design in which a behavior is measured before treatment, during treatment, and after the cessation of treatment is called a(n) ____________________ design.

(7) The reversal design involves measuring the behavior during a baseline condition, during a treatment condition, and during what is known as a(n) ____________________ to the baseline condition.

(13) A reversal design is a strong design because, if a treatment causes a change when it is introduced and the elimination of that change when it is withdrawn, the experimenter can feel safe in ruling out ____________________ explanations of the changes.

(17) A design in which two (or more) classes of behavioral observations are subjected to the same treatment at different times is called a(n) ____________________ design.

(6) If two behaviors are measured with a treatment used on each behavior at the <u>same</u> time, be sure to recognize that this is not a multiple-baseline design; it is a(n) ____________________ design.

(16) If a treatment is applied to the behavior of one person after five weeks and to the same behavior in a second person after 10 weeks, then this would be an example of a(n) ____________________ design across persons.

(21) If a treatment is applied to the behavior of a person in one situation after 17 days and then is applied to the same behavior of the same person but in another situation after 26 days, this would be an example of a(n) ____________________ design across situations.

(5) A multiple-baseline design is a strong design because, if a treatment causes a change in each of two baselines at different times, ____________________ causes of the change may be ruled out.

(4) A baseline is the record of a behavior prior to the use of a(n) ____________________ designed to modify that behavior.

(15) Meichenbaum's (1972) procedure for teaching students how to relax and be less anxious during tests is called a(n) ____________________ .

(3) Meichenbaum (1972) determined students' GPA before teaching them how to be less anxious on tests. He then determined it after. The name of the design that he used is ____________________ .

(14) Komacki and Barnett (1977) provided feedback for football play performance after 10 sessions on the option play, after 14 sessions for the power sweep, and after 18 sessions for the counter. What experimental design were they using? ____________

(20) Komacki and Barnett (1977) used a checklist to record correct performance of three football plays; they were using ____________ recording.

(2) Palmer and associates (1977) measured electrical usage by a middle-class household when not giving them cost information, for a period of time while giving them cost information, and again after no longer giving them cost information. They used what experimental design? ____________

(12) Palmer and associates (1977) determined the electricity usage of the middle-class family that they studied by reading an electric meter. What method of observation did they use? ____________ recording

(1) If two observers determine the rate of a behavior prior to some treatment being applied to change it, their agreement is a measure of what? ____________

READING QUIZ ANSWERS

(1) reliability (2) reversal (3) comparison (4) treatment (5) alternative (6) comparison (7) reversal (8) alternative (9) comparison (10) baseline (11) treatment (12) outcome (13) alternative (14) multiple baseline (15) treatment (16) multiple baseline (17) multiple baseline (18) reversal (19) treatment (20) event (21) multiple baseline

LESSON 5 EXAMPLES

Example #1

Three students formed a store specializing in "paraphernalia" and called it "Bash!" After two months they realized that they weren't getting much business, and so they decided to have a sale on pipes, papers, and posters. Their sales zoomed to the outer limits as a result.

(28) If they compared volume prior to the sale with that during the sale, they would be using what type of design? ____________

(21) If they then discontinued the sale and compared volume prior to, during, and after the sale, they would be using what type of design? ____________

(12) If they owned two stores and started the sale March 1 in one store and April 1 in the other, what type of design would they be using? ____________

Example #2

Merideth seems to initiate conversations most often in the middle of Francie's studying. Francie decided to record the interruptions for several days before discussing the situation with Merideth.

(20) What is the record of interruptions prior to the discussion called? ____________

(11) What would the discussion designed to reduce interruptions be called? ____________

(27) If the rate of interruptions were determined first prior to the discussion and then after the discussion, what experimental design would Francie be using? ____________

Example #3

Freda found that she got an average of one ticket in six months when she was driving her old VW. But now that she is driving a new sports car, she is getting an average of one ticket a month. She is considering selling her sports car and getting an old VW again just to save on tickets.

(10) If Freda sold her sports car and started driving a VW again, this would be called a(n) ______________________ to baseline condition.

(19) What experimental design would Freda be using if she compared the rate of getting tickets when she first had the VW, when she had the sports car, and again when she drove a VW? ______________________

Example #4

Sonny had asked Ann and Patsy out for a date each week for two months with no success. Sonny then had a brilliant idea—didn't that TV commercial say something like "Try wearing Rut Cologne and the girls will follow you around"? So he put on some Rut and asked Patsy out for a date each week for a month, still with no success. He still asked Ann but he never remembered to wear Rut. Finally, he started wearing Rut when asking both Ann and Patsy out. Since he got no dates when he wore Rut, he decided it was terrible stuff and decided he would try Wild Hare!

(9) What experimental design was Sonny using to determine the effectiveness of Rut? ______________________

Example #5

Regan wanted to be a more effective teacher. She decided to investigate the effect of praising her second-grade students when they were working hard. She measured Tony's study time before using praise and after she had started using praise.

(18) Her observations of Tony's rate of studying before she started praising him would be called a(n) ______________________ .

(8) Her observations of Tony's rate of study after she started praising him would be made during a(n) ______________________ condition.

(26) What experimental design would she be using? ______________________

(17) What is the weakness of this design? It can't rule out ______________________ explanations for a change in behavior.

Example #6

Marie and Harry observed the rate at which Steve played his new record.

(7) The agreement between their observations would be called ______________________.

Example #7

Mr. James was always entering Ms. Murray's office and interrupting her work. His usual comments centered on his weekend activities or the previous night's entertainment at his favorite bar. None of his comments interested Ms. Murray at all, but she wanted to be polite. She usually looked at him attentively and nodded her head. She found that he interrupted her about seven times a week. Finally she decided to get him to stop interrupting her by ignoring him. She found that his rate of interrupting decreased to less than twice a week. After several months of this she began to feel sorry for him and took to looking at him attentively and nodding when he described his weekend. His rate of interruptions increased again to over six a week.

(6) What experimental design did Ms. Murray unintentionally use? ______________________

Example #8

Dave had two friends, each of whom complained a lot about life. Dave usually listened, but he finally decided that he was only encouraging their complaints rather than helping them by listening. So he decided to do an experiment to see if ignoring them would be a help to them. He first recorded the number of complaints that they each made for a month. Then he ignored his first friend while continuing to listen to his second friend's complaints. After another month, he ignored the complaints of both. He found that ignoring their complaints did reduce the amount of complaining without any other evidence of problems.

(25) What experimental design did Dave use? ______________________________

Example #9

The library committee had charged only 5¢ a day for overdue books. They thought this might not be enough, because over 15% of their books were overdue. So they increased the fine to 25¢ a day to see if that would get the books back faster.

(16) Assuming that they kept track of the number of overdue books, what experimental design were they using? ______________________________

Example #10

Vern and his friend counted the number of times that Dee hit the tennis ball with a good level swing (and immediately told her the results). Vern counted 100 level hits while his friend counted only 87.

(5) What is the reliability of their observations? __________ Is this an acceptable level? __________

Example #11

Jimmy counted the number of headaches that he got prior to enrolling in transcendental meditation class. He got an average of five a week.

(15) His record of headaches would be called a(n) ______________________________.

Example #12

Bob was excited about the new audiovisual material he had for teaching his junior high social studies class. He found that the students' grades this year averaged 85% compared with only 77% last year.

(4) The problem with Bob's experimental design is that it cannot rule out ______________ ______________ explanations for the observed increase (such as better students this year).

Example #13

Sandra kept track of her little league batting average. After 5 weeks she was delighted to find that she had 20 hits in 50 at bats for a .400 average!

(24) What method of observing hits did she use? ______________________________ recording

Example #14

Marvin gradually became aware that he had a terrible outlook on life, negative and self-defeating. He decided to go to a class in self-actualization.

(14) The class would be called a(n) ______________________________ for his miserable outlook on life.

Example #15

Professor Brainbuster was actually a very kindly old guy. He did everything that he could to help any student who was really trying in his courses. He considered students to be trying if they came to class regularly, asked questions, did their assignments, and asked for help.

(3) The underlined statement would be called a(n) ____________________ of "trying."

Example #16

Sara normally weighed 130. She tried a new quick diet to find out how well it worked and lost 13 pounds. She then stopped using the diet and returned to 130.

(23) What experimental design was she using that would have permitted her to determine the effectiveness of the new diet? ____________________

Example #17

When Sara stopped using the diet, she was using a reversal to baseline design.

(2) This is a strong design because it effectively rules out ____________________ explanations of her weight loss.

Example #18

Hal and Sheila had been appointed umpires for the annual softball game. They decided to keep track of how they would call action plays. Here is their record of calls:

		Hal	*Sheila*
a.	play at first base	out	out
b.	attempted steal	out	safe
c.	pickoff play	safe	safe
d.	bunt	out	out
e.	inside-the-park homer	safe	safe

(22) What is their reliability? __________ Would a behavior analyst consider it acceptable? __________

Example #19

Roger had three friends who were annoying him to death. He determined that he would have a long talk with each one when he had the time. He talked with Carol in October, Steve in November, and Lacey in December. Being scientific, he kept track of instances of annoyance throughout in order to see if the investment of time in discussions had been worth the effort.

(13) What kind of design did Roger use? ____________________

Example #20

Debby had always considered herself friendly. She smiled at people, offered to do little favors, and always stopped to talk.

(1) If she were to gather evidence about whether other people considered this pattern of behaving to be "friendly" she would be trying to determine the ____________________ of her definition.

EXAMPLE ANSWERS

(1) social validity (2) alternative (3) behavioral definition (4) alternative (5) 87%; no (6) reversal (7) reliability (8) treatment (9) multiple baseline (10) reversal (11) treatment (12) multiple baseline (13) multiple baseline (14) treatment (15) baseline (16) comparison (17) alternative (18) baseline (19) reversal (20) baseline (21) reversal (22) 80%; no (23) reversal (24) event (25) multiple baseline (26) comparison (27) comparison (28) comparison

Lesson 6

Graphing Everyday Behaviors

Graphs display behavioral measurements to provide an overall visual impression of when and how frequently a certain behavior occurs. Graphs are usually drawn between two lines that are joined to form an "L." The vertical line (up and down) is the **ordinate** and is usually used to indicate the rate or amount of behavior. The horizontal line (right to left) is the **abscissa** and is usually used to indicate the time when the behavior occurred.

Each entry on the graph is a dot that simultaneously records two facts: the amount or rate of behavior and the time that the behavior occurred. The dot records these two facts by being placed directly opposite the value of the ordinate that corresponds to the amount or rate of behavior and directly above the value of the abscissa that corresponds to the time that the behavior occurred.

For example, suppose that you note the number of dorm residents who are visiting with another person at 10 o'clock in the evening (as one measure of "friendliness"). Out of the 30 residents, you might find the following number of visitors on the five days that you did your observing: 9, 6, 4, 7, and 5. To record the first observation, you would find "9" on the ordinate (the number of behaviors of visiting) and "1" on the abscissa (the day that you observed—that is, the first day of your observation) and place a dot to the right of the "9" and directly above the "1." Your next entry would be to the right of the "6" and directly above the "2." You would end up with a graph like the one in Figure 6-1.

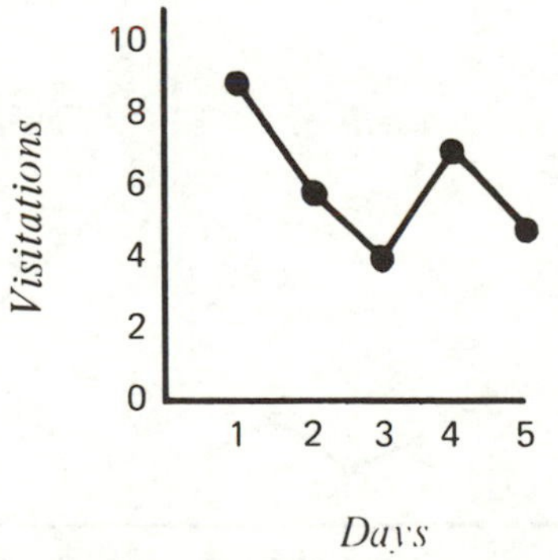

Figure 6-1. Visitations baseline (hypothetical data)

When making a simple graph (only one condition), you will have two major decisions to make: how long to make the ordinate and abscissa and what to label them.

Each graph label should be as short as possible while still describing the numbers being recorded. The abscissa is usually simple; you select a label that indicates the time factor that you are recording, such as days (as in Figure 6-1), weeks, hours, or unevenly spaced occasions (as in the first observation, second observation, and so on). The ordinate is somewhat harder to label. In general you should use a word or words that communicate the nature of the behavior being recorded. The ordinate might be short, such as "visitations" in the example above, or it might be somewhat longer, as in "percentage of cleaning done."

Selecting the most attractive proportions for a **simple graph** requires that you square the graph by making the length of the ordinate and the abscissa equal. To square a graph you should follow these six steps:

1. Find the largest value of the abscissa occurring in your entries.
2. Find the largest value of the ordinate occurring in your entries.
3. Divide the largest ordinate value by the largest abscissa value.
4. If the result is a decimal, round it off to the next larger whole number.[1]
5. Draw a horizontal line on the graph paper that crosses a number of graph lines equal to the largest abscissa value, and label it with the whole numbers from zero to the largest abscissa value.
6. Draw a vertical line upward from the left end of the abscissa and equal in length to the abscissa; label each graph line that it crosses with multiples of the result of step four up to the largest ordinate value. Thus, you should find the ratio between the ordinate and abscissa values in order to fit the largest values of each onto a square graph.

The visitations graph was squared by this process. First, we found that five observations were made; thus, the largest abscissa value would be 5. Second, we found that the largest number of visitors was nine; thus, the largest ordinate value would be 9. Third, dividing these two numbers, we get 9/5, which equals 1.8. Fourth, rounding off, we get 2.0. Fifth, we labeled the abscissa with the numbers 0 through 5. Sixth, we labeled the ordinate with the numbers 0, 2, 4, 6, 8, and 10.

When making a **complex graph** (more than one condition), you must also decide how long to make the ordinate and abscissa in order to create attractive proportions. If the numbers of observations in each condition are equal, you should square that portion of the graph that displays the condition containing the largest value of the ordinate.[2] You may use the same steps that are used in squaring a simple graph and apply the results to drawing the entire graph. The result will be a graph that is longer than it is high.

Suppose that you were using a comparison design to study the effects of a sensitivity-group session on visitation. Perhaps the data graphed in Figure 6–1 were the baseline. After the sensitivity session, the numbers of visitations were 25, 19, 15, 9, and 12. These would be observations for days 6, 7, 8, 9, and 10. To square this portion of the graph, you would find that 25 is the largest ordinate number, 5 is the number of entries during this time period, and 25/5 is 5.0, which doesn't need to be rounded off; you would draw an abscissa and label it 1 to 10 (for both conditions); and you would label your ordinate in steps of 5.0 each. As an additional step, you would divide the two conditions with a vertical line and label the conditions: "baseline," "treatment," "reversal," and so on (see Figure 6–2).

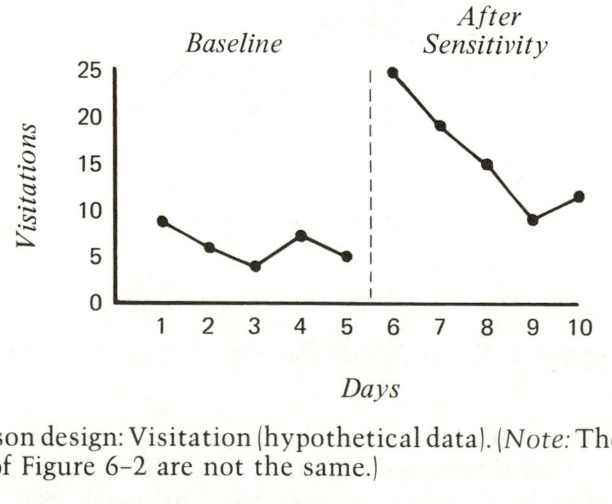

Figure 6–2. Comparison design: Visitation (hypothetical data). (*Note:* The scale of Figure 6–1 and the baseline portion of Figure 6–2 are not the same.)

When making a **multiple baseline graph,** you may use the same general strategy. In this

[1]Unless the result is a fraction less than 1.0, in which case you should round off to the next larger tenth, hundredth, and so on, whichever is appropriate. No such examples appear in the book. Percentages may be treated as whole numbers.

[2]If you are making a complex graph in which the numbers of observations in each condition are unequal, an acceptable graph will often be produced by using the average number of observations per condition in the first step. No such examples will be given in this book.

case you will make two or more graphs. For convenience we shall consider that a new condition occurs for all baselines each time the treatment is applied to the behavior displayed on one graph. Thus, if the baseline for one behavior is five weeks long, this is the first condition for all of the behaviors. If the treatment is applied to that behavior after week five, then that defines the beginning of the second condition. If the treatment is applied to the second behavior after the tenth week, then this is the beginning of the third condition. If the conditions are of equal length, then you would use the number of observations per condition as the number sought in the first step of squaring a simple graph.[3] You would look for the highest ordinate value occurring for any behavior as the number sought in the second step. You would then proceed through the remaining steps using these two numbers. The result would be applied to each of the separate graphs of the multiple baseline.

Suppose that you wished to find out whether sensitivity training increased the visitation among dorm members. You might take measurements in two dorms: Dorm A and Dorm B. The results can be put into the following table:

Day:	1	2	3	4	5	6	7	8	9	10	11	12	13	14	15
Dorm A:	9	6	4	7	5	18	19	15	9	12	8	4	6	7	5
Dorm B:	5	2	7	3	3	2	4	3	3	4	20	18	8	4	3

In this example, the sensitivity training was introduced after the observations at Day 5 for Dorm A and after the observations at Day 10 for Dorm B. Thus, for purposes of constructing a graph there are three conditions, each 5 days long.

Dorm B has the largest visitation total, 20 visitors during Day 11. Using the two numbers 20 (visitations) and 5 (days), you should get (through step four) a ratio of 4.0. You should then make two graphs with enough room on the ordinates and abscissas to record all entries (see Figure 6–3). Also, you would label the conditions at the top of the graph.

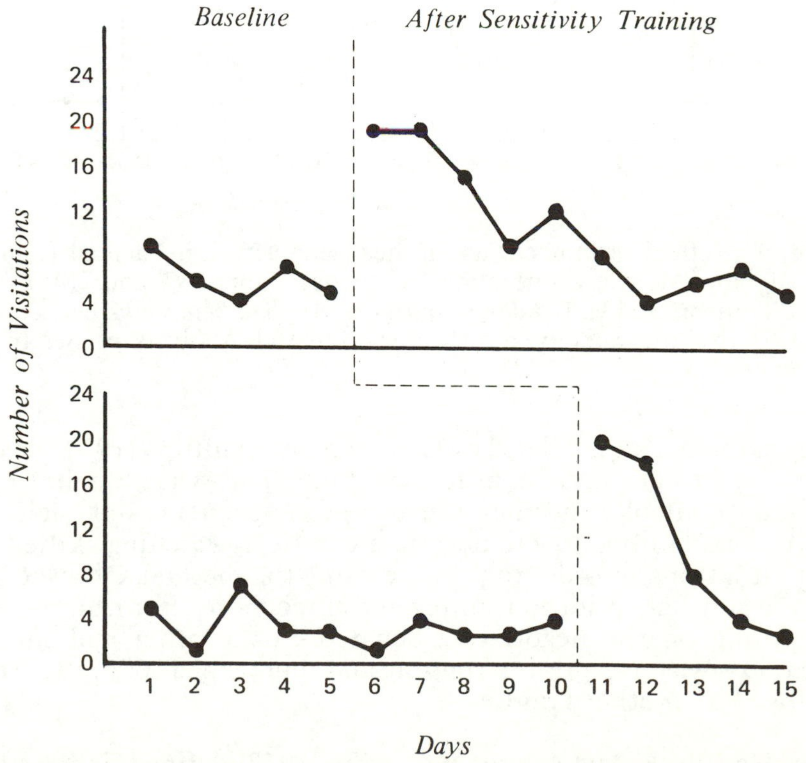

Figure 6-3. Multiple-baseline design: Visitations (hypothetical data)

[3]If the number of observations per condition varies, an acceptable graph may usually be produced by using the average length of each condition in the first step. No such examples will be used in this book.

EXAMPLES OF GRAPHS OF BEHAVIORAL EXPERIMENTS

Following are specially prepared graphs adapted from published data of three behavioral experiments. These examples are intended to illustrate how graphs help a reader to understand the effects of experiments and to illustrate how the rules of this lesson may be applied to actual data.

Headaches. Sturgis, Tollison, and Adams (1978) studied the effects of biofeedback training on the reduction of headaches in a 34-year-old laboratory technician who was almost totally incapacitated by both tension and migraine headaches. The technician described the tension headaches as a dull pain that first appeared in the forehead and later spread over her entire head. The migraines were usually accompanied by facial paralysis, slurred speech, numbness in arms and hands, and occasional nausea. In treatment, the technician was taught, during weeks 6 to 10, to relax the frontalis muscle in the forehead to eliminate the tension headaches, and, from weeks 11 to 15, to reduce the flow of blood to the brain to eliminate the migraines. The training virtually eliminated both types of headaches, as one can see in Figure 6–4. The technician reported spending less time in bed, being able to do housework, spending more time with the children, and improving her marriage. The data were gathered by asking the person to fill out a special self-report form at the time of the headache. The generality of these findings was partially confirmed by repeating the experiment with a second headache sufferer.

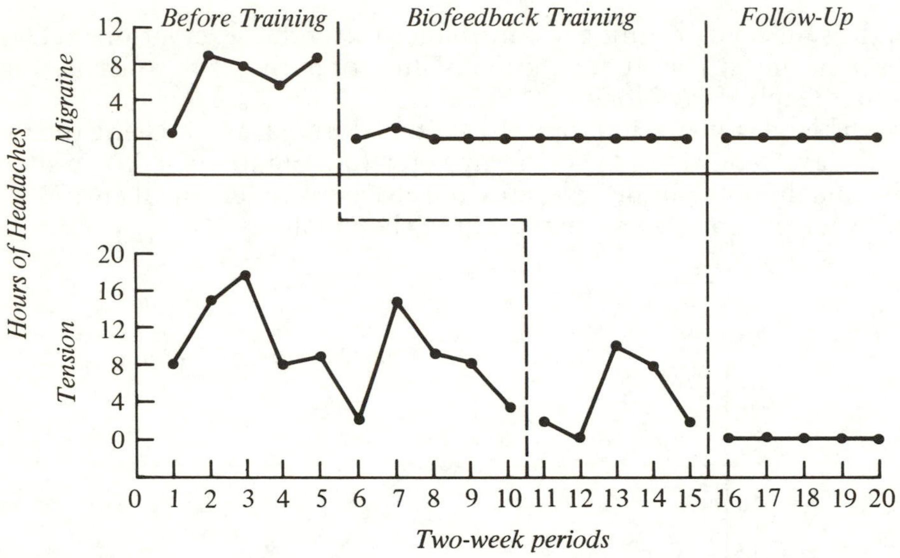

Figure 6–4. The effect of biofeedback on headache activity. Adapted from "Modification of Combined Migraine-Muscle Contraction Headaches Using BVP and EMG Feedback," by E. T. Sturgis, C. D. Tollison, and H. E. Adams, *Journal of Applied Behavior Analysis,* 1978, *11,* 215–223. Copyright 1978 by the Society for the Experimental Analysis of Behavior, Inc. Used by permission.

Negotiating family fights. Kifer, Lewis, Green, and Phillips (1974) developed a method for teaching families how to negotiate conflict situations. They were taught to describe the conflict, analyze the options available, and then specify the consequences of each option. The teaching procedure involved explaining how to negotiate conflicts, watching skilled negotiators, and role playing conflict situations in order to practice using the method. Observers were present in the home during three conflicts prior to training and three more after training. Figure 6–5 shows the effect of the training on the negotiating behaviors of a father and son. The percent of the negotiating behaviors was zero prior to training and approached 100% after training. These results were confirmed with two other families.

Depression. Hersen, Eisler, Alford, and Agras (1973) defined depression as the absence of smiling, talking, and motor activity. They observed one institutionalized patient, who had just experienced a severe loss, for four days using a time-sample recording procedure. They found that he was engaged in less than one of those behaviors on the average, as shown in Figure 6–6. They then awarded him tokens for assuming minimal responsibility, maintaining his personal hygiene,

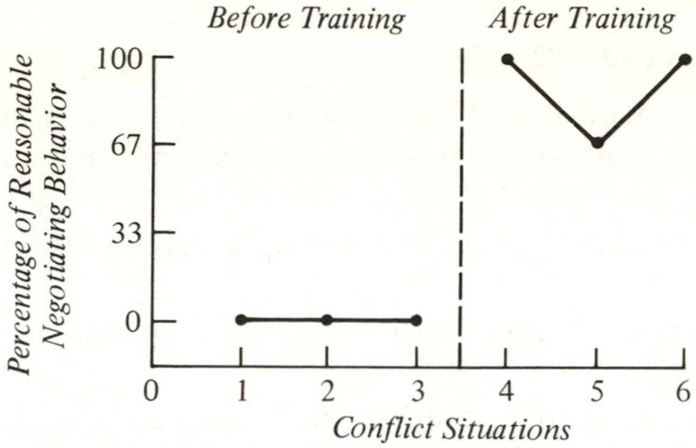

Figure 6–5. Graph of the percent of reasonable negotiating behaviors taught to family members before and after training. Adapted from "Training Predelinquent Youths and Their Parents To Negotiate Conflict Situations," by R. E. Kifer, M. A. Lewis, D. R. Green, and E. L. Phillips, *Journal of Applied Behavior Analysis,* 1974, 7, 357–364. Copyright 1974 by the Society for the Experimental Analysis of Behavior, Inc. Used by permission.

Figure 6–6. Graph of the effect of tokens on nondepressed behavior. Adapted from "Effects of Token Economy on Neurotic Depression: An Experimental Analysis," by M. Hersen, R. Eisler, G. Alford, and W. S. Agras, *Behavior Therapy,* 1973, 4, 392–397. Copyright 1973 by Academic Press. Used by permission.

and working. During this period, his rate of nondepressed behaviors increased to an average of two out of three. When the researchers discontinued the tokens, the patient's rate of nondepressed behaviors again decreased. This finding was replicated for two other depressed patients. The finding suggests that the use of behavioral procedures to increase responsible activity may be a useful treatment for depression. Hersen and associates reported that the staff had the impression that these patients were less depressed.

Note: Another type of graph that is frequently used by basic researchers and occasionally by applied behavior analysts is called a "cumulative graph" (or "cumulative record"). In this graph, each ordinate value is equal to the value of the last one plus the value of the new observation. To cumulatively plot smoking for Jack, if his daily rates were 5, 8, 3, and 4, would involve plotting a zero observation of no cigarettes: the second point would then be equal to 0 (the last value) plus 5 (the new observation) for a total of 5; the third point would equal 5 (the last value) plus 8 (the new observation) for a total of 13; the next point would equal 13 + 3 = 16. Can you figure out what the next point would be? You will not be tested on cumulative graphs but you will see several in the lessons on schedule effects (13 and 14).

ADDITIONAL READINGS

Instructions to authors: Preparation of graphs for JABA. *Journal of Applied Behavior Analysis,* 1976, 9, 24. This brief article explains how to prepare graphs for publication in *The Journal of Applied Behavior Analysis.*

Helpful hint: Draw graphs in pencil so that errors may be corrected. The following criteria will be used in grading your graphs: all lines must be drawn with a ruler; ordinate and abscissa must be correctly labeled; numbering on ordinate and abscissa must be correct; placement of data points must be correct; and all experimental conditions must be labeled. Overall neatness is important.

LESSON 6 READING QUIZ

(11) Is the ordinate the vertical or the horizontal line? ______________________

(21) The line on a graph that runs from left to right (horizontal) is called the ______________ ______________.

(10) Which line on a graph is used to record the amount of behavior? ______________ (abscissa or ordinate?)

(20) Which line on a graph is used to record the time that a behavior occurred? ______________ ______________

(9) Each entry on a graph is represented by a(n) ______________ that simultaneously records the amount of behavior and the time that the behavior occurred.

(27) Each graph label should be as ______________ as possible while still describing the numbers being recorded.

(19) If you were labeling the <u>number of people who are visiting with one another at a specific time of day</u>, you might shorten this to the one word ______________.

(8) The most attractive proportions for a simple graph require making the length of the ordinate and abscissa equal so that the graph will be ______________.

(18) To square a simple graph, divide the largest value of the ______________ by the largest value of the ______________.

(7) If the result of dividing the two numbers is a decimal, round off the resulting number to the next ______________ (larger, smaller) whole number.

(26) If the largest abscissa value in some data is 10 and the largest ordinate value is 28, what size steps should you use for the ordinate? ______________

(17) If the largest ordinate value of some data is 18 and the largest abscissa value is 5, what size steps would you use for the ordinate? ______________

(6) Mary's smiles are recorded for 5 days. You would label the ordinate ______________ ______________, and you would label the abscissa ______________. (Remember, smiles are the behavior.)

(16) When making a complex graph, you should square that portion of the graph that displays the condition containing the largest value of the ______________.

(5) To square a complex graph, you find the condition that has the largest value of the ______________, square just that portion of the graph, and then extend the abscissa to include the "time" variable for all conditions.

(25) When making a multiple-baseline graph, a new condition is considered to occur for all baselines at each time that the ______________ is applied to the behavior in one graph.

(15) To square a multiple-baseline graph, you should find the number of observations per condition and divide it into the largest value of the ______________ found for any of the behaviors.

(4) Remember, if you are graphing the number of scandals in government per year for 50 years, you would label the abscissa with the word ______________.

(24) Suppose that playing and talking are observed in a multiple-baseline design. If talking is observed prior to treatment for four days, then the first condition for both behaviors is ______________ days long. If playing is observed prior to treatment for eight days, then the second condition covers the period from the treatment of talking to the treatment of playing, or a total of ______________ days.

(14) If Behavior A is observed without treatment for three hours, and then the treatment is introduced for six hours, and if Behavior B is observed without treatment for six hours and then treatment is introduced for three hours, how long is each condition? ______________

(3) Don't forget, when labeling a complex graph, you ______________

(should, shouldn't) place labels for the baseline, treatment, and reversal (if any) at the top of the graph.

(13) Kifer and his colleagues (1974) observed the percentage of good negotiating behaviors used by a family before and after training in negotiating. They used what kind of design? ______________________

(23) Hersen and his colleagues (1973) used tokens to treat severe depression. To arrive at the scale in the graph in Figure 6-6 you should divide __________ by __________ and round (give the numbers).

(2) Hersen and his colleagues (1973) treated the depression of a patient by giving him tokens for responsible activity. They measured nondepressed behavior before, during, and after token giving. What design did they use? ______________________

(22) Sturgis and her colleagues (1978) studied the effect of biofeedback training on headache activity. Examine the graph of their results, Figure 6-4, and indicate how long each condition was. ______________________

(12) Sturgis and her colleagues (1978) studied the effect of biofeedback training on headaches. What is the largest number of hours of headaches in their graph, Figure 6-4? ______________________ To find the proper scale for their graph you should divide __________ by __________ and round.

(1) Kifer and his colleagues (1974) taught families to negotiate conflict situations. The scale for their graph, shown in Figure 6-5, was determined by dividing __________ by __________.

READING QUIZ ANSWERS

(1) 100; 3 (2) reversal (3) should (4) year (5) ordinate (6) smiles; days (7) larger (8) square (9) dot (10) ordinate (11) vertical (12) 18; 18; 5 (13) comparison (14) 3 (15) ordinate (16) ordinate (17) 4 (18) ordinate; abscissa (19) visitations (20) abscissa (21) abscissa (22) 5 (23) about 2.5 by 4 (24) 4; 4 (25) treatment (26) 3 (27) short

LESSON 6 EXAMPLES

Example #1

Frank had been trying to stop smoking for quite some time. Each time he started smoking again, his excuse was that he really didn't smoke that many cigarettes a day anyway. His roommate decided to count the number of cigarettes Frank put in his mouth and lit and then show him just how many cigarettes he was smoking when he was at home. The roommate kept track of the cigarettes smoked each day for six days. The results were 6, 8, 12, 2, 7, and 10. A conventional graph of these results is shown in Figure 6-7.

(25) The number of days for which data are plotted determines the largest unit on the abscissa; it is __________.

(12) The largest number to be plotted on the ordinate is determined by finding the largest number of cigarettes that Frank smoked; it is __________.

(37) The third step is to divide the largest ______________________ value by the largest ______________________ value to get the number __________.

(13) The fourth step is to round off the result of step three, if needed, to the next larger whole number; in this case, the number would be __________. The fifth and sixth steps are to draw and to label the graph; note how this was done.

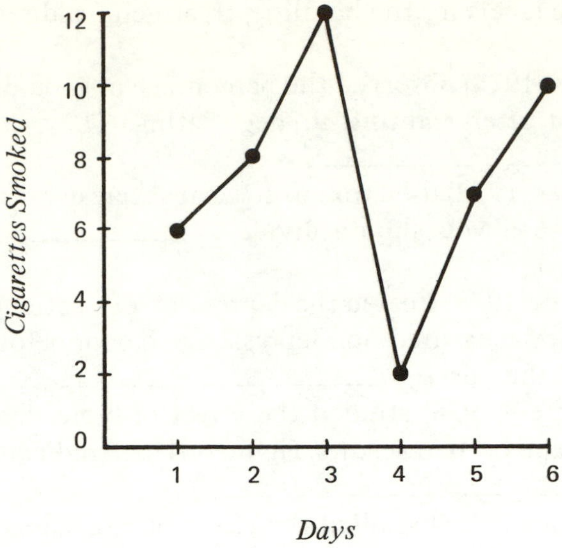

Figure 6–7. Frank's cigarette-smoking behavior (hypothetical data)

Example #2

Jamie, a brunette, took Political Science 230 because Willie had told her that the instructor favored pretty girls. On the first day of class, she noticed that the instructor spent most of his time talking with another girl, a blonde. She decided to find out during how many 30-second intervals the instructor and the blonde were talking. She observed for seven days and got the following results: 35, 65, 45, 70, 50, 45, and 60%. She stayed in the class, however, and found the instructor to be an excellent teacher. Label the graph of Jamie's observations in Figure 6–8.

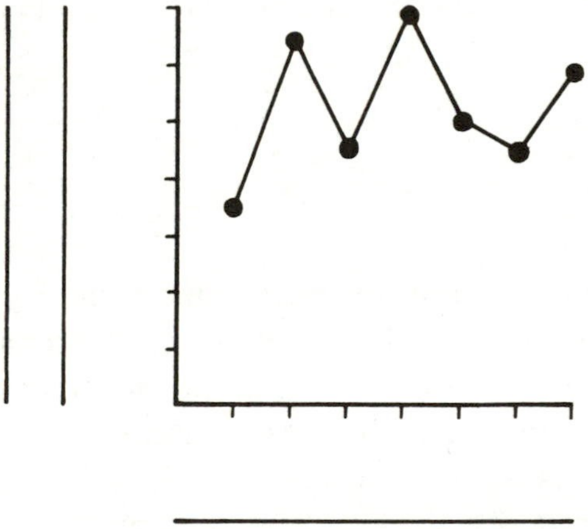

Figure 6–8. Percentage of class conversation between instructor and blonde

(24) The first step is to find the largest number of the abscissa; it is __________. The second step is to find the largest number of the ordinate; it is __________.

(11) The third step is to divide those two numbers; the result is __________. (Be sure that you are dividing by the right number.)

(36) The fourth step is to round off to a whole number, if needed; in this case, it is __________. The fifth and sixth steps are to label the abscissa and ordinate.

(35) The best label for the abscissa is the word "__________"; enter the label in the appropriate space in Figure 6–8.

Example #3

John was out of his seat causing trouble all day long in his third-grade class. The teacher decided to keep a record of his out-of-seat behavior for a school week. She recorded 10, 6, 7, 4, and 5 out-of-seat episodes. If you were to make a squared graph of the teacher's data, you would be able to answer the following:

(9) The result from step one is ____________ .
(22) The result from step two is ____________ .
(34) The procedure for step three is to divide ____________ by ____________ .
(10) The result of step three is ____________ .
(23) The result of step four is ____________ .

Example #4

Make a graph of John's out-of-seat episodes on the grid labeled Figure 6–9. Remember to number the abscissa first in one-step intervals. Then number the ordinate in steps determined by the outcome of step four in Example #3.

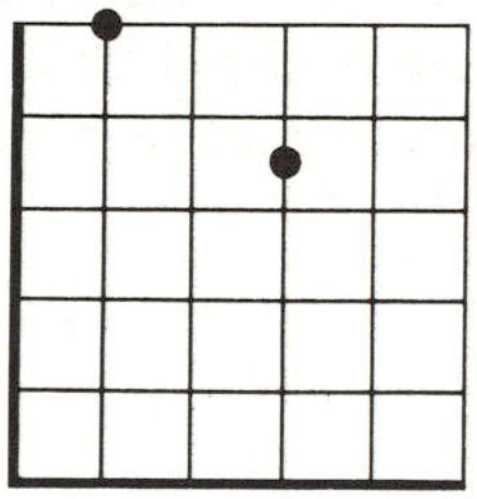

Figure 6–9. John's out-of-seat episodes

(8) Now place dots on the grid for each of the five entries. The first entry would be a "10" on day "1"; this entry has been made for you. The next entry would be a(n) ____________ on day ____________. Make this and all other entries.
(21) Label the abscissa as "________________________________."
(33) Label the ordinate as "________________________________."

Example #5

Mr. Norris collected the following information about Willie's performance on his daily assignment of ten math homework problems. The data represent the number of correctly worked problems: 4, 6, 6, 8, and 4 per day.

(7) The outcome for step three in squaring the graph of Willie's math homework would be ____________ .
(20) Step four would be to round off the result of step three to the whole number ____________.
(32) Label the abscissa "________________________________" and the ordinate "number of ________________________________ correct."

Example #6

Make a graph of Mr. Norris' data on Willie using Figure 6-10. (On following page.)

(31) Graph:

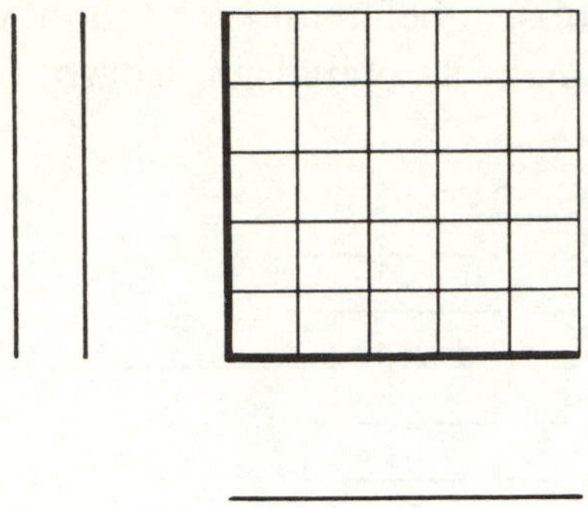

Figure 6-10. Willie's math homework scores

Example #7

Frank found that he smoked 6, 8, 12, 2, 7, and 10 cigarettes during a baseline period of observation. He decided he wanted to stop smoking, so he made a rule for himself: "Every time I take a cigarette, I will give my roommate a dollar." He found that he smoked 1, 0, 0, 1, 0, and 1 cigarettes during the next six days. His roommate suggested that he try smoking normally again without the one dollar fine. Frank then smoked 1, 4, 2, 3, 1, and 2 cigarettes. Figure 6-11 shows a graph of the experiment (notice the vertical lines between conditions).

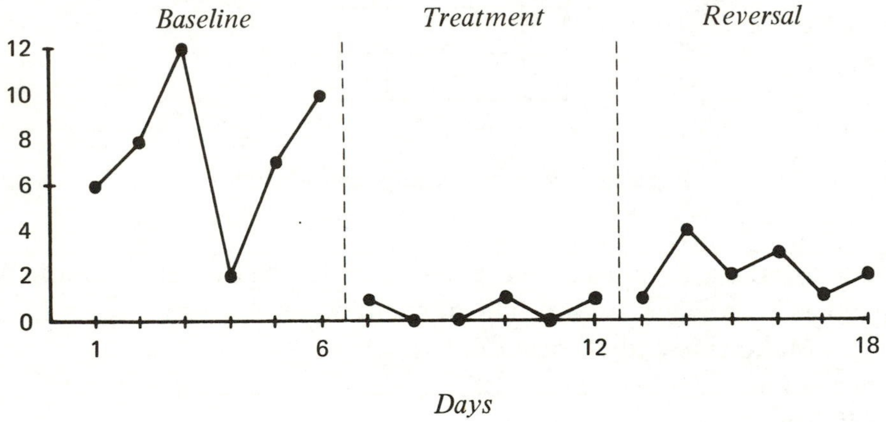

Figure 6-11. Frank's cigarette smoking during three experimental conditions

(19) To square a complex graph like this (more than one condition), find the condition with the highest value of the ordinate. In this case, the highest value of the ordinate occurred in the ________________ condition (use technical term).

(30) Now go through the six steps used to square a simple graph to find that the ordinate should increase in steps of ________.

(6) Note also the fact that each condition is labeled baseline, treatment, or ________________.

Example #8

John's out-of-seat behavior was really bothering the teacher. She spoke to John and asked him to please behave or his parents would be informed. John's out-of-seat behavior before the talk was 14, 8, 12, 14, and 8 episodes per day. After the talk, his out-of-seat behavior was 0, 1, 2, 8, and 12. Make a graph of this comparison design using Figure 6-12. (Remember, square the condition with the highest ordinate value.)

(38) Graph:

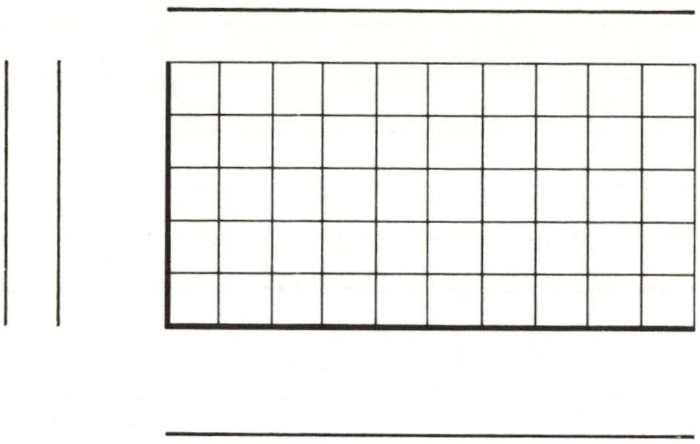

Figure 6-12. John's out-of-seat episodes

Example #9

Willie's homework in both math and social studies was poor, so Mr. Norris decided to experiment to see if he could help. First, he got a baseline on Willie's math and social-studies homework for five days. Then he announced to Willie that he could go out for a recess on any day that his math homework was 90% or better. After five more days, Mr. Norris told Willie that he could go out for an extra recess on any day that his social-studies homework was 90% or better. This lasted for five days also and meant that Willie could go out for two recesses if he got 90% or better in both subjects. The data are reported below:

Day:	1	2	3	4	5	6	7	8	9	10	11	12	13	14	15
Mathematics:	30	40	60	30	40	70	90	80	90	90	90	80	90	90	90
Social Studies:	50	40	60	30	50	20	60	50	40	20	90	70	90	80	100

(18) When making a multiple-baseline graph, you should first determine the length of each condition. The first treatment occurred after ____________ days; the next also after ____________ days. Thus each condition would be that long.

(5) The next step is to find the largest value of the ____________________________ for any behavior and proceed to square that portion of the graph and use the same scale for both graphs.

(29) For this graph the ordinate steps should increase by ____________.

Example #10

Make a graph of Mr. Norris' experiment with Willie's homework using Figure 6-13. (On following page.)

Example #11

John kept track of the number of times that his dancing partner forgot the new disco step. He counted 15 times. She disagreed, however, and said it had been only 12 times.

(17) Their reliability is ____________. If you consider this to be a new behavioral definition, then would this constitute an acceptable level? ____________

Example #12

Kevin was into jogging. For the first five weeks he jogged 1, 4, 2, 3, and 2 times. His wife then

(4) Graph:

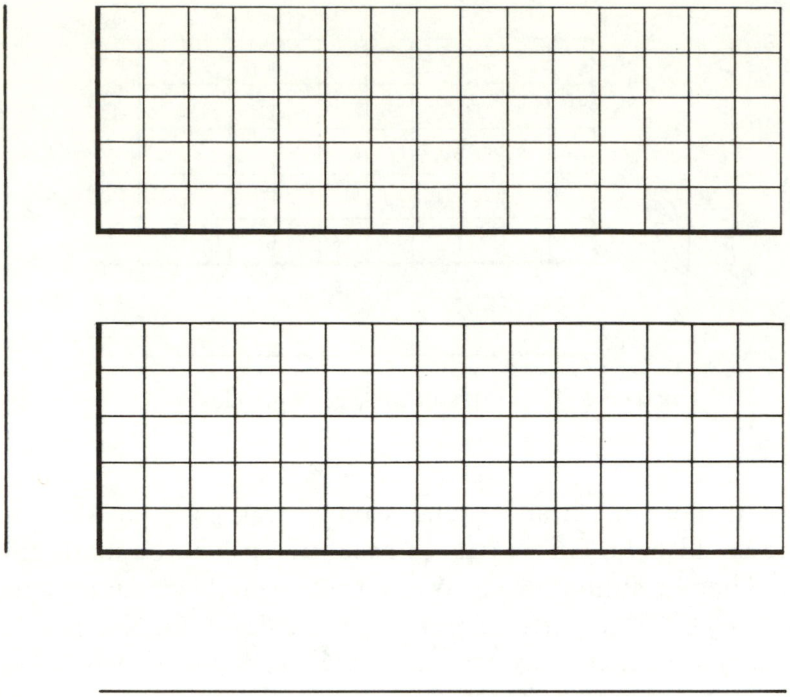

Figure 6–13. Willie's homework problems

joined him for five weeks and he jogged 3, 5, 7, 7, and 6 times. However, she got sick and for the next five weeks, jogging along, he jogged 6, 5, 3, 2, and 3 times. Graph the experiment using Figure 6–14.

(28) Graph:

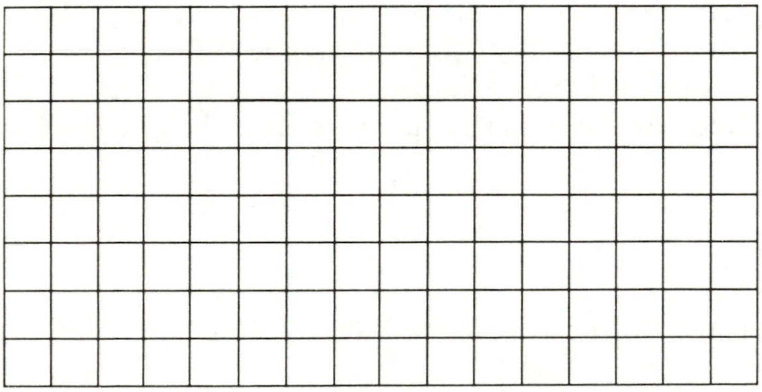

Figure 6–14. Times per week that Kevin jogged

Example #13

If a teacher is having trouble with his kids hitting each other, an observer might note whether anyone was hitting during each 30-second interval of the class.

(3) The observer would be using what method of observing? ______________________ recording

Example #14

Sam checked every 15 minutes to see whether any of his students were studying.

(16) He was using what method of direct observation? ______________________ recording

Example #15

Jane felt that the pledges were not doing enough for the seniors during their weekly Saturday work. So she made up a list of services to provide to the seniors to improve the appearance of their clothing: shine their shoes, wash their clothes, press their blouses, and so on. She also made up a list of services to keep the seniors' rooms looking nicer. For five weeks she simply observed the percentage of the clothing checklist and the percentage of the cleaning checklist completed. Then she proposed a rule that for each clothing item not done, all pledges be fined $1. She then observed the percentage of items completed for five weeks. Finally she proposed that the pledges be fined $1 for each cleaning item not done. By the way, half the pledges moved out after the "experiment." The data were

Week:	1	2	3	4	5	6	7	8	9	10	11	12	13	14	15
Clothing:	40	30	50	20	40	80	90	95	90	85	95	90	95	90	100
Cleaning:	60	50	40	60	50	40	30	50	60	40	90	95	85	90	95

Make a graph of the experiment using Figure 6-15.

(27) Graph:

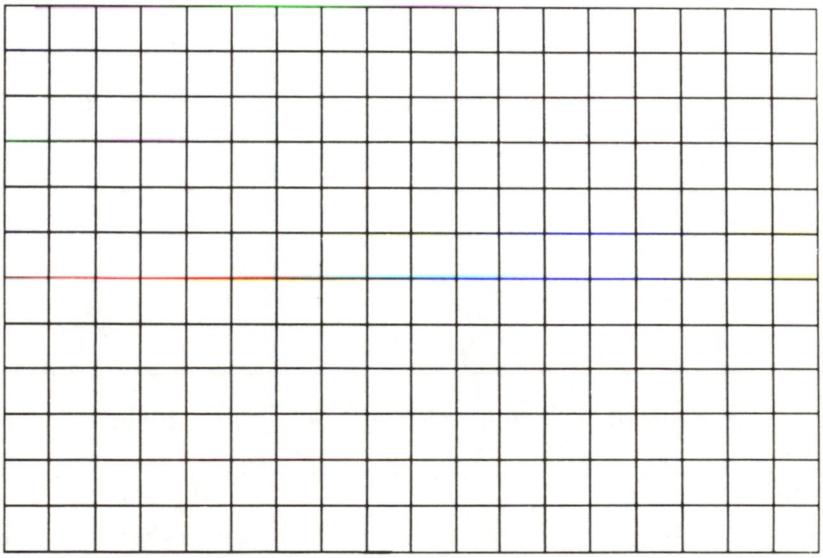

Figure 6-15. Amount of work done in a sorority

Example #16

(2) If John decided that good interview behavior is "looking the interviewer in the eye and answering each question clearly and politely," then the statement in quotes would be called a(n) ______________________.

Example #17

(15) The record of class attendance prior to the strike at Reagan College is technically a(n) ______________________.

Example #18

John burped the following number of times at dinner: 23, 15, 19, 13, 19, and 20. Make a graph of John's burps using Figure 6-16. (On following page.)

(26) Graph:

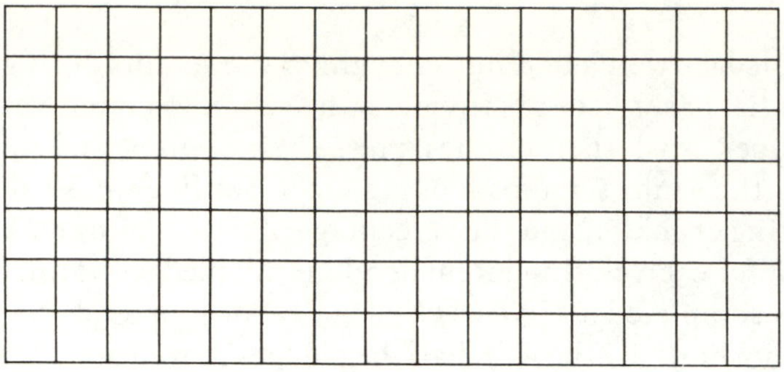

Figure 6-16. John's frequency of burping

Example #19

Delores was observed to study the following number of hours per week: 3, 7, 4, 6, and 9. Her father, concerned that his money was being wasted, insisted that she consult with the school psychiatrist in the hopes that she would take her studying more seriously. After seeing the psychiatrist she was observed to study the following number of hours: 4, 7, 6, 3, and 5. Make a graph of Delores' studying using Figure 6–17.

(1) Graph:

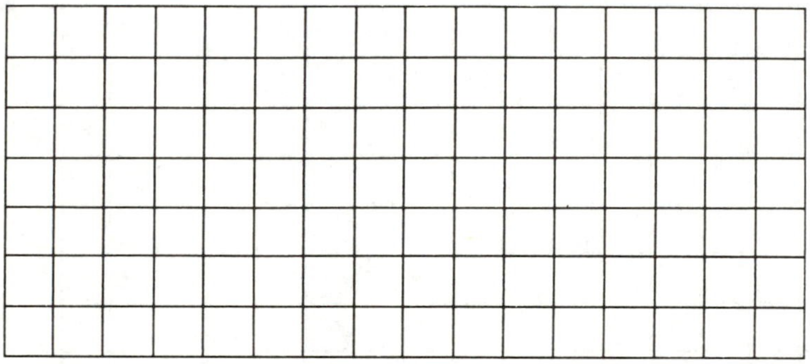

Figure 6-17. Number of hours that Delores studied

Example #20

(14) If Louise observed the interrupting behavior of Archie while she was being polite and again after she started to ignore him, she would be using a design that couldn't rule out __________ ______________________________ causes for a change in his interrupting behavior.

EXAMPLE ANSWERS

(1) see graph* (2) behavioral definition (3) interval (4) see graph* (5) ordinate (6) reversal (7) 1.6 (8) 6; 2 (see graph*) (9) 5 (10) 2 (11) 10 (12) 12 (13) 2 (14) alternative (15) baseline (16) time-sample (17) 80%; yes (18) 5; 5 (19) baseline (20) 2 (21) day (22) 10 (23) 2 (24) 7; 70 (25) 6 (26) see graph* (27) see graph* (28) see graph* (29) 20 (30) 2 (31) see graph* (32) day; problems (33) out-of-seat episodes (34) 10; 5 (35) class (or day) (36) 10 (37) ordinate; abscissa; 2 (38) see graph*

*Graphs on following pages

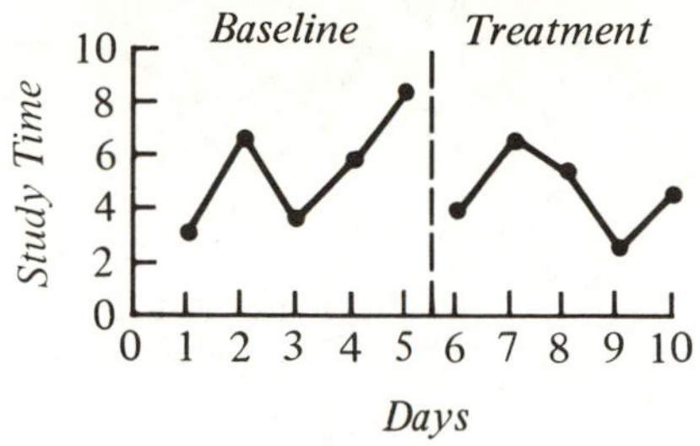
Baseline
Treatment
Study Time
10
8
6
4
2
0
0 1 2 3 4 5 6 7 8 9 10
Days

(1)

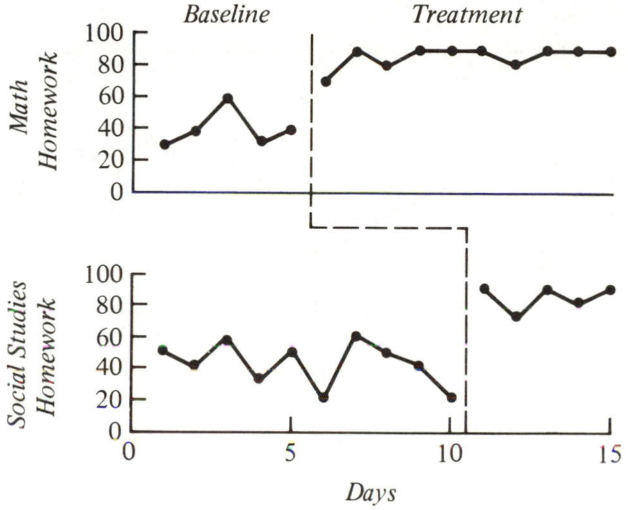
Baseline
Treatment
Math Homework
100
80
60
40
20
0
Social Studies Homework
100
80
60
40
20
0
0 5 10 15
Days

(4)

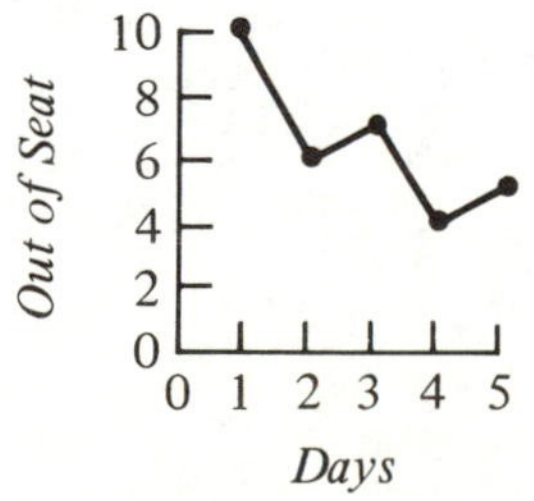
Out of Seat
10
8
6
4
2
0
0 1 2 3 4 5
Days

(8)

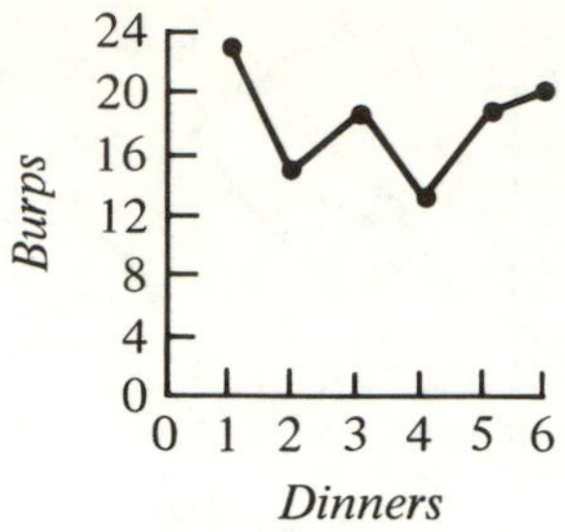
Burps
24
20
16
12
8
4
0
0 1 2 3 4 5 6
Dinners

(26)

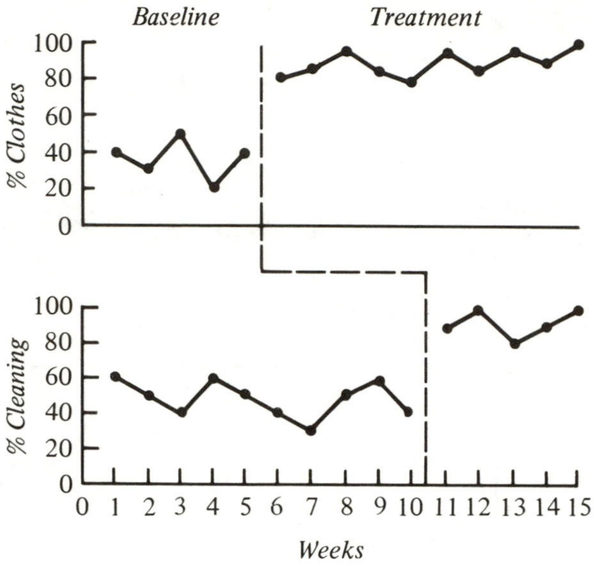
Baseline
Treatment
% Clothes
100
80
60
40
20
0
% Cleaning
100
80
60
40
20
0
0 1 2 3 4 5 6 7 8 9 10 11 12 13 14 15
Weeks

(27)

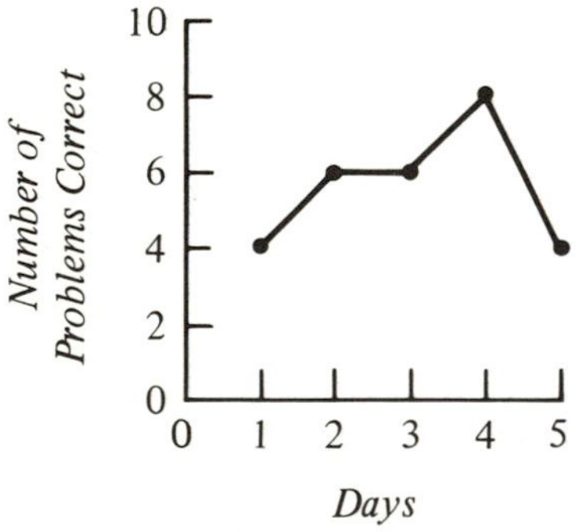
Number of
Problems Correct
10
8
6
4
2
0
0 1 2 3 4 5
Days

(31)

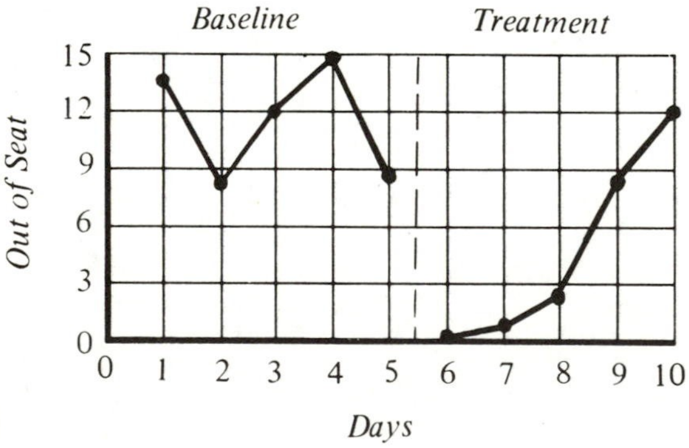
Baseline
Treatment
Out of Seat
15
12
9
6
3
0
0 1 2 3 4 5 6 7 8 9 10
Days

(38)

Lesson 7

Review of Behavioral Methods

Behavior analysis is directed toward finding practical treatment procedures that can be proven effective in changing behavior that is considered socially important. This research direction requires at least four steps. First, the human activity of interest must be defined in behavioral terms. Second, an observational procedure must be developed that is capable of measuring the behavior. Third, the behavioral definition and observation method must be capable of producing reliable observations. Fourth, a treatment that effectively modifies the behavior must be found. Fifth, the effect of the treatment procedure on the behavior must be demonstrated by means of an experimental design that can rule out alternative explanations of the behavioral change.

The first stage of behavioral analysis is to translate the ambiguous language of everyday speech concerning human activity into behavioral language. Sometimes, everyday language is already behavioral; all the behavior analyst has to do is make a more explicit definition. "Crying" is already directly behavioral; all the behavior modifier has to do is specify when a vocalization should be considered a cry (for example, how loud it must be). Sometimes, our everyday language is implicitly behavioral. "Studying" obviously describes what a person is doing. However, the behavior analyst must specify aspects of the behavior that are valid components of studying (for example, head orientation or ability to answer content questions).

Often, however, our everyday language is vague and does not seem to refer to behavior at all. For example, someone's "understanding" of an idea refers to something in his or her mind; "understanding" does not seem to relate directly to behavior. However, we can define the idea and then judge whether someone understands. Can the person explain the idea according to our definition and apply it to a new situation that hasn't been explicitly taught? Thus, if someone could explain "reliability" and could apply that idea to a situation that he or she was not taught, such as the observation of conversational skills, we would conclude that the person "understands" reliability.

Behavioral definitions are the result of behavior analysts becoming interested in a particular form of human activity and translating that activity into behavioral terms. Such translations have produced good behavioral definitions for such diverse activities as creativity (Goetz & Baer, 1973), nervous tension (Budzynski & Stoyva, 1969), and communal living (Miller & Feallock, 1974). Without doubt, many areas of human activity that are not now considered "behavioral" will be translated into behavioral terms in the years to come.

The second stage of behavior analysis is to select an effective and practical method of observation. If the behavior leaves a permanent product, then outcome recording might be an effective method of observation. If the behavior occurs in discrete episodes, then we might count the episodes as they occur. If the behavior occurs for long periods that cannot be continuously observed or if there are a number of people to be observed simultaneously, then we might use a

Note to instructors: The Instructor's Manual for this text (available from the publisher) contains four review-exam forms for this and the other unit reviews (Lessons 15, 21, and 25).

time-sampling method. Or if the behavior tends to be ongoing, we can use an interval-recording approach. Whatever approach we use, the method of observation must be capable of being directly applied to the activities specified in the behavioral definition.

The third stage of behavior analysis is to determine whether the results of the observation are reliable. If they are not, then the data are of no meaning or use to other people. If the data are reliable, then a way of viewing a human activity that may lead to results that can be useful and interesting to others will have been established. At this stage the social validity must be determined if the behavioral definition is not intuitively valid.

If the behavioral observations are not reliable enough, the behavior analyst has several options. He or she can undertake more extensive training of the observers in an attempt to resolve ambiguities in the behavioral definition or he or she can attempt to revise the behavioral definition so that it is clearer and produces higher reliability.

The fourth stage of behavior analysis requires that the analyst find a treatment that will produce desired changes in the behavior being studied. This treatment can be anything that is capable of objective specification—a sit-in, a sensitivity-training session, a reward, a new training method, or even meditation. If a treatment can be specified, it can be tested to see whether it really works. Treatments always involve some alteration of the person's physical environment.

The fifth stage of proving whether or not a treatment works requires the use of an experimental design that rules out alternative explanations for any behavioral change, such as a reversal design or a multiple-baseline design. If we find that a behavioral change disappears after the treatment is stopped or that the same behavioral change occurs in two behaviors only after the treatment has been introduced, we can be relatively sure that we have a method that will effectively change the behavior in question.

Behavior analysis research has several characteristic features. First, behavior analysts use direct observation of behavior. This observation is undertaken by trained observers who use carefully developed behavioral definitions. Behavior analysts seldom rely on information that is obtained by asking individuals to describe their own behavior, because they are not trained observers, they do not use a specified behavioral definition, and they rely on memory. Thus, questionnaires and interviews are not used to gather information about a person's behavior. It should be added that questionnaires and interviews may be used to find out what individuals say about their behavior, the behavior of others, or the procedures of behavior analysts. The use of such devices may be interpreted as a method for obtaining an outcome record of people's verbal behavior with respect to a certain question.

Second, behavior analysis research is usually characterized by the use of careful experimental designs capable of eliminating alternative explanations of any behavioral changes. The use of such controlled designs permits the evaluation of the effectiveness of behavioral procedures, which provides a constant source of information about the need to change procedures that are not effective.

GLOSSARY

Helpful hint: You can review the ideas of this unit by reading the definitions of the following 19 terms. Each term was introduced, defined, and illustrated in the preceding unit. As you review the terms, see if you can define them before looking at the definition, and see if you can think of an example for each term.

The **abscissa** is the horizontal line of a graph, used to record the time that behavior occurred.

The **baseline** is the record of a behavior prior to the use of a method to modify it.

Behavior analysis is a behavioral science that develops practical techniques for producing changes in socially significant behaviors. It has three important characteristics: (a) it focuses on behavior; (b) it studies environmental influences on behavior; and (c) it uses single-subject designs to experiment with the effect of different environmental arrangements.

A **behavioral definition** is a statement that specifies exactly what behavior is to be observed.

A **comparison design** is an experimental design in which just baseline and treatment conditions are examined. Its weakness is that it doesn't rule out alternative explanations of an effect.

A **direct observation** is an observation that is personally seen (or heard) by the observer and immediately recorded.

Event recording is a method of observation in which a response is recorded if a complete behavioral episode is observed.

Interval recording is a method of observation in which a response is recorded if some part of a behavioral episode is observed within one of a series of continuous intervals.

A **multiple-baseline design** is an experimental design in which a treatment is introduced at different times (according to a staggered schedule) to determine its effect on two or more behaviors in one individual or on two or more individuals with the same behavior.

An **ordinate** is the vertical line of a graph, used to display the amount or rate of behavior.

Outcome recording is a method of observation in which a response occurrence is recorded if the result of a behavioral episode is observed.

Reliability is the extent to which two independent observers agree on their observations, computed by the formula A/(A+D), in which A stands for the number of agreements and D stands for the number of disagreements. A quotient of 90% or more is acceptable unless the response definition is a new and difficult one, in which case 80% or more is acceptable.

A **reversal design** is an experimental design in which the behavior is compared during baseline, during treatment, and then during a reversal to baseline.

Social validity is the use of outside judges to determine whether a behavioral definition is a valid definition of a commonly used behavioral term.

Squaring a simple graph is a process performed by dividing the ordinate by the abscissa, rounding the result up to the next whole number, and labeling the ordinate with numbers that increase in steps equal to the number.

Squaring a complex graph is a process performed when making a graph with more than one condition by selecting the condition with the highest value of the ordinate and squaring the graph for that condition. Use the same scale for the rest of the graph.

Squaring a multiple-baseline graph involves squaring the condition containing the largest value of the ordinate and applying that scale to the graphs for all baselines. A condition is defined as beginning with the introduction of the treatment for any of the baselines and ending with the introduction of the treatment for another baseline.

Time-sample recording is a method of observation in which a response occurrence is recorded if some part of a behavioral episode is observed within one of a series of discontinuous intervals.

A **treatment** is any method that is used in an attempt to modify a behavior.

ADDITIONAL READINGS

Bachrach, A. J. *Psychological research: An introduction.* New York: Random House, 1962. This book is an easily read introduction to the philosophy of behavioral research.

Skinner, B. F. *Cumulative record.* New York: Appleton-Century-Crofts, 1958. This book is an excellent introduction for the advanced student to Skinner's approach to the methods of behavioral science.

UNIT ONE PRACTICE REVIEW

The following questions provide a thorough review of the concepts in Unit I. By answering these questions and checking your answers with the answer key on page 68–69 you can prepare for your review exam.

(36) Vera wasn't getting anywhere with James; he hadn't even kissed her yet. She decided to try an experiment and wear musk-oil perfume. James now kisses Vera on every date. What type of experimental design is this? ______________________

(63) Ben kept track of the number of homework questions he got right for both math and business for three weeks. He then decided that he would not watch TV until he had completed his math homework as carefully as possible. He recorded the number right for three more weeks. Finally, he made a personal rule that he would not watch TV until he had also completed his business homework as carefully as possible. The record of his experiment is:

Weeks:	1	2	3	4	5	6	7	8	9
Math:	0	1	0	8	7	9	9	8	9
Business:	2	3	1	3	2	2	7	9	8

If he were to graph his experiment, the steps on his ordinate would increase by ________ units. (Check your answer to this one!)

(44) Four children were being observed for their writing behavior. The observer divided the one-hour writing period into 240 intervals of 15 seconds each. The observer watched the first child for the first 15 seconds, the second child during the next 15 seconds, and so on. Thus, he observed each child's writing for one 15-second period per minute. His method of observing is ________________________ recording.

(29) A statement that specifies exactly what to observe is called a(n) ________________ ________ .

(51) Ken was intensely interested in nervousness. He observed his professor's displays of nervous pacing during lectures by breaking the lecture period down into 150 consecutive 20-second periods of time and recording whether any nervous pacing occurred during each 20-second period. Ken was using ________________________ recording.

(6) The method of observation that involves observing someone's behavior for 10 seconds at several randomly scheduled times is called ________________________ recording.

(2) In the field of behavior analysis, any procedure designed to change the rate of a behavior is called a(n) ________________________ .

(10) If Dave observed the amount of studying that Pam did for three weeks, then started urging her to study more while continuing to observe the amount of studying she did for another three weeks, and then finally stopped urging her to study but observed her studying for another three weeks, he would be using what experimental design? ________________

(62) Behavior analysis was founded by ________________________ .

(16) Mr. Warren, a high school teacher, was quite negative in his class. Several of his students decided to observe him to find out how much of the time he was negative. They made their observations in consecutive 15-second blocks throughout the day. They found out that he was negative 75% of the time. What method of observation did they use? ________________ ________________ recording

(8) The use of outside judges to determine whether a behavioral definition is acceptable to nonbehaviorists is called determining the ________________________ of the definition.

(14) The vertical line on a graph is called the ________________________ .

(42) Suppose that Diane developed a behavioral definition of assertiveness. She had an outside group rate the assertiveness of individuals observed by means of a videotape in which some individuals exhibited a high level of what she defined as assertive behavior and others exhibited a low level. If she compared the outside group's ratings with her own observations to see whether they were using a similar definition of assertiveness, she would be determining the ________________________ of her definition.

(30) The teacher found that Mary was near other children the following percent of the time: 5, 20, 15, 10, and 15%. She found that when she praised Mary for being near other children, the percentages rose to 25, 30, 55, 75, and 60%. And when she stopped praising Mary, she found 35, 20, 10, 20, and 15%. To square a graph of this information, the steps on the ordinate should increase by ________ .

(20) Dave studied for 15, 20, 10, 20, and 15 minutes. Then he made a rule for himself that he wouldn't go out unless he had studied at least 30 minutes. He then studied 35, 40, 30, 45, and

50 minutes. The next week he stopped using the rule, with the following results: 25, 15, 10, 5, and 15 minutes. Make a graph of this experiment using Figure 7-1 (below).

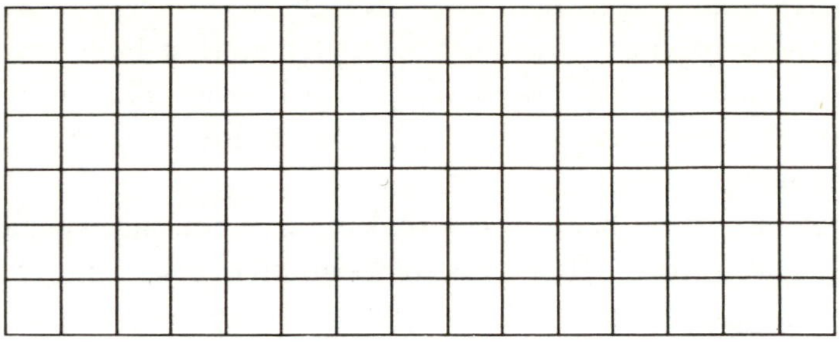

Figure 7-1. Grid for question #20

(52) If a behavior is observed before treatment and during treatment to see whether the treatment has any effect, we say that a(n) ________________ design is used.

(58) The simplest form of the time-sampling method of observation involves observing behavior during a series of ________________ intervals.

(21) To square a simple graph, you should divide the highest value of the ________________ by the highest value of the ________________.

(61) The widespread publication of behavior analysis results began in what year? ________

(15) Direct observation requires that the observer personally see the behavior and immediately ________________ it.

(53) When Damon counts the number of times that Janice compliments him, he is using what method of observation? ________________ recording

(38) If John observes Mary's smiling during 75 consecutive time periods, each of 15 seconds' duration, he is using what method of observation? ________________ recording

(31) Observing for a behavior during one brief interval at several times of the day would be called ________________ recording.

(39) Two observers are counting the number of times a person smiles. One counts 43, while the other counts 50. What is the reliability? ________ Is it acceptable? ________

(11) Dr. Petersen developed a procedure that helped people be nice to one another. The procedure approached being nice as a behavior; it programmed the people in the environment to encourage niceness through training and a reward system. Dr. Petersen used a multiple-baseline design to evaluate experimentally the success of the procedure. Dr. Petersen's work would be an example of what behavioral science? ________________

(9) The basic formula for computing reliability is ________________.

(1) John was a pretty good golfer, scoring an average of 85. He decided to see what effect daily practice would have on his score. After five weeks of practice his scores had decreased to 78 on the average. He stopped practicing when school started again and noticed that his scores slowly crept up until he was averaging about 83. What experimental design was John inadvertently using? ________________

(24) Behavior analysis is a behavioral science that develops practical techniques for producing changes in socially significant ________________.

(7) May observed Professor Brainbuster on Thursday to see how many chauvinistic comments he made. She counted 18. April observed Professor Brainbuster on Friday and found that he made 20 such comments. Can you conclude that May and April were making reliable observations of Professor Brainbuster's chauvinistic comments? ________

(5) Setting the scale of the ordinate by dividing the ordinate by the abscissa is called ______________________________________ a graph.

(12) An experimental design in which two or more behaviors are examined is called a(n) ______________________________________ design.

(47) The instructor decided to count the number of times that Dale spoke in class. She found that Dale spoke 25 times during one period. Another observer, however, counted only 19 times. Compute their reliability: ____________. If this is a new behavioral definition, is the reliability acceptable? ____________

(13) The statement that "assertive behavior is making eye contact, speaking loud enough to be clearly heard, and asking the other person to change his or her behavior" is called a(n) ______________________________________ of assertiveness.

(49) One criterion for a good behavioral definition is that the observations be based on what the observer can see and immediately record. Any procedure that incorporates those features is called ______________________________________ .

(4) Mary's teacher and another observer made the following observations of Mary's nearness to other children (where N stands for near and F stands for far):

Teacher: F N F F F F F N F F F F F F F F N N F F F F F F N
Other: F N F F F F F N N F F F F F F F N N F F N F F F F

What is the reliability of these observations? ____________ Is this an acceptable level if the behavioral definition is a new one? ____________

(48) The horizontal line on a graph is called the ______________________________________ .

(32) The method of observing that counts complete occurrences of behavior is called ______________________________________ recording.

(17) Name an experimental design that rules out alternative explanations of any observed change in behavior. ______________________________________

(40) Mary was observed to talk each day with the other children in her class the following number of times: 2, 7, 2, 9, 7, 1, and 5. Make a graph of these data on the grid in Figure 7-2.

Graph:

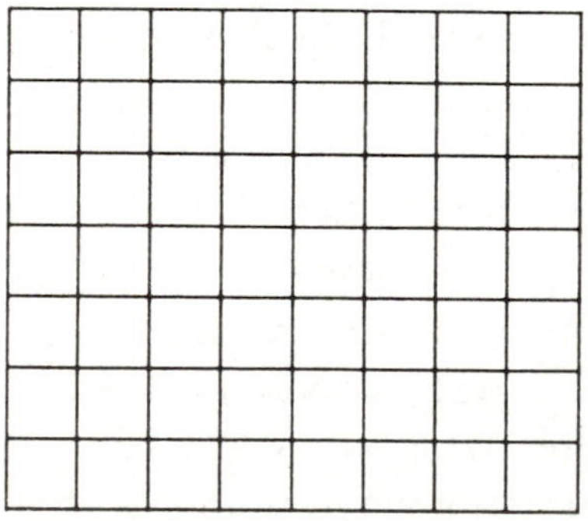

Figure 7-2. Grid for question 40

(55) When squaring a complex graph, divide the largest value of the ______________________ by the number of observations in that condition.

(3) If a behavior is observed during many consecutive short periods of time, the method of observation is called ______________________________________ recording.

(54) A good experimental design is one that can rule out ______________________________ causes of any observed change in behavior.

(33) Vera wasn't getting anywhere with James; he hadn't even kissed her yet. She decided to try an experiment and wear some musk-oil perfume to turn James on. If Vera kept a record of the number of kisses from James before she started to use the musk oil, this record would be called a(n) ________________.

(22) Professor Mills made up a checklist of behaviors that a good teaching assistant should perform every time that a student came up to obtain a quiz form. The checklist included such behaviors as greeting the student by name, asking the student if he or she has a question, and so on. The professor then watched every new assistant greet several students and recorded each behavior if it occurred. He was using ________________ recording.

(35) The abscissa of a behavioral graph is used to record ________________.

(18) Two young Black men were observing a policeman as he covered his beat to see how many times he called a brother a "boy." They wrote their observations down immediately. What method of direct observation were they using? ________________ recording

(25) A group of students, during the early 1960s, tried using "sit-ins" to desegregate a Northern suburb. Before starting their protests, however, they sent ten Black students into three restaurants every day for a week to test whether they would be served. None were served. They began a sit-in at Restaurant A, informing the manager of their intentions. They conducted their sit-ins during the lunch and dinner rush periods. Their "testers" would then go in during other periods of the day to see whether the sit-ins were having any effect. The testers continued going to the other two restaurants. After ten days Restaurant A changed its policy and served the testers. The students then went after Restaurants B and C. The design that they used is an example of a(n) ________________ design.

(50) Reliability for new behavioral definitions should equal or exceed __________ %.

(26) An experimental design that studies a behavior before the treatment, during the treatment, and after the treatment is called a(n) ________________ design.

(34) About one student per week joined the new record-buying co-op. Then the co-op decided to try a newspaper advertisement. As a result, about 20 students per week joined. The members concluded that advertising pays because the ad succeeded in getting many new members. This is not a good experimental design because it doesn't ________________ ________________.

(27) A measure of the amount of agreement between two observers is called ________________.

(56) If two observers find the following patterns of a behavior, compute their reliability: __________. Is it acceptable? __________

First observer:	O N O O O O O O O O
Second observer:	O N O O O N O O O O

(28) In a multiple-baseline design, if Behavior A is observed for 12 weeks before any procedure is used to change its rate; if Behavior B is observed for 24 weeks before the same procedure is used; and if Behavior B is observed for another 12 weeks, how long is each "condition" in this experiment? ________________

(57) Behavior analysis has the following important characteristics: (a) it focuses on <u>behavior</u>; (b) it studies the ________________ influences on behavior; (c) it uses single-subject designs to ________________ with different environmental arrangements.

(43) Data recorded for a behavior prior to an attempt to change the rate of that behavior are called a(n) ________________.

(59) Jenny decided to record the number of pieces of junk that her slobbish roommate piled on her

desk and bed for two weeks and then to confront her roommate with this information. She showed her roommate data proving that an average of 12 objects per day had been left in Jenny's part of the room. Her roommate was surprised by the data, said that she was really sorry, and promised to stop. What is Jenny's talking with her roommate called? ______________________________

(19) If we had to graph the data 18, 8, 6, 3, 9, 2, and 14, we should make the numbers of the vertical divisions increase in steps of ____________ units.

(37) Name an experimental design that does not rule out alternative explanations of any observed change in behavior. ______________________________

(45) Harry, a poor reader, read 25, 15, 30, 20, and 10% of the time during the first week of observation. During the next week, Harry was told that he could stay at recess for an extra ten minutes on any day that he read a lot. He read 60, 85, 80, 95, and 85% of the time that week. During the third week, Harry was not permitted extra recess time. He read 55, 35, 10, 25, and 15% of the time that week. If the third week of the experiment had not been conducted, the first and second weeks would be an example of a(n) ______________________________ design.

(41) The method that observes a result of behavior is called ______________________________ recording.

(46) Wade observed Tom's rate of smiling and his rate of making positive comments for a week. Wade then had a long talk with Tom about the importance of trying to be happy and smiling once in a while. Wade observed Tom's smiling after their talk, and he continued to observe Tom's positive comments for a second week. Finally, Wade had a long talk with Tom about the importance of looking for the good side of things and telling others your positive feelings. Wade then observed Tom's rate of making positive comments after their talk and he continued observing Tom's smiling behavior for a third week. Tom is a changed person due to those two talks. What experimental design did Wade use to investigate the effect of his two talks on Tom's smiling behavior and on his behavior of making positive comments? ______________________________

(23) The teacher and another observer decided to measure the amount of time that Mary was studying. Since they weren't able to make continuous observations, they checked Mary every half hour and noted whether she was studying. Their observations the first day were:

Teacher:	Y Y N N N N N N Y N
Other:	N Y N N N N N N Y Y

What is the reliability? ____________ Is this acceptable for a new behavioral definition? ____________

(60) Mary's teacher did an experiment on Mary's studying and puzzlemaking. The percent of studying during baseline was 20, 5, 15, 25, and 10. The treatment observations were 45, 75, 80, 70, 85, 85, 90, 85, 100, and 80%. The percent of time spent puzzlemaking during baseline was 5, 20, 30, 40, 15, 20, 40, 30, 20, and 40%. The treatment observations were 60, 75, 90, 95, and 85%. Make a graph of this experiment using the grid in Figure 7-3. (On opposite page.)

PRACTICE REVIEW ANSWERS

(1) reversal (2) treatment (3) interval (4) 88%; yes (5) squaring (6) time sample (7) no (8) social validity (9) A/(A+D) (10) reversal (11) behavior analysis (12) multiple baseline (13) behavioral definition (14) ordinate (15) record (16) interval (17) reversal or multiple baseline (18) event (19) 3 (20) see graph (21) ordinate; abscissa (22) event (23) 80%; yes (24) behavior (25) multiple baseline (26) reversal (27) reliability (28) 12 (29) behavioral definition (30) 15 (31) time sample (32) event (33) baseline (34) rule out alternatives (35) time (36) comparison (37) comparison (38) interval (39) 86%;

no (40) see graph (41) outcome (42) social validity (43) baseline (44) time sample (45) comparison (46) multiple baseline (47) 76%; no (48) abscissa (49) direct observation (50) 80% (51) interval (52) comparison (53) event (54) alternative (55) ordinate (56) 90%; yes (57) environmental; experiment (58) discontinuous (59) treatment (60) see graph (61) 1970 (62) Skinner (63) 3

(60) Graph:

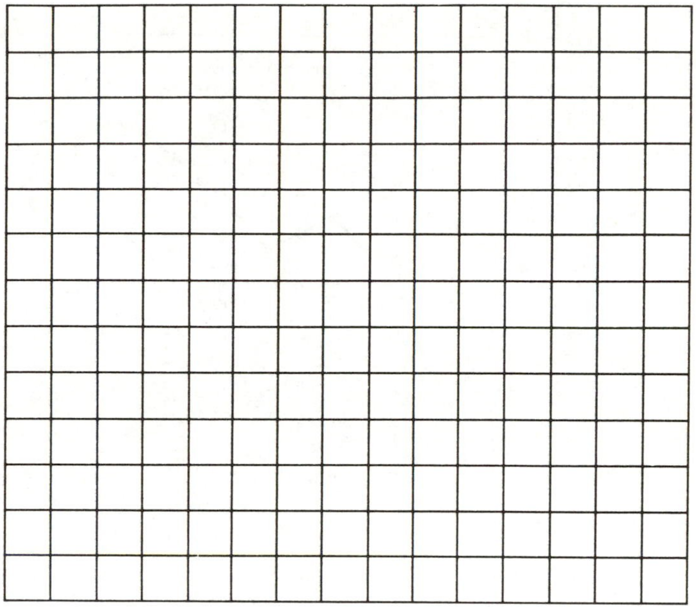

Figure 7-3. Grid for question 60

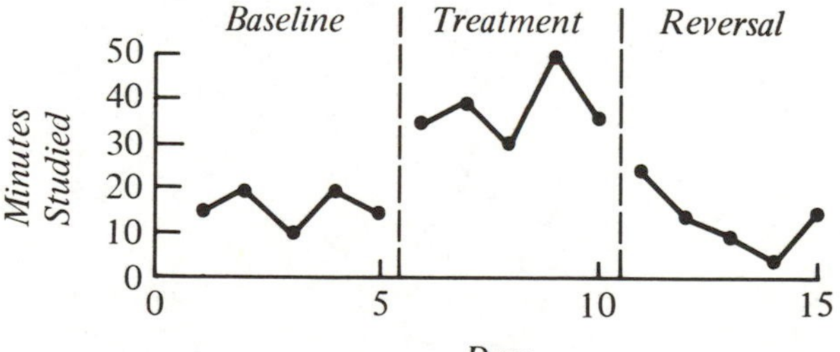

(20)

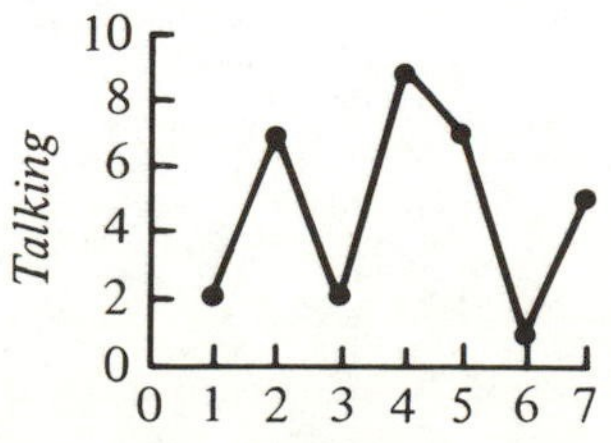

(40)

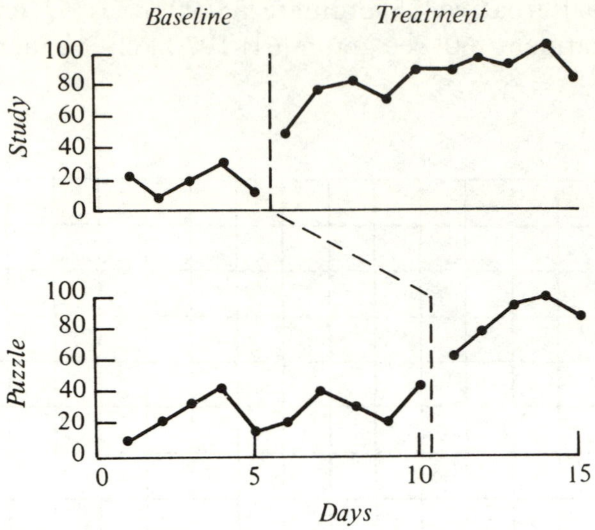
Baseline
Treatment
Study
100
80
60
40
20
0
Puzzle
100
80
60
40
20
0
0
5
10
15
Days

(60)

UNIT TWO
Reinforcement Control

Lesson 8

Reinforcement of Everyday Behaviors

In an earlier part of the book it was stated that behavior analysis is characterized by the fact that it studies environmental influences on behavior. This lesson introduces "reinforcement," the major concept that lies at the heart of most environmental influences that create and maintain behavior. Other lessons in Unit 2 will help you to fully understand complex characteristics of reinforcement and related concepts. Unit 3 will explain how reinforcement can cause other aspects of the behavioral environment to become powerful determinants of behavior. Finally, Unit 4 will teach you about the concept of "punishment," a major concept that lies at the heart of many environmental influences that reduce and destroy behavior. Thus, with this lesson you move from studying the methodology of behavior analysis to studying the scientific knowledge about everyday human behavior that has resulted from employing that methodology.

The term *reinforcer* is similar in meaning to the everyday word "reward" except that it is used in a precise technical sense that makes it different in an extremely important way. Unlike "reward," which refers to any event that, in the speaker's subjective opinion, should be liked by its recipient, "reinforcer" refers only to an event that has been proven through observation to effectively modify the behavior of its recipient. You might think of a reinforcer as a "proven reward."

The behavioral definition of **reinforcer** is any event that (1) follows the occurrences of a behavior and (2) increases the probability (or rate) of that behavior.[1] The first part of the definition stresses that a reinforcer must be a consequence—it must come after the behavior. The second part of the definition stresses that a reinforcer must be effective—it must cause the person to produce more of the event through an increase in how often he or she responds. It is this second part that makes a reinforcer like a proven reward.

Reinforcement refers to the procedure used to increase the probability (or rate) of a behavior by arranging for a reinforcer to follow it. Thus reinforcement refers to the procedure in

[1]When you read the second part of the definition you should understand it to mean two things that are not specified. It means that the probability of the behavior is increased over its baseline level when the event was not following the behavior. And it means that the probability is increased for the duration of the period during which the event follows the behavior, thereby ruling out temporary increases due to factors other than a reinforcing effect.

> DON'T BE A NIXON—USE REINFORCEMENT CORRECTLY
>
> The former president [Nixon] and Kissinger were sitting in the Oval Office of the White House discussing policy matters when King Timahoe, Nixon's Irish setter, came in and began chewing on the rug. The president commanded him to stop. King Timahoe kept right on chewing. The president commanded again. More chewing. Finally, Nixon opened his desk drawer, took out a dog biscuit and gave it to King Timahoe.
>
> "Mr. President," said Kissinger, "you have taught that dog to chew the rug." (Valariani, R. Pet journal: That Kissinger dog. *Ladies' Home Journal,* January 1976, 93, 126–129. Noted by Michael C. Roberts and David A. Santogrossi, Department of Psychological Sciences, Purdue University.)

which a reinforcer is scheduled to follow the occurrence of a behavior. This is an important distinction and one that will appear throughout the book, so be sure that you understand it.

We can use the example of parents giving their child a dessert for eating spinach to illustrate the meaning of these two terms. If the child eats spinach more often in the future, then the dessert would be called a "reinforcer." The procedure of giving the child dessert after he or she eats spinach (knowing that the dessert is a reinforcer) would be called "reinforcement."

There are a limitless variety of reinforcing events. There are social reinforcers such as a smile, a word of praise, agreement, and attention. There are edible reinforcers such as candy, snacks, and beer. There are manipulatable reinforcers such as toys, airplanes, and Frisbees. There are activity reinforcers such as disco dancing and jogging. And there are generalized reinforcers such as money and points. Although there is often widespread agreement on what constitutes a reinforcer, there are reinforcers that are unique to small groups or even single individuals. Even painful stimuli can be reinforcing, as is attested to by the existence of masochists.

Reinforcement may be deliberately contrived or it may be naturally occurring. Teachers may deliberately use praise to increase the studying of their pupils. But the world may naturally produce a beautiful sunset that just happens to increase the rate at which a person goes outside at sunset to view future sunsets.

It is important to use the term *reinforcer* precisely. When an event is seen to follow instances of a behavior and to increase the rate of that behavior, we can say that the event is a reinforcer for that behavior for that person. We cannot be sure that the event would reinforce other behaviors of that person, although it is reasonably likely to. Nor can we conclude that the event would reinforce the same behavior of another person, although this will be highly likely for some reinforcers, such as food and sex. The cartoon in Figure 8-1 makes this point eloquently. It has been summed up in the old hippie motto: "different strokes for different folks." Be careful to depart from this very precise usage of the term *reinforcer* only with good reason, as it represents the very essence of the meaning of the concept.

Behavior analysts have been guided by the concept of *reinforcer* to help individuals who otherwise would not engage in a particular behavior that would be beneficial to them. For example, severe retardates have been taught simple language skills by following correct responses with a sweet treat (for example, Garcia, Guess, & Bynes, 1973). Disruptive grade school children who study very infrequently have had their study behavior improved by having the teacher praise them and pay attention to them when they were studying (for example, Hall, Lund, & Jackson, 1968). Students in a communal living arrangement who tend to let their residence become messy produced high levels of housework when points (exchangeable for rent reductions) were given for such work (Feallock & Miller, 1976). And members of a little league football team who frequently missed their assignments improved their performance considerably simply because they were provided with immediate feedback (Komacki & Barnett, 1977). As you can see, the application of the concept can be useful not only for severely dependent populations such as retardates and young children, but also for adults.

The significance of reinforcement extends far beyond its usefulness for psychologists interested in helping people improve their behavior. Behavioral psychologists claim that reinforcement is the basic building block of all human behavior. Everything that we do is ultimately the result of reinforcement. If we engage in a new behavior and it leads to a reinforcer, we will be more likely to engage in it again. If we engage in a behavior and it does not lead to a reinforcer, we will be less

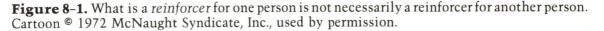

"Boy! What do you do with all that swell stuff?"

Figure 8-1. What is a *reinforcer* for one person is not necessarily a reinforcer for another person. Cartoon © 1972 McNaught Syndicate, Inc., used by permission.

likely to do it again. Thus, reinforcement is the basic motor of all human learning and hence of everything that we are and do.

The importance of reinforcement is evident in the results of the attention that an adult gives a child. If a child does something at home, such as cleaning his or her room thoroughly, the parents will often pay a lot of attention to the child, thereby increasing the probability that the child will clean his or her room in the future. The attention is a reinforcer for room cleaning. It is thought that many behaviors are caused through this kind of reinforcing mechanism. Thus, children are reinforced for talking clearly, using new words, studying in school, washing themselves, wearing neat clothes, saying "thank you," and so on.

However, the results of attention don't always work out so nicely. Children will often pester a parent around dinnertime for a snack. Frequently the parent will reprimand the child or lecture him or her about not eating just before dinner. Such attention, although unpleasant, may be reinforcing to a child, particularly if the parent pays little attention otherwise, and can lead to all sorts of pestering behavior on the part of the child.

Behavior analysts have found that the use of attention without a knowledge of reinforcement is often the cause of undesirable behavior. Two studies have found that the attention of most teachers is directed at disruptive behavior almost three times more frequently than it is directed at constructive behavior (Thomas, Presland, Grant, & Glynn, 1978; White, 1975). Psychiatric aides in mental hospitals often pay attention to the "crazy" behavior of patients, thereby increasing the probability of further crazy behavior (for example, Ayllon & Michael, 1959). In a study of one family typical of those with problem children, Patterson (1977) found that the parents frequently reinforced hostile behavior from their child through attention. There are innumerable examples of well-meaning individuals who pay attention to, and thereby reinforce, behavior that they find undesirable.

Reinforcers have the capability of drastically modifying behavior, causing both desirable and undesirable outcomes. Thus, in the hands of an incompetent or unscrupulous person, they can be very dangerous. They could be used to promote conformity, hard work for someone else's benefit, or even criminal behavior. On the other hand, used by competent people within the framework of democratic and accountable institutions, this tool can solve many behavioral problems. Children can be reinforced for doing well in school; parents can be reinforced for learning how to raise their children with care; individuals can be reinforced for doing things that they feel will be beneficial; and members of groups can be reinforced for working for the common good.

BEHAVIOR ANALYSIS EXAMPLE

Creative word use. Glover and Gary (1976) investigated the possibility of increasing the creative use of words by fourth- and fifth-grade students. To do so, they created a game situation in which a noun was put on the blackboard and students were given ten minutes to list all possible uses they could think of for the object named. The investigators then observed four aspects of the students' responses: the number of different responses, which meant the number of uses listed that were different from all previous uses listed by the student (including those listed for previous nouns); the number of verb forms (for example, "throwing", "pitching," and "flinging" would count as only one while "throwing," "hitting," and "containing" would count as three); number of words per response, which meant the number of words used by the students in explaining the uses of the noun; and number of infrequent verbs, which meant the number of verbs employed in describing a use that had never before been suggested by the student.

For the initial phase of the experiment, the researchers observed the frequency of each of these behaviors daily. During the experimental phase, one behavior was selected and each student earned a point for each response. The group was divided into two teams that competed against each other for the highest score. The team with the highest point total went to recess early. However, both teams could win if the lower team got 80% of the points earned by the higher team.

Figure 8–2 shows the results. The number of different responses increased from a baseline level of about 10 to about 13 when points were awarded; the behavior decreased gradually to about 11 after points were no longer awarded. The number of different verb forms increased from about 1 per day to about 5 per day when points were awarded; the rate decreased again when points were no longer awarded. The number of words per response increased from about 3 to over 13 when points

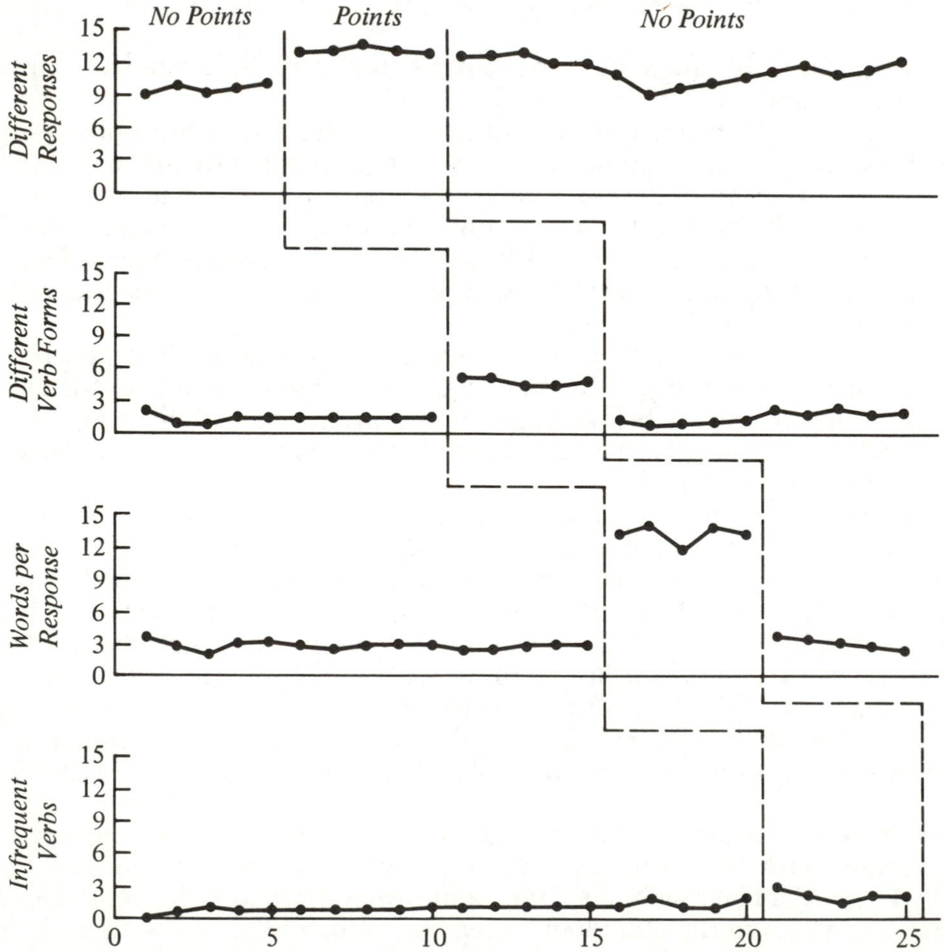

Figure 8–2. The effect of awarding points in a game situation to students for four different aspects of creative word usage. Adapted from "Procedures to Increase Some Aspects of Creativity," by J. Glover and A. L. Gary, *Journal of Applied Behavior Analysis*, 1976, 9, 79–84. Copyright 1976 by the Society for the Experimental Analysis of Behavior, Inc. Used by permission.

were being awarded and then decreased again to around 3 afterward. And the number of infrequent verbs increased from about 1 per day to almost 3 when points were awarded. Thus, for each aspect of creativity, when points were awarded the behavior increased—sometimes dramatically.

To determine whether the behaviors that they taught these students would increase their creativity scores on a standardized test of creativity widely used by psychologists, Glover and Gary administered the test before and after the experiment. The students' scores increased about 13% after their training. This suggests that the behaviors that were observed and increased are related to what other psychologists consider creativity.

Note #1: In the following pages you will come across frequent examples in which people inadvertently reinforce other people for talking about their problems. These examples do not imply that talking with people about their problems or listening to their complaints is without value and is not done by behavior analysts. In fact, talking with people is an important aspect of most applications of behavior analysis and is even the major component in a number of therapeutic procedures. These examples simply illustrate that talking with people about their problems, just like any other application of reinforcement, can produce undesirable effects if it is done without an understanding of the principle of reinforcement.

Note #2: This book will refer to the delivery of an event after a behavior, when it is not known if the event is a reinforcer, as "reinforcement procedure." It will never use that term if the event is known not to be a reinforcer. You will not be tested on this term.

Note #3: The definition of a reinforcer requires that we observe an increase in behavior that is caused by the event in question. Observing that the rate of a particular response increases after we initiate a certain event following a certain response of the individual does not prove that the increase was caused by that event. The results could have been caused by an alternative factor that happened to begin at the same time as the potential reinforcer. For example, suppose that after the teacher gives John an M & M each time he raises his hand in class instead of just blurting his question out, John raises his hand more often. Without further research, the new behavior pattern doesn't prove that the teacher caused this increase by delivering the M & M. John's mother might have just previously told him to always raise his hand in class—or else!

The most rigorous way to prove that an event is a reinforcer is to use a reversal design. You would observe the rate of a behavior during a baseline condition; then you would institute the reinforcement condition to see whether the rate of the behavior increased. Finally you would stop reinforcing responses during a reversal to baseline condition to see whether the rate would return again to the lower baseline level. If it did, then you would have firm evidence that the event was a reinforcer.

A slightly less rigorous way to determine whether an event is a reinforcer is to use a multiple-baseline design across two or more behaviors of the same person. If the rate of each behavior increased after the introduction of the reinforcement condition, then you would have evidence that the event was reinforcing. However, if the rate did not increase for one of the behaviors, the event might still be a reinforcer for the other behaviors. Likewise, you could use a multiple-baseline design across different situations or different individuals.

If you observed increases after the introduction of reinforcement for all individuals or situations, you could reasonably conclude that the event is a reinforcer. But again the absence of an effect does not rule out the possibility that the event is a reinforcer for some individuals and not others or in some situations and not others. Since the practical application of a reinforcer demands that it be effective for most individuals and situations, the multiple-baseline design is particularly reasonable if you are seeking a practical method for changing behavior.

For convenience, we will assume in the examples in this book that the apparent cause of a change in behavior is, in fact, the real cause. However, don't forget that to obtain scientific proof would require careful experimentation with the situation.

ADDITIONAL READINGS

Allen, K. E., Hart, B. M., Buell, J. S., Harris, F. R., & Wolf, M. M. Effects of social reinforcement on isolate behavior of a nursery school child. *Child Development,* 1964, 35, 511–518. This article refers to an early behavior-analysis experiment in which teacher attention was used to reinforce an "isolate" child for playing with other children.

Homme, L. E., DeBaca, P. C., Devine, J. V., Steinhorst, R., & Rickert, E. J. Use of the Premack Principle in controlling the behavior of nursery school children. *Journal of the Experimental Analysis of Behavior*, 1963, *6*, 554. This article discusses an interesting use of reinforcement that illustrates the Premack Principle for finding reinforcers. The Premack Principle states: "If behavior B is of higher probability than behavior A, then behavior A can be reinforced by making permission to engage in behavior B depend upon the occurrence of behavior A." In this example, the authors noted that preschool children ran and screamed at a high rate but did not often sit and look at the blackboard when the teacher was at it. When permission to run and scream occurred only after the children sat and looked at the blackboard, the rate of sitting and looking increased dramatically. Other reinforcing events included kicking the wastebasket and pushing the instructor around the room in his caster-equipped chair.

Osborne, J. G. Free-time as a reinforcer in the management of classroom behavior. *Journal of Applied Behavior Analysis*, 1969, *2*, 113–118. This article reports the effective use of free time as a reinforcer. Children in a normally rowdy classroom were permitted to have extra free time if they stayed in their seats during study time. The number of children staying seated increased dramatically as a result of this reinforcement procedure.

Helpful hints: The remainder of this lesson is designed to teach you how to apply the concept of "reinforcer" to everyday situations familiar to you. There are a number of situations in which it is often difficult to decide whether or not there is a reinforcer.

Helpful hint #1: Perhaps the most difficult situation involves instructions to perform a behavior. Since such an instruction may follow an instance of the behavior and may lead to an increase in the rate of the behavior, it is easily confused with a reinforcer. In those cases where an instruction follows an incorrect performance of the behavior and leads to an increase in the correct performance of the behavior, the situation should be absolutely clear. It can't be a reinforcer because it did not follow an instance of the correct performance of the behavior. For example, suppose that an employee comes in late to work and the boss tells him to be prompt from then on. Even if the employee is prompt from then on, the boss's admonition cannot be a reinforcer because it did not follow an instance of promptness. Thus it cannot have reinforced promptness. Technically, behavior analysts consider an instruction to influence the behavior that it precedes rather than the behavior that it follows—thus it is not considered to be an event that follows a behavior.

In those cases where an instruction follows a low-rate behavior and leads to an increase, the situation is murkier. In a later lesson (19), it will be shown how much an instruction depends for its effectiveness on the response being followed by reinforcement. In any event, you cannot go wrong if you simply remember that an instruction (usually) cannot be a reinforcer. Consider any verbal behavior, including written material, to be an instruction if it even indirectly implies that there will be a positive or negative consequence for performing the behavior. However, verbal behavior that follows some other behavior and is not instructional may be a reinforcer if it increases the rate of the other behavior.

Helpful hint #2: Often an "unpleasant" event will follow a behavior and, surprisingly, the behavior will increase in probability: A person may engage in stupid arguments and be put down. Instead of shutting up, the person may start more stupid arguments. In these cases, the "unpleasant" event would be termed a reinforcer because it follows the behavior and increases its probability.

Helpful hint #3: Sometimes an event will occur concurrently with the behavior, and the rate of the behavior will increase. A teacher may watch while a child works a problem, and the rate of working problems may increase. The attention would be a reinforcer, because "follows" can refer to following the start of the behavior as well as its end.

Helpful hint #4: The situations on the following pages contain examples of each concept in this lesson: reinforcer and reinforcement. They also contain some examples that don't fall into either of those categories. If an example does not fall into either category, label it "unknown." Do not use the labels in the "helpful hints" sections (instructions, unpleasant event, and so on).

Helpful hint #5: Throughout the rest of the book you will be asked to distinguish between "reinforcer" and "reinforcement." It will help you in doing so if you always remember that a reinforcer is a stimulus that follows a behavior and increases the rate of the behavior whereas reinforcement is the procedure of delivering that event following the behavior. For example, if you read that the rate of a behavior increases after a stimulus follows it, you may be asked two kinds of questions. You might be asked something like "What is the stimulus called?" (or "the stimulus is called a(n) ______") in which case you should label it a "reinforcer." Or you might be asked something like "What behavioral procedure was used to increase the behavior?" in which case you should label it "reinforcement."

LESSON 8 READING QUIZ

(18) The major concept that lies at the heart of most environmental influences that create and maintain behavior is the behavioral procedure called ______.

(9) The term *reward* refers to any event that should be liked by the recipient—in the speaker's subjective ______.

(27) If you wish to use a synonym for *reinforcer* do not use the term *reward*; however, you may use the phrase ______ reward.

(17) A reinforcer is any event that ______ a behavior and that ______ the probability of that behavior.

(8) When you read the phrase "increases the probability of a behavior" you should understand that it means "increases the probability of the behavior over what it would be if the event ______ follow the behavior" (see footnote to the definition).

(26) The term *reinforcement* is used to refer to the procedure of arranging for an event to follow a behavior, knowing that the event will ______ the rate of the behavior.

(25) If a child eats spinach in the future because he or she was given dessert after eating spinach in the past, then the dessert would be called a(n) ______.

(16) If the rate of eating spinach is increased by delivering a dessert after spinach is eaten, then this procedure is called ______.

(29) If a person's statements on religion always lead to an argument from her friends, and if her rate of making such statements increases, then we are dealing with both reinforcement and reinforcer. The event consisting of another person's stating an argument would be an example of a(n) ______; the procedure involving the delivery of an argument after the person's religious statement would be an example of the behavioral procedure called ______.

(15) Remember, if we discover that an event is a reinforcer for a particular behavior and person, we cannot conclude that it will reinforce a different ______ in the same person.

(7) Behaviorists have been guided to help individuals who otherwise would not engage in a functional behavior by the behavioral procedure called ______.

(24) Behavioral psychologists claim that reinforcement is the basic building block of all human ______.

(14) Behavior analysts have found that the use of attention without a knowledge of reinforcement is often the cause of ______ behavior.

(6) If a person says kind things to other people after they have just griped, and their rate of griping increases, you would call this procedure ______.

(23) Glover and Gary (1976) investigated the possibility of increasing the ______ use of words by fourth and fifth graders.

(5) The statement "the number of infrequent verbs means the number of verbs used in describing a use that had never before been used by the student" is called a(n) ______ ______.

(20) If an unpleasant event follows a behavior and increases the probability of that behavior, then the event would be termed a(n) ______________________________ .

(22) Examine Figure 8-2, which reported the results of the experiment on creativity. The experimental design for "different responses" alone could be called a(n) ______________________________ design. However, if you look at all four behaviors you can see that the overall design is called a(n) ______________________________ design.

(13) In the study by Glover and Gary (1976), points were awarded for creative responses. The points would be called a(n) ______________________________; awarding the points to increase creativity would be called ______________________________ .

(4) To scientifically prove that an event is a reinforcer would require the researcher to use either a(n) ______________________________ design or a(n) ______________________________ design.

(21) We will assume in the examples given in this book that the apparent cause of an increase in behavior—if it follows the behavior and if the behavior increases in probability—is actually a(n) ______________________________, even without scientific proof.

(12) If someone asks another person to do something and he or she does it, the event is not classified as a reinforcer even though the behavior increases. This is because a(n) ______________________________ cannot be a reinforcer.

(3) If people are asked to do something and their rate of doing it increases, this would not be an example of a reinforcer because an instruction cannot be a reinforcer. If you are asked in the following examples to name this you should write ______________________________ .

(11) If a pleasant event follows a behavior and doesn't increase the probability of that behavior, the event ______________ (is, isn't) a reinforcer.

(2) An event can qualify as a reinforcer if it follows the end of the behavior or if it follows the ______________________________ of the behavior.

(19) If a person sees a sign that says "speed up" and his or her rate of responding increases, you would call this a(n) ______________________________ . (Check your answer!)

(10) If an event occurs while someone is making a response, it is considered to be the same as an event following the response. Therefore, if the event also increases the probability of the behavior, we would call that event a(n) ______________________________ .

(28) If an event follows a behavior and increases the probability of that behavior, that event is called a(n) ______________________________ .

(1) If a question asks you to name a particular event and you can't name it because it is not a reinforcer, you should write the word ______________________________ .

READING QUIZ ANSWERS

(1) unknown (2) start (beginning) (3) unknown (4) reversal; multiple-baseline (5) behavioral definition (6) reinforcement (7) reinforcement (8) did not (9) opinion (10) reinforcer (11) isn't (12) instruction (13) reinforcer; reinforcement (14) undesirable (15) behavior (16) reinforcement (17) follows; increases (18) reinforcement (19) unknown (20) reinforcer (21) reinforcer (22) reversal; multiple-baseline (23) creative (24) behavior (25) reinforcer (26) increase (27) proven (28) reinforcer (29) reinforcer; reinforcement

LESSON 8 EXAMPLES

Example #1

Carla sometimes smiled at men that she passed on campus. One day she smiled at a guy who then came right up and asked her for a date. Carla now smiles at many of the guys whom she passes on campus and frequently gets asked out for interesting dates.

(25) After she started getting dates, the rate at which Carla smiled ______________ (decreased, remained the same, increased).
(13) Frequently when Carla smiled, getting a date ______________ (preceded, followed).
(35) In this example, "getting a date" is an event that follows smiling and that increases the rate of smiling. Therefore, "getting a date" is a(n) ______________.
(36) The occurrence of "getting a date" after Carla smiles is an example of what behavioral procedure? ______________

Example #2

Alma liked Grant a lot. He rarely did favors for her, however (like opening the door, offering her a cigarette, and so on), so she decided to reward him by saying "thank you" immediately after a favor. After a month, Alma decided that her program hadn't worked because Grant still rarely did favors for her.

(11) She said "thank you" immediately ______________ the response.
(24) Did the rate of the behavior increase? ______________
(12) Because the "thank you" followed the behavior but did not increase the rate of doing favors, it should be labeled a(n) ______________.

Example #3

Joe's TV set went on the blink during the NFL playoffs, so he tapped it with the palm of his hand. Immediately, the picture cleared up. Now, whenever the picture goes bad, he taps the set.

(23) The TV picture cleared up immediately after Joe tapped the set, and subsequently Joe's rate of tapping the set ______________.
(34) Therefore, having the picture clear up is an example of a(n) ______________. (Don't hesitate to state "unknown" when applicable.)
(37) The occurrence of the event "the picture cleared up" after Joe tapped his TV would be an example of what behavioral procedure? ______________

Example #4

Sam was a fourth grader who liked to wander around town after school. His mother worried about him, especially after he described what the underside of a train looked like. She therefore told him to come straight home from school. Sam started coming home earlier after his mother told him to.

(33) The rate of Sam's coming right home after school ______________ after his mother told him to.
(10) This cannot be an example of a reinforcer because of the rule "A(n) ______________ cannot be a reinforcer."
(22) When answering questions in this book, you should label such an event a(n) ______________.

Example #5

Dave was a slob; he would rip off his clothes at night and just throw them down. Shawn, his roommate, didn't like living with the resulting mess, so she asked Dave to please hang up his stuff. No result. So she then started looking carefully for any time that Dave did hang up even one article of clothing. When he did so, she gave him a special hand-printed ticket that read: "This ticket good for one special gift of your choosing."

(9) If Dave started picking up his clothes, then you would call the procedure that Shawn used ______________________ .

(21) If Dave started picking up his clothes, then the ticket would be called a(n) ____________ .

Example #6

Verna decided that her child Tom interrupted her too often. She started punishing him every time he interrupted by giving him a good spanking. She was disappointed, however, because Tom seemed to interrupt much more often than before. She concluded that punishment just doesn't work with some children.

(20) In this example, Verna's spanking of Tom occurred ____________ Tom's interruptions, and the rate of Tom's interruptions ____________ .
(32) This situation involves an "unpleasant" event that was a(n) ____________ .
(8) What is the name of the procedure of giving Tom a spanking? ____________ .
(38) What is the name of the event called a "spanking"? ____________ .

Example #7

Elvis used to be a safe and sane driver. One day he was in a hurry to get to a movie that supposedly had a torrid opening love scene, so he drove fast. He noticed that as soon as he increased his speed, his girlfriend appeared frightened and leaned on him much more than usual. Elvis frequently drove fast after that.

(6) The rate of Elvis' speeding ____________ as a result of having his girlfriend lean on him.
(19) However, his girlfriend did not lean on him ____________ the completion of his speeding but rather while he was still speeding.
(31) You should view this as an instance of an event (leaning on) that followed the ____________ ____________ of the behavior, not the end of it.
(7) Therefore, you should call the event "leaning on" for speeding a(n) ____________ .
(39) And you should call the delivery of "leaning on him" for speeding a(n) ____________ .

Example #8

The teacher firmly told Francie to start doing her homework. Immediately thereafter, Francie started doing her homework all the time.

(30) What behavioral procedure did the teacher use? ____________ .

Example #9

Marty was in second grade. One day during spelling he laid his head on the desk. The teacher asked him what was the matter, and he said, "Teacher, I have a terrible headhurt." The teacher, a kind woman, soothed him by saying, "That's too bad, Marty. Why don't you just lay your head down until it feels better?" It was noted that Marty frequently complained about headaches after that, even though he had never had any in the previous year, and that Marty's schoolwork became much poorer.

(29) The teacher allowed Marty to put his head down on the desk ____________ his complaints of a headache.
(5) Marty's rate of complaining about headaches ____________ .
(18) Therefore, we can say that the teacher ____________ Marty for complaining about a headache.

Example #10

Linda didn't talk with her roommate Priscilla very often. However, whenever Priscilla complained about how badly life was going for her, Linda would talk with her about it for a long time. She had just had a course in psychotherapy, and she realized that she could help Priscilla by discussing her problems with her. After several months, however, she decided that psychotherapy was a "bunch of junk" because Priscilla was talking about how awful life was even more often than before.

(16) In this case Linda's verbal behavior does not constitute instruction. Therefore, Linda's procedure would be an example of ______________________ .

Example #11

May came home from school on Monday and told her parents that she had finally beaten up the little boy who had been tormenting her every day. On Friday, May's father took her out for ice cream and told her it was a special treat for beating up the awful little boy. May now beats up the boy more often.

(4) What is the ice cream an example of? ______________________

Example #12

Bill almost never welcomed Jane home when she finished her late evening class. So Jane decided on a new strategy. When Bill did welcome her, she kissed him. Naturally, Bill's rate increased.

(28) What behavioral procedure did Jane use? ______________________

Example #13

Professor Reynolds was dissatisfied with the rate of participation by his students in his discussion class. So he announced that he would award all students who presented good ideas during discussion with a bonus point toward their grade and they would know they got it because he would write it in his book as soon as it happened. Professor Reynolds was disheartened to discover that none of his students participated more often as a result of his new rule.

(15) What procedure did he use? ______________________

Example #14

Gail felt that her 6-year-old son Jimmy was not expressive enough. So she decided to give him a special treat every time that he spontaneously hugged her. She found that Jimmy gradually became more expressive.

(3) Gail used what behavioral procedure? ______________________

Example #15

Leslie had long regretted being so remote from her parents. She had tried talking with them about it to no avail. So she decided that she would give them a really nice compliment any time they shared something intimate with her. Their rate slowly increased.

(27) One of Leslie's compliments would be an example of a(n) ______________________ .

Example #16

Dollie was really turned off by the table manners of her friends. So she asked them if they wouldn't please ask people to pass things to them rather than just grabbing them. To her surprise, her friends started asking others to pass things.

(17) Dollie used what behavioral procedure? ______________________.

Example #17

Carla sometimes went to the disco for a little dancing. The trouble was she was a super dancer and was bored dancing with most of the guys who usually hung out there. One day Steve asked her to dance and she found out that he was also a super dancer. She started dancing a lot more after Steve started asking her.

(2) Dancing with Steve is a(n) ______________________.

Example #18

John complained of problems every once in a while. One day his friend had a long talk with him. After that, John complained more often of his problems and thus had more talks with his friend.

(26) His friend inadvertently used what procedure to increase John's rate of complaining? ______________________

Example #19

Larry sometimes commented that he liked long hair. His friends always agreed with him and they frequently discussed how stupid was the reaction of many older people to long hair. Larry's rate of commenting about long hair remained unchanged.

(14) What behavioral procedure did his friends' agreement exemplify? ______________.

Example #20

Stuart spontaneously trimmed the front hedge around his home one day. His parents were delighted and took him out for a steak dinner to reward his spontaneous helping around the house. His spontaneous helping increased.

(1) What behavioral procedure did his parents use? ______________________

EXAMPLE ANSWERS

(1) reinforcement (2) reinforcer (3) reinforcement (4) reinforcer (5) increased (6) increased (7) reinforcer (8) reinforcement (9) reinforcement (10) instruction (11) following (12) unknown (13) followed (14) unknown (15) unknown (16) reinforcement (17) unknown (18) reinforced (19) following (20) following (after); increased (21) reinforcer (22) unknown (23) increased (24) no (25) increased (26) reinforcement (27) reinforcer (28) reinforcement (29) following (30) unknown (31) beginning (32) reinforcer (33) increased (34) reinforcer (35) reinforcer (36) reinforcement (37) reinforcement (38) reinforcer (39) reinforcement

Lesson 9

Extinction of Everyday Behaviors

The last lesson introduced reinforcement, a behavioral procedure for increasing the rate of a behavior. This lesson discusses extinction, a procedure for decreasing the rate of a behavior.

Extinction is defined as (1) stopping the delivery of a reinforcer that has followed a behavior in the past and (2) causing a decrease in the future probability or rate of the behavior. For a procedure to be termed *extinction*, it must possess both of these characteristics.[1]

This definition of extinction states that the event being stopped is a reinforcer. This is necessary because the rate of the behavior would decrease only if it had been previously increased by that event. In fact, when the reinforcing properties of an event are studied in a reversal design, the reversal to baseline (during which the delivery of the event is stopped) would be called an "extinction" condition.

Due to the widespread ignorance of reinforcement, behavior analysts continually encounter cases where very undesirable behaviors have been reinforced and are occurring at a high rate. For example, Lovaas and Simmons (1969) guessed that the frequent occurrence of self-destructive behaviors found among retarded children who had been placed in institutions was actually a method for those children to obtain attention from their attendants. They approached two state hospitals in southern California and asked them to point out their two worst cases of self-destructive behavior. They were given two children known from among several thousand as the worst cases. These children were then put into a special room and totally ignored when they engaged in self-destructive behaviors. One of the children, John, was an 8-year-old with an IQ of 24 who struck his forehead with his fists and knuckles, giving himself bruises and contusions. To keep him from hurting himself, the hospital had kept him in arm and leg restraints continuously for six months prior to the study. During the first hour-and-a-half session out of the restraints, John struck himself over 2500 times, or once every two seconds! Extinction was carried out by placing John in a room and ignoring all self-destructive acts. His rate of striking himself dropped to zero by ten days, during which time he had struck himself a total of almost 9000 times. By the end of ten days, however, John could be permitted to sit in the room without the restraints that had been previously required, thereby becoming a bit more normal and certainly freer. Incidentally, this is one of the few types of situations in which behavior analysts sometimes recommend the use of punishment because, by reducing the self-destructive acts more quickly than extinction, it is more humane.

A related but far milder example with a normal child living with its parents was described by C. Williams (1959), who consulted with the family of a 2-year-old child. The parents comforted the child anytime that he cried after being put to bed. As a result, the child cried and raged whenever he was put to bed and typically took several hours to go to sleep. Williams advised the parents to put the child to bed and then firmly ignore the crying. Figure 9–1 graphs the resulting crying. On the first day the child cried for a total of 45 minutes before quieting and going to sleep. The second day the child did not cry at all and on several successive days cried only a few minutes, finally stopping

[1]The act of applying extinction to a behavior is called "extinguishing" the behavior.

crying on the seventh day. An unexpected reversal (not shown on the graph) occurred when the child's aunt babysat one night and the child cried and was comforted by her. The next night the parents ignored the child's crying, which lasted for almost an hour. The crying rapidly decreased in the following days, finally stopping altogether.

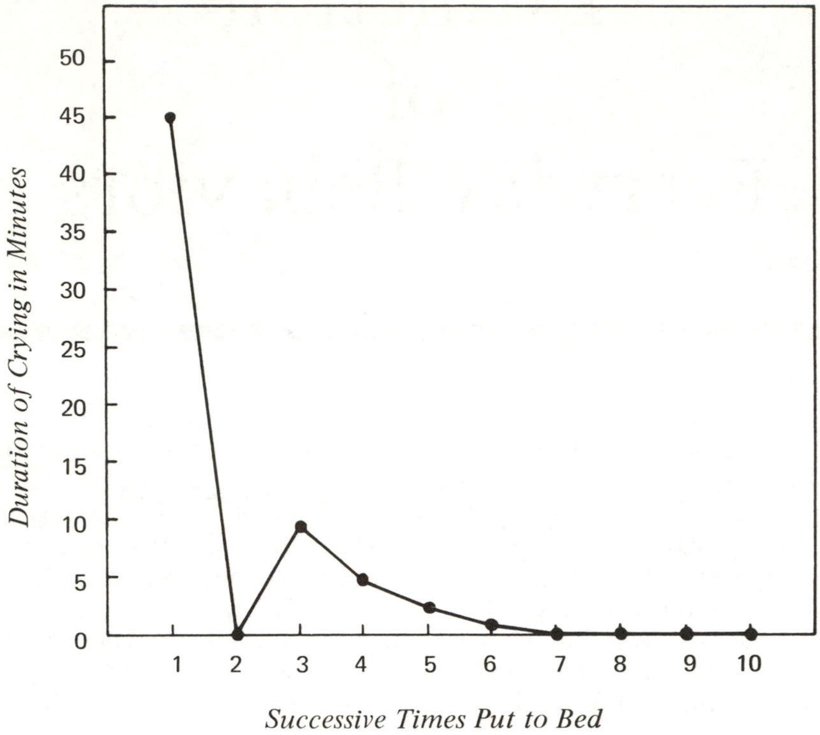

Figure 9-1. Number of minutes a chronic crier cried after being put to bed and ignored on ten successive nights. The child had previously been attended to if he cried. Adapted from "The Elimination of Tantrum Behavior by Extinction Procedure," by C. D. Williams, *Journal of Abnormal and Social Psychology*, 1959, *59*, 269. Copyright 1959 by the American Psychological Association. Reprinted by permission.

As was noted in Lesson 8, public-school teachers pay far more attention to undesirable behaviors in their classrooms than they do to desirable behavior. It may be that the widespread existence of disruptive and nonlearning responses in grade schools results from this pattern of teacher attention. In one study, Allen, Turner, and Everett (1970) described a child who had tantrums lasting five minutes apiece that were unwittingly reinforced by the teacher. When the teacher started ignoring them, only two more occurred—although the first one lasted over 25 minutes! A large number of studies in classrooms have shown that when teachers are taught to stop attending at a high rate to undesirable behaviors, those behaviors decrease sharply. It is likely that a great deal of disruptive and pointless behavior in many everyday situations is inadvertently maintained by individuals who are ignorant of the reinforcing properties of attention—and the constructive influence of well-placed extinction.

For example, a group may unconsciously reinforce one of its members for doing "funny" or disruptive things by laughing at that member, or a teacher will reinforce disruptive behavior of her students by paying attention to them only when they are goofing off. By stopping that poor use of reinforcement, the person can usually eliminate the undesirable behavior.

Extinction, like reinforcement, can also be used incorrectly. When parents ignore a child's good behavior because they are "too busy," they are decreasing the probability of the child's acting that way in the future. When any of us have a fit of shyness and act embarrassed at the compliment that we just received, we are likely to decrease the rate at which we get compliments. Parents who complain about the absence of communication with their teenager probably extinguished conversational behavior sometime in the past. The teacher who spends all his or her time trying to discipline disruptive students will probably be extinguishing the study behavior of good students.

And a government that ignores the legitimate complaints of its citizens may later be faced with open rebellion and an inability to communicate with those same citizens. Extinction, then, is a powerful tool with which to change behavior, and, like reinforcement, it can be used wisely or unwisely.

BEHAVIOR ANALYSIS EXAMPLE

Aggression in young children. Pinkston, Reese, LeBlanc, and Baer (1973) investigated the case of Cain, a 3½-year-old child of well-educated parents. Cain was bright and often had long discussions with the teachers in his preschool. However, when he tried to play with other children it was a disaster. The investigators noticed that he would stand on the edge of the play area with his fists clenched and after a few minutes move onto the play area and attack other children indiscriminately. If the teachers intervened, they were bitten, scratched, struck and told "I hate you."

Pinkston and her colleagues carefully defined aggression so that it included both physical and verbal aggression. Physical aggression "included any physically negative behavior directed toward peers and/or materials being used by them." Specific definitions were then given for eight categories of physical aggression including choking, head pushing, biting, pinching, pushing, poking, hitting, and kicking. Verbal aggression was defined as any verbalization that threatened, forbade an activity, or indicated negative judgments about persons, their relatives, or their property. Observations were made during consecutive ten-second intervals. Reliability was found to be 92%.

Figure 9–2 shows the results of this experiment. During the first period of observation the teachers continued reacting as they had in the past to aggression, that is, by attending to it. Aggression averaged almost 30% of all interactions with other children during that time. The teachers were then instructed to ignore all aggression. By the last four days of this condition, aggression had decreased to an average of only 6% of all interactions. During the third condition, the teachers were instructed to react as they had in the past to aggression by once again attending to it. The rate of aggression once again rose and during the last three days averaged about 30% again. Subsequent withdrawal of attention and reinstatement of it produced similar results. In a long period of observation not shown on this figure, the teachers continued to ignore aggressive acts and they remained between 0 and 5% for another 30 days.

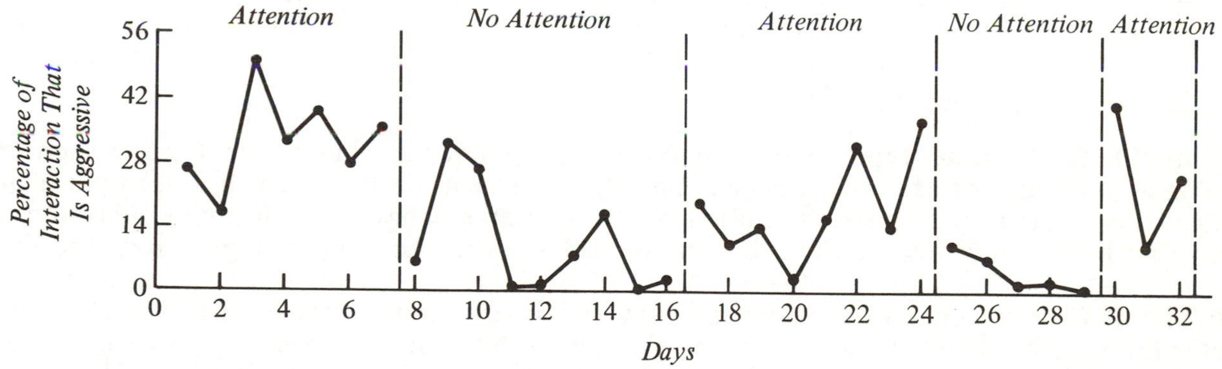

Figure 9–2. The effects of attention and elimination of attention on the aggressive behavior of Cain. Adapted from "Independent Control of a Preschool Child's Aggression and Peer Interaction by Contingent Teacher Attention," by E. M. Pinkston, N. M. Reese, J. M. LeBlanc, and D. M. Baer, *Journal of Applied Behavior Analysis,* 1973, 6, 115–124. Copyright 1973 by the Society for the Experimental Analysis of Behavior, Inc. Used by permission.

The results of this carefully designed and executed study show that the aggressive behaviors of Cain could easily be eliminated by ignoring them.

Note #1: You will encounter a number of examples in which someone's complaining behavior is ignored and perhaps decreases. You should not conclude that behavior analysts solve behavioral problems by ignoring them. This approach is appropriate only when the complaining behavior is the problem—when the complaint is not legitimate and when some other well-meaning individual inadvertently reinforced that behavior. As noted in Lesson 8, behavior analysts frequently talk with individuals about their problems as a critical aspect of the treatment procedure. This lesson should lead you to be wary in deciding when that is the appropriate approach and when extinction is appropriate.

Note #2: Behavior analysts often refer to the procedure of stopping the delivery of an event, even when it is not known that this will be effective, as an "extinction procedure." By adding the word *procedure* to the term, they call attention to the fact that only the procedural aspect of extinction exists and the behavioral effect of a reduction in rate is not yet known to exist. The term will be occasionally used in this manner in this book; it will never be used when the procedure is known not to produce the behavioral effect. You will not be tested on this term.

ADDITIONAL READINGS

Ayllon, T., & Michael, J. The psychiatric nurse as a behavioral engineer. *Journal of the Experimental Analysis of Behavior*, 1969, 2, 323–334. This article consists of a series of case studies in the use of behavioral principles to change the behavior of mental patients. One case involves Lucille, a mental defective who continually entered the nurses' office and disrupted their work. The nurses had in the past usually taken her by the hand and led her out of the office. This reaction seemed only to increase the rate of office entering. When the nurses totally ignored Lucille's visits, the office entering dropped from an average of 16 per day to two per day within two months.

Wolf, M. M., Birnbrauer, J., Lawler, J., & Williams, T. The operant extinction, reinstatement, and re-extinction of vomiting behavior in a retarded child. In R. Ulrich, T. Stachnik, & J. Mabry (Eds.), *Control of human behavior*, Vol. II. Glenview, Ill.: Scott, Foresman, 1970. This article shows how extinction can be used to eliminate severe behavior problems in retarded children. In this case, a retarded girl vomited most days when she was in a class; the teacher immediately sent her to her residence. By having the child remain in the class regardless of her vomiting behavior, the teacher's attention and the child's removal from class were eliminated. This procedure virtually eliminated the vomiting. This case also illustrates how easy it is to unintentionally reinforce certain behaviors.

Helpful hints: There are two types of situations in which the rate of a response decreases and that may be confused with extinction.

Helpful hint #1: If an instruction to perform a behavior is stopped and the rate of the behavior decreases, this would not be an example of extinction. The reason is that instructions do not usually act as reinforcers; therefore the delivery of a reinforcer is not being stopped. Just remember: <u>stopping an instruction cannot be extinction.</u>

Helpful hint #2: An easier type of situation to analyze is where verbal behavior contains the word *stop* or a synonym. For example, a person may threaten to stop some event if a behavior is not reduced. Or a person may instruct another person to stop a behavior. In neither situation is an event that had been following the behavior stopped—so these are not examples of extinction.

Helpful hint #3: If you encounter an example in which instructions were used to reduce the rate of a behavior, you should label it as "unknown." Also, if you encounter an example in which an event following a behavior is stopped and the behavioral rate is <u>not</u> decreased, you should label it as "unknown."

Helpful hint #4: Remember, you should refer to the act of applying extinction to a behavior as "extinguishing" the behavior.

LESSON 9 READING QUIZ

(7) Extinction is defined as (a) ________________________ a reinforcer that has followed a behavior in the past and (b) causing a(n) ________________________ in the rate of that behavior.

(14) Thus, extinction applies only to stopping events that occur ________________________ a behavior. (When)

(13) The term *extinction* involves stopping an event that conforms to the definition of a(n) _______________ .

(19) The act of applying extinction to a behavior is called _______________ the behavior.

(12) When studying the reinforcing properties of an event in a reversal design, the reversal to baseline condition can also be called the _______________ condition.

(6) Behavior analysts frequently encounter situations in which extinction seems to be the way to eliminate very disruptive behaviors that have been _______________ inadvertently by some well-meaning person.

(18) Lovaas and Simmons (1969) found that John, a severely self-destructive child, hit himself over _______________ times, presumably as a result of prior inadvertent reinforcement in a state hospital.

(5) Lovaas and Simmons (1969) ensured that no one attended to the child's self-destructive acts, and they totally disappeared within _______________ days.

(11) C. Williams (1959) consulted with a family that had comforted their child anytime that he cried after being put to bed. They inadvertently _______________ crying by doing so.

(10) C. Williams (1959) proposed to the family that they stop attending to the child's crying. The rate of his crying _______________ .

(4) Pinkston and her colleagues (1973) instructed the preschool teacher to stop paying attention to the child when he was being aggressive. The rate of the child's aggressive acts decreased to zero. What procedure were they employing? _______________

(17) Pinkston and her colleagues (1973) instructed the teacher to attend to the child's aggressive behavior as one normally would during the reversal condition. The child's rate of aggressive behavior increased. What procedure was the teacher using in this condition? _______________

(3) If an instruction to perform a behavior is stopped and the rate of the behavior decreases, this _______________ (would, wouldn't) be an example of extinction.

(9) If an instruction is given to stop a behavior, and the rate of the behavior decreases, this _______________ (would, wouldn't) be an example of extinction.

(16) If a threat is made that an event will be stopped if a behavior is not decreased, and the behavior decreases, this _______________ (would, wouldn't) be an example of extinction.

(2) Suppose that you stop giving your spouse a kiss after he or she does you a favor and his or her rate of doing favors decreases. What behavioral procedure are you using? _______________

(8) Suppose that you tell others to stop smoking and they do. What behavioral procedure is this an example of? _______________

(15) Suppose that you stop giving your spouse a kiss after he or she does a favor for you and his or her rate of doing favors does not change. What behavioral procedure are you using? _______________

(1) Suppose that you stop telling your roommates to clean the room and they stop. This would be an example of what behavioral procedure? _______________

READING QUIZ ANSWERS

(1) unknown (2) extinction (3) wouldn't (4) extinction (5) 10 (6) reinforced (7) stopping; decrease (8)

unknown (9) wouldn't (10) decreased (stopped) (11) reinforced (12) extinction (13) reinforcer (14) following (15) unknown (16) wouldn't (17) reinforcement (18) 9000 (19) extinguishing

LESSON 9 EXAMPLES

Example #1

Martha's 5-year-old son frequently pinched his mother for no apparent reason. Martha felt that there must be something troubling her son for him to do such a thing, so when he pinched her she would immediately stop whatever she was doing, explain that pinching was not nice, and ask him why he had pinched her. He usually said "I don't know" and later would pinch her again.

Martha finally explained the situation to her husband. He suggested that she ignore the pinches no matter how irritating they were. She did this for several weeks and noticed that the pinching stopped.

(20) You might guess that the event of "talking to her child about the pinching" was actually an example of a(n) ________________________________ .

(12) Did Martha eventually stop talking to her son about the pinching? ____________

(21) Did the frequency of the behavior decrease? ____________

(30) Because Martha <u>stopped</u> paying attention to the pinches and the rate of pinching decreased, ignoring pinching is called ________________________________ .

Example #2

Lora was taking a biology course from a rather conservative professor. Each class period she would ask one silly question, such as "Why do dogs mate only twice a year? Don't they like it?" The professor usually got mad, turned red, and said, "That will be enough, Miss Smith." Her classmates noticed that she usually asked one question like that every class period. After talking with a behavior analyst, the professor started handling Lora's questions differently. He didn't get mad or turn red, he just followed her question with "Are there any other questions?" After 12 class periods of the professor's new technique, Lora was still asking one silly question every class period.

(31) Initially, after each silly question, the event ("the professor got mad and turned ____________ ________________________") occurred.

(10) The professor then changed tactics. When he stopped getting mad and turning red, did the rate of Lora's behavior change? ____________

(29) Because the only feature relating to the extinction of Lora's behavior possessed by this example is (write whichever phrase fits: "stop event" or "behavior decreases") ____________ ________________________, this is not an example of extinction.

(11) The procedure used by the professor should be labeled ________________________.

Example #3

Bobby often whispered to his friends in English class. To stop this behavior, the teacher told the class: "I will tolerate no more whispering in this class. I want it stopped as of today!" Bobby never whispered in class again after that.

(28) In this example the teacher did not stop an event ________________________ (preceding, following) whispering, although the rate of whispering did decrease.

(9) Therefore, this is not an example of ________________________________ .

Example #4

Mary had been drinking with her friends on Wednesday nights for the past few months. She enjoyed their company, and they liked hers except for one habit: she interrupted the conversation (particularly when Sally was talking). She always had something interesting to say, however, so they would pay attention to her interruptions.

Sally finally became angry with Mary for interrupting her all the time. She asked Mary to stop doing it, and Mary apologized and said she would stop. But she didn't, so Sally told her feelings to the other members of the group. They all agreed to ignore Mary whenever she interrupted Sally. Sally was to continue to talk, and the other members would continue to pay attention to her and to ignore Mary. After several Wednesday nights of this procedure, Mary had completely stopped interrupting.

(8) Sally got her group to try a procedure. What characteristic(s) of extinction does it eventually possess? ____________

(19) What behavioral procedure is this an example of? ____________
(Don't hesitate to write "unknown" if this is not an example of a behavioral procedure that you've already learned.)

Example #5

Jimmy and his dad had trouble getting along with each other. Whenever his dad would ask him how things were, Jimmy always explained at great length how bad his life was. Not wanting to make the boy's sad state worse, his dad always paid attention to him and tried to comfort him. One evening Jimmy's mother suggested that perhaps Dad should stop all the attention to such sad talk. Dad stopped the attention, and Jimmy's rate of sad talk decreased.

(7) Jimmy's dad ____________ paying attention to sad talk.

(18) The rate of sad talk ____________.

(27) Since an event following the behavior was stopped and the rate of the behavior decreased, the procedure used by Jimmy's dad would be labeled ____________.

Example #6

James kept interrupting Don's work by visiting him. Eventually, Don told James that he could visit and read *Playboy* or use the tape deck but that Don wouldn't be able to stop his studies to talk. Soon, James almost stopped visiting.

(26) Don's refusal to talk is an example of what procedure? ____________

Example #7

Ben, the star pledge in his fraternity, was in charge of vacuuming the pledge dormitory. As long as Skoog, the frat president, asked him every Saturday to do it, Ben did an excellent job. However, Skoog finally stopped asking Ben to do it, feeling that Ben should be responsible enough to do it without being asked. Ben's rate of vacuuming the dorm dropped to nearly zero.

(17) To analyze this example you must remember the rule that "stopping a(n) ____________ ____________ cannot be an example of extinction."

(6) Therefore you would label the procedure used by Skoog as ____________.

Example #8

Connie was becoming extremely irritated with her husband's habit of throwing his clothes around. She had asked him and threatened him repeatedly about this habit, but the chair in the bedroom was still his favorite storage place. One morning Connie saw him actually hanging up his clothes, so she fixed him a large breakfast (his usual breakfast was oatmeal and toast). Connie thought this was such a good idea that she made a rule to fix a large breakfast whenever the clothes were hung up. She noticed that they were hung up most of the time from then on.

(25) What procedure did Connie use? ____________________

Example #9

Darwin, a publicity-seeking student posing as a radical, came up with a sensational new tactic for disrupting the campus. The disruption was followed by the news media, and Darwin was interviewed on TV. He used that same tactic frequently thereafter.

(5) What behavioral procedure were the news media unwittingly applying to Darwin? ____________________

Example #10

At the beginning of the semester, Gary, the new instructor of philosophy, told his students that he would give them a bonus if they handed their weekly papers in by Thursday. Everyone in the class did so. After several weeks Gary figured that the problem of late papers was solved and stopped giving bonuses. The students stopped handing their papers in on time.

(24) What behavioral procedure did Gary start using when he dropped the bonus? ____________________

Example #11

Gary wanted to get his students to turn their papers in on time each week, so he reminded them on Thursday to be sure to have them in by Friday. Everyone did so. Midway through the semester he stopped reminding them, and, to his surprise, they stopped handing them in on time.

(16) What behavioral procedure did he use when he stopped reminding them? ____________________

Example #12

Tom liked compliments a lot. So anytime that he got one he beamed and profusely thanked the person for the compliment. Tom noticed that this increased the number of compliments that he got from each person that he had thanked.

(4) What behavioral procedure did Tom use by thanking people? ____________________

Example #13

At first Mary tried to be nice to Fred. But she did not like the kind of attention that he gave her, so she finally just totally ignored his attention and he stopped paying attention to her.

(3) What behavioral procedure was she using by ignoring him? ____________________

Example #14

Galen had finally gotten fed up with the teasing that he was getting from Ben for going to church. So he decided to totally ignore all teasing. Ben continued teasing as much as before.

(15) What behavioral procedure did Galen use? ____________________

Example #15

Willie was unhappy with the slow pace at which Sonny was carrying rocks for the wall. So he started asking Sonny to carry the rocks faster and sure enough Sonny did.

(23) What behavioral procedure did Willie use to increase Sonny's rate of carrying rocks? ______________________________

Example #16

Pat teased Carol incessantly about her weight. At first Carol took it all very seriously. Then later she stopped taking it so seriously and just laughed it off.

(2) Pat stopped teasing her. What behavioral procedure did Carol use? ______________________________

Example #17

Ward liked Bev a lot and so he went out of his way to find things about her to compliment. At first Bev liked this and smiled and thanked him. However, after she got engaged to Tom she felt embarrassed by Ward's compliments. As a result she invariably ended up ignoring them. Ward doesn't compliment her anymore.

(14) What behavioral procedure did Bev use when she ignored Ward's compliments? ______________________________

Example #18

Whenever Pam took Clara with her in the car, Clara would continually ask "How long until we get there?" At first Pam would explain carefully, but later she decided that Clara was just pestering her so she did not answer these questions. Clara continued to ask the question afterwards.

(22) What procedure was Pam using? ______________________________

Example #19

Dan had a fantastic smile. Anyone who did a favor for him and received a thank-you accompanied by that smile was much more likely to do another favor for him in the future.

(1) One of Dan's smiles is termed a(n) ______________________________ .

Example #20

Professor Jones disrupted faculty meetings with insane ideas. His colleagues used to argue vehemently with him. However, the chairman finally convinced them to simply ignore Jones. Soon, Jones wasn't disrupting meetings anymore.

(13) The faculty's ignoring Jones's insane ideas is an example of what behavioral procedure? ______________________________

EXAMPLE ANSWERS

(1) reinforcer (2) extinction (3) extinction (4) reinforcement (5) reinforcement (6) unknown (7) stopped (8) stop event; behavior decreases (9) extinction (10) no (11) unknown (12) yes (13) extinction (14) extinction (15) unknown (16) unknown (17) instruction (18) decreased (19) extinction (20) reinforcer (21) yes (22) unknown (23) unknown (24) extinction (25) reinforcement (26) extinction (27) extinction (28) following (29) stop event (30) extinction (31) red

Lesson 10

Differential Reinforcement of Everyday Behaviors

Lessons 8 and 9 dealt with reinforcement and extinction, both procedures for altering the rate of a single behavior. This lesson introduces a procedure for altering the relative rates of two or more different behaviors.

Differential reinforcement refers to a procedure in which one behavior is reinforced while other behaviors are extinguished. The ultimate goal is to increase the rate of that behavior relative to the others. The term **differential reinforcement** is applied to any procedure that has the following three characteristics: (1) two or more physically different behaviors occurring in one situation are involved; (2) one behavior is reinforced; and (3) the other behaviors are extinguished. All three characteristics must be present before the procedure can be called "differential reinforcement."

Differential reinforcement is most often used to increase the rate of a desirable behavior while decreasing the rate of closely related but undesirable behaviors. For example, when teaching someone to sing a particular note, differential reinforcement would probably be employed to increase the singing of the desired note while decreasing the singing of notes that are close to the desired one but not close enough. Similarly, differential reinforcement would be used to teach the correct pronunciation of difficult English words to a child, pronunciation of foreign words to a student, throwing a curve ball, and coordinating the movement of clutch and accelerator when shifting a car.

We met up with a good example of the application of differential reinforcement to normal people earlier. Goetz and Baer (1973) differentially reinforced Mary, a preschool child, for creative blockbuilding. They did this by praising any form that she had not previously built and ignoring those forms that she had previously built. Figure 10-1 shows the result of that experiment. As you can see, Mary built many new forms when they were differentially reinforced, but built few new ones when they were not. It may be that creative behavior can be encouraged by the systematic use of differential reinforcement.

We gave other examples of differential reinforcement earlier in the book. For example, Komacki and Barnett (1977) helped the coaches of a little league football team differentially reinforce the young players for carrying out their part of a set play correctly. They reported an increase in the correct carrying out of those plays by all of the members of the team. Budzynski and Stoyva (1969) differentially reinforced relaxation behaviors in adults that led to a decrease in the muscular tension in the forehead muscles. Differential reinforcement of relaxation behavior may be a behavioral method for producing meditation skills, as suggested by Karlins and Andrews (1972). Differential reinforcement has proven useful in teaching such widely diverse behavioral skills as creativity, executing football plays, and relaxation. We can expect that behavior analysts will demonstrate that differential reinforcement can be used to teach many other skills useful in everyday life.

BEHAVIOR ANALYSIS EXAMPLE

One of the most unpleasant jobs in a modern urban society is that of garbage collector. The job is made unnecessarily unpleasant by the lack of citizens' cooperation in packaging their trash

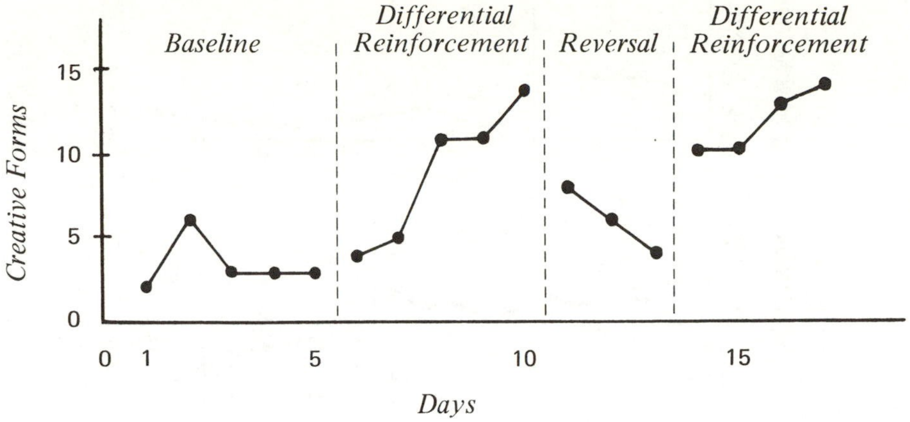

Figure 10–1. This graph shows the outcome of an experiment designed to increase 4-year-old Mary's creativity. During the periods marked "differential reinforcement," Mary was given social attention only when she built a new, creative structure with her building blocks. During the reversal period, Mary was reinforced only when she built noncreative forms similar to ones that she had already built. Thus differential reinforcement can be used to improve a child's creativity. Adapted from "Social Control of Form Diversity and the Emergence of New Forms in Children's Blockbuilding," by E. M. Goetz and D. M. Baer, *Journal of Applied Behavior Analysis,* 1973, *6,* 209–217. Copyright 1973 by the Society for the Experimental Analysis of Behavior, Inc. Used by permission.

carefully. Stokes and Fawcett (1977) investigated the possibility of improving the packaging of trash by the citizens of one city. The city ordinance specified a number of rules to be followed by citizens when they put out their garbage. These rules were designed to make the work of the sanitation personnel safer and pleasanter. These rules included: place containers conveniently near the curb; don't overfill the containers; tie plastic bags and use only untorn ones; don't use containers that fall apart when wet; tie yard trimmings into easily manageable bundles; and pick up loose litter at collection point. Stokes and Fawcett developed behavioral definitions that would permit the observation of violations of these standards. They measured reliability on four days and found it to be 95%. Their observations suggested that almost half of all residences violated the standards before treatment.

They then developed a simple treatment procedure in which the households being studied were notified of the standards and told that any trash not correctly packaged would not be collected. In addition, the sanitation crews wrote out a ticket to be placed on any container not collected which explained the reason(s) that it was not being collected. In other words, those packaging behaviors that met the city standards were followed by collection of the trash while those packaging behaviors that did not meet city standards were followed by no collection.

The experiment was conducted by studying two neighborhoods, one middle class and the other working class. Figure 10–2 shows that in the middle-class neighborhood the percent of households violating one or more of the standards was about 40% under normal conditions. After five days, the noncollection policy was implemented and the percentage of households making one or more violations fell to about 12%. In the working-class neighborhood, the percentage of violating households was about 45% under normal conditions. After ten days the noncollection policy was implemented and the percentage fell to 23%. Thus, for both neighborhoods, the effect of the noncollection policy was a sharp drop in packaging behaviors that violated the standards.

To determine whether the packaging standards were relevant to the sanitation crews, they were asked to rate the neighborhoods before and after the new policy was put into effect. These ratings indicated that the packaging was considered by the crews to be much better done after the start of the policy and that the collections were easier and safer to make.

This study suggests that differential reinforcement may be relevant not only to individual skill acquisition but also to the broader societal process of social change.

Note: The term *differential reinforcement* is used to refer to a behavioral procedure that has a specified effect on behavior. If you wish to refer only to the procedure because the effect is not yet known, you would use the term *differential reinforcement procedure,* because this emphasizes

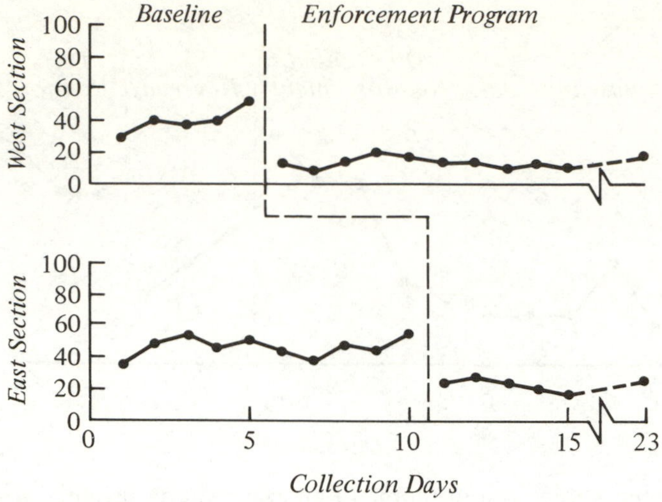

Figure 10-2. Percentage of residences violating the trash packaging standards of a midwest city. From "Evaluating Municipal Policy: An Analysis of a Refuse Packaging Program," by T. F. Stokes and S. B. Fawcett, *Journal of Applied Behavior Analysis,* 1977, *10,* 391–398. Copyright 1977 by the Society for the Experimental Analysis of Behavior, Inc. Used by permission.

that you are talking about the procedure. This term would never be applied if the behavioral effect was known not to exist. This term will be used occasionally in the rest of this book, but you will not be tested on it.

ADDITIONAL READINGS

Schwartz, G. J. College students as contingency managers for adolescents in a program to develop reading skills. *Journal of Applied Behavior Analysis,* 1977, *10,* 645–655. Schwartz organized a tutorial program for 260 seventh-grade students with important reading deficits. She used 42 college students as the tutors. They carried out a careful program in which special remedial materials were made available to the grade schoolers, who entered into written contracts agreeing to complete specified amounts of work relevant to their problems. They awarded points to the students based on carrying out the contracts. The seventh-grade students advanced during the ten-week program an average of about two school years on the Gates-MacGinitie Reading Test. In an interesting addition to this experiment, the tutors were instructed to differentially reinforce the students for expressing positive comments about reading, the learning process, and their abilities. The ratio of positive to negative comments changed from 50% positive before the program to about 85% positive afterwards. Thus it appears that differential reinforcement, coupled with the effective training of reading skills, improved the attitudes of the students toward reading and also toward themselves!

Helpful hints: To apply the concept of differential reinforcement to everyday situations, you must first determine whether there are at least two different behaviors involved. If not, then you can rule out the possibility that differential reinforcement is involved. This step is particularly important because there is another behavioral procedure to be introduced in Lesson 16 that involves the reinforcement and extinction of one or more behaviors in differing situations. Thus, determining whether there are at least two behaviors will permit you to easily make a very difficult distinction. Examples of this other procedure will be introduced in this lesson to help you learn how to tell the difference—for now you will label them as examples of an "unknown" procedure.

Helpful hint #1: To determine whether an example contains two or more different behaviors you must analyze whether the individual makes different physical movements of his or her muscles. If the same muscles are moved in the same way, then only one behavior is involved no matter what else may differ in the surrounding situation.

The following are some common examples in which there is only one behavior.

(1) Making and not making a response: not making a response is the absence of behavior. So it cannot be considered to be a second behavior.
(2) The same muscles in two locations: digging a hole in the front yard does not involve

different muscular movements than digging a hole in the back yard. You don't shovel differently just because you are in the back yard.

(3) The same muscles at different times: pointing at a cardinal does not involve a different movement of the finger muscles than pointing at a robin.

(4) Reading different materials: your eyes focus in the same way and scan from left to right no matter what you are reading. Although there may be slight differences in line length, print size, illustrations, and even type arrangement (as in a comic book), the minor variations in movement required usually do not justify regarding the behaviors as different.

(5) Saying the same word to different people: your vocal cords, lips, tongue, and lungs move in the same way to say "stop" to John as to Sam.

The following are examples of different behaviors.

(1) The same muscles at different speeds: sprinting and running involve similar movements of the leg muscles. However, the greater speed of sprinting clearly requires a different length stride, a stronger push off, and even landing on a different portion of the foot.

(2) The same muscles at different strengths: whispering "stop" exerts the vocal muscles differently than screaming it. Driving a nail with one blow requires a longer backswing, more wrist action, and a stronger pull than driving it with ten blows.

(3) Talking about different topics: talking about different topics requires the use of different words that in turn involve different movements of the vocal apparatus. Talking about poetry would be a different behavior than talking about cars.

(4) Pronouncing a word correctly and incorrectly: this would be the same as saying two or more different words since differing pronunciation will result in differing sounds.

Helpful hint #2: Verbal behavior can present problems in analysis. If two individuals are talking, it is helpful to focus on one individual's talking as a series of responses whose rate might be increased or decreased. Then the talking of the other individual can be analyzed as a possible reinforcing event for the first person. For example, if Jean talks about how tough her job is and Larry listens sympathetically, he could well be reinforcing her. That is, each comment that Jean makes about her job (the response) may be followed by comments from Larry such as "Gee, that's too bad!" or "You ought to do something about that." If these comments by Larry increase the rate of Jean's negative job statements, they can be viewed as reinforcing events because they follow and increase the rate of Jean's comments. When you read examples involving conversations, be sure to read into the example this type of dyadic interaction between the two individuals.

LESSON 10 READING QUIZ

(11) One characteristic of differential reinforcement is that two or more physically ________________ behaviors are involved.

(26) The different behaviors occurring in an example of differential reinforcement must occur in one ________________.

(22) A second characteristic of differential reinforcement is that one of those behaviors is ________________.

(10) The third characteristic of differential reinforcement is that one or more other behaviors are ________________.

(21) The three characteristics of differential reinforcement are: two or more physically ________________ behaviors (occurring in one situation) are involved; one behavior is ________________; other behaviors are ________________.

(20) To teach the correct pronunciation of a difficult English word to a child, one could use the behavioral procedure of ________________.

(9) Zimmerman and her colleagues (1969) used differential reinforcement to teach retarded children to follow ________________.

(19) Goetz and Baer (1973) used differential reinforcement to teach a preschool child to engage in ________________ blockbuilding.

(18) Komacki and Barnett (1977) taught the coaches to use differential reinforcement to improve

the correct carrying out of assignments by members of a little league ________________ ________________ team.

(8) Budzynski and Stoyva (1969) used differential reinforcement to teach adults how to ________________ the forehead muscles.

(17) Stokes and Fawcett (1977) studied the correct and incorrect packaging of trash by the residents of a city. Correct and incorrect packaging of trash ________ (is, isn't) an example of physically different responses.

(7) Stokes and Fawcett (1977) found that correct packaging behaviors increased when they were followed by collection and that incorrect packaging behaviors decreased when they were not followed by collection. We can conclude that collection as a stimulus is a(n) ________ ________________ for everyone whose packaging behavior improved.

(6) Stokes and Fawcett (1977) found that correct packaging behaviors increased and incorrect packaging behavior decreased when only correct packaging was followed by collection. Therefore, their procedure would be labeled ________________ ________________.

(16) By asking the sanitation workers to rate the packaging of trash before and after the new rules were imposed, Stokes and Fawcett (1977) were determining the ________________ ________ of the behavioral definition implied by the rules.

(5) There is a behavioral procedure not covered in this lesson that involves the reinforcement and extinction of a single ________________ occurring in more than one situation.

(25) If a single behavior is reinforced in one situation and extinguished in another, you should label the procedure as ________________.

(15) To determine whether an example contains two or more different behaviors you must analyze whether the individual makes different physical movements of his or her ________.

(4) Making and not making a response ________________ (is, isn't) considered to be an example of two different behaviors.

(24) Performing the same behavior (that is, using the same muscles) in two different places ________________ (is, isn't) considered to be two behaviors.

(14) Using the same muscles at different speeds ________________ (is, isn't) considered to be two different behaviors.

(3) Using the same muscles at different times ________________ (is, isn't) considered to be different behaviors.

(13) Reading different materials ________________ (is, isn't considered to constitute different behaviors.

(2) Using the same muscles with different strength ________________ (is, isn't) considered different behaviors.

(23) Talking about different topics ________________ (is, isn't) considered to be different behaviors.

(12) Saying the same word to different people ________________ (is, isn't) considered to constitute different behaviors.

(1) If two individuals are having a conversation, it is helpful to focus on the talking of ____ ________________ individual(s) as a behavior whose rate may be increased or decreased by the response of the other individual.

READING QUIZ ANSWERS

(1) one (2) is (3) isn't (4) isn't (5) behavior (6) differential reinforcement (7) reinforcer (not reinforcement) (8) relax (9) instructions (10) extinguished (11) different (12) isn't (13) isn't (14) is (15) muscles (16) social validity (17) is (18) football (19) creative (20) differential reinforcement (21) different; reinforced; extinguished (22) reinforced (23) is (24) isn't (25) unknown (26) situation

LESSON 10 EXAMPLES

Example #1

A baby boy makes many vocalizations such as "ba," "glub," "goo-goo," and eventually "da" or "da-da." When parents first hear a vocalization similar to "da," they immediately pay a lot of attention to the child, pet him, hold him, make nice sounds back at him, and generally ignore the other vocalizations. As a result the child starts saying "da" more often.

(12) To determine whether this is an example of differential reinforcement, you must first decide whether there are at least two ______________ behaviors involved. Are there? ______

(26) Next determine whether one behavior is being ______________. Is it? ______

(13) Finally, determine whether other physically different behaviors are being ______. Are they? ______

(35) Since the example involves two or more different behaviors one of which is being reinforced and the other extinguished, this is an example of ______________.

Example #2

A baby boy may say "dada" to many males other than his father. His parents, by reserving their attention for those occasions when the child says "dada" to his father, will eventually teach the child not to say "dada" to any other males.

(24) Does saying "dada" to the father involve a behavior that is physically different from saying "dada" to other males? ______

(11) By paying attention to the child when he says "dada" to the father, thereby causing the rate of saying "dada" to increase, the parents are using what procedure? ______________

(34) By ignoring the child when he says "dada" to other males, thereby causing the rate of saying "dada" to decrease, the parents are using what procedure? ______________

(25) In this example, although reinforcement and extinction are used, the situation does not involve two responses. Therefore this ______________ (is, isn't) an example of differential reinforcement.

Example #3

Roger watched everything on TV from cartoons to *Sesame Street*. However, his father started reinforcing him when he watched *Sesame Street* and ignoring him when he watched cartoons. Soon Roger was watching only *Sesame Street*.

(33) Does watching cartoons involve a physically different behavior from watching *Sesame Street*? ______

(23) You can therefore conclude that this is not an example of ______________.

(10) You should therefore label it as a(n) ______________ procedure.

Example #4

Frank's dad noticed that his son's habit of tuning the radio had changed considerably. At first his son would usually twirl the knob very quickly and then complain of not being able to find his favorite radio station. However, the few times that he turned it slowly, he was able to find the station. As time went on, Frank turned the knob slowly more often.

(22) First, does turning the knob quickly constitute a different behavior from turning it slowly? ______

(8) Is turning the knob slowly reinforced by any event? ______

(32) Is turning the knob quickly extinguished? ______

(9) The procedure being followed by the natural operation of the tuner on the radio would be called ______________________________.

Example #5

Billy was pretty good at using a hammer and screwdriver. However, his mother saw him sometimes hammer a screw in rather than use the screwdriver. She even saw him try to screw in a nail a couple of times. His mom decided to help Billy by telling him whenever his use of the tools was correct and by letting him struggle otherwise. Soon Billy was using the tools correctly.

(20) Remember to determine whether there are two ______________________ behaviors;

(31) whether one of them is ______________________;

(7) whether the other is ______________________.

(21) Then you must read the example carefully to see if the behavioral effect of the procedure is stated. In the present example, you would label the procedure used by the mother as ______________________________.

Example #6

Faith was learning the language of radical politics. For some reason she had trouble pronouncing "imperialism." So her boyfriend Imamu delighted in helping her learn the correct pronunciation. When she was right he praised her, when she was wrong he didn't. She soon learned to pronounce it correctly.

(30) You must read into this example that because Faith had trouble pronouncing "imperialism" means that she sometimes said something different; this something different would constitute a physically different ______________________ from the correct pronunciation.

(6) What behavioral procedure is Imamu using in this example? ______________________________

Example #7

Marcie was tired of Dave watching the baseball game on TV every weekend. She told him about her feelings and asked him to stop watching it. He agreed and now no longer watches the weekend game.

(19) What procedure did Marcie use to reduce Dave's rate of watching the game? ______________________

Example #8

Garvey liked the meetings of the Young Republicans, and he also liked the meetings of the Humanists' Club. But he found that if he talked about the dignity of all humans, including poor people, the Republicans didn't seem too interested, while the Humanists seemed overjoyed. Without even noticing it, Garvey found himself talking less about the dignity of poor people with the Republicans and more about it with the Humanists.

(5) What procedure were these two organizations unintentionally applying to Garvey's behavior? ______________________________

Example #9

Gary and Lois frequently visited Gary's parents during breaks from the university. The vacations were nice; however, Gary's parents seemed to talk incessantly about the "hippies" who attended college. They made comments such as "I wish those hippies would wash once in a while" and "If you don't learn to get up earlier in the morning, you're going to become another damned hippie."

Gary and Lois finally decided to do something about it. They both agreed that they would be very nice to the parents when they made comments like that and that they would carefully explain to them why the youth movement is a good thing. They vowed that they would win the parents over. After they had done this for several vacations, they found that Gary's parents were making even more comments about hippies.

(29) What behavioral procedure is involved with the parents' comments about hippies? ______ ________________________

Example #10

John and Darrin were in the cafeteria having an important discussion about their social action meeting that night. Lee came over and sat down with them. John and Darrin both said "hello" and immediately included Lee in their conversation. After this incident Lee sat with John and Darrin more often during lunchtime and they always included him in their conversations.

(18) What behavioral procedure is at work determining how often Lee sat with John and Darrin? ________________________

Example #11

Bob's coach helped him to improve his hitting. Prior to every at-bat, he would remind Bob to keep his eye on the ball. Bob usually did. Then the coach decided that Bob now could do it on his own so he stopped reminding him. Bob does not keep his eye on the ball very often now.

(4) What procedure did the coach use that resulted in the decrease in Bob keeping his eye on the ball? ________________________

Example #12

David Jaynes was the new psychiatrist for Mrs. Brooke. She became annoyed at Jaynes's habit of discussing his own problems but never trying to find out what help Mrs. Brooke needed. So Mrs. Brooke started ignoring all discussions about his problems and paid attention only when her own problems came up. He soon talked about her problems.

(17) What behavioral procedure was Mrs. Brooke using? ________________________

Example #13

Mr. Howard taught a ninth-grade geography class. It was his conviction that the students would learn more about geography if they participated in class discussion. For the most part, the students appeared to enjoy the discussion classes and to willingly enter into discussions. However, one boy, Ben, said very little. Mr. Howard decided that, rather than continue to put him on the spot by constantly asking him questions, he would compliment him profusely whenever he did say anything.

(3) Mr. Howard tried to change Ben's behavior by using what behavioral procedure? ______ ________________________

Example #14

Grace wanted desperately to learn how to dance, but she had little sense of rhythm. Her roommate volunteered to help by dancing in rhythm to the radio. Grace would dance at the same time and, by watching whether she was moving at the same time as her roommate, determine whether she was in rhythm or not. She was happy when her movements coincided and unhappy when they did not. Gradually her movements were in time with her roommate's.

(28) What procedure is built into this situation encouraging Grace to move in rhythm? ____________________

Example #15

Many new parents are unhappy that their baby cries so often. For example, they may change a baby's diapers, attend to all his or her physical needs, and put him or her to bed for the night. However, they will then answer the baby's cries for hours even though there is nothing wrong with the child. They would be advised by a behavior analyst to ignore all crying after the baby is put to bed properly cared for. The child will cry a lot for the first part of a few nights but will gradually stop crying.

(16) This method of changing the baby's crying after he or she is put to bed is called what? ____________________

Example #16

Gary found that if he smiled when he was with Jane, she would pay a lot of attention to him. However, if he smiled when he was with Gloria, she would ignore him. Naturally, Gary started smiling a lot when he was around Jane and hardly at all when he was around Gloria.

(2) What behavioral process is at work changing his pattern of smiling? ____________________

Example #17

Carole had a friend who was helping her learn to jog. Whenever she took a long smooth stride, her friend praised her; when she took a shorter stride or a rougher stride, her friend made no comment. She was soon the smoothest runner around.

(27) What procedure is her friend using to teach Carole how to jog? ____________________

Example #18

If a child starts to read the comics out loud, his or her parents usually make a big fuss about this suddenly displayed reading skill.

(15) What behavioral procedure would account for any increase in the child's reading from the comics? ____________________

Example #19

Faith has learned about radical politics from her friend Imamu. After she had read parts of *Das Kapital* Imamu would talk with her excitedly about it; after she had read parts of *The Rise and Fall of the Roman Empire,* however, he was very quiet. Faith came to read *Das Kapital* more and more often.

(1) What behavioral procedure was Imamu using? ____________________

Example #20

Kurt wanted to learn to speak German really well but he was having trouble in his language class learning to say "ch" as the Germans do. He found that it was a guttural sound that combined some aspects of the English "k" and the English "ch." His instructor praised him strongly when he got it right but ignored him the rest of the time.

(14) If Kurt's pronunciation of "ch" improved, what procedure was his instructor using? ______
____

EXAMPLE ANSWERS

(1) unknown (2) unknown (3) reinforcement (4) unknown (5) unknown (6) differential reinforcement (7) extinguished (8) yes (9) differential reinforcement (10) unknown (11) reinforcement (12) different; yes (13) extinguished; yes (14) differential reinforcement (15) reinforcement (16) extinction (17) differential reinforcement (18) reinforcement (19) unknown (20) different (21) differential reinforcement (22) yes (23) differential reinforcement (24) no (25) isn't (26) reinforced; yes (27) differential reinforcement (28) differential reinforcement (29) reinforcement (30) behavior (31) reinforced (32) yes (33) no (34) extinction (35) differential reinforcement

Lesson 11

Shaping Everyday Behaviors

In previous lessons you learned that a person's performance of existing behaviors can be improved through the appropriate use of reinforcement. Thus, if children can already build structures with blocks, differential reinforcement can be used to teach them to build more creative structures. If students can describe various uses of an object, reinforcement can be used to increase their rate of suggesting novel uses. In both cases, the function of reinforcement is to increase the rate of an existing behavior. In this lesson, we shall introduce the concept of shaping, in which differential reinforcement can be used to literally mold a new behavior that previously did not exist in the person's abilities. The basic idea involves selecting a behavior that the person can do that is in some way related to the desired but nonexistent behavior and differentially reinforcing those aspects that are related to the desired behavior. By then shifting the criterion of reinforcement to aspects of the behavior that are more closely related to the desired behavior, an entirely new behavior can be gradually shaped.

The term **shaping** should be used only when both (1) a target behavior has been specified and (2) differential reinforcement has been (or is being) applied to a series of successive approximations to that target behavior. The term *shaping* can also be applied to accidental situations, even though a target behavior has not been explicitly defined in advance, if the behavioral change produced by the differential reinforcement moves toward an end result that could be thought of as an "unintentional target behavior."

The desired behavior that does not now occur is called the "target behavior." A **target behavior** is a specified behavior to be produced through shaping. The shaping procedure involves selecting a behavior that in some way approximates the target behavior and then differentially reinforcing that behavior until it occurs frequently. Once a high frequency is established, the criterion for reinforcement is changed slightly to produce another behavior that is a somewhat closer approximation to the target behavior. This technique is continued until the target behavior is produced and can be reinforced. Each behavioral approximation to the target behavior is called a **successive approximation.**

For example, suppose that you wished to teach people how to shoot a bow and arrow accurately. You would teach them the preliminaries of how to grip the bow, how to hold the arrow, how to sight the target, how to draw the arrow back and how to release it. Once you had taught these mechanics, you might have them shoot from a very short distance so that they could practice the basic method with little need for the strength and steadiness required to shoot from a distance. Then you would have them move back a few steps and differentially reinforce accurate shooting. You would continue this until they were able to shoot accurately from the desired distance. In this example, the target behavior would be accurate shooting from a long distance. The successive approximations would consist of shooting accurately from first short and then longer distances. Accurate shooting at each distance would be differentially reinforced in order to create a high level of accuracy. Figure 11-1 illustrates how a concerned father might start with a very easy first approximation.

The importance of shaping in producing complicated human behavior cannot be overestimated. Many complex skills are acquired through accidental or intentional shaping. Playing an instrument, writing poetry, making a speech, building a house, speaking a foreign language,

Figure 11-1. When using *shaping* to teach someone a new skill, you should start by differentially reinforcing behavior that he can do successfully. Cartoon copyright © 1973 King Features Syndicate. Reproduced by permission.

pleasing a sweetheart—virtually everything we do starts from a simple behavior that is built on until it becomes an extensive behavioral skill.

Accidental shaping often results from natural contingencies that exist in our environment. For example, mothers often shape up very obnoxious pestering behaviors in their children. Often a mother will give her sweet young child a cookie just before dinner the first few times that he or she asks. Later, the mother may decide that it isn't such a good idea to do that and will refuse to give the cookie. But the child may persist and pretty soon the mother gives it a cookie to shut it up. At a later time the mother may again resolve to stop this pattern, whereupon the child may raise his or her voice and continue nagging, perhaps breaking down the mother's resolve. In such a situation, the mother's natural, unprogrammed response is to differentially reinforce first sweet requests, then persistent requests, then loud and obnoxious requests—each being a successive approximation to some unintended target behavior that might best be described as "brat" behavior.

Intentional shaping involves the deliberate effort of a behavior analyst or other person to create a new behavior by differentially reinforcing a series of successive approximations. A good example is the program devised by Jackson and Wallace (1974) to teach a 15-year-old, mildly retarded girl to speak loudly enough to be heard. Alice had been diagnosed as extremely withdrawn since age 7; she had no social skills, no friends, and learned little in school. A primary characteristic of her withdrawal was that she spoke in a soft whisper that generally could not be heard. Jackson and Wallace, using very sensitive electronic equipment, differentially reinforced Alice for whispering one-syllable words appearing on a card in front of her. Once she was doing that, they required her to whisper louder before reinforcing her. They continued to slowly increase the loudness requirement as she mastered each stage until she was reading the words in a normal tone of voice. The investigators then went through a series of additional steps, including having her read words of more than one syllable, having her say things to other people, and so on. Jackson and Wallace also undertook a series of steps to help Alice transfer her new found voice loudness to the classroom situation. After this training, Alice changed quite dramatically. She talked with other kids, she did quite well in a normal classroom, and she obtained a job as a waitress.

Another example of intentional shaping is given by Horner (1971), who taught Dennis, a 5-year-old, moderately retarded child, to walk with crutches. Dennis was moderately retarded with a birth defect that left his legs paralyzed. He was said to function with his muscular movements at the level of a 10-month-old child. He could sit up and pull himself along the floor with his arms. Horner differentially reinforced Dennis for a series of approximations to using the crutches. The first step was to have Dennis place the crutch tips on two dots on the floor while they were secured to his hands with Ace bandages. The next step was to place the crutch tips on the dots and swing his body to an erect crutch-supported position. The very gradual increase in the behavior required for differential reinforcement occurred through ten steps until Dennis was able to walk unassisted with the crutches. He learned to walk to and from all programs and activities in the hospital within 15 days. The treatment permitted Dennis the dignity of controlling when and where he went.

Intentional shaping has been used to develop complex behaviors in many situations where normal psychiatric or medical procedures have been ineffective. For instance, it has been used to teach electively mute psychotics to resume talking by first reinforcing eye contact, then nodding, then grunting, and finally the production of verbal behavior (for example, Isaacs, Thomas, & Goldiamond, 1960; Sherman, 1963). In an extensive series of experiments, behavior analysts have identified and taught many of the component skills of verbal communication to retarded children. Retardates have been taught such verbal skills as the correct use of plurals (Guess, Sailor, Rutherford, & Baer, 1968), the correct use of adjectives (Baer & Guess, 1971) and even the appropriate asking of questions (Twardosz & Baer, 1973). These studies not only show the promise of using behavioral methods to shape complex communication skills but they also may help us understand normal language acquisition and use from a behavioral perspective.

The belief in the "magic" of shaping has made many behavior analysts into radical egalitarians. Some believe that any skill can be taught through shaping if sound behavioral definitions of the successive approximations can be determined and if appropriate reinforcers can be discovered (Skinner, 1948b). We may find some day that no person is inferior to any other person in potential.

The term *shaping* should not be applied to just any gradual change related to a person's behavior. For example, the gradual increase in response rate that results from reinforcement shouldn't be described as shaping. Nor should the change in an outcome of a person's behavior without a change in the technique itself be described as shaping. For example, if a person were to gradually buy more expensive books, his or her actual buying behavior (that is, picking out the book, carrying it to the counter, writing a check, and so on) will not have changed. Be sure that some physical aspect of the person's movements changes through a series of approximations.

BEHAVIOR ANALYSIS EXAMPLES

Proper use of asthma therapy equipment. Renne and Creer (1976) investigated the possibility of using behavior analysis methods to help young asthmatic children learn how to use inhalation therapy equipment properly. When properly used, the equipment gave the children immediate relief from asthma symptoms. If the children did not use the equipment properly, they frequently required additional medication that relieved their symptoms more slowly, or sometimes they even required hospitalization. Although simple instructions from a nurse usually sufficed to teach the children to use the equipment properly, a small percentage did not learn in this way. This description will focus on one of the children helped by Renne and Creer, whom we shall call David.

Renne and Creer identified three behaviors that were involved in successful use of the equipment: (1) eye fixation, which consisted of looking at the pressure gauge indicating air pressure; (2) facial posture, which consisted of holding the mouthpiece at the right angle and keeping the lips motionless and secured to the mouthpiece; and (3) deep breathing, which consisted of extending the stomach when inhaling and contracting it when exhaling.

Prior to teaching David proper eye fixation, Renne and Creer observed him during three baseline trials, each consisting of 15 breaths. They counted the number of breaths during which he looked at the air pressure dial for the full duration of each breath. They found that he looked at the dial during 4, 4, and 3 breaths for these baseline trials. They then explained to him that he could earn tickets that could be applied toward a surprise gift. To earn the first ticket, he had to look at the dial without interruption for the duration of at least 4 breaths—his best baseline score. They then followed the rule that if he surpassed the criterion, they would increase it to his new best score. As you can see from Figure 11–2[1] he surpassed his best baseline score of 4 by looking at the dial for all 15 breaths. Except for the very next trial, he looked at the dial for all 15 breaths on every subsequent trial.

By the end of the sixth trial it was clear that eye fixation had been taught. Renne and Creer turned their attention to teaching David correct facial posture. Prior to trial seven, they told him that to earn a ticket he now had to do two things. First, he had to maintain his eye fixation performance; second, he had to at least match his best baseline performance of the correct facial posture. That was easy since his best baseline performance was that he maintained the correct posture only one breath out of 15. He maintained it 13 out of 15 breaths on the next trial, so they changed the criterion so that he had to maintain correct facial posture on 13 of 15 breaths. As you can see, he improved in several trials to the point where he was maintaining the correct facial posture and eye posture for virtually every breath.

At the end of the 12th trial, Renne and Creer told David he could now earn tickets by maintaining his performance on eye fixation and facial posture and by matching his best baseline

[1]This figure is actually the average of the scores for David and three other children.

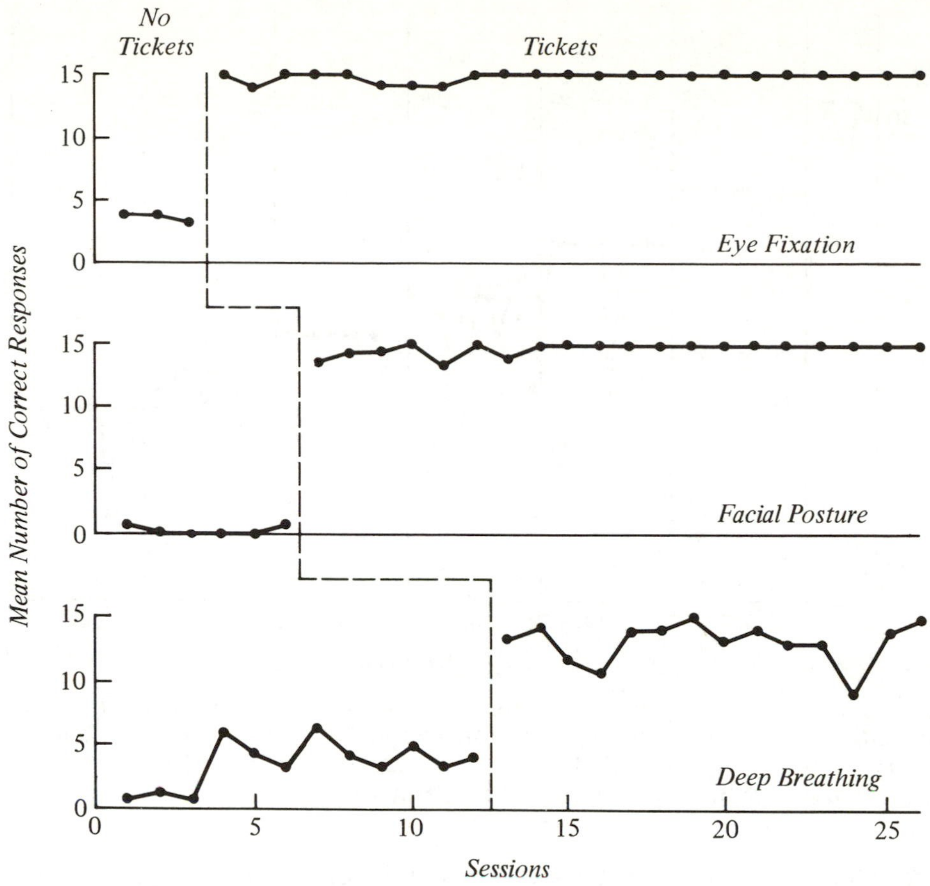

Figure 11–2. Training asthmatic children in the correct use of inhalation therapy equipment. Adapted from "Training Children With Asthma to Use Inhalation Therapy Equipment," by C. M. Renne and T. L. Creer, *Journal of Applied Behavior Analysis*, 1976, 9, 1–11. Copyright 1976 by the Society for the Experimental Analysis of Behavior, Inc. Used by permission.

performance for deep breathing. The figure shows that it was somewhat harder to develop correct deep breathing responses, but there was a notable improvement to an average of about 13 out of 15 breaths correct.

The validity of the behavioral definition was obtained in an interesting way for this experiment. When David did not use the equipment properly, he often needed supplementary medication within 2 hours of the inhalation treatment. In fact, sometimes he would have to be hospitalized as a result. Renne and Creer used the occurrence of such a situation as an indication that under normal, nonexperimental conditions David was using the equipment incorrectly. They found that he used the equipment incorrectly about 60% of the time prior to training but only 20% after training. This suggests that the trained behaviors were those needed to use the equipment properly.

Reducing cigarette smoking. Hartmann and Hall (1976) developed a behavioral procedure to help a heavy smoker, whom we shall call Paul, reduce his rate of smoking. The first step in their procedure was to determine Paul's initial rate of smoking. His rate averaged 46 cigarettes per day. They then imposed a monetary contingency that paid Paul 10¢ for smoking one less, 20¢ for two less, 30¢ for three less, and so on. In addition, a fine was imposed for smoking more than 46 cigarettes per day. After Paul's rate had held steady at 46 or fewer cigarettes per day, Hartmann and Hall changed the criterion to 43 cigarettes per day and used the same payment schedule. They continued to reduce the criterion through a series of 21 steps until the rate was under 15 per day. Figure 11–3 shows the gradual decrease in smoking through the first six criteria. Paul's smoking decreased from 46 cigarettes smoked per day to less than 15 per day. The entire course of treatment extended over a period of one year.

Note #1: Martin and Pear (1978) suggest several guidelines for effective applications of shaping. First, select a target behavior that is as specific as possible and that will be maintained by naturally

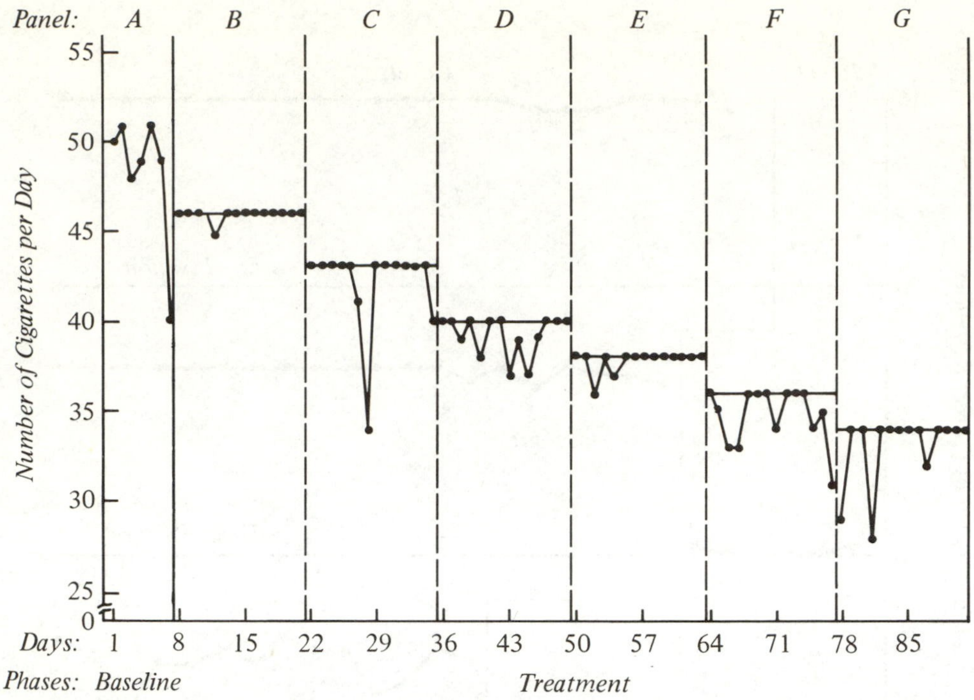

Figure 11-3. The number of cigarettes smoked per day during a shaping program designed to reduce smoking. From "The Changing Criterion Design," by D. P. Hartmann and R. V. Hall, *Journal of Applied Behavior Analysis,* 1976, *9,* 527–532. Copyright 1976 by the Society for the Experimental Analysis of Behavior, Inc. Used by permission.

occurring reinforcers after it has been shaped. Second, select an appropriate reinforcer that is readily available, that can be delivered immediately after the behavior, can be consumed quickly, and that the person won't tire of rapidly. Third, select an initial behavior that occurs at least once during the observation period and that resembles the target behavior as closely as possible. Fourth, if possible, explain to the person the goals of shaping, move from one approximation to the next after it has been performed correctly 6 out of 10 times, and, if the person has difficulty with a step, reassess your program, because if the program is properly designed you can produce the new behavior.

Note #2: The creation of complex behaviors with many components can also be referred to as "chaining" (see Lesson 20). For example, teaching the child to walk with crutches involves a number of components that are joined together into a smoothly functioning unit. This book will conform to general usage and refer to these procedures as "shaping."

ADDITIONAL READINGS

Baer, D. M., Peterson, R. F., & Sherman, J. A. The development of imitation by reinforcing behavioral similarity to a model. *Journal of the Experimental Analysis of Behavior,* 1967, *10,* 405–416. This classic article demonstrates the use of shaping for training severely retarded children to imitate progressively more complex behaviors demonstrated by others. Such imitation makes it possible for the children to learn new skills by observing the people around them.

Hingtgen, J. N., Sanders, B. J., & DeMeyer, M. K. Shaping cooperative responses in childhood schizophrenics. In L. Ullman & L. Krasner (Eds.), *Case studies in behavior modification.* New York: Holt, Rinehart & Winston, 1965, pp. 130–138. Six subjects diagnosed as early childhood schizophrenics were taught to engage in cooperative responses through shaping. At first, either of two children was permitted to push a button for coins whenever he wanted, then only when the signal light was on, then only when the one member of the pair turned on the signal light for the other. This procedure resulted in a simple cooperative response between the two children.

Isaacs, W., Thomas, J., & Goldiamond, I. Application of operant conditioning to reinstate verbal behavior in psychotics. *Journal of Speech and Hearing Disorders,* 1960, *25,* 8–12. This article illustrates the use of shaping procedures to get mute mental patients to begin talking. The patients were reinforced with a stick of gum, first when they moved their lips, then only when they made a noise, and finally only when they imitated a word. As a result the patients quickly learned to engage in conversation.

Skinner, B. F. *Walden Two.* New York: Macmillan, 1948. This is a Utopian novel based on the principles of behavior modification. The novel presents a statement of how man can control his own behavior and develop a more perfect community. The use of shaping to develop new behavioral skills plays a prominent part in the novel.

Wolf, M. M., Risley, T. R., & Mees, H. L. Application of operant conditioning procedures to the behavior problems of an autistic child. *Behavior Research and Therapy,* 1964, *1,* 305–312. This paper reports the use of shaping to teach a severely autistic child to wear corrective glasses, thereby permitting him to see. The problem was that the child would not wear the glasses, would not permit anyone to touch him, and would throw the glasses down if handed them. Shaping this response proceeded from picking them up, holding them, carrying them about, and bringing them toward his eyes. Food was used as the reinforcer.

Helpful hint: In examples of shaping, the extinction part of differential reinforcement is often not explicitly described. However, if the example states that a person is reinforced <u>only</u> when he makes a particular response, you should assume that he is extinguished for all other responses.

LESSON 11 READING QUIZ

(20) The term *shaping* is used to denote a particular use of what behavioral procedure that you have already studied? ______________________

(10) Behavior analysts use shaping to mold a(n) ______________________ behavior.

(28) The behavior that is the goal of a shaping program is called the ______________________.

(19) A behavior that is similar to the target behavior in a shaping program is called a(n) ______________________.

(9) Shaping involves the differential reinforcement of a behavior that ______________________ the target behavior.

(18) In shaping, once differential reinforcement has increased the rate of the first approximation, differential reinforcement is then applied to a second, closer approximation to the ______________________.

(8) If you wanted to teach someone to shoot a bow and arrow accurately from a distance of 30 feet, you might differentially reinforce him for shooting accurately from 5 feet on the theory that shooting from that close is a(n) ______________________ to the ultimate goal of shooting from 30 feet.

(27) Many complex skills are acquired through the accidental or intentional use of what behavioral procedure? ______________________

(17) The term *shaping* can also be applied to accidental or unintentional situations in which no ______________________ has been explicitly defined in advance.

(7) An example of accidental shaping might consist of the parent who differentially reinforces a series of successive ______________________ to the unintended target behavior of loudly and obnoxiously requesting a snack.

(26) Jackson and Wallace (1974) used shaping to help a 15-year-old girl learn to talk loudly enough to be heard by others. Talking loudly enough would be called a(n) ______________________.

(16) They selected barely audible whispering to start with. Such whispering would be called their first ______________________ to talking loudly enough.

(6) To encourage barely audible whispering, Jackson and Wallace (1974) reinforced such whispers and extinguished inaudible whispers. That involves the use of what behavioral procedure? ______________________

(25) Jackson and Wallace (1974) differentially reinforced first soft whispers, then louder and

louder whispers, in order to teach a retarded girl to talk loudly enough to be heard. What behavioral procedure did they use to develop "talking loudly enough"? ______________

(15) Horner (1971) developed a procedure to teach Dennis how to walk with crutches. Walking with crutches would be called Horner's ______________________.

(5) Horner first differentially reinforced placing the tips of the crutches on two circles on the floor while they were attached to his hands. This would be called the first ______________ to walking with crutches.

(24) By differentially reinforcing a series of successive approximations to walking with crutches, Horner (1971) was using what behavioral procedure? ______________

(14) The term *shaping* should be used only when both a(n) ______________ has been specified and differential reinforcement has been applied to a series of ______________________.

(4) Should all gradual changes in a person's behavior be classified as shaping? ______________

(23) Renne and Creer (1976) attempted to teach the correct use of inhalation equipment to asthmatic children. The correct use of the equipment would be called the ______________________ in their experiment.

(13) Renne and Creer at first gave David a ticket good for a prize only if he looked at the dial for at least 4 breaths out of 15. By giving the ticket only if he looked at the dial, but not if he looked elsewhere, they were using what behavioral procedure? ______________

(3) Looking at the dial 4 times out of 15 would be called a(n) ______________ to the ultimate goal of looking at it for all 15 breaths.

(22) Later in their program, they required David to breathe deeply at least 7 of 15 times (and to also look at the dial and maintain the correct facial posture). This would be a more advanced ______________________ to using the equipment properly.

(12) By giving tickets to David only when he met a behavioral criterion related to using the equipment properly and then changing that criterion until completely correct use was developed, Renne and Creer were using what behavioral procedure? ______________

(2) Hartmann and Hall (1976) developed a procedure to help Paul reduce his rate of smoking. A reduced rate of smoking is called a(n) ______________________.

(21) By paying Paul 10¢ for smoking less than 46 cigarettes a day and not paying him for smoking 46 or more, they were using what behavioral procedure? ______________

(11) By paying Paul first for smoking slightly less than 46 cigarettes a day, they were establishing a(n) ______________________ to greatly reduced smoking.

(1) When Hartmann and Hall (1976) paid Paul only when smoking less than 46 cigarettes a day, then only when smoking less than 43 per day, and continued decreasing the criterion until it was less than 15 per day, they were using what behavioral procedure? ______________

READING QUIZ ANSWERS

(1) shaping (2) target behavior (3) approximation (4) no (5) approximation (6) differential reinforcement (7) approximations (8) approximation (9) approximates (10) new (11) approximation (12) shaping (13) differential reinforcement (14) target behavior; approximations (15) target behavior (16) approximation (17) target behavior (18) target behavior (19) approximation (20) differential reinforcement (21) differential reinforcement (22) approximation (23) target behavior (24) shaping (25) shaping (26) target behavior (27) shaping (28) target behavior

LESSON 11 EXAMPLES

Example #1

Dean was teaching his son Jason how to play badminton. Jason learned the rules quickly and developed a good stroke, but he kept hitting the birdie right to Dean, even though Dean told him to hit it at least two steps away. To change this, Dean started praising Jason anytime that he hit the birdie at least one step away from him. When that had worked, Dean started praising Jason only when he hit the birdie two steps away from him. Pretty soon Jason was hitting his shots away from Dean as often as possible.

(14) Hitting the birdie at least two steps away from Dean would be called the ______________ ______________.

(28) Hitting the birdie one step away would be called a(n) ______________ to the ultimate goal.

(36) When the example states that Dean praised Jason *only* when Jason hit the birdie at least one step away, it means that Dean praised him when he did that and did not praise him when he didn't. Since this procedure increased the rate at which Jason hit the birdie one step away, it would be called ______________.

(13) Dean's total procedure is called ______________.

Example #2

Charlie Brown wants the little redheaded girl to sit by him. One day last month, he smiled at her, and she smiled back. Charlie decided to stop being wishy-washy and to try to get her to sit near him at lunch. At first, each time she looked in his direction, he smiled at her. After a while, he smiled only when she sat within 5 feet of him. Then, he smiled only when she sat within 2 feet of him. Finally, the little redheaded girl sat right next to Charlie Brown at lunch. (It was on that day that she said "Hi there, smiley.")

(26) For Charlie Brown, having the little redheaded girl sit next to him would be an example of a(n) ______________.

(11) Charlie Brown reinforced the little redheaded girl by ______________ at her.

(34) At first, he reinforced her only when she ______________ at him.

(12) Next, he reinforced her only when she sat within ______________ feet.

(25) Reinforcing her <u>only</u> when she sat that close is called ______________.

(24) Each change in the criterion for reinforcing her is a successive ______________ to the ultimate target behavior of having her sit next to him.

(10) The behavioral procedure used in this example is called ______________.

Example #3

Mr. Baker had taken on the job of teaching Tone Deaf Tony to sing on key. He decided to start by teaching Tony to sing middle C. He first played the note on the piano and asked Tony to hum the same note. After many repetitions Tony couldn't do it consistently, so Mr. Baker decided to praise him whenever he came within a half tone of middle C and simply ignore him and play the note over again when he missed it. Pretty soon Tony could sing within a half tone of middle C.

(27) Mr. Baker used what behavioral procedure? ______________

Example #4

Ralph was helping his brother learn to hit a fast-pitched ball. He started by throwing not-so-fast pitches. Each time that Bob got a hit, Ralph gave him a swig of beer. After many hits, Ralph threw medium-fast pitches and continued to give Bob a swig after each hit. Finally, Ralph threw fast pitches and still gave Bob a swig of beer after every hit. Bob learned to hit a fast ball pretty well in the process. But further practice had to be put off, because after 147 hits Bob couldn't stand up anymore.

(33) Hitting a fast-pitched ball in this example would be called the ______________ ______________.

(9) Giving Bob a swig of beer after he got a hit increased the rate of good swings and decreased the rate of poor swings. Therefore Ralph was using what behavioral procedure? ______________ ______________

(8) Hitting medium-fast pitches is a(n) ______________ to hitting fast pitches.

(23) What procedure did Ralph use to teach his brother to hit a fast pitch? ______________

Example #5

Janice's parents wanted her to be more assertive, so they talked with her about it and found that she too wished to be more assertive. They decided to teach her through role playing to be able firmly to say "no thank you" if a boy asked her to go to a movie she wasn't interested in. At first, if she said "no thank you" during the role playing they praised her. Later, they praised her only if she said "no thank you" firmly.

(32) Being able to say "no thank you" firmly would be called the ______________.

(35) Simply saying "no thank you" whether or not it was firm would be called a(n) ______________.

(7) The women's movement claims that many "masculine" traits are taught to boys and are not linked to the physical sex of the person. What procedure did Janice's parents use to teach her elementary assertiveness? ______________

Example #6

Tad wanted to take up jogging. He decided to build up to running a mile a day in under 6 minutes slowly. He set as his goal during the first week to run the mile in under 12 minutes. When he made it he bought himself a Super Sundae. The next week he tried to run it in under 11 minutes and again rewarded himself when he made it. Each week he lowered his goal until he was running the mile in under 6 minutes.

(22) Tad's weekly goals would be termed ______________.

(15) What behavioral procedure was Tad using to learn to run the mile in under 6 minutes? ______________

Example #7

James decided to teach his best friend to do the new disco step—the Twirling Chicken. For one particularly difficult part of the step he always praised her when she did it well and said nothing when she didn't. She started doing it much better.

(6) Doing the difficult part of the step well and doing it not so well would definitely be considered to be at least two ______________ behaviors.

(31) Therefore James' procedure would be an example of ______________.

Example #8

His mother told Sammy to bring out the garbage every night and he did so. When he was 12, she stopped telling him to bring out the garbage and he quit doing it.

(21) What behavioral procedure did she inadvertently employ to reduce his rate of bringing out the garbage? ______________

Example #9

John lived in a coed living group with eight other people. He used to sit in the living room looking, as someone put it, "very miserable." Since one reason for starting the group was to bring people together, Mary would sit down next to John whenever she saw him in the living room and would talk with him. At first, during these conversations, John complained about school, so John and Mary would talk about these problems. Later, John complained of many problems. The conversations began occurring more often.

(30) What behavioral procedure is involved here? ______________________

Example #10

Kerr went to the New West Freedom Preschool, where he was the brat of the school. He yelled, he broke things, he pushed into line, he spilled paint, he even wet his pants. The staff had a meeting and decided that instead of paying attention to him as they had done, they would henceforth ignore Kerr's brat behavior. Unfortunately, he kept doing it.

(5) What behavioral procedure did they use? ______________________

Example #11

Clarence is a skilled carpenter. One day he was reminiscing about how he had learned to hammer in a 16-penny nail with one thump. At first his father had praised him only when he hit the nail with each tiny tap—taking many taps to drive the nail in. His father had then praised him only when he drove it in with several rough raps. Finally his father had praised him only when he drove it in with one thunderous thump.

(29) What behavioral procedure was his father using? ______________________

Example #12

Mrs. Upton's 9-year-old stepdaughter, Betty, complains of illness much of the time. Mr. Upton recalls a time before his remarriage two years ago when his daughter was not so "sickly." Mrs. Upton loves Betty and has been observed to pay close attention to her stepdaughter's health. On school mornings, she often greets Betty with the question "How do you feel, dear?" If Betty reports that she is not feeling well, Mrs. Upton usually asks further questions, frequently suggesting that her daughter stay home that morning to "make sure that she is okay." At the same time, Mrs. Upton generally ignores other things that Betty says. Betty's attendance at school has decreased markedly in the past year as compared with the two previous years.

(4) What behavioral procedure is involved in making Betty a hypochondriac? __________ ______________________

Example #13

Five-year-old John was a loner. His preschool teacher noticed that John seldom interacted with other children during play periods, preferring to play alone in a far corner of the room. Recognizing the importance of social interaction in development, the teacher decided to attempt to increase the incidence of John's cooperative play.

The teacher's plan called for attending to John (looking or smiling at him and making positive comments to him) as a consequence of specific responses by John. At first, he attended to John whenever he looked toward other children. Next, he attended to him only if he moved toward other children; for example, he might say "I like that. John and Mary are playing together." It was observed that after a few weeks of this special teacher attention, John's time spent in cooperative play increased.

(20) Name the procedure employed by the teacher in modifying John's play behavior. __________ ______________________

Example #14

Yancey wanted Fran to smile more often. So every time that she smiled he told her how good she looked. Fran didn't smile any more often even after a month of compliments.

(19) What behavioral procedure was Yancey using? ____________________

Example #15

Bobby was a pretty good chess player who liked to win. When he played with Dan he won most of the time and as a result he started playing with Dan more often. But when he played with Shelly he lost most of the time. As a result he almost completely stopped playing with Shelly.

(3) What behavioral procedure accounts for Bobby playing more with Dan and less with Shelly? ____________________

Example #16

Marie helped Fred learn to not get angry over a minor annoyance. She taught him to count to 10 if an annoying event occurred. She continued to praise him during future annoyances until he was doing it all the time. Next she would praise him only when he counted to 20, which he soon mastered. In this way she finally got him to count to 100, at which time he was no longer angry.

(18) What is counting to 100 called? ____________________

Example #17

Jean wanted Sam to offer to help more often so she wouldn't have to do all the work. Every time that he offered to help, she made sure to get him a cold beer immediately. As a result, he started helping more often.

(17) What procedure did she use? ____________________

Example #18

Mary wanted to teach John how to do really good, fast disco dancing. She decided to start by teaching him some very slow steps.

(2) Slow dancing would be a(n) ____________________ to fast dancing.

Example #19

Frank was a pretty unattentive boyfriend. Finally Marsha told him to start opening doors for her. From then on he always opened the door for Marsha.

(16) What behavioral procedure did Marsha employ? ____________________

Example #20

At first Dave swam the 100 in about 75 seconds. His coach praised him only when he swam it in under 75 seconds. Then his coach praised him only when he swam it in under 70 seconds. Using this same approach, the coach eventually got Dave swimming the 100 in under 50 seconds.

(1) What behavioral procedure did his coach use? ____________________

EXAMPLE ANSWERS

(1) shaping (2) approximation (3) unknown (4) differential reinforcement (5) unknown (6) different (7) shaping (8) approximation (9) differential reinforcement (10) shaping (11) smiling (12) 5 (13)

shaping (14) target behavior (15) shaping (16) unknown (17) reinforcement (18) target behavior (19) unknown (20) shaping (21) unknown (22) approximations (23) shaping (24) approximation (25) differential reinforcement (26) target behavior (27) differential reinforcement (28) approximation (29) shaping (30) reinforcement (31) differential reinforcement (32) target behavior (33) target behavior (34) looked (35) approximation (36) differential reinforcement

Lesson 12

Factors Influencing the Reinforcing Effectiveness of Events

In Lesson 8 you learned that some events, called "reinforcers," are capable of producing an increase in the rate of a behavior that they consistently follow. You also learned that what is a reinforcer for one person may not be a reinforcer for another person. In this lesson you will learn that the same event may be a reinforcer when it is delivered to a person in one way but that it may not be if delivered in another way. By studying the factors that maximize the potential reinforcing ability of events, you can improve your ability to effectively reinforce behavior.

There are four main factors that determine the effectiveness of an event as a reinforcer. The event must be delivered contingent on the behavior occurring (that is, only when the behavior occurs); the event should be delivered immediately after the behavior has occurred; the size of the reinforcer should be enough to be worthwhile; and the event should be something that the person is deprived of (that is, doesn't have too much of). The effectiveness of an event as a reinforcer will be defined as the extent to which it increases the rate of the behavior.

The **Principle of Contingency** states that the effectiveness of an event will be maximized if it is delivered only when the desired behavior occurs but never when an alternative behavior that is not desired occurs. If the event is sometimes delivered for the alternative behavior, then the rate of this behavior will increase, thereby decreasing the time available to make the desired behavior—in fact, it may totally crowd out the desired behavior. (Stealing an object, rather than buying or making it, is a classic example of alternative behavior.) Alternative behaviors may also be inadvertently reinforced when events are delivered sloppily. If you ask your little brother to vacuum your room while you are at a dance, you might come home, glance at the room, conclude that it was vacuumed, and give him a box of chocolate-covered raisins. If he actually only picked up but didn't vacuum, then your reinforcer will not be very effective in increasing the rate of vacuuming. Thus, the principle points to exercising care that the event be delivered only when the desired behavior occurs—guarding against unauthorized responses like stealing and sloppy performance.

The Principle of Contingency does not imply that you can deliver the event for only one desired behavior. You could give your brother chocolate-covered raisins for vacuuming your room, for playing nicely with his toys, and for just being a sweet kid. Just don't give them out for alternative behaviors that are not desired.

To decide whether the Principle of Contingency was followed in a specific case, ask "Was the event given only if the desired behavior occurred?"

The immediacy with which an event is delivered after the behavior occurs is a very powerful determinant of the event's effectiveness. The **Principle of Immediacy** states that the more immediate the delivery of an event after the occurrence of the desired behavior, the more effect it will have on the rate of the behavior. If you want to get your brother started vacuuming your room, watch him when he does it and give him his chocolate-covered raisins while he is doing it or right after he is done; if you wait until you get home from the dance, or maybe even until tomorrow, it will have less effect. In general, the event should be delivered as soon after the behavior as possible—within seconds is the most effective timing. (One exception to this is when you "signal" immediately that the event will be delivered later—in which case the signal will be a "conditioned reinforcer." This will be covered in Lesson 20.)

To decide whether the Principle of Immediacy was followed, ask "Was the event delivered within a minute of the behavior (or while the behavior was still occurring)?"

The amount of the event delivered is also an important determinant of the event's effectiveness. The **Principle of Size** states that the more of the event that is delivered after the desired behavior, the more effect it will have on the rate of the behavior. Your goal should be to deliver just enough of the event to the subject to be effective but not so much of it that the subject never has to emit the desired behavior again. This optimum amount will vary depending on such factors as the difficulty of performing the behavior, the amount of behavior required, and other opportunities for reinforcement that may exist in the environment. If your little brother vacuumed your room, one chocolate-covered raisin probably wouldn't be effective. But a case of packages might last him for a year so that he needn't ever vacuum the room again. Rather you need to decide how hard it is for him to operate the vacuum, how long it takes, and whether mom just offered him a slice of chocolate cake. In any event, this principle indicates that the more of an event that is delivered, the more effective it will be.

To decide whether the Principle of Size was followed, ask "Was the amount of the event used worthwhile?"

The final principle involves the opposite concepts of "satiation" and "deprivation." **Satiation** refers to how recently the person has received the event—the more recently, the more satiation. If you have just had a quart of ice cream you are more satiated on ice cream than if you had not had it for a month. The opposite of satiation is deprivation. **Deprivation** refers to how long it has been since the person has received the event—the longer it has been, the more deprivation. If you have not had ice cream for a month you are more deprived of it than if you have had it recently.

The state of deprivation of the person with respect to a particular event is a powerful determinant of the event's effectiveness. The **Principle of Deprivation** states that the more deprived the person is with respect to the event, the more effective it will be. If your little brother has not had any chocolate-covered raisins for a week, they will be more effective than if he just had a box of them a half hour ago. The event you hope to use as a reinforcer should be carefully examined with respect to the level of deprivation that exists for that event.

To decide whether the Principle of Deprivation was followed, ask "Has the reinforcer been delivered too recently (or too often)?"

The Principle of Contingency and the Principle of Immediacy are sometimes confused. If an event is delivered immediately after the desired behavior occurs, this means that both the Principle of Immediacy and the Principle of Contingency are used. If the event is delivered immediately after alternative, undesired behavior, the Principle of Contingency is not being observed, and, if the event is delivered long after the desired behavior occurred, the Principle of Immediacy is not being used.

The Principle of Size and the Principle of Deprivation are also often confused. If a reinforcement is large, it might satiate the subject. The size principle refers to whether the amount of the reinforcer on any one given delivery is large enough to be worthwhile. The deprivation principle refers to whether the reinforcer recently has been delivered so often that the subject has had enough of that reinforcer. Thus, the distinction is between the amount of a single delivery and the number and timing of deliveries.

These four principles can be the difference between the success and failure of behavior analysis attempts. If behavior analysts don't deliver their reinforcers contingently and immediately, or if they use too little reinforcement or give their subjects something that they already have too much of, their modification attempts may not work. All four factors are important tools for improving the effectiveness of a reinforcer.

There are several other factors that should be taken into account when selecting reinforcers. For example, the reinforcers should be convenient to dispense, inexpensive, and not simultaneously available from another source. In addition, they should not generate behaviors that are incompatible with the behavior that is being reinforced (for example, giving gum for saying words clearly).

BEHAVIOR ANALYSIS EXAMPLES

Basic research uncovered the importance of these four principles; the complexity of applied situations often obscures their importance. The following examples have been drawn from the literature of applied behavior analysis to give you an idea of what is known about applied situations.

Teaching handwriting. Brigham, Finfrock, Bruenig, and Bushell (1972) sought to increase the accuracy with which six kindergarten children made responses in a program designed to teach beginning handwriting. They developed a very carefully organized set of materials for the children to use. However, the children made only about 50% correct responses during baseline observation. The investigators decided to give the children tokens good for a variety of fun activities. They first tried giving them tokens at the beginning of the session with no respect to accuracy of work. The children's accuracy decreased to around 40% correct. They then gave the tokens to the children only for accurate responses; the children's accuracy increased until it was over 60%. Thus, when tokens were given regardless of the accuracy, the accuracy decreased below baseline; when they were given only for accurate responses, accuracy increased.

Wearing orthodontic braces. Hall, Axelrod, Tyler, Grief, Jones, and Robertson (1972) consulted with the mother of an 8-year-old boy who needed braces to straighten his teeth. Despite spending about $3000 with four dentists over a period of eight years, Jerry's teeth were not any better. The problem was that Jerry could not remember to wear his braces. Observations during this baseline period indicated that he was wearing them during only 25% of the five times that he was checked each day. Hall and his colleagues suggested that the mother give Jerry 25¢ for each time that he was wearing them during those five checks. A record was kept of the money owed, which was to be paid at the end of the month. This procedure increased the rate of wearing the braces to about 60%. As a further improvement, Hall recommended giving Jerry the money immediately after any check during which he was wearing them. This increased his rate to nearly 100%. Thus you can see that when the money was given at the end of the month the rate was better than baseline but not nearly as good as when the money was given as soon as the desired behavior was observed. Eight months after the study was initiated, the dentist indicated that there had been great progress in Jerry's mouth structure.

Towel hoarding. A patient whom we shall call Doris had been a resident in a mental hospital for nine years. One of her behaviors was particularly bothersome to the staff: she hoarded towels. This required the staff to enter her room twice a week and remove some of the towels, which were needed for the rest of the hospital. During a period of baseline observation lasting seven weeks, Ayllon (1963) observed that the patient had about 25 towels in her room even though they were continually removed. In an attempt to solve the problem, Doris was given all the towels she wanted. Within four weeks she was keeping over 600 towels in her room. At first she patted the towels, folded, and stacked them. During the first week of this treatment, when the nurses brought her some towels she said "Oh, you found it for me, thank you." The second week she said "Don't give me no more towels. I've got enough." The third week she said "Take them towels away . . . I can't sit here all night and fold towels." The fourth week she said "Get these dirty towels out of here." The sixth week she had started to remove the towels from her room herself and she told the nurse "I can't drag any more of these towels, I just can't do it." Within 16 weeks, Doris had removed all the towels from her room and no longer kept them. This observation was followed by over a year during which towel hoarding never reappeared.

The nurses had felt that hoarding towels reflected a deep seated need for love and security and guessed that this approach would not work because it did not treat that underlying need. Not only did it work, but no other behavior problems were observed to develop that might have replaced hoarding.

ADDITIONAL READINGS

Ayllon, T., & Michael, J. The psychiatric nurse as a behavioral engineer. *Journal of the Experimental Analysis of Behavior,* 1959, *2,* 323-334. Several mental patients who hoarded magazines were treated through satiation by giving them as many as they would accept. Within a few weeks they were no longer hoarding magazines.

Schroeder, S. R. Parametric effects of reinforcement frequency, amount of reinforcement, and required response force on sheltered workshop behavior. *Journal of Applied Behavior Analysis*, 1972, *5*, 431–441. This article reports a study in which the amount of money paid to retardates for a job was increased. Unlike the expected finding that they would work harder for the larger amount, they actually worked less. No satisfactory explanation was offered for this contradictory finding.

Schwartz, M. L., & Hawkins, R. P. Application of delayed reinforcement procedures to the behaviors of an elementary school child. *Journal of Applied Behavior Analysis*, 1970, *3*, 85–96. This article reports the use of delayed feedback that was effective in teaching a 12-year-old girl to stop slouching and picking at her face, and to start talking loudly enough to be heard. The researchers showed her videotape records of her behaviors in class, but they showed them to her 5 hours later. In spite of the lack of immediacy, their procedure was very effective at improving her behaviors. And her self-image soared as a result. The delayed consequences may have worked in this case because of the powerful impact of videotaping.

Sulzer, B., & Mayer, G. R. *Behavior modification procedure for school personnel.* Hinsdale, Ill.: Dryden Press, 1972. This book contains many practical tips for teachers wishing to use behavior-modification procedures. Chapter 2, "Reinforcement," reviews some of the principles covered in this lesson with respect to selecting an effective and practical reinforcer.

LESSON 12 READING QUIZ

(9) The effectiveness of an event as a reinforcer is defined as the extent to which it __________ __________ the rate of the behavior.

(24) The Principle of Contingency states that the reinforcer must be delivered to the person __________ if he or she emits the desired behavior.

(8) The Principle of Contingency states that the effectiveness of an event will be maximized if it is delivered only when the desired behavior occurs but never when an alternative behavior that is not __________ occurs.

(17) Does the Principle of Contingency imply that you can deliver an event for only one desired behavior? __________

(7) To determine whether the Principle of Contingency is being used, ask "Was the reinforcer given __________ if a desired behavior occurred?"

(23) The Principle of Immediacy states that the more __________ the delivery of a reinforcer, the more effective the reinforcer will be.

(16) To determine whether the Principle of Immediacy was used, ask "Was the reinforcer delivered within a(n) __________ of the behavior?"

(25) If an event is delivered to a person while he or she is performing a behavior, the Principle of Immediacy __________ (would, wouldn't) be followed.

(6) The Principle of Size states that the __________ of the reinforcer delivered after a behavior, the more effective the reinforcer will be.

(15) Does the Principle of Size imply that you should give just as much of the reinforcer as possible in order to maximize its effectiveness? __________

(22) To decide whether the Principle of Size was followed, ask "Was the amount of the reinforcement used __________?"

(5) Satiation refers to how __________ the person received the reinforcer.

(14) Deprivation refers to how __________ since the person received the reinforcer.

(21) The opposite of deprivation is __________.

(13) The Principle of Deprivation states that the more __________ a person is of the reinforcer, the more effective it will be.

(4) To determine whether the Principle of Deprivation was followed, ask "Has the reinforcer been delivered too __________ (or too __________)?"

(20) If the amount of a reinforcer was worthwhile, then the Principle of __________ was being used correctly.

(3) If a person is reinforced within a minute of his or her response, the Principle of ______________ is being used.

(19) The principle of reinforcer effectiveness that deals with how recently (or how much) a person has had a particular reinforcer is called the Principle of ______________.

(12) If a reinforcer is given only when a particular desired behavior is made, the Principle of ______________ is being used correctly.

(2) Brigham and his colleagues (1972) delivered tokens to children immediately after they sat down for their handwriting lessons. The tokens could be traded for activities that they enjoyed but that they did not get to participate in too often. If Brigham and his colleagues wished to increase the rate of correct handwriting behaviors, then this example would clearly violate which principle of effective reinforcement? ______________

(18) Brigham and his colleagues (1972) delivered tokens for a time contingent on accurate handwriting and for another time noncontingent on correct handwriting. Which procedure produced a higher rate of accurate behaviors? ______________

(11) Hall and his colleagues (1972) gave Jerry 25¢ at the end of the month for every time he was wearing his braces when they checked him (and only for wearing his braces). The money permitted him to buy things he wanted and he never got too much of it. What principle of effective reinforcement did they violate? ______________

(1) Hall and his colleagues (1972) tried two procedures for giving Jerry 25¢ for each time that he was observed wearing his braces. The first procedure involved observing him every day and paying him at the end of the month. The second procedure involved observing him every day and paying him every time that he was wearing them. Did the first or the second procedure result in a higher rate of wearing the braces? ______________

(10) Ayllon (1963) gave Doris towels only when she was in her room. She had hoarded towels for nine years. By the time she had 600 of them, she started taking them out of her room. Ayllon used what principle of effective reinforcement to <u>reduce</u> the reinforcing properties of towels? ______________

READING QUIZ ANSWERS

(1) second (2) contingency (3) Immediacy (4) recently; often (5) recently (6) more (7) only (8) desired (9) increases (10) deprivation (satiation) (11) immediacy (12) Contingency (13) deprived (14) long (15) no (16) minute (17) no (18) contingent (19) Deprivation (20) Size (21) satiation (22) worthwhile (23) immediate (24) only (25) would

LESSON 12 EXAMPLES

Example #1

Lora wanted to increase the amount of reading that her daughter, Mary, did. So she had Mary read out loud and gave her a cookie as soon as a page was completed. As a result, Mary would read from the book for quite a while. Eventually, however, she would get fidgety and stop reading. Lora decided that Mary should do more reading. Analyze this example to see if Lora delivered cookies according to the principles of effective reinforcement.

(13) First, determine whether the Principle of Contingency was followed by asking "Was the reinforcer given ______________ when the desired behavior occurred but not when an alternative undesired behavior occurred?"

(26) Next determine whether the Principle of Immediacy was followed, by asking "Was the reinforcer given within a(n) ______________ of the behavior of reading a page?"

(14) Then determine whether the Principle of Size was followed, by asking "Was the amount of the reinforcer given ________________________?"

(36) Finally determine whether the Principle of Deprivation was followed by asking "Was the reinforcer delivered too recently or too ________________________?" Ask this question for both the beginning and end of the session.

(27) No principles were violated at the beginning of the reading session. What principle, if any, was violated near the end of the session? ________________________
(Write down just the applicable key word, "contingency," "immediacy," "size," or "deprivation," if one of the principles was violated, and write "none" if none of them were violated.)

Example #2

Sarah tried to help her friend John overcome his shyness by signaling him with a wink every time that he acted assertively during a social gathering. She never winked at him for undesired alternative behaviors. John was elated each time that she winked at him and he never tired of earning a wink.

(11) You should ask "Was the reinforcer given only if the desired behavior occurred?" to determine whether the Principle of ________________________ was followed.

(24) You should ask "Was the reinforcer given within a minute of the desired behavior?" to decide whether the Principle of ________________________ was followed.

(35) You should ask "Was the amount of the reinforcer given worthwhile?" to determine whether the Principle of ________________________ was followed.

(12) You should ask "Was the reinforcer delivered too recently or too often?" (at the beginning and at the end of the session) to determine whether the Principle of ________________________ was followed.

(25) What principles, if any, were ignored by Sarah when she was helping John become more assertive? ________________________ (Remember, write either the key word or "none.")

Example #3

Judy encouraged her son Tom to read by bringing him a delicious snack often while he was reading. Tom appreciated the snacks immensely, as they were always his favorite foods. Judy was careful never to give him too much. Judy also gave Tom snacks if he was sitting quietly, helping her with her work, playing nicely with his sister, or any of several other behaviors, but she never gave them so often that he got tired of them. Tom's rate of reading increased.

(22) Decide whether Judy made her snacks contingent on the desired behavior. ____________
(yes, no)

(9) Decide whether Judy delivered the snacks immediately. ____________

(34) Decide whether Judy's snacks were a big enough reinforcer. ____________

(23) Decide whether Judy used a reinforcer that Tom was deprived of. ____________

(10) What principle of effective reinforcement, if any, did Judy fail to employ? ____________
(Write "none" if she failed to employ none!)

Example #4

Ben and Hal loved to go fishing. Usually they went to a lake and found that they would catch a fish every 20 casts or so. This time they went to an artificial lake that had been stocked. Here they caught a fish almost every cast. They quit after a little while because it wasn't any fun.

(32) If their casting was reinforced by catching a fish, then the fact that the fish was caught right

after a cast occurred means that the Principle of ____________________________
was operating.

(7) Because they caught fish only by casting—grabbing with their hands in the water didn't work too well—the Principle of ____________________________ was operating.

(21) The fact that they usually loved to catch a fish meant that the Principle of ____________
was operating.

(33) The fact that they quit after catching a lot of fish meant that the Principle of ____________ __________________ was breaking down at the artificial lake and weakening the effectiveness of the reinforcer.

(8) What principles, if any, were not operating and therefore led to a decrease in the effectiveness of catching fish as a reinforcer? ____________________________

Example #5

Members of the Utopian Commune rely on expressions of respect to maintain work behaviors in their community. These expressions of respect were given immediately after work behavior but on no other occasion. They weren't given too often, but members did not seem too thrilled when they got them.

(20) What principle of effective reinforcement, if any, is being ignored by this community? ____________________________

Example #6

Barb had been really thoughtful of Ken. Every time that he complained about how poorly his relationship with friends was going, she had listened and asked questions, hoping to help him. However, he had gotten to complaining more and more often. So she decided to just plain quit listening—in fact she would get up and walk away when the complaining started. Barb was disappointed to find that Ken just kept right on complaining as frequently as ever.

(6) What behavioral procedure did Barb use? ____________________________

Example #7

Jerry told his mother that he wanted to learn how to sew. His mother did not have a stereotyped view of children's sex roles, so she welcomed Jerry's interest and patted him on the head when he was sewing skillfully. She patted his head only when he was sewing skillfully. She didn't pat him on the head too frequently. However, Jerry soon lost interest in sewing.

(19) What principle of effective reinforcement, if any, did his mother fail to employ? ____________

Example #8

Chester took his children for a rare ice cream treat on the Sunday of any week during which they brought home a good school paper for him to see.

(31) What principle probably accounts for the fact that this is an ineffective reinforcer for schoolwork? ____________________________

Example #9

Dave got interested in meditation. To try it out he tried very brief (5-minute) meditation periods during the day. He felt so good after each meditation that he started doing more of them during the day.

(5) Meditation as a stimulus event would be called a(n) ____________________________.

Example #10

Carey had Dave, the star football tackle, compose poems and hand them to her during class. She read them, wrote her praise on them, and returned them during the next class period. She gave Dave praise only for the good aspects of his poems. And she was careful not to give him too much praise. Surprisingly, her praise was very important to Dave. However, in spite of her careful procedure, Dave's poetry writing did not improve.

(18) What principle of effective reinforcement, if any, did Carey fail to use in her procedure? ______________________

Example #11

Dad wanted to help Bobby improve his math skills. So right after dinner they sat down and Dad gave Bobby problems orally ("What is 4 times 9?"). For every correct answer Dad gave Bobby a potato chip immediately. Bobby could not earn potato chips during this session in any other way. Normally, Bobby loved potato chips and would do almost anything to get one. However, Dad's procedure didn't work too well.

(4) What principle of effective reinforcement, if any, did Dad ignore? ______________________

Example #12

Marvin was determined to teach his daughter Bee how to do math problems. He bought a math workbook and insisted that every morning she do all the problems in one chapter before being allowed to play. He then graded her problems and had her correct the ones that were wrong. When she was done she could play for the rest of the day. She could soon do the problems very rapidly but still didn't seem to know any more than before. It was then that he noticed the correct answers listed in the back of the book.

(30) If Bee was copying the answers, then the delivery of the opportunity to play would violate what principle of effective reinforcement? ______________________

Example #13

Senor Jimenez taught 4-year-old Janice to say his name by telling her one day "Say HEE-MAY-NAYZ."

(17) From then on she said it correctly. What behavioral procedure did he use? ______________

Example #14

Dave didn't like Timmy to play with his model cars because Timmy usually played too rough and damaged them. One day Dave had the idea that he would reinforce Timmy for playing nicely by giving him several M & M's whenever he played nicely with the models for 5 minutes. Timmy loved M & M's and Dave never gave him any if Timmy started to get a bit too rough. The procedure worked really well for several hours, but finally Timmy started getting too rough.

(3) What principle of effective reinforcement, if any, would you guess had finally been violated after several hours? ______________________

Example #15

He was every employee's dream—he praised you if you did your work well no matter what your prior mistakes had been. He didn't load you down with praise; the way he did it made you feel important. He gave it right after you finished the job, and he never gave it otherwise.

(29) What principle of effective reinforcement, if any, did he neglect? ____________

Example #16

Hal did not invite Dana to parties very often. On those occasions when Hal did extend an invitation, Dana would immediately say "thank you very much" as enthusiastically as he knew how. He did not say "thank you very much" at any other time he was around Hal. And he certainly did not overdo the amount of thanks he gave Hal.

(16) What principle of effective reinforcement, if any, did Dana ignore in his attempt to get Hal to invite him to more parties? ____________

Example #17

Bob had two really tough classes that were required for his degree. One day he went up to Professor Barnes and asked him a question after lecture. The professor was very friendly and encouraged Bob to ask his question. Bob frequently did so in the future and was always greeted warmly by Professor Barnes. Bob tried the same thing with Professor Mead but he was not at all friendly or encouraging. Bob didn't ask questions of Professor Mead very often.

(2) What behavioral procedure would be used to explain why Bob asked more questions of Professor Barnes and fewer of Professor Mead? ____________

Example #18

Mary didn't like the way that Vera treated her—Vera was usually very unpleasant. But Mary had heard about reinforcement and decided to try it. She kept track of any pleasant behavior that Vera engaged in and then mentioned those things to her on Sunday night. Vera seemed genuinely delighted at the praise, did not seem to get too much of it, and was praised only for pleasant behaviors. Vera did not get any nicer as a result.

(28) If you could talk with Mary, what principle of effective reinforcement would you tell her she was neglecting in her method? ____________

Example #19

Alice liked Rich very much, but he was a bit backward. So she was very warm and friendly when he held her hand. Then she was warm and friendly only when he kissed her. Next she was warm and friendly only when he embraced her passionately. You can guess what Alice's target behavior was.

(15) What procedure was she using to get there? ____________

Example #20

Professor Brainbuster asked his students to formulate literary criticisms of the novel that they had just read. Every time that Fred made a good point, the professor praised him lavishly, hoping to reward such critical thinking. Fred, knowing that his grade was going up, was very pleased about each occurrence of praise and never got too much of it. Little did the professor know that Fred was simply parroting the notes from his frat brother.

(1) What principle of effective reinforcement, if any, was not followed in this example? ____________

EXAMPLE ANSWERS

(1) Contingency (2) unknown (3) Deprivation (4) Deprivation (5) reinforcer (6) unknown (7) Contingency (8) Deprivation (9) yes (10) none (11) Contingency (12) Deprivation (13) only (14) worthwhile (15) shaping (16) Size (17) unknown (18) Immediacy (19) Size (20) Size (21) Size (22) yes (23) yes (24) Immediacy (25) none (26) minute (27) Deprivation (28) Immediacy (29) none (30) Contingency (31) Immediacy (32) Immediacy (33) Deprivation (34) yes (35) Size (36) often

Lesson 13

Ratio Schedules

This lesson and the next will introduce you to an aspect of reinforcement that is usually referred to as the schedule of reinforcement. In previous lessons, you have learned about two schedules of reinforcement. In one of them, the delivery of a reinforcer was scheduled for every occurrence of the behavior. That is referred to as a continuous schedule of reinforcement. In the other one, the delivery of a reinforcer was not scheduled to follow occurrences of the behavior. This is referred to as an extinction schedule. In this and the next lesson you will learn about four specific types of schedules in which a reinforcer is scheduled to follow only some occurrences of the behavior. Such schedules are generally referred to as intermittent schedules.

There are two common intermittent schedules of reinforcement that are based on counting the number of responses that have occurred since the last reinforcement. A **fixed-ratio** schedule requires that a person be reinforced every time he or she completes a fixed number of responses. For example, if the person is on a fixed ratio of 3, then he or she will be reinforced for every third response. A common example of this schedule is the piece-rate system of wage payments sometimes used in factories. The worker is paid for making a fixed number of responses. Thus a worker on an assembly line might be paid 25¢ for making five spot welds on an auto body. This schedule would be referred to as a "fixed ratio of 5" or abbreviated "FR–5."

People tend to work rapidly on fixed-ratio schedules, and, usually, a fixed-ratio schedule will generate a higher rate of responding than will a simple continuous-reinforcement schedule (which can be thought of as a fixed ratio of 1, because the person is reinforced for every response). However, people tend to pause in their responding right after they have earned their reinforcer. So the fixed-ratio schedule is characterized by alternating periods of responding and periods of rest.

This pattern of rapid responding followed by rest is best displayed in a "cumulative record" graph. Figure 13–1 is an example. The graph shows the response pattern of a high school boy whose vocal responding was reinforced after every 50 responses. Usually the boy made 50 vocal responses in less than 20 seconds to earn his reinforcer. Then after he had consumed it he would pause for up to 3 minutes before starting to make the vocal responses that would earn him another reinforcer.

In general, behavior analysts have found that people's response rates increase as the ratio requirement is increased—until they reach some upper limit, at which point the response rate decreases again. For example, Stephens, Pear, Wray, and Jackson (1975) studied the effect of different ratio requirements on the rate at which severely retarded children learned correctly to name the objects shown in pictures. The names of the objects were taught using a complex procedure in which the child was first taught to look at the picture and repeat the name given by the experimenter, then taught to give the name of the picture without help, and finally to name it when it was interspersed among other already known pictures. Later, the newly learned picture was interspersed with other known pictures during the learning of another picture. If at any point an error was made, the child was placed back in the 24-step sequence to improve his or her mastery of the name. This elaborate procedure was required because these children had very little learning ability. The investigators then reinforced responses in the learning sequence on different ratios. Four out of 5 children learned more rapidly when reinforced once in 5 (FR–5) or once in 12 (FR–12) times than when continuously reinforced. They also learned more rapidly as the ratio was increased until they were reinforced only once in 25 times (FR–25), at which point their rates decreased. This example illustrates the typical finding in this area of research, but other variables

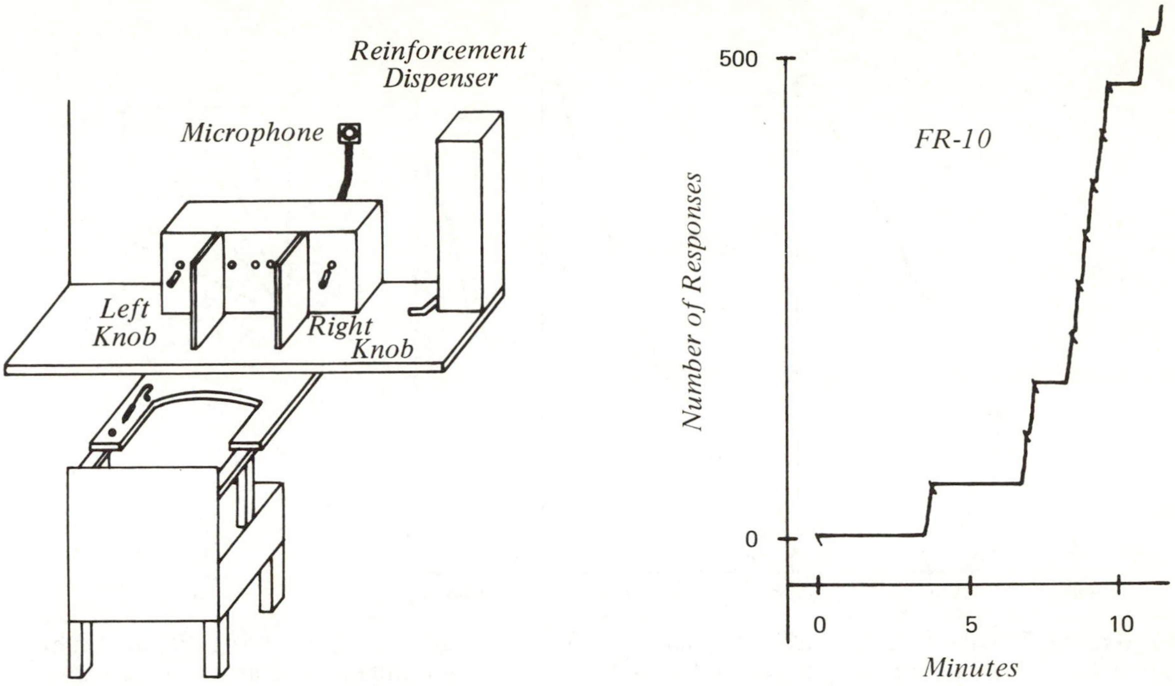

Figure 13–1. An experiment with a fixed-ratio schedule. A high school boy made vocal responses into the microphone. These responses are shown on the "cumulative record" graph on the right. When he was responding rapidly, the graph went up; when he was pausing, the graph went to the right. The subject could earn nickels by pulling either the right or the left knob. The right knob required a pull of 50 pounds. If he made 50 vocal responses, he was permitted to pull with the left knob for 1 minute. The left knob required only 1 pound of pull and was therefore much easier than the right. Thus, he was reinforced for his vocal responses on a fixed-ratio schedule of 50 by being permitted to pull the easier knob for the nickels.

Notice that he worked at a high rate until he got the reinforcement (indicated by the slash mark). Then, he paused for a while. Adapted from "Escape From an Effortful Situation," by L. K. Miller, *Journal of the Experimental Analysis of Behavior*, 1968, *11*, 619–627. Copyright 1968 by the Society for the Experimental Analysis of Behavior, Inc. Used by permission.

affect the relationship. Several studies are referred to in the Additional Readings section that illustrate some of the complexities of the area.

NOVEL WRITING—A CASE OF FIXED RATIO SCHEDULING?

Joseph Pear has suggested (Wallace & Pear, 1977) that novel writing may be viewed as an instance of responding under a fixed-ratio schedule. He suggested that the total novel is a fixed ratio—the novelist must complete a fixed number of pages to complete the novel.

Figure 13–2 shows a cumulative graph of the number of pages written by Irving Wallace on his novel *The Prize*. The graph shows that Wallace wrote less than 10 pages a day when he started but increased to over 20 pages a day near the completion of the novel.

Pear has suggested that each chapter may serve as a fixed ratio within the overall book. The graph shows a pause in writing after many of the chapters were completed (for example, Chapter 1). Furthermore, the author's records indicate that he stopped writing for the day after completing all but one of the 12 chapters (the missed one is Chapter 8, indicated by an asterisk). This pattern suggests that each chapter served as a fixed-ratio schedule. Thus, the laws of behavior extend even into that most creative and "subjective" process of writing a novel.

The other common intermittent schedule based on counting is called a "variable-ratio" schedule. A **variable-ratio** schedule requires that a person be reinforced when he or she

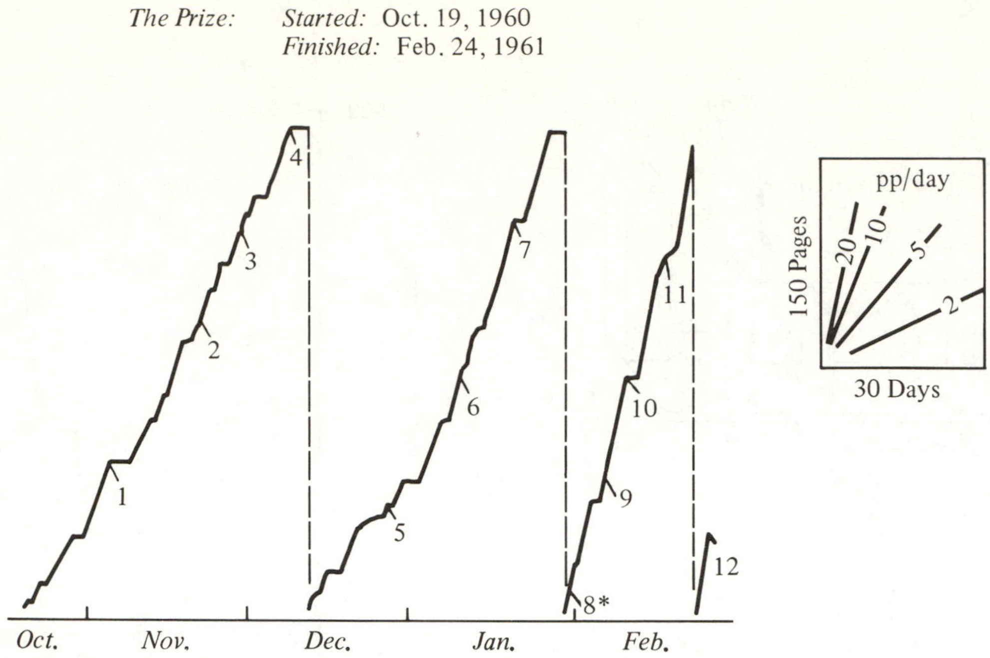

Figure 13–2. This is a cumulative graph of the number of pages written by Irving Wallace on his novel *The Prize* taken from his own self-recording diary. The numbers indicate which chapters were finished. The dotted lines are used to indicate when the number of written pages was too much for the size of the graph and it had to be started over again—without this convention the graph would be three times as high. Adapted from "Self-Control Techniques of Famous Novelists," by I. Wallace and J. J. Pear, *Journal of Applied Behavior Analysis*, 1977, *10*, 515–525. Copyright 1977 by the Society for the Experimental Analysis of Behavior, Inc. Used by permission.

completes a variable number of responses; the number of responses required for reinforcement varies every time. For example, if a person is given reinforcement after 3 responses, then after 1 response, then after 2 responses, he or she is being reinforced according to a variable-ratio schedule that averages a reinforcement after two responses (the average of 3, 1, and 2). In behavior analysis experiments, the experimenter delivers each reinforcer after a predetermined number of responses where the number varies from one delivery to the next. A common example is mechanical gambling devices. A "one-armed bandit" is programmed to pay off a certain percentage of the time. The player might have to make 100 plays for the first payoff, 50 for the second, and so on. In this case, the machine is programmed to deliver the reinforcer a certain percentage of the time, thereby resulting in varying numbers of responses being required to hit a payoff.

The rate of responding on a variable-ratio schedule is as rapid as the rate of responding on a fixed-ratio schedule, but the variable-ratio schedule does not lead to any pauses after reinforcement. Some have speculated that the no-pause effect is caused by the fact that the very next response may produce a reinforcement, so people keep responding. In any event, variable-ratio schedules produce the highest rate of responding of any schedule of reinforcement considered in this book. I include a graph illustrating responding on a variable-ratio schedule in connection with a behavior-analysis example later in this lesson.

To summarize, the fixed-ratio schedule delivers a reinforcer after a fixed number of responses, producing a high rate of responding prior to reinforcement and a pause after reinforcement. The variable-ratio schedule delivers a reinforcer after a variable number of responses, producing a high rate of responding with no pauses. Overall, the variable ratio produces a higher rate of responding because of the absence of pauses.

Ratio schedules have a number of advantages for behavior analysts, which I will outline below.

Resistance to extinction. Ratio schedules may be used to increase a person's resistance to extinction. Often, behavior analysts know that someone's behavior will be put on extinction at some point—usually after a training procedure ends and the person returns to a normal environment. By devoting some portion of the training period to reinforcing the person on an intermittent ratio schedule, they can lengthen the time that the person will continue to respond. This may provide a longer period of time for the natural environment accidentally to reinforce the behavior and eventually maintain it.

Koegel and Rincover (1977) provide a dramatic illustration of this effect. They taught severely retarded children to imitate behaviors that a therapist demonstrated—quite an accomplishment when the children's IQs were so low that they were untestable! They then had another adult, in a different setting, demonstrate the same behavior but provide no reinforcement for imitation. They found that the children stopped imitating after 20 trials if they had been trained with continuous reinforcement. They stopped after 60 to 100 trials if trained with reinforcement on every other response (FR–2). And they showed no signs of stopping if trained with reinforcement on every fifth correct response (FR–5)—they were still responding after as many as 500 trials. The use of a ratio schedule resulted in the children maintaining the behavior in the natural environment even with no one reinforcing that behavior. Thus, the simple skill of imitating the behavior of another person, an important source of learning, was maintained after training with a fixed-ratio schedule.

An experiment by Kazdin and Polster (1973) also confirmed this effect. They reinforced two retarded adults who were social isolates for having a social conversation with another person in their workplace. One of these individuals received a token every time that he interacted with another person. The other individual received a token for only one of three interactions. When token reinforcement was discontinued, the individual who had been reinforced every time decreased interactions to less than 1 per day; the individual who had been intermittently reinforced maintained the high rate of about 10 interactions per day.

One would suppose that continuous reinforcement gives a person's behavior little resistance to extinction because once it is stopped it is easy for the person to recognize that he or she is no longer being reinforced. Several responses without reinforcement should be enough to make it clear. Even with continued occasional testing to determine whether reinforcement is still missing, people make few responses during extinction after having been trained on continuous reinforcement. The situation is, of course, just the opposite if a ratio schedule of reinforcement is suddenly stopped. The person has not been reinforced after every response so many more responses must be emitted to recognize that it has been stopped. If these intermittent reinforcements are on a variable schedule, that recognition is even more difficult.

Variable-ratio schedules produce greater resistance to extinction than do fixed-ratio schedules

Decreased satiation. Ratio schedules also have the advantage that fewer reinforcers are used to generate the same amount of behavior. For instance, if the behavior analyst is delivering one reinforcer for ten responses (FR–10 or VR–10), ten reinforcers will be used for a hundred responses. With continuous reinforcement, 100 reinforcers would have to be delivered. As a result, ratio schedules may be used to reduce the problem of the person becoming satiated on the reinforcer and then no longer responding. Both fixed-ratio and variable-ratio schedules of the same size are equally good at opposing satiation.

Ratio schedules also have several disadvantages.

Continuous schedule for shaping. When shaping a new response, it is necessary to ensure that the approximation that is being differentially reinforced is consistently reinforced. The best way to increase its rate is to reinforce it every time that it occurs. Thus, continuous reinforcement is used during shaping.

Ratio strain. If a person's behavior is reinforced too infrequently, the behavior may fall apart and become very irregular. Normally, a ratio schedule is introduced by small steps. First the person is reinforced for every response, then for every other one, then for one in five, and so on. Using this gradual approach, behavior analysts can gradually build up very sizable ratios. However, at some point, no matter how gradually the schedule is changed, the ratio simply becomes too large and responding is not maintained. There is no predictable point at which this happens because it depends on how effortful the response is, how valuable the reinforcer is, how much is delivered, and how gradually the increase in ratio requirement was introduced. Thus, at some point "ratio strain" occurs. **Ratio strain** occurs when the person is placed on such a large ratio that he or she isn't reinforced often enough to maintain responding.

BEHAVIOR ANALYSIS EXAMPLE

Teaching reading. Staats, Finley, Minke, and Wolf (1964) developed a behavioral approach to teaching reading under controlled conditions so that the process could be carefully studied. They first attempted to analyze the process of reading acquisition from a behavioral point of view. They determined that to acquire a reading response meant that people could name the word that they were looking at. In order to acquire it, they had to begin by looking at the word. Next they had to either hear how that word sounded or sound it out for themselves. They then had to repeat that sound. Finally they had to discriminate that word from other words and say its name. Each step involves a response on the part of the learner and those responses could be increased in probability by reinforcing them. Based on this analysis, Staats developed an apparatus permitting the measurement of each component behavior and the reinforcement of the total reading acquisition response.

Figure 13-3 shows the apparatus that Staats developed to study the reading acquisition behaviors. It consisted of a working area in front of where the child sat and a reinforcer area to the right.

Figure 13-3. The Staats apparatus for studying the reading acquisition process. From "Reinforcement Variables in the Control of Unit Reading Responses," by A. W. Staats, J. R. Finley, K. A. Minke, and M. Wolf, *Journal of the Experimental Analysis of Behavior*, 1964, 7, 139-149. Copyright 1964 by the Society for the Experimental Analysis of Behavior, Inc. Used by permission.

The working area was designed so that each component behavior could be separately observed. To begin the process of learning a word, the child pressed a button on the table in front of him or her. The word was then projected onto the square window. The experimenter then named that word. The child was required to name the word while pressing that window. Pressing the window ensured that the child would attend to the word, and it provided a way to observe that attending response. Next, the child was required to repeat the word and to press the rectangular windows below that contained the same word but not those that displayed different words. This step required the child to practice naming the word without the help of the experimenter while picking that word out from other similar words.

If the child made the wrong response, he or she was required to repeat the sequence. If the child made the correct response, he or she received a marble from the dispenser on the right. The child could apply that marble toward the purchase of any of the toys on the right by placing it in the tube below his or her choice. When the tube was filled, the child earned the toy.

Staats and his colleagues have undertaken many experiments to investigate the development of reading behavior. These studies included an examination of different schedules of reinforcement. Figure 13-4 shows a cumulative graph of responding under two conditions. The bottom record shows the rate of responding when the child was reinforced for every correct response. The top record shows the rate when the child was reinforced on a variable-ratio schedule in which a reinforcer was earned on the average after every five correct responses (VR–5). This experiment demonstrates that the rate of responding is more rapid with variable-ratio than with continuous reinforcement. The series of experiments illustrates that as complex a human behavior as the acquisition of reading behavior occurs according to behavioral principles.

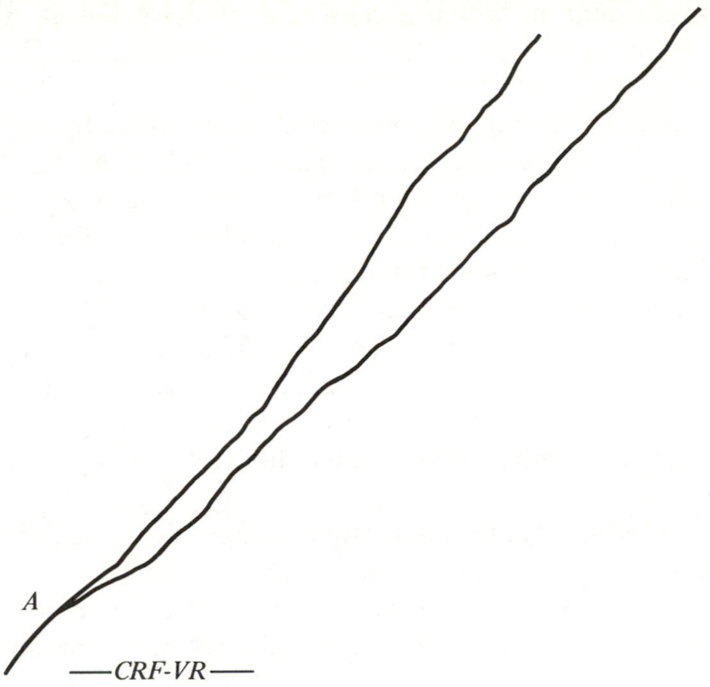

Figure 13–4. A cumulative graph of reading acquisition responses in the Staats experiment. The line on the left shows the rate of reading responses when every fifth correct response on the average was reinforced; the one on the right shows the rate of reading responses when every correct response was reinforced. From "Reinforcement Variables in the Control of Unit Reading Responses," by A. W. Staats, J. R. Finley, K. A. Minke, and M. Wolf, *Journal of the Experimental Analysis of Behavior*, 1964, 7, 139–149. Copyright 1964 by the Society for the Experimental Analysis of Behavior, Inc. Used by permission.

ADDITIONAL READINGS

Ferster, C. B., & Skinner, B. F. *Schedules of reinforcement.* New York: Appleton-Century-Crofts, 1957. This advanced book is the original and most comprehensive source of information on schedules. It is the "bible" of operant psychology.

Lovitt, T. C., & Esveldt, K. A. The relative effects on math performance of single versus multiple ratio schedules: A case study. *Journal of Applied Behavior Analysis*, 1970, 3, 261–270. This study involved a disturbed child having problems learning math. The researchers found that his response rate did not increase when the schedule was changed from an FR–5 to an FR–20.

Schroeder, S. R. Parametric effects of reinforcement frequency, amount of reinforcement, and required response force on sheltered workshop behavior. *Journal of Applied Behavior Analysis*, 1972, 5, 431–441. Schroeder found that retardates made more electrical components per hour when reinforced on a higher fixed-ratio or variable-ratio schedule (up to FR–600), but only if the effort required in making the response was easy. If the effort was great, then they worked more slowly at the higher ratios.

Helpful hint #1: When asked what schedule describes a situation, always use the most specific name. If a person is reinforced every five responses, describe the situation as a "fixed-ratio," not an "intermittent," schedule.

Helpful hint #2: You may abbreviate fixed ratio as "FR" and variable ratio as "VR." These abbreviations are widely used by behaviorists.

Helpful hint #3: If an example states that a reinforcer was delivered after an average of four responses, you should assume that the number of responses varies from reinforcement to reinforcement but that it averages four responses. Thus this would identify a variable-ratio schedule.

LESSON 13 READING QUIZ

(11) The schedule of reinforcement in which a reinforcer is delivered after every response is called a(n) ______________________ schedule of reinforcement.

(22) A schedule of reinforcement in which a reinforcer is delivered after only some of the responses is called a(n) ______________________ schedule of reinforcement.

(32) A schedule of reinforcement in which a reinforcer is not delivered for any of the responses is called a(n) ______________________ schedule.

(10) A fixed-ratio schedule requires that the person be reinforced when he or she completes a(n) ______________________ number of responses.

(21) A fixed-ratio schedule usually produces a ______________________ (higher, lower) rate of responding than does a continuous schedule.

(31) A fixed-ratio schedule causes people to respond at a high rate prior to reinforcement, but they tend to ______________________ after reinforcement.

(9) When the high school boy was reinforced for every 50 responses, he made the responses in less than 20 seconds. Then, after he had consumed the reinforcer, he ______________________ for up to 3 minutes.

(12) Behavior analysts usually find that people's response rates ______________________ as the ratio requirement increases (up to some limit).

(20) Stephens and his associates (1975) found that retarded children learned to name pictures. Did they learn more rapidly when continuously reinforced or when reinforced on a fixed ratio of 5?

____

(30) Pear suggested that writing a novel is reinforced on a(n) ______________________ schedule.

(8) According to Irving Wallace's record, he paused in his writing every time that he completed the writing of one ______________________ in his book.

(19) A variable-ratio schedule is one in which the person is reinforced when he or she completes a(n) ______________________ number of responses.

(29) The variable-ratio schedule produces a(n) ______________________ rate of responding.

(7) Does a variable ratio usually produce a pause after reinforcement? ____________

(18) What schedule produces the highest rate of responding? ______________________

(28) What schedule produces rapid responding alternating with pauses? ______________________

(6) If a person receives a reinforcer after every six responses exactly, then he or she is on what schedule? ______________________

(17) If a person receives a reinforcer on the average of every six responses, what schedule is involved? ______________________

(27) Ratio schedules may be used to increase a person's resistance to ______________________.

(5) Koegel and Rincover (1977) found that, at the request of an adult who never reinforced them, retarded children would imitate for much longer when they had been trained on what type of schedule: continuous or fixed ratio of 5? ______________________

(33) Kazdin and Polster (1973) found that an individual who was reinforced for one in three interactions maintained a high rate of interaction when reinforcement was discontinued, compared to another individual who had been reinforced for every interaction. Thus, they found that intermittent reinforcement leads to greater ______________________.

(16) If a response has been reinforced every time it occurs and that is suddenly stopped, it should take only a few responses for the person to discover that responding is on what schedule of reinforcement? ______________________

(26) Which of the following schedules produces the greatest resistance to extinction: continuous, fixed ratio, variable ratio? ______________________

(4) Ratio schedules produce more responding per reinforcement; therefore they are useful in combatting ______________________ .

(15) What type of schedule should be used when shaping a new response? ______________________

(25) When a ratio is made so high that the person receives few reinforcers, his or her responding may break down. This occurrence is known as ______________________ .

(3) Staats and associates (1964) defined an attending response as pressing a window with a word displayed on it. This would be called a(n) ______________________ of "attending."

(14) Staats and associates found that reading-acquisition responses could be increased in rate by delivering a marble after every response. What schedule of reinforcement were they using? ______________________

(24) Staats and associates sometimes delivered reinforcers after every response and sometimes after an average of five responses. Name the schedule that would have been least likely to satiate the child. ______________________

(2) Staats and associates delivered a reinforcer after a varying number of reading-acquisition responses that averaged 5. What is the name of the schedule that they were using? ______________________

(13) Staats and associates studied the rate of making reading-acquisition responses when children were given a reinforcer after every response and when they were given a reinforcer after varying numbers of responses that averaged five. Name the schedule that produced the highest rate of responding. ______________________

(23) When a reinforcer is delivered after every response, the schedule is called a(n) ______________________ schedule; when a reinforcer is delivered after only some responses, the schedule is called a(n) ______________________ schedule; when a reinforcer is never delivered after a response, the schedule is called a(n) ______________________ schedule.

(1) If a person is reinforced for every 30 responses, would it be better to describe this as an intermittent schedule or as a fixed-ratio schedule? ______________________

(34) If a reinforcer is delivered after every seventh response on the average, you should assume that it is delivered after ______________________ numbers of responses averaging 7. Thus the schedule would be ______________________ .

READING QUIZ ANSWERS

(1) fixed ratio (FR–30) (2) variable ratio (VR–5) (3) behavioral definition (4) satiation (5) fixed ratio (6) fixed ratio (FR–6) (7) no (8) chapter (9) paused (10) fixed (11) continuous (12) increase (13) variable ratio (VR–5) (14) continuous (15) continuous (16) extinction (17) variable ratio (VR–6) (18) variable ratio (19) varying (20) fixed ratio (21) higher (22) intermittent (23) continuous; intermittent; extinction (24) variable ratio (25) ratio strain (26) variable ratio (27) extinction (28) fixed ratio (29) high (or uniform) (30) fixed-ratio (31) pause (32) extinction (33) resistance to extinction (34) varying; variable ratio (VR–7)

LESSON 13 EXAMPLES

Example #1

Johnny found that if he nagged his mother long enough, she would eventually give him a cookie. Sometimes she wouldn't give it to him until he had asked for it 20 times, but other times she would give him one the first time that he asked.

(29) Johnny's asking behavior is reinforced with a cookie after varying numbers of responses; therefore his behavior is on a(n) ______________ schedule of reinforcement.

(11) Suppose that his mother stopped giving him cookies. Would his nagging stop faster with the schedule described in the example or with a schedule in which he was given a cookie every time that he asked for it? ______________ (name the schedule)

(19) Would Johnny's rate of nagging be higher under the schedule described or would it be higher if he had been given a cookie every time he asked? ______________

Example #2

Mr. James encouraged his daughter Carol's study of third-grade math by looking at her work after every problem and praising it. After she began doing her homework reliably, he shifted and checked her work after every second problem for a while. Later, he worked it up to checking after every 5 problems.

(9) When Mr. James was reinforcing Carol's studying after fixed numbers of responses, the schedule would be called a(n) ______________ schedule of reinforcement.

(27) Would Carol work her problems faster when praised after every problem or would she work them faster when praised after every five problems (not counting checking time)? ______________ (name the schedule)

(18) Would Carol be likely to continue working longer without her father's praise if she had previously been praised after every problem or if she had been praised after every five problems? ______________ (name the schedule)

(10) Carol's rate of working when praised after every five problems would probably show a slight pause right after being ______________ by her father.

(28) Suppose that Mr. James checked Carol's problems after different numbers of problems averaging five. Would Carol work faster on this schedule compared to the one described in the example? ______________

Example #3

Angie seemed to have a hearing problem. She never answered a question the first time it was asked of her. She always said "What?" to the questioner and then would answer the question the second time it was asked.

(26) What is the technical name for the schedule of reinforcement that Angie had put the questioners on? ______________

Example #4

When Tom got home from work he would always check to see if there was any mail for the day. He found that there was mail on the average of one day in 3.

(17) What schedule of reinforcement is he on for looking for the mail? ______________

(8) If he found mail only once in 100 days he might stop looking. What is the name for this phenomenon? ______________

Example #5

John praised and hugged his infant daughter Lou when she tried to say "dada." At first he praised her only when she said something that started with "da"; later only when she said both the "da" and a following "da."

(16) Saying "dada" would be called the ______________________________ .

(7) John is using what procedure to get Lou to say "dada"? ______________________________

(25) What schedule of reinforcement would you recommend that John use when he tries to teach Lou to say "dada"? ______________________________

Example #6

Jeanie was a 6-month-old baby. She was just learning to feed herself with a spoon. Since she was a bit clumsy, she dropped an average of three out of four spoonfuls. Fortunately, Jeanie kept trying.

(6) What intermittent schedule of reinforcement was Jeanie on for operating her spoon? ______________________________ (Ask yourself if the reinforcement occurred after a fixed number of spooning responses or after a varying number of spooning responses.)

Example #7

Professor Brainbuster required each of his students to turn in an essay every week on ancient history. Ken did so but was totally appalled that he never found out his grade on the essay or had the essay returned.

(24) Ken's essay-writing behavior is on what schedule of reinforcement? ______________________________

Example #8

Marge let little Timmy earn some money by pulling weeds. She paid him 1¢ per weed pulled. She gave him the money as soon as he reported the number of weeds. Timmy never had any money so his earnings were welcome to him. The pay of 1¢ per weed seemed to add up fast enough so that Timmy wanted to weed. However, his mother found that he was pulling weeds from the field and counting them, that he counted when he pulled a leaf but didn't get the whole weed, and worst of all that he pulled some flowers and counted them.

(5) The effectiveness of the reinforcer was undermined because Marge ignored the Principle of ______________________________ .

Example #9

When Don was 14, he was always reading science-fiction stories. His father was also a science-fiction fan, so when Don had finished reading a chapter, he would immediately go to his father and describe all the interesting events in the story. Don's father seemed to have endless interest in hearing about the latest adventures in Don's books.

(23) What schedule of reinforcement is Don on? ______________________________ (Assume that reading a single chapter is one "response.")

(15) If Don's father started listening to Don's accounts of the science-fiction stories only when Don had completed a whole book (no matter how many chapters were in it), Don would be on a(n) ______________________________ schedule of reinforcement. (Assume each chapter is one response.)

Example #10

Rich had talked Fran into washing the windows of their house, but Fran needed encouragement. At first Rich made it a point to come by after every window Fran completed. Soon, however, Rich just didn't have the time, so he came by after Fran had completed 3, 1, 8, and 4 windows. Fran seemed to finish the windows faster then.

(4) What schedule was Fran on for her last 16 windows? ______________________

Example #11

In Dr. Smith's course, each student used to take a daily quiz that had six questions on it. Any student who got all six questions correct advanced one step toward an A.

(30) What schedule is having to make six correct responses for one step toward an A an example of? ______________________

Example #12

Walter's mother was teaching him to sew. At first, she praised him for any kind of job that he did. After that, she praised him only when he made the right kind of stitch and made it well. Finally, she praised him only when he cut his pattern himself and then sewed it properly.

(22) What behavioral concept is this an example of? ______________________

Example #13

Jake "gets off" after 2, 5, 4, 6, or 3 puffs on a joint on different occasions.

(14) What schedule of reinforcement is his puffing on? ______________________

Example #14

Sam thanked his roommate for taking a phone message only when the roommate wrote down all the details carefully. His roommate's message taking improved as a result.

(3) What behavioral procedure did Sam use? ______________________

Example #15

Bob lived near the phone in the dorm, so he had to answer it much of the time. Furthermore, most of the dorm members didn't bother to thank him for answering it. He found that, on the average, he got thanked once in every four times.

(21) What behavioral concept is the rate of thank-you's an example of? ______________________

Example #16

At first, Horace's teacher praised him lavishly whenever he wrote a short poem. He wrote several poems one stanza long. Later, she praised him whenever he wrote a poem two stanzas long and paid no attention to his shorter poems. By this method, the teacher eventually got him writing 20-stanza poems.

(13) What behavioral procedure did the teacher use to teach Horace to write 20-stanza poems? ______________________

Example #17

Have you ever played "the dozens"? "The dozens" involves insulting someone's mother in a funny way. After you say something such as, "You know, Joe is the ugliest person I ever saw," the other person says "Who's Joe?" You answer "Joe (your) Momma." Then it's his turn to trick you into getting an insult. After a while, everyone gets tired of the game.

(2) Getting tired of "the dozens" is probably an example of what principle of reinforcement? ______________________

Example #18

Mr. Potts couldn't decide whether to reinforce his son's behavior every time that he took out the trash or only after every 5 times.

(20) Under which schedule would his son continue longest to take out the trash if he was never again reinforced (name the schedule that is the correct answer)? ______________

Example #19

One criticism of the idea "Most of what people do is because of reinforcement" is that most people are constantly doing all kinds of things without reinforcement.

(12) One possible defense against this criticism is that people were, in the past, on a(n) ______________ schedule of reinforcement that still hasn't been extinguished.

Example #20

(1) Many people who try to use the principles of reinforcement don't realize that the reinforcement won't be effective if it is not delivered ______________ after the response has occurred.

EXAMPLE ANSWERS

(1) immediately (2) deprivation (or satiation) (3) reinforcement (4) variable ratio (VR–4) (5) Contingency (6) variable ratio (VR–4) (7) shaping (8) ratio strain (9) fixed-ratio (FR–5) (10) praised (or reinforced) (11) continuous (12) intermittent (13) shaping (14) variable ratio (VR–4) (15) variable-ratio (16) target behavior (17) variable ratio (VR–3) (18) fixed ratio (FR–5) (19) variable ratio (20) fixed ratio (FR–5) (21) variable ratio (VR–4) (22) shaping (23) continuous (24) extinction (25) continuous (26) fixed ratio (FR–2) (27) fixed ratio (FR–5) (28) yes (29) variable-ratio (30) fixed ratio (FR–6)

Lesson 14

Interval Schedules of Reinforcement

The last lesson described the concept of an intermittent schedule of reinforcement as well as two intermittent schedules (fixed ratio and variable ratio) that deliver the reinforcement after a specified number of responses have been counted.

This lesson describes two intermittent schedules that are based on the passage of time. They are referred to as interval schedules.

The simplest interval schedule is called a "fixed-interval" schedule. A **fixed-interval** schedule is one in which the person must (1) wait for a fixed time to pass (during which responses are not reinforced); and (2) make a response after that time that will be reinforced. For example, if people are reinforced for the first response that they make after 5 minutes have elapsed, then for the first response after another 5 minutes, and so on, they are on a fixed-interval (of 5 minutes) schedule. Theoretically, people could wait for the passage of the fixed time without making any responses and then be reinforced for making a single response. Of course they would have to know in advance how long the interval was and be able to time it accurately—which is seldom the case. It is crucial to realize that a person will not receive a reinforcer simply for the passage of time; he or she must make a response after that time has passed.

Typically, people work at an increasingly rapid rate as the time period passes until they are working at a high rate at the moment of reinforcement. Then, after reinforcement, they pause or rest for a while. The pattern is somewhat similar to a fixed-ratio pattern in that there is an alternation between responding and resting. However, the overall rate of a fixed-interval schedule is lower, because there is a gradual increase in rate rather than an abrupt increase as in the fixed-ratio schedule.

An example of a fixed-interval schedule might be Jean's sitting every day in the student union waiting from 12:50 for Bill, who always arrives at 1:00 P.M. If Jean is reading a book, she will probably look up from time to time to see whether Bill is coming. Furthermore, if Jean is like most of us, she will look up only infrequently at first (say at 12:55), but then her rate of looking up will increase as the time approaches 1:00. If Bill is on time, the first look that Jean takes after 1:00 will be reinforced by the sight of Bill.

In this example, Jean's looking responses will not be reinforced by the sight of Bill until a fixed period of time has elapsed (from 12:50 until 1:00 P.M.). The first looking response after that time will be reinforced.

Note that this is not an example of a fixed-ratio schedule because there is no fixed number of looking responses that will somehow produce sight of Bill. Jean must simply wait for the passage of a certain amount of time; by looking more often, she cannot cause Bill to appear.

Figure 14–1 shows a graph of legislation passed by Congress, which Weisberg and Waldrop (1972) interpret as resulting from a fixed-interval schedule of reinforcement for Congresspersons.

The other common interval schedule is called a "variable-interval" schedule. A **variable-interval** schedule is one in which the person (1) must wait for a varying time to pass (during which responses have no effect); and (2) must make a response after that time that will be reinforced. For example, if a person is reinforced for the first response after 3 minutes, then for the

EVEN CONGRESS OBEYS THE LAWS OF BEHAVIOR

Weisberg and Waldrop (1972) investigated the rate at which Congress passed bills. They found that Congress started at the beginning of a legislative session passing very few bills, but that as they approached adjournment, the rate gradually increased. Figure 14–1 shows this pattern on a cumulative graph for the years 1951, 1952, 1953, and 1954. Weisberg and Waldrop suggested that adjournment was a reinforcer that was delivered only after the pending legislation was disposed of, usually through passage of the bill. This reinforcer was delivered on a fixed-interval schedule and therefore would be expected to produce a pattern of responding in which the behavior occurred at a low rate initially and then at an increasing rate as the interval passed. It is interesting to note that this same pattern occurs for pigeons responding for food reinforcement and is considered to be a universal behavioral law.

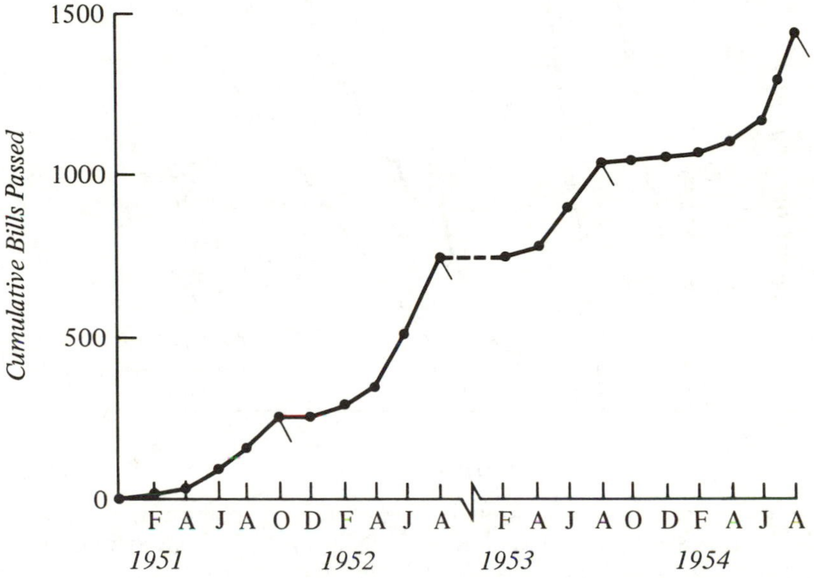

Figure 14–1. The cumulative number of bills passed by Congress in four years. The diagonal deflections indicate adjournment of Congress. Adapted from "Fixed Interval Work Habits of Congress," by P. Weisberg and P. B. Waldrop, *Journal of Applied Behavior Analysis*, 1972, 5, 93–97. Copyright 1972 by the Society for the Experimental Analysis of Behavior, Inc. Used by permission.

first response after 7 minutes, then 5, and so on, his responding would be on a variable-interval (averaging 5 minutes) schedule. Theoretically, he could wait for the passage of one of these differing intervals, make only one response, and receive reinforcement. Of course, he would have to know in advance how long each interval was and be able to accurately time it—which is seldom the case. It is important to realize that the person will not receive the reinforcer simply after the passage of time; he must make a response after the time has passed.

Typically, people on a variable-interval schedule work at a uniform rate. There is no rate increase near reinforcement, probably because the reinforcement is not predictable. The actual rate of responding, however, is considerably lower than for a variable-ratio schedule.

An example of a variable-interval schedule might be Alice's waiting in the student union every day from 12:50 for Steve, who arrives anytime from 12:50 to 1:15. If Alice is reading the student paper while she waits, she will probably look up from time to time to see if Steve is coming. She will probably look up fairly often from the time that she arrives because Steve could show up at any time. The first time that she looks up after he shows up, her looking will be reinforced by the sight of Steve.

Note that this is an example of a variable-interval schedule, not a variable-ratio schedule, because there is not some varying number of looking responses that will somehow produce the sight of Steve; by looking more often Alice cannot cause Steve to appear.

Interval schedules have some of the advantages of ratio schedules: they can be used to reduce the problem of satiation and they produce increased resistance to extinction. They also suffer from the problems of not being useful in shaping a new response and in sometimes delivering too little reinforcement to maintain responding (that is, "ratio" strain).

Figure 14-2 illustrates the patterns and comparative rates of the four simple schedules of reinforcement. As you can see, variable ratio produces the fastest rate of responding with fixed ratio somewhat less. The two interval schedules produce response rates that are lower than the ratio schedules. In fact, data from Staats and his associates (1964) on reading acquisition suggest that interval schedules produce response rates that are below even that of continuous reinforcement. Notice that the variable-interval and variable-ratio schedules both produce uniform rates of responding. The fixed ratio and fixed interval both produce pauses after reinforcement. However, the fixed ratio tends to produce a brief pause that switches abruptly to high-rate responding. Fixed interval produces a long pause that switches very gradually to high-rate responding—this pattern is called a "scallop."

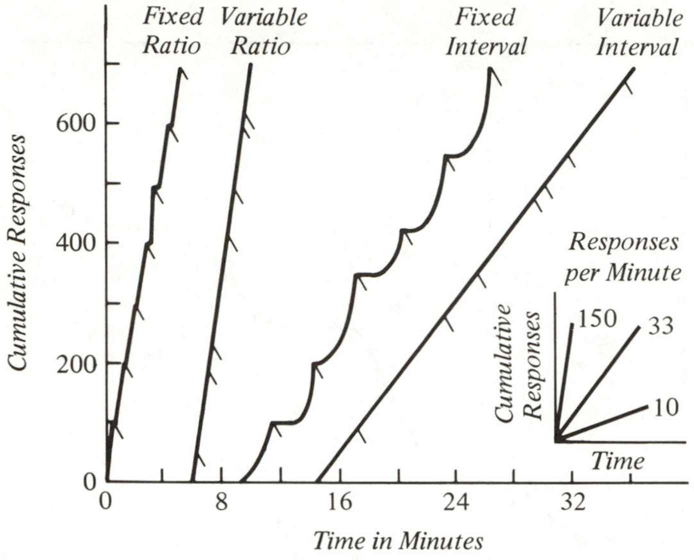

Figure 14-2. Stylized cumulative graphs of the pattern of responding produced by the four simple schedules of reinforcement. The diagonal slash marks indicate the delivery of reinforcement. From *Operant Learning: Procedures for Changing Behavior,* by J. L. Williams. Copyright © 1972 by Wadsworth, Inc. Reprinted by permission of the publisher, Brooks/Cole Publishing Company, Monterey, California.

The unique patterns of responding associated with each schedule are of immense importance to behavioral science. They provide powerful examples that behavior is lawful. In fact, these patterns are often described as behavioral laws applicable to many species and many behaviors. As you have seen, these laws apply to many complex forms of human behavior, from passing Congressional legislation to novel writing.

BEHAVIOR ANALYSIS EXAMPLE

Study behavior. Mawhinney, Bostow, Laws, Blumenfeld, and Hopkins (1971) studied the pattern of university-student study behavior. They taught a class in which the reading material was available only in a library room and had to be checked out for use in that room. They stamped the time out and time in on a recording clock and kept track of the total amount of time that each student had the material for study in that room. At first, they scheduled a test for each day of the class. As you can see from the cumulative graph in Figure 14-3, during this portion of the semester the students studied the material roughly an equal amount of time each day. The researchers then shifted to a schedule of testing every 3 weeks. The students studied very little for the first part of the 3-week period but gradually started studying more and more as the time of the test approached. They next reversed to daily tests and found equal studying each day. And finally, they once again tried a 3-week testing period and, although there was a less dramatic effect, they once again found little studying at the beginning of the period and an increasing rate as the test date approached.

This experiment produced a pattern of responding that is like that in fixed-interval studies. It

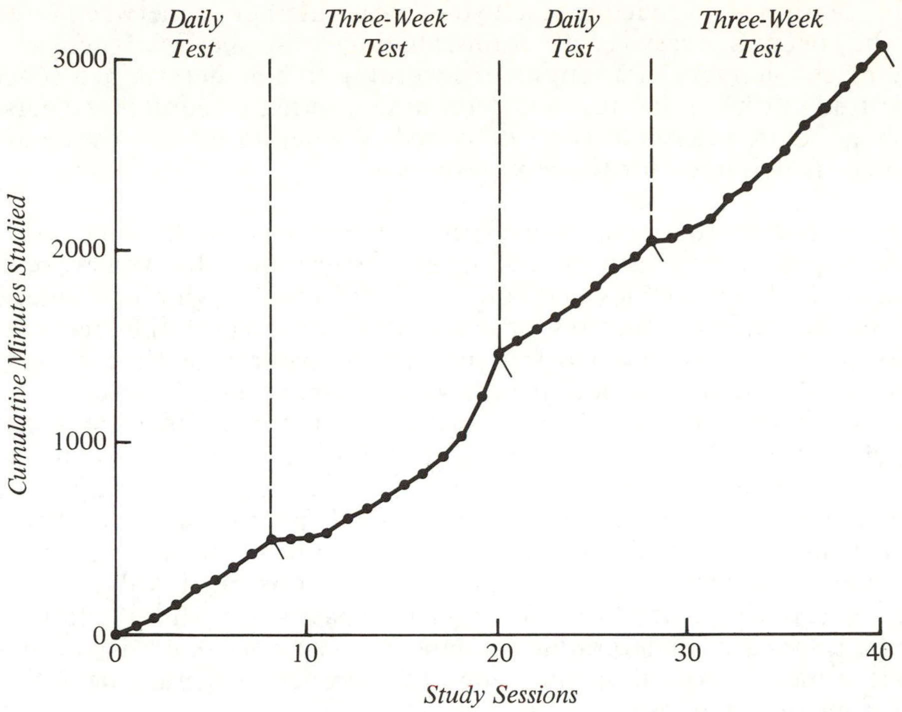

Figure 14-3. The cumulative study hours by college students when different testing schedules are in effect. Adapted from "A Comparison of Students' Studying Behavior Produced by Daily, Weekly, and Three-Week Testing Schedules," by V. T. Mawhinney, D. E. Bostow, D. R. Laws, G. J. Blumenfeld, and B. L. Hopkins, *Journal of Applied Behavior Analysis*, 1971, *4*, 257–264. Copyright 1971 by the Society for the Experimental Analysis of Behavior, Inc. Used by permission.

is possible to view the test as a reinforcing event that can be scheduled in different ways. When scheduled daily, it approximates a continuous schedule of reinforcement, which would be expected to result in continuous and relatively uniform responding. When scheduled for long intervals, it is similar to a fixed-interval schedule and would be expected to produce a scalloped rate of responding. These results indicate that even the complex intellectual behavior involved in studying follows predictable and lawful patterns observed in other behaviors.

Note: If a person is reinforced after a fixed period of time no matter what he or she is doing at the time, then the situation would be called superstitious reinforcement. This situation was named by B. F. Skinner (1948a), who delivered food to pigeons for 5 seconds every 15 seconds no matter what the pigeons were doing. The pigeons developed a variety of superstitious behaviors—such as turning in a full circle, swaying the body like a pendulum, and hopping from one foot to the other. These behaviors were called "superstitious" because the pigeons acted as if their behavior caused the reinforcement even though it did not. People display many superstitious behaviors—like swearing at their cars when they won't start—that may well be caused by the same kind of coincidental reinforcement. Notice carefully that superstitious reinforcement differs from fixed-interval reinforcement in that it is delivered after a fixed period of time regardless of whether the person emits a specified behavior.

ADDITIONAL READINGS

Holland, J. G. Human vigilance. *Science*, 1958, *128*, 61–67. Also reprinted in R. Ulrich, T. Stachnik, & J. Mabry (Eds.), *Control of human behavior* (Vol. 1). Glenview, Ill.: Scott, Foresman, 1966. This article reports one of the earliest demonstrations of schedule effects with human subjects. Holland showed that the "looking response" is one that is influenced by its consequences (that is, seeing a reinforcing scene), and that, depending on the schedule of seeing what one is looking for, the pattern of looking will vary.

Reese, E. P. *Human behavior: Analysis and application.* Dubuque, Iowa: William C. Brown, 1978. This book is a fine introduction to operant psychology applied to the analysis of human behavior. It contains an excellent description of schedule effects and many citations to research illustrating these effects.

Helpful hints: This section is intended to teach you how to distinguish between interval and ratio schedules when they occur in everyday situations. Distinguishing between them when a behavior analyst is arranging the delivery of a reinforcer according to a predetermined schedule is quite simple. You must find out his or her rule and determine whether it requires the person to make a number of responses before the reinforcer is delivered, or whether it requires the passage of time before the reinforcer is delivered for the next response.

Helpful hint #1: In everyday situations, however, the distinction is a lot harder to make since we do not have someone to put the rule into words. Suppose, for example, that you are operating a slide projector and you are looking at slides that you took (only a few of which are interesting). What type of schedule is your slide advance response on? Some responses will be reinforced by seeing interesting slides, some will not be. Does it involve the passage of time during which your responding makes no difference? Or does it involve the number of responses?

Here's how you should analyze this. You must realize that the slides are in some unknown sequence in which you may have to advance many slides before coming to an interesting one. Suppose the first interesting one occurs after seven slides. There is no amount of time that you must wait before your next advancing response will suddenly produce the interesting slide. In fact, if you make no responses for a fixed period of time, you will be no closer to the interesting slide than you were when you started. Thus the passage of time is not involved in getting to the reinforcer. Rather you must advance the slide projector past seven slides before you get to the reinforcer. That is, there is a predetermined number of responses, even if you don't know the number—or, for that matter, even if no one knows the number. You must make those responses before the interesting slide arrives.

If you think that an example involves an interval schedule, you may check your conclusion by asking the question "If the person makes no response at all, will there eventually arrive a time at which <u>one response</u> will produce the reinforcer?" Or if the behavior is an <u>ongoing</u> behavior, ask "If the person does not emit the behavior for a time, will there eventually arrive a time when emitting it for a <u>brief time</u> will produce the reinforcer?"

If you think that an example involves a ratio schedule, you may check your conclusion by asking "If the person makes the responses very rapidly (or very often) will the next reinforcer arrive <u>sooner</u> (than if the responses are made slowly)?"

In other words, the rapidity of reinforcement for an interval schedule is <u>time-controlled</u> (although you still must make at least one response), and it is <u>response-controlled</u> for a ratio schedule.

Helpful hint #2: The slide projector example can also be analyzed from the point of view of people watching slides that are being advanced by someone else. In that case, their looking response would be reinforced by the sight of an interesting slide only after the passage of the amount of time that it takes the operator to get around to advancing the projector seven slides. Thus, the viewer, unlike the operator, is on a variable-interval schedule. Watching a movie would be analyzed in a similar manner. Remember to determine whether the person's response advances the slide or whether it involves looking at a slide whose delivery depends on someone else.

Helpful hint #3: You may abbreviate fixed interval as "FI" and variable interval as "VI." These abbreviations are widely used by behaviorists.

LESSON 14 READING QUIZ

(20) A fixed-interval schedule is one in which the person must (a) ________________ for a fixed period of time to pass and (b) make a(n) ________________ after that time.

(10) Theoretically, a person on a fixed-interval schedule of reinforcement could wait for the passage of the fixed interval without making any responses and then be reinforced for making ________________ response.

(29) Will a person on a fixed-interval schedule be reinforced at the end of the fixed interval even if he or she does not respond? ________

(19) Typically, people on a fixed-interval schedule of reinforcement pause just after reinforcement

and then their rate of responding ____________________ as the time for reinforcement approaches.

(9) A fixed-interval schedule is one in which the person is reinforced for the first response made after a(n) ____________________ period of time passes.

(28) The pausing and working pattern of the fixed-interval schedule is similar to the pattern for another schedule called ____________________.

(30) When the behavior of someone is being reinforced on a fixed-interval schedule, not every response is reinforced. Therefore, the person is being reinforced according to a(n) ____________________ (intermittent, continuous) schedule.

(18) Weisberg and Waldrop (1972) pointed out that Congress passes legislation during the several-month-long period of time set for a legislative session, and that their behavior is then reinforced by adjournment. If legislative sessions are always of the same length, passing legislation is on what schedule of reinforcement? ____________________

(8) A variable-interval schedule is one in which the person must (a) ____________________ for a varying time to pass, and (b) make a(n) ____________________ after that time.

(27) Theoretically, a person reinforced on a variable-interval schedule could wait for the passage of the time without responding and then be reinforced for making __________ (how many) response(s) after that time.

(17) Will a person on a variable-interval schedule be reinforced at the end of the different-length intervals even if he or she doesn't respond? __________

(7) Typically, people on a variable-interval schedule work at a(n) ____________________ rate for the entire period of time that the schedule is in effect.

(26) The pattern of uniform responding for the variable-interval schedule is similar to the pattern for what other schedule (not counting continuous reinforcement)? ____________________

(16) A variable-interval schedule of reinforcement is one in which the person is reinforced for the first response after ____________________ periods of time.

(31) If a person's behavior is being reinforced according to a variable-interval schedule, not every response is reinforced. Therefore, the behavior is being reinforced according to a(n) ____________________ (continuous, intermittent) schedule.

(6) Is the responding rate higher in a variable-ratio schedule or a variable-interval schedule? ____________________

(25) Is the overall rate of responding higher for a fixed-interval schedule or a fixed-ratio schedule? ____________________

(15) Pauses after reinforcement are characteristic of the response pattern produced by what two schedules of reinforcement? ____________________ and ____________________

(5) The pattern of responding produced by a fixed interval—pause after reinforcement and then gradually increasing response rate—is called a(n) ____________________.

(32) A common feature of fixed-<u>interval</u> and fixed-<u>ratio</u> schedules is that not every response is reinforced. Therefore, both schedules are examples of ____________________ schedules.

(24) The unique patterns of responding produced by schedules of reinforcement provide powerful examples that behavior is ____________________.

(14) Interval schedules can be used to reduce the problem of ____________________ and to increase resistance to ____________________.

(4) Interval schedules are not suitable for use when ____________________ a new response, and they may end up delivering too few ____________________ to maintain responding.

(23) Mawhinney and associates (1971) might have given tests unannounced but occurring either

on the average of every 3 weeks or exactly every 3 weeks. Which schedule of test giving would result in a more uniform pattern of studying? ______________

(13) Mawhinney and associates (1971) studied student study patterns when tested daily and when tested at 3-week intervals. If the professor no longer reinforced studying, which schedule would lead to greater studying? (Name the correct schedule used in their study.) ______________

(3) Mawhinney and associates (1971) tested students at 3-week intervals. Their study behavior would be on what schedule of reinforcement? ______________

(22) If a person is reinforced after a fixed period of time no matter what he or she is doing at the time, the schedule would not be called a(n) ______________ but rather would be called ______________ reinforcement.

(12) If you think that an interval schedule is involved, ask "If the person makes no responses will a time arrive when only ______________ response will produce the reinforcer?"

(2) If you think that an example involves interval reinforcement and the behavior is an ongoing one, ask "If the person does not emit the behavior for a time, will there eventually arrive a time when emitting it for a(n) ______________ time will produce the reinforcer?"

(21) If you think that a schedule is a ratio schedule, ask "If the person makes the responses very rapidly, will the next reinforcer arrive ______________?"

(11) In which type of schedule is the rapidity of reinforcement response-controlled? ______________ In which type is it time-controlled? ______________

(1) If people can speed up the delivery of a reinforcer by working harder, they are on what type of schedule? ______________

(33) Name four intermittent schedules of reinforcement. ______________, ______________, ______________, and ______________

READING QUIZ ANSWERS

(1) ratio (2) brief (3) fixed interval (FI-3) (4) shaping; reinforcers (5) scallop (6) variable ratio (7) uniform (8) wait; response (9) fixed (10) one (11) ratio; interval (12) one (13) fixed interval (FI-3) (14) satiation; extinction (15) fixed ratio; fixed interval (16) varying (17) no (18) fixed interval (19) increases (20) wait; response (21) sooner (22) fixed interval; superstitious (23) variable interval (24) lawful (25) fixed ratio (26) variable ratio (27) one (28) fixed ratio (29) no (30) intermittent (31) intermittent (32) intermittent (33) fixed ratio, fixed interval, variable ratio, variable interval

LESSON 14 EXAMPLES

Example #1

Dave met Doris for lunch at the corner of Market and Fifth every day. Doris was supposed to show up at 1:00 but she came anywhere from 10 minutes early to 10 minutes late. If Dave looks at each passerby to see if he or she is Doris, and if seeing Doris reinforces him, decide what schedule his looking behavior is on.

(11) Suppose that you guessed that this was a ratio schedule. You could check your guess by asking "If Dave looks more often at people, will Doris arrive ______________?" You could conclude that this is not a ratio schedule because the answer to that question is ______________.

(31) You might then conclude that the schedule was an interval schedule. You could check this by asking "If Dave does not look at all, will there eventually arrive a time when ______________

__________ looking response will sight Doris?" This example illustrates an interval schedule because the answer to that question is __________.

(22) What type of interval schedule is this an example of? __________
(Notice that Doris comes at different times each day.)

Example #2

Ron and Betty were watching a movie containing a few scenes showing disco dancing. Since they were interested in learning some new steps, these scenes were the only ones that were of interest to them. Suppose that the scenes were 2 minutes long and the first one occurred after 15 minutes had elapsed, the second after another 5 minutes, the third after another 25 minutes and the last after another 15 minutes.

(30) Suppose that you guess that this may be a ratio schedule. To check your guess you should ask "If Ron and Betty look at the movie more often, will the disco scenes arrive __________?" The answer to that question is __________.

(21) If you now conclude that the schedule must be an interval schedule, you should check your answer. First, you must recognize that looking at a movie is an ongoing behavior and ask "If Ron and Betty do not look for a time, will there eventually arrive a time when looking for a(n) __________ will result in seeing the disco dancing?" The answer to that question is __________.

(10) Since the time between scenes varies from 5 to 25 minutes, this example illustrates a(n) __________ schedule.

Example #3

Martha worked on an assembly line at the Ford plant. It was her job to tighten 13 nuts on each car frame. Every time that she did this, a supervisor would check the job and record her work. She got paid 50¢ for every 13 nuts tightened.

(20) To determine whether this is a ratio schedule, ask "If Martha makes the response very fast or very often, will the next reinforcer arrive __________?" The answer is __________.

(29) It is usually wise to also check to see whether this might be an interval schedule by asking "If Martha makes no response at all, will there eventually arrive a time at which __________ response will produce the reinforcer?" The answer is __________.

(9) Because Martha must make 13 responses per reinforcer, her work is on a(n) __________ __________ schedule of reinforcement.

Example #4

George worked in a factory. His supervisor came by to check on him every 30 minutes. (Assume that it is reinforcing for George to be found working.)

(7) To check whether this is a ratio schedule ask "If George works faster will the supervisor arrive __________?" The answer is __________.

(19) To check whether this is an interval schedule, first notice that this is an ongoing behavior and ask "If George does not work at all for a time, will there eventually arrive a time when working for a(n) __________ will result in the supervisor seeing him working?" The answer is __________.

(8) Since the supervisor comes by every 30 minutes, this is an example of a(n) __________ __________ schedule.

Example #5

When reading a book, one might find many passages or scenes that are boring. However, most people keep reading with the hope that a really exciting passage will come along soon. Such a scene may occur on the average of only once every 20 pages.

(6) This can be a confusing example because you might think it is like the movie. However, the movie goes on whether or not you look. Unless you are going to skip pages, which will destroy the plot and make no passages exciting, you must read on. Thus, when you guess interval and ask "If the person does not read for a period of time, will there arrive a time when emitting the behavior for a brief time will produce the reinforcer (the exciting passage)?" The answer must be ____________.

(18) If you ask "Can the reader make the exciting scene arrive sooner by reading faster?" the answer is ____________. Thus, since the exciting scenes are after different numbers of pages, this would be an example of a(n) ________________________ schedule.

Example #6

John was very clothes conscious. He liked to have on his hip clothes whenever anyone stopped by his room to visit. On an ordinary day, John had a visitor on the average of once every 93 minutes. The visitors came between 7:00 and 11:00 P.M. Having a visitor when he had his hip clothes on was a reinforcer for John.

(5) By asking the question "If John makes the response more often (for example, by staying in his hip clothes for the full 4 hours), will the next reinforcer arrive sooner?" you can determine whether this is a(n) ________________________ schedule.

(17) By asking the question "If John does not make the response for a time, will there arrive a time when he could make it for a brief time and produce the reinforcer?" you can determine whether this is a(n) ________________________ schedule.

(28) In this example, John's dressing in hip clothes is being reinforced according to a(n) ________________________ schedule.

Example #7

Marty's teacher wanted him to do more math problems for less reinforcement. She decided to reinforce him an average of once every five times that he completed a problem. She kept track of where he started and then complimented him after he completed 3, 8, 5, and 4 problems.

(27) The teacher was giving out compliments on a(n) ________________________ schedule. (Be sure to check your answer by asking both questions.)

Example #8

Believe it or not, Gloria is a peeper. She can see into Dave's room from her own room. She starts watching his room at 11:30 each night. Dave comes into his room and starts undressing at exactly 11:40 every night.

(16) What schedule of reinforcement is Gloria's peeping behavior on? ________________________ (Be sure to check your answer by asking both questions.)

Example #9

John had been trying to teach his son to bring his plate into the kitchen and put it in the sink immediately after dinner. During the first month, John gave his son an ice cream dessert each time he brought his plate into the kitchen. In the second month, John started giving his son an ice cream dessert when he brought his plate to the kitchen for several meals in a row, averaging four.

(4) What schedule of reinforcement is the son on during the second month? ______________

Example #10

Alice was a radar scanner in Alaska. She was supposed to scan the radar screen continually for an 8-hour period looking for unidentified (and possible hostile) planes. Alice spotted an average of two unidentified planes per night. Usually they were American planes that were off course.

(15) What schedule of reinforcement is Alice's scanning on? ______________
(Be sure to ask the questions.)

Example #11

Chester took his children for a rare ice cream treat on Sunday of any week during which they brought home a good school paper for him to see. He never gave them an ice cream treat for anything else. It seemed like they would do anything for such a treat.

(26) What principle of effective reinforcement accounts for the fact that Chester's procedure did not result in higher grades for his children? ______________

Example #12

Darlene's clock radio always woke her at exactly 6:45. As she dressed she would occasionally listen to see if the 7:00 news had come on yet.

(3) What schedule of reinforcement is her listening behavior on? ______________

Example #13

Daisy continued to cry every night after being put to bed. Her parents would go into her room to see what was the matter and they always spent some time comforting her. They never found any physical problems such as wet diapers. After some months, they decided that they should simply ignore the crying. They found that within several days Daisy no longer cried after being put to bed.

(14) What schedule of reinforcement did her parents eventually place her crying on? ______________

Example #14

Stan wanted everyone around him to be happy and cheerful. Anytime that Susan said something cheerful he was happy and smiled. Anytime that she said something down, he was unhappy and glum. Susan began saying cheerful things more often.

(25) What behavioral procedure did Stan unconsciously apply to Susan's behavior? ______________

Example #15

The Kramers had a light switch that didn't work right. The first time that you moved the switch the lights did not come on. In fact, you had to turn the switch three times before the lights would come on.

(13) Operating the light switch was on what schedule of reinforcement? ______________

Example #16

Porno Pete had reduced the writing of pornographic books to a science. He had a chart that told him how many pages to wait before creating one of the filthy scenes for which he was famous. He made his reader wait for 1 page to get to the first one, then 11, then 5, then 23 more, and so on.

(2) If reading a page is one response, what schedule of reinforcement is that response on? ______________________

Example #17

Timmy discovered that if you hold a magnifying lens between an ant and the sun, and focus it properly, the ant will burn up with a popping sound. Timmy's rate of focusing the magnifying glass increased dramatically after this discovery.

(24) Frying ants as a stimulus would be called a(n) ______________________.

Example #18

Kay was always thrilled when she saw a deer. She used to sit by the hour on her favorite hill waiting to see one.

(23) What schedule of reinforcement is her deer-looking behavior on? ______________________

Example #19

Willis was fascinated by comets. He watched patiently to catch sight of Alpha 13, which was visible at 4 A.M. on August 24 every two years.

(1) What schedule of reinforcement was his watching for Alpha 13 on? ______________________

Example #20

Tillie was difficult to engage in a conversation and, in particular, she was difficult to get started talking about herself. Frank found out that if you asked her enough questions about herself she would eventually open up. Sometimes it took only a couple of questions, but other times it took many more.

(12) What schedule of reinforcement is Frank's questioning on if "opening up" is the reinforcer? ______________________

EXAMPLE ANSWERS

(1) fixed interval (FI–2 years) (2) variable ratio (VR–10) (3) fixed interval (FI–15 minutes) (4) variable-ratio (VR–4) (5) ratio (6) no (7) sooner; no (8) fixed-interval (FI–30 minutes) (9) fixed-ratio (FR–13) (10) variable-interval (VI–15) (11) sooner; no (12) variable ratio (13) fixed ratio (FR–3) (14) extinction (15) variable interval (VI–4 hours) (16) fixed interval (FI–10) (17) interval (18) yes; variable-ratio (VR–20) (19) brief time; yes (20) sooner; yes (21) brief time; yes (22) variable interval (23) variable interval (24) reinforcer (25) differential reinforcement (26) Immediacy (27) variable-ratio (VR–5) (28) variable-interval (VI–93 minutes) (29) one; no (30) sooner; no (31) one; yes

Lesson 15

Review of Reinforcement

This unit has focused on reinforcement—the procedure in which an event follows a behavior and increases the probability or rate of that behavior. The lessons have included examples of many varied kinds of reinforcing events, most of which stem directly from the behavior of other people, including such strong reinforcers as attention, encouragement, and compliments. The lessons have also mentioned a wide variety of behaviors, both desirable and undesirable, that may be the result of reinforcement—such as studying, talking about problems, and nagging.

The important point to be made about the reinforcement of behavior is that it is a social—a very human—concept. Most reinforcement relates to how people treat each other. Under the best of circumstances, the behaviors that two people engage in are mutually reinforcing—an ideal situation, whether the two people be married, friends, or roommates. Each person benefits, and the benefits can maintain the relationship.

However, most people don't understand the concept of reinforcement and, thus, frequently engage in self-defeating behaviors. They give in to the nagger to get him or her out of their hair but, in the process, guarantee that he or she will keep nagging. They try to be nice to people by listening to their problems but thereby guarantee that they will continue to complain. Or they let people who aren't doing their share of some common task have the same privileges as those who are, thereby increasing the probability that others will fail to do their share in the future.

Reinforcement is a powerful tool that an individual or a group can use to set up a beneficial social system. By reinforcing desired behavior and extinguishing undesirable behavior, it is possible to create a happy, comfortable environment. B. F. Skinner's novel *Walden Two* illustrates how reinforcement principles might be used to set up a utopian society; it emphasizes how individuals and small groups can use behavioral principles to modify their own behavior in ways agreeable to all. Reinforcement has been used by behavior therapists to help individuals solve self-identified behavior problems (Cautela, 1969), it has been used to set up a democratically controlled student commune (Miller & Feallock, 1974), and it has been used to teach individuals to apply behavioral principles to solving their own problems (Watson & Tharp, 1972).

To use reinforcement effectively, you should ask a series of questions related to the situation that you want to change. First, determine exactly what is the desired behavior in that particular situation. In specifying this goal, don't use vague descriptions involving attitudes, feelings, or thoughts—such as "being nice" or "working hard"—that do not point to physical acts. Decide on your goals and state them in behavioral terms. Then develop behavioral definitions that tell you how to observe the behavior, and test these definitions by measuring the reliability of observations based on them.

Second, decide whether the rate of the behavior should be increased or decreased. If an increase is desirable, look for potential reinforcers that the person has been deprived of and that can be delivered immediately after the behavior, in sufficient amounts, and contingent on the behavior. If a decrease in the behavior is desirable, decide what events are currently maintaining the behavior and attempt to stop them. Don't make assumptions about the effectiveness of those events. Measure their effect on behavior and make sure that they do, in fact, increase or decrease the behavior.

Third, decide whether you can directly reinforce the behavior that you want to increase. If the behavior doesn't occur naturally (that is, the person doesn't "know" how to do it), create a series of behavioral approximations to the desired behavior and use the process of shaping. Or, if the behavior is part of a broader response class that is undesirable, differentially reinforce the desired behavior. The procedures of shaping and differential reinforcement are powerful tools that, in skillful hands, can be used to develop almost any new behavior.

Fourth, consider what kind of schedule you want. If the behavior occurs at a low rate (but doesn't have to be shaped), start with continuous reinforcement to increase its rate. When you have increased its rate, switch to intermittent reinforcement in order to save reinforcers, conserve the energy of the person(s) giving the reinforcers, avoid satiation, and develop a greater resistance to extinction. Furthermore, by selecting a schedule of reinforcement similar to one provided by the real environment, you may be able to discontinue your program and have the behavior maintained by natural reinforcement.

Fifth, evaluate the effectiveness of your program. Design an experiment to see whether your program works. If you are increasing a behavior by means of an event, reverse the behavior (by stopping the delivery of the event) to make sure that the event is really producing the effect, or try a second behavior or a second person. Be sure to rule out coincidences, and keep in mind that merely the decision to try a new program is often sufficient to increase the behavior.

In summary, the five basic steps that are involved in the application of reinforcement to behavior are:

1. Specifying the behavior
2. Determining the reinforcing event that you will manipulate and measure
3. Deciding whether you need to shape a new behavior
4. Deciding on a schedule of reinforcement
5. Designing an experiment to evaluate the success of your program

It is not necessary to manipulate others in order to use the tool of reinforcement. This tool can be used to change your own behavior (usually the program should be arranged through a second person, because you might find it more immediately reinforcing simply to adjust your rules rather than your behavior), or it can be used by a democratic group to establish a certain set of behaviors or a social system that will succeed (you should decide what behaviors are necessary, who should do what, and how the group will arrange suitable consequences for the behavior).

It is, however, possible that this tool can be used to manipulate others. For instance, when you have to interact with someone who will not or cannot voluntarily change a behavior that is annoying to you, you are faced with a decision. You can tolerate the behavior, avoid the person, leave the situation, or attempt to modify the behavior. In another situation, you may be faced with an enemy who is trying to control your behavior. By understanding the principles of reinforcement, you have a better chance of not being controlled.

The problem of *countercontrol*—that is, of one person resisting the control of another person—is a complicated one. For example, if reinforcement principles are used by industrial owners to make workers work harder and faster, how can workers fight that control? The traditional tool of the worker has been unions, yet unions are sometimes weak and incapable of resisting the control of owners. One possibility is using behavioral principles to develop a stronger union capable of stronger resistance. Thus, a knowledge of behavioral principles can potentially aid any group in resisting the control of another group (see also Skinner, 1953).

Behavior analysis is not manipulative; people are manipulative. Reinforcement is simply a tool that an individual or a group can use to effectively modify the social environment for a happier and more productive life.

GLOSSARY

Helpful hint: The definitions of all terms introduced in this unit of the book are presented below. You can review the unit and prepare for your exam by testing yourself on the definitions and correlated facts presented for each term. You might use a piece of paper as a mask and leave only the term exposed; see if you can formulate a reasonable definition and any other facts about that term. Then move the mask and check on yourself.

A (successive) **approximation** is any behavior similar to a target behavior; it is usually one of a series of behaviors differentially reinforced in a program of shaping toward the goal of producing the target behavior.

Continuous reinforcement is a schedule of reinforcement in which every response is reinforced. This technique is usually used when a person is first learning a behavior, particularly in shaping procedures.

Deprivation is the frequency with which a person has received a particular reinforcer in the recent past—the less frequent the reinforcer, the more deprived the person.

Differential reinforcement involves two or more physically different behaviors; one behavior is reinforced, and all others are extinguished.

Extinction is the procedure by which an event that followed a behavior in the past is stopped, and the probability (or rate) of the behavior decreases.

Fixed interval is a schedule in which a person is reinforced for the first response after a fixed period of time has passed since the previous reinforcement. This schedule usually causes people to pause after a reinforcer and then to gradually increase their response rate until they are working at a high rate at the moment they receive the next reinforcer.

Fixed ratio is a schedule in which people are reinforced for making a response only after they have made a fixed number of those responses without reinforcement. This schedule usually causes people to pause after reinforcement and then work at a very high rate until the next reinforcement. The overall rate is higher than continuous reinforcement but lower than variable ratio.

Intermittent reinforcement applies to schedules of reinforcement in which only some responses are reinforced; ratio and interval schedules are common examples. A person trained on an intermittent schedule of reinforcement will continue making a response during extinction for a longer period of time than a person trained on a continuous schedule. Intermittent reinforcement also produces more responding for fewer reinforcers, thus reducing the problem of satiation.

The **Principle of Contingency** states that a reinforcer will be maximally effective if the reinforcer is delivered only when the desired behavior has occurred. To decide whether this principle has been followed, ask the question "Was the reinforcer given only when the desired behavior occurred?"

The **Principle of Deprivation** states that the more deprived a person is of a certain reinforcer, the more effective that reinforcer will be. To decide whether the principle has been followed, ask "Has the reinforcer been delivered too often?"

The **Principle of Immediacy** states that the more immediate the delivery of the reinforcer after the occurrence of the behavior, the more effective the reinforcer. To decide whether this principle has been followed, ask the question "Was the reinforcer delivered within one minute of the behavior (or while the behavior was still occurring)?"

The **Principle of Size** states that the larger the amount of any single reinforcer, the more effective the reinforcement. To decide whether the principle has been followed, ask the question "Was the amount of reinforcement worthwhile?"

Ratio strain describes the fact that a behavior that is seldom reinforced (for instance, once every 1000 responses) may slow or stop altogether.

A **reinforcer** is any event that follows a behavior and increases the probability (or rate) of that behavior.

Satiation is the opposite of deprivation. The more frequently a person has received a particular reinforcer in the recent past, the more satiated he or she is.

Shaping is the use of differential reinforcement on a series of successive approximations to a target behavior.

A **target behavior** is the ultimate goal of a program of shaping.

Unknown is the term used in this book to describe a behavioral procedure for which a name and definition have not yet been taught.

Variable interval is a schedule in which a person is reinforced for the first response after a varying period of time has passed since the previous reinforcement. This schedule usually causes a person to respond at a uniform rate.

Variable ratio is a schedule in which people are reinforced for making a response only after they have made a varying number of those responses without reinforcement. This schedule usually causes people to work at a high and uniform rate of speed. It produces the highest rate of responding of the simple schedules.

ADDITIONAL READINGS

Wheeler, H. (Ed.). *Beyond the punitive society.* San Francisco: W. H. Freeman, 1973. This book is a collection of writings by economists, philosophers, and social scientists on the social and political aspects of behavior analysis.

UNIT TWO PRACTICE REVIEW

The following material has questions over every concept studied in Unit 2 as well as review questions from Unit 1. By answering the questions and checking your answers, you can prepare yourself for the Review Exam. The Review Exam will contain questions from both units.

(56) At first Kevin liked to have Alice hang around him all the time and he always tried to be friendly. Finally, however, it got to be a drag, so he stopped being friendly to her. To his surprise, she kept hanging around him anyway. What behavioral procedure did Kevin use?

____

(50) The record of a behavior prior to an experimental manipulation is called the __________.

(71) If a person is reinforced for emitting a behavior in one situation and is extinguished for emitting it in another situation, his behavior is being modified by what behavioral procedure?

____

(16) Pam told the other members of her sorority that they were far too interested in materialistic things like clothes, money, and cars. At first her sisters ignored her but later they started arguing with her. As a result her rate of making such comments increased. Her sisters' arguments as stimulus events would be called ____________________.

(10) Compute the reliability of these two observations. __________ Is it acceptable?

____

Observer 1:	X O X O O O O O O X
Observer 2:	O O X O O O O O O X

(53) If a behavior produces a reinforcer every second time that it occurs, the behavior is said to be reinforced on a(n) ____________________ schedule.

(4) The behavioral procedure of extinction is being used if the delivery of a reinforcing event is ____________________ and the rate of the behavior __________

____________________.

(45) If people are reinforced only when they emit a specified behavior, the reinforcer will be effective as a result of the Principle of ____________________.

(65) Ben and Sue were building up their endurance for the disco marathon. They began by setting the goal of dancing continuously for 3 hours. When they got so they could do that, they set their goal at 4 hours. They were aiming for 35 hours. Dancing for 3 hours straight is called a(n) ____________________ to dancing for 35 hours.

(39) Jim and Pete had trouble getting along even though they were brothers. Jim kept teasing Pete and Pete would get upset and cry. One day, Pete realized that his brother was simply trying to get him to cry. So he decided he would never again cry when he was teased. Jim teased Pete just as often. What behavioral procedure did Pete use on Jim? ____________________

(36) What specific schedule of reinforcement produces the highest average rate of responding?

____

(22) Ben and Sue were building up their endurance for the disco marathon. They began by setting the goal of dancing for 3 hours. When they could do that they set their goal at 4 hours. They were aiming at 35 hours. Dancing for 35 hours would be called the ________________ ________________.

(33) What two intermittent schedules produce a uniform rate of responding? ________________ ________________

(29) The horizontal line on a graph is called the ________________.

(73) Any method that is used to try to change a behavior is called a(n) ________________.

(61) Behaviors that successively approximate a target behavior are differentially reinforced in the procedure called ________________.

(31) One factor that increases the effectiveness of a reinforcer is having the reinforcer occur as soon as possible after a response has been made. This is called the Principle of ________________ ________________.

(27) The vertical line on a graph is called the ________________.

(58) Sarge decided to find out once and for all how often Beetle was asleep. So he observed <u>the amount of time that Beetle did not move</u>—whether or not his eyes were open! The underlined words are called a(n) ________________.

(7) Suppose that someone fails to do something that he or she has agreed to do. If you then tell the person to do it and he or she does, what behavioral procedure are you using? ________________ ________________

(60) Sam's teacher tried to come by his desk after different periods of time to see if he was working on his spelling lesson. If it was reinforcing for Sam to be found working, what schedule was his studying on? ________________

(72) If one behavior is extinguished and another behavior is reinforced, we say that the procedure of ________________ is being used.

(62) John was interested in the effect of attempting to reinforce compliments on the rate of getting compliments. So he observed the rate of compliments that he got for several weeks when he did not reinforce them. He then started reinforcing compliments from Mary while still not reinforcing them from Bev. After 2 weeks he started reinforcing them from Bev also. He found large increases after he started using reinforcement. What experimental design did he use? ________________

(51) Bernie told Professor Jacobs that he studied so hard in sociology because he was terribly interested in social problems, although he had never explained it that way before. The professor nodded in agreement and then spent a long time discussing social problems with Bernie. After that, Bernie always explained his extensive studying of sociology as resulting from his interest in it. What behavioral procedure did the professor use, probably without realizing it, to increase Bernie's rate of explaining his studying as resulting from a strong interest in sociology? ________________

(32) If a person is reinforced after differing numbers of responses, he or she is on a(n) ________________ ________________ schedule of reinforcement.

(14) Two observers counted the number of times that Fearsome Freddy hit another child. Observer 1 counted 15 hits, while Observer 2 counted 20 hits. Compute their reliability. ________________ Is this acceptable if it is a new definition? ________________

(47) Interval recording involves dividing the observation period into a series of ________________ intervals.

(74) Intermittent schedules of reinforcement create a greater resistance to ________________ than do continuous schedules. ("Satiation" is not the desired response here.)

(28) Behavior analysis is a behavioral science that develops practical techniques for producing changes in socially significant ________________.

(59) John counted the number of times that Professor Brainbuster said the word "orthogonal" because he was interested in the professor's tendency to use big words that his students did not understand. What method of observation was he using? ______________ recording

(34) If only some responses are reinforced, then the behavior is said to be on a(n) ______________ schedule of reinforcement.

(44) Alice was a third grader who liked to take long bike rides after school. Her father worried about this, particularly after Alice described how she almost got run over by a heavy truck. He therefore told her to come straight home after school. She started coming straight home after that. What behavioral procedure did her father use to increase her rate of coming right home? ______________

(63) Claire was interested in whether ignoring complaining behavior would reduce it. She started observing the rate of complaints uttered by Bill for 3 weeks and she tried to appear sympathetic. She then totally ignored complaints for 3 weeks. And finally she again appeared sympathetic to his complaints. She noted a substantial drop during the time when she ignored them. What experimental design was she using? ______________

(30) Dave found that he could get a date for dancing if he asked enough single women outside the disco. Sometimes the first woman he asked agreed to go dancing, other times he asked as many as 30 before scoring. What schedule of reinforcement is his date-asking behavior on? ______________

(21) What schedule of reinforcement produces a pause after reinforcement and then very rapid responding until the next reinforcement? ______________

(35) If a behavior is reinforced every time that it occurs, what schedule is it on? ______________

(26) A complex graph can be squared by selecting the condition with the highest value of the ______________ and squaring the graph for that condition.

(23) Professor Clark wanted her students to turn in a two-page essay every Friday, so for the first part of the semester she reminded them every Thursday to hand in an essay by Friday. Midway through the semester she stopped reminding them, and to her surprise they stopped handing them in on time. What behavioral procedure did she use to decrease their rate of handing their essays in on time? ______________

(20) Willie helped her friend Sarah learn to be more assertive by providing her with feedback during parties. Anytime that Sarah was properly assertive, Willie nodded her head so that Sarah could see. She nodded her head immediately after Sarah was assertive and only when she was assertive. Sarah seemed to thrive on the feedback and certainly never got too many nods from Willie. What principle of effective reinforcement, if any, did Willie neglect in her procedure? ______________

(37) An event is called a reinforcer if it both ______________ a behavior and ______________ the future probability of the behavior.

(25) The use of outside judges to determine whether a definition is valid is called investigating its ______________.

(38) One way to increase the effectiveness of a reinforcer is to make sure the person doesn't receive any of that type of reinforcer for a long time. This technique involves the Principle of ______________.

(64) Differential reinforcement involves two basic behavioral procedures. They are ______________ and ______________.

(40) If a behavior decreases in rate or even stops after it has been placed on a very high ratio of responses to reinforcers, we say that ______________ has occurred.

(18) One experimental design involves determining the effect of a treatment on two or more behaviors at different times. This is called a(n) ______________ design.

(66) If you stop telling someone to do something and he stops, what behavioral procedure is this an example of? ______________

(46) Time sampling involves observing whether a behavior is occurring during each of a series of ______________ intervals.

(19) Two intermittent schedules of reinforcement that produce a high rate of responding prior to reinforcement and a low rate just after reinforcement are ______________ and ______________.

(24) If an event that usually follows a behavior is stopped and there is no change in the rate, the procedure involved is ______________.

(67) The term used to refer to the procedure of delivering an event following a behavior that will increase the rate of the behavior is ______________; the term used to refer to the event itself is ______________.

(41) The swallows come back to Capistrano on exactly March 21st of every year. Mr. Peterson watches all year round for their return. What schedule of reinforcement is his swallow-watching behavior on? ______________

(3) When Damon was first learning to play Ping-Pong, he hit every shot too hard; those hard shots never worked. Gradually, he hit a few shots softly with good results. If the rate of his hard shooting decreased while the rate of his soft shooting increased, what behavioral procedure would this be an example of? ______________

(75) The use of a second observer to determine if your observations are in agreement is called ______________; the use of outside judges to determine if your definition is in agreement with theirs is called ______________.

(52) If a person is reinforced for many responses in a row, the effectiveness of the reinforcer may decrease because the person has been ______________ with respect to that reinforcer.

(68) Harvey (the con man) Miller once told Jim a fantastic story about how he could arrange for Jim to buy a small jet airplane worth $100,000 for only $5000 if he could just get the money this hour. Jim believed him and got the money. Naturally, Harvey took the money and left town never to be heard of again. He told many stories of this sort in the future. The money is clearly a(n) ______________ for Harvey's con jobs.

(17) A secretary recorded each day the number of times that her employer was late for an appointment. He was late for the following number of appointments: 8, 3, 7, 4, 4, 7, 8, 2, 1, and 6. Each division on the ordinate should be labeled with numbers that increase by steps of ______.

(69) Fran tried to increase the amount of study time put in by her daughter by giving her a special snack whenever she studied for more than a half hour. She looked in on Melanie often and made a mental note to give her a snack later if she had been studying more than a half hour. She gave the snack before bedtime. She did not give her a snack unless she was pretty sure that Melanie had been studying all that time. Melanie loved the snack and never seemed to get too much of it. But she didn't seem to increase her studying. What principle of effective reinforcement, if any, did Fran fail to employ? ______________

(5) The Principle of Size states that the larger the ______________ of a reinforcer, the stronger its effect on behavior.

(42) At first, little Janie called everyone "mama." But her parents hugged and petted her when she called her mother "mama" and ignored her when she called anyone else "mama." Gradually, Janie called only her mother "mama." What behavioral procedure did her parents use to teach her to call only her mother by the name? ______________

(9) Mr. Davis helped his daughter with her math homework by checking her work after every seven problems. If having her homework checked is a reinforcer, what schedule is doing homework on? ______________

(15) At the Freedom Food Co-op, the bookkeeper's work was observed by auditing his books. Assuming that his entries in the books are the result of the behavior of interest, what method of observation is this? ______________ recording

(12) What schedule of reinforcement should be used when shaping a new response? ______________

(43) Les had long regretted that he was so distant from his parents. He had tried talking with them about the problem to no avail. So he decided to give them a really nice compliment anytime that they shared something intimate with him. Their rate of intimacy did not change. What behavioral procedure was Les using? ______________

(48) If some behavior is never reinforced, what schedule is it on? ______________

(11) If you reinforce the first response that occurs after varying periods of time, the behavior is on a(n) ______________ schedule.

(6) Most researchers aim for a reliability figure that is ______________ or better (except for new behavioral definitions).

(70) Differential reinforcement involves two or more physically ______________ behaviors.

(49) An event that follows a behavior and leads to no change in the rate of that behavior is called a(n) ______________.

(2) Computing the agreement between two independent observations results in a measure of the ______________ of the observers.

(54) What schedule of reinforcement produces very rapid, uniform responding? ______________

(8) Wanda rarely did any work at the Freedom Food Co-op. If you worked at the Co-op, your hours were immediately recorded on the bulletin board; if you had 5 hours a month, you could buy the food at wholesale price. Wanda needed the financial savings and could never get enough savings. However, anyone could just write up the number of hours he or she worked, and many people cheated. Wanda found that she could work an hour and record 5 hours. What principle of effectiveness was at work weakening the privilege of buying at wholesale as a reinforcer for working for the Co-op? ______________

(55) Suppose that you wanted to engineer a classroom in which ghetto children learned basic skills more effectively. If they didn't possess those skills at all, you might find some skills they did possess that were related to your target skills and differentially reinforce these simpler skills. You might gradually progress to the more difficult skills. This technique would be called ______________ the complex skills.

(57) If you reinforce the first response that occurs after a fixed amount of time has passed, you are following a(n) ______________ schedule.

(76) One experimental design involves studying a behavior before and after the initiation of the treatment. This design is called a simple ______________ design.

(1) Shaping involves the differential reinforcement of a series of behaviors that are ______________ to a target behavior.

(13) Shaping involves the differential reinforcement of a series of behaviors that are successive approximations to a(n) ______________.

PRACTICE REVIEW ANSWERS

(1) approximations (2) reliability (3) differential reinforcement (4) stopped; decreases (5) amount (6) 90% (7) unknown (8) Contingency (9) fixed ratio (FR-7) (10) 90%; yes (11) variable interval (12)

continuous (13) target behavior (14) 75%; no (15) outcome (16) reinforcers (17) 1 (18) multiple-baseline (19) fixed interval; fixed ratio (20) none (21) fixed ratio (22) target behavior (23) unknown (24) unknown (25) social validation (26) ordinate (27) ordinate (28) behavior (29) abscissa (30) variable ratio (31) Immediacy (32) variable-ratio (33) variable ratio and variable interval (34) intermittent (35) continuous (36) variable ratio (37) follows; increases (38) Deprivation (39) unknown (40) ratio strain (41) fixed interval (FI–1 year) (42) unknown (43) unknown (44) unknown (45) Contingency (46) discontinuous (47) continuous (48) extinction (49) unknown (50) baseline (51) reinforcement (52) satiated (53) fixed-ratio (FR–2) (54) variable ratio (55) shaping (56) unknown (57) fixed-interval (58) behavioral definition (59) event (60) variable interval (61) shaping (62) multiple baseline (63) reversal (64) reinforcement; extinction (65) approximation (66) unknown (67) reinforcement; reinforcer (68) reinforcer (69) Immediacy (70) different (71) unknown (72) differential reinforcement (73) treatment (74) extinction (75) reliability; social validity (76) comparison

UNIT THREE
Stimulus Control

Lesson 16

Stimulus Discrimination and Everyday Behavior

STIMULUS CONTROL

This unit examines the behavioral principles that determine how stimulus situations affect behavior. In the unit on reinforcement, we focused on how to increase or decrease rates of behaviors, but now we will focus on how to get behavior to occur in the appropriate stimulus situations.

A **stimulus** is any physical event, object, or change in the environment that is related to a person's behavior. The plural of *stimulus, stimuli,* might refer to objects such as doors, windows, other people, parts of one's own body, clothing, and hair; vocal sounds such as words, sighs, and laughter; and visible configurations such as words on a page, colors, length, and width.[1] The term might also refer to a broader situation, such as an entire room, although we then usually use the term *stimulus situation.*

This unit deals with how people learn to behave in ways that are appropriate for their stimulus situation. The lessons include procedures for distinguishing among different situations (discrimination), procedures for grouping similar situations into general categories (generalization), procedures for teaching discrimination (fading), and communication (verbal behavior). In general, this unit describes a behavioral approach to intellectual behavior.

Discrimination

People act differently in the presence of different stimulus situations. They act differently toward the friendly professor than they do toward the pompous one; they act differently in a library than they do in a bar; and they act differently when driving toward a red light than they do when driving toward a green light. The basic process at work in developing these behavioral differences is the reinforcement of a behavior in the presence of one stimulus and the extinction of the same behavior in the presence of another stimulus. Behaviorists call this procedure discrimination training.

[1]As you can see from this definition, all reinforcers are also stimuli. A reinforcing stimulus is one that follows a behavior. This unit will deal primarily with stimuli that precede a behavior.

Discrimination training consists of reinforcing a behavior in the presence of a particular stimulus and extinguishing that same behavior in the presence of another stimulus. Examples of discrimination training in everyday life are common. Consider, for example, the person wandering around a modern building while trying to get out. Each time he or she goes through a door with the sign "Exit" over it, he or she will be reinforced by getting out of the building. On the other hand, going through doors marked with signs such as "Women," "Library," "223," and "Psychology Department" will not be reinforced by getting out of the building; that is, these stimuli will be associated with extinction with respect to getting out of the building. Eventually, the person will learn to go through the door marked "Exit" when he or she is trying to get out of the building. Notice that the same response (opening a door) is occurring in the presence of different stimuli (the different signs). The stimulus associated with reinforcement is called an S^D (the raised "*D*" standing for discriminative and the "*S*" for stimulus), and the stimulus associated with extinction is called an *S*-delta.

A **discriminative stimulus** (or S^D) is a stimulus that precedes the behavior and is present only if reinforcement will occur for that behavior. For example, the sign "Exit" indicates that the behavior of going through the door will be reinforced by getting out of the building.

An **S-delta** is a stimulus that precedes the behavior and is present only if extinction will occur for that behavior. For example, the sign "Library" would indicate that the behavior of going through that door will not be reinforced by getting out of the building.

If discrimination training is successful, it will cause a behavior to occur more frequently in the presence of one stimulus than in the presence of other stimuli. Behavior analysts have found it convenient to be able to talk about the components of this outcome. They refer to the behavior as "discriminated behavior"; and they refer to the effect of the stimulus (that is, the S^D) as "stimulus control." This is clarified by the next two definitions.

Discriminated behavior is a behavior that is more likely to occur in the presence of the S^D than in the presence of the *S*-delta. Producing discriminated behavior may take anywhere from just one trial to hundreds or even thousands of trials. For example, people learning to get out of a modern building may require only a few trials before they will always go through the door marked "Exit" when trying to get out of the building and never go through the doors with other markings. Their door-opening behavior (with respect to getting out of the building) would then be considered a discriminated behavior.

Stimulus control is the increased probability of a discriminated behavior that is produced by a stimulus (S^D). Thus, the increased probability of the door-opening behavior that is produced by the "Exit" sign would be called stimulus control. The "Exit" sign literally controls this behavior. We usually say that the stimulus exerts stimulus control over the behavior.

Thus if you wish to refer to the behavior that results from discrimination training, you would designate it as "discriminated behavior"; if you wish to talk about the effect of the stimulus involved in discrimination training, you would call it "stimulus control."

Discrimination training has been widely used by behavior analysts in the development of educational behaviors, particularly in programmed instruction. It has also been used to teach rudimentary skills to retarded and autistic children—such as imitating someone else's behavior or following simple instructions. And it has been used to produce generalization of behaviors outside of the training situation. Because these procedures all involve modifications of the basic discrimination-training procedure, they will be described in greater detail in succeeding lessons. A behavior analyst or any other person may inadvertently provide discrimination training when he or she starts reinforcing a behavior in order to increase its frequency. Although the behavior analyst may reinforce assertive behavior, everyone else may continue to ignore it. The behavior analyst may then become an S^D for the assertive behavior so that the person will be assertive in his or her presence. But everyone else may become (or remain) an *S*-delta for assertiveness, so that the person will not be assertive around others. Obviously such a limited change in behavior would not be particularly helpful to a person who wishes to become generally assertive. The next lesson will describe a variety of techniques to overcome the limitations of such unintended discrimination training and produce behavioral changes of greater generality.

Many everyday examples of discrimination training are easy to analyze. When teachers ask a number of historical questions, they will probably employ discrimination training to increase the probability of their students' giving the correct answers. For example, they will attempt to reinforce students for stating "December 7, 1941" when asked "When did the Japanese bomb Pearl Harbor?" However, they will attempt to extinguish that same response when asking "When did the

Japanese formally surrender in World War II?" The question "When did the Japanese bomb Pearl Harbor?" would be called the discriminative stimulus (S^D), or cue, for "December 7, 1941," and any other question would be called the *S*-delta for that response. If we learn to give the correct answer, then that response is called a discriminated behavior, and the question is said to exert stimulus control over it.

Other simple examples of discrimination training occur when we learn to call a particular person "Laverne" but not to call others by that name; when we learn to yell at a football game but not in a library; when we learn to enter the men's room but not the women's room (or vice versa); and when we learn that "81" is the answer to 9 × 9 but not to 8 × 8.

All these examples share two basic components. First, there is only one behavior being considered (Laverne, yelling, entering, or 81). Second, the behavior will be reinforced in the presence of only one stimulus situation (a particular person, a football game, a "men's-room" sign, or a question) but not in the presence of other stimulus situations (other persons, libraries, "ladies'-room" signs, or other questions).

There are other everyday examples that are much more difficult to analyze. These are examples in which the behavior and the stimulus are closely interrelated. For example, reading Freud's *Interpretation of Dreams* may seem like a different behavior from reading Skinner's *Walden Two*. However, as was discussed in Lesson 11, the act of reading is basically the same no matter what is read. In the same way, learning to read historical novels instead of science fiction is an example of developing a discriminated behavior. The same analysis also applies to watching TV or movies—the same behavior is occurring in the presence of different stimulus situations.

BEHAVIOR ANALYSIS EXAMPLES

Teaching reading to a culturally deprived Chicano. Staats and Butterfield (1965) undertook to teach a 14-year-old Chicano boy, whom we shall call Carlos, how to read. Carlos had a long history of school failure prior to the study. His reading ability was at about the second-grade level, he had never passed a course in school, and he was a persistent behavioral problem to the teachers. He was one of 11 children; his four older brothers had been referred to juvenile court. His parents attempted to discipline him through physical and verbal abuse, not knowing any other way to influence his behavior.

Staats and Butterfield approached the problem using the same method that Staats had developed for teaching reading to preschool children (described in Lesson 13). In this case, they used a set of specially developed reading materials that are widely used in public schools. They consist of a very large number of brief stories that have been carefully sequenced to start with a first-grade reading level and progress very slowly to a higher level. Each story has a set of questions associated with it to test for comprehension. To reinforce the associated reading behaviors, Staats and Butterfield awarded tokens that could be traded in for toys, special events, and money.

The procedure involved presenting to Carlos each new word that was to appear in a story and awarding him a token if he read it correctly. If he did not, he was told what the word was and given additional chances later on to read it correctly. Once these words were mastered, he then read the story out loud paragraph by paragraph. He was given a token for each time he read a paragraph with no errors. If he made an error he was corrected and given another chance later. Finally, he was given the whole story on a single page along with the questions. He was instructed to read it silently and answer the questions. He was reinforced for attending to the materials by a token given on a variable interval averaging 15 seconds. When he had completed the questions, he was given a token for each correct answer. He was notified of errors and permitted to reread the story to find the correct answer. Finally, every 20 stories he was presented with a review of all the new words that he had had trouble with. He was given a token for correct answers.

The training resulted in remarkable improvements in his reading. Figure 16-1 shows the results of reading-achievement tests given to him. Carlos had attained a reading level at the second grade after 8½ years in public school. In just 6 months of special training he improved to a grade level of 4.3. Further, during that term he passed all of his courses—the first time that he had passed even one course! And his misbehavior in the classroom had decreased to near zero.

Carlos made a total of about 65,000 oral responses to words during the training period. The training required about 40 actual contact hours and the reinforcers cost about $20. Thus, the procedure accomplished as much in 40 hours as had been accomplished by public school methods in over 8 years.

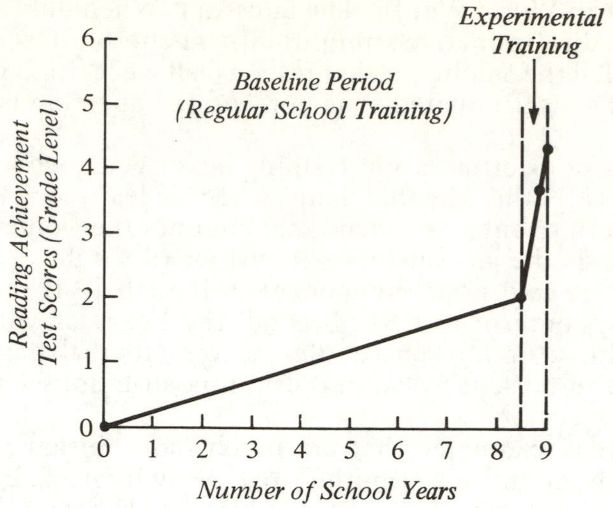

Figure 16-1. The reading-achievement level of Carlos with regular school training and special training using discrimination training methods. Adapted from "Treatment of Non-Reading in a Culturally Deprived Juvenile Delinquent: An Application of Reinforcement Principles," by A. W. Staats and W. H. Butterfield, *Child Development*, 1965, 36, 925–942. Copyright 1965 by The Society for Research in Child Development, Inc. Used by permission.

The effects of different adults on a child's behavior. Redd and Birnbrauer (1969) studied the effects of two different adults on the cooperative play behavior of a 14-year-old retarded boy. This child was selected because he did not engage in cooperative play. The experimenters were interested in whether the child would learn to behave differently in the presence of the two adults if one of them reinforced cooperative play and the other did not.

The child and four other children were brought into a playroom containing a wide variety of toys. Two observers sat behind a one-way mirror and recorded whether the child was engaging in cooperative play every 2½ seconds. In the absence of any adults in the room, the child engaged in no cooperative play.

One adult, whom we shall call Bill, then proceeded to shape cooperative play by giving an edible reinforcement (M & M's, bites of ice cream, and sips of Coke) and saying "good boy" contingent upon approximations. When such play was established, Bill gradually reduced the reinforcement to a fixed interval of 45 seconds, which was sufficient to maintain it.

The other adult, whom we shall call Grundy, was present in the room at other times than Bill. Grundy gave as many edibles as did Bill, but he did not give them contingent on cooperative play.

The child very soon adopted a very distinctive pattern of cooperative play. If neither adult was in the room, he did not engage in cooperative play. If Bill came into the room, he immediately started playing cooperatively and continued to do so as long as Bill remained. If Bill left the room, the child stopped playing cooperatively. If Grundy then came into the room, the child continued to not play cooperatively. Thus, Bill came to be a "signal" to play cooperatively.

To make sure that this result was not produced by some personality difference between Bill and Grundy, the experimenters had them exchange roles so that Grundy was awarding reinforcers contingently for cooperative play and Bill was not. With this reversal, the child started to play cooperatively the moment that Grundy entered the room but not when Bill entered the room.

This study shows that attempting to change the cooperative play behavior of the child resulted in a very limited change. The child's behavior changed only in the presence of the adult who reinforced it but did not occur more generally than that. The child had not learned to play cooperatively with other children in general. The next lesson will discuss procedures for producing such general changes.

This study also has implications for all of us. If a person acts in an undesired way in our presence but in desired ways in the presence of others, we should question whether we are reinforcing the behaviors that we desire rather than blaming it on the person's "personality."

Note #1: The S^D, or discriminative stimulus, is sometimes confused with a reinforcer. For any specific response they are different. The S^D is present before the response is made. It is associated with reinforcement, but it is not reinforcement. It should be viewed as a cue to what behavior will be reinforced. To say "Please pass the butter" is not a reinforcer; it is a discriminative stimulus (S^D) that indicates that you will be reinforced (thanked) for passing the butter but not for passing anything else. The request is the S^D, and the "thanks" is the reinforcer. The S^D always occurs before the behavior; the reinforcer always occurs after the behavior.

Note #2: There is one type of situation in which differential reinforcement and discrimination training can be easily confused. If there are two or more stimulus situations and two or more behaviors, then either term would be appropriate according to the definitions given in this book. Usage by behavior analysts on this point is quite murky. The underlying tendency, derived from operant psychology, is to use *differential reinforcement* when a new behavior is being "differentiated" and to use *discrimination* when an existing behavior is being "discriminated." But this is a tricky and unreliable distinction. Therefore, this book will adopt the simple convention of always referring to this complex procedure as discrimination training.

You may sometimes run across descriptions of a procedure that suggest to you that differential reinforcement is involved but where this convention requires that you designate it as discrimination training. If saying "red" is reinforced when a red card is shown to a child and saying "blue" is extinguished, you would normally call the procedure differential reinforcement. However, if the context makes it clear that saying "red" is extinguished when a blue card is shown to the child and saying "blue" is reinforced, then the situation is different. Such a situation could also be described as: saying "red" is reinforced in the presence of the red card but extinguished in the presence of the blue card (and vice versa for saying blue). Such a rewording, while describing the same situation, makes it clear that we are dealing with discrimination training.

For example, if a teacher asks his students "What is 2 × 2?" he will reinforce "4" and extinguish "6." If he asks at about the same time "What is 2 × 3?" he will reinforce "6" and extinguish "4." In these and similar situations, the teacher's procedure will be termed discrimination training.

ADDITIONAL READINGS

Barrett, B. H., & Lindsley, O. R. Deficits in acquisition of operant discrimination and differentiation shown by institutionalized retarded children. *American Journal of Mental Deficiency*, 1962, *67*, 424–436. Also reprinted in L. P. Ullman & L. Krasner (Eds.), *Case studies in behavior modification*. New York: Holt, Rinehart & Winston, 1965. This article reports the use of operant psychology to measure the ability of retarded children rapidly to form a variety of discriminations.

Neale, D. H. Behavior therapy and encopresis in children. *Behaviour Research and Therapy*, 1963, *1*, 139–149. Discrimination training was used as part of the procedure for treating four disturbed children with encopresis (the children defecated in their pants rather than in the toilet). The success of the procedure permitted the children to be released from the hospital and develop normal lives.

Simmons, M. W., & Lipsitt, L. P. An operant discrimination apparatus for infants. *Journal of the Experimental Analysis of Behavior*, 1961, *4*, 233–235. Chimes were used as a reinforcer to teach a 10-month-old girl a simple discrimination.

Staats, A. W., Staats, C. K., Schutz, R. E., & Wolf, M. M. The conditioning of textual responses using "extrinsic" reinforcers. *Journal of the Experimental Analysis of Behavior*, 1962, *5*, 33–40. This article describes a procedure to systematically teach young children to discriminate written words from one another through a complex discrimination-training procedure. This procedure provides a systematic way to teach young children to read.

Helpful hint: As you have probably guessed by now, "discrimination training" is the name for the procedure mentioned in Lesson 11 that is easy to confuse with differential reinforcement. At that time you were taught to label it as "unknown." From this lesson on you should label it as "discrimination training." Remember, differential reinforcement involves two or more different behaviors occurring with only one stimulus. Discrimination training involves two or more different stimuli and, in the simple case, only one behavior. Complex cases involving two or more stimuli and two or more behaviors should also be labeled discrimination training.

LESSON 16 READING QUIZ

(20) Any physical event or object in a person's environment that is related to his behavior is termed a(n) ______________________ .

(10) The plural of *stimulus* is ______________________.

(29) A stimulus that follows a behavior and increases its rate is called a(n) ______________.

(19) Behaviorists call the procedure by which people learn to behave in ways that are appropriate for their stimulus situations ______________________.

(9) Discrimination training consists of reinforcing a behavior in the presence of one stimulus and ______________________ that same behavior in the presence of another stimulus.

(28) Increasing the rate of a behavior in one situation and decreasing the rate of another behavior in that same situation is called ______________________.

(18) Any stimulus that precedes the behavior and is present only if reinforcement will occur for that behavior is called a(n) "______________________ stimulus" and is abbreviated ______________________.

(8) Any stimulus that precedes a behavior and is present only if extinction will occur for that behavior is called a(n) ______________________.

(27) If a behavior has a higher probability of occurring in the presence of an S^D than it does in the presence of an *S*-delta, then it is called ______________________ behavior.

(17) The increased probability of a discriminated behavior that is produced by the stimulus (S^D) is called ______________________.

(30) When referring to the effect of the stimulus on a behavior (as a result of discrimination training) we say that the stimulus exerts ______________________ over the behavior; when referring to the behavior that occurs more frequently in the presence of the S^D than the *S*-delta we call it ______________________.

(7) Discrimination training has been widely used by behaviorists in the development of ______________________ behavior.

(26) A person may inadvertently receive discrimination training when the behavior analyst reinforces a desirable behavior while other people continue to ______________ that same behavior.

(16) Staats and Butterfield (1965) gave Carlos a token when he said "inspect" and that was the word on the card; they gave him nothing when he said "inspect" and that was not the word on the card. What behavioral procedure were they employing? ______________

(6) Staats and Butterfield (1965) repeatedly presented to Carlos any word that he got wrong until he could say its name correctly when that was the word on the card but not when some other word was on the card. The increased probability of saying the correct word would be called ______________________.

(25) Staats and Butterfield (1965) reinforced the behavior of saying the name of the word on the card. If that behavior was more likely to occur in the presence of the word on the card than it was in the presence of some other word, then we would call it ______________ behavior.

(15) Staats and Butterfield (1965) presented Carlos with a card containing the word "whenever." They gave him a token if he said that word. The written word "whenever" would be called a(n) ______________________ for the spoken word "whenever;" it would be called a(n) ______________________ for any other spoken word.

(5) After 8 years of school, Carlos had a second-grade reading level. After 6 months (40 hours) of training by Staats and Butterfield (1965) he had a reading level beyond the ______________ -grade level.

(24) Redd and Birnbrauer (1969) had Bill give a child edibles for playing cooperatively with other children; Grundy did not reward the child for cooperative play. Bill would be called a(n) ______________________ for cooperative play whereas Grundy would be called a(n) ______________________.

(14) Redd and Birnbrauer (1969) studied the results of having one behavior analyst give a retarded child edibles when he played cooperatively with other children while a second behavior analyst did not. The child learned to play cooperatively when the adult who reinforced him was present but not when the other adult was present. What behavioral procedure accounts for this result? ____________________

(4) When the retarded child is observed to play cooperatively in the presence of an adult who reinforced him for such play but to not play cooperatively in the presence of a second adult who did not reinforce him for such play, we say that the adults have come to exert ____________________ over the child's play behavior.

(23) When a retarded child was observed to play cooperatively in the presence of an adult who reinforced such play but not in the presence of a second adult who did not, we say that cooperative play has become a(n) ____________________.

(13) Staats and Butterfield (1965) showed Carlos a card with the word "inspect" on it; they gave him a token if he said "inspect" but nothing if he said any other word. They repeated this for about 700 new words. What behavioral procedure did they use? ____________________

(3) If a stimulus increases the probability of a behavior and occurs before the behavior, that stimulus is called a(n) ____________________. If a stimulus increases the probability of a behavior and occurs after the behavior, the stimulus is called a(n) ____________________.

(22) If reinforcement and extinction are being applied to one behavior in two or more stimulus situations, the total behavioral procedure is termed ____________________.

(12) If reinforcement and extinction are being applied to two or more behaviors in one stimulus situation, the total procedure is termed ____________________.

(2) If reinforcement and extinction are being applied to two or more behaviors in two or more stimulus situations, then this book has adopted the convention of referring to the total procedure as ____________________.

(21) A discriminated behavior is one that has a higher probability of occurring in the presence of a(n) ____________________.

(11) Stimulus control is defined as the ____________________ probability of a discriminated behavior produced by a stimulus (S^D).

(1) Increasing the probability of a behavior in one situation and decreasing its probability in another situation through the use of reinforcement and extinction would be called ____________________.

READING QUIZ ANSWERS

(1) discrimination training (2) discrimination training (3) S^D; reinforcer (4) stimulus control (5) fourth (6) stimulus control (7) educational (8) *S*-delta (9) extinguishing (10) stimuli (11) increased (12) differential reinforcement (13) discrimination training (14) discrimination training (15) S^D; *S*-delta (16) discrimination training (17) stimulus control (18) discriminative; S^D (19) discrimination training (20) stimulus (21) S^D (22) discrimination training (23) discriminated behavior (24) S^D; S-delta (25) discrimionated (26) extinguish (27) discriminated (28) differential reinforcement (29) reinforcer (30) stimulus control; discriminated behavior

LESSON 16 EXAMPLES

Example #1

Ms. Yablonski often asks Ward "What does 2 + 2 equal?" She always praises him when he says "4." However, when Ms. Yablonski asks the question "What does 2 + 3 equal?" she ignores him when he answers "4." Ms. Yablonski's procedure has increased the probability that Ward will answer "4" when asked the first question but not when asked the second question.

(14) The first step in analyzing an example of this kind is to determine whether it is discrimination training or differential reinforcement. For it to be differential reinforcement would require that there be two behaviors and one stimulus. Is this an example of differential reinforcement? __________

(27) Since there are two stimuli ("What does 2 + 2 equal?" is one stimulus and "What does 2 + 3 equal?" is another), this must be an example of ____________________.

(40) Because the behavior of saying "4" will be reinforced in the presence of the question "What does 2 + 2 equal?", this stimulus is called the "discriminative stimulus" and abbreviated ____________________.

(13) Because the behavior of saying "4" will be extinguished in the presence of the question "What does 2 + 3 equal?", this stimulus is called a(n) ____________________.

(39) When referring to the behavior of saying "4" after this training has been successful, behavior analysts call it ____________________ behavior.

(26) When referring to the effect of the stimulus on saying "4" after the training has been successful, we say that the stimulus "What does 2 + 2 equal?" exerts __________ __________ over the behavior.

Example #2

Sammy had trouble pronouncing dates in his American History class. He just couldn't seem to say "1492" clearly. When the teacher asked him "When did Columbus discover America?" Sammy would answer "forty nineteen two," "forty-nine two," or "fourteen nineteen two." The teacher ignored Sammy when he made these responses. Sometimes Sammy answered "fourteen ninety-two," and the teacher immediately praised him.

(12) The teacher used the behavioral procedure of ____________________ when Sammy responded to the stimulus question with "fourteen ninety-two." But when he responded to the same stimulus question with "forty ninety-two" or any of the other similar responses, she used the procedure of ____________________.

(38) Does this situation involve one behavior and two or more stimuli? __________ Does this situation involve two or more behaviors and one stimulus? __________

(25) Therefore, the procedure involved is ____________________.

Example #3

Jeff and his friends swear a lot around the dorm. They swear at each other, they laugh at their more outrageous swearing episodes, and, in general, they pay a lot of attention to one another's swearing behavior. When Jeff goes home, however, it is a different situation. His parents do not reinforce him for swearing. As a result, Jeff does not swear much at home.

(11) Where is Jeff's swearing reinforced? ____________________ Could you call this a stimulus situation? __________

(37) Where is Jeff's swearing extinguished? ____________________ Could you call this a stimulus situation? __________

(24) Does this situation involve one behavior and two or more stimuli? __________ Does this situation involve two or more behaviors and one stimulus? __________

(10) Jeff's friends and parents accidentally used a procedure to "train" him. What would you call this procedure? ____________________

(36) Think of Jeff's friends as stimuli in his environment. Since Jeff's swearing behavior will be reinforced in their presence (it does not matter for this purpose that they will be doing the reinforcing), they would be called ____________________ (use abbreviation). By the same token, his parents would be called __________ __________.

(23) If Jeff starts swearing more in the presence of his friends than he does in the presence of his parents, his swearing behavior would be called ______________.

(9) The increased probability of swearing produced by his friends' presence would be described by saying that his friends, as a stimulus, exert ______________ over his swearing behavior.

Example #4

When Jeff first lived in the dorm, he would often loudly and angrily say things such as "gosh," "darn," and "x@#!" His friends ignored "gosh" and "darn," but they paid attention when he said "x@#!" Gradually, Jeff said "x@#!" more often than "gosh" or "darn."

(35) Jeff's friends reinforced the word ______________ and extinguished the words ______________ and ______________.

(22) Does this situation involve one behavior and two or more stimuli? ________ Does this situation involve two or more behaviors and one stimulus? ________

(8) Therefore, the change in Jeff's swearing behavior is the result of the behavioral process of ______________.

Example #5

Mr. Campbell frequently asked Dave multiplication questions. When Mr. Campbell asked "What does 7 × 8 equal?" he praised Dave for answering "56" but ignored him for saying anything else. Mr. Campbell asked many other multiplication questions and followed the same procedure.

(34) If Mr. Campbell used his procedure only for that one question, then your analysis would reveal that there is one stimulus and more than two behaviors. This would lead you to refer to his procedure as ______________.

(21) However, Mr. Campbell used that same procedure for many stimulus questions. Since reinforcement and extinction are used with more than two behaviors and more than two stimuli, this book follows the convention of calling the procedure ______________.

Example #6

Johnny's parents ignored most of his "baby noises." However, when Johnny first said "dada," his parents paid a lot of attention to him, and they ignored most other sounds that he made. As a result, Johnny said "dada" at a much higher rate than he said any other sound.

(7) What behavioral procedure is this an example of? ______________

Example #7

When Johnny first said "dada," his parents got excited and showered him with attention. Soon afterwards, they praised him when he said "dada" to his actual father and ignored him when he said "dada" to anyone else.

(33) What behavioral procedure is this an example of? ______________

Example #8

Johnny's parents paid a lot of attention when he called his mother "mama" but ignored him when he called his mother "dada." They of course paid a lot of attention when he called his father "dada" but ignored him when he called his father "mama."

(20) What behavioral procedures were Johnny's parents using? ______________________
(Check your answer on this one!)

Example #9

Martha had two teachers in her kindergarten class. Ms. Smith praised Martha anytime that she was appropriately assertive around the other children while Mrs. Warner ignored Martha's assertive behavior. Pretty soon Martha was assertive when Ms. Smith was around but was not when Mrs. Warner was around.

(6) The two teachers were unwittingly using what behavioral procedure with respect to Martha's assertive behavior? ______________________

(32) Ms. Smith would be called a(n) ______________________ for assertive behavior; Mrs. Warner would be called a(n) ______________________ for assertive behavior.

(19) The effect that Ms. Smith exerts on Martha's assertive behavior is called ______________________.

(5) Because assertive behavior occurs more frequently around Ms. Smith than it does around Mrs. Warner, it would be called ______________________.

Example #10

Mary has always been an avid reader; she reads anything that she can get her hands on. For a time, Mary's dad thought that she would not follow in his footsteps and become an archeologist, but he has begun to change his mind lately; Mary has started reading books on the archeological history of ancient Egypt and Mesopotamia. This change came about because Mary's father started going into her room after coming home from the university to see what she was reading. If she was reading archeology books, he got very interested and held long discussions with her; if she was reading anything else, he usually went off to read the paper.

(31) In this example, since reading occurred more frequently in the presence of archeology books, we would say that archeology books exert ______________________ over Mary's reading behavior.

(18) Mary's reading behavior, now that it occurs more frequently in the presence of archeology books, would be called ______________________.

Example #11

When Frank started hanging around with the gang, he found that the tall red-headed guy answered him when called "Bob" but ignored him if called "Jim," "Ken," or "Dave." Similarly, the short muscular dude answered him when called "Jim" but not when called anything else.

(4) What behavioral procedure is at work in this group situation affecting Frank's choice of names for each person? ______________________

Example #12

Doris usually acted in a happy mood around Fran because Fran got into the spirit and they had a good time together. Doris usually did not act in a happy mood around Kay because Kay remained serious and did not get into the happy mood.

(30) In this situation we would say that Fran exerted ______________________ over Doris' happy behavior.

Example #13

When Flora first moved into the sorority, she found that she could get to the bathroom by going down her hall and turning left at the corner.

(17) If you consider the corner of the hall to be a stimulus, then it would be considered a(n) ______________________ with respect to getting to the bathroom.

Example #14

When Karen was learning how to use this book, she discovered that the answers to the example questions could be found by looking under the heading Example Answers rather than under Reading Quiz Answers.

(3) If her answer-looking-up behavior for examples came to occur more frequently under the first than the second heading, we would call her behavior ______________________.

Example #15

Bob tried to boogie with Alice every chance that he had because she was such a good dancer. She easily followed any complicated turn that Bob tried but she felt awkward when he tried a dip. He gradually came to perform many complicated turns but no dips.

(29) What behavioral procedure did her dancing skills impose on Bob's selection of steps? ______________________

Example #16

(16) If Carol frowned at Lenny, you would guess that this would be a(n) ______________________ for asking her out for a date.

Example #17

Barb showed little Wanda a picture of a dog and praised her when she said "doggie," but not when she said "kitty." Of course, Barb also showed Wanda pictures of cats, snakes, and gila monsters and followed the same procedure.

(2) What procedure did Barb use to teach Wanda the names of the animals? ______________________

Example #18

(28) If a person always stops his or her car at any sign that says "stop" because of earlier training, we would say that the stop sign exerts ______________________ over his or her stopping behavior.

Example #19

Mrs. Niles praised her son Larry for using unusual words when describing events; unfortunately his friends ignored him when he used unusual words around them.

(15) In this situation we would call Mrs. Niles a(n) ______________________ for using such words and Larry's friends a(n) ______________________ for using such words.

Example #20

Dennis learned that anytime that he was out past the curfew (everyone in his town under 18 was supposed to be home by 11:00 P.M.) and was stopped by a policeman, if he acted very courteously and apologized for losing track of the time, the policeman would let him go. He did not act this way at other times.

(1) His polite behavior was more likely to occur after 11:00 so it is therefore referred to as ______________________.

EXAMPLE ANSWERS

(1) discriminated behavior (2) discrimination training (3) discriminated behavior (4) discrimination training (5) discriminated behavior (6) discrimination training (7) differential reinforcement (8) differential reinforcement (9) stimulus control (10) discrimination training (11) dorm; yes (12) reinforcement; extinction (13) *S*-delta (14) no (15) S^D, *S*-delta (16) *S*-delta (17) S^D (18) discriminated behavior (19) stimulus control (20) discrimination training (21) discrimination training (22) no; yes (23) discriminated behavior (24) yes; no (25) differential reinforcement (26) stimulus control (27) discrimination training (28) stimulus control (29) differential reinforcement (30) stimulus control (31) stimulus control (32) S^D; *S*-delta (33) discrimination training (34) differential reinforcement (35) x@#!; gosh; darn (36) S^D; *S*-delta (37) home; yes (38) no; yes (39) discriminated (40) S^D

Lesson 17

Generalization Training of Everyday Behaviors

Discrimination training is a procedure for increasing the probability of a behavior in one situation and decreasing it in other situations. In a sense, it draws a boundary between two situations so that the behavior does not spread from one to the other. This lesson will introduce a procedure designed to do just the opposite—to eliminate boundaries between several situations so that the behavior does spread spontaneously from one to the other. The name of this procedure is "generalization training."

Generalization training is a procedure in which a behavior is reinforced in each of a series of situations until it generalizes to other members of that same stimulus class. An example drawn from this book is reinforcing the reader for applying the label "extinction" to each of a series of everyday stories until the reader spontaneously labels most such stories as extinction without any further reinforcement. By using this procedure, the boundaries between examples of extinction are eliminated so that the reader's labeling behavior spreads to most of them.

Generalization is the occurrence of a behavior in the presence of a novel stimulus. A novel stimulus would be any stimulus in whose presence the person's behavior has not been reinforced. In the above example, new stories illustrating extinction would constitute novel stimuli for readers because they had not previously tried to analyze the stimuli and they had not received feedback (reinforcement) for their behavior.

A **stimulus class** is a set of related stimuli. In the above example, the stories illustrating extinction are all related to the fundamental definition of that procedure and to each other through it. Other examples of related stimuli would be red objects, behavior analysts, differential equations, or students.

The importance of generalization and generalization training is difficult to overemphasize. Without them the reader of this book would have to laboriously learn whether every possible instance was or was not "extinction." There could be no such thing as "understanding," only training and memorization. The child who learned the words in one sentence would not know how to create other novel sentences. Human behavior would come to a virtual standstill because we would always be helpless in the face of the constant bombardment by novel stimuli.

I should point out that the occurrence of a behavior in a novel situation may not lead to reinforcement. Calling someone's infant a pretty little girl just because it is wrapped in a pink blanket could be very embarrassing if the parents are particularly proud of their handsome little baby boy! This process, sometimes called "overgeneralization" although it is a valid instance of generalization, can be counteracted through discrimination training. Thus, the procedures of discrimination training and generalization training are often used together.

Generalization of behavior change is an important issue in behavior analysis. As we pointed out in the last lesson, if a person's behavior is reinforced by a behavior analyst, it may remain on extinction by the person's friends and family. The result could be a discrimination such that the new behavior will occur with increased frequency only in the presence of the behavior analyst. Such a result would be of little value to most people, who wish that behavior to occur in their normal everyday lives. The person wishing to become more assertive doesn't want to become more assertive only around the behavior analyst. As a result, many behavior analysis studies have measured the behavior after treatment is completed or in other situations to see if generalization has occurred.

The most frequent approach to generalization by behavior analysts has been dubbed by Stokes and Baer (1977) as "train and hope." That is, the desired behavioral change is produced in a training situation but the behavior analyst does not employ generalization training or any other systematic procedure to produce generalization to everyday situations. The train-and-hope approach usually results in the not very surprising failure to produce generalization, although it may sometimes succeed to a greater or lesser extent. An example of limited success using this approach is the study of racial integration in a first-grade classroom reported by Hauserman, Walen, and Behling (1973). They measured social contacts between five Black children and 20 White children in two situations: sitting in the lunchroom and playing together on the playground. During treatment, they reinforced any child who sat with a new friend during lunch by giving him or her a snack later in the day. This increased the rate of integrated seating from about 20% to about 60%. As can be seen in Figure 17-1, the amount of playing together on the playground increased by about 100% even though such playing was not reinforced. Notice, however, that this generalized increase stopped when sitting together in the lunchroom was no longer reinforced.

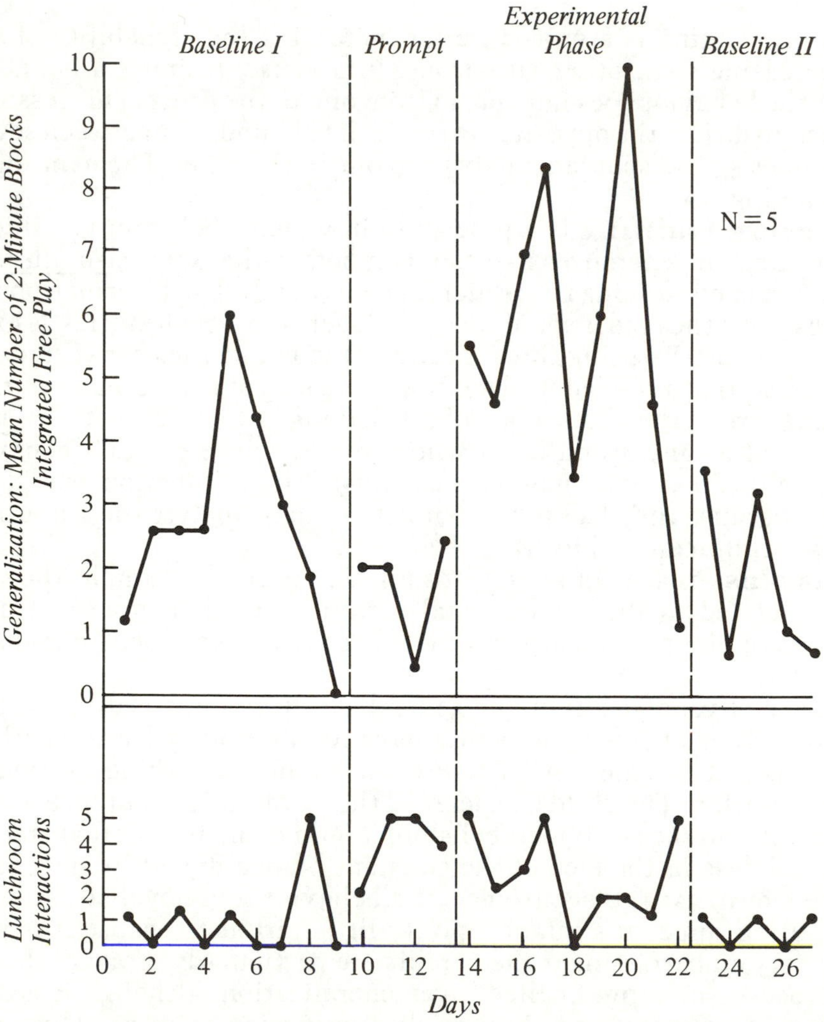

Figure 17-1. The amount of social interaction between five Black and 20 White first graders. Children were given snacks for sitting with "new friends" (of either race) in the lunchroom during the "prompt" and "experimental phase" but nothing for playing together on the playground during free play. Adapted from "Reinforced Racial Integration in the First Grade: A Study in Generalization," by N. Hauserman, S. R. Walen, and M. Behling, *Journal of Applied Behavior Analysis*, 1973, 6, 193–200. Copyright 1973 by the Society for the Experimental Analysis of Behavior, Inc. Used by permission.

Thus, this study showed generalization of the reinforcement effect from the lunchroom to the playground, but not from the reinforcement period to the more normal nonreinforcement period.

Several other studies described earlier in this book have also shown some limited success with the "train and hope" approach. The study by Hersen and his colleagues (1973) described in Lesson 6 reported that several depressed patients continued emitting nondepressed behavior above baseline levels after the token-reinforcement program was discontinued. However, this level still represented a major decrease from token-reinforcement levels. The study by Sturgis and her colleagues (1978) described in Lesson 6 reported a continuing lack of headaches after biofeedback training was discontinued. This study also observed decrements in headaches at home even though the training occurred in a psychological clinic. The small generalization effect reported for the nondepressed behavior is more typical of results using the train and hope approach than is the generalization effect reported for headaches. In general, some systematic approach must be used to increase generalization if it is to occur with any consistency.

Generalization may be mildly encouraged by using the observation that a behavior that has been reinforced in the presence of a stimulus will tend to occur spontaneously in the presence of similar stimuli (Skinner, 1953). Thus, most behavior analysis studies that are at all concerned about generalization of the behavioral effect attempt to maximize the similarity between the training situation and the "natural" situation. They may do this by training in the natural situation or structuring the training situation so that it is similar to the natural situation. For example, Walker and Buckley (1972) trained severely disruptive elementary school children in a special classroom to engage primarily in appropriate behavior. These children increased their rate of appropriate behavior from about 40% in their regular classroom to about 90% in the special classroom. Walker and Buckley arranged for the regular classrooms of some of the children to be similar to the training classroom while not doing that for others. The children returned to similar classrooms maintained over 50% of their improved behavior but the other children maintained only about 30% of their improvement.

A more effective way to encourage generalization is to deliberately train it. Stokes, Baer, and Jackson (1974) used this approach when teaching an institutionalized retarded child to greet people. Observation indicated that even after one experimenter had taught the child to greet him the child did not greet others. However, after a second experimenter had taught the child to greet him, the behavior generalized and the child greeted other staff members and even visitors to the institution without having been trained to do so. Garcia (1974) used a similar approach to teach two retarded children to engage in basic conversational behaviors. The children readily learned to engage in the behaviors in the presence of the trainer, but the behavior did not generalize until a second trainer also reinforced them for the behaviors. A slightly different approach was used by Griffiths and Craighead (1972), who reinforced a 30-year-old retarded woman to correctly articulate her words in a special classroom setting. She continued to misarticulate her words in other settings until the researchers also reinforced her correct articulations at her residence. She then began to articulate correctly in all situations.

Generalization training may be used in connection with many behavioral procedures other than reinforcement. Thus, an undesirable behavior could be extinguished in a series of situations in an attempt to produce generalized extinction. For example, Allen (1973) used such an approach to reducing the rate of bizarre verbalizations in an 8-year-old child attending a summer camp. The boy's parents reported that he fantasized about penguins for up to 8 hours a day. At camp his talk was constantly centered on penguins in general and on his imaginary pet penguins "Tug-Tug," "Junior Polkadot," and "Super Penguin." Using a multiple-baseline analysis, the camp counselors found that extinguishing penguin verbalizations while walking on a trail resulted in a decrease from about 40 such verbalizations per day to none; there was no decrease in other settings. However, when penguin verbalizations were extinguished also in the dining hall, where they immediately decreased, generalization was also observed in the cabin and in an educational setting. Thus, extinguishing the behavior in two settings produced generalized extinction in other settings.

A particularly important behavioral process occurs when discrimination training is generalized so that a person can make a discrimination as to whether a stimulus is within or outside of a stimulus class. The outcome of this is called "concept formation" and is the basis of all complex intellectual activity, thinking, and ideas. Any type of understanding beyond memorizing must involve this process. One of the behavior analysis examples used in this lesson illustrates this procedure.

BEHAVIOR ANALYSIS EXAMPLES

Teaching assertiveness. Bornstein, Bellack, and Hersen (1977) sought to help Jane, an 8-year-old girl. She had difficulty relating to her peers, was described as passive, had difficulty expressing anger when appropriate, was unable to refuse unreasonable requests, was oversensitive to criticism, and rarely volunteered in class.

Bornstein and his colleagues used nine role-playing scenes to observe assertiveness in Jane. These scenes were similar to ones that she might encounter in her everyday life, and they required assertive behavior. For example, Jane was first told to imagine the following scene: "You are part of a small group in science class. Your group is trying to come up with an idea for a project to present to class. You start to give your idea when Amy begins to tell hers also." Then another person pretended to be Amy and said "Hey, listen to my idea." Jane was then supposed to behave in the way that she thought most appropriate. Six scenes were used as part of the training procedure; the other three were used to observe whether changes in assertiveness in the training scenes would occur spontaneously in these scenes.

Bornstein and his colleagues selected three behaviors that they felt would assist Jane in being more assertive. They defined eye contact as looking at the other person while speaking. Loudness of speech was rated on a scale of 1 to 5 with appropriate loudness rated 5. Requests for new behavior was defined as asking the other person to change some behavior (for example, "Amy, please be quiet while I finish my idea.") Reliability was computed for each measure. It ranged from 85% to 100%. In addition to these behavioral observations, two independent judges provided a rating of overall assertiveness without knowing these behaviors were being treated and without knowing the purpose of the study.

A detailed training procedure was used for treatment. The therapist presented a scene, the other person engaged in the undesirable behavior (like Amy interrupting Jane), and then Jane responded in whatever way she thought was appropriate. Then the therapist provided feedback with reference to the specific target behavior (for example, "Jane, you failed to look at Amy for the whole time!") and discussed it. The correct behavior was then modeled for Jane. Finally, the therapist instructed Jane in what she should do, and she was given another opportunity to respond. This form of training continued until the behavior was correct for that scene; training then moved on to the next scene.

Figure 17–2 shows the results of the experiment with Jane in the three untrained scenes. As you can see, the baseline observations were taken for different numbers of sessions for each of the three treated behaviors. Eye contact increased from near zero to 100% after training. Loudness increased from very low to close to appropriate. And number of requests during the three test scenes increased from zero to two out of three.

The judges rated Jane's assertiveness as very unassertive before treatment. This increased slightly when Jane had learned to make eye contact; a little further increase may have occurred with the increase in her loudness; but the real increase came with her learning to request that the other person change a behavior. When she was doing that, the judges rated her as "moderately" to "very" assertive. In follow-up tests two and four weeks later, her behavioral changes were maintained and the judges' rating was very high.

The results with Jane were replicated with three other unassertive children.

These results indicate that a straightforward behavioral training procedure can be used to increase assertive behaviors in untrained situations. The judges' ratings also suggest that these behaviors are recognized by other people as constituting assertiveness.

Understanding. One experimental analysis that will probably be of interest to readers of this book was undertaken by myself and Hal Weaver several years ago (Miller & Weaver, 1974). We were concerned with the effectiveness of the procedure used in this book at training the readers' concept identification responses so that they would generalize to other novel instances of the concepts. To examine this effect, we developed a test containing 48 novel examples totally unrelated to any examples contained in the book. The test consisted of four parts, each defining a baseline corresponding to each unit of the book. We then administered this test at the beginning of every week during the semester, and computed the percentage of the examples in each baseline that had been correctly identified.

We used a multiple-baseline design because reading and passing quizzes on the material within each unit constituted the treatment condition for each of the four baselines. In this

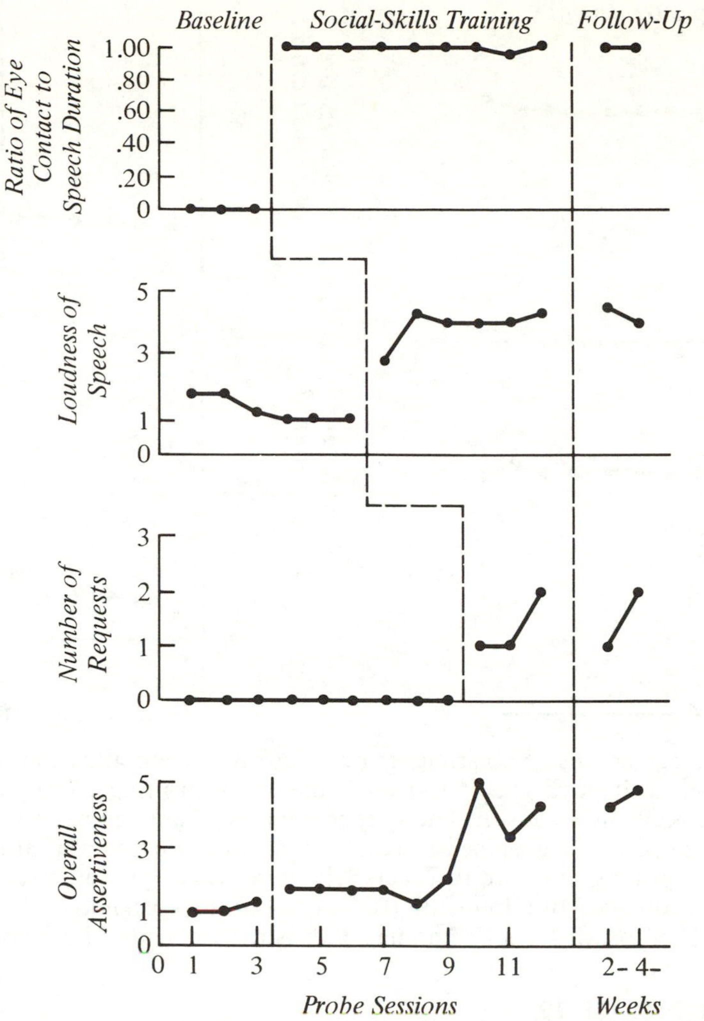

Figure 17-2. The amount of three assertive behaviors observed in Jane. The bottom graph reports the overall assessment of "assertiveness" by outside judges not aware of the experimental treatment. Adapted from "Social Skills Training for Unassertive Children: A Multiple Baseline Analysis," by M. R. Bornstein, A. S. Bellack, and M. Hersen, *Journal of Applied Behavior Analysis*, 1977, *10*, 183–195. Copyright 1977 by the Society for the Experimental Analysis of Behavior, Inc. Used by permission.

experiment, the quizzes were given by the instructor in class on a certain date, so that we could control when the treatment was introduced.

Figure 17-3 shows the results of the experiment. As you can see, after the treatment for Research Methods had been completed, the scores for that baseline increased. But during that same time, they did not increase for the other three baselines. Further, after the treatment for Reinforcement Control had been completed, the scores for only that baseline increased. The same effect was present for each baseline, thereby demonstrating that the method in the book is an effective generalization training procedure.

Note: Generalization may also occur among behaviors. For example, when teaching someone to make positive statements to other people, one might begin by teaching first one positive statement, then another, and another. At some point, the individual will generalize to the class of all positive statements. This process is often referred to as "induction" or "response generalization."

ADDITIONAL READINGS

Stokes, T. F., & Baer, D. M. An implicit technology of generalization. *Journal of Applied Behavior Analysis*, 1977, *10*, 349–367. This article reviews 270 behavior analysis studies in order to establish what is known about generalization. The authors suggest seven strategies for promoting generalization.

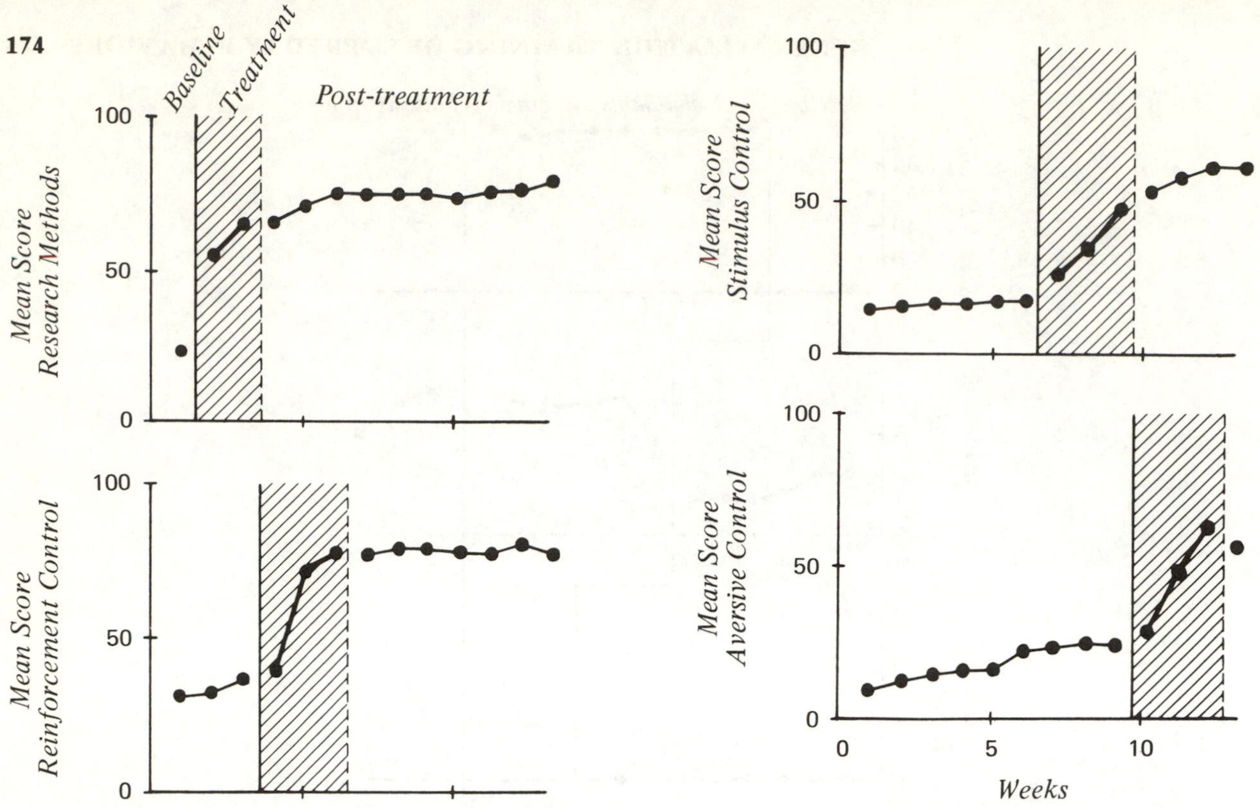

Figure 17-3. The average scores of 50 students on a four-part generalization test designed to determine whether each unit in the book assisted students in forming concepts. The test was administered every week of the semester. The striped bars represent the period of time that the students were studying each unit designed to teach them the concepts in that part of the test. From "The Use of 'Concept Programming' to Teach Behavioral Concepts to University Students," by L. K. Miller and F. H. Weaver. In J. Johnston (Ed.), *Behavior research and technology in higher education.* Copyright 1974 by Charles C Thomas, Publisher. Reprinted by permission.

LESSON 17 READING QUIZ

(9) What behavioral procedure can be said to draw boundaries between two or more stimulus situations? ______________________

(25) What behavioral procedure can be said to eliminate boundaries between stimulus situations? ______________________

(17) Generalization training is a procedure in which a behavior is reinforced in each of a series of situations until it ______________________ to other members of that same stimulus class.

(8) Generalization training has the goal of causing a behavior to generalize to other members of the same ______________________ class.

(24) To produce generalization, generalization training reinforces the same behavior in a(n) ______________________ of situations.

(16) Generalization is the occurrence of a behavior in the presence of a(n) ______________ stimulus.

(7) A novel stimulus is any stimulus in whose presence the person's behavior has not been ______________________ .

(23) A stimulus class is a set of ______________________ stimuli.

(15) Without generalization human behavior would come to a virtual standstill because we would always be helpless in the face of the constant bombardment by ______________ stimuli.

(6) The occurrence of generalization to a novel situation where it does not lead to reinforcement is sometimes called ______________________ .

(22) Many behavior analysis studies have measured the behavior after treatment or in other settings to see if __________________ has occurred.

(14) In the most common approach to generalization by behavior analysts, the desired behavioral change is produced and generalization training ________ (is, isn't) employed to ensure that generalization occurs.

(5) Generalization may be mildly encouraged by using the observation that a behavior that has been reinforced in the presence of one stimulus will tend to occur spontaneously in the presence of __________________ stimuli.

(21) To produce reliable generalization of behavioral change it is necessary to employ what behavioral procedure? __________________

(13) Allen (1973) produced generalized extinction of penguin talk in a little boy by extinguishing his behavior in __________________ (one, more than one) situation(s) in the summer camp.

(4) Bornstein and his colleagues (1977) used six situations to teach Jane how to be assertive. They used an additional three situations, in which they never reinforced Jane for being assertive, to see whether she would be. These situations would be called __________________ .

(20) Bornstein and associates (1977) taught Jane to be assertive in response to being interrupted by another person. They then taught her to be assertive in several other types of situations. When they tested her assertiveness in three other untrained situations, they found her to be quite assertive. What behavioral procedure did they use? __________________

(12) Miller and Weaver (1974) reinforced students for correctly labeling the examples in this book. They then observed that the students could correctly label examples that they had not seen before. What behavioral procedure did they use to produce this result? __________________

(3) Miller and Weaver (1974) reinforced students for correctly labeling the examples contained in this book. They then observed that the students could correctly label examples that they had not seen before. The occurrence of the students' labeling behavior in the presence of the new examples would be called __________________ .

(19) Miller and Weaver (1974) showed students a series of examples of extinction. The collection of all examples of extinction would be termed a(n) __________________ .

(11) A procedure in which a behavior is reinforced in each of a series of situations until it generalizes to other members of that stimulus class is called __________________ .

(2) The occurrence of a behavior in the presence of a novel stimulus is called ________ .

(18) A set of related stimuli is called a(n) __________________ .

(10) If a person's behavior is changed in one situation, a procedure for ensuring that the change appears in other situations would be __________________ .

(1) Just because a person's behavior is reinforced, and thereby increased in one situation, does not ensure that the behavior will __________________ to other situations.

READING QUIZ ANSWERS

(1) generalize (2) generalization (3) generalization (4) novel stimuli (5) similar (6) overgeneralization (7) reinforced (8) stimulus (9) discrimination training (10) generalization training (11) generalization training (12) generalization training (13) more than one (14) isn't (15) novel (16) novel (17) generalizes (18) stimulus class (19) stimulus class (20) generalization training (21) generalization training (22) generalization (23) related (24) series (25) generalization training

LESSON 17 EXAMPLES

Example #1

Professor Brainbuster had a talent for bringing students into his discussions. He was so successful that he even managed to get Sweet Sue to talk in class and express her opinions. Ken thought that this was great, that the professor was making an important change in Sue's behavior. Lisa disagreed, however, pointing out that Sue still didn't express her opinions in other classes.

(36) Through the use of reinforcement, Professor Brainbuster had become a(n) ______________ for Sue's talking; the professors in other classes remained a(n) ______________ ______________ for her talking.

(24) If Sue's talking occurred in other classes after Professor Brainbuster had reinforced her, this would be an instance of what behavioral process? ______________

(12) All university classes would be called a(n) ______________ because they are related stimuli.

(35) If someone had wanted badly enough to change Sweet Sue's talking behavior in all classes, he or she could have tried arranging for several professors to reinforce talking in class. What procedure would be used by the combined group to increase her talking in all classes? ______________

Example #2

Steve began speaking with a beautiful rhythm and sound to his words when he was around Marcia, and she loved it. When he was around Ken he started speaking the same way but Ken looked at him real funnily and split. Eventually Steve spoke poetically around Marcia but not around Ken.

(23) The temporary spread of poetic speaking from the presence of Marcia to the presence of Ken would be an example of ______________ (because Ken had never reinforced or extinguished him for it before and would therefore be a novel stimulus with respect to this behavior).

(11) The procedure that the combined reaction of Ken and Marcia represents would be called ______________.

(34) If Ken had, instead of splitting, praised poetic speaking, then the combined reaction of Ken and Marcia would have been at least a start toward using what procedure to produce poetic talking in Ken for many situations? ______________

Example #3

After Dave had been going with Bad Bertha for 3 months, she started being really nice to him. She had a gentle streak in her that no one else could have even guessed about. Dave mentioned to several friends how nice Bertha was. They thought Dave was crazy since they rather enjoyed her tough behavior.

(22) In Dave's presence, gentle behavior was reinforced and tough behavior was extinguished; he would be a(n) ______________ for acting gently.

(10) In his friends' presence, Bertha's tough behavior was reinforced and gentle behavior extinguished. Their presence would be a(n) ______________ for gentle behavior.

(33) Between them, Dave and his friends were using what behavioral procedure to encourage Bertha to act gently in one place and tough in the other? ______________ (Remember how to handle complex situations like this.)

(21) If Dave convinced all of his friends to change their reaction to Bertha and to reinforce

gentleness, they would be using what behavioral procedure to make Bertha into a gentle person? ______________________

Example #4

Arnie teased all of the pets in the neighborhood, including his own. He chased cats and dogs and sprayed them with water. This behavior upset Arnie's parents. They would yell at him and plead with him to stop, but he continued to tease the pets. Finally, in desperation, Arnie's parents listened to the advice of a behavior analyst. He told them to totally ignore Arnie's behavior. After a month, Arnie's parents discovered to their delight that he had indeed stopped teasing their pets. They were bragging about this one night at a cocktail party given by a neighbor. The neighbor disagreed violently and called behavior analysis "a stupid waste of time." She told Arnie's parents that Arnie hadn't stopped teasing her pets even though she had chased him away, pleaded with him, and done everything else she could think of to stop him.

(9) The procedure that Arnie's parents and their neighbors applied to him would be called ______________________ .

(32) The procedure that they should have applied to him would be the analogue of generalization training except that they should have used what procedure instead of reinforcement? ______________________

Example #5

Calvin was undergoing training as a salesperson for a company that makes and sells encyclopedias. They of course started by explaining to him the virtues of their product; next, they explained the tricks of being a good salesperson. But then started the fun part. They had him enter a special room at their factory that was made up to look like someone's living room. He was greeted at the "door" by a trainer who played the role of the homeowner. Calvin was to use what he had learned to try to "sell" the trainer a set of encyclopedias. The trainer had a checklist of behaviors that Calvin was supposed to perform, which he quietly checked off as they went along. If Calvin forgot to mention the special sale price, or if he forgot to have the trainer sign a contract, then he was told about it. This training was repeated until Calvin got it all right three times in a row. Then another different trainer was brought in, one who was a "harder sell" and acted quite differently. Again the training was repeated until Calvin got it right. Several other trainers were then brought in as the final part of the process. Calvin is now an ace salesperson.

(20) What method of observation was used? ______________________ recording

(8) When Calvin saw the trainer make a check mark indicating that he had done the right thing, this probably served as a(n) ______________________ for Calvin.

(31) The training room was made to look like a living room to increase the probability that Calvin's selling ability would ______________________ to real living rooms.

(19) Calvin had to sell a number of trainers, each of whom reinforced his good sales behaviors by checking them off. What procedure was the company using by employing the series of trainers? ______________________

Example #6

Professor Forsyth had recently worked in the State Department under President Nixon, but he now taught political science at the University. He taught his classes that "imperialism" was when one country took over the government of another. He gave as an example the takeover of Lithuania by the Soviet Union in 1939. He then asked John to give three other examples. John delighted the professor by citing Czechoslovakia's take-over by the Soviet Union in 1948; he also won approval from the professor for citing North Korea in 1945. But when he suggested that American intervention in Vietnam was imperialism, the professor turned bright red, marked down a bad grade, and shouted "You are a damned Communist!"

(7) The occurrence of labeling the Vietnam intervention as "imperialistic" would be an example of what behavioral process? ______________________

(30) By reinforcing John for labeling as "imperialism" any intervention by the Soviet Union but not reinforcing such a label when the United States was involved, the professor was using what behavioral procedure? ______________________

Example #7

Ms. Lucci is an eighth-grade English teacher. She taught her students the meaning of the word "alliteration"—the repetition of a sound that begins several words in a series. She asked Michael of what the sentence "Peter Piper picked a peck of pickled peppers" is an example. She praised him profusely when he said "alliteration." Several days later she asked Michael of what poetic concept Poe's line "In the clamor and the clangor of the bells!" is an example. He said "alliteration."

(18) Michael's second response is an example of what behavioral concept? ______________

(6) In this example, Michael's identification of an instance of alliteration was ______________ by Ms. Lucci's praise only once.

(29) If his behavior had not generalized after one reinforcement, Ms. Lucci could have introduced more examples and reinforced his behavior many times. She would then be using what behavioral procedure? ______________________

Example #8

Margo complained when Danny wouldn't go out because he was studying and she complained when Danny wouldn't go out because he was going to a football game. Danny decided that she had a right to complain when he put football ahead of her, but not when he put studying ahead of her, and he explained his conclusions to her. Thereafter, every time that she complained that he wouldn't go out with her because of a football game he canceled plans to attend the game and went out with her instead. However, when she complained about his studying, he totally ignored her. After six months, Margo was complaining about his putting football ahead of her but not studying.

(17) After his initial talk, what procedure did Danny use to alter Margo's pattern of complaining?

____

Example #9

A self-control procedure for studying used by many students is to set aside a specific place to do schoolwork and to make sure that no other behavior is reinforced there. Thus, they never bring magazines, food, a radio, or other potential reinforcers to their study area.

(5) Eliminating reinforcement for other behaviors would make the study area a(n) ______________ ______________________ for nonstudy behaviors. If studying succeeded there, the area could become a(n) ______________________ for studying.

(28) If study behavior began to occur in the study area and nowhere else, we would say that the study area exerted ______________________ over study behavior.

Example #10

One day Corbin complained of his unhappiness to his mother. She listened sympathetically and told him that he didn't have to do his chores that day. Corbin frequently complained of his unhappiness to his mother after that and she let him stop any chores that he was doing. Corbin complained to his teacher one day that he was unhappy. She excused him from the classwork that he was engaged in.

(16) What behavioral process describes Corbin's complaining about his unhappiness to his teacher? ________________

Example #11

Raney was in second grade. One day during spelling she laid her head on the desk. The teacher asked her what was the matter and she said "Teacher, I have a terrible headhurt." The teacher soothed her by saying "That's too bad, Raney, why don't you just lay your head down until it feels better?" Raney frequently complained of headhurts after that. She also complained of headhurts to her third-grade teacher the next year. That teacher didn't buy it. She gave Raney an aspirin and told her to get back to work.

(4) These two teachers were applying what procedure to Raney's complaints of headhurts? ________________

Example #12

(27) If we consider Diane's friends as stimuli, then the collection consisting of all of her friends would be called a(n) ________________.

Example #13

(15) If Janice swears in the presence of her friends at school but not in the presence of her parents, her swearing behavior would be called ________________.

Example #14

Frank made a joke when asked by his English teacher to define "noun" and everyone in class laughed uproariously. As a result he made a joke in his social studies class the next hour.

(3) The occurrence of his joking behavior in the second class is an example of what behavioral process? ________________

Example #15

The taxonomy class was interesting but terribly difficult for Clara. She got a correct score when she remembered to apply the label "invertebrate" to a crab but not to a rat; likewise she got a correct score for applying the label "vertebrate" to a rat but not to a crab.

(26) The course instructor is applying what behavioral procedure to her behavior? ________________

Example #16

Janice carefully typed a course paper for the first time in college. She received her first "A" ever for that paper. She then typed a paper for another course and got another "A." This happened in several other courses.

(14) What procedure are those course instructors unknowingly applying to Janice's typing behavior to increase its occurrence in many other courses? ________________

Example #17

After much trial and error, Janice learned to call the big planet "Jupiter" and the little one "Venus," but not vice versa.

(2) Her labeling behavior of calling the big planet "Jupiter" would be called ______________ ______________ .

Example #18

(25) When Janice had finally learned to call a picture of the biggest planet "Jupiter," we would say that the picture had developed ______________ over her planet-naming behavior.

Example #19

Dr. Feelgood reacted positively when Felix accepted compliments happily but ignored him when he did not. Gradually Felix learned to accept compliments happily.

(1) What behavioral procedure did Dr. Feelgood employ? ______________

Example #20

Grant was usually pretty stingy with his favors. However, every time that he did something nice for Alma she immediately thanked him and often did something even nicer for him. His rate of doing favors for Alma gradually increased. One day he did a very nice thing for Karen and she was so surprised that she thanked him profusely. This same pattern occurred with several other friends of Grant. He gradually started doing favors for many people.

(13) What behavioral procedure was being unknowingly employed by Grant's friends to increase his favor doing for everyone? ______________

EXAMPLE ANSWERS

(1) differential reinforcement (2) discriminated behavior (3) generalization (4) discrimination training (5) *S*-delta; S^D (6) reinforced (7) generalization (8) reinforcer (9) discrimination training (10) *S*-delta (11) discrimination training (12) stimulus class (13) generalization training (14) generalization training (15) discriminated behavior (16) generalization (17) discrimination training (18) generalization (19) generalization training (20) event (21) generalization training (22) S^D (23) generalization (24) generalization (25) stimulus control (26) discrimination training (27) stimulus class (28) stimulus control (29) generalization training (30) discrimination training (31) generalize (32) extinction (33) discrimination training (34) generalization training (35) generalization training (36) S^D; *S*-delta

Lesson 18

Programming and Fading

This lesson introduces the behavioral procedures of "fading" and "programming." The effects of these procedures on stimulus control are similar to the effects of shaping on reinforcement control. Shaping starts with an existing behavior and, using differential reinforcement on a series of successive approximations, develops a target behavior. That is, shaping is a technique for developing new behaviors. Fading and programming are techniques that use an established discrimination to develop a new one. A stimulus that a person has already discriminated is temporarily paired with a stimulus in a new discrimination situation. The added stimulus (the one that has already been discriminated) is called a prompt (or hint). If the prompt works—that is, if the person responds correctly to this new situation—then it is gradually withdrawn so that the person learns to respond correctly to the new discrimination without help. Thus, a **prompt** is an added stimulus that increases the probability that a person will make the correct response in a discriminative situation.

Fading is the temporary use of a prompt to assist in establishing a specific discrimination involving the gradual withdrawal of the prompt so that the discrimination can be made without the prompt. Fading solves the problem that may be present when trying to establish a discrimination: what happens if the behavior never occurs in the presence of the S^D? If that were to happen, the behavior analyst could never reinforce it and begin the process of discrimination training. However, if the behavior can be increased in probability by the use of a prompt, then it can be made to occur in the presence of the S^D where it can be reinforced. By gradually eliminating the prompt, the behavior analyst tries to shift stimulus control solely to the S^D. For example, if you wish to teach children to label colors, you might show them a red spot and ask "What color is this?" If they cannot answer, you might give them a hint such as "Is it red?" or "Say red." Using such a prompt you can get the behavior started so that it can be reinforced. Since you don't want to have to give them hints all the time, you must then gradually withdraw the hint.

It should be understood that fading is a particular kind of discrimination training—a kind that involves the use of a prompt. Everything else about discrimination training remains the same, however, except that stimulus control may develop more rapidly.

Examples of prompts and fading abound in everyday life. Each time parents give a hint to a child and then gradually withdraw it, they are using prompting and fading. For example, if they show a child a picture of a cow and ask "What is this, Suzie? You know, moo," the added phrase is a prompt. If they then show the child a picture of a dog, ask what it is, and use the sound "bowwow," they are again using a prompt. These prompts will help the child to make the discrimination between the picture of the cow and the picture of the dog.

Once this initial discrimination is established, the parents may start to eliminate the prompts. For example, the next time they show the child the picture of the cow, they may only say "moo." The time after that, the parents may silently mouth the "moo" sound. And finally, they will eliminate the prompt altogether so that the child responds solely to the visual stimulus of the cow. A similar gradual elimination of the "bowwow" prompt for the dog picture would also be an example of fading. While it is not spelled out in the example, you should understand that the prompted behavior must be reinforced.

Notice in this example that the parents used prompts to establish a discrimination between two distinct pictures; that is, prompts were used to establish a discrimination.

It is important to realize that fading will be ineffective if a prompt is used with a single stimulus. If the parents always showed their child the picture of a dog, the child would not even need a prompt—he or she could just remember to say "dog." However, if the picture of the dog is alternated with a picture of a cow, then remembering only "dog" would not work. The hint could then help the child learn which animal is which. When using two stimuli, prompts can be used with each picture, but a prompt with just one of them would probably be enough. If the parents provide the hint "You know, bowwow" for the dog, then the absence of that hint will help the child learn which animal is the cow. Or the parent could also provide a hint with the picture of the cow. Either approach is probably about equally effective.

Initially, presenting the S^D will not produce the desired behavior, so the behavior analyst selects as a prompt another stimulus that already tends to produce that behavior. For fading out of the prompt to be meaningful, it is necessary that the S^D gradually develop stimulus control. Transferring stimulus control from a prompt to the desired discriminative stimulus can be the most difficult aspect of fading. For it to work, it is necessary somehow to get the person gradually to shift his or her attention from the prompt to the S^D. If the prompt is totally unrelated to the S^D, this can be even more difficult (Schreibman, 1975). Managing this process remains a largely unspecified and artistic process at this time.

"Programming" is a more complex use of prompts. **Programming** is the temporary use of prompts with the prompts gradually withdrawn to establish a generalization. The use of programming is particularly important where you are attempting to establish a generalization but the behavior never occurs in the presence of the novel stimulus. In such a case, you can use a prompt to initiate the behavior so that it can be reinforced in the presence of the novel stimulus. Once you have done that, you can begin to eliminate the prompt so that the person learns to perform the behavior solely as a result of the (once novel) stimulus. For example, if a child has learned to call a big red round object, but nothing else, a "ball," you might use a prompt to initiate the generalization to other round objects. You might hold up a golf ball and ask "What is this?" and if you get no response, you might ask "Is it a ball?" or say "Say 'ball'" and reinforce the resulting response. Then by eliminating the prompt very slowly, you may be able to teach the child to call the golf ball a "ball" with no prompting.

Programming occurs often in everyday life. In the example of the parents' teaching their child to discriminate between a picture of a cow and a picture of a dog, suppose they were to use several pictures of each animal, differing in color, size, background, and the like. If the parents were to use prompts to establish these discriminations and then gradually withdraw the prompts, this procedure would be an example of programming. If enough different animals were used, this procedure might produce generalization of the responses.

It should be understood that programming is a particular kind of generalization training—a kind that employs prompts. Everything else is the same about the two procedures except that the generalization may develop more rapidly with the use of prompts.

The difference between fading and programming, then, is whether prompts are used to establish a discrimination between two specific stimuli or whether prompts are used to establish a generalization to a class of stimuli.

Figure 18–1 illustrates an innovative program designed to teach German to people while they read a series of short stories by Edgar Allan Poe. In this illustration, the student is taught to understand the meaning of a number of German words from the context of the story. The context provides the prompt. This is a program because the student is being taught to recognize the word in a number of contexts. For example, the word *ich* appears in four different contexts in this illustration. Thus recognition of it will hopefully generalize to other contexts.

Programmed instruction is a common use of programming. It consists of a series of statements, each of which requires a written response. Typically these statements are sentences with one word to be filled in. Sometimes longer units of reading are used (such as a paragraph) before the fill-in sentence occurs. The originators of this form of teaching feel that three features are particularly important: (1) programmed instruction requires an overt response, which serves as a measure of reading comprehension; (2) it provides immediate feedback on the accuracy of the response, which may serve as a reinforcement when the answer is correct; and (3) it uses small

True!—nervous, very very dreadfully nervous, *ich*, had been, and am; but why will you say that *ich* am mad? The disease had sharpened *mein* senses—not destroyed, not dulled them. Above all was *der* sense of hearing acute. *Ich* heard all the things in *dem* heaven and *der* earth. I heard many things in hell.

Der second *und* third day went by *und* yet showed himself *mein* tormenter *nicht*. Again could *ich* as a free man breathe. *Das* monster was apparently in great terror ran away! Never again would *ich es* see!

Die slope *seiner Wande wurde von Moment zu Moment* smaller, *und der* bottom *der Vortex* seemed *sich* gradually *zu* lift. *Der* sky *war klar, die Winde Hatten sich* died, *und der* moon went brightly *im Westen* down, *als ich mich auf dem* surface *des Ozeans* facing *die* coast *von Lofden* found, exactly *über der* place,...

Figure 18–1. Illustrations of three phases used in teaching German by replacing redundant words in three short stories by Edgar Allan Poe. In phase one, "skeletal" words (a, the, and, but, in, out, have) are replaced by their German equivalents in those places where the student can guess their meaning from the context of the story. In phase two, few new words are introduced but the sentences are couched in the grammatical structure of German. In phase three, common words (such as table, boy, floor, and so on) are introduced into sentences containing skeletal words cast in the German grammatical structure. Using this method the student learns German while reading an entertaining short story. From "A Vocabulary Program Using 'Language Redundancy,'" by H. H. Schaefer, *Journal of Programmed Instruction*, 1963, 2, 9–16. Reprinted by permission.

steps so that the person is asked to learn only a small amount of new information at one time. Programmed instruction usually involves the development of complex verbal behavior. There are programs to teach children to read, to work arithmetic problems, and to write. It is also used at higher levels of education to teach language, algebra, history, and psychology.

Figure 18–2 shows a simple sequence from one example of programmed instruction, titled *Programmed Reading* (Buchanan, 1973). This sequence is designed to teach children to be able to write the word "bag." Initially the children are given the prompt "ba__" to draw their attention to the "g." Then the prompt is shortened to "b____." Next the "b" is omitted and the children must write out the whole word. Of course, they can still see the complete word in previous questions so that part of the prompt still remains. At a later stage, they will be required to fill in the whole word with no prompts. At that point they will have a pretty good grasp of the word and its meaning.

Notice that this example possesses the features of programmed instruction. The children must make a written response; they can obtain immediate feedback by looking at the correct answer on the left, which is hidden under a mask until that point; and they must learn only the amount contained in each of the small steps. Although one's first reaction might be that they will never learn very much with such a method, in fact the program takes them from no reading level to a sixth-grade reading level and can do so faster than alternative teaching methods. Also, this method works extremely well even with children who have severe learning disabilities.

Figure 18–2 would be an example of fading if it showed a picture of a bag and stated "This is a ba__" and later "This is a ___." In such a simplified situation, the children would not be learning the word in relation to other words like "pig" and "big" or in relation to a variety of pictures. They would be learning a simple discrimination (labeling this picture "bag" and not other pictures). The

no
Is that a pig in the bag? yes no
bag
That is Ann in the ba__.
bag
It is a big b___.
bag
The sandman has a __ag.
sand
bag
His _____ has sand in it.

Figure 18–2. Five items from a sequence designed to teach the word "bag." The children use this program by covering the answers on the left with a mask. They then circle either "yes" or "no" in answering the first question, move the mask down far enough to reveal the answer to that question, and proceed to the next question. This sequence is taken from the second of 23 books designed to teach children with no prior reading ability how to read. The last books involve reading complete stories at the sixth-grade reading level and answering questions about them. These books have been demonstrated to be extremely effective in teaching reading to all children; they are particularly useful in teaching reading to children who do not respond to traditional teaching methods. For example, they can produce gains in low-income children that are equivalent to or even greater than those attained by middle-class children using traditional reading instruction materials. From *Programmed Reading, Book 2* (3rd ed.), by W. Sullivan and C. D. Buchanan. Copyright 1973 by McGraw-Hill, Inc. Reprinted by permission.

example as it stands, since it does teach a generalized response, would be an example of programming.

The implications of fading and programming are revolutionary, not only for our educational system but also for our society. One implication is that specific intellectual skills can now be taught to segments of society that seemed incapable of learning by standard teaching methods. For example, these methods have been used to teach new skills to preschool children (Moore & Goldiamond, 1964), retarded children (Birnbrauer, Bijou, Wolf, & Kidder, 1965), and low-income children (Miller & Schneider, 1970). Extensions of these data indicate that the complex intellectual skills that are now characteristic of the educated elite may soon be effectively taught to a much broader range of people.

BEHAVIOR ANALYSIS EXAMPLE

Teaching toddlers triangles. Moore and Goldiamond (1964) used fading to teach young children to discriminate between triangles that matched and did not match a "sample" triangle. We will describe the results with one 3-year-old girl whom we shall call Sarah. The researchers sat Sarah in front of a discrimination-training machine that had a sample triangle with a light illuminating it. During normal operation, when the light went off for the sample triangle, three other triangles were lit up. One of those triangles matched the orientation of the sample and the other two did not. If Sarah pressed the button below the matching triangle, she was given an edible treat. If she pressed the button below the other two triangles, she was given nothing.

Moore and Goldiamond tried two approaches to teaching Sarah to find the matching triangle. One approach involved trial and error learning similar to that used in all discrimination training. If she was correct, she received a reinforcer; otherwise she received nothing. The other approach involved the use of a prompt and a fading procedure. In this approach, when the light went off of the sample triangle, only the correct matching triangle was lit up; the nonmatching triangles were dark. Thus, the light was the prompt for a correct answer. They then faded this prompt out very gradually by illuminating the two nonmatching triangles, at first slightly and then gradually increasing their illumination until they were as bright as the matching triangle.

Figure 18-3 shows a simple graph of the results. When they first used trial and error with no prompt, Sarah got the correct answer about 20% of the time. When they started the use of a prompt and fading, she got the correct answer 100% of the time. During this time they faded the prompt until the nonmatching triangles were 60% as bright as the matching triangle. They then returned to trial and error condition with no prompt, and less than 20% of Sarah's responses were correct. They again returned to the use of the prompt and fading and almost 90% of her responses were correct. The interesting thing about this was that by the end of this condition they faded the prompt out completely by making the nonmatching triangles as bright as the matching triangle. The last condition was one more return to the use of no prompt. Because of the training that involved the prompt and fading, Sarah could now always pick the correct triangle. Interestingly, even though normally she made many errors while learning very poorly through trial and error, she made virtually no errors while learning through fading.

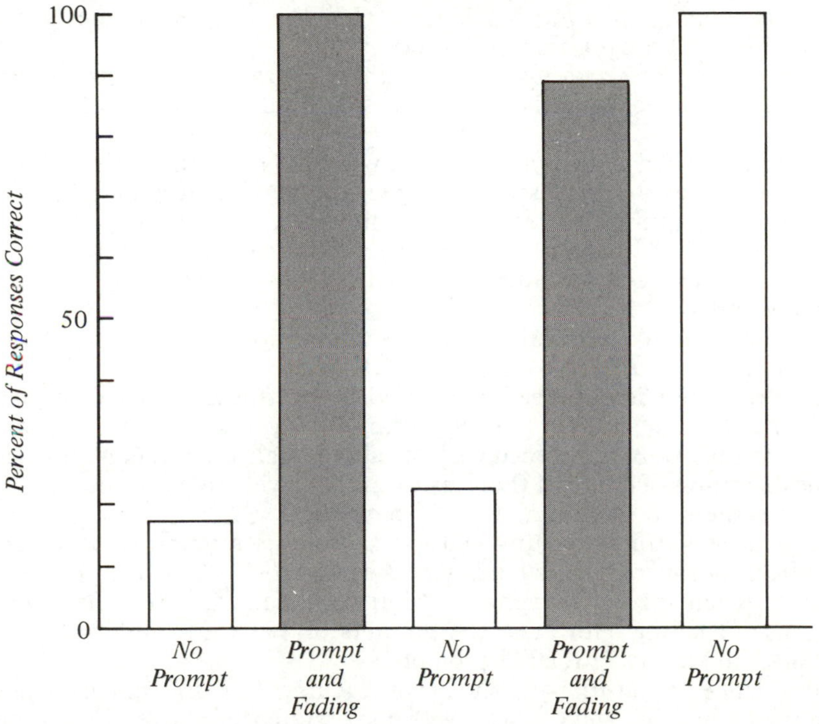

18-3

Figure 18–3. Sarah's accuracy in matching triangles with different orientations when no prompt is given and when a prompt is used but gradually faded out. The last bar shows the performance after the prompt had been completely faded out. Without the prior use of the prompt and fading, this performance would have been only about 20% accurate. Adapted from "Errorless Establishment of Visual Discrimination Using Fading Procedures," by R. Moore and I. Goldiamond, *Journal of the Experimental Analysis of Behavior*, 1964, 7, 269–272. Copyright 1964 by the Society for the Experimental Analysis of Behavior, Inc. Used by permission.

These results, in common with other results often obtained when using fading or programming procedures, suggest that learning can be both faster and almost error free when behavioral procedures are used.

Note #1: Programming has a rather unfortunate history. It was first developed by B. F. Skinner in the mid 1950s and it showed great promise of improving educational technology. Skinner wrote a series of articles promoting its use (for example, Skinner, 1954). The idea, particularly in the form of teaching machines, was picked up by the book publishers and by a number of psychologists and educators who did not understand behavior analysis. It was promoted by them without adequate research and many programs were developed quickly, without sufficient care and published in order to make money. The results were disastrous. Many educators exposed to these products concluded that programs were boring and ineffective. It may be many years before the ill effects of this history are overcome.

Note #2: The book will ask you to identify several examples of programmed instruction. In these cases, you may label the example either as "programmed instruction" or simply as "programming," since programmed instruction is a type of programming.

ADDITIONAL READINGS

Birnbrauer, J. S., Bijou, S. W., Wolf, M. M., & Kidder, J. D. Programmed instruction in the classroom. In L. P. Ullman and L. Krasner (Eds.), *Case studies in behavior modification.* New York: Holt, Rinehart & Winston, 1965. This article describes the use of programmed instruction to advance the academic scores of retarded children with no previous record of academic achievement. Gains were made in the children's writing, reading, and math skills.

Holland, J. G. Teaching machines: An application of principles from the laboratory. *Journal of the Experimental Analysis of Behavior,* 1960, *3,* 275–287. This article is an early description of the principles of teaching machines and programmed instruction.

Lumsdaine, A. A., & Glaser, R. *Teaching machines and programmed learning.* Washington, D.C.: National Education Association, 1960. This book is a collection of early articles that discuss programmed instruction.

Markle, S. *Good frames and bad: A grammar of frame writing.* New York: Wiley, 1969. This is a programmed how-to-do-it book. It explains in simple language how to write programmed materials, gives many examples, and then requires the reader to try his or her knowledge.

Miller, L. K., & Schneider, R. The use of a token system in Project Head Start. *Journal of Applied Behavior Analysis,* 1970, *3,* 213–220. An early study using fading procedures to teach low-income children simple printing skills.

Newsom, C. D., & Simon, K. M. A simultaneous discrimination procedure for the measurement of vision in non-verbal children. *Journal of Applied Behavior Analysis,* 1977, *10,* 633–644. Severely retarded and psychotic children often do not receive proper vision testing and needed eyeglasses because they don't follow the instructions necessary in such testing. To adequately test such children, a procedure was devised in which they were reinforced with an edible (such as an M & M) for selecting one of two cards that could be discriminated only if their vision at that level was adequate. A fading procedure was used to initially train them to select one type of card.

Schreibman, L. Effects of within-stimulus and extra-stimulus prompting on discrimination learning in autistic children. *Journal of Applied Behavior Analysis,* 1975, *8,* 91–112. This study demonstrates that it is possible to teach severely psychotic children to make very fine discriminations without errors through the use of fading. However, the prompts must be integrally related to the discriminative stimuli rather than simply unrelated prompts.

Skinner, B. F. The science of learning and the art of teaching. *Harvard Educational Review,* 1954, *24.* Also reprinted in the Lumsdaine and Glaser (1960) book referenced above. This is the earliest statement by Skinner of the concepts lying behind programmed instruction.

Wulbert, M., Nyman, B. A., Snow, D., & Owen, Y. The efficacy of stimulus fading and contingency management in the treatment of elective mutism: A case study. *Journal of Applied Behavior Analysis,* 1973, *6,* 435–441. This study concerns a 6-year-old child who did not speak or follow instructions in kindergarten. However, she reacted normally at home in the presence of her mother. The mother was used as a prompt to maintain normal responding and an experimenter was faded into the situation in gradual steps until the child responded normally in her presence. This was repeated with five experimenters until the child responded normally to the sixth and to her teacher. At this point the mother's presence was not required and the child became a well-adjusted student in her class.

Helpful hints: Shaping and fading are sometimes confused. Shaping involves the gradual change of behavior; the stimulus situation remains the same, but the rules of reinforcement, and therefore the behaviors, are changed. Fading involves the gradual change of the stimulus; the behavior stays the same, but the prompt is gradually withdrawn, and the stimulus situation is changed.

Fading is used to gradually change the stimulus; shaping is used to gradually change the behavior.

LESSON 18 READING QUIZ

(9) Fading and programming are procedures that use established ______________ to develop new ones.

(25) An added stimulus that increases the probability that a discrimination will be formed is called a(n) ______________.

(17) The gradual withdrawal of a prompt used to teach a specific discrimination is called ______________.

(8) If the correct behavior never occurs in the presence of the S^D during discrimination training, then you can try to increase its probability by using a(n) ______________.

(24) Fading is a particular kind of ______________ that employs prompts.

(16) Suppose that you show a young child a picture of a dog and ask her "What is this? You know, bowwow!" The underlined words would be called a(n) ______________.

(7) Suppose that you show a young child a picture of a dog (interspersed with pictures of a cat) many times during the day, each time asking him or her what it is. What behavioral procedure would you be using if you first add "You know, bowwow," next add it more softly, then only silently mouth the bowwow, and finally omit it altogether? ______________

(23) When teaching the discrimination between two stimuli, the use of a prompt with only one picture ______________ (is, isn't) about equally effective as the use of a different prompt with each picture.

(15) The gradual withdrawal of prompts used to teach a generalization is called ______________.

(6) If the correct behavior never occurs in the presence of a novel stimulus during generalization training, then you can try to increase its probability by using a(n) ______________.

(22) Generalization training that temporarily employs prompts is called ______________.

(14) Suppose parents show their young child a series of pictures of dogs, some big, some small, and ask "What is this? You know, bowwow." If they gradually eliminate the "bowwow" for all of the pictures, they are using what behavioral procedure to teach their child to label all of the pictures as a "dog" (but not other pictures)? ______________

(5) Schaeffer (1963) used the German word *ich* to replace the English "I" in several short stories by Poe. The context of redundant sentences was enough to serve as an effective prompt for correct translation. By replacing the German word in many different sentences, including some that did not prompt correct translation, students learned to always recognize that word. What behavioral procedure did Schaeffer use to teach the meaning of *ich*? ______________

(21) Using a prompt to teach a generalization is called ______________; using a prompt to teach a specific discrimination is called ______________.

(13) Programmed instruction is a common use of what behavioral procedure? ______________

(4) Programmed instruction involves three important features: (1) it requires an overt ______________ (as a measure of reading); (2) it provides immediate ______________ (hopefully as a reinforcer); and (3) it uses small ______________.

(20) In *Programmed Reading*, the child is shown a picture of a bag and is then required to fill in a blank like "That is Ann in the ba____." Showing one or more letters contained in the correct answer would be called a(n) ______________.

(12) If prompts are used (and then withdrawn) to teach a child to correctly label a picture of a boy and a picture of a girl, the situation is an example of what behavioral procedure? ______________

(3) If a prompt is used to help establish a discrimination between a specific S^D and a specific *S*-delta, then the name of the procedure is ______________.

(19) A prompt is a(n) ______________________ that increases the probability of making the correct response.
(11) Fading involves the gradual ______________________ of a prompt to teach a specific discrimination.
(2) Shaping is a behavioral procedure that involves the gradual changing of the __________; fading is a behavioral procedure that involves the gradual changing of the __________.
(18) Moore and Goldiamond (1964) had the correct answer light up while the incorrect answers remained dark. They then gradually increased the brightness of the incorrect answers until they were as bright as the correct answer. What behavioral procedure were they using? ______________________
(10) Programming is a particular kind of ______________________ that temporarily employs prompts.
(1) Discrimination training that temporarily employs prompts to establish a specific discrimination is called ______________________.

READING QUIZ ANSWERS

(1) fading (2) behavior; stimulus (3) fading (4) response; feedback; steps (5) programming (6) prompt (7) fading (8) prompt (9) discriminations (10) generalization training (11) withdrawal (12) fading (13) programming (14) programming (15) programming (16) prompt (17) fading (18) fading (19) added stimulus (20) prompt (21) programming; fading (22) programming (23) is (24) discrimination training (25) prompt

LESSON 18 EXAMPLES

Example #1

Professor Smith was trying to teach 18-month-old Tracey the concepts of "above" and "below" so that she could be the smartest child in Kansas. She started by placing her hand over the table and asking "Where is my hand? You know, above" and giving Tracey a bite of strained applesauce if she repeated it. She did this several times until Tracey copied the word right off. Then she put her hand over the table and asked "Where is my hand? You know, abuh," being careful not to say the "v" sound in above. Again she reinforced Tracey for saying "above." In this way she gradually taught Tracey to say "above" when asked where the hand was. Professor Smith interspersed instances of placing her hand below the table and asking Tracey where it was, using a similar hint and gradually eliminating it. In several days, Tracey could answer either question correctly with no hints.

(27) The phrase "You know, above" is an added stimulus that is called a(n) __________.
(18) Shortening the amount of the word "above" that was said is called __________.
(9) Teaching the specific discrimination between the hand over and the hand under the table by the temporary use of the phrase "You know, above" is called __________.

Example #2

Professor Smith wanted Tracey to learn to use "above" correctly for any situation. So she next placed her hand over a dish and asked Tracey "Where is my hand? You know, above" and gave Tracey a bite if she repeated "above." She then gradually eliminated the hint. Next, she put a ball over the dish and asked Tracey "Where is the ball?" To her surprise, before she could give the hint, Tracey blurted out "above." Professor Smith tried placing the dish on top of the ball and asking where it was. Again Tracey said "above." Tracey could always tell you whether an object was above or below from then on.

(26) When Tracey said "above" when asked where the ball was with respect to the dish, the

occurrence of this behavior in this situation would be called ______________.

(17) The temporary use of the phrase "You know, above" with novel instances in which one object is located above another is an example of the behavioral procedure called ______________ ______________.

Example #3

Mr. Franklin had just about given up on teaching his ninth-grade students the principles of algebra. Then he heard about a new type of book that presented only small amounts of information at a time, required the students to write answers, and let them look up the answers for immediate feedback on their responses. He tried it and found that his students really started to learn algebra well.

(8) The new type of book would be an example of ______________.

Example #4

Terry attempted to increase her vocabulary by writing out the definition of every previously unknown word that she came across. She studied the definition and, with it before her, wrote several sentences using the word. She then wrote out a very shortened version of the definition and wrote several sentences with that before her. Next, she looked at a definition consisting only of a synonym or key word. Finally, she wrote sentences with no help from a definition. By the time she had done all of this, she could use the word fluently in both speech and writing.

(25) Terry's goal was to be able to use the new word in any novel situation that might come along. Her production of the world in a novel situation would be called ______________.

(16) The written definitions of different lengths served as a(n) ______________ for correct use of the new words.

(7) By using a written definition at first and gradually relying less and less on it, in order to acquire the skill of using the word in any situation, Terry was using what behavioral procedure? ______________

Example #5

Bob had just taken a behavior analysis course. He decided that he could use his new understanding of behavior to teach himself to wake up at 7:00 A.M. without an alarm clock. To do this, he set his alarm radio softer and softer every morning until he finally could not hear it when it came on. That was the morning he overslept, missed an hour exam, flunked his business course, and decided he didn't understand behavior as well as he had thought.

(24) What procedure was Bob trying to use to teach himself to wake up without an alarm clock?

____

Example #6

James held up a tennis ball for his sister to see and asked her what it was. When she said "ball" he gave her a big smile and praised her. When she didn't, he ignored her. After she had learned to call the tennis ball a "ball," he showed her a basketball and asked her what it was, again repeating the same procedure used on the tennis ball. After she had learned to call it a ball, he showed her a golf ball and she immediately said "ball."

(15) What behavioral procedure did he use? ______________

(6) If he had given her a hint for each ball that he gradually withdrew, what behavioral procedure would he be using? ______________

Example #7

Fred learned the definition of "reinforcer" from a specially designed book. In the book he was first given a specific definition of "reinforcer" with the key words underlined. The first question had the same words underlined: "An event that <u>follows</u> a behavior and <u>increases</u> its probability is called a(n) ________________________." The next wording of the question, which occurred after several intervening questions about other procedures, left the underlining out but used the same words. The next wording used different words but meant the same: "An event that occurs after a behavior such that its frequency increases is called a(n) ________________________." Fred was able after that to label the definition of a "reinforcer" no matter what wording was used.

(23) What behavioral procedure did the book use to develop this skill? ________________

Example #8

When Roger learned to always say the "pl" part of "playing" correctly, the behaviorist decided to reinforce him only if he got the "a" sound also. When Roger said "play" correctly, the behaviorist next insisted on Roger's saying the "ing" distinctly.

(14) Teaching Roger to say "playing" correctly used what behavioral procedure? ____________

Example #9

Darlene held up a picture of a crow, asked her daughter "What is this?" and then said "This is a large bird." Later she simply said "large"; still later she made a movement with her hands to indicate "large"; and finally she did nothing. If the child said "crow," Darlene praised her lavishly. However, if Darlene held up a picture of a blackbird and the child said "crow," Darlene ignored her. The daughter quickly learned to call the larger bird a crow but not the smaller one.

(5) What behavioral procedure was Darlene using? ________________________

(22) If Darlene did not provide the hint about size, what procedure would she be using? ________________________

Example #10

Mr. Janes taught Robert to draw a map of Kansas by first praising any rectangle that was twice as long as it was high. He then praised the map only if the Missouri River was shown, and finally he praised the map only if Wichita, Kansas City, and Topeka were shown.

(13) The behavioral procedure by which Mr. Janes taught Robert to draw the map is called ________________________.

Example #11

Professor Smart pointed to a complex differential equation and asked Mary "What is that?" She immediately said "That is a differential equation" and was rewarded with a broad smile from the professor.

(4) The differential equation would be called a(n) ________________________ for the response "That is a differential equation." It would be called a(n) ________________ for the response "That is a matrix."

Example #12

Professor Smart pointed to a linear equation ($12x + 7 = y$) that no one had seen before. He asked Jane what kind of equation it was. She said "That is a linear equation."

(21) The occurrence of her behavior in the presence of this new equation would be called ______________________.

Example #13

Pete's dad tutored him in the identification of football plays by showing him diagrams of many kinds of playes and asking him to name them. He praised Pete for calling the first one a "power sweep" but not a "flea flicker." He praised him for calling the second diagram a "line buck" but not for calling it a "power sweep."

(12) What behavioral procedure was his dad using? ______________________

Example #14

The coach praised Bruiser Bob for tackling the practice dummy low, but ignored him when he tackled it high. Soon, Bob only tackled it low.

(3) What behavioral procedure was the coach using? ______________________

Example #15

A special tutor was used to teach Bruiser Bob, not the smartest of students, to learn his blocking assignments for the power sweep and end run. At first the tutor let Bob read from a crib sheet "power sweep—block opposing tackle to left." Later he had him use a crib sheet that had only "power sweep—tackle" and later, no crib sheet. Bruiser learned his assignment perfectly.

(20) What behavioral procedure did the tutor employ? ______________________

Example #16

Mrs. Livermore taught her kindergarten pupil, Francie, to label a large circular line as a "circle" by asking "Francie, what is this? You know, a circle" and praising her when she said "circle." Next, she gave as a hint only "You know, a cirk" but did not say the "l." Pretty soon, Francie could label the drawing as a circle with no hint. Then, Mrs. Livermore showed Francie a small solid circle and used the same procedure. With that training, Francie started to label all circular patterns as "circles."

(11) What behavioral procedure did Mrs. Livermore use to teach that skill? ______________

Example #17

Carol was taught to add by a teacher who let her see two sets of matches that corresponded to the addition problem. When he asked "How much is 4 + 7?" the teacher would arrange a pile of four matches and a pile of seven matches. As Carol learned to answer the question, the teacher would gradually move the match piles out of sight. Eventually, Carol could add "4 + 7" without the help of the matches.

(2) What behavioral procedure did the teacher use? ______________________

Example #18

Ray was a loner, never playing with the other preschool children. Ms. Gray started trying to change this by praising Ray whenever he was playing with Jane; after several days he started playing quite a bit with Jane. Then she started praising Ray when he was playing with Billy. In a few days he was playing with Billy and Jane. In addition, he started playing with Mary.

(19) What behavioral method had Ms. Gray used to produce this result? ______________
____

Example #19

Eleanor praised her daughter for saying "dog" when shown a picture of a dog and ignored her for saying "dog" when shown a picture of a cat.

(10) What behavioral procedure was she using? ______________________

Example #20

Frank thought he had just discovered a fundamental principle of education. In the lower grades, everything he did was directly supervised by the teacher. When the teacher was present he worked, when she was not, he goofed off. During junior high he had to do a little bit of homework, about 2 hours for every 8 hours in class. In high school, he had to do still more work on his own. In college, he learned you were supposed to do 2 hours of homework for every hour in class. In graduate school, most work was on your own. Thus, the role of direct teacher supervision was gradually reduced.

(1) Frank had discovered that what behavioral procedure was being used by the educational system to teach students to work on their own? ______________________

EXAMPLE ANSWERS

(1) fading (2) fading (3) differential reinforcement (4) S^D; S-delta (5) fading (6) programming (7) programming (8) programmed instruction (or programming) (9) fading (10) discrimination training (11) programming (12) discrimination training (13) shaping (14) shaping (15) generalization training (16) prompt (17) programming (18) fading (19) generalization training (20) fading (21) generalization (22) discrimination training (23) programming (24) fading (25) generalization (26) generalization (27) prompt

Lesson 19

Instructions and Imitation

This lesson introduces two widely used methods for modifying behavior: imitation training and instructional training. Imitation training involves demonstrating to another person how to perform a behavior. Instructional training involves describing to another person how to perform a behavior. In everyday life both methods can be extraordinarily complex. The so-called "exemplary behavior" of revolutionaries is an attempt to demonstrate to other people how to behave and is therefore potentially a very complex example of imitation training. Programmed instruction is an attempt to describe to other people how to behave and is therefore potentially an example of the complex use of instructional training.

Imitation training consists of three parts: (1) the teacher provides a behavioral demonstration (called the imitative stimulus) of what the learner is supposed to do; (2) the learner produces imitative behavior; and (3) the teacher arranges some kind of reinforcement for the learner's imitative behavior. An example might be when a teacher says *gut* with the correct German accent, the learner says *gut* in a similar way, and the teacher reinforces the correct response.

Imitation training is used frequently in everyday situations. When a parent shows a child how to hold a football, or how to sauté onions, he or she is using imitation training. Frequently, people who do not fully understand behavioral principles do not let learners try to produce the imitative behavior themselves. This abbreviated form of imitation training may result in learning, although it is not likely to be as effective as the full procedure. This more passive portion of imitation training is sometimes referred to as "observational learning," because the learner simply observes the imitative stimulus and only later tries to produce the imitative behavior.

Imitative training has been widely used by behavior analysts, particularly with individuals who have very limited verbal skills. Interestingly, the very skill of imitating itself has been found to be very limited among autistic, psychotic, and retarded children. Behavior analysts have therefore sought to learn how to teach the skill of imitating, hypothesizing that such a skill is fundamental to the ability of such children to learn basic everyday behaviors. The approach has usually involved selecting a very simple form of imitation initially and, if necessary, actually shaping it. After a simple imitation has been developed and reinforced, further simple forms of imitation are taught. The goal has been to teach enough imitations that generalized imitative behavior develops and the child then starts to imitate additional behaviors spontaneously. Many investigators have used such an approach successfully.

The procedure for teaching an imitation may usually be viewed as an example of complex discrimination training. The teacher will reinforce the learner for saying "two" if the imitative stimulus was "two" but not if it was "three." Thus, the imitative stimulus is an S^D for the corresponding imitative behavior. Since, generally, many imitative responses are taught, the child is being taught to discriminate between them.

Instructional training also consists of three parts: (1) the teacher provides a verbal description of the desired behavior; (2) the learner produces the instructed behavior; and (3) the teacher arranges for reinforcement of the instructed behavior. An example might be when a teacher says to a child, "Pass the butter," the child passes the butter, and the teacher says "Thank you" or provides some stronger reinforcement.

The training procedure for teaching by instruction is also usually a discrimination training procedure. The teacher reinforces the learner for putting the ball on the table only if the instruction was "put the ball on the table," but not if it was "put the ball on the floor." Thus the instruction is an S^D for the described behavior. Since the learner is usually being taught a number of instructions, the situation involves complex discrimination training.

Instructional training is probably the most widely used form of behavior modification employed in everyday settings. We are all constantly engaged in talking, telling people what to do, when to do it, how to do it, and why to do it. Unfortunately, the nonbehavior analyst frequently fails to follow through by observing the instructed behavior and then supplying reinforcement. As a result, following instructions is frequently placed on a schedule of extinction.

Instructional training is one component of most behavior analysis procedures. The learner is instructed on what behavior is expected, as well as what consequences will follow successful instructed behavior. This holds true for almost every type of person worked with toward the goal of any form of behavioral change. Thus it is not surprising to find behavior analysts also attempting to establish generalized instruction-following behavior in nonverbal individuals such as autistic and retarded children. The strategy is similar to that employed to develop a generalized imitative behavior: a simple instruction is used first and then a number of instructions are used to develop generalized instruction following. Such a procedure has been successful in establishing this skill with such individuals.

An experiment by Ayllon and Azrin (1964) illustrates the importance of reinforcement in developing and maintaining instruction-following behavior in long-term adult psychotics. As Figure 19-1 shows, Ayllon and Azrin observed during a baseline period that such patients rarely bother to use eating implements during meals—even when eating soup! They tried instructing the patients to pick up and use such implements and found that this resulted in about a third of the patients complying. It wasn't until they started awarding tokens that virtually all the patients started following the instructions. Reinforcing instruction-following behavior is crucial in maintaining such behavior.

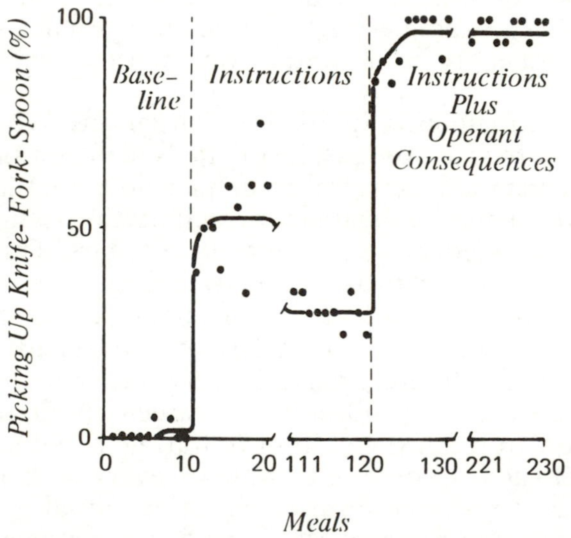

Figure 19-1. Chronic schizophrenic patients in many mental hospitals eat their food with their hands (including soup). This figure shows the number of patients who picked up the knife, fork, and spoon during a baseline period, during a period when they were instructed to pick these items up, and then during a period when they were instructed plus reinforced for picking them up. Notice that instructions helped but tended to lose their effect over time. And notice that when reinforcement was added, almost all the patients always picked up the implements. This example shows the necessity of using reinforcement along with instructions in many applications of instruction training. Adapted from "Reinforcement and Instructions With Mental Patients," by T. Ayllon and N. H. Azrin, *Journal of the Experimental Analysis of Behavior*, 1964, 7, 327–331. Copyright 1964 by the Society for the Experimental Analysis of Behavior, Inc. Used by permission.

One interesting implication of instructional training has been widely explored by behavior therapists working with relatively normal adults with "problems." Behavior therapists frequently diagnose the problems as resulting from these individuals developing instructions that they repeat to themselves that influence their behavior in ways that are not functional. For example, if some people constantly tell themselves that they must have something to eat, they may literally instruct themselves to become obese. Alcoholism, depression, anxiety, drug dependence, and many other problems may ultimately be the result of such faulty "self-instructions." Behavior therapists regard these instructions as behavior; that is, the person's verbal behavior contains the instructions and therefore is susceptible to the behavioral processes of reinforcement, extinction, and punishment. There are frequent reports that therapeutic approaches based on such an analysis have been far more successful than attempts to find the sources of such problems in the childhood history of the patients—an approach associated with traditional psychotherapy and psychoanalysis.

Both imitation training and instructional training are methods for modifying behavior that are simpler and more direct thatn procedures that rely exclusively on reinforcement. For example, if a teacher wishes to increase the rate of students' talking in class, then instructing them to talk more (and reinforcing their talking) is surely simpler and faster than waiting for them to talk and reinforcing them. Similarly, instructing people to hit their Ping-Pong shots more softly is quicker and easier than painstakingly reinforcing soft shots and extinguishing hard shots. Similar examples can be drawn that relate to virtually every concept that has been covered in this book, including discrimination training and generalization training.

However, it often is not possible to use instructional training because it requires verbal skills. For example, it would not be effective with infants, retarded children, autistic children, or anyone whose verbal skills are not advanced enough considering the nature of the instructions. Similarly, many forms of behavior (for instance, singing) cannot be described well enough to lend themselves to instructional training. And many forms of behavior cannot be easily demonstrated for imitation training (for example, correctly applying the definition of role). In any event, if the person's verbal skills are sufficient, instructional training should be used as a quick and convenient method of generating behavior. And if the skill can be conveniently and adequately demonstrated, imitation should be used.

BEHAVIOR ANALYSIS EXAMPLE

Teaching a college graduate how to get a job. A recent experiment by Hollandsworth, Glazeski, and Dressel (1978) demonstrates how effective the combined use of instructions and imitation training can be in teaching an extremely nervous college graduate to obtain a job. The college graduate, whom we will call Herbert, had sought employment during the 5 months after graduation with a General Business degree. He had participated in over 60 job interviews without a single offer. In desperation he finally accepted a part-time sales job in a men's clothing store at $1.50 per hour.

The behavior analysts determined that Herbert was losing his opportunity for employment through extreme nervousness in the interview situation. His speech was incoherent, he lost his train of thought, and he stared into space silently for long periods. They therefore specified three behaviors which would improve his interview performance: focused responses to the interviewer's questions, coping statements, such as "excuse me" and "let me start over," to be made when he goofed, and asking questions that requested additional information, feedback, or clarification of a question.

The behavior analysts designed a role playing situation in which one of them played the role of an interviewer while another observed the interview. Figure 19–2 shows Herbert's baseline performance level for each of the three interviewing behaviors. As you can see, his performance was very poor.

Prior to session 7, the behavior analysts trained Herbert in a simple method for making focused (or clear) responses to an interviewer's questions. They first defined "clear responses" and explained why they were important. They then explained to him how to make clear responses. This involved using a "pause-think-speak" paradigm. When the interviewer asked a question, Herbert was to break eye contact and pause while looking at a spot on the wall behind the interviewer; he was then to attend to one or two key words in the question and generate one or two key words to be used in his response; finally he was to make eye contact and initiate a clear

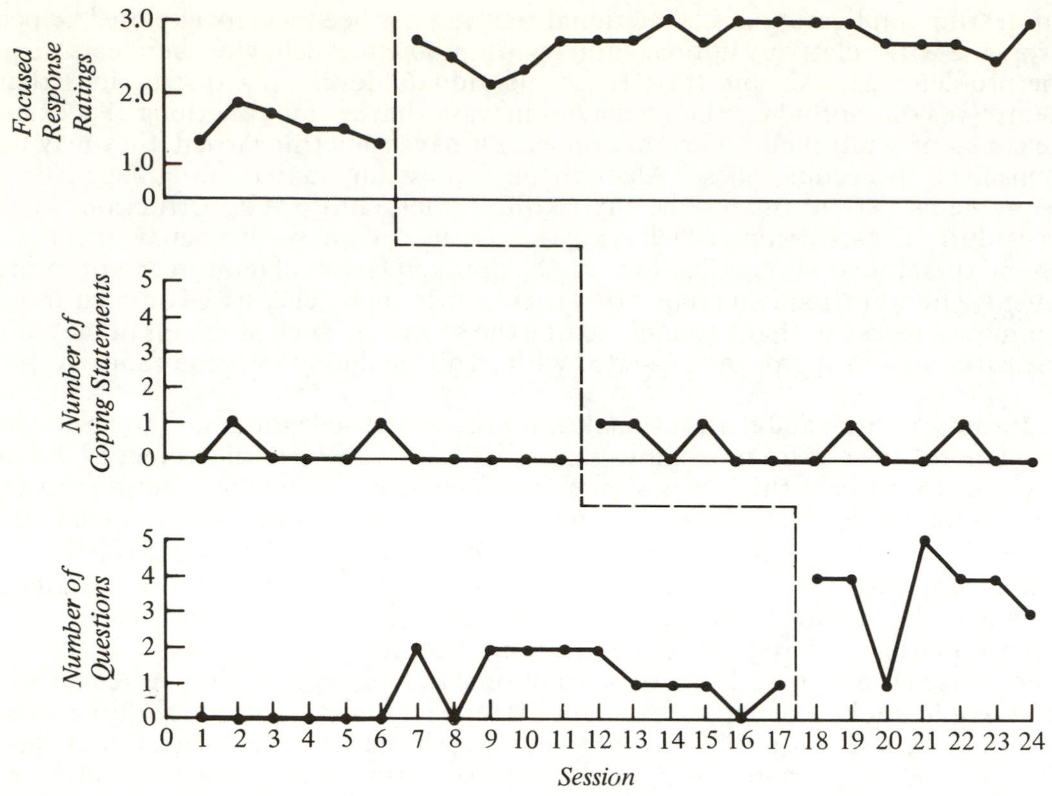

Figure 19–2. The average rating of focused responding, frequency of coping statements, and questions for Herbert during training for job interviews. From "Use of Social Skills Training in the Treatment of Extreme Anxiety and Deficient Verbal Skills in the Job Interview Setting," by J. G. Hollandsworth, R. C. Glazeski, and M. E. Dressel, *Journal of Applied Behavior Analysis*, 1978, *11*, 259–269. Copyright 1978 by the Society for the Experimental Analysis of Behavior, Inc. Used by permission.

response to the interviewer's question. After practice, Herbert appeared very natural using this approach.

In addition to presenting Herbert with an explanation of the desired behavior the investigators showed him a videotape recording of another person actually using that method. Herbert was then given the opportunity to practice what he had learned in response to five questions commonly asked by job interviewers. The trainer provided feedback on his performance.

As you can see by looking at Figure 19–2, Herbert's performance improved dramatically after this training for "focused responses." A similar training procedure was used prior to session 12 for coping statements, and there was a modest improvement in performance. Finally, training in asking questions of the interviewers (to clarify their questions) was given prior to session 17. Again a dramatic increase in performance resulted.

Additional data were gathered during the experiment. The number of stutters emitted by Herbert during each role-playing session was measured as an indication of nervousness. Stutters decreased from a baseline level of about 20 per session to about 2 or 3. But the most important outcome of the experiment was that Herbert went for three interviews after training and was offered three jobs. He took one as an Administrative Assistant in a hospital for about $4.00 per hour.

Note #1: Examples in which a single imitative stimulus is presented and imitative behavior that is highly similar is reinforced may sometimes be analyzed as differential reinforcement. That is, correct imitation is reinforced and incorrect imitation is extinguished. However, imitative stimuli are seldom presented singly. Rather, the learner is taught to imitate several imitative stimuli, making the procedure an example of complex discrimination training (that is, many stimuli and many behaviors).

Note #2: Programming and fading may involve imitation training during the initial portion of training, prior to the withdrawal of the prompt. For example, if a fading sequence involves asking the question "What is this, (a tree)?" the person can simply imitate the word "tree." However, since that imitative stimulus is eventually withdrawn, this would not be classified as an example of imitation training. So in any example involving the withdrawal of an imitative stimulus used as a prompt, the only acceptable answer is programming or fading.

ADDITIONAL READINGS

Baer, A. M., Rowbury, R., & Baer, D. M. The development of instructional control over classroom activities of deviant preschool children. *Journal of Applied Behavior Analysis*, 1973, *6*, 289–298. This article describes the use of reinforcement procedures to teach a group of severely disturbed children to comply with instructions given by the teacher.

Bandura, A. *Psychological modeling: Conflicting theories.* Chicago: Aldine-Atherton, 1971. This is an excellent source book for a broader understanding of imitation training and various psychological theories of imitation.

Brawley, E. R., Harris, F. R., Allen, K. E., Flemin, R. S., & Peterson, R. F. Behavior modification of an autistic child. *Behavioral Science*, 1969, *14*, 87–97. Systematic reinforcement procedures were used to strengthen appropriate behaviors, such as talking and following instructions. Extinction was used to weaken inappropriate behaviors, such as the child's hitting himself and throwing a tantrum. These procedures were used with effectiveness in therapy sessions three times a week. Generalization was programmed by involving ward personnel in the reinforcement and extinction procedures.

Garcia, E., Guess, D., & Byrnes, J. Development of syntax in a retarded girl using procedures of imitation, reinforcement, and modeling. *Journal of Applied Behavior Analysis*, 1973, *6*, 299–310. This article describes the effectiveness of using imitation training for developing complex speech patterns in a severely retarded child.

Kennedy, D. A., & Thompson, I. The use of reinforcement techniques with a first grade boy. *Personality and Guidance Journal*, 1967, *46*, 366–370. In this case report, a child taught to pay attention in a counselor's office also paid attention more closely in the classroom. This example involved spontaneous generalization in that the behavior modifier did not have to reinforce the child for paying attention in the classroom.

Helpful hints: Imitation training and instructional training are sometimes confused, because in both cases the teacher engages in some form of behavior designed to influence another person. The distinction lies in whether the teacher's behavior is identical (or highly similar) to the desired behavior. If it is identical or similar, then the teacher is using imitation training. If the teacher's behavior is different, but somehow describes the desired behavior, then the teacher is using instructional control. For example, if the teacher says *Guten Tag* and reinforces the student for saying *Guten Tag*, then the technique used is imitative training. If the teacher says "Say the German phrase for hello" and reinforces the student for saying *Guten Tag*, the technique used is instructional training. Usually you can clarify which type of training is involved by asking: "Did the teacher describe the correct behavior (instruction), or did the teacher demonstrate the correct behavior (imitation)?"

LESSON 19 READING QUIZ

(14) Imitation training involves showing a person how to do something. The behavioral demonstration is called the ______________________ stimulus.

(7) If the person copies the demonstration, his behavior is called ______________ behavior.

(20) In addition to the demonstration, the trainer must be sure to ______________ the person's response if it is correct.

(13) When a father demonstrates to a child how to hold a football in order to throw it, the father is producing a(n) ______________________ stimulus.

(6) If a learner is presented with an imitative stimulus but does not attempt to imitate it, this portion of imitative training is sometimes referred to as ______________ learning.

(19) If the learner is reinforced for producing imitative behavior 1 in the presence of imitative stimulus 1 but not in the presence of imitative stimulus 2, then this form of imitation training

would be an example of what behavioral procedure? ______________

(12) Instructional training involves explaining to someone how to do something. That explanation is called a(n) ______________.

(5) If the person follows the instructions correctly, his behavior is called ______________ ______________.

(18) In addition to the instructions, a trainer using instructional training must be sure to ______________ the person's correct responses.

(11) From the point of view of discrimination training, both the imitative stimulus and the verbal description would be ______________ for the correct behavior on the part of the learner.

(4) If the teacher describes to learners how to do something and watches them try to do it, but fails to reinforce them, what schedule of reinforcement are the learners on? ______________

(17) Aylon and Azrin (1964) instructed long-term mental patients to pick up and use eating utensils at meals. This was largely ineffective until what behavioral procedure was used in addition to providing a verbal description of the desired behavior? ______________

(10) Behavior therapists have diagnosed many of the problems experienced by "normal" adults as resulting from faulty self- ______________.

(3) Behavior therapists regard self-instructions as verbal behavior. Therefore they assume that undesirable self-instructions can be reduced in frequency through the use of what behavioral procedure? ______________

(16) Hollandsworth and colleagues (1978) demonstrated for Herbert how to ask questions designed to clarify interview questions. They then watched his ability to ask questions in a simulated interview situation and reinforced correct performance. What behavioral procedure were they using? ______________

(9) Hollandsworth and his colleagues (1978) provided a verbal description to Herbert of how to make clear responses to interview questions. They then observed his performance in a simulated interview session and reinforced correct performance. The behavior analysts used what behavioral procedure? ______________

(2) The three parts of imitation training are a(n) ______________, the ______________, and reinforcement.

(15) The three parts of instructional training are a(n) ______________, the ______________, and reinforcement.

(8) If you think that an example is imitative training, you may check your analysis by asking the question "Did the teacher ______________ the correct behavior?" If so, it is imitative training.

(1) If you think that an example is instructional training, you may check your analysis by asking the question "Did the teacher ______________ the correct behavior?"

READING QUIZ ANSWERS

(1) describe (2) imitative stimulus; imitative behavior (3) extinction (4) extinction (5) instructed behavior (6) observational (7) imitative (8) demonstrate (9) instructional training (10) instructions (11) S^Ds (12) verbal description (13) imitative (14) imitative (15) verbal description; instructed behavior (16) imitation training (17) reinforcement (18) reinforce (19) discrimination training (20) reinforce

LESSON 19 EXAMPLES

Example #1

One night at dinner, Tiny Tim's father said "Pass the salt." Since Tiny Tim did not yet speak very well, his father was surprised when he passed the salt. But he managed to say "Thank you" and act pleased enough to make Tim feel like a hero. After that, Tiny Tim always passed the salt when asked to and he always looked very grown up and pleased about doing so.

(14) When Father said "Pass the salt" he gave a verbal ________________ of the desired behavior.
(40) By passing the salt, Tim performed the instructed ________________.
(27) His father's pleased reaction clearly was a(n) ________________ for Tim.
(13) This is clearly an example of instructional training because Father ________________ (demonstrated, described) the desired behavior.
(39) Instructional training involves: (1) a(n) ________________ description of the desired behavior; (2) the ________________ behavior; and (3) ________________ of that behavior.

Example #2

Tiny Tim got a wooden puzzle of different geometric shapes. However, he didn't have much luck putting the right shape into the right hole, so his mother showed him where to put each piece. She took the piece from Tim, put it into the right hole, and then gave it back to Tim. Tim put the right piece into the right hole immediately. Mother beamed at him, gave him a kiss, and said "Good, Timmy." She continued this procedure with each piece.

(26) Tim's mother showed him where each puzzle piece went. Her behavior is called the imitative ________________.
(12) Tim then placed the puzzle piece correctly. This behavior is called the imitative ________________
(38) Having the puzzle piece go right into the puzzle hole was probably a(n) ________________ for Tim. If it wasn't, his mother's smile, kiss, and praise probably were.
(25) Imitation training consists of three parts: (1) Mother's showing Tim where to put the puzzle piece—called the ________________ stimulus; (2) Tim's putting the puzzle piece in correctly—called the ________________ behavior; and (3) Tim's getting the piece to go in or his being praised—called the ________________.
(11) Two different technical terms can be used to describe the behavior of Tim's mother when she showed Tim where the puzzle piece went. First, because the behavior demonstrates to Tim where the piece goes, it is called an imitative stimulus. And second, because the mother's behavior is associated with reinforcement for Tim's imitative behavior, the mother's behavior is called a(n) ________________.
(37) If the mother's behavior of showing Tim where to put the piece were not reinforced, it would be on what schedule? ________________ Having Tim put the piece correctly into the puzzle would probably be a(n) ________________ for his mother's behavior.

Example #3

The first time Tom heard someone say "right on," he didn't know what it meant. He heard the phrase a few more times and got the idea that it could mean something like "good idea." Tom then started saying it and found that people listened to him a lot more closely and seemed to approve of him for using this phrase.

(24) The other people that Tom heard saying "right on" were providing Tom with a demonstration

of a new behavior. Their behavior, from Tom's point of view, was a(n) ________________
________________.

(10) When Tom said "right on," this was an example of ________________.

(36) The fact that Tom's friends started listening more closely to him would provide a ________________ for saying "right on."

(23) Tom's learning to say "right on" is an example of what behavioral procedure? ________________ (Did Tom's friends demonstrate the behavior, or did they describe it?)

Example #4

Marcia came to the university from a small rural high school. She didn't know the new clothing styles, and, as a result, she looked "old-fashioned." Even though she was pretty and smart, she wasn't getting any dates. She asked her roommate for help in learning the new styles. Her roommate explained what styles of clothes were "in," how to apply makeup, and how to style her hair. Marcia then bought some new clothes and tried the new makeup styles. Her first try produced quite a change, and her roommate told her how nice she looked. Marcia had succeeded in changing her look to fit the university. After this change she got many dates.

(9) The explanations given to Marcia by her roommate are an example of a(n) ________________
________________.

(35) Marcia's behaviors of buying some new clothes and applying makeup are examples of ________________.

(22) Getting dates would be an example of a ________________ that kept Marcia following her roommate's instructions.

(8) Marcia's roommate may have been reinforced by seeing how successful her instructions were in helping Marcia to get dates. If not, and there were no other reinforcers, then the rate at which the roommate would give instructions to Marcia would probably ________________.

(34) The method of changing Marcia's behavior is called ________________.

(21) On the other hand, if Marcia had copied the clothing and the way that her roommate put on makeup, the method of changing Marcia's behavior would have been called ________________
________________.

Example #5

Mrs. Morris always worked an example of the latest type of math problem on the board before she asked her class to work any problems. By doing this, she taught them how to organize their answer—where to write the different parts of the answer and how much of the answer to show. She then gave the children an assignment of similar problems to work in class. As they worked, she walked around the room and indicated to them whether they were doing the problems correctly.

(42) This method of teaching the children how to organize their answers would be called ________________. (Did she demonstrate or describe how to work the problems?)

(41) The children's behavior is called ________________.

Example #6

Tiny Tim's mother showed him a picture of a robin and asked him "What is that? Is it a bird?" Tim agreed and said "bird" to his mother's obvious delight. She showed him the picture of the robin later and repeated the question but said "bird" much more softly. Tim said "That's a bird." He could still identify the picture as a bird after his mother stopped saying "bird." She then showed him a picture of a bluejay and repeated the same procedure. After she had stopped giving the hint, Tim could still identify the bluejay as a bird. His mother then showed him many other pictures of birds and he always labeled them as birds.

(7) What behavioral procedure did his mother use to teach him the identification of birds? ______________________

Example #7

John had to cut some wood to make a doghouse for his new collie. He asked his father whether he might be permitted to do the cutting with the power saw, and his father agreed. First, however, John's father had to show him how to use the saw. He went to the garage with John and cut the first piece of wood for him. In the process, he demonstrated how to measure the wood, how to set the saw blade at the right height, how to guide the wood through safely, and several other aspects of correct use of the saw. John then cut a piece with his father watching. His father praised John's efforts and left him to cut the rest of the wood.

(33) John's father used what method to train John to use the power saw? ______________________

Example #8

Jan wanted some new clothes for her vacation trip. She asked her mother to show her how to use the sewing machine. Her mother didn't have time to show her but did explain in some detail how to use it. Jan followed her mother's explanation and sewed several articles of clothing for her vacation.

(20) What method is Jan's mother using to change Jan's behavior with respect to the sewing machine? ______________________

(6) Successfully sewing the clothing would probably be the ______________________ for Jan's following her mother's explanation.

(32) The mother's explanation would be called a(n) ______________________.

Example #9

Henry was writing a book. He typed a rough draft of each chapter himself and then gave that copy to a typist to produce a polished copy. However, he found that the polished copy wasn't always perfect. If he left any abbreviations in the copy that he gave the typist, the typist did not complete the abbreviation (as a whole word) but, rather, just copied it. Thus he found that he had to type the entire word if that was the way it was to appear in the final copy. So Henry started typing the entire word and stopped using abbreviations.

(19) Henry's use of abbreviations was ______________________, and his typing full words was ______________________ by getting back a correct final manuscript.

(5) Henry's typing behavior changed in that he started typing whole words and stopped typing abbreviations. What behavioral procedure accounted for this change? ______________________

Example #10

Children often learn cursive writing by seeing examples of the properly formed letters and words. Then the children are required to copy these letters over and over again. The teacher usually praises correct copies.

(31) The examples that the children copy would be called ______________________.

(18) This method of teaching writing would be an example of ______________________.

Example #11

Ada was a little-league baseball coach. To help the children learn to field ground balls, she had them hit balls to her while she demonstrated the essential elements of fielding. These elements included getting her body in front of the ball, kneeling to one knee, keeping her eye on the ball, and so on. Then she hit some balls and had the children try to field them. When they fielded the ball correctly, she praised them.

(4) What method for changing behavior was Ada using? ______________________

Example #12

Ada had a lot of trouble teaching Billy to field the ball. He kept jerking his head up and taking his eye off the ball. Ada hit several balls right to him. When he kept his eye on the ball, she praised him. When he took his eye off the ball, she stopped hitting balls to him for a while. Billy started keeping his head down more and more often.

(30) Ada used what method to teach Billy to keep his eye on the ball? ______________________

Example #13

Sam was the best pitcher on the team, but he tended to take his eye off the catcher's mitt when he was throwing. This behavior often led to his missing the strike zone. So Ada patiently explained to Sam exactly where to look when he was pitching. She then had him throw several pitches while she was watching and praised him when he did it right.

(17) What method of changing Sam's behavior did Ada use? ______________________

Example #14

Gordie was a good hitter, but Ada felt that he could be much better. His main problem was that he swung at bad pitches—pitches that were not thrown over the plate. So Ada got out on the mound and threw several pitches. Sometimes she threw pitches right over the plate, and sometimes she threw bad pitches. She had Gordie stand at the plate and call "strike" for the good ones. She praised him when he called a good pitch a strike and ignored him when he called a bad pitch a strike. She hoped this method would teach him which pitches were worth swinging at.

(3) What method was she using to teach Gordie to call out "strike" correctly? ______________________

Example #15

Tiny Tim's mother often showed him a picture of a sailboat and asked him "What is that?" She praised him when he said "boat." She later showed him a picture of the Queen Mary and asked him what it was. She praised him when he said "boat." Later she showed him pictures of many other boats and he always labeled them as "boats."

(29) What behavioral procedure had she used? ______________________

Example #16

(16) An owl would be called a(n) ______________________ for the behavior of calling it an "owl." However, a chicken would be called a(n) ______________________ for the behavior of calling it an "owl."

Example #17

Mrs. Price praised Gladys for saying "81" when asked "What does 9^2 equal?" but not for saying anything else. She also praised Gladys for saying "49" when asked "What does 7^2 equal?" but not for saying anything else.

(2) What behavioral procedure did Mrs. Price use? ______________________

Example #18

Mrs. Price asked Gladys "What does 8^2 equal?" and permitted her to see a set of eight rows of eight dots. She praised Gladys if she answered "64." Subsequently, Mrs. Price permitted Gladys to look at dots that were harder and harder to see. Eventually Gladys "knew" that 8^2 was 64 even without looking at the dots.

(28) What behavioral procedure did Mrs. Price use to teach Gladys the value of 8^2? __________

Example #19

After Gladys had learned the value of 7^2, 8^2, and 9^2, Mrs. Price asked her "What is 10^2?" Gladys thought a moment, realized that she had simply multiplied 7×7 to get the value of 7^2 and that she had done the same for 8^2 and 9^2, and simply multiplied 10×10 to get 100.

(15) The occurrence of Gladys multiplying the number by itself to find its square for a new number would be an example of what behavioral process? ______________________

Example #20

Turning around while on skis can be a very complicated process unless you know how to do it. Debby showed Felix how to do it. First you take your right ski and kick it in the air right in front of you with the back end dug into the snow. Then you pivot it to the right so that the tip is pointing backwards and you are standing with your right foot pointed backwards. Then you simply bring your left ski around and place it parallel to your right ski and you are turned around. (This is a situation where imitation training is far superior to instructional training, as you now realize!) Felix tried it and was reinforced by turning around easily.

(1) What behavioral procedure did Debby use? ______________________

EXAMPLE ANSWERS

(1) imitation training (2) discrimination training (3) discrimination training (4) imitation training (5) differential reinforcement (6) reinforcer (7) programming (8) decrease (9) verbal description (10) imitative behavior (11) *SD* (12) behavior (13) described (14) description (15) generalization (16) *SD*; *S*-delta (17) instructional training (18) imitation training (19) extinguished; reinforced (20) instructional training (21) imitation training (22) reinforcer (23) imitation training (24) imitative stimulus (25) imitative; imitative; reinforcer (26) stimulus (27) reinforcer (28) fading (29) generalization training (30) differential reinforcement (31) imitative stimuli (32) verbal description (33) imitation training (34) instructional training (35) instructed behavior (36) reinforcer (37) extinction; reinforcer (38) reinforcer (39) verbal; instructed; reinforcement (40) behavior (41) imitative behavior (42) imitation training

Lesson 20

Conditioned Reinforcers and Everyday Situations

When we are born, our behavior is influenced by certain reinforcing events that seem to be rooted in our biological nature. These events, referred to as primary reinforcers, include the delivery of food, water, sex, and reasonable temperatures. The events that serve as primary reinforcers tend to be pretty much the same for everyone.

In addition to primary reinforcers, we learn through our individual experience to react to other, previously unimportant, events as reinforcers. These events, referred to by behavior analysts as conditioned reinforcers (or sometimes secondary reinforcers), might include such events as mother's smile, the opportunity to wear blue jeans, or first prize in a contest. The list of such events varies enormously from individual to individual and society to society. Conditioned reinforcers are important to behavior analysts because many behavioral problems are the result of an absence of appropriate conditioned reinforcers for a particular individual. To solve such problems, the behavior analyst has had to learn how to establish certain events as conditioned reinforcers. This lesson will introduce you to three behavioral procedures designed to create conditioned reinforcers.

First, it is important to understand the behavioral definition of a primary reinforcer. A **primary reinforcer** is any reinforcing event that loses its effectiveness only temporarily through satiation. In other words, a primary reinforcer is any event that is always reinforcing unless someone has had too much of it recently. The effectiveness of such reinforcers is not based on learning, but rather seems to be based on the unlearned biological effects they produce in us.

Conditioned reinforcers. The other major class of reinforcers are those that have arisen through our experience. It is thought that such reinforcers become effective because they have in some manner been paired with other events that are already established reinforcers. If your mother always smiled at you before she gave you milk when you were an infant, then the smile comes to "signal" the delivery of milk. Once this relationship has become established, your behavior will be reinforced by the smile alone. While the necessary and sufficient conditions capable of creating conditioned reinforcers have not been fully established by basic research, it is widely believed that some association between existing reinforcers and a neutral event is a necessary part of the process.

Thus, a **conditioned reinforcer** has been defined as any reinforcing event that will permanently lose its effectiveness if it is presented to an individual unpaired with backup reinforcers. In Lesson 12 you learned about an experiment designed to treat a woman who hoarded towels. It was thought that the towels signaled for her the coming of the attendants to take them back. Since this required some interaction and therefore attention from the attendants, hoarding towels and attention from attendants became paired. If this was the only way that the patient could obtain any attention from the attendants, and anyone understanding the sad conditions that exist in mental hospitals will readily realize that it may have been, then such attention could be quite reinforcing. The effectiveness of the towels was overcome simply by giving the woman all the towels she wanted and no longer coming to pick them up—thereby no longer pairing attention with them. This, then, is a good example of the mechanism underlying the establishment and elimination of events as conditioned reinforcers.

The reinforcer that is paired with a conditioned reinforcer and is therefore responsible for its effectiveness is called a **backup reinforcer** because the person receives it after the conditioned reinforcer. So it "backs up" the conditioned reinforcer and makes it effective. The effectiveness of the towels as conditioned reinforcers depended on being "backed up" by the attention of the attendants.

I should note that the effectiveness of a conditioned reinforcer is affected by the degree of deprivation of the person with respect to the backup reinforcer. It may be that had the attendants given the towel hoarder an ample amount of attention for more constructive behavior, the towels would have been much less effective as reinforcers.

Perhaps the most important point to be made about conditioned reinforcers is that they generally end up being events that occur immediately after the person has made a response and they indicate the later delivery of long-delayed events. Thus, while they are not powerful reinforcers for an individual, they are very effective because of the immediacy of their occurrence. Behavior analysts often create conditioned reinforcers that they can deliver immediately after a behavior to thereby signal long-delayed reinforcers. The advantage of doing so, of course, is that the behavior analysts can then deliver the conditioned reinforcer according to the Principle of Immediacy. A good example occurs when the behavior analyst provides praise immediately after the occurrence of a desired behavior and then later delivers a more valuable backup reinforcer.

Generalized reinforcers. Behavior analysts have extensively explored the creation and use of very powerful reinforcers called "generalized reinforcers." A generalized reinforcer is a specific kind of conditioned reinforcer. A **generalized reinforcer** is any conditioned reinforcer that is paired with many backup reinforcers. Thus, it is a particular kind of conditioned reinforcer, for if it were unpaired with all of those backup reinforcers, it would permanently lose its effectiveness. Money is the most obvious example of a generalized reinforcer. It is associated with any reinforcer that can be purchased. If it could no longer be used to purchase desired items, it would permanently lose its effectiveness. Such a calamity occurred when the money issued by the Southern Confederacy lost its value after the Civil War.

Generalized reinforcers are particularly effective because it is very unlikely that a person will become satiated with respect to all of the backup reinforcers at the same time. Although you might buy food and become satiated on food, you are likely to still be interested in a drink, the movies, or a new car. Thus, while any primary reinforcer or any conditioned reinforcer associated with only one other reinforcer may frequently become ineffective due to satiation, generalized reinforcers are likely to be effective virtually continuously. It is hard to get too much money!!

A more subtle example of a generalized reinforcer is social approval. If someone approves of you, you can expect a wide variety of favors from that person. These might include sexual favors, loans of money, invitations to parties, and general assistance. Because social approval can be associated with so many other reinforcers, it fits the definition of a generalized reinforcer.

As with other conditioned reinforcers, an advantage of generalized reinforcers is that they can be delivered immediately after the behavior occurs. The various backup reinforcers could not readily be delivered immediately. Therefore, the generalized reinforcer can enhance the effectiveness of the backup reinforcers by utilizing the Principle of Immediacy.

Token systems and point systems backed up by many reinforcers are increasingly being used by behavior modifiers. Such a token system may be viewed as a local monetary system. An actual object or "token" is given to a person performing desirable behaviors. These tokens can then be exchanged at a fixed rate for other reinforcers. This system has been used to assist chronic mental patients in learning self-care and productive work behaviors (Ayllon & Azrin, 1965). It has been used in settings such as institutions for retarded children (Birnbrauer, Bijou, Wolf, & Kidder, 1965), Head Start programs (Miller & Schneider, 1970), and self-help groups for poor people (Miller & Miller, 1970).

A POINT SYSTEM 1787 STYLE

Alexander Maconochie, born in 1787, was a captain in the Royal Navy of England and a noted geographer. He was appointed to run one of the worst British penal colonies, located on Norfolk Island, 1000 miles from Australia. The prisoners were two-time losers who had committed crimes in both England and Australia.

Maconochie installed a point system by which each prisoner was debited, based on the seriousness of his crime. The notion was that each person redeemed himself through appropriate task and social behaviors. As Maconochie put it: "When a man keeps the key of his own prison, he is soon persuaded to fit it into the lock."

Unfortunately, Maconochie knew naught of baselines but, in the spirit of that important measure, may be judged by his well-founded remark: "I found Norfolk Island a hell but left it an orderly and well regulated community."

In the equally well-founded spirit of keeping things the way they are, Maconochie's superiors were distrubed by his lack of orthodoxy and openly repudiated his successes. Maconochie was soon recalled to England.

From "Behavior Modification—1978," by C. Pitts, *Journal of Applied Behavior Analysis*, 1976, 9, 147–152.

Point systems are like a credit-card economy. No actual token or object changes hands, but someone records points earned and spent and maintains a running balance for each person. Point systems have been used in a variety of settings, such as Achievement Place, a family-style alternative to reform school for delinquent youths (Phillips, 1968). Figure 20–1 outlines the point system used by Achievement Place. Youths who watched the news on TV (300 points), read 20 pages of a book (200 points), and did their homework (500 points) would earn a privilege, such as permission to come home late from school (1000 points). Numerous experiments have shown that this system encourages a wide range of constructive behaviors among a group of youth generally lacking in such behaviors. They did better in school, stayed out of trouble and got jobs that led to a constructive and law-abiding role in the community (for example, Fixsen, Phillips, Phillips, & Wolf, 1976).

These systems of generalized reinforcers have become an extremely powerful tool for producing behavioral change. The tokens or points maintain their effectiveness as reinforcers due to their association with a wide range of other reinforcers. They are simple to use with large numbers of individuals. And they can accommodate enough different events to ensure that almost everyone in the group will be deprived of some potential reinforcer associated with the points or tokens.

An increasing number of groups are using a system of generalized reinforcement to develop a structure to their social environment. Instead of allowing outside influences to dictate what is desired behavior, these groups are learning to use this tool to develop behavior that they themselves define as desirable. Thus, we are seeing the emergence of democratically controlled systems of reinforcement. For example, welfare recipients have used systems of generalized reinforcement to get people to come to meetings, to teach other recipients how to get help from the Welfare Department (Miller & Miller, 1970), and to start various self-help projects such as a co-op food store. And students have used this approach to build communal living arrangements that really work. Points are used to encourage members of the commune to clean the house, to prepare food, to learn more about the operation of the house, and even to learn behavior-modification techniques so that they can more effectively design a pleasant commune (Miller & Feallock, 1974).

Stimulus/response chains. Up to this point, we have restricted our attention to situations in which only one response is analyzed. But most of our behavior is far more complex than that. We usually make many related responses in some kind of sequence. We don't take just one step; we walk somewhere. We don't say just one word; we ask questions, make speeches, and engage in conversations. And we don't just hit a baseball; we hit the ball, run toward first base, watch where the ball went, and maybe try for second base. Thus, in most situations we don't engage in just one response over and over again; we engage in a series of responses, each one of which is influenced by the prior response.

Sequences of related responses are called "stimulus/response chains" (often shortened to just

Privileges for the Week	*Price in Points*
Allowance	1000
Bicycle	1000
TV	1000
Games	500
Tools	500
Snacks	1000
Permission to go downtown	1000
Permission to stay up past bedtime	1000
Permission to come home late after school	1000

	Behaviors That Earned Points	*Points*
1.	Watching news on TV or reading the newspaper	300 per day
2.	Cleaning and maintaining neatness in one's room	500 per day
3.	Keeping one's person neat and clean	500 per day
4.	Reading books	5 to 10 per page
5.	Aiding house-parents in various household tasks	20 to 1000 per task
6.	Doing dishes	500 to 1000 per meal
7.	Being well dressed for an evening meal	100 to 500 per meal
8.	Performing homework	500 per day
9.	Obtaining desirable grades on school report cards	500 to 1000 per grade
10.	Turning out lights when not in use	25 per light

Figure 20–1. Privileges that could be earned each week are listed in the top part of the figure, and behaviors and the number of points they earned in the botton. These two tables summarize part of the point system at Achievement Place, a family-style rehabilitation center for predelinquent youths at the University of Kansas. A judge assigns youths to Achievement Place instead of sending them to a reform school. As an example of how the system works, if a boy cleans his room (2), he earns 500 points; if he also grooms himself (3), he earns another 500 points. With this 1000 points, he can buy an allowance, bicycle privileges for a week, or other items on the list. Extensive research has shown that this program improves each boy's social skills, school achievement, and lawful behavior at a much higher rate than reform school. Because the points can be exchanged for a variety of backup reinforcers (listed in the table), the points are considered generalized reinforcers. Adapted from "Achievement Place: Token Reinforcement Procedures in a Home-Style Rehabilitation Setting for 'Pre-Delinquent' Boys," by E. L. Phillips, *Journal of Applied Behavior Analysis*, 1968, *1*, 213–224. Copyright 1968 by the Society for the Experimental Analysis of Behavior, Inc. Used by permission.

"chains"). A **stimulus/response chain** is a sequence of two or more responses in which the last response leads to a reinforcer, and in which the result of each prior response produces a discriminative stimulus (*SD*) for the following response. Suppose that a person is solving arith- If he writes "2 + 2," those numbers serve as an *SD* for the response of "4." If someone sings "Oh say can you . . . ," these words serve as an S^D for the final word "see." Often, if a chain of many responses, such as *The Star-Spangled Banner*, is reduced to just one of the responses in the middle, that word will no longer serve as an S^D. For example, do you immediately know what word comes right after "early" in *The Star-Spangled Banner*? (Most people have to go back and start from the beginning.) In fact, virtually all verbal behavior consists of long chains of individual responses. Many other types of behavior are chains also. For example, walking is a chain of individual steps with the result of getting to one place serving as a discriminative stimulus for the next step or set of steps.

One feature of the chain is that each response (except the last one) produces an effect on the environment that acts as a conditioned reinforcer for that response as well as a discriminative stimulus for the next response. Each of these responses enables the person to move closer to the final response that produces the reinforcer, and thus each response is reinforced by its increasing nearness to the goal. For example, opening a refrigerator, taking out some milk, filling a glass, and drinking constitute a four-response chain. The last response in the chain, drinking, is obviously reinforced by consumption of the milk. However, drinking the milk can't be done unless the milk is in the glass. Therefore the full milk glass is a discriminative stimulus for drinking as well as a conditioned reinforcer for the filling response, because it brings you a step closer to drinking the milk.

BEHAVIOR ANALYSIS EXAMPLES

Modifying teacher behavior. Students and teachers often have a clash of personalities that interferes in the educational process. A study by Polirstok and Greer (1977) deals with an eighth-grade student, who was regarded as a discipline problem, and a teacher of Spanish. The teacher had an M.A. degree and 15 years of experience. The student came from a poor family; she was referred to the administration for disciplinary action at a mean rate of five times per week. She was also referred for more serious offenses on an average of twice a month. Her achievement level was about a year behind her grade placement.

The experimenters decided to teach Jean to show appropriate approval of the teacher's desirable behaviors in an attempt to increase those teacher behaviors. This was done by having Jean decide what were desirable teacher behaviors and then role play showing approval of them. Jean was then given a tape player that frequently cued her to show approval. And the experimenters gave her tokens each day after class based on how many approvals she gave out. The tokens could be traded in for popular music tapes, extra gym, lunch with a favorite teacher, and extra English credit.

Figure 20–2 shows the results. Prior to the use of tokens, Jean averaged about 6 approvals per class. After tokens were introduced, Jean averaged 13 approvals per class. When tokens were no longer given out, Jean's rate of approval fell to a little more than 8 per day. When tokens were again awarded, Jean averaged 13 approvals per class once again.

The experimenters also taught Jean to withhold a disapproval of the Spanish teacher. Her rate of disapproval did decrease. At the same time, the Spanish teacher's behavior also changed radically: she showed more approval and less disapproval of Jean. This same procedure was used on three other teachers with similar results. After the experiment, Jean often commented on how nice her teachers had become. Her teachers indicated that they were pleased with her remarkable socialization and newfound maturity. She was referred for discipline only once after the experiment. The experimenters interpreted these results as indicating that a mutually unpleasant interaction pattern had been broken and turned into a mutually pleasant one, which then sustained Jean's behavioral change even after the experiment was over. (This final phase is not shown on the graph.)

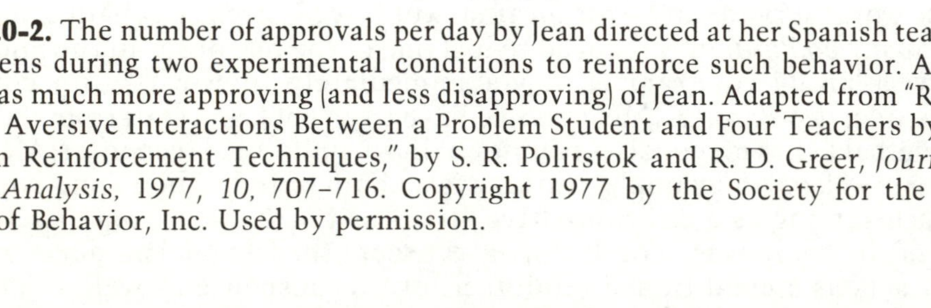

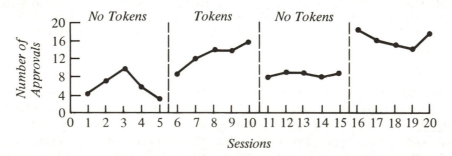

Figure 20-2. The number of approvals per day by Jean directed at her Spanish teacher. Jean was given tokens during two experimental conditions to reinforce such behavior. As a result, the teacher was much more approving (and less disapproving) of Jean. Adapted from "Remediation of Mutually Aversive Interactions Between a Problem Student and Four Teachers by Training the Student in Reinforcement Techniques," by S. R. Polirstok and R. D. Greer, *Journal of Applied Behavior Analysis,* 1977, *10,* 707–716. Copyright 1977 by the Society for the Experimental Analysis of Behavior, Inc. Used by permission.

A token economy for self-control. Whitman and Dussault (1976) reported the use of a token economy by a student whom we shall call James to control his own behavior. James was a 21-year-old undergraduate who had trouble organizing his time. He had a part-time job, a full class load, and a girlfriend. He had begun spending more time on his job and with his girlfriend at the expense of school. This led him to feel "guilty and depressed." He had lost 20 pounds in a period of 6 months and his personal habits, such as bathing, were deteriorating.

Whitman and Dussault suggested that James organize his behavior by setting up a token system that he would apply to his own behavior. The result was that he specified a large number of behaviors and assigned them points depending on how important they were. Thus, studying for one of his courses at least 4 to 6 hours a week would earn 20 points class attendance for all courses would earn 20 points, writing home would earn 20 points, washing dishes once a day 5 points, washing hair once a week 10 points and so on. Visiting his girlfriend would cost him 25 points per day, watching TV 10 points, walking for pleasure 5 points, and so on. James was to record all points as he earned them. He agreed not to obtain any reinforcers unless he had previously earned sufficient points to afford them.

As you can see from Figure 20–3, James achieved about 30% of his goals during a baseline period of observation. However, once the token system was introduced, he steadily improved until he was achieving about 70% of his goals. A reversal to baseline and subsequent reversal to the token economy confirmed the impact of the token economy on his behavior.

The data suggest that James found it useful to formulate his personal targets in terms of how many points he should earn for achieving them and to formulate his reinforcing activities in terms of how much they were worth to him. He could then keep records that permitted him to more judiciously balance these two aspects of his life.

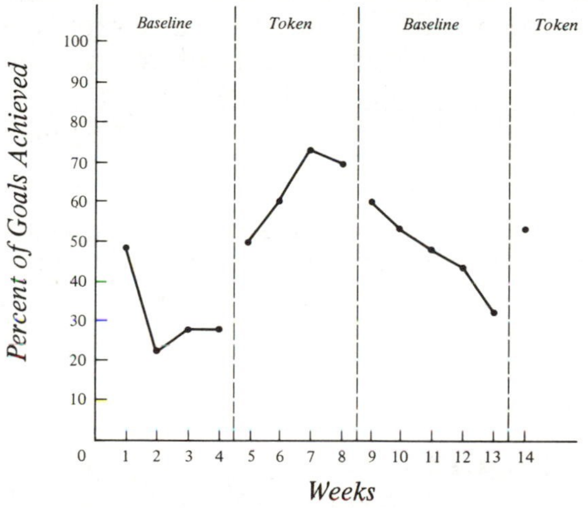

Figure 20–3. The percent of goals earned by a student having trouble maintaining studying, class attendance, and personal cleanliness. He used a token system to balance these goals with seeing his girlfriend and other reinforcing activities. From "Self Control Through the Use of a Token Economy," by T. L. Whitman and P. Dussault, *Journal of Behavior Therapy and Experimental Psychiatry*, 1976, 7, 161–166. Copyright 1976, Pergamon Press, Ltd. Reprinted by permission.

Note #1: Token economies have sometimes been criticized because they do not always lead to permanent behavioral change; that is, the behavioral change does not generalize to other situations or even the same situation without the tokens (Levine & Fasnacht, 1974). This, of course, is built into the very concept of reinforcement of any kind. If you stop reinforcing a behavior, and there is no other source of reinforcement, the behavior will eventually disappear. If the use of a token economy produces a desired behavior, and the natural environment provides enough reinforcement to maintain it (even though it might not have produced enough to create it in the first place), then we would not expect the removal of a token system to stop the behavior. If the natural environment does not provide such reinforcement, then it must be redesigned. A token economy would be a simple and effective procedure to implement on a permanent basis in that "natural" environment.

Note #2: Stopping the delivery of the backup reinforcer while continuing the delivery of the conditioned reinforcer is not an example of extinction. Stopping the delivery of both the backup and the conditioned reinforcer is an example of extinction.

ADDITIONAL READINGS

Ayllon, T., & Azrin, N. H. The measurement and reinforcement of behavior of psychotics. *Journal of the Experimental Analysis of Behavior*, 1965, 8, 357–383. This classic article reports a series of experiments evaluating the effectiveness of a token system to develop and maintain self-care and self-help behaviors among chronic psychotics.

Ayllon, T., & Azrin, N. H. *The token economy.* New York: Appleton-Century Crofts, 1968. This book was designed as a token-economies handbook. It contains a great deal of practical information on how to select and define target behaviors, how to select reinforcers, and many other important aspects of designing and using a token economy.

Kelleher, R. T., & Gollub, L. R. A review of positive conditioned reinforcement. *Journal of the Experimental Analysis of Behavior*, 1962, 5, 543. This article is a highly technical review of the concept of conditioned reinforcement. It discusses many of the theories about the conditions necessary to make an event into a conditioned reinforcer.

Helpful hint #1: Students sometimes confuse "generalization" and "generalized reinforcer." Remember that the occurrence of a behavior in a novel situation is called "generalization," but a reinforcer that is paired with <u>many</u> other reinforcers is called a "generalized reinforcer." Be sure to carefully distinguish between these two concepts.

Helpful hint #2: Students sometimes fail to distinguish properly between a conditioned reinforcer and a generalized reinforcer. When you are asked a question concerning one of these concepts, be sure to answer with the most specific answer. If you are asked the name of a reinforcer that is paired with <u>many</u> other reinforcers, don't call it a "conditioned reinforcer"—tell us what kind of conditioned reinforcer. If you are asked the name of a reinforcer that is paired with only <u>one</u> other reinforcer, or if the example <u>does not specify</u> that it is paired with many reinforcers, then you should answer "conditioned reinforcer." Your answers will be considered wrong if you answer in any other way.

Helpful hint #3: You should keep in mind that tokens and points are not necessarily generalized reinforcers. They are generalized reinforcers only if they are paired with many backup reinforcers. If they are paired with only one backup reinforcer, then they would be simple conditioned reinforcers.

LESSON 20 READING QUIZ

(33) A primary reinforcer is a reinforcing event that loses its effectiveness only temporarily through ______________________________ .

(22) Some reinforcers gain their effectiveness by being <u>paired</u> with other established reinforcers. The name for <u>all</u> such reinforcers is ______________________________ .

(11) A conditioned reinforcer is any reinforcer that loses its effectiveness permanently if it is presented ______________________________ with backup reinforcers.

(32) For example, the towels were no longer hoarded by the woman in the Ayllon and Michael (1959) study when they were no longer paired with ______________________________ from the attendants.

(21) A reinforcer that is paired with a conditioned reinforcer to make it effective is called a(n) ______________________________ reinforcer.

(10) It should be noted that a conditioned reinforcer will no longer be effective if a person is ______________________________ with respect to its backup reinforcer.

(31) An important advantage of conditioned reinforcers, particularly for behavior analysts, is that they can readily be delivered according to the Principle of ______________________________ and thereby increase reinforcer effectiveness.

(20) A generalized reinforcer is a reinforcer that is associated with ______________________________ backup reinforcers.

(9) A reinforcer that is paired with either a conditioned reinforcer or a generalized reinforcer is called a(n) ______________________________ .

(30) A generalized reinforcer is one type of conditioned reinforcer because it would lose its effectiveness if it were presented to a person ______________ with all of its backup reinforcers.

(19) What is the most obvious example of a generalized reinforcer? ______________

(8) One reason that a generalized reinforcer is so effective is that the person is likely to be ______________ with respect to at least one of the backup reinforcers.

(29) Which of the following reinforcers are most likely at any time to be effective (primary, conditioned, generalized)? ______________

(18) Since social approval is paired with many other reinforcers, it should be considered a(n) ______________ reinforcer.

(7) Generalized reinforcers can enhance the effectiveness of the backup reinforcers by utilizing the Principle of ______________ .

(28) Behavior analysts frequently use "token systems" or "point systems" to reinforce desired behaviors. What type of reinforcer are they? ______________

(17) One of the most successful point systems is used in Achievement Place. This program is designed to help what kind of people become more constructive citizens? ______________

(6) Groups of poor people and students have created democratically controlled systems of reinforcement. What type of reinforcer do these groups use? ______________

(27) A stimulus/response chain is defined as a <u>sequence</u> of two or more responses in which the last response leads to ______________ and each prior response serves as a(n) ______________ for the following response.

(16) The recitation of *The Star-Spangled Banner* without looking at the words would technically be called a(n) ______________ .

(5) One feature of the stimulus/response chain is that each behavior produces an effect on the environment that acts as a conditioned reinforcer for that behavior and also as a(n) ______________ for the next behavior.

(26) Suppose that a particular behavior has been increased in one situation through the use of token reinforcement. If that behavior is not reinforced by tokens (or any natural reinforcers) in another situation, what schedule of reinforcement would it be on? ______________ What is the likely effect on the rate of that behavior? ______________

(15) It is not an example of "extinction" if you stop the delivery of a backup reinforcer but ______________ (do, do not) stop the delivery of the conditioned reinforcer.

(4) Whitman and Dussault (1976) helped James set up a point system in which he earned points by such behaviors as studying and attending class, and he spent them on such activities as visiting his girlfriend and watching TV. Visiting his girlfriend and watching TV would be considered ______________ reinforcers for the points.

(25) Polirstok and Greer (1977) gave Jean a token for each approval she directed at her teachers. The tokens could be exchanged for music tapes, extra gym, lunch with a favorite teacher, or extra credit in English. These tokens would be considered to be ______________ reinforcers.

(14) A reinforcer paired with one backup reinforcer is called a(n) ______________ reinforcer.

(3) A sequence of responses that leads to reinforcement and in which each prior response is a discriminative stimulus for the following response is called a(n) ______________ .

(24) A reinforcer that loses its effectiveness only temporarily through satiation is called a(n) ______________ reinforcer.

(13) A reinforcer that is associated with many other reinforcers is called a(n) ______________ reinforcer.

(2) A reinforcer that is paired with a conditioned reinforcer and that is responsible for the conditioned reinforcer's effectiveness is called a(n) ______________ reinforcer.

(23) A reinforcer that is paired with many backup reinforcers is the specific type of conditioned reinforcer called a generalized reinforcer. If you were asked to label it, the correct label would be ______________.

(12) Would it be correct to refer to a reinforcer that is paired with many backup reinforcers as a "generalization"? __________ What is the correct label for it? ______________

(1) If a token is backed up only by M & M's, then it would be called a(n) ______________ reinforcer.

READING QUIZ ANSWERS

(1) conditioned (2) backup (3) stimulus/response chain (4) backup (5) S^D (6) generalized (7) Immediacy (8) deprived (9) backup (reinforcer) (10) satiated (11) unpaired (12) no; generalized reinforcer (13) generalized (14) conditioned (15) do not (16) stimulus/response chain (17) delinquents (18) generalized (19) money (20) many (21) backup (22) conditioned reinforcers (23) generalized reinforcer (24) primary (25) generalized (26) extinction; decrease (27) reinforcement; S^D (28) generalized (29) generalized (30) unpaired (31) Immediacy (32) attention (33) satiation

LESSON 20 EXAMPLES

Example #1

When Harry did something pleasant for the family, his father awarded him Reinforcer A. Harry could trade in Reinforcer A for cookies later on. If Reinforcer A is unpaired with cookies, it permanently loses its effectiveness (until again paired with cookies).

(15) Since Reinforcer A loses its effectiveness permanently when unpaired with cookies, it is called a(n) ______________ reinforcer.

(42) The cookies are called ______________ reinforcers for Reinforcer A.

(28) You should be aware that the effectiveness of Reinforcer A would also temporarily decrease if Harry were to eat many cookies and become ______________ with them.

(14) An advantage of Reinforcer A over cookies may be that it can be delivered more quickly after a pleasant behavior than could a cookie (think of "thank you"). Thus, it may have a more powerful effect on pleasant behaviors due to the Principle of ______________ .

Example #2

When Harry read the daily news or read a good book, his father delivered Reinforcer B, which could be traded in by Harry for a trip to the movies, allowance, a late night snack, or a game of Frisbee with his father.

(41) Since Reinforcer B is paired with a trip to the movies, allowance, a late snack, or a game of Frisbee, it is called a(n) ______________ reinforcer.

(27) Such events as a trip to the movies or a game of Frisbee are both called ______________ reinforcers for Reinforcer B.

(13) One advantage of Reinforcer B is that Harry is likely at any given time to be ______________ of at least one of its backup reinforcers.

(40) Another advantage of Reinforcer B is that it can more readily than its backup reinforcers take

advantage of the Principle of ________________ by being given to Harry during or right after he has done some reading.

Example #3

When Harry did household chores, his father gave him Reinforcer C. Reinforcer C was always an effective reinforcer for Harry except temporarily when he got too much of it.

(26) Since Reinforcer C lost its effectiveness only when Harry got too much of it, it is called a(n) ________________ reinforcer.

Example #4

Marla was being taught to cube the number 3. She was given two cards with stimuli on them. The first card had $3 \times 3 = A$ written on it and the second card $A \times 3 = B$. Marla's job was to write down the values of A and B. She immediately saw that she couldn't determine the value of B until she knew the value of A, so she wrote on the first card "$A = 9$." Then she rewrote the second card with the value of A filled in to get a new second card: $9 \times 3 = B$. Finally, she wrote "$B = 27$"—that is, "$3^3 = 27$."

(12) The first response would consist of Marla's writing "________________;" however, this response also creates the written product "9," which is a stimulus.

(39) When Marla wrote a "9" in place of the A on the second card, she ended up with the stimulus "$9 \times 3 = B$." This stimulus would be called a(n) ________________" for the response of "$B = 27$."

(25) When the teacher praised Marla for writing "$B = 27$," she probably ________________ Marla's response.

(11) This example involves a sequence of two responses, in which the outcome of the first response served as a reinforcer for that response and an S^D for the second response. Then the teacher reinforced the last response by praise. Therefore, Marla's responses to solving the problem are an example of what behavioral concept? ________________

Example #5

Bobby was a messy little boy. He was a menace to the preschool because he always left his toys strewn around after he was through playing with them. They got in other people's way, caused accidents, and resulted in the teachers' having to do more work. As a result, the teachers got together to figure out how to teach Bobby to pick up his toys and to put them away after playing with them. They decided to give him a poker chip each time he picked up a toy after playing with it. The poker chip would then be used by Bobby to get a snack, to have a teacher tell him a story, or to permit him to go for a long walk outside. Bobby learned to pick up his toys within a week. The poker chips seemed to always be reinforcing to Bobby.

(38) The poker chip was effective because it could be exchanged for many other events called "________________" reinforcers, such as snacks, stories, and walks.

(24) The poker chip is a particular kind of conditioned reinforcer called a(n) ________________ reinforcer, because it is associated with many other reinforcers.

(10) The poker chip is likely to be an effective reinforcer most of the time because Bobby will probably be in a state of ________________ with respect to at least one of the reinforcers that it is associated with.

(37) The poker chips would probably lose their effectiveness if they were presented to Bobby ________________ with the backup reinforcers.

(23) If the poker chips were backed up with only long walks, then the poker chips would be called ________________ reinforcers.

Example #6

Ten-year-old Sarah was a big eater. She always ate at a rapid rate for the first 10 minutes of a meal. Then she would relax, as though she knew she would get enough to eat that night, and finish the meal slowly.

(9) As Sarah ate a meal, she gradually stopped making eating responses. This decrease in response rate occurred because she had become ______________________ with respect to food.

(36) Because food lost its reinforcing ability only temporarily through satiation and always regained the effectiveness that it lost, food would be classified as a(n) ______________ reinforcer.

Example #7

Carey was having trouble in school. She had not learned to read at the fourth-grade level during the regular school year. To avoid her having to repeat the grade, her parents had volunteered to get her to finish three books in the *Sullivan Reading Series* during the summer.

Like any other 9-year-old girl, Carey wasn't too interested in reading, especially during summer vacation. So her parents arranged to give Carey one point for each page she completed (by filling in the four answers on that page). Carey was told that she could exchange ten points for an ice cream cone.

Carey read about five pages a day in her reading book. This accomplishment meant that she got an ice cream cone an average of once every other day.

(22) If Carey's parents stopped giving her points (and therefore ice cream) for her work, Carey might stop reading. If she did, the decrease in her reading rate would be the result of what behavioral procedure? ______________________

(8) If her parents continued to give her points but no longer allowed her to exchange them for ice cream, her rate of reading would decrease as the points became ineffective. They would become ineffective because of not being ______________________ with ice cream.

(35) If her parents gave Carey so many points that she could have ten ice creams a day, her reading might decrease because she would become ______________________ on the backup of ice cream.

(21) The points would be an example of what type of reinforcer? ______________

(7) If her parents allowed Carey to exchange the points for ice cream, a ride, watching TV, or visiting a friend, then the points would be an example of what type of reinforcer? ______________________

Example #8

Sociology 71 was a unique course. Instead of working for a grade, the students earned "credits" by reading materials for the course. The credits could be exchanged for a variety of learning experiences, including movies, guest speakers, discussions, field trips, parties, and special meetings with the instructor. It was found that 50% of the students earned enough credits to "buy" several learning experiences.

(34) The events, such as movies, guest speakers, and discussions, back up the credits and make them effective. Therefore, they are called ______________________ reinforcers.

(20) The "credits" are called ______________________ reinforcers.

Example #9

Kim decided to hike along the railroad track to the old abandoned station 5 miles away. She thought that she might find interesting old artifacts at the station, and it seemed like an interesting way to spend a slow summer day.

To keep track of her progress, she wore a pedometer, which measured the distance she walked. Walking (by itself) usually isn't too reinforcing; however, walking to go somewhere interesting can be reinforcing. In this case, the pedometer measured the rate at which Kim was walking somewhere interesting.

(6) Clicks of the pedometer might have been an effective reinforcer, because they indicated to Kim that she was getting closer to the abandoned station. Thus "getting to the abandoned station" would be a(n) ______________________ reinforcer for the pedometer clicks.

(33) The pedometer clicks would be an example of what type of reinforcer? ____________

Example #10

Grades for a course are usually given long after the student's work. Even grades on test and term papers are usually given days after the actual writing. One way to help overcome this long delay is to develop conditioned reinforcers that occur immediately after the behavior; for example, getting correct answers on a "self-quiz" over material that students have just finished studying may be such a conditioned reinforcer (if they can easily answer all of the questions).

(19) Correct answers to a self-quiz would probably be only mildly reinforcing by itself. However, if it is used as the basis for a class quiz later, the grade on the class quiz will be paired with the results of the self-quiz. In this case, it is likely that the results of the self-quiz could be classified as a(n) ______________________ reinforcer.

(5) If the grade on the class quiz is the backup reinforcer, it is likely that such a weak conditioned reinforcer as the result of a self-quiz is effective because it occurs ______________ ________ after the study behavior.

Example #11

Willie's mother, Fay, encouraged Willie to do at least one thoughtful act a day. When she noticed him doing something particularly thoughtful, she would immediately say "thank you" and, as soon as possible, give him an M & M. Willie did many thoughtful things each day with this kind of reinforcement. One week, however, disaster struck. The grocery store was out of M & M's and there were no more at home. Fay decided to continue reinforcing by saying "thank you." She noticed that Willie gradually did fewer and fewer thoughtful things around the house so that by the end of a week he was doing almost none.

(32) Because the M & M is paired with the "thank you," the M & M is called a(n) ________ reinforcer.

(18) The effectiveness of the "thank you" decreased due to the fact that it was presented ______________________ with the M & M's.

(4) Therefore, the "thank you" is considered to be a(n) ______________________ reinforcer.

Example #12

John found that if he talked about politics when he was with Mary she would get involved in a conversation with him, but if he talked about politics with Carol she ignored him. Pretty soon he talked about politics a lot when he was with Mary but not at all when he was with Carol.

(31) What behavioral procedure did Mary and Carol unwittingly use to affect when John talked politics? ______________________

Example #13

Martin wore a wrist counter to count the number of times he said something positive to someone. On any day that he counted at least 15 positive statements, he permitted himself to have a beer with dinner.

(17) The counts on the counter would probably be a(n) ____________________;
the beer would be a(n) ____________________.

Example #14

Berry's teacher asked him to complete the sentence "Any event that follows a response and increases the future probability of that response is called what?"

(3) If the teacher praised Berry for his answer, this sentence would technically be called a(n) ____________________ for the response "reinforcer."

Example #15

When a person has been trained to make a response in the presence of one stimulus and not in the presence of another stimulus, he or she will sometimes emit that same response in the presence of a novel stimulus.

(30) This is called ____________________.

Example #16

Claire wanted to learn to study every afternoon after getting home from high school from 4 to 6. So she made a giant sign for her room that said "If you study from 4 to 6, you can take a bike ride." She left it up until she was studying every day from 4 to 6. Then she made a smaller sign for her desk saying the same thing. When she found that she was still studying from 4 to 6 she took all signs away and found that she studied every day from 4 to 6.

(43) What behavioral method was involved in the use of the signs and their gradual elimination?
____

Example #17

It took a long time for Ed to learn how to shift smoothly. He learned to take his foot off the accelerator at the same time that he pushed the clutch in, then to move the lever from one gear position to the next, and finally to let the clutch out as he again depressed the accelerator.

(2) What is the name of the set of behaviors that he learned? ____________________

Example #18

For every 15 minutes of chores, Calvin was given one point by his mother. At the end of the week, Calvin could turn the points in for allowance at the rate of 25¢ per point.

(29) What type of reinforcer are the points? ____________________ (Check!)

Example #19

If a chronic stutterer were reinforced by his best friend for saying complete words and sentences without stuttering, his "cure" might carry over to other friends and acquaintances.

(16) We would say that his nonstuttering behavior with his best friend ____________________
to situations with other people present.

Example #20

Flora was careful to always thank anyone who did her a favor. Unlike many people, however, she was extremely careful to ultimately back her thank you with a return favor.

(1) Therefore we would refer to her "Thank you" as what kind of a reinforcer? ______________

EXAMPLE ANSWERS

(1) conditioned (or generalized) (2) stimulus/response chain (3) S^D (4) conditioned (5) immediately (6) backup (7) generalized (8) paired (9) satiated (10) deprivation (11) stimulus/response chain (12) 9 (13) deprived (14) Immediacy (15) conditioned (16) generalized (17) conditioned reinforcer; backup (18) unpaired (19) conditioned (20) generalized (21) conditioned (22) extinction (23) conditioned (24) generalized (25) reinforced (26) primary (27) backup (28) satiated (29) conditioned (30) generalization (31) discrimination training (32) backup (33) conditioned (34) backup (35) satiated (36) primary (37) unpaired (38) backup (39) S^D (40) Immediacy (41) generalized (42) backup (43) fading

Lesson 21

Review of Stimulus Control

This unit has introduced a variety of ways in which stimulus situations can influence a person's behavior. Such influence is frequently related to the most complex forms of human behavior—language, intellectual behavior, long sequences of behavior, and innovative behavior.

Discrimination training is the basic behavioral process that produces such influence of stimulus situations on behavior. Discrimination training occurs everywhere we turn. We are reinforced for a behavior by the individuals in one situation and extinguished for the same behavior by the individuals in another situation. The most important aspect of these situations is the individuals in them; they become S^Ds for those behaviors that they consistently reinforce and *S*-deltas for those behaviors that they extinguish.

Frequently, discrimination training is continued until we generalize to whole classes of situations. At this point, we begin to form concepts, probably the most fundamental intellectual process. Most fields of learning are identified by their concepts; all language is based on concepts, and even basic behavior observations are based on concepts. Thus, the systematic use of behavioral procedures to produce concept formation may well become one of the most important areas for behavioral research in the future. An understanding of how "ideas" are created and taught would be of immense importance to society.

The advent of fading and programming procedures makes it possible to teach discrimination and generalization quickly and with few errors. These procedures (such as programmed instruction) have already been used effectively not only to teach children in normal educational settings but to teach children with behavioral and cultural deficits. There is hope that the systematic use of these procedures will improve the educational attainment of most Americans.

Imitation training and instructional training are also important tools for behavioral change, once they are properly understood. For example, teaching severely retarded children how to imitate other people (Baer, Peterson, & Sherman, 1967) makes it possible for those children to learn new behaviors much more easily. In fact, imitation training is a basic step in teaching these children the necessary behaviors to survive in a normal environment. Similarly, teaching oppositional children (Baer, Rowbury, & Baer, 1973) and adult schizophrenics (Ayllon & Azrin, 1965) to follow verbal instructions is a crucial step toward helping these individuals operate in a normal environment. Although there are undoubtedly many other skills that such individuals need in order to function in a reasonably normal manner, being able to imitate the behavior of another individual and being able to follow verbal instructions are certainly of great importance.

Finally, a better understanding of conditioned reinforcers and generalized reinforcers permits the behavior analyst to use reinforcement more readily and more conveniently. Most of our everyday behaviors are not immediately reinforced with primary reinforcers. Rather, we learn to respond to the immediate consequences of our behavior that are associated with delayed (often long-delayed) primary reinforcement. A major activity of behavior analysts is to use the principles of conditioned reinforcement and generalized reinforcement to ensure that immediate consequences support those behaviors that lead to long-delayed reinforcers that we might not otherwise obtain.

GLOSSARY

Helpful hint: The definitions of all terms introduced in this unit of the book are presented below. You can review the unit and prepare for your exam by testing yourself on the definitions and correlated facts presented for each term. You might use a piece of paper as a mask and leave only the term exposed; see if you can formulate a reasonable definition and any other facts about that term. Then move the mask and check on yourself.

A **backup reinforcer** is any reinforcing event that makes a conditioned reinforcer or a generalized reinforcer effective. When a person obtains a conditioned or generalized reinforcer, he or she can exchange it for other reinforcers. These reinforcers are called backups.

Chain is the most commonly used term for "stimulus/response chain."

A **conditioned reinforcer** is any reinforcing event that loses its effectiveness permanently through unpaired presentations (that is, the presentation of the event without its being associated with any other reinforcers). It is generally assumed that conditioned reinforcers are caused by a previously nonreinforcing event being frequently paired with a reinforcing event (perhaps as a discriminative stimulus) until that stimulus becomes a reinforcer itself.

Discriminated behavior is a behavior that is more likely to occur in the presence of the S^D than in the presence of the *S*-delta in a discrimination-training procedure.

Discrimination training is the procedure in which a behavior is reinforced in the presence of one stimulus and extinguished in the presence of another stimulus. It is also used to label more complex situations where one behavior is reinforced in stimulus A and extinguished in stimulus B and where another behavior is extinguished in stimulus A and reinforced in stimulus B.

Fading is the procedure by which an added stimulus (prompt) is gradually withdrawn. Fading is used to help establish a simple discrimination.

Generalization is the occurrence of a behavior in the presence of a novel stimulus. Usually the novel stimulus is similar to the S^D in a discrimination-training procedure.

Generalization training is the reinforcement of a behavior in a series of stimulus situations until it generalizes to other members of that stimulus class.

A **generalized reinforcer** is a conditioned reinforcer that is associated with many other reinforcers. This kind of reinforcer is effective because the person is usually deprived with respect to at least one of the backup reinforcers.

Imitation training consists of three parts: (1) the teacher demonstrates what behavior the learner is to engage in (called the imitative stimulus); (2) the learner is called on to produce a similar behavior (called the imitative behavior); and (3) the teacher arranges for some type of reinforcement for the imitative behavor. The imitative stimulus is an S^D for the imitative behavior.

Instructional training consists of three parts: (1) the teacher provides a verbal description of the desired behavior; (2) the learner produces the instructed behavior; and (3) the teacher arranges for some form of reinforcement for the instructed behavior. The verbal description is an S^D for the instructed behavior.

A **primary reinforcer** is any reinforcing event that loses its effectiveness only temporarily through satiation.

Programming is the use of prompts (and their withdrawal) to establish a generalization.

A **prompt** is an added stimulus in a discrimination-training procedure designed to increase the probability of a person's making the correct response.

S^D is a symbol for "discriminative stimulus"—a stimulus associated with reinforcement of a particular behavior in discrimination training.

***S*-delta** is a stimulus associated with extinction for a particular response.

A **stimulus** is any physical object or event in the environment in which a person is behaving.

A **stimulus class** is a set of related stimuli.

Stimulus control is the increased probability of a discriminated behavior that is produced by a stimulus (S^D).

A **stimulus/response chain** (also called "chain" or "S-R chain") is a sequence of two or more behaviors in which each behavior produces a result that is the discriminative stimulus for the next behavior and in which the last behavior is reinforced. Most of our behavior consists of such stimulus/response chains.

UNIT THREE PRACTICE REVIEW

(13) Generalization training involves reinforcing a behavior in each of a series of situations until ______________________ occurs to other members of that same stimulus class.

(37) Harold's mother praised him when he was good. When he had been praised many times in a day, she would arrange for a special event, such as a trip to the zoo or ice cream. If we think of the mother's praise as a generalized reinforcer, these other events would be called ______________________ for the praise.

(25) When reinforcement and extinction are related to two different behaviors and one stimulus, we call the procedure ______________________. When reinforcement and extinction are related to two different stimuli, we call the procedure ______________________.

(12) Martha's mother frequently explained how to do chores around the house. If Martha did them, her mother always reinforced her. This would be an example of what behavioral procedure? ______________________

(36) If a behavior occurs more frequently in the presence of the S^D than the S-delta, it is called ______________________.

(24) Maria listened to Lefkowitz when he referred to female persons as "women" but ignored him when he called them "chicks." However, she listened to him when he referred to baby chickens as "chicks" and ignored him when he called them "women" (naturally). What behavioral procedure was she using? ______________________

(11) One reason that a generalized reinforcer is so effective is that the person is likely to be ______________________ with respect to at least one of the backup reinforcers.

(48) If you want to increase the resistance of a person's responding to extinction, you would use what type of reinforcement? ______________________ (continuous or intermittent)

(35) A reinforcer that is paired with a conditioned reinforcer and that is responsible for the conditioned reinforcer's effectiveness is called a(n) ______________________ reinforcer.

(23) Danny held up one object and gave Marty an M & M when he said "one"; Danny held up two objects and ignored Marty when he said "one." What behavioral procedure was Danny using? ______________________

(10) Fading is a method for gradually changing the ______________________ in a situation. Shaping is a method for gradually changing the ______________________ in a situation.

(47) If an event follows a behavior and the ______________________ of that behavior increases, the event is called a reinforcer.

(34) If a person learns a certain behavior in one situation and later emits that behavior in a new situation without being trained to do so, ______________________ is said to have occurred.

(22) Eli taught his friend to say "hi" when greeted with "Yassou," the Greek word for "hi," by also waving at him at the same time. However, after his friend started saying "hi," Eli delayed the wave for a longer period until his friend was saying "hi" before the wave was made—and it was no longer necessary. What behavioral procedure was Eli using to teach his friend to say "hi" when greeted with "Yassou"? ______________________

(9) When dealing with two responses, if the result of the first response serves as a discriminative stimulus for the second and if the last response is reinforced, we have what is called a(n) ______________________.

(46) If a teacher starts the year by making class attendance optional and later makes it required, he or she would be using a(n) ______________________ design.

(33) One method for attempting to produce generalization of a behavior involves the temporary use of a prompt. The method is called ______________________.

(21) Kay didn't give compliments to people very often. One day, however, she complimented Alice. She was delighted at the positive response she got. As a result, she frequently complimented Alice in the future. A bit later she complimented Norma. The occurrence of Kay's complimenting behavior around Norma would be an example of what behavioral process? ______________________

(8) If the many backup reinforcers for poker chips are stopped, and if the rate of responding previously maintained by the poker chips declines, then the poker chip was an example of what type of reinforcer? ______________________

(45) What two types of intermittent schedules produce a tendency for people to work at a uniform rate? ______________________

(32) If you are not sure whether a specific example is imitative training or instructional training, ask the question "Did the teacher ______________________ to the person what to do, or did the teacher ______________________ to the person what to do?"

(20) If people touch the top of their heads while saying that, if you also touch the top of your head, they will reinforce you, then technically their touching the top of their head is called the ______________________ stimulus.

(7) The increased probability of a discriminated behavior that is produced by a stimulus (S^D) is called ______________________.

(44) If a person is required to make a high number of responses for each reinforcement, his or her responding may decrease because of what is called ______________________.

(31) A stimulus associated with extinction for a particular response is called a(n) __________.

(19) An added stimulus that increases the probability that a person will make the correct response in a discriminative situation is called a(n) ______________________.

(6) If Gloria peeps only when the light in Todd's room is on, then we say that the light exerts ______________________ over Gloria's peeping.

(43) Fran and Willie observed how often someone played a game in the lounge. They used 60-second intervals and recorded the following:

X X X O X X O X X X
X X O O X X O O X X

Compute their reliability. __________ Is it acceptable if this is a new behavioral definition? __________

(30) In the process of teaching Marty to say "one," Danny would show Marty how to say "one" by saying it himself. Danny would then reinforce Marty if he correctly said "one." The method that Danny used to teach Marty to say "one" is called ______________________.

(18) A stimulus/response chain is several related responses in which the results of one response serve as a(n) ______________________ for the next response.

(5) A set of related stimuli is called a(n) ______________________.

(42) Dan gets pleasantly high after different numbers of beers. Sometimes it only takes one, but other times it takes 2, 3, or 4; once it took 47! If getting pleasantly high is a reinforcer, what schedule is Dan's beer drinking on? ______________________

(29) Many people can say the "Lord's Prayer" from beginning to end. Such a verbalization would technically be called a(n) ______________________.

(17) Every time that Tabby visited them, Sally asked her baby son Marty "What is that? Is that a

kitty?" and praised him if he said "kitty." Each time she said the word "kitty" a bit softer until Marty could identify Tabby as a kitty with no help. She then followed the same procedure with Fluffy until Marty could identify any kitty that happened to come by. What behavioral procedure did Sally use? ____________________

(4) A primary reinforcer is a reinforcing event that loses its effectiveness only through ____________________.

(41) Marsha kept track of the number of times that her lover, Francois, was late for a date: 3, 5, 11, 7, 3, and 5 per month. The ordinate should be labeled so that it increases in steps of ____________________ for these data.

(28) Two methods of modifying behavior that use discriminative stimuli (S^Ds) produced by another person are ____________________ and ____________________ training.

(16) If the tall guy will answer you only when addressed as "Marvin" and the short guy will not answer you when addressed as "Marvin," we would call the tall guy a(n) ____________________ for the response "Marvin."

(3) A generalized reinforcer is a reinforcer that is associated with ____________________ other reinforcers.

(40) Believe it or not, Shecky counted every step that Tom took while jogging and praised him after every 100th one. What schedule of reinforcement was Tom's running on? ____________________

(27) When a person copies the demonstration of a behavior, his or her copying behavior is called ____________________ behavior.

(15) Mrs. Keller gave Janie a cookie if she said "two" when two marbles were held up and she was asked the question "How many marbles are there?" But Janie could not answer the same question when two books were held up until one day she guessed "two" and got a cookie. After that she could answer that question no matter what kind of objects were held up. What behavioral procedure did Mrs. Keller use? ____________________

(2) If Kelly answers "5" when asked "4 + 1 = ?" but not when asked "4 − 1 = ?" then we call her behavior of answering "5" ____________________.

(39) Danny was trying to teach Marty to say "one." Every time Marty said something like "one," Danny said "Very good." At first Marty had a high rate of saying something close to "one." Then he slowed down, and finally he quit altogether. Marty probably quit because Danny violated what principle of effective reinforcement? ____________________

(26) Which type of reinforcer gains its effectiveness through repeated pairings with another reinforcer? ____________________

(14) A prompt is a(n) ____________________ stimulus that increases the probability of a person's making the correct response in a discriminative situation.

(1) A reinforcing stimulus occurs ____________________ (when) the response; a discriminative stimulus occurs ____________________ (when) the response.

(38) Tom was teaching Mona to play the guitar. He first praised her only when she held it correctly, next only when she strummed it correctly, and finally only when she strummed a particular chord. What behavioral procedure was Tom using? ____________________

PRACTICE REVIEW ANSWERS

(1) after; before (2) discriminated behavior (3) many (4) satiation (5) stimulus class (6) stimulus control (7) stimulus control (8) generalized (conditioned) (9) stimulus/response chain (10) stimulus; behavior (11) deprived (12) instructional training (13) generalization (14) added (15) generalization training (16) *SD* (17) programming (18) *SD* (19) prompt (20) imitative (21) generalization (22) fading (23) discrimination training (24) discrimination training (25) differential reinforcement;

discrimination training (26) conditioned (27) imitative (28) imitation; instructional (29) stimulus/response chain (30) imitation training (31) *S*-delta (32) demonstrate; describe (33) programming (34) generalization (35) backup (36) discriminated behavior (37) backups (38) shaping (39) deprivation (40) FR (FR–100) (41) 2 (42) VR (43) 80%; yes (44) ratio strain (45) VR; VI (46) comparison (47) rate (48) intermittent

UNIT FOUR
Aversive Control

Lesson 22

Punishment by Contingent Stimulation

The last part of this book discusses the topic of "aversive control." Aversive control refers to the use of so-called "unpleasant" events to control behavior. The next three lessons will examine punishment, escape, and avoidance. These behavioral procedures have a profound influence on daily behavior, and therefore your understanding of them is important to your understanding of everyday behavior. Some behaviorists, however, tend to play down the importance of these processes because of their negative connotations.

Because positive control can be highly effective, it is the dream of many behaviorists (including the founder of behavioral analysis, B. F. Skinner) to build a world in which aversive control is minimized. It is a noble dream and perhaps attainable. However, aversive control appears to be necessary and useful as a tool of behavioral change in today's world.

Punishment is often thought of as doing something unpleasant to someone because he or she did something you didn't like. To behaviorists, however, punishment is a highly technical term. **Punishment** is the procedure in which a punisher is administered contingent on an undesired behavior. A **punisher** is an event that (1) follows a behavior and (2) decreases the frequency of that behavior. It is therefore exactly the opposite in terms of its behavioral effect from a reinforcer. Because of the behavioral definition of punishment, it is possible for an unpleasant event not to be a punisher and it is possible for a pleasant event to be a punisher.

There are two types of punishment. This lesson will deal only with that type of punishment that involves the delivery of a stimulus contingent on the behavior. This form of punishment is often referred to as "punishment by contingent stimulation." (The second type of punishment will be introduced in the next lesson.) Both punishment and extinction are procedures that may be used to reduce the rate of a behavior. These two methods are easily distinguished. When punishment by contingent stimulation is used, an aversive event is delivered to the person contingent on performing a particular behavior. When extinction is used, the established reinforcing event is no longer delivered.

For example, suppose that Bobby keeps asking for a cookie just before dinner (his mother has reinforced this behavior in the past by eventually giving him the cookie). She might decide to eliminate his behavior by spanking him each time he asks for a cookie. This would be an example of contingent punishment, since she is now delivering an aversive event after the behavior. Or she might decide to eliminate the behavior by no longer giving him the cookie. This would be an example of extinction, because the reinforcing event is no longer delivered.

Another example of punishment might occur if Tommy often hits Sally. If Sally turns around and gives Tommy a black eye, she might succeed in eliminating that hitting behavior, as shown in Figure 22–1.

"Now I know why a gentleman shouldn't hit a lady."

Figure 22–1. Teaching little gentlemen to stop hitting little ladies is an excellent example of the use of punishment. Cartoon copyright 1973 by Cartoon Features Syndicate. Reproduced by permission.

The everyday world punishes much of our physical behavior. For example, if you forget to take your finger out of the door, the closing door will serve as a punisher. Or if you look away from where you're going, an approaching wall might deliver a punisher.

Punishment has most frequently been used in behavior analysis to eliminate behavior that is dangerous or highly disadvantageous to the people being helped or to others around them. Thus the self-mutilation of the autistic child is sometimes directly punished in order to rapidly eliminate a behavior that could result in permanent damage to the child (Tate & Baroff, 1966; Risley, 1968). Smoking (Powell & Azrin, 1968) and stuttering (Flanagan, Goldiamond, & Azrin, 1958) have also been reduced by punishment procedures for clients wishing to reduce these behaviors. Mild forms of punishment are sometimes used for less serious behavioral problems. For example, Greene and Hoats (1969) punished hyperactivity in a mildly retarded girl by distorting the TV picture she was watching.

It is likely that punishment will continue to be used to deal with behavior that is strongly reinforced by events not under the direct control of others. For example, stealing, a behavior quite reinforcing to the thief, can be checked by some form of punishment designed to decrease the rate of that behavior. The usual form of punishment, imprisonment, violates many of the rules of punishment effectiveness, particularly by being delivered after a long delay. However, in our everyday lives, most of us use more direct and immediate punishment for stealing.

Punishment also plays a role in everyday discussions. Proving a person wrong through logical argument should be considered a form of punishment that is useful and will undoubtedly continue (unless the wrong behavior is increased due to the attention associated with arguing).

A related example of great importance to behavior therapy might involve discussing your friends' problems with them. If you encourage them to talk about their problems, a few careful questions on your part may lead them to suddenly realize that they were thinking about the problem incorrectly. They may discover that it is not as serious as they thought; they may discover that they had overlooked an obvious solution; or they may realize that they had a silly hang-up. They might even come to laugh at the problem as a result of such a gentle and loving discussion, and stop labeling it as a "problem." Their insight might very well consist of a new way of describing the situation that would serve to completely terminate the previous behavior of labeling it as a problem and perhaps feeling very bad about it. In spite of the gentleness of this situation, it might be appropriate to label your behavior as punishment!

One of the dangers of punishment is that its use is too reinforcing—for the person administering it! If you punish a child for nagging, his or her nagging is likely to stop immediately. If you think of the cessation of the nagging as an event that follows the behavior of punishing it, then clearly it is likely to be reinforcing for the parent. Its effectiveness, furthermore, is enhanced through the principle of immediacy. The positive results of punishment are immediate. Furthermore, the negative results, such as the person not liking you as much, are delivered later. It is a wonder that we are not all punishers!

Contrast this immediacy of effectiveness with the delayed effects of reinforcement. If the parent praises the child for playing nicely (instead of nagging) while the parent is fixing dinner, there is no change in behavior that is immediately reinforcing to the parent for praising. The results are there—the child will continue playing and not nagging, but there is no obvious event that reinforces the parent's taking time out from cooking to go praise the child. In fact, since the parent has to leave the cooking process to praise the child, there is even a slight negative outcome for praising. No wonder so few people learn to use the positive and constructive approach of reinforcing desired behavior rather than punishing undesired behavior.

THE ANCIENT GREEKS UNDERSTOOD BEHAVIOR ANALYSIS

Thales, the "Father of Greek Mathematics," may have understood the basic principle of by contingent stimulation, long before the time of Skinner (or Christ, for that matter). The following story is told about him.

> On one occasion as a merchant, he was transporting several large sacks of salt by donkeys to a neighboring town. While crossing a shallow river, one of the donkeys slipped and fell. Naturally, some of the salt dissolved in the water, resulting in a lighter load. When the same donkey came to the second water crossing, it purposely fell in an effort to further lighten its load. At the next seaboard town, Thales purchased a large quantity of sponges and loaded them on the donkey's back. At the next water crossing, the donkey again went into its stumbling act, needless to say, for the last time.

From *Modern Geometry*, Jurgensen, R. C., Donnelly, A. J., & Dolciani, M. P. (Meder, A. E., Editorial Advisor). Boston: Houghton Mifflin, 1965. Noted in "Thales on Behavior Modification," Talsma, T. *Journal of Applied Behavior Analysis*, 1976, 9, 178.

ANALOGUES BETWEEN REINFORCEMENT AND PUNISHMENT

Many of the concepts associated with reinforcers have analogues with punishers. Thus there are punishers that seem to have a physical basis for their effectiveness—such as shock, hitting, pinching, and extreme heat or cold. There are punishers that seem to gain strength from association with other punishers. And there are even punishers that seem to gain strength from association with many other punishers.

In addition, if a particular behavior is decreased through punishment in one situation, this effect may not generalize to other situations any more than the effect of reinforcement generalizes to other situations.

A **primary punisher** is a punisher that loses part of its effectiveness (temporarily) only through satiation (an effect commonly called adaptation when referring to punishment). Primary punishers include events such as a spanking, an electric shock, or a beating. These events are effective for most people most of the time as a method for reducing the rate of some behavior on which these events have been made contingent. However, if a person is subjected to these stimuli frequently in a short period of time, they lose part of their effectiveness. The effectiveness can be regained, however, after a period of time without the punishment. This effect is analogous to the effects of satiation and deprivation with reinforcing events and will be referred to by these terms in this book.

A **conditioned punisher** is a punisher that permanently loses its effectiveness through repeated unpaired presentations, in which the conditioned punisher is not paired with another punisher. Conditioned punishers are events such as warning children that you may punish them with a spanking. Events such as a loud yell or a bad grade are also conditioned punishers called "symbolic" punishers. These punishers can lose part of their effectiveness by being used too often, as is the case with primary punishers, but they can also lose their effectiveness by being used without being paired with another effective punisher. Thus, if you warn a child that you are going to spank him or her but never do, soon your warning won't serve as a punisher.

A **generalized punisher** is a conditioned punisher that is associated with many other punishers. Generalized punishers are events, such as social disapproval, in which the person stands to have many punishing things happen as a result of the disapproval. Generalized punishers are effective as punishers because usually one or more of the "backup" punishers will be effective for the person.[1]

Punishment can also enter into discriminative processes. It is possible for a stimulus to be consistently associated with punishment so that it becomes a discriminative stimulus for punishment. We will refer to such a stimulus as an S^P or **discriminative stimulus for punishment.** The function of an S^P in discrimination and concept training is similar to that of the *S*-delta. They are both associated with a low rate of responding as compared with the S^D, which is associated with a high rate of responding.

Discriminative stimuli for punishment can be used in a punishment-based form of instructional training. If an undesirable behavior is described before it occurs and if the teacher punishes that behavior each time it occurs, this situation would be an example of instructional training. In fact, people will often stop making a response just on the basis of the description (perhaps because of their long history of being reinforced for following instructions and punished for not following them). An example of an instruction that might reduce the rate of a behavior might be when a boy tells his girlfriend "Please stop digging your fingernails into my back when we're kissing."

Verbal stimuli can act as instructions (or, more generally, as discriminative stimuli for punishment), and they can also act as punishers. The phrase "don't talk" could be either an S^P or a punisher, depending on when the phrase occurs. If it is said before a behavior that would be punished, it would be called an S^P; if it occurs quickly after the behavior and the rate of the behavior decreases, it would be a punisher.

Finally, the principles of effective reinforcement also apply to punishment. To be maximally effective, the punisher should be contingent on the behavior, it should follow the response immediately, and the person should be deprived of the punisher. The greater the size of the punisher (its intensity), the more effective it will be.

BEHAVIOR ANALYSIS EXAMPLES

Curing smoking. Smoking has been one of the most difficult behaviors for psychologists to assist people in modifying. Dericco, Brigham, and Garlington (1977) reviewed the many attempts to modify cigarette smoking by various behavior techniques and found indications of little effect, resumption of smoking after treatment, and methodological errors making it impossible to rule out alternative explanations of observed effects in many studies. The difficulty in treating cigarette smoking is quite dramatic, considering the fact that the long-term effects of smoking include heart disease, cancer, and a variety of other very serious medical complications. Even people wishing to quit to avoid these medical consequences have great trouble doing so.

Dericco and her associates examined the effectiveness of using contingent shock punishment with two volunteers (whom we will name Jane and Don), who wished to quit smoking and agreed to the treatment. Jane and Don answered a newspaper ad, were medically screened to ensure

[1]It should be pointed out that these distinctions (primary, conditioned, and generalized punishers) are not common in the field of behavior analysis. Basic research with animals has documented the satiation effect of punishment and the creation of conditioned punishers, but behavior analysts working with people seldom use or study these procedures. Their emphasis is on the use of reinforcement whenever possible. However, since the real world is full of examples of these behavioral processes, I have included them in this book so that you may understand those everyday situations better.

that the treatment would not adversely affect their health, and had the treatment procedure fully explained to them so that they could personally determine whether they thought it would be helpful to them. Jane and Don then self-recorded their rate of smoking for a baseline period. Jane's level was over 50, and Don's around 15, cigarettes per day. At critical stages in the experiment, friends, spouses, children, and employers assisted in taking reliability. Reliability by the counting method averaged 96%.

The treatment procedure required that Jane and Don determine what shock intensity was painful to them. Each was separately seated in a small room with the experimenter, who engaged them in discussion about various topics excluding only smoking. They were encouraged to smoke normally during this discussion; painful shock was delivered at 26 times during the conversation contingent on lighting a cigarette, holding a lit cigarette, and smoking.

Figure 22–2 (see p. 230) shows the results of the experiment for both smokers. Jane's baseline was 21 days and Don's 42 days. Treatment continued until smoking in their everyday life decreased to zero for five straight days for both Jane and Don. Furthermore, additional observations 6 months later showed that they had not resumed smoking. Further follow-up data (Dericco, 1977) revealed that they were still abstinent one year later. These results were replicated with six additional smokers, who also remained abstinent one year later.

These results indicate that a very strongly persistent behavior that is medically disastrous can be effectively treated through the use of contingent shock.[2] The justification for the use of aversive control in this case rests on the harmful effects of the behavior and on the fact that the smokers sought the treatment and consented to its use. This experiment is particularly important on a methodological level. Prior studies did not use sound single-subject designs and therefore did not provide scientifically useful results.

This experiment has another interesting aspect to it. The treatment consisted of shocking cigarette smoking in a special setting while observing the behavior in its everyday setting. The reduction of smoking observed in the special setting generalized very well to the everyday setting. It may be that the casual conversations during which the smoking was punished were similar to the everyday settings so that generalization was to a similar stimulus situation.

Shoplifting. Shoplifting is a major problem; it was estimated in 1973 that shoplifting cost the average American family $150 in hidden costs of the merchandise. McNees, Egli, Marshall, Schnelle, and Risley (1976) developed a simple method for reducing the shoplifting of young women's clothing. They developed an ingenious system for observing the rate of shoplifting for clothing. They wanted to observe the daily rate at which women's jeans were shoplifted. The store procedure was to tear off a portion of the price tag on any pair of jeans that were sold. The experimenters simply stapled a yellow tag on the back of that portion of the price tag for every pair of jeans in stock. By counting the number of tags on jeans in the morning, they then knew that at the close of business there should be the same number of jeans with tags minus all yellow tags collected by the cashier. If there were fewer jeans than that, the balance had to have been stolen.

The experimenters observed the number of women's pants and the number of young women's tops stolen. Figure 22–3 (see p. 231) shows the results of these observations. Tops were taken at the rate of 0.66 per day while pants were taken at the rate of 0.50 per day. After 34 days, a sign was posted in the clothing department stating: "Attention shoppers and shoplifters. The items you see marked with a red star are items that shoplifters frequently take." Stars were about 5 inches across; six were mounted on the pants racks. After 47 days, six red stars were also posted on racks containing young women's tops. The rate of shoplifting dramatically decreased for both items.

ADDITIONAL READINGS

Alford, G. S., & Turner, S. M. Stimulus interference and conditioned inhibition of auditory hallucinations. *Journal of Behavior Therapy and Experimental Psychiatry*, 1976, 7, 155–160. A 32-year-old woman, who was hospitalized because she frequently heard voices and responded to them, was given an apparatus with which she could give herself a shock when she heard the voices. This procedure resulted in the woman no longer reporting hearing the voices and no longer responding to them. She was dismissed from the hospital and has lived a normal life since.

Flanagan, B., Goldiamond, I., & Azrin, N. H. Operant stuttering: The control of stuttering behavior through

[2]One of the authors (Brigham) has indicated in a personal communication to me that there may be a problem in the replicability of this study.

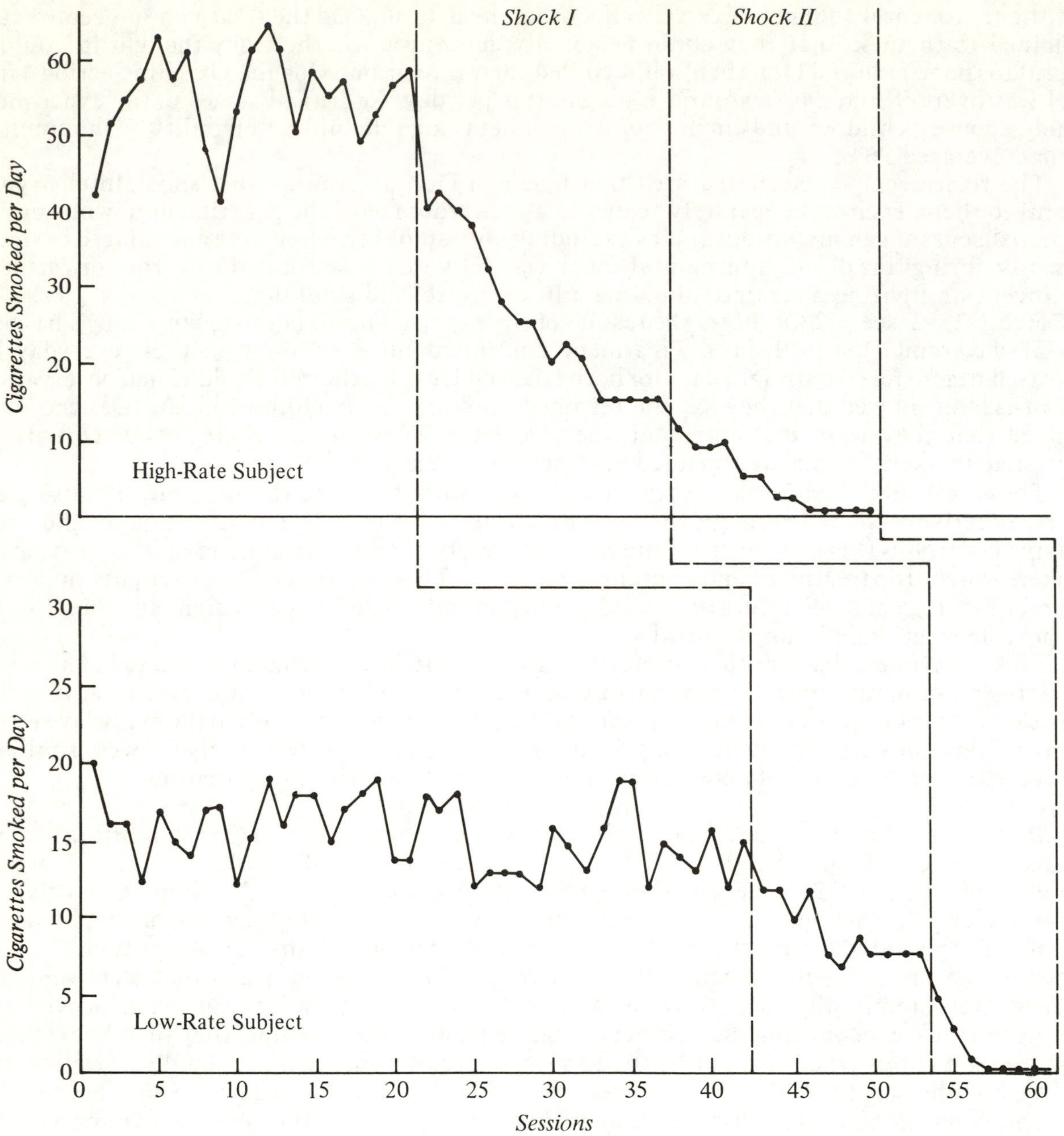

Figure 22-2. The number of cigarettes smoked daily by Jane and Don during an experiment. During contingent shock, they were shocked for smoking while involved in a casual conversation with the therapist in a special room. The clients requested this treatment because of their strong desire to quit smoking. No smoking recurred even a year later. From "Development and Evaluation of Treatment Paradigms for the Suppression of Smoking Behavior," by D. A. Dericco, T. A. Brigham, and W. K. Garlington, *Journal of Applied Behavior Analysis*, 1977, *10*, 173–181. Copyright 1977 by the Society for the Experimental Analysis of Behavior, Inc. Used by permission.

response contingent consequences. *Journal of the Experimental Analysis of Behavior*, 1958, *1*, 173–177. Chronic stutterers read from a book into a microphone while an observer counted the number of disfluencies. When every disfluency was followed by a blast of noise delivered to the stutterers through earphones, their rate of stuttering decreased markedly.

Greene, R. J., & Hoats, D. L. Reinforcing capabilities of television distortion. *Journal of Applied Behavior Analysis*, 1969, *2*, 139–141. A hyperactive, mildly retarded girl of 18 was seated in a room watching TV. Her hyperactivity was observed, and during baseline it averaged about 22 responses per minute. During treatment, the TV picture was mildly distorted contingent on her hyperactive behavior. Her rate decreased to an average of about 3 responses per minute. Thus, the distortion served as a successful punisher of hyperactive responding.

Holz, W. C., & Azrin, N. H. Punishment. In W. K. Honig (Ed.), *Operant behavior: Areas of research and*

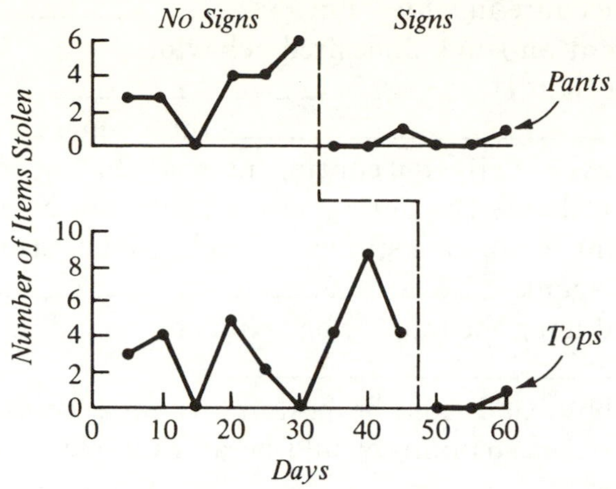

Figure 22-3. Number of women's pants and tops shoplifted. Adapted from "Shoplifting Prevention: Providing Information Through Signs," by M. P. McNees, D. S. Egli, R. S. Marshall, J. F. Schnelle, and T. R. Risley, *Journal of Applied Behavior Analysis*, 1976, *9*, 399–406. Copyright 1976 by the Society for the Experimental Analysis of Behavior, Inc. Used by permission.

application. New York: Appleton-Century-Crofts, 1966. This article provides an excellent overview of the concept of punishment, the side effects of using punishment, a comparison of punishment with other methods for reducing behavior, and the ethical considerations involved in using punishment.

Powell, J., & Azrin, N. H. The effect of shock as a punisher for cigarette smoking. *Journal of Applied Behavior Analysis*, 1968, *1*, 63–71. Individuals who wished to stop smoking were given a harness device that was hooked up to a special cigarette case. Each time they opened the pack, they were shocked. This procedure decreased their smoking, but the individuals began to wear the harness for only short periods of time.

Risley, T. R. The effects and side effects of punishing the autistic behaviors of a deviant child. *Journal of Applied Behavior Analysis*, 1968, *1*, 21–34. A hyperactive, autistic child frequently engaged in climbing behaviors that resulted in falls and serious physical damage to the child (such as knocking out teeth). To eliminate such behaviors, shock punishment was used at the start of each climbing episode. This eliminated the dangerous climbing behavior.

Tate, B. G., & Baroff, G. S. Aversive control of self-injurious behavior in a psychotic boy. *Behavior Research and Therapy*, 1966, *4*, 281–287. A psychotic boy engaged in such serious head-banging behavior that he was in danger of losing his eyesight. The use of electric shock contingent on the head-banging response quickly eliminated this self-injurious behavior.

Wilson, G. T., Leaf, R. C., & Nathan, P. E. The aversive control of excessive alcohol consumption by chronic alcoholics in the laboratory setting. *Journal of Applied Behavior Analysis*, 1975, *8*, 13–26. Shock was used to punish the consumption of alcohol by chronic alcoholics. The alcoholics were permitted to drink as much as they wished. During baseline they drank over 20 ounces of alcohol per day! During treatment, they were shocked each time they took a drink. This resulted in nearly complete elimination of drinking.

Helpful hint #1: Both punishment and extinction reduce the rate of a response. If you are asked to label the behavioral process that produces a decreased rate of behavior, you must determine whether an event follows the behavior or whether some usually reinforcing event fails to follow the behavior. If an event fails to follow the behavior, the behavioral process involved is extinction, not punishment by contingent stimulation.

Helpful hint #2: An instruction not to perform a behavior will usually not be a punisher. You should use the general rule suggested for reinforcers and instructions in the case of punishment also: "An instruction cannot be a punisher."

LESSON 22 READING QUIZ

(9) Aversive control refers to the use of so-called "______________________" events to control behavior.

(25) A dream of behavior analysts is to create a world in which the need for ______________ control is minimized.

(17) Punishment is the procedure in which a(n) ______________________________ is administered contingent on some undesired behavior.

(8) A punisher is an event that (1) ______________________________ a behavior and (2) ______________________________ the frequency of that behavior.

(24) Must an "unpleasant" event delivered contingent on a behavior be a punisher? __________

(16) May a "pleasant" event delivered contingent on a behavior be a punisher? __________

(7) The type of punishment in which a stimulus is delivered contingent on a behavior is called "punishment by contingent ______________________________."

(23) Two procedures for reducing the rate of a behavior are ______________________________ and ______________________________.

(15) If Mother spanks Bobby each time he pesters her for a cookie and his rate of pestering decreases, then the use of spanking would be an example of what behavioral procedure?

____

(6) If Mother simply never gives Bobby a cookie when he pesters her, and his rate of pestering decreases, she would be using what behavioral procedure? ______________________________

(22) If a behavior modifier shocked severely disturbed autistic children each time that they attempted to injure themselves and the rate of such self-injury decreased, what behavioral method would the administration of shock be an example of? ______________________________

(14) If a person's undesirable behavior is strongly reinforced by events whose delivery you cannot personally stop, you cannot use extinction to reduce the rate of that behavior. What behavioral procedure could you use? ______________________________

(5) If your proving someone wrong in a discussion reduces the rate at which he or she continues to hold that wrong opinion, then you have used what behavioral method? ______________________________

(21) If you are discussing something with a friend and the friend helps you see that your labeling of it as a problem is incorrect and even laughable, and if your rate of labeling that as a problem decreases, then your friend's gentle assistance might appropriately be considered to involve what behavioral procedure? ______________________________

(13) An important danger of punishment is that it produces a change in the environment of the person administering the punishment immediately after the punishment-delivering behavior. This change may turn out to be a very effective reinforcer due to the Principle of ______________________________, thereby increasing the person's use of punishment.

(4) A primary punisher is a punisher that loses its effectiveness only through __________.

(20) A conditioned punisher loses its effect permanently through ______________________________ presentations.

(12) A generalized punisher is a punisher that is associated with ______________________________ other punishers.

(3) A stimulus associated with the punishment for a particular behavior is called a(n) ______________________________ stimulus for punishment and abbreviated as ______________________________.

(19) A stimulus that decreases the rate of a response that it precedes is called a(n) __________; a stimulus that decreases the rate of a response that it quickly follows is called a(n) ______________________________

(11) To have maximum effectiveness, when should a punisher occur in relation to the behavior?

____

(2) An event that decreases the rate of a behavior that it follows is called a(n) __________ .

(18) The use of "unpleasant" events to control behavior is called ______________________________ control.

(10) Dericco, Brigham, and Garlington (1977) shocked Jane each time she puffed on her cigarette while engaged in casual conversation. Her rate of smoking decreased. What behavioral concept should be used to label the shock? ______________

(26) Dericco, Brigham, and Garlington (1977) shocked Jane each time that she puffed on a cigarette while engaged in casual conversation. Her rate of smoking decreased. Giving her a shock each time she puffed on a cigarette is an example of what behavioral procedure? ______________

(1) McNees and his associates (1976) posted stars identifying clothing items that were often stolen. Customers stole much less after the posting than before. If the customers stole less because they had been punished in the past for stealing in similar situations, then the star would technically be called a(n) ______________ .

READING QUIZ ANSWERS

(1) discriminative stimulus for punishment (S^P) (2) punisher (3) discriminative; S^P (4) satiation (5) punishment (6) extinction (7) stimulation (8) follows; decreases (9) unpleasant (10) punisher (11) immediately after (12) many (13) Immediacy (14) punishment (15) punishment (16) yes (17) punisher (18) aversive (19) S^P; punisher (20) unpaired (21) punishment (22) punishment (23) punishment; extinction (24) no (25) aversive (26) punishment

LESSON 22 EXAMPLES

Example #1

Tom teased his little sister constantly. He would take her toys away from her, tell her that she couldn't play anymore, and make believe that he was going to run away and leave her. Tom's mother took a dim view of his teasing. She decided she would warn him to stop teasing his sister and then spank him every time she detected his teasing. Tom's rate of teasing decreased quickly.

(28) Did Mom's spanking follow Tom's teasing behavior? ______________

(14) Did Tom's rate of teasing decrease? ______________

(41) Mom's spanking is technically called a(n) ______________ .

(27) Mom found that her spanking wasn't effective, because she had to spank Tom many times during a day. Toward the end of the day, it seemed as though Tom didn't mind being spanked. However, the next day the spanking worked as well as ever. If Tom's acceptance of spanking during a given day is viewed as satiation (or adaptation), this pattern of effectiveness indicates that spanking should be viewed as a(n) ______________ punisher.

(13) A year later, Mom decided that Tom was too old to spank, so she started simply admonishing him to stop his teasing. At first this worked as long as she spoke to him only a few times a day. However, over time, she discovered that the statement became less and less effective. If these warnings are considered to be unpaired presentations because the warning is no longer followed by (or paired with) the spankings, this pattern of effectiveness would indicate that the warning was a(n) ______________ punisher.

(40) If Mom spanked Tom for teasing and Dad didn't, Mom would be associated with punishment for teasing. Technically, she would be called a(n) ______________ stimulus for punishment of teasing.

(20) If Mom waited to spank Tom until after dinner, the effectiveness of the spanking would be decreased due to her failure to follow the Principle of ______________ (think of the corresponding principle of effective reinforcement).

Example #2

Mary got very hungry during the afternoon. By the time her mother was fixing dinner, Mary thought that she would die of hunger, so she would beg her mother for a snack. Her mother would tell her she couldn't have a snack because it would spoil her dinner. Then Mary would nag her mother. Soon her mother would scream "No!" every time Mary asked for a snack. Her mother thought that a scream would punish Mary for asking. However, Mary continued to beg and nag for a snack even after her mother started screaming at her.

(12) Did Mother's scream follow Mary's request? ____________

(39) Did the rate of nagging decrease? ____________

(25) Is this an example of punishment? ____________

(11) One way Mary's mother could have made her "No!" an effective punisher of Mary's request would be for her to always follow her "No!" with another, more powerful ____________.

Example #3

Fred was one of the newest commune members. Unlike the other members, Fred wasn't political. He just liked living with a friendly group of people. One of his more annoying habits to the other members was his repeated racial slurs. The members of the group simply ignored his comments, knowing that his attitude was the result of the kind of family he was brought up in. However, his comments didn't decrease (perhaps because friends outside the group reinforced him for such talk). One day he commented to another commune member "Look at that Black buck! He's the tallest guy I've ever seen." The other member said "It's disrespectful of Black people to call them 'bucks.'" Fred looked surprised, but he never used that word again around other members of the commune.

(38) Was Fred's use of the word "buck" followed immediately by the other member's comment? ____________

(24) Did the rate of Fred's use of the word decrease? ____________

(10) Is this an example of punishment? ____________

(37) Suppose that such comments by other members of the group were never followed by other, more powerful punishers. If the rate of Fred's racial slurs was no longer reduced by such comments after a while, this would be evidence that these comments should be classified as what kind of punisher? ____________

(23) If one member of the group was a racist and encouraged Fred to make such comments, that member would be classified as a(n) ____________ with respect to racial slurs.

(9) The other members would be classified as a(n) ____________ with respect to racial slurs, because they punished such behavior.

Example #4

Mr. Tubbs, the sixth-grade math teacher, was angry with Gerald for always talking with his neighbor when Mr. Tubbs was presenting the daily lesson. So Mr. Tubbs spoke with Gerald after school one day and told him not to whisper to his neighbor anymore. Gerald never whispered in Mr. Tubbs's class again.

(36) To analyze this example, remember the rule: "An instruction can never be a(n) ____________ ____________."

(22) If Mr. Tubbs praised Gerald for listening to the daily lesson and scolded him when he whispered, he would be using what behavioral procedure? ____________

(8) If Mr. Tubbs's warning indicated that Gerald would be punished for any whispering, the warning would technically be called a(n) ____________.

Example #5

Professor Brainbuster had high standards for class discussions. He wanted his students to discuss only really important ideas. As a result, he would immediately ridicule anyone who made a comment on, or asked a question about, what he considered a trivial problem. Most students stopped participating in the class discussion within 2 weeks.

(35) The decrease in student participation suggests that, for many students, Brainbuster's ridicule was a(n) ______________________________ .

(21) One semester, Brainbuster, in a "radical" mood, assured everyone in his class that he no longer believed in grades. He therefore gave everyone an "A" at the beginning of the semester. To his surprise, he found that the students no longer shut up after he ridiculed them; many argued back, and some even ridiculed *him.* The results of his ridicule unpaired with poor grades indicate that ridicule is a(n) ______________________________ punisher.

(7) Professor Brainbuster learned that semester that he wasn't truly a radical, so he went back to giving contingent grades. However, he stopped using ridicule. Instead, he warmly praised everyone who expressed an important idea and ignored those who discussed trivia. This is an example of what behavioral procedure? ______________________________

Example #6

Lou frequently insulted people with comments such as "That was a dumb idea" or "That is a terrible-looking shirt." The response of Lou's friends to these insults was to look annoyed and to argue with him about his assertion. One day, several of Lou's friends decided that they had had enough of his insults. They agreed to maintain a neutral look when Lou insulted them and to pretend that he hadn't said anything. Lou's rate of insults decreased quite rapidly after his friends started this behavior.

(34) Did Lou's friends start delivering an aversive event after his insults as a way of reducing the rate of his insults? __________

(26) Did the friends stop the delivery of some event after his insults as a way of reducing his rate of insults? __________

(6) This is not an example of punishment; it is an example of ______________________________ .

Example #7

The group had a written rule "No complaining about dinner during the dinner period." Bob complained one night about the dinner, and two other members of the group immediately responded by saying "Hey, you're not supposed to complain about the meals during dinner time." Bob never broke that rule again.

(33) The decrease in Bob's complaining is an example of the behavioral procedure called ______________________________ .

(19) The fact that Bob no longer complains during the dinner period means that the written rule now functions as a(n) ______________________________ for punishment with respect to Bob's complaining behavior. (Remember that the rule is a stimulus.)

(5) If there was an increased probability that Bob would not complain as a result of the written rule, we would say that the rule had developed ______________________________ over his complaining.

Example #8

Barbara broke the rule "No complaining about the food during the dinner period." Another member immediately responded by saying "Barbara, we have a rule that you're not supposed to complain during the dinner period." Barbara continued to break the rule from time to time. Several members became annoyed enough with Barbara's complaining to bring the problem up at the next house meeting. Someone suggested that the "reminder" that the other members were giving Barbara when she complained wasn't strong enough and that Barbara (or any other complainer) should be assessed a fine of 25¢ when she had to be given a "reminder."

(18) If the reminder served as a punisher when it was associated with the 25¢ fine but quickly lost its effectiveness when it was not paired with the fine, it would be classified as what type of punisher? ______________________

Example #9

Carol told her little son, Lenny, not to touch the steering wheel while she was driving. The next time that he touched the wheel, she spanked him. He rarely touched the wheel after that and always got a spanking when he did.

(43) The spanking considered as a stimulus following a behavior would be called a(n) ______________________; the administration of a spanking after every touch of the steering wheel, that is, the procedure of giving a spanking, is called ______________________.

Example #10

Jane was teaching her daughter to count to ten. Her daughter would start counting and, whenever she said the wrong number, Jane would say "No, that's wrong." The daughter rarely made the same error more than once.

(32) Jane's statement "No, that's wrong" would be called a(n) ______________________ for incorrect responses.

(42) Notice that this procedure stops the daughter from making a specific wrong response again, but she still may make another incorrect response. (Instead of "one, two, three, *five*," she may say "one, two, three, *house*.") Nor does it directly encourage the daughter to make the correct response a second time. To increase the probability of correct responses, Jane should also use ______________________ for correct responses.

Example #11

Frank ran a red light one day when he was in a hurry to get to class. A police officer caught him and gave him a ticket. Frank didn't go through a red light again after that.

(4) The ticket was an example of a(n) ______________________.

Example #12

Yvonne told everyone in class that she didn't think President Nixon should have gotten us out of the Vietnam War until the United States had won. Several people immediately gasped "Yvonne!! You can't mean that!" Yvonne never mentioned her feelings about the war again in class.

(31) The reactions of Yvonne's classmates to her remark would be an example of what behavioral procedure? ______________________

Example #13

Bob went home on his first vacation from the university convinced that the poor people in this country are treated badly. He mentioned this idea several times to his father, a stockbroker. His father ignored him. Bob never brought the subject up again.

(17) Bob's decreased rate of talking about the problems of poor people is the result of what behavioral procedure? ______________________

Example #14

Professor Young encouraged his sociology students to express ideas about U.S. social problems, but he ridiculed them if they talked about abstract theory. Professor Old encouraged his students to express ideas about abstract sociological theory and scolded them if they expressed ideas about actual social problems. Dan was a student of both professors. He soon learned to talk about social problems in Professor Young's class and not to talk about them in Professor Old's class.

(3) The changes in Dan's behavior would be the result of what behavioral procedure? ______________________

Example #15

Donny frequently made disparaging remarks about Dale's figure in front of their friends. As soon as they were alone, Dale always became very angry at Donny's remarks. However, Donny continued to make such remarks in front of their friends.

(30) What principle of punishment may have reduced the effectiveness of Dale's anger as a punisher? ______________________

Example #16

Whenever there was a group around, everyone paid a lot of attention to Donny, because he was always arguing. Soon Donny's friends decided to reduce his rate of arguing by ignoring those arguments that seemed designed to get attention but reacting to his reasonable ones. Donny's rate of arguing for attention decreased drastically; his rate of reasonable arguing increased.

(16) What behavioral procedure accounts for this reduction? ______________________

Example #17

Sam hit Bobby a few months ago because Bobby was being a terrible pest. Bobby immediately started acting nice to Sam. Since then, Sam has hit Bobby whenever he was being a pest.

(2) The <u>increase</u> in the rate of Sam's hitting response is a result of what behavioral procedure? ______________________

Example #18

Gladys spanked Danny for bothering her but immediately felt sorry for the child. She picked him up, soothed the tears, sat him on her lap, and paid a lot of attention to him. If Danny started getting into more trouble, rather than less, we would guess that the attention was more reinforcing than the spanking was punishing. Furthermore, if Danny got spanked, he knew that Gladys would then pay a lot of attention; therefore a spanking by Gladys was always associated with a lot of attention.

(29) The spanking could actually become a(n) ______________________ reinforcer.

Example #19

(15) Instructional training was previously defined in terms of asking someone to do something (instructions), observing the requested behavior (instructed behavior), and reinforcing that behavior. However, if a person is asked to stop doing something, the instructional training

would consist of requesting a stop to the behavior, observing the undesired behavior, and then not reinforcing the behavior but rather ________________________________ it.

Example #20

Terry was the newest member of the food co-op's staff. During the regular Thursday staff meetings, Terry would frequently launch into a discourse on the evils of the local merchants. Needless to say, this subject had nothing to do with what order the Food Co-op was going to place next week or who was going to work what hours. Consequently, the other staff members paid no attention to Terry's irrelevant rhetoric. After a month, he confined himself to the issue of running the co-op.

(1) What behavioral procedure was at work decreasing Terry's rate of rhetoric? ________________

EXAMPLE ANSWERS

(1) extinction (2) reinforcement (3) discrimination training (4) punisher (5) stimulus control (6) extinction (7) differential reinforcement (8) S^P (9) S^P (10) yes (11) punisher (12) yes (13) conditioned (14) yes (15) punishing (16) differential reinforcement (17) extinction (18) conditioned (19) discriminative stimulus S^P (20) Immediacy (21) conditioned (22) differential reinforcement (23) S^D (24) yes (25) no (26) yes (27) primary (28) yes (29) conditioned (30) Immediacy (31) punishment (32) punisher (33) punishment (34) no (35) punisher (36) punisher (37) conditioned (38) yes (39) no (40) discriminative (41) punisher (42) reinforcement (43) punisher; punishment

Lesson 23

Punishment by Contingent Withdrawal

This lesson introduces a second type of punishment, in which something considered pleasant is taken away from people each time that they emit an undesirable behavior. For example, treating a pinball machine too roughly will cause a "tilt" light to go on, thereby taking away the privilege of playing the machine any longer. This form of punishment, **punishment by contingent withdrawal,** is defined as the procedure in which an event is withdrawn contingent on the occurrence of a behavior, thus producing a decrease in the rate of that behavior.

Thus we have two types of punishment. In one type, an event (often unpleasant) is delivered to people when they emit a certain behavior (and the rate of the behavior decreases). In the other type of punishment, an event (most often pleasant) is withdrawn when a person emits a certain behavior (and the rate of the behavior decreases).

There are two forms of punishment by withdrawal. In one form, something is permanently taken away from a person. An example would be a fine; a person permanently loses money. Other examples might include the permanent withdrawal of tokens, toys, or even a friendship.

Fines consisting of token losses are quite common in behavior analysis. For example, Phillips, Phillips, Fixsen, and Wolf (1971) punished coming late to dinner by taking away points from predelinquent boys in Achievement Place. Perhaps more remarkably, Winkler (1970) effectively reduced tantrums and acts of violence among chronic psychiatric patients solely by removing tokens for their occurrence.

An interesting example of the use of punishment by permanent withdrawal that occurred in the natural environment is given in Figure 23-1. Ma Bell initiated the practice of charging customers 20¢ for each local directory assistance call made in Cincinnati in 1973. Since the charge immediately followed the placing of such a call and since the rate of such calls decreased, this would be an excellent example of such punishment.

The other form of punishment by withdrawal involves the temporary loss of a privilege contingent on making a certain response. If a child steals something from the refrigerator and the mother decrees that the child cannot go out to play the rest of that day, this would be an example of the temporary withdrawal of a privilege (and an example of punishment if the future rate of stealing decreased). This form of punishment by withdrawal is usually called time out, referring to the fact that some activity that was reinforcing to people is denied them for a period of time after they emit the behavior.

"Time out" is widely used by behavior analysts to reduce the rate of undesirable behaviors. Its precise form varies widely. For example, Hall and his colleagues (1972) withdrew the privilege of watching TV to reduce extreme dressing times in a 5-year-old girl. Baer (1962) reduced thumbsucking behavior in young children by interrupting a cartoon when the children sucked their thumbs. In these examples, a reinforcing activity is denied to the person contingent on making the undesired response.

Another more common use of time out involves removing people from the reinforcing environment when they emit the undesirable behavior. For example, the aggressive behavior of one child was reduced by his parents when they simply removed him from the room and placed

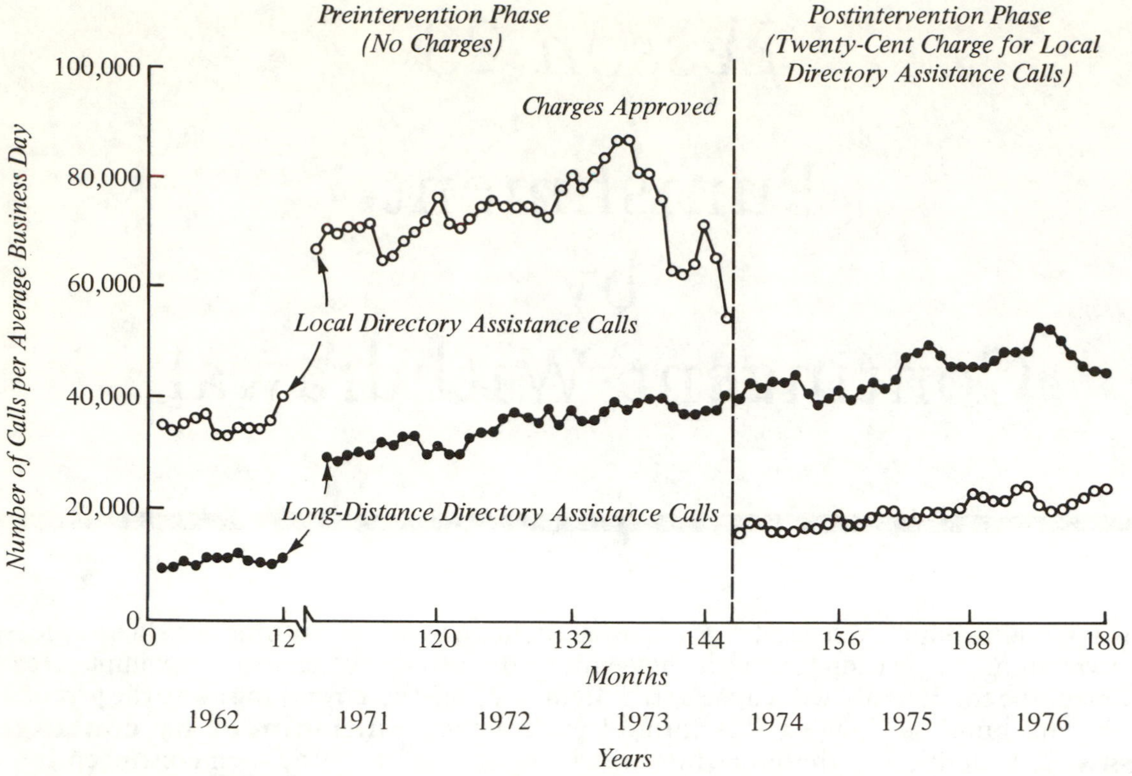

Figure 23-1. The number of local and long-distance directory assistance phone calls made in Cincinnati before and after introduction of a charge for local directory assistance calls. Since the charges amount to withdrawing an amount of money for the behavior, they can be conceptualized as punishment by contingent withdrawal. From "Effects of Response Cost on the Behavior of a Million Persons: Charging for Directory Assistance in Cincinnati," by A. J. McSweeny, *Journal of Applied Behavior Analysis*, 1978, *11*, 47–51. Copyright 1978 by the Society for the Experimental Analysis of Behavior, Inc. Used by permission.

him in a specially modified room that had no toys in it (Zeilberger, Sampen, & Sloan, 1968). The child was kept in the time-out room for 2 minutes unless he continued screaming, in which case he was kept there for 2 minutes past the termination of his screaming. While this type of isolation may seem unusually harsh, the child's aggressive behavior was also extreme, consisting of hitting, kicking, throwing, biting, and scratching.

One final point about punishment should be made. Behaviorists do not speak of "punishing" not making a response. For example, if a child forgets to make his or her bed and the parent spanks the child, this spanking would not be called punishment. It is an example of an "avoidance" schedule and will be discussed in the next lesson.

BEHAVIOR ANALYSIS EXAMPLE

Rule following in a recreation center. Pierce and Risley (1974) investigated the maintenance of rule following in an urban youth center. This center was frequented by young Black men aged 7 to 25. The center offered facilities for pool, Ping-Pong, and table games for 2 hours at night. Typically the facilities were not kept in reasonable order by the participants. Pool cues were broken, fights occurred, and trash was thrown around, thereby reducing the desirability of the facility for the participants.

The experiment proceeded in two phases. First, a list of rules was posted. Each rule specified a group penalty consisting of closing the center 1 to 15 minutes early per violation. The more severe violations were strictly enforced and problems like fighting, breaking equipment, and crowding into line were virtually eliminated. However, the less severe violations were not consistently enforced at first by the director because, as he explained, "I'm here to help the kids. I want to show them that I'm a nice guy." Three weeks later he agreed that they had to be enforced also.

To enforce rule violations, the director walked through the center every 15 minutes and looked for violations. For every violation that he observed, he wrote it and a penalty on the blackboard. He then followed through by closing the center by the number of minutes of accumulated penalties indicated on the blackboard. Thus, the individuals attending the center lost the privilege of using the center when one or more of their group violated the rules.

To observe the minor violations, an observer walked through the center every 30 minutes and counted rule infractions occurring in each area of the center. The observer never enforced the rules or showed his observations to the director. At various times a second observer recorded rule violations at the same time but independently of the primary observer. Reliability averaged 96%.

Figure 23–2 shows the results of the study. When the rules were only enforced occasionally, each rule was broken most of the time. After consistent enforcement was implemented, the rate at which the three rules were violated decreased dramatically. The amount of time lost in penalties averaged 10 minutes. The number of participants did not change over the period of the experiment.

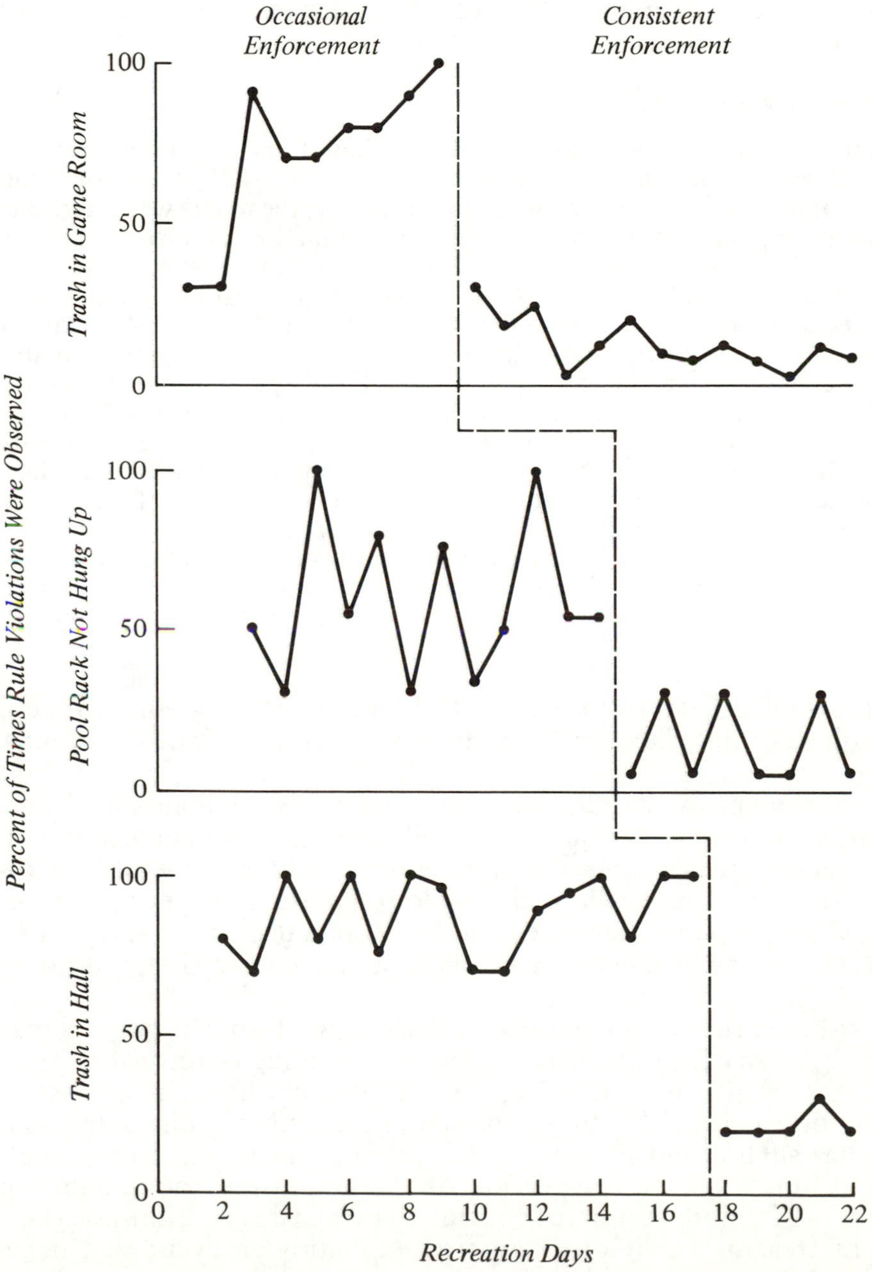

Figure 23–2. The effect of consistent rule enforcement on disruptive behavior in an inner-city recreational facility. Adapted from "Recreation as a Reinforcer: Increasing Membership and Decreasing Disruptions in an Urban Recreation Center," by C. H. Pierce and T. R. Risley, *Journal of Applied Behavior Analysis*, 1974, 7, 403–411. Used by permission.

The group contingency used in this experiment seemed particularly well suited to this situation. By being a group contingency it did not require personal and possibly abrasive confrontations between director and participants. Instead, it seemed to generate prompting of appropriate behavior by the older participants to younger ones who were breaking the rules. The result of the procedure was a cleaner, better-operating recreation center that left the director more time to plan constructive activities and improve the facility.

Note: At least two experiments have demonstrated that removing autistic children from a presumably reinforcing environment may be reinforcing rather than punishing! Solnick, Rincover, and Peterson (1977) used time out in an attempt to reduce the tantrums of a 6-year-old autistic girl. This procedure increased the rate of tantrums. The authors concluded that placing the child in isolation permitted her to engage in autistic self-stimulation, the opportunity for which was apparently reinforcing. Similar results were obtained by Plummer, Baer, and LeBlanc (1977). These findings point out once again that it is crucial to determine empirically whether an event that is presumed a punisher or reinforcer actually affects behavior in the predicted manner.

ADDITIONAL READINGS

Baer, D. M. Laboratory control of thumbsucking by withdrawal and re-presentation of reinforcement. *Journal of the Experimental Analysis of Behavior*, 1962, *5*, 525–528. Thumbsucking children were shown a cartoon movie. Whenever they sucked their thumb, the movie was interrupted for as long as they sucked their thumb. When they pulled their thumb from their mouth, the cartoon was turned on again. The rate of thumbsucking was drastically reduced by this procedure.

Clark, H. B., Rowbury, T., Baer, A. M., & Baer, D. M. Time-out as a punishing stimulus in continuous and intermittent schedules. *Journal of Applied Behavior Analysis*,1973, *6*, 443–455. Time out was used to suppress the rate of extremely disruptive behaviors (including physical aggression) in a retarded child. The article also contains references to many other studies using time-out procedures.

Hall, R. V., Axelrod, S., Tyler, L., Grief, E., Jones, F. C., & Robertson, R. Modification of behavior problems in the home with a parent as observer and experimenter. *Journal of Applied Behavior Analysis*, 1972, *5*, 53–64. Elaise, a 5-year-old girl, took an average of over 3 hours to get dressed in the morning during baseline. Treatment consisted of withdrawing TV-watching privileges if she took longer than 30 minutes. This reduced her dressing time to an average of 23 minutes.

Winkler, R. C. Management of chronic psychiatric patients by a token reinforcement system. *Journal of Applied Behavior Analysis*, 1970, *3*, 47–55. Chronic psychiatric patients were fined by loss of tokens for tantrumming, screaming, and acts of violence. These behaviors increased rather sharply when the fines were discontinued.

Helpful hint #1: It is not necessary to use the full label describing which type of punisher or punishment is involved. Simply label the procedure as "punishment" and the event as a "punisher."

Helpful hint #2: Punishment by withdrawal must be carefully distinguished from extinction. In punishment by withdrawal, an event that is normally in the person's environment is withdrawn contingent on the person's making an undesirable response. In other words, the event is there as long as the person does not make the undesirable response. In extinction, an event that was previously produced by a person's response is no longer produced by that response. The event is not withdrawn only when the response is made, as in punishment; rather, it is no longer delivered for the response.

For example, suppose that Danny teases his little sister, Kim. His parents may use either of two approaches. If they can determine what has been reinforcing Danny's teasing behavior, and if they can control that event, then they might try extinction. It might be that they have paid attention to Danny for teasing, either by yelling at him or possibly by discussing his behavior with him. If they feel that such attention was reinforcing the teasing, then they might simply stop paying attention to him when he teases Kim. At the same time, they might continue to pay attention to him for other, more desirable behaviors. Their goal is to eliminate the reinforcer that was maintaining his teasing behavior. They are eliminating an event that occurs in Danny's environment only after his undesirable behavior.

The other approach might be to select some event that Danny likes and withdraw it from him for a period of time when he teases his sister. Again the parents might select their own attention to him, but this time not because it was reinforcing the teasing behavior but rather because he likes to receive attention from them. And they might simply eliminate all attention for 5 minutes after any teasing behavior occurs. In this case, they would not be eliminating attention paid to teasing, but all attention paid to Danny for any reason whatever. The parents' goal in this procedure is to take something nice away from Danny for a period of time whenever he performs the undesirable behavior. In this case, they are withdrawing an event that occurs in his environment before (or without respect to) his undesirable behavior.

To distinguish between the two procedures, ask the question "Is the event normally in the person's environment before the response or after the response (and contingent on making the response)?" If the event is normally in the environment before the person makes the response, and if the event is now withdrawn from the environment every time he or she makes the response, then the procedure is punishment by contingent withdrawal. If the event is normally in the person's environment after the response and dependent on making the response, and if the event is now no longer produced by the response, then the procedure involved is extinction.

Helpful hint #3: Remember to distinguish between punishment and punisher in all questions. If you do not, your answer will be marked as incorrect. Punishment is the procedure of using a punisher.

LESSON 23 READING QUIZ

(6) Punishment by contingent withdrawal is the procedure in which an event is ________ contingent on the occurrence of a behavior, thereby producing a decrease in the rate of that behavior.

(16) Punishment by contingent stimulation, as studied in the last lesson, involves the ________________ of an event contingent on the occurrence of a behavior and a decrease in the rate of that behavior.

(11) In punishment by contingent withdrawal, an event that is normally in the person's environment is ________________ when he or she emits a particular behavior.

(5) If you decide that a procedure is punishment by contingent stimulation, you should label it as ________________; if you decide that a procedure is punishment by withdrawal, you should label it as ________________.

(15) If a person is denied access to some reinforcing situation temporarily when he or she emits a behavior, this is a form of punishment by contingent withdrawal that is called ________ ________________.

(10) If a mother spanks a child for not brushing his or her teeth and the rate of not brushing teeth decreases, would the spanking be an example of punishment? ________

(4) Delivering an aversive event when a person does not emit a particular behavior ________ (is, isn't) an example of punishment.

(14) Pierce and Risley (1974) observed trash in the game room for 10 days before enforcing the rules strictly. They observed how often the pool rack was not hung up for 14 days before enforcing the rules strictly. What type of experimental design were they using? ________ ________________

(9) When Pierce and Risley (1974) posted a list of rules and the penalties for breaking them, but did not always enforce the penalties, the rate of rule-violating behavior ________ (did, didn't) decrease.

(3) Pierce and Risley (1974) marked the number of minutes that a recreation center would have to close each time a rule violation was observed. This procedure reduced rule violation dramatically. If these numbers were no longer paired with the actual early closing of the center, they would probably lose their effect. If they did, what type of punisher would they be? ________________

(13) If Pierce and Risley (1974) had ignored all rule-violating behavior and the rate of such behavior had decreased, what procedure would they have been using? ________

(8) Pierce and Risley (1974) withdrew the privilege of playing in the recreation center when a rule

was violated. The rule-violating behavior decreased dramatically. What behavioral procedure did they use? ______________________

(2) An event that was previously produced by a behavior is no longer produced by it in the procedure called ______________________.

(12) If an event is normally in the environment before one emits a behavior and is withdrawn when the person emits the behavior, what procedure is involved? ______________________

(7) If an event is normally in the environment only after one emits a behavior and now the person's behavior no longer produces the event, what behavioral procedure is this? ______________________

(1) To distinguish between punishment by withdrawal and extinction, ask the question "Is the event in the person's environment ______________________ the response, or is it normally in the person's environment ______________________ the behavior (and contingent on it)?"

READING QUIZ ANSWERS

(1) before; after (2) extinction (3) conditioned (4) isn't (5) punishment; punishment (6) withdrawn (7) extinction (8) punishment (or time out) (9) didn't (10) no (11) withdrawn (12) punishment (13) extinction (14) multiple baseline (15) time out (16) delivery

LESSON 23 EXAMPLES

Example #1

Six-year-old Bobbie treated his toys roughly. He would take his toy soldiers and make them have a war. He would then decide who had been shot during the war, and he would break that soldier into little pieces. He also played demolition derby with his toy cars and had them crash into one another. Many of his cars were broken in this manner.

Bobbie's parents were upset by his destructiveness and decided to teach Bobbie to stop being destructive. So every time Bobbie played too roughly with his toys, his parents simply took the toys away for a short period of time (usually about 15 minutes). They would also explain to him why the toys were being taken away. After the 15 minutes were up, Bobbie would get his toys back again. Bobbie had almost stopped his destructive play within 2 weeks.

(33) Were the toys withdrawn following Bobbie's destructive behavior? ______________

(22) Did the rate of Bobbie's destructiveness decrease? ______________

(11) If you think this might be an example of extinction, you should ask the question "Are the toys normally in Bobbie's environment before he is destructive, or are they in his environment after he is destructive (and as a result of his destructiveness)?" The answer in this case is ______________________ (before, after).

(32) Therefore, because the toys are normally in Bobbie's environment before his destructiveness and they are then removed when he is destructive (and the rate of destructiveness decreases), this is an example of ______________________ by contingent withdrawal.

Example #2

Dora was mean to her little brother Rickie all the time. She grabbed toys away from him and wouldn't let him have them back. She called him names and humiliated him in front of other children. Dora's parents were upset about her behavior. They felt that her meanness was harmful to Rickie, so they decided to put a stop to it. Each time they caught her being mean to her brother, they took away her "outside-play" privilege by keeping her inside for 1 hour. Soon Dora had almost stopped being mean to her little brother.

(21) They took away Dora's "________________" privilege when she mistreated her brother.

(10) Soon Dora's rate of meanness ________________.

(31) To determine whether the decrease in Dora's meanness resulted from punishment or extinction, ask "Is outside play normally in Dora's environment before she is mean, or is it in her environment after she is mean (and because she is mean)?" In this case, it is in her environment ________________ (before, after) her meanness.

(20) Therefore, this is an example of ________________.

Example #3

John's comments about bad food were gross. When the fraternity served a meal that he didn't like, he likened the food to every undesirable form of organic material he could think of. Naturally, this had a terrible effect on everyone's appetite. One day several members decided that John's gross comments were being reinforced because of everyone's outraged reactions. They decided that no one would act outraged for these kinds of statements again. John's rate of griping gradually decreased over a period of about 6 weeks so that everyone could eat his meal in peace again.

(9) This might be an example of either extinction or punishment because John's rate of griping ________________.

(30) To decide which it is, ask "Is outrage normally in John's environment before his griping, or is it after griping and as a result of griping?" In this case, it is ________________.

(19) Therefore, this is an example of what behavioral procedure? ________________

Example #4

Every time Tad pouted, his parents took away some of his play time by immediately sending him to his room for 10 minutes. At the end of the 10 minutes, they would go to his room and tell him his time was up. They usually had a useful discussion about Tad's pouting at that time. Tad's pouting went on at about the same rate for the next few months.

(8) Tad's parents used neither extinction nor punishment because Tad's pouting did not ________________ in rate.

(29) If Tad's pouting had decreased, you could determine whether the decrease resulted from extinction or punishment by asking "Did Tad normally have play privileges before pouting, or did play privileges arise only after Tad's pouting?" The answer is ________________.

(18) If Tad's pouting had decreased, the parents' behavior would have been an example of what behavioral procedure? ________________

Example #5

Mary burped frequently at the dinner table. Usually when Mary burped, her parents admonished her and explained that it wasn't polite to burp at the dinner table. Recently, however, Mary's parents decided that they were encouraging Mary's burping behavior by arguing with her when she burped. Mary has been burping less and less since her parents instituted their new policy of not arguing with her.

(7) This situation might be an example of either punishment or extinction because the parents' procedure produced a(n) ________________ in the rate of Mary's burping.

(28) To decide which procedure is involved, ask "Is arguing normally in Mary's environment before she burps, or is it normally in Mary's environment after she burps and as a result of her burping?" ________________

(17) Because Mary's rate of burping decreased and because arguing was normally in her environment only after a burp, the stopping of arguments is an example of what behavioral procedure? ____________________

Example #6

Clarence frequently gossiped about the other members of the group—which ones smoked dope, who was sleeping with whom, and who didn't like whom. At first the members of the group listened to Clarence and took his gossip seriously. Later, however, they decided that it was creating bad feelings in their group. They therefore decided to suspend him from membership for a week each time he gossiped. Clarence was suspended only once; he never gossiped after that.

(6) What behavioral procedure is this an example of? ____________________
(Is membership present before or after gossiping?)

Example #7

Marcie and Fran had a nice friendship. Both were interested in learning how to set up a utopian commune. In long talks with Marcie about how to do this, Fran frequently took an anarchist position: if one just had faith in people, everything would work out by itself. Marcie didn't believe that philosophy, however, and always disagreed with Fran. She used her knowledge of behavior analysis to point out sources of unintentional reinforcement and punishment that would defeat Fran's anarchistic solution. Marcie's alternative was to have faith in the ultimate capabilities of people if they understood behavior and went about setting up a system that would develop the kind of behavior that everyone wanted. Marcie's disagreements were always convincingly stated, and soon Fran stopped proposing anarchistic solutions.

(27) The decrease in Fran's rate of proposing anarchistic solutions caused by Marcie's convincing arguments would be an example of what behavioral procedure? ____________________

Example #8

Barbara was both the school artist and the school bully. She did beautiful art, but she tended to beat up her schoolmates whenever she felt like it. The teachers felt that Barbara's behavior severely disrupted the recess and class periods, so they decided to take action. Every time they caught Barbara fighting, they immediately told her that she could not take part in the art period that day. They observed that Barbara's rate of fighting decreased.

(16) Is Barbara's opportunity to take part in the art period present <u>before</u> she bullies someone, or is it present <u>after</u> she bullies someone (and as a result of bullying someone)? ____________________

(5) Stopping Barbara from taking part in the art period when she beats up another child would be an example of what behavioral procedure? ____________________

Example #9

Bud had the bad habit of griping about the evening meal almost every night no matter what food was served. The other members of the commune became increasingly annoyed by this behavior and tried to explain to Bud why his griping was bad for the group (especially the cooks). But Bud persisted in his griping. Finally everyone decided to stop explaining to Bud why he shouldn't gripe. So each time Bud started to gripe about the food, everyone just acted as though he hadn't said anything. Bud's griping gradually disappeared.

(26) The decrease in Bud's griping is an example of what behavioral procedure? ____________________
(Are the members' explanations present before or after Bud's griping?)

Example #10

Bob used to flirt with all the other women that he met. This greatly angered Barb, who finally decided to withhold all affection from him on any day that he flirted with someone else.

(15) Bob no longer flirts with other women. What behavioral procedure did Barb use to stop his flirting? ______________________

Example #11

Fred was a radical and Ruth was a liberal. Both of them were very aggressive in arguing their points of view. In spite of their differences, however, Fred and Ruth got along beautifully. One rule that helped them get along was that they never talked about politics. Ruth obeyed the rule all the time, but Fred frequently broke it. So whenever Fred started a political harangue or made a political joke, Ruth got mad at him and told him to knock it off. Within 2 weeks, Fred was obeying the "no-politics" rule also.

(4) The decrease in Fred's political talk is the result of what behavioral procedure? ________

Example #12

Larry often took extreme positions just for the sake of an argument. When he did so, Jim gave him a certain kind of look that made Larry feel very uncomfortable. The rate at which he took extreme positions decreased as a result of Jim's looks.

(25) What behavioral procedure did Jim use? ______________________

Example #13

Larry took extreme positions with Frank just for the sake of an argument. Later Frank just ignored all such arguments. Larry's rate of taking extreme positions for the sake of an argument decreased.

(14) What behavioral procedure did Frank use? ______________________

Example #14

Larry took extreme positions with Theresa just for the sake of an argument. Theresa always broke off the conversation in a very gentle way as soon as this started to happen. Larry's rate of taking extreme positions with Theresa decreased soon afterwards.

(3) What behavioral procedure did Theresa use? ______________________

Example #15

(24) If each of three people decreased Larry's rate of argumentative behavior with them by soon stopping the conversation, and if Larry stopped being argumentative with any other people, what behavioral procedure did these three people use to change Larry's behavior in all situations? ______________________

Example #16

Dr. Brunner met with Tim three times a week to help him learn to live without his true love, Ann, who broke up with him last week. Every time that Tim said something like "I just can't live without her!" Dr. Brunner would ask "Why?" Tim soon came to recognize that he did not have any valid reasons for feeling that he could not live without Ann. His rate of saying "I just can't live without her" decreased rapidly during several sessions with Dr. Brunner.

(13) What behavioral procedure did Dr. Brunner use to reduce the rate at which Tim said that?
____

Example #17

When Steve and Maria were talking, Maria usually looked directly at Steve with a nice little smile. However, anytime that Steve talked about Maria's lack of belief in God, she stopped looking at him for at least a minute. Pretty soon Steve stopped talking about Maria's beliefs.

(2) What behavioral procedure did Maria use? ____________________

Example #18

Anytime that Steve brought up the question of the disadvantages of socialism, Maria argued with him. However, recently she decided that she would not argue with Steve. She would just ignore his comments until he changed topics. Steve does not bring up that issue much any more.

(23) What behavioral procedure did Maria use to reduce Steve's rate of discussing socialism?
____

Example #19

Little Kathy sometimes threw a temper tantrum if she could not have a cookie when she wanted it. Every time that she threw a temper tantrum, her father carried her upstairs to her room and made her stay there until well after she had finished her tantrum. Kathy no longer throws temper tantrums when she can't have a cookie.

(12) What behavioral procedure did her father use? ____________________

Example #20

Little Kathy sometimes threw temper tantrums when she couldn't stay up late. Her parents, wanting to be kind, would usually let her stay up late. However, lately, they have ignored her temper tantrums and just made her go to bed. Kathy has stopped throwing temper tantrums.

(1) What behavioral procedure did her parents use to eliminate temper tantrums?____________

EXAMPLE ANSWERS

(1) extinction (2) punishment (3) punishment (4) punishment (5) punishment (6) punishment (7) decrease (8) decrease (9) decreased (10) decreased (11) before (12) punishment (13) punishment (14) extinction (15) punishment (16) before (17) extinction (18) punishment (19) extinction (20) punishment (21) outside-play (22) yes (23) extinction (24) generalization training (25) punishment (26) extinction (27) punishment (28) after (29) before (30) after (31) before (32) punishment (33) yes

Lesson 24

Escape and Avoidance

This lesson introduces a new kind of reinforcer—the negative reinforcer. A **negative reinforcer** is any event that is terminated or prevented by a behavior and that causes the rate of that behavior to increase. An example of a negative reinforcer changing parental behavior would be when a child starts crying and doesn't stop until one of his or her parents pays attention and when the parent then pays more attention to the child in the future. The crying is called the negative reinforcer, because it is terminated by the attending behavior and the attending behavior then increases in the future (when the child cries).

In distinguishing a negative reinforcer from a positive reinforcer, a **positive reinforcer** (any event whose delivery following a response increases the rate of that behavior) would be thought of as a pleasant event, while a negative reinforcer would usually be thought of as an unpleasant event. But delivering the positive reinforcer and terminating (or postponing) the negative reinforcer produce the same behavioral results.

When people speak of "punishing" another person for not doing something, they are speaking of using negative reinforcement. For example, if a mother spanks her son because he didn't clean up his room, she is creating a situation in which the child can prevent such a spanking by making the cleaning response the next time. If the rate of the child's cleaning behavior increases because it prevents the spanking, the spanking would be a negative reinforcer. Thus, what many people refer to as "punishing" a nonresponse is called by behavior analysts "negative reinforcement" of that same behavior.

If you have any doubt about whether an event that follows a behavior is a punisher or a negative reinforcer, just ask "Did the rate of the behavior increase, or did it decrease?" If the rate of the behavior increased, you are dealing with a reinforcer. If it decreased, you are dealing with a punisher.

Remember, a negative reinforcer is not a punisher. Traditional psychologists equate "negative reinforcer" with "punisher," thus emphasizing the "negative" in negative reinforcer. Behavior analysts, however, emphasize the "reinforcer" in negative reinforcer. The term *reinforcer*, whether modified by a "positive" or a "negative," is always used by behavior analysts to refer to an event that follows and increases the rate of a behavior. Usually a stimulus that can be used as a negative reinforcer can also be used as a punisher, but this is not always the case.

Behavior analysts distinguish between the situation in which a negative reinforcer is terminated by the behavior and the situation in which it is prevented by a behavior. **Escape** is the name of the procedure in which a negative reinforcer is present until the person makes a response to terminate it; such a response is called an escape response. **Avoidance** is the name of the procedure in which a negative reinforcer is prevented from occurring because the person makes a response; such a response is called an avoidance response.

With an escape response, the negative reinforcer is physically present in the environment until the response is made. Thus the response terminates the negative reinforcer. For example, if a father lends his son $5 but the son fails to thank him, the father may scowl until he is thanked. As soon as the son says "thanks" the father stops scowling, and the son escapes the dirty look.

Azrin and Powell (1969) used an escape procedure to increase the frequency of taking medication at the prescribed time. They developed a timed pill holder that caused a loud buzzer to sound when it was time to take a pill. The buzzer could be turned off only by turning a handle and thereby dispensing a pill. Supplementary observation indicated that such pills were usually taken if dispensed in this manner. Thus, the patient could terminate the buzzer by dispensing the pill—a good example of escape behavior.

With an avoidance response, the negative reinforcer is not physically present at the time of the response, but it is scheduled to be delivered if the response is not made. Thus, the response prevents the negative reinforcer from occurring. For example, if the son immediately thanked his father for the $5, his "thanks" would be an avoidance response because "thanks" prevents the scowl from occurring. Of course, we must have some knowledge that the father would have scowled if the son had not thanked him. Figure 24–1 shows a more humorous example of avoidance as Beetle Bailey executes a brilliant avoidance response to avoid work!

Figure 24–1. "Work" is always a negative reinforcer for some people. Notice the avoidance response! Cartoon copyright 1973 King Features Syndicate. Reproduced by permission.

Fichter, Wallace, Liberman, and Davis (1976) used an avoidance procedure to increase the social interaction skills of chronic schizophrenics. They found that a typical patient, whom we will call Joe, spoke too softly to be easily heard, made the briefest possible comments, and bit his fingernails. They taught him more appropriate behaviors by engaging him in simple conversations and nagging him if he failed to engage in those behaviors. The nagging consisted of instructing him to engage in those behaviors. If he engaged in the behaviors during the conversations, no nagging was employed. Thus Joe could prevent the occurrence of the nagging by engaging in the behavior. This would be a good example of avoidance behavior.

Escape and avoidance procedures are often combined to produce a more powerful procedure. Azrin, Rubin, O'Brien, Ayllon, and Roll (1968) used such a procedure to teach improved posture to normal adults. The subjects wore a simple device that could detect slouching during their normal daytime activities. They could prevent the device from operating a loud buzzer by maintaining good posture. Thus, maintaining good posture was an avoidance behavior. If, however, the subjects slouched, the buzzer would sound and could be terminated only by adopting good posture. Thus adopting good posture was also an escape behavior.

Negative reinforcement can be used in place of positive reinforcement in any of the procedures that you studied earlier in the book. For example, stopping the termination or prevention of a negative reinforcer and observing a decrease in the rate of the behavior is an example of extinction. If you will remember that positive and negative reinforcement are both reinforcement, then it should be clear that any procedure or principle that applies to positive reinforcement will also apply to negative reinforcement. There follows a brief review of the major reinforcement procedures from the point of view of negative reinforcement.

Extinction of a behavior maintained by a negative reinforcer. Stopping the withdrawal or termination of an event following a behavior and observing a decrease in the behavior is called extinction. For example, if the father no longer stops scowling when his son borrows $5 and thanks him, the son's thanking behavior is on extinction.

Differential reinforcement using negative reinforcement. If one behavior is followed by the termination or prevention of an event, while other behaviors are not, then the procedure would be called "differential reinforcement." For example, if the father stops scowling only if the son says "thank you, sir" but not if thanked in any other way, then the behavior of saying "thank you, sir" is being differentially reinforced.

Shaping with the use of negative reinforcement. If each of a series of successive approximations to a target behavior is differentially reinforced by terminating or preventing an event following the desired approximation, then the procedure is called "shaping." For example, if the father terminated his scowl originally only if the son said "thanks," later if he said "thank you," and finally only if he said "thank you, sir," this would be an example of shaping.

Intermittent negative reinforcement. If only some instances of a behavior lead to the termination or prevention of an event, then the schedule of reinforcement is called "intermittent." Specifically, if people must make a response five times to eliminate a shock, then their behavior is being (negatively) reinforced according to a fixed-ratio schedule. If the people must make differing numbers of responses averaging five, then their behavior is being reinforced according to a variable-ratio schedule. If the people can eliminate the shock only through the first response occurring after 5 seconds, then their behavior is being reinforced according to a fixed-interval schedule. And, if the intervals differ but average 5 seconds, then their behavior is being reinforced according to a variable-interval schedule.

The various effects of different schedules are the same for positive and negative reinforcement. For example, a fixed ratio of negative reinforcement will produce a pause after reinforcement and then a rapid rate of responding until reinforcement occurs again. The longer scalloping effect of fixed-interval schedules will be the same. The more uniform rates produced by variable-interval and variable-ratio schedules will also be produced by negative reinforcement, with the variable ratio producing the highest rate of responding.

Likewise, resistance to extinction will be greater with an intermittent schedule; satiation will be less likely; ratio strain may occur if the ratio is too high; and shaping will occur more readily if a continuous schedule of negative reinforcement is used.

Principle of contingent negative reinforcement. The termination or prevention of an event will be a more effective (negative) reinforcer if it occurs only when the behavior is emitted. For example, the father's scowl will be most effective if it is terminated only when the son says "thank you, sir." If the father sometimes stops scowling for a "thank you," it will be less effective in reinforcing the desired behavior of "thank you, sir."

Principle of immediate negative reinforcement. The more immediately after the behavior an event is terminated or prevented, the more effective it will be as a negative reinforcer. For example, if Father stops scowling only several minutes after his son has said "thank you, sir," the negative reinforcement will not be as effective.

Principle of the size of a negative reinforcer. The larger the amount (or intensity) of a negative reinforcer, the more effective it will be. If Father makes only a slight grimace when not thanked, it will not be as effective as if he makes a very obvious scowl. Better yet would be to yell and hit the son until he thanks his father.[1]

Principle of deprivation of a negative reinforcer. The less recently an event has been terminated or prevented, the more effective it will be. Thus the father that scowls only very rarely and the rest of the time is positive and supportive will have more of an effect than the father who scowls frequently.

Discrimination training using negative reinforcement. If a behavior leads to the termination or prevention of an event in one situation but not another, then the procedure being used is called "discrimination training." Thus, saying "thank you, sir" may terminate the scowl after borrowing money, but not after Father has said "Son, it is your turn to do the dishes."

[1]It should be obvious that a behavior analyst would not recommend such a procedure, but you should realize that this statement is true. In fact, most behavior analysts would question the father's target behavior and help father and son to adopt a more mutually reinforcing pattern of behavior.

BEHAVIOR ANALYSIS EXAMPLE

Taking prescribed medication. The failure of patients to take medication at the times prescribed by their doctor is a major medical problem. This failure can undermine the medical treatment of a wide range of illnesses. Studies have estimated that as many as 35% of all patients fail to take their medication correctly. A review of about 100 medical research articles studying 34 different strategies not involving behavioral methods for improving patient compliance with prescribed pilltaking schedules, such as education of the patient, revealed little effect.

Epstein and Masek (1978) analyzed the compliance of 20 patients in taking a 100 mg dose of vitamin C four times a day. They approached compliance as a behavioral problem by devising a simple method for observing whether their patients took the medication as scheduled. Their method involved adding 200 mg of phenazopyridine as a "tracer" medicine to three of the 28 tablets to be taken in a week. The tracer pills looked and tasted just like the regular vitamin C pills. All 28 pills were placed in a dispenser so that they would be taken in a fixed order; the tracer pills were placed in a random order known only to the doctors.

The patients were then required to report any time that they noticed a discoloration in their urine caused by the tracer. Compliance was measured by determining whether the reports of discoloration occurred within 12 hours of the time that patients were scheduled to take the randomly scheduled tracer pills. Since the patients did not know which pills contained the tracer medicine and could not taste or see the difference, their report could be correct only if they took their pills on time. Thus, the patients could prevent the occurrence of a fine by taking their pills as prescribed.

Figure 24-2 shows the results of observations during baseline. The patients reported taking on the average only one of their three tracer pills at the correct time. The doctors then required half of the patients to pay $1 if they did not correctly report taking at least two of the three tracer pills. The patients who had to pay the fine reported taking well over two of the three tracer pills at the correct time. But the patients who still did not have to pay the fine continued at baseline level.

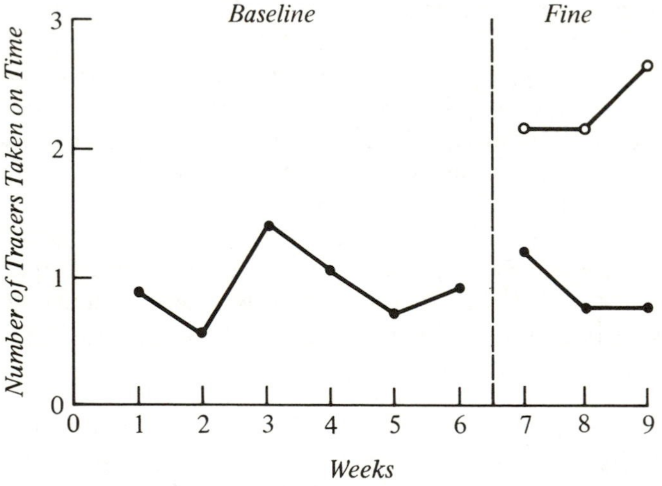

Figure 24-2. The number of pills taken at the prescribed time. The filled circles represent patients operating with no special consequences. The open circles represent patients who were fined $1 for failing to take at least two out of three tracer pills at the prescribed time. From "Behavioral Control of Medicine Compliance," by L. H. Epstein and B. J. Masek, *Journal of Applied Behavior Analysis*, 1978, *11*, 1-9. Copyright 1978 by the Society for the Experimental Analysis of Behavior, Inc. Used by permission.

Note #1: Michael (1973) has taken the position that the distinction between positive and negative reinforcement is often impossible to make objectively and in any event is not a useful distinction. He also provides an interesting description of the history of the distinction.

ADDITIONAL READINGS

Ayllon, T., & Michael, J. The psychiatric nurse as a behavioral engineer. *Journal of the Experimental Analysis of Behavior*, 1959, *2*, 323-334. Two psychiatric patients who refused to feed themselves and thus required spoonfeeding by a nurse were exposed to an avoidance procedure. The researchers observed that both patients were extremely concerned about their appearance, so the nurse continued to feed both patients but now dropped a bit of food on the patients' clothing. The patients soon learned to feed themselves in order to avoid the spilled food.

Lovaas, O. I., Schaeffer, B., & Simmons, J. Q. Building social behavior in autistic children by use of electric shock. *Journal of Experimental Research in Personality*, 1965, *1*, 99–109. This study deals with two autistic children. Psychiatric treatment had been totally ineffective in bringing them into contact with other individuals, so a program was started in which they were shocked for any self-stimulating behaviors. The shock was turned off if they approached the therapist (escape). This procedure rapidly increased the social behaviors of the children and provided a starting point for further behavioral therapy.

Helpful hint #1: To decide whether a response is an escape response or an avoidance response, ask "When the response was made, was the negative reinforcer present (escape), or was the negative reinforcer scheduled to be delivered later if the response was not made (avoidance)?" That is, "Was the negative reinforcer present or absent at the moment of responding?"

Helpful hint #2: You do not have to name an event as a "negative" reinforcer; just to note that it is a reinforcer is sufficient. Also be sure that an event that is terminated by a behavior leads to an increase in the rate of that behavior. Otherwise it is an "unknown," not a negative reinforcer.

Helpful hint #3: Sometimes a procedure can be viewed as being either punishment or negative reinforcement depending on the perspective that you adopt. For example, if a child is spanked for being dirty, you would normally label the spanking procedure as punishment—punishment for getting dirty. However, this situation can also be viewed as the child being spanked for not having cleaned up. This you would normally label as negative reinforcement of cleaning behavior. This type of alternative will arise whenever the person must make one of two responses (for example, getting dirty or cleaning up). In such cases, be sure to answer the question as it is stated. If the question is "What do you call the procedure of spanking a child for getting dirty?" the correct answer is "punishment." If the question is "What do you call the procedure of spanking a child for failing to clean up?" the correct answer is "negative reinforcement" or "avoidance." Your answer will be considered incorrect if you do not answer the question as stated.

LESSON 24 READING QUIZ

(7) Any event that is terminated or prevented by a behavior and that causes the rate of that behavior to increase is called a(n) ______________________.

(19) A negative reinforcer is any event that, when it is ______________________ or ______________________ by a behavior, produces an increase in the rate of that behavior.

(13) The similarity between a positive reinforcer and the termination or prevention of a negative reinforcer is that they both follow the behavior and produce a(n) ______________________ in the rate of that behavior.

(6) Traditional psychology equates the two terms *negative reinforcer* and ______________; behavior analysts do not.

(18) If a person is "punished" for not making a response, behavior analysts would refer to this as an example of what behavioral procedure? ______________________

(12) A punisher leads to a(n) ______________________ in the rate of a behavior; a negative reinforcer leads to a(n) ______________________ in the rate of a behavior.

(5) Escape is the procedure in which a negative reinforcer is present until a response is made that ______________________ that stimulus.

(17) Avoidance is the procedure in which a negative reinforcer is scheduled until a response is made that ______________________ that stimulus from occurring.

(11) Azrin and Powell (1969) developed a pill dispenser that sounded a buzzer at the prescribed time for taking a pill. The buzzer could be turned off only by dispensing a pill. The behavior of dispensing the pill would be an example of a(n) ______________________ behavior.

(4) Fichter and his colleagues (1976) nagged Joe anytime that he failed to engage in acceptable social behavior. Engaging in acceptable social behavior would be a(n) ______________ behavior.

(16) Azrin and his colleagues (1968) developed an apparatus that sounded a loud buzzer any time that a person slouched. Maintaining good posture would be an example of a(n) ______________ behavior. If the person did slouch, he or she could turn the buzzer off only by adopting good posture. Adopting good posture would be an example of a(n) ______________ behavior.

(10) If each of a series of successive approximations to some target response terminates a negative reinforcer (while nonapproximations do not), the procedure would be called ______________.

(3) In order to be most effective, a negative reinforcer should be terminated ______________ (when) after the behavior occurs.

(15) To decide whether a behavior is an escape behavior or an avoidance behavior, ask "Was the negative reinforcer ______________ at the moment of responding (if so, it is escape), or was the negative reinforcer ______________ at the moment of responding (if so, it is avoidance)?"

(9) Epstein and Masek (1978) required that their patients pay a $1 fine if they failed to take their medication at the prescribed time. The patients' rate of taking their medication at the correct time increased as a result. The patients' behavior of taking the medication at the prescribed time would be called a(n) ______________ response.

(2) Epstein and Masek (1978) required their patients to pay a $1 fine if the medication was not taken at the prescribed time. The patients' rate of taking their medication at the prescribed time increased as a result. The $1 fine would be called a(n) ______________.

(14) If you decide that a procedure involves the termination or prevention of an event following a behavior and the rate of the behavior increases, you should label it as ______________; if you decide that a procedure involves the delivery of an event following a behavior and the rate increases, you should label the procedure as ______________.

(8) If a behavior prevents an event from occurring and the rate of the behavior increases, the behavior is called a(n) ______________ response.

(1) If a behavior terminates an event and the rate of the behavior increases, the behavior is called a(n) ______________ response.

READING QUIZ ANSWERS

(1) escape (2) negative reinforcer (3) immediately (4) avoidance (5) terminates (6) *punisher* (7) negative reinforcer (8) avoidance (9) avoidance (10) shaping (11) escape (12) decrease; increase (13) increase (14) reinforcement; reinforcement (don't need negative or positive) (15) present; absent (16) avoidance; escape (17) prevents (18) negative reinforcement (or avoidance) (19) terminated; prevented

LESSON 24 EXAMPLES

Example #1

When 4-year-old Mary got out of bed on a cold morning, she "froze" her feet. One morning she put on her slippers as soon as she began to feel the cold. This action kept her feet warm. From then on she put on her slippers any morning that she felt the cold.

(30) The cold feeling was ______________ (terminated or prevented?) immediately after Mary put on her slippers.

(15) Mary's behavior of putting on slippers on cold mornings ________ in rate after that first time.

(44) Because the cold feeling was terminated by putting on the slippers and because Mary's rate of putting on the slippers increased in frequency, coldness would be classified as a(n) ________ reinforcer.

(29) Because Mary's behavior of putting on the slippers <u>terminates</u> the stimulus of the coldness, behavior analysts say that Mary's behavior is a(n) ________ behavior. (Was the cold <u>present</u> or <u>absent</u> when the slippers were put on?)

Example #2

One day Mary put on her slippers before she put her feet on the floor. In this way, she prevented the coldness from reaching her feet. From that day on, Mary put her slippers on before getting out of bed.

(14) In this example, the cold feeling was ________ (terminated or prevented?) by putting on the slippers.

(43) The rate of Mary's putting on the slippers before getting out of bed ________.

(28) Therefore the cold feeling is called a(n) ________.

(13) However, because putting on the slippers before getting out of bed prevented the coldness from affecting Mary's feet, Mary's putting on slippers before getting out of bed is called a(n) ________ behavior. (Is the cold present or absent?)

(42) When Mary put on the slippers <u>after</u> she felt the cold (thereby terminating the cold), the behavior of putting on the slippers is called a(n) ________ behavior. When Mary put on the slippers <u>before</u> she felt the cold (thereby preventing the coldness), the behavior of putting on the slippers is called a(n) ________ behavior.

Example #3

Hamm and Carey had been friends for quite a while. But Hamm had a bad habit. Somehow he would just lose track of time when talking with one of his friends and, as a result, would show up late for his dates with Carey. Carey got depressed each time Hamm was late and always looked sad by the time he got there. Whenever he was on time, though, she looked her usual self—not at all sad. In effect, by showing up on time, Hamm could keep Carey from looking sad. Soon Hamm noticed the difference in Carey when he was on time and when he was late, so he started showing up on time.

(27) Carey's looking sad was ________ (terminated, prevented) by Hamm's showing up on time.

(12) The rate of Hamm's showing up on time ________.

(41) Carey's sad look is called a(n) ________.

(26) Hamm's behavior of being on time is called a(n) ________ behavior. (Is the stimulus present or absent at the moment of responding?)

(11) When Hamm did not come on time, Carey looked sad; therefore Hamm started coming on time. Is this an example of Carey's punishing Hamm? ________

Example #4

Sally never did her homework for Ms. Mann's social studies class, so Ms. Mann started keeping Sally after class every day she failed to do her homework. Thus, Sally could get out of having to stay after school by simply doing her homework. Ms. Mann found after 2 months that Sally still never did her homework.

(40) Sally could ______________________ (terminate, prevent) herself from being kept after school by doing her homework.

(25) The rate of Sally's doing her homework during the 2 months that Ms. Mann tried keeping her after school ______________________.

(10) Is being kept after school a negative reinforcer for Sally? __________

(39) Keeping Sally after school did not effectively change her behavior, perhaps because the effectiveness of the event was reduced when its delivery did not follow the Principle of ______________________.

Example #5

Gene had a beautiful Siamese cat. However, the cat would run around the apartment knocking over lamps and small tables and climbing crazily up curtains, sometimes pulling them down. Gene started putting his cat in the basement to keep him out of trouble. Unfortunately, after several weeks, the cat started to howl and cry when locked in the basement. Gene found that the cat would stop howling the moment he was let out of the basement. After discovering this, Gene always let the cat out of the basement as soon as he heard the cat's howls.

(24) Gene could ______________________ (terminate, prevent) the cat's crying and screaming by letting him out of the basement.

(9) The rate at which Gene let the cat out of the basement, after discovering that this action would stop the screaming, ______________________.

(38) The stimulus "stopping the screams and cries of the cat" is an example of a(n) __________ __________.

(23) Gene's behavior of letting the cat out of the basement is called a(n) __________ behavior. (Is the stimulus absent or present at the moment of responding?)

(8) By letting the cat out of the basement, Gene ______________________ the rate at which the cat screamed and howled.

Example #6

Ken wasn't doing well in his sixth-grade math class. When his mother and father had their regular conferences with the teacher, she informed them of the situation, adding that Ken handed in fewer than half of his homework assignments. Ken's parents then made the rule that, for any day that Ken did not hand in his homework, he would be sent to bed early as a "punishment." It was observed that, during the next few months, Ken handed in all of his homework assignments.

(37) Ken could ______________________ being sent to bed early by handing in his homework.

(22) Ken's behavior of doing his homework would be classified as a(n) __________ __________ behavior. (Is the stimulus absent or present?)

(7) What behavioral procedure produced Ken's increased rate of doing his homework? ______________________

Example #7

Eight-year-old Dan had trouble pronouncing "refrigerator," so his parents decided to teach him to pronounce it correctly. They asked Dan to repeat the word each time he said it incorrectly. The first time, they had Dan repeat the word 20 times before he finally got the correct pronunciation. When he had said it right, his parents said "Good" and immediately stopped asking him to repeat it. After a while, Dan started pronouncing "refrigerator" correctly on his own.

(36) By pronouncing "refrigerator" correctly on his own (without being asked by his parents to do

so), Dan could ______________________ his parents from asking him to pronounce it.

(21) Because the repeated requests by Dan's parents increased the rate of correct pronunciations by Dan, they would be an example of what behavioral procedure? ______________________

(6) Dan's correct pronunciation of "refrigerator" on his own is an example of what type of behavior? ______________________

(35) This approach has a serious drawback frequently overlooked by parents; that is, the rate at which Dan said words incorrectly might actually increase if attention were more of a(n) ______________________ reinforcer than being asked to repeat a word was a(n) ______________________ reinforcer.

Example #8

Jerry didn't do his homework often enough in his social studies class. His teacher, Mr. Johnson, decided that he would embarrass Jerry every day until he started to do his homework. During the first day of this new procedure, he called on Jerry first for every question on the assignment. Naturally, Jerry didn't know the answers to any of them. Mr. Johnson repeated this same pattern every day for a week. Jerry got called on an average of 10 to 15 times each day, and he never had the correct answer. Finally, Jerry did his homework, so the teacher didn't ask him any questions. From then on, Jerry usually did his homework. On the few days that he didn't, the teacher again asked him many questions in class.

(20) The increase in Jerry's homework behavior is due to the teacher's use of what behavioral procedure? ______________________

Example #9

The students at a big Midwestern university were angry that their administration had refused to immediately hire more female faculty members while a special committee was "studying the problem." They decided to sit in the president's office until he changed his mind. They sat there for 3 days, but the president still would not agree to immediately hire any female faculty members. Finally they gave up and went home.

(5) Is the sit-in an example of negative reinforcement? ____________

(34) What behavioral procedure accounts for the students' giving up? ______________

Example #10

The children on the corner frequently got into arguments with Mr. Ryker, the candy-store owner. Mr. Ryker contended that they were reducing his business by standing there and bothering people that walked by. The children replied that they were among his best customers, and they had a right to stay there. One day Mr. Ryker got angrier than usual. In spite of his outburst, the children remained on the corner, so Mr. Ryker called the police. The children left before the police arrived, but they were angry. As a result, they threw a rock through the candy-store window. Mr. Ryker never called the police again.

(19) What behavioral procedure did the children use to modify Mr. Ryker's police-calling behavior? ______________________

(4) By throwing the rock through the window, the children prevented Mr. Ryker from calling the police again. If the effect of "preventing further calls to the police" on the behavior of throwing a rock was to increase that behavior in the future, then the event, "calls to the police," would be called a(n) ______________________ .

Example #11

The behavioral commune, like all communes, had a problem with getting its members to do the basic work needed to keep the house going. To solve the problem, the membership voted to fine any members who didn't do their share of the work during a given week. After this rule was instituted, everyone started doing his or her share of the work.

(33) What behavioral procedure is the fining an example of? ____________________

Example #12

(18) When a parent punishes a child for pestering him or her, the child stops immediately. The parent's behavior is called a punisher for the child, but, in this situation, a behavior analyst would also call it a(n) ____________________ behavior for the parent because it terminated the pestering.

Example #13

In some courses, if students don't score high enough on the daily quiz, they must take it over again.

(3) If this procedure gets the student to work hard to pass the quiz on the first try, the quiz repetition would be an example of what behavioral procedure? ____________________

Example #14

(32) Mrs. Marlowe often reprimanded Ken for not doing his daily chores. If this reprimand is given quite a while after Ken should have done the chores, then it is likely that the effectiveness of the reprimand will be reduced due to the fact that it did not occur ____________________ after his response-failure.

Example #15

Dave didn't like waiting for Carol to come home late at dinnertime without calling him. Finally, one day when she came home late without calling, he explained his feelings to her. From then on Carol prevented Dave's complaint by calling when she was going to be late.

(45) Carol's calling behavior would be called ____________________ behavior.

Example #16

Jane hated it when Bob put his cigarette out on his dinner plate. Finally, she explained her feelings to him. He usually did not put his cigarette out that way in the future and when he did, Jane again explained her dislike for the practice. Eventually, Bob completely stopped doing it.

(17) What behavioral procedure did Jane use to stop Bob's annoying behavior? ____________________

Example #17

People learn to use escape and punishment procedures more rapidly and more easily than they learn to use reinforcement procedures. When a person uses either escape or punishment, the change in another person's behavior is likely to occur immediately. When a person uses reinforcement techniques, he or she reinforces a behavior that has already happened and that may not be appropriate again for a long time. Thus, any change resulting from the reinforcement can't be seen until that later time.

(2) Which principle of reinforcer effectiveness suggests that such a long delay may radically reduce the reinforcing effectiveness of any resulting behavioral change? ____________________

Example #18

(31) Fining people for complaining about the communal food (if the fine is effective) would be an example of what behavioral procedure? ______________________
On the other hand, fining people for not doing their share of the work would be an example of what behavioral procedure? ______________________

Example #19

Kip had the bad habit of talking in the weekly dorm meetings without putting up his hand. Maryanne, the chairperson of the meeting, finally started yelling at him each time he failed to raise his hand. Kip soon started to raise his hand.

(16) Kip's behavior of raising his hand would be called ______________________ behavior.

Example #20

Paul got to thinking about his driving behavior one day. He looked in the rear view mirror frequently to prevent accidents; he looked carefully at side streets, parked cars, and moving cars to prevent being hit; he stopped at traffic lights and signs to prevent accidents.

(1) He concluded that most of his driving behavior should be classified as ______________ behavior.

EXAMPLE ANSWERS

(1) avoidance (2) immediacy (3) (negative) reinforcement (or avoidance) (4) (negative) reinforcer (5) no (6) avoidance (7) (negative) reinforcement (or avoidance) (8) increased (9) increased (10) no (11) no (12) increased (13) avoidance (14) prevented (15) increased (16) avoidance (17) punishment (18) escape (19) punishment (20) (negative) reinforcement (or avoidance) (21) (negative) reinforcement (22) avoidance (23) escape (24) terminate (25) stayed same (26) avoidance (27) prevented (28) (negative) reinforcer (29) escape (30) terminated (31) punishment; (negative) reinforcement (or avoidance) (32) immediately (33) (negative) reinforcement (or avoidance) (34) extinction (35) positive; negative (36) prevent (37) prevent (38) (negative) reinforcer (39) Immediacy (40) prevent (41) (negative) reinforcer (42) escape; avoidance (43) increased (44) negative (45) avoidance

Lesson 25

Review of Aversive Control

This unit has covered the basic elements of aversive control. In general, aversive control involves either withdrawing something that most people would judge "pleasant" or delivering something that most people would judge "unpleasant." The three techniques of aversive control are thus sharply different from the use of positive reinforcement.

The relationships among these four procedures are shown in Table 25-1. As shown in this table, the procedure in which an event follows a behavior and increases the rate of the behavior is called reinforcement. The term *reinforcement* is applied whether the procedure involves presenting a stimulus (positive reinforcer) or whether the procedure involves withdrawing a stimulus (negative reinforcer). The table also shows that the procedure in which an event follows a behavior and decreases the rate of the behavior is called a punishment. The term *punishment* is applied whether the procedure involves presenting a stimulus or withdrawing a stimulus. Thus, the distinction between punishment and reinforcement is the effect that the procedure has on behavior.

Table 25-1. Procedures for Delivering Contingent Stimuli

	Presentation	*Withdrawal*
Rate Increase	Positive reinforcement	Negative reinforcement
Rate Decrease	Punishment	Punishment

GLOSSARY

Helpful hint: The definitions of all terms introduced in this unit of the book are presented below. You can review the unit and prepare for your exam by testing yourself on the definitions and correlated facts presented for each term. You might use a piece of paper as a mask and leave only the term exposed; see if you can formulate a reasonable definition and any other facts about that term. Then move the mask and check on yourself.

Avoidance is any behavior that prevents a negative reinforcer from occurring.

A **conditioned punisher** is a punisher that loses its effectiveness through unpaired presentations.

A **discriminative stimulus** for punishment (S^P) is any stimulus that is associated with the punishment of a particular behavior.

Escape is any behavior that terminates a negative reinforcer.

A **generalized punisher** is any conditioned punisher that is associated with many other punishers.

A **negative reinforcer** is any event that, when terminated or prevented by a behavior, increases the rate of that behavior. A negative reinforcer is simply another form of a reinforcer and thus can be used in shaping, discrimination training, and conditioned reinforcement.

A **primary punisher** is any punisher that loses its effectiveness only through satiation (adaptation). Primary punishers are usually basic physical events such as hitting, shock, pinching, and so on.

A **punisher** is any event that follows a response and decreases the rate of that behavior. This definition of a punisher also applies to the withdrawal of an event following a behavior such that the rate of the behavior decreases—for instance, fining people or "timing them out" of a reinforcing activity.

UNIT FOUR PRACTICE REVIEW

Note: The following questions offer a review of all four units.

(63) If a behavior analyst reinforces a particular behavior, the behavior analyst will probably become a(n) ______________________ for that behavior.

(126) The use of unpleasant events to control behavior is called ______________________ control.

(125) If a response prevents a negative reinforcer, it is termed a(n) ______________________ response.

(62) A primary reinforcer is one that is weakened only temporarily by ______________.

(187) Tom frequently looks in his rearview mirror so that he won't have an accident. Looking in his rearview mirror is an example of a(n) ______________________ behavior.

(124) If a teacher shows students how to do something, observes to see whether they do it the same way, and then reinforces them, we say that the teacher is using the method of ______________________.

(61) If an event is withdrawn whenever a particular response is made and the rate decreases, this procedure is an example of ______________________. If an event is no longer delivered when a particular response is made and the rate decreases, this procedure would be called ______________________.

(186) Instructional training involves explaining to someone how to do something. That explanation is called a(n) ______________________.

(123) The attention that one person pays to another is frequently associated with many other reinforcers. Therefore it can be termed a(n) ______________________ reinforcer.

(60) If a reinforcer is produced by the first response that occurs after a fixed period of time, we say that it is b eing reinforced according to a(n) ______________________ schedule.

(185) A stimulus associated with reinforcement for a particular response is called a(n) ______________________.

(122) A stimulus/response chain is a sequence of responses in which the occurrence of one response serves as the ______________________ for the next response. (Note carefully the order of events implied by this question.)

(59) To determine whether the Principle of Size was followed, ask "Was the amount of the event used ______________________?"

(184) A conditioned reinforcer is any reinforcer that is weakened permanently by ______________________ presentations.

(121) People will continue to imitate the behavior of someone else only if they are ______________________ for doing so.

(58) The method of observation based on dividing the observational period into many continuous intervals and observing whether the behavior occurs during each interval is called ______________________________.

(183) If Brad is praised for saying "9" when asked "What is the sum of 5 + 4?" but ignored for saying anything else; and if he is praised for saying "12" when asked "What is the sum of 8 + 4?" but ignored for saying anything else, we have agreed to label this as an example of what behavioral procedure? ______________________________

(120) Mr. Cosgrove explained to his eighth graders exactly how to find the square of a number. He then asked them to find the square of the number. He praised each student who got the right answer. What behavioral procedure was he using? __________________________

(57) The baseline is a record of a behavior before the ______________________________ condition.

(182) Mr. Cosgrove worked out an example of how to find the square of a number. He then erased his example and asked his students to find the square of that same number. He examined each student's work and praised him or her if it was correct. What behavioral procedure did he use? ______________________________

(119) The person who is consistently nice to other people may be reinforced by the smile of the other person. If the smile is usually associated with many other reinforcers from that other person, it would be an example of what type of reinforcer? ________________________

(56) A punisher is defined as any event that (1) ______________________________ a response and (2) ______________________________ the rate of that response.

(181) If a response is reinforced after a fixed number of occurrences of the response, this procedure is an example of a(n) ______________________________ schedule.

(118) Any conditioned reinforcer that is paired with many backup reinforcers is called a(n) ______________________________ reinforcer.

(55) Barb and Scott were pretty good friends. But Scott annoyed Barb greatly when he tried to convert her to Hare Krishnaism. However, when she started simply getting up and leaving the conversation whenever he would start talking about religion, he quickly stopped doing it. What behavioral procedure did Barb use to eliminate the conversion attempts? ______________________________

(180) If a behavior occurs more frequently in the presence of one stimulus and less frequently in the presence of another stimulus, we call that behavior __________________________.

(117) When civil-rights groups measure the number of shoppers at a store prior to undertaking a boycott, the resulting data are called a(n) ______________________________.

(54) To determine whether a schedule is actually an interval schedule, ask "If the person makes no response at all, will there eventually arrive a time at which ______________________________ will produce the reinforcer?" or, if the behavior is ongoing, "Will there eventually arrive a time when emitting the behavior for a(n) ______________________________ time will produce the reinforcer?"

(179) If a behavior analyst reinforced someone for chewing gum but not for smoking cigarettes, the analyst's actions would be an example of what behavioral procedure? ______________________________

(116) To decide whether the Principle of Immediacy was followed, ask "Was the event delivered within a(n) ______________________________ of the behavior (or while it was still occurring)?"

(53) If Tommy has learned to call the funny-shaped little car a "beetle" but not the long sleek car, we say that the funny little car exerts ______________________________ over his behavior of calling it a "beetle."

(178) Husbands and wives often point out one another's thoughtless acts. If this pointing them out decreases the rate of thoughtless acts, it would be an example of what behavioral procedure? ______________________________

(115) Shaping involves ________________ of a series of successive ________________ to some target behavior.

(52) If people have not received a particular reinforcer for a while, we say that they are ________________ with respect to that reinforcer.

(177) Two kinds of experimental designs that rule out alternative explanations are the ________________ design and the ________________ ________ design.

(114) Larry wondered if Kevin's stuttering was decreasing so he recorded each time that Kevin emitted a stuttered word in his presence. What method of observation was he using? ________________ recording

(51) A stimulus event that occurs prior to a response and increases the frequency of that response is called a(n) ________________; a stimulus event that occurs after a response and increases the frequency of that response is called a(n) ________________ .

(176) The more immediate the delivery of an event after the occurrence of the desired behavior, the more effective the reinforcer, according to the Principle of ________________.

(113) A snerkel is a card that can be exchanged for a wide range of privileges in the commune. A reinforcer of this type is effective because at least one of the backup reinforcers is likely to be an effective reinforcer at any given time due to what principle? ________________

(50) If one behavior is reinforced in the presence of a stimulus while another is extinguished, and if the first behavior is extinguished in the presence of another stimulus while the second is reinforced, we have decided to label this as an example of what behavioral procedure? ________________

(175) The design in which a behavior is observed during baseline and then during treatment would be called a(n) ________________ design.

(112) If the delivery of an event following a behavior is stopped and the rate of that behavior decreases, then this procedure is called ________________ .

(49) Fred and Charlie observed Murray's study behavior using the same definition but on different days. Is their agreement a measure of the reliability of their observations? ________

(174) Frank argued long and loud against the idea that only club members should be allowed to buy at reduced prices. If no one paid any attention to him, it is likely that this verbal behavior (arguing) would decrease. What behavioral procedure would be involved? ________________

(111) A procedure for gradually changing a behavior is called ________________.

(48) Mr. Jackson observed five students to determine whether they were studying. He first observed Diane for 12 seconds, then shifted to Ken and observed him for 12 seconds, and so on for the other three students. He started over again with Diane after having observed the others. What method of observation is he using? ________________

(173) Paul praised Kim every time that she acted assertively with others. Kim's rate of acting assertively did not change. What behavioral procedure did Paul use? ________________

(110) Extinction involves stopping the delivery of a reinforcer for a behavior and observing a(n) ________________ in the rate of that behavior.

(47) Any response that terminates a negative reinforcer is called a(n) ________________ behavior.

(172) When you arrange to deliver an event after each instance of a behavior, thereby increasing the rate of the behavior, you refer to the procedure as ________________ and the event as a(n) ________________ .

(109) A positive reinforcer must have two characteristics: it must ________________ a behavior, and it must ________________ the frequency of the behavior.

(46) Ruby's rate of smoking during the experiment was 13, 17, 18, 12, and 15 before shock, 2, 5, 3, 6, and 7 during shock, and 20, 15, 18, 17, and 19 after shock. Using Figure 25–1, make a graph of the experiment.

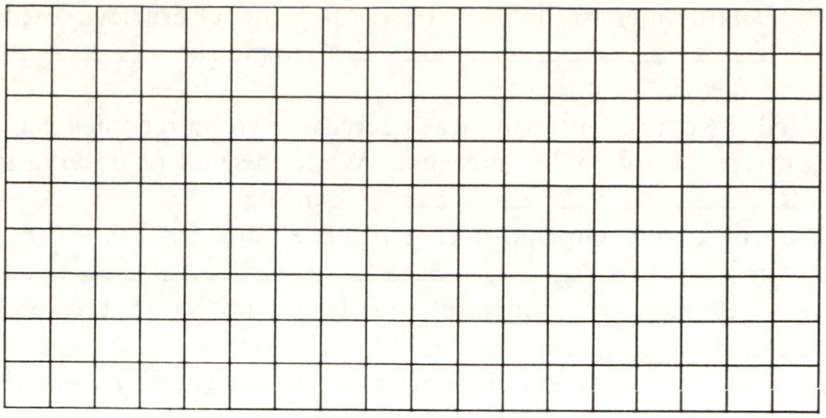

Figure 25–1. Graph of Ruby's smoking behavior

(171) Reinforcing a behavior in the presence of one stimulus and extinguishing that same behavior in the presence of another stimulus is called ________________.

(108) Tom's only problem was that he was always griping about the food at the commune. When he griped, people argued with him. The more they argued, the more he griped. What behavioral procedure did the other members use to increase his rate of griping? ________________

(45) Squaring a simple graph is done by dividing the ________________ by the ________________ and labeling the ordinate with the next larger whole number.

(170) Prior to the introduction of a special grading system, Claire read the following number of pages in English: 23, 14, 17, and 10; and the following number in history: 8, 5, 19, and 12. After the new grading system was introduced in English she read: 45, 73, 80, and 36; and she read the following number in history, where the system had not been introduced: 17, 2, 19, and 3. Finally, the special grading system was in effect in both courses and Claire read the following number of pages in each: English: 73, 69, 46, and 68; History 60, 55, 51, and 60. The ordinate for English would increase by ________ and for history by ________.

(107) An escape response is any response that ________________ a negative reinforcer; an avoidance response is any response that ________________ a negative reinforcer.

(44) If a stimulus signals the contingent withdrawal of a reinforcer, that stimulus is called a(n) ________________.

(169) If Tommy is praised for calling the funny little car a "beetle" but not for calling other cars "beetles," then what behavioral procedure is being used? ________________

(106) An experimental design in which two behaviors are observed over different-length baselines prior to the introduction of the treatment is called a(n) ________________ design.

(43) If a person is reinforced after varying numbers of responses, what schedule of reinforcement is being used? ________________

(168) Outcome recording involves observing some relatively lasting ________________ of the response.

(105) Larry was assertive prior to training the following number of times out of 10 situations: 1, 0, 3, 2, 0, and 1 on successive days. After training, he was assertive the following number of

times: 9, 10, 10, 8, 10, and 9. To make a graph of this experiment you should label the ordinate with steps that increase by ________ .

(42) The differential reinforcement of a series of successive approximations to some target behavior is called ________________ .

(167) Generalization training consists of reinforcing a behavior in each of a series of situations until it ________________ to other members of that same stimulus class.

(104) The funny-shaped little car would be called a(n) ________________ for calling it a "plane."

(41) Any behavior that prevents a negative reinforcer is called a(n) ________________ behavior.

(166) Differential reinforcement is a procedure in which one response is ________________ and other responses are ________________ .

(103) May studied the child-rearing practices of college graduates by asking a random sample of 25 of them to answer such questions as "How many times last week did you tell your child to finish the rest of the food on his or her plate?" Since the parents did not record the observations immediately, this is not an example of ________________ .

(40) Tom was teaching Mona how to play a particular chord on the guitar step by step. He first praised her only when she held it correctly, next only when she strummed it correctly, and finally only when she strummed a particular chord. Playing a particular chord is called the ________________ that Tom was trying to teach.

(165) Henry helped Carol move by going to her old place with her, loading up his pickup truck with her possessions, driving them to her new place and carrying them up to her apartment. She thanked him right after the last box was brought from his truck and gave him a beer. He loved beer but could never afford it himself. Even though it took three trips to move all her stuff, he didn't tire of drinking the beer she offered. What principle of effective reinforcement, if any, did Carol neglect? ________________

(102) A stimulus associated with extinction for a particular response is called a(n) ________________ .

(39) Time-sample recording involves observing whether or not a behavior occurs during each of a series of ________________ intervals.

(164) Dr. Gold observed Maria's assertiveness prior to assertiveness training and after assertiveness training. What experimental design was he using? ________________

(101) If a response is reinforced every time it occurs, it is said to be on a(n) ________________ schedule of reinforcement.

(38) Name the four principles of effective reinforcement: ________________, ________________, ________________, and ________________

(163) Suppose Bob Behaviorist found that any time Ruby wasn't shocked for taking a cigarette, she smoked at her normal rate. This discovery would indicate that the effect of the shock on her rate of smoking did not ________________ to situations in which she wasn't shocked.

(100) The principle of effective reinforcement that states "The more deprived a person is with respect to the event, the more effective it will be" is called ________________ .

(37) Event recording involves recording the occurrence of ________________ behavioral episodes.

(162) If Tommy has learned to call the funny-shaped little car a "beetle" but not other cars, then we would call his behavior of calling it a "beetle" ________________ behavior.

(99) Reliability is a measure of the ________________ between the records of two independent observers.

(36) If a reinforcer is delivered to people for their first response after differing periods of time, they are said to be on a(n) ______________________ schedule.

(161) The person who was to be the main observer for the experiment and Mary's teacher observed Mary's nearness to other children during the first day of observations. The following are their results (where F stands for further than two feet or not facing, and N stands for nearness):

Teacher: F F N F F F F N F F F F F F N N F F F F F F F

Other: F F F F F F N N F F F F F F F N N N F F F F F F F

Compute reliability. __________

Is the reliability of these observations acceptable? __________

(98) If you think that an example involves a ratio schedule, check your conclusion by asking "If the person makes the responses very rapidly (or very often) will the next reinforcer arrive ______________________ (than if the responses were made slowly)?"

(35) An *S*-delta is a stimulus that is associated with the ______________________ of a particular response.

(160) Fred felt that it was important to determine whether the behaviors that he was observing and calling "studying" would be regarded by others as studying. He had a panel of individuals observe several students who were studying according to his definition and several who were not to see if they would agree with his definition. Fred is attempting to determine the ______________________ of his definition of studying.

(97) To decide whether the public areas of a dorm are clean enough, you might make up a checklist of things that should be clean (floors, ashtrays, trash baskets, and so on) and check once a day to see whether they are clean. You would be using what method of observing? ______________________ recording

(34) An observation that is personally seen (or heard) by the observer and is immediately recorded is called a(n) ______________________.

(159) If you show someone how to do something, your behavior is called the ______________ stimulus.

(96) Differential reinforcement involves two basic behavioral procedures. They are ______________________ and ______________________.

(33) The weakness of a simple comparison design is that it does not rule out __________ causes of an observed change in the behavior.

(158) Programming is the temporary use of a prompt to produce ______________________.

(95) The design in which a behavior is observed during a baseline, during a treatment condition, and, finally, during a return to baseline, is called a(n) ______________________ design.

(32) Students listening to a lecture are often regarded as being "attentive" if their heads are pointed toward the speaker with their eyes looking at the speaker. If this was a statement of how to observe attentive behavior, it would be called what? ______________________

(157) Carol wished to change several of her own behaviors. She decided to try the method of counting her own behaviors with a wrist counter to see if the increased awareness would reduce their frequency. Prior to starting, she asked her friend to count the number of times that she interrupted him and the number of times that she argued with him. Then she started counting interruptions. Later, she also counted arguing behaviors. She was happy to find that both decreased. What experimental design was she using? ______________________

(94) Henry was particularly interested in pictures of birds. When he looked through a book of photos, he skipped the pictures that were not of birds. What schedule was his picture-looking behavior on? ______________________

(31) Observation based on some physical result of a response rather than observation of the response itself is called ________________ recording.

(156) If Jan's mother showed her a picture of a cow to help her learn to read the word "cow," the picture of the cow would be called a(n) ________________.

(93) Mr. James awarded Tom a token for every ten multiplication problems he got correct. What schedule of intermittent reinforcement is Mr. James using? ________________

(30) The vertical line on a graph is called the ________________; it is used to record the ________________.

(155) A statement that specifies the exact behavior to be observed is called a(n) ________________.

(92) Fading is a procedure used to help teach a specific ________________ that involves gradually withdrawing a stimulus called a prompt.

(29) If a person's behavior occurs in the presence of a novel stimulus, we say that his or her behavior has ________________.

(154) Interval recording involves recording whether or not a behavior occurs during each of a series of ________________ intervals.

(91) Tom the Peeper has to wait different lengths of time for Gloria to enter her room and begin disrobing, but it averages 45 minutes. What schedule of reinforcement is his peeping on? ________________

(28) Sarah wanted to help Ken build his stone fireplace, so she volunteered to wheel the very heavy wet concrete from the mixer to the fireplace for Ken. Each time she brought a load, he said "thanks" as soon as she arrived. He thanked her only for hauling the concrete. Sarah certainly did not get thanked too often for her work. What principle of effective reinforcement, if any, did Ken neglect in his treatment of Sarah's help? ________________

(153) Mr. Janes taught Robert to draw a map of Kansas by first praising any rectangle that was twice as long as it was high. He then praised the map only if the Missouri River was shown; finally he praised the map only if Wichita, Kansas City, and Topeka were shown. The behavioral procedure by which Mr. Janes taught Robert to draw the map is called ________________.

(90) If you hit people every time they tell you "Your Momma's feet stink," and they start saying it even more often, you should probably conclude that hitting them is what is technically known as a(n) ________________.

(27) To decide whether the Principle of Deprivation was followed, ask "Has the reinforcer been delivered too ________________ (or too often)?"

(152) Mr. Warren, a high school teacher, was always negative in his class. Several of his students decided to observe him to find out how much of the time he was negative. They made their observations in 15-second blocks throughout the day and found that he was negative 75% of the time. What method of observation did they use? ________________ recording

(89) The procedure of having an event follow a behavior and increase its rate is called ________________.

(26) Any time a response is not reinforced after every occurrence, we say that the response is being ________________ reinforced.

(151) The use of outside judges to determine whether a behavioral definition is acceptable to non-behaviorists is called determining the ________________ of the definition.

(88) Bev did a meticulous job with her homework for math last Friday. Her teacher was so pleased that he showed her homework to everyone in class as the way to do your homework. Bev then did a meticulous job with her English homework. The occurrence of such a careful job

in a second class would be an example of what behavioral process? ____________

(25) A response will take longer to extinguish if it has been on a(n) ____________ schedule of reinforcement.

(150) Remember, if you tell people to do something and they do, this ____________ (is, isn't) an example of reinforcement.

(87) The longer the delay in providing reinforcement for a response, the ____________ (more, less) effective the reinforcer.

(24) The observation of a behavior prior to introducing a treatment is called the ____________ ____________ condition.

(149) Four basic methods of observation of behavior are ____________, ____________, ____________, and ____________ recording.

(86) Reinforcing one response while extinguishing a different response is called ____________ ____________.

(23) A generalization may occur when a response has been reinforced in the presence of a stimulus so that the person emits the same response in the presence of a(n) ____________ stimulus.

(148) A stimulus that consistently signals the occurrence of punishment is called a(n) ____________.

(85) Danny was trying to teach Marty to say "one." Every time Marty said something like "one," Danny said "Very good." At first Marty had a high rate of saying something close to "one." Then he slowed down, and finally he quit altogether. Marty probably quit because Danny was saying "Very good" too often. What principle of effective reinforcement did Danny violate? ____________

(22) Tom was teaching Mona to play the guitar. He first praised her only when she held it correctly, next only when she strummed properly, and finally only when she struck a particular chord. Holding the guitar properly is called a(n) ____________ to playing it correctly.

(147) The goal of shaping is to produce a specified behavior called a(n) ____________ ____________.

(84) A procedure in which a person's response prevents a(n) ____________ reinforcer from occurring is called avoidance.

(21) If an event follows a behavior and increases its rate, it is called a(n) ____________.

(146) To decide if the Principle of Contingency was followed, ask "Was the event given ____________ if the desired behavior occurred?"

(83) Ace burped often at dinner. In fact, a record of his burps showed that he burped the following number of times per dinner: 58, 25, 40, 23, 37, and 42. On a graph of Ace's burps, you would label the divisions on the ordinate with numbers that increase by steps of ____________.

(20) Recording whether or not a behavior occurs during each of a series of discontinuous intervals is called ____________ recording.

(145) The horizontal line of a graph is called the ____________. It is used to record ____________.

(82) Bob really liked Kay when she acted assertively so he always made it a point to praise such behavior. After a while Kay always acted assertively around Bob, but for some reason her assertiveness did not spill over into her other relationships. However, after David also started reinforcing assertiveness, Kay began acting assertively with everyone she knew. What behavioral procedure did her friends use to change her behavior in this way? ____________

(19) Reinforcing a behavior in the presence of a series of situations until it generalizes to other members of that same stimulus class is called ____________.

(144) The collection of all works of art would be considered a(n) ____________________ ____________.

(81) The agreement between the observations of two independent observers is called the ____________________ of those observations.

(18) Mrs. Whalen observed Penny's study behavior prior to praising it, while she praised it, and after she had stopped praising it. What experimental design was she using? ____________________

(143) As soon as Susie felt her feet get cold on the cold floor, she put her slippers on. Her rate of putting her slippers on increased over time. Putting her slippers on to stop the cold is called a(n) ____________________ behavior.

(80) Punishment can occur in two ways: a response can lead to the delivery of a punisher, and the rate of the response decreases; or a response can lead to the ____________________ of a reinforcer, and the rate of the response decreases.

(17) When Thurmond moved up north, no one paid any attention to his racially prejudiced statements. However, they did not decrease in rate. What behavioral procedure was being applied to his prejudiced behavior? ____________________

(142) Behavior analysis has three important characteristics: (1) it focuses on ____________ ____________; (2) it studies ____________________ influences on behavior; and (3) it uses single-subject designs to ____________ ____________ with the effect of different environmental arrangements.

(79) Lenny's mother was very interested in increasing his rate of comments reflecting a positive outlook on life. So she watched very carefully for such comments to occur and noted them to herself. She then would praise Lenny for each comment at a special meeting that they held every Sunday. She never praised comments that were not positive. Her praise was very important to Lenny and he never seemed to get too much of it. What principle of effective reinforcement, if any, did his mother neglect? ____________________

(16) Pete designed the world's best token system for his third-grade pupils. They could trade tokens for snacks, TV lessons, meeting with the principal, having a story read, and lots of neat things. Pete never gave them so many tokens that they didn't want them any more. And he always gave the tokens immediately after the behavior that he desired. When he tried to reinforce them for pronouncing difficult words accurately, however, he had little success because he was hard of hearing. Thus, he gave them tokens for both right and wrong pronunciation. What principle of effective reinforcement, if any, did he neglect? ____________________

(141) The effectiveness of an event will be maximized if it is delivered only when the desired behavior occurs, according to the Principle of ____________________.

(78) The temporary use of a prompt to produce a generalization is called ____________.

(15) Each of a series of behaviors that are similar to some target behavior is called a(n) ____________________.

(140) Eleanor learned to read the word "dog" from a special book that showed a picture of a dog when the word was first presented but gradually showed less and less of the dog—until Eleanor had to read the word without the help of the picture. What behavioral procedure did the book use? ____________________

(77) Is a generalized reinforcer defined as an event that can be used to reinforce a response as it generalizes to new situations? ____________

(14) Tommy's mother wanted to teach him the idea of "boy" so she showed him a picture of Ken and asked "What kind of person is this—you know, like Daddy?" and reinforced him when he said "boy." She then gave less and less of the hint until Tommy always said "boy" when showed a picture of Ken. She then repeated the procedure with a picture of Joe until he learned to call Joe a boy. By this time, Tommy could label any picture of a young male as a

boy. What behavioral procedure did his mother use? ______

(139) Mary was observed by the primary observer to talk with other children in her class 7 times. A reliability observer noted 10 instances of talking. Compute the reliability of these observations. ______ Is it acceptable? ______

(76) The reliability of a new behavioral definition should be at least ______.

(13) An added stimulus, used to help learn a discrimination, is called a(n) ______.

(138) A set of related stimuli is called a(n) ______.

(75) What two schedules of reinforcement produce low rates of responding right after reinforcement and a higher rate as the time for the next reinforcement approaches? ______ ______

(12) Writing the date, the store's name, and the amount on a check usually precedes the signing of the check and the receiving of the store's merchandise. If signing the check is reinforced by receiving the merchandise, the sequence of writing behaviors is what is called a(n) ______.

(137) A stimulus class consists of a set of ______ stimuli.

(74) Schedules of reinforcement based on time are called ______ schedules; schedules based on number of responses are called ______ schedules.

(11) A negative reinforcer is any event that is ______ by a behavior and that causes the rate of the behavior to increase.

(136) Satiation of the reinforcer, extinction, and punishment all have the effect of ______ ______ the rate of a response.

(73) Reinforcing one response and extinguishing a different response is called ______ ______; reinforcing a response in one situation and extinguishing the same response in a different situation is called ______.

(10) A procedure used to help teach a specific discrimination that involves gradually changing the stimulus is called ______.

(135) If observers check for 5 seconds every 14 minutes to see if a certain behavior is occurring, they are using the ______ method of observation. (Don't give a schedule.)

(72) An intermittent schedule of reinforcement will produce a greater resistance to ______ than will a continuous schedule.

(9) The principle of effective reinforcement that states "The more of an event that is delivered after the desired behavior, the more effective it will be" is called ______.

(134) A method of observation based on counting complete behaviors is called ______ recording.

(71) Escape is a procedure in which a negative reinforcer is ______ following a response.

(8) A sequence of responses in which the prior response serves as the stimulus for the succeeding response is called a(n) ______.

(133) Suppose that two observers were recording the occurrence of nervous looks by witnesses at the Watergate hearings. If the first observer observed N N N N N and the second observer observed N N C N N (where N stands for nervous and C stands for calm), compute the reliability. ______ If this is a new definition, is the reliability acceptable? ______

(70) To make a negative reinforcer most effective in increasing the rate of response, be sure that the negative reinforcer is withdrawn ______ after the response.

(7) Ms. Whalen wanted to increase the amount of studying in her fourth grade so that the

children would learn faster. She decided that she would walk through the room while the children were working on their math and would grade their work right then and there. Each child would then be allowed to play outside for 10 minutes after he or she had completed ten problems correctly. She found that the rate of work in the class went up dramatically as a result of this approach. The conditioned reinforcer in this example is probably her ______________________; the backup reinforcer is the right to ______________________.

(132) Any event that follows a response and reduces the probability of that response's occurring is called a(n) ______________________.

(69) A punisher that loses its effectiveness through unpaired presentations is called a(n) ______________________ punisher.

(6) People will continue to follow instructions only if they are ______________________ for doing so.

(131) What two schedules of reinforcement produce uniform rates of responding? ______________________ and ______________________

(68) What is the best schedule of reinforcement to use when attempting to shape a new behavior? ______________________

(5) Reinforcing events that make conditioned reinforcers and generalized reinforcers effective as a result of being paired with them are called ______________________ reinforcers.

(130) In order for punishment to be most effective, it should follow the response __________.

(67) If people are reinforced only every 500 responses, their responding may become erratic and slower. This consequence is known as ______________________.

(4) Quite frequently, we can't reinforce someone immediately after the behavior we would like to encourage. The important thing about conditioned reinforcers, such as a smile or a thank-you, is that they can be delivered ______________________, which enhances their effectiveness.

(129) An S^D is a stimulus that precedes a behavior and is present only if that behavior will be ______________________; an S-delta is a stimulus that precedes a behavior and is present only if that behavior will be ______________________.

(66) Carol didn't like football but she did like the interviews with the players. So she tuned in exactly at the start of half time. The interviews always started 5 minutes after the start of half time. What schedule of reinforcement is her TV viewing on? ______________________

(3) Any reinforcer that is weakened permanently by unpaired presentations is called a(n) ______________________ reinforcer.

(128) The procedure of reinforcing a desired behavior that has been verbally described to a person is called ______________________.

(65) A generalized reinforcer is any conditioned reinforcer that is paired with ______________________ backup reinforcers.

(2) Mike's parents "punished" him by sending him to bed early on any day that he hadn't done his homework for school. Mike started doing his homework. What behavioral procedure modified Mike's rate of doing homework? ______________________

(127) If you withdraw an event contingent on a behavior and if the rate of that behavior decreases, the procedure is called ______________________.

(64) Any reinforcer that is weakened temporarily only by satiation is called a(n) ______________________ reinforcer.

(1) Behavior analysts don't consider "negative reinforcement" and "______________________" to be the same.

PRACTICE REVIEW ANSWERS

(1) punishment (2) reinforcement (avoidance) (3) conditioned (4) immediately (5) backup (6) reinforced (7) grade; play (8) (stimulus/response) chain (9) Size (10) fading (11) prevented or terminated (12) (stimulus/response) chain (13) prompt (14) programming (15) approximation (16) Contingency (17) unknown (18) reversal (19) generalization training (20) time-sample (21) reinforcer (22) approximation (23) novel (24) baseline (25) intermittent (26) intermittently (27) recently (28) Size (29) generalized (30) ordinate; behavior (31) outcome (32) behavioral definition (33) alternative (34) direct observation (35) extinction (36) variable-interval (37) complete (38) Contingency, Immediacy, Size, and Deprivation (39) discontinuous (40) target behavior (41) avoidance (42) shaping (43) variable ratio (44) discriminative stimulus for punishment (or S^P) (45) ordinate; abscissa (46) steps should increase by 4 (47) escape (48) time sampling (49) no (50) discrimination training (51) S^D; reinforcer (52) deprived (53) stimulus control (54) one response; brief (55) punishment (56) follows; decreases (57) treatment (58) interval recording (59) worthwhile (60) fixed-interval (61) punishment; extinction (62) satiation (63) S^D (64) primary (65) many (66) fixed interval (FI–5 minutes) (67) ratio strain (68) continuous (69) conditioned (70) immediately (only) (71) terminated (72) extinction (73) differential reinforcement; discrimination training (74) interval; ratio (75) fixed ratio; fixed interval (76) 80% (77) no (78) programming (79) Immediacy (80) withdrawal (81) reliability (82) generalization training (83) 10 (84) negative (85) Deprivation (86) differential reinforcement (87) less (88) generalization (89) reinforcement (90) reinforcer (91) variable interval (VI–45 minutes) (92) discrimination (93) fixed ratio (FR–10) (94) variable ratio (95) reversal (96) reinforcement; extinction (97) outcome (98) sooner (99) agreement (100) Deprivation (101) continuous (102) *S*-delta (103) direct observation (104) *S*-delta (105) 2 (106) multiple-baseline (107) terminates; prevents (108) reinforcement (109) follow; increase (110) decrease (111) shaping (112) extinction (113) Deprivation (114) event (115) differential reinforcement; approximations (116) minute (117) baseline (118) generalized (119) generalized (120) instructional training (121) reinforced (122) S^D (123) generalized (124) imitation training (125) avoidance (126) aversive (127) punishment (128) instructional training (129) reinforced; extinguished (130) immediately (131) variable interval; variable ratio (132) punisher (133) 80%; yes (134) event (135) time-sample (136) decreasing (137) related (138) stimulus class (139) 70%; no (140) fading (141) Contingency (142) behavior; environmental; experiment (143) escape (144) stimulus class (145) abscissa; time (146) only (147) target behavior (148) discriminative stimulus for punishment (or S^P) (149) outcome; event; interval; time-sample (150) isn't (151) social validity (152) interval (153) shaping (154) continuous (155) behavioral definition (156) prompt (157) multiple baseline (158) generalization (159) imitative (160) social validity (161) 88%; no (162) discriminated (163) generalize (164) comparison (165) none (166) reinforced; extinguished (167) generalizes (168) result (169) discrimination training (170) 20; 20 (they should be the same) (171) discrimination training (172) reinforcement; reinforcer (173) unknown (174) extinction (175) comparison (176) Immediacy (177) reversal; multiple-baseline (178) punishment (179) differential reinforcement (180) discriminated behavior (181) fixed-ratio (182) imitation training (183) discrimination training (184) unpaired (185) S^D (186) verbal description (187) avoidance

REFERENCES

Agnew's blast at behaviorism. *Psychology Today*, January 1972, pp. 4; 84; 87.

Alford, G. S., & Turner, S. M. Stimulus interference and conditioned inhibition of auditory hallucinations. *Journal of Behavior Therapy and Experimental Psychiatry*, 1976, *7*, 155–160.

Allen, G. J. Case study: Implementation of behavior modification techniques in summer camp settings. *Behavior Therapy*, 1973, *4*, 570–575.

Allen, K. E., Hart, B. M., Buell, J. S., Harris, F. R., & Wolf, M. M. Effects of social reinforcement on isolate behavior of a nursery school child. *Child Development*, 1964, *35*, 511–518.

Allen, K. E., Turner, K. D., & Everett, P. M. A behavior modification classroom for Head Start children with problem behaviors. *Exceptional Children*, 1970, *37*, 119–127.

Allport, G. W., & Postman, L. F. The basic psychology of rumor. *Transactions of the New York Academy of Sciences*, 1945, Series II, 61–81.

Ayllon, T. Intensive treatment of psychotic behavior by stimulus satiation and food reinforcement. *Behavior Research and Therapy*, 1963, *1*, 53–61.

Ayllon, T., & Azrin, N. H. Reinforcement and instructions with mental patients. *Journal of the Experimental Analysis of Behavior*, 1964, *7*, 327–331.

Ayllon, T., & Azrin, N. H. The measurement and reinforcement of behavior of psychotics. *Journal of the Experimental Analysis of Behavior*, 1965, *8*, 357–383.

Ayllon, T., & Azrin, N. H. *The token economy*. New York: Appleton-Century-Crofts, 1968.

Ayllon, T., & Michael, J. The psychiatric nurse as a behavioral engineer. *Journal of the Experimental Analysis of Behavior*, 1959, *2*, 323–334.

Azrin, N. H., & Powell, J. Behavioral engineering: The use of response priming to improve prescribed self-medication. *Journal of Applied Behavior Analysis*, 1969, *2*, 39–42.

Azrin, N., Rubin, H., O'Brien, F., Ayllon, T., & Roll, D. Behavioral engineering: Posture control by a portable operant apparatus. *Journal of Applied Behavior Analysis*, 1968, *1*, 99–108.

Bachrach, A. J. *Psychological research: An introduction*. New York: Random House, 1962.

Baer, D. M. Laboratory control of thumbsucking by withdrawal and re-presentation of reinforcement. *Journal of the Experimental Analysis of Behavior*, 1962, *5*, 525–528.

Baer, D. M. Perhaps it would be better not to know everything. *Journal of Applied Behavior Analysis*, 1977, *10*, 167–172. (a)

Baer, D. M. Reviewer's comments: Just because it's reliable doesn't mean that you can use it. *Journal of Applied Behavior Analysis*, 1977, *10*, 117–119. (b)

Baer, D. M., & Guess, D. Receptive training of adjective inflections in mental retardates. *Journal of Applied Behavior Analysis*, 1971, *4*, 129–140.

Baer, D. M., Peterson, R. F., & Sherman, J. A. The development of imitation by reinforcing behavioral similarity to a model. *Journal of the Experimental Analysis of Behavior*, 1967, *10*, 405–416.

Baer, A. M., Rowbury, T., & Baer, D. M. The development of instructional control over classroom activities of deviant preschool children. *Journal of Applied Behavior Analysis*, 1973, *6*, 289–298.

Baer, D. M., Wolf, M. M., & Risley, T. R. Some current dimensions of applied behavior analysis. *Journal of Applied Behavior Analysis*, 1968, *1*, 91–97.

Bandura, A. *Principles of behavior modification*. New York: Holt, Rinehart & Winston, 1969.

Bandura, A. *Psychological modeling: Conflicting theories*. Chicago: Aldine-Atherton, 1971.

Barrett, B. H., & Lindsley, O. R. Deficits in acquisition of operant discrimination and differentiation shown by institutionalized retarded children. *American Journal of Mental Deficiency*, 1962, *67*, 424–436. Also reprinted in L. P. Ullman & L. Krasner (Eds.), *Case studies in behavior modification*. New York: Holt, Rinehart & Winston, 1965.

Bellack, A. S., & Hersen, M. *Behavior modification*. Baltimore: Williams and Wilkins, 1977.

Bereiter, C., & Midian, K. *Were some Follow Through models more effective than others?* Paper presented at American Educational Research Association, Toronto, March 30, 1978.

Bijou, S. W., Peterson, R. F., & Ault, M. H. A method to integrate descriptive and experimental field studies at the level of data and empirical concepts. *Journal of Applied Behavior Analysis*, 1968, *1*, 175–191.

Birnbrauer, J. S., Bijou, S. W., Wolf, M. M., & Kidder, J. D. Programmed instruction in the classroom. In L. P. Ullman & L. Krasner (Eds.), *Case studies in behavior modification*. New York: Holt, Rinehart & Winston, 1965.

Bornstein, M. R., Bellack, A. S., & Hersen, M. Social skills training for unassertive children: A multiple baseline analysis. *Journal of Applied Behavior Analysis*, 1977, *10*, 183–195.

Brandt, R. M. *Studying behavior in natural settings*. New York: Holt, Rinehart & Winston, 1972.

Brawley, E. R., Harris, F. R., Allen, K. E., Flemin, R. S., & Peterson, R. F. Behavior modification of an autistic child. *Behavioral Science*, 1969, *14*, 87–97.

Brigham, T. A., Finfrock, S. R., Bruenig, M. K., & Bushell, D. The use of programmed materials in the analysis of academic contingencies. *Journal of Applied Behavior Analysis*, 1972, *5*, 177–182.

Buchanan, C. D. *Programmed Reading.* New York: McGraw-Hill, 1973.

Budzynski, T. H., & Stoyva, J. M. An instrument for producing deep muscle relaxation by means of analog information feedback. *Journal of Applied Behavior Analysis,* 1969, *2,* 231–237.

Burgess, R. L., & Bushell, D., Jr. *Behavioral sociology.* New York: Columbia University Press, 1969.

Bushell, D., Jr. An engineering approach to the elementary classroom: The Behavior Analysis Follow Through Project. In T. A. Brigham & A. C. Catania (Eds.), *The handbook of applied behavior research: Social and instructional processes.* New York: Irvington Press/Halstead Press, 1978.

Campbell, D. T., & Stanley, J. C. *Experimental and quasi-experimental designs for research.* Chicago: Rand McNally, 1963.

Cautela, J. R. Behavior therapy and self-control: Techniques and implications. In C. M. Franks (Ed.), *Behavior therapy: Appraisal and status.* New York: McGraw-Hill, 1969.

Clark, H. B., Rowbury, T., Baer, A. M., & Baer, D. M. Timeout as a punishing stimulus in continuous and intermittent schedules. *Journal of Applied Behavior Analysis,* 1973, *6,* 443–455.

Cronbach, L. J. *Essentials of psychological testing.* New York: Harper & Row, 1960.

Dericco, D. A. Suppression of smoking behavior: A one year follow up. *Journal of Applied Behavior Analysis,* 1977, *10,* 706.

Dericco, D. A., Brigham, T. A., & Garlington, W. K. Development and evaluation of treatment paradigms for the suppression of smoking behavior. *Journal of Applied Behavior Analysis,* 1977, *10,* 173–181.

Epstein, L. H., & Masek, B. J. Behavioral control of medicine compliance. *Journal of Applied Behavior Analysis,* 1978, *11,* 1–9.

Eysenck, H. J. The effects of psychotherapy. In H. J. Eysenck (Ed.), *Handbook of abnormal psychology.* London: Pitman Medical Publishers, 1960.

Fawcett, S. B., & Miller, L. K. Training public speaking behavior: An experimental analysis and social validation. *Journal of Applied Behavior Analysis,* 1975, *8,* 125–135.

Feallock, R. A., & Miller, L. K. The design and evaluation of a work-sharing system for experimental group living. *Journal of Applied Behavior Analysis,* 1976, *9,* 277–288.

Ferster, C. B., & Skinner, B. F. *Schedules of reinforcement.* New York: Appleton-Century-Crofts, 1957.

Fichter, M. M., Wallace, C. J., Liberman, R. P., & Davis, J. R. Improving social interaction in a chronic schizophrenic using discriminated avoidance ("nagging"): Experimental analysis and generalization. *Journal of Applied Behavior Analysis,* 1976, *9,* 377–386.

Fixsen, D. L., Phillips, E. L., Phillips, E. A., & Wolf, M. M. The teaching-family model of group home treatment. In W. E. Craighead, A. E. Kazdin, & M. J. Mahoney, *Behavior modification.* Boston: Houghton Mifflin, 1976.

Flanagan, B., Goldiamond, I., & Azrin, N. H. Operant stuttering: The control of stuttering behavior through response contingent consequences. *Journal of the Experimental Analysis of Behavior,* 1958, *1,* 173–177.

Garcia, E. E. The training and generalization of a conversational speech form in non-verbal retardates. *Journal of Applied Behavior Analysis,* 1974, *7,* 137–150.

Garcia, E., Guess, D., & Byrnes, J. Development of syntax in a retarded girl using procedures of imitation, reinforcement, and modelling. *Journal of Applied Behavior Analysis,* 1973, *6,* 299–310.

Glover, J., & Gary, A. L. Procedures to increase some aspects of creativity. *Journal of Applied Behavior Analysis,* 1976, *9,* 79–84.

Goetz, E. M., & Baer, D. M. Social control of form diversity and the emergence of new forms in children's blockbuilding. *Journal of Applied Behavior Analysis,* 1973, *6,* 209–217.

Goodall, K. Shapers at work. *Psychology Today,* November 1972, pp. 53–63.

Green, R. R., & Hoats, D. L. Reinforcing capabilities of television distortion. *Journal of Applied Behavior Analysis,* 1969, *2,* 139–141.

Griffiths, H., & Craighead, W. E. Generalization in operant speech therapy for misarticulation. *Journal of Speech and Hearing Disorders,* 1972, *37,* 485–494.

Guess, D., Sailor, W., Rutherford, G., & Baer, D. M. An experimental analysis of linguistic development: Productive use of the plural morpheme. *Journal of Applied Behavior Analysis,* 1968, *1,* 297–306.

Hall, R. V., Axelrod, S., Tyler, L., Grief, E., Jones, F. C., & Robertson, R. Modification of behavior problems in the home with a parent as observer and experimenter. *Journal of Applied Behavior Analysis,* 1972, *5,* 53–64.

Hall, R. V., Lund, D., & Jackson, D. Effects of teacher attention on study behavior. *Journal of Applied Behavior Analysis,* 1968, *1,* 1–12.

Hartmann, D. P. Considerations in the choice of interobserver reliability estimates. *Journal of Applied Behavior Analysis,* 1977, *10,* 103–116.

Hartmann, D. P., & Hall, R. V. The changing criterion design. *Journal of Applied Behavior Analysis,* 1976, *9,* 527–532.

Hartmann, D. P., & Peterson, L. A neglected literature and an aphorism. *Journal of Applied Behavior Analysis,* 1975, *8,* 231–232.

Hauserman, N., Walen, S. R., & Behling, M. Reinforced racial integration in the first grade: A study in generalization. *Journal of Applied Behavior Analysis*, 1973, *6*, 193–200.

Hersen, M., Eisler, R., Alford, G., & Agras, W. S. Effects of token economy on neurotic depression: An experimental analysis. *Behavior Therapy*, 1973, *4*, 392–397.

Hingtgen, J. N., Sander, B. J., & DeMeyer, M. K. Shaping cooperative responses in childhood schizophrenics. In L. Ullman & L. Krasner (Eds.), *Case studies in behavior modification*. New York: Holt, Rinehart & Winston, 1965.

Holland, J. G. Human vigilance. *Science*, 1958, *128*, 61–67.

Holland, J. G. Teaching machines: An application of principles from the laboratory. *Journal of the Experimental Analysis of Behavior*, 1960, *3*, 275–287.

Holland, J. G. Research on programming variables. In R. Glaser (Ed.), *Teaching machines and programming learning, II: Data and directions*. Washington, D.C.: National Education Association, 1965.

Hollandsworth, J. G., Glazeski, R. C., & Dressel, M. E. Use of social-skills training in the treatment of extreme anxiety and deficient verbal skills in the job interview setting. *Journal of Applied Behavior Analysis*, 1978, *11*, 259–269.

Holz, W. C., & Azrin, N. H. Punishment. In W. K. Honig (Ed.), *Operant behavior: Areas of research and application*. New York: Appleton-Century-Crofts, 1966.

Homme, L. E., DeBaca, P. C., Devine, J. V., Steinhorst, R., & Rickert, E. J. Use of the Premack Principle in controlling the behavior of nursery school children. *Journal of the Experimental Analysis of Behavior*, 1963, *6*, 544.

Hoon, P. W., & Lindsley, O. R. A comparison of behavior therapy and traditional therapy publication activity. *American Psychologist*, 1974, *29*, 694–697.

Hopkins, B. L., & Hermann, J. A. Evaluating interobserver reliability of interval data. *Journal of Applied Behavior Analysis*, 1977, *10*, 121–126.

Horner, R. D. Establishing use of crutches by a mentally retarded spina bifida child. *Journal of Applied Behavior Analysis*, 1971, *4*, 183–189.

Instructions to authors: Preparation of graphs for *JABA*. *Journal of Applied Behavior Analysis*, 1976, *9*, 24.

Isaacs, W., Thomas, J., & Goldiamond, I. Application of operant conditioning to reinstate verbal behavior in psychotics. *Journal of Speech and Hearing Disorders*, 1960, *25*, 8–12.

Jackson, D. A., & Wallace, R. F. The modification and generalization of voice loudness in a fifteen year old retarded girl. *Journal of Applied Behavior Analysis*, 1974, *7*, 461–471.

Jones, R. R., Vaught, R. S., & Weinrott, M. Time series analysis in operant research. *Journal of Applied Behavior Analysis*, 1977, *10*, 151–166.

Jones, R. R., Weinrott, M. R., & Vaught, R. S. Effects of serial dependency on the agreement between visual and statistical analysis. *Journal of Applied Behavior Analysis*, 1978, *11*, 277–283.

Jourard, S. I-thou relationship versus manipulation in counseling and psychotherapy. *Journal of Individual Psychology*, 1959, *15*, 174–179.

Kagel, J. H., & Winkler, R. C. Behavioral economics: Areas of cooperative research between economics and applied behavioral analysis. *Journal of Applied Behavior Analysis*, 1972, *5*, 335–342.

Karlins, M., & Andrews, L. H. *Biofeedback*. New York: Lippincott, 1972.

Kazdin, A. E. The impact of applied behavior analysis on diverse areas of research. *Journal of Applied Behavior Analysis*, 1975, *8*, 213–229.

Kazdin, A. E. Artifact, bias, and complexity of assessment: The ABC's of reliability. *Journal of Applied Behavior Analysis*, 1977, *10*, 141–150. (a)

Kazdin, A. E. Assessing the clinical or applied importance of behavior change through social validation. *Behavior Modification*, 1977, *1*, 427–452. (b)

Kazdin, A. E., & Polster, R. Intermittent token reinforcement and response maintenance in extinction. *Behavior Therapy*, 1973, *4*, 386–391.

Kelleher, R. T., & Gollub, L. R. A review of positive conditioned reinforcement. *Journal of the Experimental Analysis of Behavior*, 1962, *5*, 543.

Kelly, M. B. A review of the observational data-collecting and reliability procedures reported in *The Journal of Applied Behavior Analysis*. *Journal of Applied Behavior Analysis*, 1977, *10*, 97–101.

Kennedy, D. A., & Thompson, I. The use of reinforcement techniques with a first-grade boy. *The Personality and Guidance Journal*, 1967, *46*, 366–370.

Kifer, R. E., Lewis, M. A., Green, D. R., & Phillips, E. L. Training predelinquent youths and their parents to negotiate conflict situations. *Journal of Applied Behavior Analysis*, 1974, *7*, 357–364.

Koegel, R. L., & Rincover, A. Research on the difference between generalization and maintenance in extra-therapy responding. *Journal of Applied Behavior Analysis*, 1977, *10*, 1–12.

Komaki, J., & Barnett, F. T. A behavioral approach to coaching football: Improving the play execution of the offensive backfield on a youth football team. *Journal of Applied Behavior Analysis*, 1977, *10*, 657–664.

Krasner, L. On the death of behavior modification. *American Psychologist*, 1976, *31*, 387–388.

Kratochwill, T. R., & Brody, G. H. Single subject designs: A perspective on the controversy over employing statistical inference and implications for research and training in behavior modification. *Behavior Modification*, 1978, *2*, 291–307.

Kulik, J. A., Kulik, C., & Carmichael, K. The Keller plan in science teaching. *Science*, 1974, *183*, 379–383.

Levine, F. M., & Fasnacht, G. Token rewards may lead to token learning. *American Psychologist*, 1974, *29*, 816–820.

Levitt, E. E. Psychotherapy with children: A further evaluation. *Behavior Research and Therapy*, 1963, *1*, 45–51.

Lindsley, O. R. A reliable wrist counter for recording behavior rates. *Journal of Applied Behavior Analysis*, 1968, 1, 77.

Loos, F. M., Williams, K. P., & Bailey, J. S. A multi-element analysis of the effects of teacher aides in an open style classroom. *Journal of Applied Behavior Analysis*, 1977, *10*, 437–448.

Lovaas, O. I., Schaeffer, B., & Simmons, J. Q. Building social behavior in autistic children by use of electric shock. *Journal of Experimental Research in Personality*, 1965, *1*, 99–109.

Lovaas, O. I., & Simmons, J. Q. Manipulation of self-destruction in three retarded children. *Journal of Applied Behavior Analysis*, 1969, *2*, 143–157.

Lovitt, T. C., & Esveldt, K. A. The relative effects on math performance of single versus multiple ratio schedules: A case study. *Journal of Applied Behavior Analysis*, 1970, *3*, 261–270.

Lumsdaine, A. A., & Glaser, R. *Teaching machines and programmed learning*. National Education Association, Washington, D.C.: 1960.

Mager, R. F. *Preparing instructional objectives*. Belmont, Calif.: Fearon, 1962.

Markle, S. *Good frames and bad: A grammar of frame writing*. New York: Wiley, 1969.

Martin, G., & Pear, J. *Behavior modification: What it is and how to do it*. Englewood Cliffs, N.J.: Prentice-Hall, 1978.

Mawhinney, V. T., Bostow, D. E., Laws, D. R., Blumenfeld, G. J., & Hopkins, B. L. A comparison of students studying-behavior produced by daily, weekly, and three week testing schedules. *Journal of Applied Behavior Analysis*, 1971, *4*, 257–264.

McMichael, J. S., & Corey, J. R. Contingency management in an introductory course produces better learning. *Journal of Applied Behavior Analysis*, 1969, *2*, 79–84.

McNees, M. P., Egli, D. S., Marshall, R. S., Schnelle, J. F., & Risley, T. R. Shoplifting prevention: Providing information through signs. *Journal of Applied Behavior Analysis*, 1976, *9*, 399–406.

McSweeny, A. J. Effects of response cost on the behavior of a million persons: Charging for directory assistance in Cincinnati. *Journal of Applied Behavior Analysis*, 1978, *11*, 47–51.

Meichenbaum, D. Cognitive modification of test anxious college students. *Journal of Consulting and Clinical Psychology*, 1972, *39*, 370–380.

Michael, J. Positive and negative reinforcement, a distinction that is no longer necessary; or a better way to talk about bad things. In E. Ramp & G. Semb (Eds.), *Behavior analysis*. Englewood Cliffs, N.J.: Prentice-Hall, 1973.

Michael, J. Statistical inference for single subject research: Mixed blessing or curse? *Journal of Applied Behavior Analysis*, 1974, *7*, 647–653.

Miller, L. K. Escape from an effortful situation. *Journal of the Experimental Analysis of Behavior*, 1968, *11*, 619–627.

Miller, L. K., & Feallock, R. A behavioral system for group living. In E. Ramp & G. Semb (Eds.), *Behavior analysis: Areas of research and application*. Englewood Cliffs, N.J.: Prentice-Hall, 1973.

Miller, L. K., & Miller, O. L. Reinforcing self-help activities of welfare recipients. *Journal of Applied Behavior Analysis*, 1970, *3*, 57–64.

Miller, L. K., & Schneider, R. The use of a token system in Project Head Start. *Journal of Applied Behavior Analysis*, 1970, *3*, 213–220.

Miller, L. K., & Weaver, F. H. The use of "concept programming" to teach behavioral concepts to university students. In J. Johnston (Ed.), *Behavior research and technology in higher education*. Springfield, Ill.: Charles C Thomas, 1974.

Minkin, N., Braukmann, C. J., Minkin, B. L., Timbers, G. D., Timbers, B. J., Fixsen, D. L., Phillips, E. L., & Wolf, M. M. The social validation and training of conversational skills. *Journal of Applied Behavior Analysis*, 1976, *9*, 127–139.

Moore, R., & Goldiamond, I. Errorless establishment of visual discrimination using fading procedures. *Journal of the Experimental Analysis of Behavior*, 1964, *7*, 269–272.

Neale, D. H. Behavior therapy and encopresis in children. *Behavior Research and Therapy*, 1963, *1*, 139–149.

Newsom, C. D., & Simon, K. M. A simultaneous discrimination procedure for the measurement of vision in non-verbal children. *Journal of Applied Behavior Analysis*, 1977, *10*, 633–644.

Osborne, J. G. Free-time as a reinforcer in the management of classroom behavior. *Journal of Applied Behavior Analysis*, 1969, *2*, 113–118.

Palmer, M. H., Lloyd, M. E., & Lloyd, K. E. An experimental analysis of electricity conservation procedures. *Journal of Applied Behavior Analysis*, 1977, *10*, 665–671.

Parsonson, B. S., & Baer, D. M. The analysis and presentation of graphic data. In T. R. Kratochwill (Ed.), *Single-subject research: Strategies for evaluating change.* New York: Academic Press, 1978.

Patterson, G. R. A performance theory for coercive family interaction. In R. Cairns (Ed.), *Social interaction: Methods, analysis, and illustrations.* Society Research Child Development Monograph, 1977.

Phillips, E. L. Achievement Place: Token reinforcement procedures in a home-style rehabilitation setting for "pre-delinquent" boys. *Journal of Applied Behavior Analysis,* 1968, *1,* 213–224.

Phillips, E. L., Phillips, E. A., Fixsen, D. L., & Wolf, M. M. Achievement Place: Modification of the behaviors of pre-delinquent boys within a token economy. *Journal of Applied Behavior Analysis,* 1971, *4,* 45–59.

Pierce, C. H., & Risley, T. R. Recreation as a reinforcer: Increasing membership and decreasing disruptions in an urban recreation center. *Journal of Applied Behavior Analysis,* 1974, *7,* 403–411.

Pinkston, E. M., Reese, N. M., LeBlanc, J. M., & Baer, D. M. Independent control of a preschool child's aggression and peer interaction by contingent teacher attention. *Journal of Applied Behavior Analysis,* 1973, *6,* 115–124.

Plummer, S., Baer, D. M., & LeBlanc, J. M. Functional considerations in the use of procedural timeout and an effective alternative. *Journal of Applied Behavior Analysis,* 1977, *10,* 689–705.

Polirstok, S. R., & Greer, R. D. Remediation of mutually aversive interactions between a problem student and four teachers by training the student in reinforcement techniques. *Journal of Applied Behavior Analysis,* 1977, *10,* 707–716.

Powell, J., & Azrin, N. H. The effect of shock as a punisher for cigarette smoking. *Journal of Applied Behavior Analysis,* 1968, *1,* 63–71.

Redd, W. H., & Birnbrauer, J. S. Adults as discriminative stimuli for different reinforcement contingencies with retarded children. *Journal of Experimental Child Psychology,* 1969, *7,* 440–447.

Reese, E. P. *Human behavior: Analysis and application.* Dubuque, Iowa: William C. Brown, 1978.

Renne, C. M., & Creer, T. L. Training children with asthma to use inhalation therapy equipment. *Journal of Applied Behavior Analysis,* 1976, *9,* 1–11.

Repp, A. C., Roberts, D. M., Slack, D. J., Repp, C. F., & Berkler, M. S. A comparison of frequency, interval, and time-sampling methods of data collection. *Journal of Applied Behavior Analysis,* 1976, *9,* 501–508.

Risley, T. R. The effects and side effects of punishing the autistic behaviors of a deviant child. *Journal of Applied Behavior Analysis,* 1968, *1,* 21–34.

Risley, T. R., & Wolf, M. M. Strategies for analyzing behavioral change over time. In J. Nesselroade & H. Reese (Eds.), *Life-span developmental psychology: Methodological issues.* New York: Academic Press, 1972.

Rosenthal, R., & Rosnow, R. L. *Artifact in behavioral research.* New York: Academic Press, 1969.

Schaefer, H. H. A vocabulary program using "language redundancy." *Journal of Programmed Instruction,* 1963, *2,* 9–16.

Schreibman, L. Effects of within-stimulus and extra-stimulus prompting on discrimination learning in autistic children. *Journal of Applied Behavior Analysis,* 1975, *8,* 91–112.

Schroeder, S. R. Parametric effects of reinforcement frequency, amount of reinforcement, and required response force on sheltered workshop behavior. *Journal of Applied Behavior Analysis,* 1972, *5,* 431–441.

Schwartz, G. J. College students as contingency managers for adolescents in a program to develop reading skills. *Journal of Applied Behavior Analysis,* 1977, *10,* 645–655.

Schwartz, M. L., & Hawkins, R. P. Applications of delayed reinforcement procedures to the behaviors of an elementary school child. *Journal of Applied Behavior Analysis,* 1970, *3,* 85–96.

Sherman, J. A. Reinstatement of verbal behavior in a psychotic by reinforcement methods. *Journal of Speech and Hearing Disorders,* 1963, *28,* 398–401.

Sidman, M. *Tactics of scientific research.* New York: Basic Books, 1961.

Simmons, M. W., & Lipsitt, L. P. An operant discrimination apparatus for infants. *Journal of the Experimental Analysis of Behavior,* 1961, *4,* 233–235.

Skinner, B. F. "Superstition" in the pigeon. *Journal of Experimental Psychology,* 1948, *38,* 168–172. (a)

Skinner, B. F. *Walden Two.* New York: Macmillan, 1948. (b)

Skinner, B. F. *Science and human behavior.* New York: Macmillan, 1953.

Skinner, B. F. The science of learning and the art of teaching. *Harvard Educational Review,* 1954, *24.*

Skinner, B. F. *Cumulative record.* New York: Appleton-Century-Crofts, 1958.

Solnick, J. V., Rincover, A., & Peterson, C. R. Some determinants of the reinforcing and punishing effects of timeout. *Journal of Applied Behavior Analysis,* 1977, *10,* 415–424.

Staats, A. W., & Butterfield, W. H. Treatment of non-reading in a culturally deprived juvenile delinquent: An application of reinforcement procedures. *Child Development,* 1965, *36,* 925–942.

Staats, A. W., Finley, J. R., Minke, K. A., & Wolf, M. Reinforcement variables in the control of unit reading responses. *Journal of the Experimental Analysis of Behavior,* 1964, *7,* 139–149.

Staats, A. W., Staats, C. K., Schutz, R., & Wolf, M. M. The conditioning of textual responses using "extrinsic" reinforcers. *Journal of the Experimental Analysis of Behavior,* 1962, *5,* 33–40.

Stephens, C. E., Pear, J. L., Wray, L. D., & Jackson, G. C. Some effects of reinforcement schedules in teaching

picture names to retarded children. *Journal of Applied Behavior Analysis,* 1975, *8,* 435–447.
Stokes, T. F., & Baer, D. M. An implicit technology of generalization. *Journal of Applied Behavior Analysis,* 1977, *10,* 349–367.
Stokes, T. F., Baer, D. M., & Jackson, R. L. Programming the generalization of a greeting response in four retarded children. *Journal of Applied Behavior Analysis,* 1974, *7,* 599–610.
Stokes, T. F., & Fawcett, S. B. Evaluating municipal policy: An analysis of a refuse packaging program. *Journal of Applied Behavior Analysis,* 1977, *10,* 391–398.
Sturgis, E. T., Tollison, C. D., & Adams, H. E. Modification of combined migraine-muscle contraction headaches using BVP and EMG feedback. *Journal of Applied Behavior Analysis,* 1978, *11,* 215–223.
Sulzer, B., & Mayer, G. R. *Behavior modification procedures for school personnel.* Hinsdale, Ill.: Dryden, 1972.
Tate, B. G., & Baroff, G. S. Aversive control of self-injurious behavior in a psychotic boy. *Behavior Research and Therapy,* 1966, *4,* 281–287.
Thomas, J. D., Presland, I. E., Grant, M. D., & Glynn, T. L. Natural rates of teacher approval and disapproval in grade-7 classrooms. *Journal of Applied Behavior Analysis,* 1978, *11,* 91–94.
Twardosz, S., & Baer, D. M. Training two severely retarded adolescents to ask questions. *Journal of Applied Behavior Analysis,* 1973, *4,* 655–661.
Ullman, L. P., & Krasner, L. *Case studies in behavior modification.* New York: Holt, Rinehart & Winston, 1965.
Walker, H. M., & Buckley, N. K. The use of positive reinforcement in conditioning attending behavior. *Journal of Applied Behavior Analysis,* 1968, *1,* 245–250.
Walker, H. M., & Buckley, N. K. Programming generalization and maintenance of treatment effects across time and settings. *Journal of Applied Behavior Analysis,* 1972, *5,* 209–224.
Wallace, I., & Pear, J. J. Self control techniques of famous novelists. *Journal of Applied Behavior Analysis,* 1977, *10,* 515–525.
Watson, D. L., & Tharp, R. G. *Self-directed behavior: Self-modification for personal adjustment.* Monterey, Calif.: Brooks/Cole, 1972.
Weisberg, P., & Waldrop, P. B. Fixed interval work habits of Congress. *Journal of Applied Behavior Analysis,* 1972, *5,* 93–97.
Wheeler, H. (Ed.). *Beyond the punitive society.* San Francisco, Calif.: W. H. Freeman, 1973.
White, M. A. Natural rate of teacher approval and disapproval in the classroom. *Journal of Applied Behavior Analysis,* 1975, *8,* 367–372.
Whitman, T. L., & Dussault, P. Self control through the use of a token economy. *Journal of Behavior Therapy and Experimental Psychiatry,* 1976, *7,* 161–166.
Williams, C. D. The elimination of tantrum behavior by extinction procedure. *Journal of Abnormal and Social Psychology,* 1959, *59,* 269.
Williams, J. L. *Operant learning: Procedures for changing behavior.* Monterey, Calif.: Brooks/Cole, 1972.
Willis, J., & Giles, D. *Great experiments in behavior modification.* Indianapolis: Hackett, 1976.
Wilson, G. T., Leaf, R. C., & Nathan, P. E. The aversive control of excessive alcohol consumption by chronic alcoholics in the laboratory setting. *Journal of Applied Behavior Analysis,* 1975, *8,* 13–26.
Winkler, R. C. Management of chronic psychiatric patients by a token reinforcement system. *Journal of Applied Behavior Analysis,* 1970, *3,* 47–55.
Wolf, M. M. Social validity: The case for subjective measurement or how applied behavior analysis is finding its heart. *Journal of Applied Behavior Analysis,* 1978, *11,* 203–214.
Wolf, M. M., Birnbrauer, J., Lawler, J., & Williams, T. The operant extinction, reinstatement, and re-extinction of vomiting behavior in a retarded child. In R. Ulrich, T. Stachnik, & J. Mabry (Eds.), *Control of human behavior, Vol. II.* Glenview, Ill.: Scott, Foresman, 1970.
Wolf, M. M., & Risley, T. R. Reinforcement: Applied research. In R. Glaser (Ed.), *The nature of reinforcement.* New York: Academic Press, 1971.
Wolf, M. M., Risley, T. R., & Mees, H. L. Application of operant conditioning procedures to the behavior problems of an autistic child. *Behavior Research and Therapy,* 1964, *1,* 305–312.
Wright, H. Observational child study. In P. Mussen (Ed.), *Handbook of research methods in child development.* New York: Wiley, 1960.
Wulbert, M., Nyman, B. A., Snow, D., & Owen, Y. The efficacy of stimulus fading and contingency management in the treatment of elective mutism: A case study. *Journal of Applied Behavior Analysis,* 1973, *6,* 435–441.
Zeilberger, J., Sampen, S. E., & Sloane, H. N., Jr. Modification of a child's problem behaviors in the home with the mother as therapist. *Journal of Applied Behavior Analysis,* 1968, *1,* 47–54.
Zimmerman, E. H., Zimmerman, J., & Russell, C. D. Differential effects of token reinforcement on instruction following behavior in retarded students instructed as a group. *Journal of Applied Behavior Analysis,* 1969, *2,* 101–112.

LESSON 1 **FORM A** **GRADE:** ____________

NAME: ______________________ **DATE:** ______________

NOTE: Do not write on this page until your instructor has given you directions.*

(1) Who is often considered to be the founder of behavior analysis? ____________________

(2) The second characteristic of behavior analysis is that it studies the ________________ ________________ influences on people's behavior.

(3) The emphasis of the book is to demonstrate the relevance of behavior analysis concepts to understanding and improving everyday ____________________________.

(4) Behavior modification is a very young discipline that did not begin large-scale publication of its results until about __________.

(5) This book will not use the term *behavioral modification* but rather will use the term ______________________________.

(6) The first characteristic of behavior analysis is that it focuses on ______________.

(7) Behavior modification has been found to be more effective in the area of psychiatry than traditional "____________________________ therapy."

(8) Behavior analysis is a behavioral science that develops and experimentally analyzes practical procedures for producing changes in socially significant ____________________.

(9) The third characteristic of behavior analysis is that it uses single-subject designs to ______________________________ with different environmental arrangements.

(10) The name of the behavioral science that develops and experimentally analyzes practical procedures for producing changes in socially significant behaviors is ________________ ________________.

Write three sentences similar to those found in the text that describe the major characteristics of behavior analysis. (The sentences must contain the key words underlined in the text.)

*The teacher's Manual that accompanies this text contains answer keys for these lesson quizzes.

LESSON 2 **FORM A** **GRADE:** ____________

NAME: ______________________ **DATE:** ____________

(1) The observers in the Goetz and Baer study recorded a novel block structure as soon as they saw it. While they did not record the behavior of blockbuilding but rather the resulting structures, this would be an example of direct observation because they recorded a physical ______________________ of blockbuilding behavior as soon as they saw it.

(2) The subject matter of behavior analysis includes all ______________________ aspects of human conduct.

(3) Suppose that "understanding" a word is defined as meaning that the person can correctly define the word. If Vince asked his fellow students if they could define the term *behavioral definition* without hearing their definition, was he using direct observation? ____________

(4) A statement that specifies exactly what behavior is to be observed is called a(n) ____________ ______________________.

(5) Using a wrist counter to record times when you say "yes" or "no" to a request ____________ ______________ (would, would not) be an example of direct observation.

(6) When Professor Lown recorded his students' visits to his personal library as they occurred, he was using ______________________ observation.

(7) Direct observation involves an observer who personally can ______________________ ____________ the behavior and ______________________ his observation immediately.

(8) When Minkin and his colleagues found a high correlation between (1) those individuals judged by a cross section of adults to be good conversationalists and (2) those individuals exhibiting a high rate of behaviors specified by other definitions of skilled conversational behaviors, they were establishing the ______________________ of their definition.

(9) The behavioral commune has developed a list that helps the inspector to determine when the living room is clean. The list includes a clean floor, emptied ashtrays, and a vacuumed rug. This specification of what is meant by "cleanness" is called a(n) ______________.

(10) Ann stated that "understanding" a word meant that a person could define it orally or in writing. Ann's statement would be called a(n) ______________________.

Give two reasons why it is important for behavior analysts to formulate specific behavioral definitions.

LESSON 2 **FORM B** **GRADE:** ____________

NAME: ______________________ **DATE:** ____________

(1) The statement by Budzynski and Stoyva that tension is "a high level of electrical activity in the forehead muscles" would be called a(n) ______________________.

(2) Direct observation does not apply only to situations in which the observer personally sees the behavior occurring. The one exception is when the observer sees the physical ______________________ of some behavior.

(3) Abe wrote down the number of calories he had eaten right after the meal was finished. Was he using direct observation? __________

(4) In forming a behavioral definition, the behavior analyst must specify exactly what behavior is to be ______________________.

(5) Skinner considered learning to be: the production of overt behaviors that correctly respond to a series of progressively more difficult educational questions. Underline the first two and last two words in the behavioral definition of learning.

(6) If an observer personally <u>sees</u> (or hears) a behavior and records it immediately, this is an example of ______________________.

(7) John weighed all human-made objects bigger than a quarter inch left at a picnic area by his family. He immediately wrote down the weight. Is this an example of direct observation? __________

(8) Observing aggression by writing down each time that your son hits or pushes another child would be an example of ______________________ observation.

(9) A friend studied whether Marge initiated conversations with men. He meant by "initiated conversations" whether she "approached a man and was the first to speak." The latter phrase in quotes would be called a(n) ______________________.

(10) The statement "Studying is when a student has a book in front of him and is looking at it" is called a(n) ______________________.

Give one reason why behavior analysts usually rely on direct observation, rather than on observations that involve memory, such as questionnaires or interviews.

LESSON 3 **FORM A** **GRADE:** ____________

NAME: ______________________ **DATE:** ______________

(1) Heddy watched Family A for 15 seconds to see if they dropped litter; she then turned to Family B and watched them for 15 seconds; she also watched Families C and D each for 15 seconds. Every minute she would return to Family A and start the routine over again. She was using ______________________ recording.

(2) Event recording is based on counting the number of times that some ______________ ______________ behavioral event occurs.

(3) When the Bakers checked their son's room each day to see whether it had been cleaned, they were using what method of direct observation? ______________________ recording

(4) Three important characteristics of behavior analysis are: (a) it focuses on behavior; (b) it studies ______________________ influences on behavior; and (c) it uses single-subject designs to ______________________ with different environmental arrangements.

(5) The observation of whether or not a behavior occurs during a series of continuous intervals is called ______________________ recording.

(6) If you use a self-recording procedure in which you note the number of times that you say something positive to another person during the day, you are using what method of observation? ______________________ recording

(7) The observation of behavior during a series of discontinuous intervals is called ________ ______________________ recording.

(8) If a mother wanted to find out how much of the day her child spent studying in school, she might go to the school and observe whether her child was studying during each 20-second period during the day. She would be using what method of observation? ______________ ______________ recording

(9) Walker and Buckley (1968) analyzed the study behavior of a fourth grader by recording when he was "looking at the assigned page, working problems, and recording responses." This statement would be called a(n) ______________________ .

(10) One of the behaviorists observing John's study behavior in spelling noted the number of times that he was studying during 15-second intervals spaced 3 minutes apart. What method of observation was the observer using? ______________________ recording

Define time sampling. Explain how it differs from interval recording.

LESSON 3 **FORM B** **GRADE:** ____________

NAME: ________________________ **DATE:** ______________

(1) The method that involves observation of behavior during continuous periods of time is called ____________________________________ recording.

(2) When a teacher gives a written test, he or she is using the method of observation called ____________________________________ recording.

(3) To find out how often Tom is watching TV each day, you might check once every 15 minutes to see whether he is watching or not and compute the percentage. You would be using what method of observation? ____________________________________ recording

(4) Outcome recording, event recording and interval recording all involve the immediate recording of behavior seen or heard by the observer. Therefore they would all be classified as examples of ____________________________________ .

(5) When Dee observed the number of times any child struck another child at the free school, she was using what method of observation? ____________________________________ recording

(6) Outcome recording is based on observing a(n) ____________________________________ of behavior, rather than observing the behavior itself.

(7) Lindsley (1968) recommended the use of a simple wrist counter so that people could count the number of cigarettes they smoked, the number of smiles, and so on. These would be examples of ____________________________________ recording.

(8) Willie noted the number of 30-second intervals during which his professor in political science talked to the pretty blonde. He was using what technique of direct observation? ____________________________________ recording

(9) Time sampling involves the observation of behavior during a series of brief intervals that are ____________________________________ .

(10) Being a bit of a gossip, you want to know what percent of the time John has his girlfriend in his room, so you check once every hour to see whether she is there. You would be using what method of observation? ____________________________________ recording

Describe two roles of behavioral observation.

LESSON 3 **FORM C** **GRADE:** ____________

NAME: ______________________ **DATE:** ____________

(1) When Tom and Mona recorded whether Bob was talking during each 15-second period of their ecology committee meeting, they were using ______________________ recording.

(2) Counting the occurrence of a complete behavior is called ______________________ recording; observing a behavior for a brief time several times a day is called ______________________ recording.

(3) When John counted the number of times during the lecture that his English professor split his infinitives, he was using what method of direct observation? ______________________ recording

(4) What two methods involve dividing the period of observation into smaller units of time? ______________________ and ______________________ recording

(5) The checklist covering the results of cleaning behavior used by Feallock and Miller (1976) would be an example of ______________________ recording.

(6) When Fran checked for 15 seconds at the end of every five-minute interval to see whether Professor Young was putting down a student, she was using what method of observation? ______________________ recording

(7) The method of observation that involves the results of behavior rather than the behavior itself is called ______________________ recording.

(8) To compare the level of violence of two TV shows, you might note how many 15-second intervals contain some form of violence for each show. You would be using what method of observation? ______________________ recording

(9) Interval recording involves dividing the observation period into a series of ______________________ intervals and noting whether a particular behavior occurs during that interval.

(10) Maria checked on her son ten times an evening, at randomly selected times, to see whether he was studying. What method of observation was she using? ______________________ recording

Explain how you can tell whether an observation involves outcome recording or event recording.

LESSON 4 **FORM A** **GRADE:** ____________

NAME: ________________________ **DATE:** ______________

(1) Dan counted the number of consecutive 15-second intervals during which his baby sister was smiling. He was using ______________________ recording.

(2) If two observers disagree on their observations, you cannot conclude that their observations are unreliable unless they were made at the same ______________________.

(3) Three members of the ecology committee were worried that they talked too much, so they asked two other members to observe the number of 10-second intervals during which they did most of the talking. The first ten observations were (with "T" indicating the trio and "O" indicating others):

(1)	O T T T T O T O T O
(2)	O T T T T O T O T T

What is their reliability? ____________ Does this evidence indicate that the observations are reliable? ____________

(4) Reliability is a measure of the extent to which there is ______________________ between two independent observers.

(5) Kim and José counted shooting stars one night. Kim saw 17 and José saw 20. Compute their reliability. ____________ Is it acceptable? ____________

(6) You and your friend both measure the accuracy of your observations about Johnny Carson's behavior by observing it at the same time and then comparing the results. This is called a test of ______________________.

(7) Alice and Jane watched ten commercials shown on late-night TV to determine how many of them were advertising products that were ecologically harmful. Their results were (where "H" stands for harmful commercials):

Alice:	H N H N H H H N N H
Jane:	H N H N H H H H H H

Compute their reliability. ____________ If they were using a new behavioral definition would this be acceptable? ____________

(8) Meecham was a born observer. He counted 23 robins on the first day of spring. Corinne was a born skeptic. She counted only one robin on the second day of spring. She concluded, in her skeptical way, that Meecham was a poor observer. Was she correct to do so? ____________

(9) Eileen checked to see whether her lazy roommate was studying at 19 random times during the day. What method of observation was she using? ______________________ recording

(10) Researchers generally shoot for a reliability figure of ____________.

Describe how you determine the reliability of two observers using interval recording to observe the same behavior at the same time.

LESSON 4 **FORM B** **GRADE:** ____________

NAME: ______________________ **DATE:** ____________

---

(1) Two instructors separately grade a multiple-choice and an essay test. Their greater reliability with the multiple-choice test is probably a result of using the same ______________ ______________ of a correct response for that test.

(2) Dave and Pat were assigned to check on the bookkeeper in the Food Co-op. They weren't as concerned with his cheating as they were with his not doing all the necessary work. Therefore, they made a checklist of 20 aspects of his job that he should do. They found:

Dave:	X X O X O O O O X X X O O O X O O X O X
Pat:	X X X X O X O O X X X O O O X X O X O O

What is their reliability? ____________ Is their agreement acceptable? ____________

(3) When Kim counts the number of typing errors made by her secretary, she is using what method of observation? ______________________________ recording

(4) Bob and Gary wanted to find out how much time the children at Yellow Brick Road Free School were spending learning to read, write, and do arithmetic. They observed in 30-second blocks of time using a new behavioral definition. Their first 20 intervals were (S = studying; N = not studying):

Bob:	N S S N S N N N N N N N S N N N N N N S
Gary:	S S S N N N N N N N N N S N N S N N N S

What is their reliability? ____________ Is their reliability acceptable? ____________

(5) Reliability can be measured only when two people observe the same behavior, using the same definition, at the same ______________________________ .

(6) Joan counted the number of times Professor Brainbuster said "uhh" during Monday's lecture and found that he said it 50 times. If Nel counts 50 "uhhs" during Wednesday's lecture, is this reliability? ____________

(7) Larry observed how often Professor Green encouraged students to make comments in his discussion class. Larry decided to record only agreements by the professor with the comment and direct praise of the comment. Larry's decision about what to record would be called a(n) ______________________________ .

(8) With a new behavioral definition, researchers will accept a reliability figure of ____________ .

(9) The agreement between two sets of observations is called their ______________ ______________ .

(10) Owen and Mary recorded gripes during dinner. Owen counted nine, and Mary counted ten. Compute their reliability. ____________ Is their reliability acceptable? ____________

Suppose that one observer using event recording counts 25 responses, and a second observer counts 20. Describe the assumption that permits you to determine agreements and disagreements in this case. What would reliability be in this case?

LESSON 4 **FORM C** **GRADE:** ____________

NAME: ________________________ **DATE:** ______________

(1) Dolores and Rick noted how many times, at five selected inspection intervals, the Ping-Pong table was being used. They came out with the following data:

Dolores:	O O O X O
Rick:	O O O X X

What is the reliability? ____________ Is it acceptable? ____________

(2) When Morgan weighs himself as a measure of his eating behavior, he would be using what method of observation? ____________________________________ recording

(3) If two observers agree on their observations, you cannot conclude that their observations are reliable unless they were made at the ____________________________________ time.

(4) To find out how many of Roger's students fall asleep during his lectures, you might have an observer count the number of students who fall asleep. To measure reliability, you would assign at least ____________ people to do the counting.

(5) Dom observed each story on the evening news for a week. He found that 46 of the news items were biased toward the status quo. John watched the evening news during the same week and, using the same definition of "biased toward the status quo," found that 50 of the items were biased. He decided that Dom's observations were accurate. If you translate "accurate" as "reliable," do you agree with his conclusion? ____________

(6) Marge felt that good teaching involved a great deal of personal contact. She observed the number of personal contacts that Tom made with his students by means of an event-recording approach and found it to be very low. She then explained her observations to Tom and suggested that he engage in more personal contact with his pupils, which he was observed to do. Marge then had 10 parents view a videotape of Tom's teaching before and after her discussion with Tom and asked them to rate the quality of his teaching. They rated Tom low before and high after the discussion, in quality of teaching. These results indicated to Marge that her definition of good teaching had ____________________________________.

(7) When calculating the reliability of event recording, if one observer counts five events and the other four events, the reliability is ____________.

(8) Barb inspected the cleaning jobs according to a 50-item checklist at 8:00 Thursday night. She found that 46 items had been done. Vince inspected the same cleaning jobs according to the same checklist at 9:00 Thursday night and found only 30 of them done. Is this evidence that they are not reliable? ____________

(9) The general formula for calculating reliability is ____________________________________.

(10) Marc and Anna felt that their teacher was biased in Anna's favor. They conspired to write down exactly the same answers on a ten-question short-answer test. The teacher's grades for the two tests were:

Marc:	O O O C O C C O O O
Anna:	O O O C C C C O O C

Compute the reliability. ____________ If this is a new definition, is the grading reliable? ____________

What are acceptable limits of reliability for old and new behavioral definitions?

LESSON 5 **FORM A** **GRADE:** ____________

NAME: ______________________ **DATE:** ____________

(1) If two students measure the amount of time that another student, Nate, dominates the discussion, before trying to get him to change, their agreement is a measure of the ______________________ of these data.

(2) Meichenbaum (1972) measured the students' GPA before teaching them how to be less anxious while taking tests; he then measured their GPA after teaching them. What experimental design did he use? ______________________

(3) Dave observed the cleaning behavior of his children. If he started giving cookies for a clean room to one of them after one week, to the second one after two weeks, and to the third one after three weeks, he would be using a(n) ______________________ design.

(4) Professor Brainbuster had used the text *Moldy History* for years. He decided to change to the new text, called *Hip History*, and found that his enrollment increased. If he used *Moldy History* again to see if the new book was what caused the increase, he would be using what experimental design? ______________________

(5) Steve and Cleo agreed to determine whether their friend was reciting his lines loud enough to be heard in the last row. Since they were also reading their own scripts, they agreed to listen to his loudness at random times throughout his recitation. They were using ______________________ recording.

(6) The Cornucopia Food Co-op assigned a clerk to count the number of customers prior to their advertising campaign. The data they obtained are called ______________________ data.

(7) The strength of a reversal design is that it can rule out ______________________ explanations of an observed behavior change.

(8) Brune was negative, and he interrupted others. First he had a friend observe both behaviors. Then he started counting (with a wrist counter) instances of being negative. A few weeks later he started observing instances of interrupting others on a second wrist counter. If the use of a wrist counter is a treatment, this is an example of a(n) ______________________ design.

(9) The name of the experiment in which two or more behaviors are subjected to the same treatment starting at different times is ______________________ design.

(10) The purpose of an experiment is to find out whether a treatment changes the rate of a behavior above or below its ______________________ level.

Define baseline and treatment.

LESSON 5 **FORM B** **GRADE:** ____________

NAME: ______________________ **DATE:** ______________

(1) If parents change their two children from a public school to a free school in order to see whether the children will be more willing to go to school, the parents would be using a(n) ______________________ design.

(2) Observing how well a student does in math for a period of time while he or she is being tutored gives you his or her behavior rate during a(n) ______________________ condition.

(3) The name of the design in which you measure the behavior for three periods of time, one before, one during, and one after the treatment is a(n) ______________________ design.

(4) Komacki and Barnett (1977) provided feedback for football play performance after 10 sessions for the option play, after 14 sessions for the power sweep, and after 18 sessions for the counter. What experimental design did they use? ______________________

(5) Observing how well a student does in math before he or she starts receiving help from a tutor would be called determining the student's ______________________ rate of behavior.

(6) Steve recorded during consecutive 15-second intervals whether his friend was reciting his lines loud enough during play practice to be heard in the last row. What method of observation did Steve use? ______________________ recording

(7) If a teacher makes class attendance optional for one student and then a week later makes it optional for a second student (to see whether it affects their participation), the teacher would be using a(n) ______________________ design.

(8) The antipollution committee was recruiting new members. After trying without much success for several months, they took out an ad in an underground newspaper for several weeks. They later stopped the ad to see what would happen to their rate of recruitment. This would be an example of a(n) ______________________ design.

(9) Steve and Cleo were both supposed to record during 15-second intervals whether their friend was talking loud enough during his play practice to be heard in the last row. The first ten observations were (where L stands for loud enough, and S for too soft):

Steve:	L L L L S L L S L S
Cleo:	L L S L S L L S L L

What is the reliability of their observations? ____________ Is it acceptable? ____________

(10) Any method that is designed to modify the rate of a behavior is called a(n) ______________________ .

Explain why a comparison design is a weak design.

LESSON 5 **FORM C** **GRADE:** ____________

NAME: ______________________ **DATE:** ____________

(1) If the teacher introduced Old West material to Bernie in his history and literature classes at the same time and compared his performance using Old West material with his performance using the regular material, the teacher would be using a(n) ______________ ______________ design.

(2) Observing a student's grades on math homework before, during, and after he or she has had a tutor is a strong research design because it can rule out ______________ ______________ causes of any improvement in his or her grades during the time he or she had the tutor.

(3) The multiple-baseline design gets its name from the fact that baselines are determined for ______________ (how many) or more classes of behavioral observations.

(4) The record of a behavior prior to some attempt to change it is called a(n) ______________ ______________.

(5) Suppose that three people have been annoying you. If this week you ask the first one to stop annoying you, next week the second one, and a week later the third one, you would be using a(n) ______________ design.

(6) Palmer and associates (1977) measured electrical usage by a middle-class household when not giving them cost information, for a period of time while giving it, and for a period of time after no longer giving them the information. They used what experimental design? ______________

(7) Frank counted 17 tics in President Nixon's face while he was talking about Watergate, and Stella counted 20. What is the reliability of their observations? ______________ Is it an acceptable level for a new definition? ______________

(8) If Marie's living group had someone observe the amount of cleaning that was done for a period of time, then assigned jobs to members to see what effect a schedule would have on cleaning, and finally stopped assigning jobs for a time, they would be using a(n) ______________ design.

(9) In a simple comparison design, we compare the rate of a behavior during two periods of time called the ______________ and the ______________ ______________ conditions.

(10) You observe the amount of time that your roommate interrupts you while you are studying. Then you ask him or her to stop doing it. The record of interruptions prior to your talking with him or her is called a(n) ______________.

Name the conditions in a reversal design.

LESSON 6 **FORM A** **GRADE:** ____________

NAME: ______________________ **DATE:** ____________

(1) Kifer and associates (1974) observed the percent of reasonable negotiating behaviors used before and after training. They found the following three observations before training: 0, 0, 0. After training they found 100, 67, and 100%. A limitation of this type of experiment is that it cannot rule out ______________________ explanations of the increase.

(2) Matty was observed to say negative statements to people the following number of times per day: 3, 7, 4, 6, and 9. If you made a graph of these data, you would label the abscissa "______________________."

(3) The labels on your graph for behavior and time should be as ______________________ ____________ as possible while still describing the numbers recorded.

(4) A secretary recorded the number of times that her employer was late for an appointment. He was late for the following number of appointments: 8, 3, 7, 4, 4, 7, 8, 2, 1, and 6. Each division on the ordinate should be labeled with numbers that increase by steps of ________.

(5) Bonnie used a new counseling technique called "empathy-self-actualization" last week with George. This week she asked George to compare how depressed he was before and after the new approach to counseling. He said he was a lot less depressed after the counseling. George's observation method for his earlier depression would not be an example of ______________________ because he did not record it immediately.

(6) Dave graphed the following number of compliments he gave per day: 16, 18, 22, 13, 17, and 10. Therefore, the ordinate divisions would be in steps of ____________.

(7) In squaring a complex graph, find the condition that has the largest value of the ____________ ______________________, and divide by the number of observations per condition (that is, the largest value of the abscissa).

(8) Frank's smoking bothered him. During a week of observation he recorded smoking the following number of cigarettes: 10, 16, 12, 15, 14, and 10. He decided to fine himself for every smoke during the next week and observed the following: 1, 0, 0, 1, 0, and 1. Then he quit fining himself and observed 1, 4, 2, 3, 1, and 2. The ordinate would be labeled in steps of ____________.

(9) Step three in making a graph square is to divide the largest value of the ____________ ____________ by the largest value of the ______________________.

(10) Bob Behaviorist observed the percentage of cleaning and cooking jobs that were completed for five weeks. He then talked the other members of the commune into assessing fines for inadequate cleaning performance for the next five weeks. Finally, the commune assessed fines for inadequate cooking for the final five weeks. Here are the results:

Week:	1	2	3	4	5	6	7	8	9	10	11	12	13	14	15
Cleaning:	40	30	50	20	40	80	90	95	90	85	95	90	95	90	100
Cooking:	60	50	40	60	50	40	30	50	60	40	90	95	85	90	95

Make a graph of the results using the grid in Figure 1.

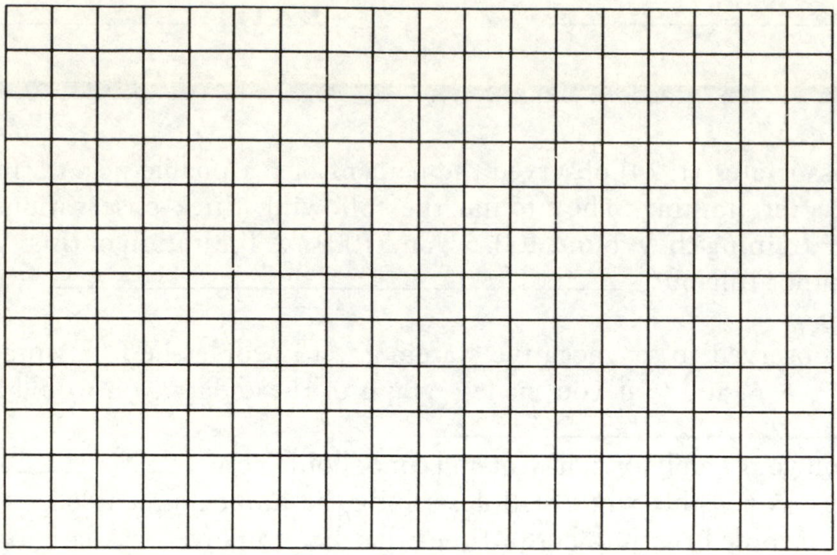

Figure 1. Amount of housework done at a commune.

Name the horizontal and vertical coordinate lines used in a graph and what behavioral data each corresponds to.

LESSON 6 **FORM B** **GRADE:** ____________

NAME: ______________________ **DATE:** ____________

(1) Sturgis and her colleagues (1978) observed the number of hours that a woman had tension and migraine headaches. After the fifth week, they trained her using biofeedback to eliminate migraines. After the tenth week they trained her to eliminate tension headaches. The number of hours of headaches during each week of the experiment were:

Weeks:	1	2	3	4	5	6	7	8	9	10	11	12	13	14	15
Migraines:	0	9	8	6	9	0	1	0	0	0	0	0	0	0	0
Tension:	8	15	18	8	8	2	15	10	9	3	2	0	10	8	2

For example, the woman had 0 hours of migraine headaches but 8 hours of tension headaches during the first week. The ordinate of this graph should increase by steps of ____________.

(2) The vertical line of a graph is used to record what aspect of a behavioral experiment? ______________________

(3) A secretary recorded the number of times that her employer was late for appointments. The boss was late for the following number of appointments: 3, 5, 2, 4, 1, 3, 5, 2, 3, and 4. You would label the ordinate of the graph "number of times ______________________."

(4) Matty is observed to say positive things to people the following number of times per day: 7, 14, 12, 5, and 10. To make a graph of these data, you would label the ordinate with numbers that increase by steps of ____________.

(5) Behavior analysis is characterized as follows: (a) it focuses on behavior; (b) it studies ______________________ influences on behavior; and (c) it uses single-subject designs to ______________________ with different environmental arrangements.

(6) Suppose that you are squaring the graphs for a multiple baseline experiment with two behaviors. If the treatment is introduced after 7 sessions and runs for 14 with the first behavior, and if the treatment is introduced after 14 sessions and runs 7 more for the second behavior, then each condition has ______________________ (how many) observations?

(7) Jamie recorded the following percentages of discussions between the professor and the pretty blonde: 35, 25, 15, 20, 15, and 20 percent. The ordinate should be labeled in steps of ____________ units.

(8) If Hersen and his colleagues (1973) had asked a group of psychiatrists to observe their patient in order to rate his depression before and after the use of tokens, they could find out whether the psychiatrists' ratings and their behavioral observations correlated. If they did, then Hersen and his colleagues would have provided evidence that their behavioral definition of nondepressed behavior had ______________________.

(9) When making a graph you should try to make the ordinate and the abscissa the same length. This is called making the graph ______________________.

(10) Roberta noted the number of times each week that her husband had meals ready on time. For the first five weeks, she noted the following times: 5, 7, 4, 10, and 6. She then made a rule that she would make a special contribution to the meal (like a dessert) if he had it ready on time. She noted the following results: 15, 19, 20, 18, and 21. Finally, she reverted to her old method of being nice all the time. She noted the following results: 17, 13, 9, 5, and 6. Make a graph of Roberta's experiment using Figure 2.

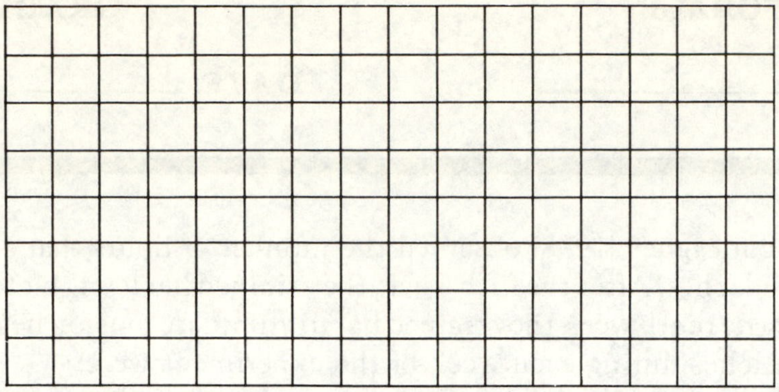

Figure 2. Frequency that Roberta's husband had meals ready on time

Summarize the first four steps of squaring a simple graph.

LESSON 6 **FORM C** **GRADE:** ____________

NAME: ______________________ **DATE:** ______________

(1) On successive days, Karen correctly worked the following number of problems on her English homework: 14, 16, 18, 18, and 14. You would label the abscissa "________________."

(2) The horizontal line of a graph is used to record what aspect of a behavioral experiment? ______________________________

(3) Hersen and his colleagues (1973) could have measured the reliability of their observations of smiling (part of nondepressed behavior) by having a second observer. They might then have the following results:

Primary observer:	S S S S N S S S N S
Secondary observer:	S N S S N S S S N N

What is the reliability of these observations? ____________ Is it acceptable? __________

(4) Mr. Norris did an experiment to help Willie improve his math and social-studies homework. For the first five days, Mr. Norris let Willie play at recess no matter how many homework problems he got correct in these subjects. For the next five days, however, Mr. Norris let Willie play only if he got more than seven math homework problems correct (regardless of how many social-studies problems were correct). And for the final five days, he let Willie play only if he got seven or more problems correct in both subjects. Below are the data for Willie:

Day:	1	2	3	4	5	6	7	8	9	10	11	12	13	14	15
Mathematics:	2	4	3	2	4	7	6	8	7	7	8	7	8	8	7
Social Studies:	3	5	4	3	6	4	5	3	5	3	6	7	7	6	8

The ordinates for this experiment would increase by steps of ____________.

(5) The vertical line on a graph is called the ______________________________.

(6) John caused trouble by hitting other kids. He hit 10, 16, 17, 14, and 15 times per day. The ordinate should be labeled in steps of ____________.

(7) Willie correctly worked the following number of problems on his math homework: 14, 16, 18, 17, 18, and 14. You would label the ordinate in steps of ____________.

(8) Hersen and associates (1973) measured nondepressed behavior by counting the number of times they observed a patient smiling, talking, and engaging in motor activity. "Smiling, talking, and engaging in motor activity" would be a(n) ______________________________ of nondepressed behavior.

(9) When graphing an experiment, put a vertical line of dots (or dashes) between the baseline and the ______________________________ condition.

(10) Matty was observed to say positive things to people the following number of times per day: 1, 0, 2, 0, and 3. Her father sent her to a psychiatrist so she would learn to be more positive. After her treatment, she was positive the following numbers of times per day: 0, 2, 1, 1, and 3. Make a graph of this experiment with psychiatry using Figure 3.

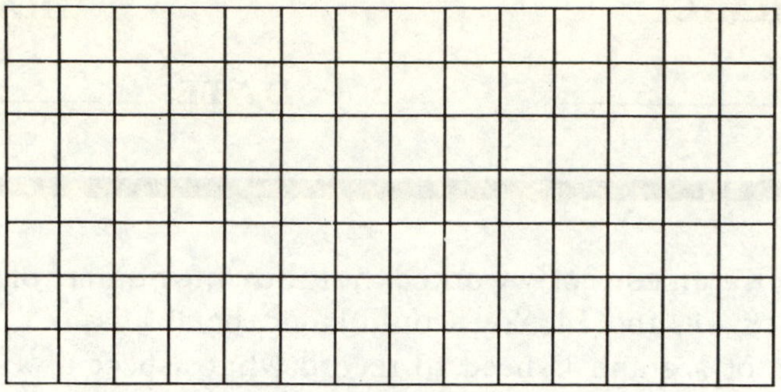

Figure 3. Matty's frequency of making positive statements.

How does squaring a complex graph differ from squaring a simple graph?

LESSON 7 **FORM A** **GRADE:** ____________

NAME: ______________________ **DATE:** ____________

(1) Ben decided to self-record the number of compliments that he gave each day and the number of compliments that he reacted positively to. After doing this for 3 days, he then discussed how to give compliments with a psychologist. After another 3 days he discussed how to react positively to compliments. He continued to record for another three days. The results of his self-recording are:

Days:	1	2	3	4	5	6	7	8	9
Give compliments:	2	5	3	5	8	6	7	9	8
Accept compliments:	1	3	9	2	1	9	6	9	8

If Ben were to graph his experiment, what size steps should he use on the ordinate? ______________________

(2) An experimental design that studies a behavior before the treatment, during the treatment, and after the treatment is called a(n) ______________________ design.

(3) Any method that attempts to change the rate of a behavior is called a(n) ______________________.

(4) June observed Professor Brainbuster on Thursday and Friday to see how many chauvinistic statements he made. She counted 18. Fay observed Professor Brainbuster on Thursday and Friday also and counted 20 such comments. Can you conclude that their observations are reliable? ____________

(5) A group of students, during the early 1960s, tried using "sit-ins" to desegregate a northern suburb. Before starting their protests, however, they sent ten Black students into three restaurants every day for a week to test whether they would be served. None were served. They then began a sit-in at Restaurant A, informing the manager of their intentions. They conducted their sit-ins during the lunch and dinner rush periods. Their "testers" would then go in during other periods of the day to see whether the sit-ins were having any effect. The testers continued going to the other two restaurants. After ten days Restaurant A changed its policy and served the testers. The students then went after Restaurants B and C. The design they used is an example of a(n) ______________________ design.

(6) To compare the amount of sexual stereotyping on two TV shows, you might record each 15-second interval that contains some form of sexual stereotyping. You would be using what method of observation? ______________________ recording

(7) A measure of the amount of agreement between two observers is called ______________________.

(8) One characteristic of behavior analysis is that it ______________________ with different environmental arrangements, using single-subject designs.

(9) When Minkin and his colleagues (1976) investigated the correlation between (1) ratings of conversational skills by a cross-section of adults and (2) the rate of three behaviors defined as constituting conversational skills, they were evaluating the ______________________ of their definition.

(10) Name an experimental design that rules out alternative explanations of any observed change in behavior: ______________________

LESSON 7 **FORM B** **GRADE:** ____________

NAME: ________________________ **DATE:** ______________

(1) Mary's teacher and another observer made the following observations of Mary's nearness to other children (where N stands for near and F stands for far). What is their reliability? ____________ Is this an acceptable level of reliability? ____________

Teacher: F N F F F F F N F F F F F F F F N N F F F F F F N
Other: F N F F F F F N N F F F F F F F N N F F N F F F F

(2) Dr. Foster developed a procedure for improving the understanding that students have of psychology. He approached understanding as an aspect of the students' behavior; he increased understanding by creating a better textbook and by rewarding his students for good performance; and he used a reversal design to determine whether the procedure worked. Dr. Foster's activity would be an example of what behavioral science? ____________________

(3) Dave observed the cleaning behavior of his children. He started giving cookies for a clean room to one of them after one week, to the second after two weeks, and to the third one after three weeks. He was using what kind of design? ________________________

(4) Name an experimental design that doesn't rule out alternative explanations of any observed change in behavior: ____________________________________ design

(5) Step three in making a graph square is to divide the ______________________________ by the ______________________________.

(6) The method of observing that counts complete occurrences of behavior is called __________ ______________________ recording.

(7) John burped often at dinner. In fact, a record of his burps showed that he burped the following number of times: 23, 15, 19, 13, 19, and 20. To make a graph, you would label the ordinate "______________________________."

(8) John's study behavior was observed during a series of randomly picked intervals 5 seconds long. What method of observation was used? ________________________ recording

(9) Harry was a poor reader. He read 25, 15, 30, 20, and 10 percent of the time during the first week of observation. During the second week, he was told that he could stay at recess for an extra ten minutes on any day that he read more than 70% of the time. That week he read 60, 85, 80, 95, and 85 percent of the time. What experimental design was being used to determine the effectiveness of the extra recess time? ______________________________

(10) Vera wasn't getting anywhere with James; he hadn't even kissed her yet. She decided to try an experiment and wear some musk-oil perfume to turn James on. If Vera kept a record of the number of kisses from James before she started to use the musk oil, this record would be called a(n) ______________________________.

LESSON 7 **FORM C** **GRADE:** ____________

NAME: ________________________ **DATE:** ______________

(1) The vertical line on a graph is called ____.

(2) If a behavior is observed for a brief time several times a day, we would call this method of observation ____.

(3) If a teacher makes class attendance optional for one student and then a week later makes it optional for a second student (to see whether this affects their attendance), the teacher is using a(n) ____ design.

(4) Professor Barton counted the number of students who dozed off in both of his classes: Persian poetry and Syrian poetry. After four weeks he started giving pop quizzes in Persian poetry at the end of his lecture. Four more weeks and he did the same thing in Syrian poetry. His results are given below:

Weeks	1	2	3	4	5	6	7	8	9	10	11	12
Persian:	17	27	12	18	11	7	3	5	1	3	2	0
Syrian:	29	37	18	21	17	31	22	28	9	2	3	1

If he graphed the results of his experiments, he should use what size steps for his ordinate?
____

(5) When someone applies for a driver's license and is requested to take a written test, the Department of Motor Vehicles is using the method of direct observation called ____________ ________________________ recording.

(6) Frank counted the number of times that the President referred to a human rights violation in another country and the number of times that he referred to the mistreatment of American Indians in the United States. He found 123 mentions for other countries and no mention of Indians. He concluded that these data constituted a classic example of hypocrisy. What method of observation was he using? ____ recording

(7) About one student per week joined the new record-buying co-op. Then the co-op decided to try a newspaper advertisement. As a result, about 20 students per week joined. The members concluded that advertising pays because the ad succeeded in getting new members. This is not a good experimental design because it doesn't ____.

(8) The basic formula for computing reliability is ____.

(9) Behavior analysis has three major characteristics: (1) It focuses on ____________ ________________; (2) it studies ____ influences on behavior; and (3) it ____ with different environmental arrangements using single-subject designs.

(10) If Hersen and his colleagues (1973) had asked a group of psychiatrists to observe their patient in order to rate his depression before and after the use of tokens, they could find out whether the psychiatrists' ratings and their behavioral observations were correlated. If they were, then Hersen and his colleagues would have provided evidence that their behavioral definition of nondepressed behavior had ____.

LESSON 8 **FORM A** **GRADE:** ____________

NAME: ______________________ **DATE:** ______________

(1) Kay was the only person in the group who supported war. She always said things in favor of war, and the other group members would always argue with her. She gradually said more and more things supporting war. When another member of the group said something like "I think that war is immoral," this statement would be an example of a(n) ____________ ______________________ for statements favoring war.

(2) Increasing the rate of a behavior by delivering a reinforcer after it occurs is called ______________________.

(3) Glover and Gary (1976) gave points to students following each word they used in describing functions of an object. Since this procedure increased the number of words they used, you would term the procedure of delivering points a(n) ______________________.

(4) Professor Brainbuster gave excellent lectures, but the few jokes that he told were greeted by a deafening silence. Recently, however, some of the poorer students started laughing uproariously at his jokes. Professor Brainbuster now tells many jokes during his lectures. The sound of laughter following one of the jokes would be an example of a(n) ____________ ______________________.

(5) Frank was given $10 by his dad for cleaning the garage. During the next year Frank's dad asked him to clean the garage again, but he never did. The $10 is an example of what? ____________ ______________________

(6) When Priscilla complained about life, Linda tried to cheer her up by talking with her. But the more often she talked with Priscilla, the more often Priscilla complained about life. By talking with Priscilla after she complained, Linda was using what behavioral procedure? ______________________

(7) If an event follows a behavior and the frequency of that behavior becomes greater, the event is called a(n) ______________________.

(8) Linda paused after giving a customer his coin change and before giving him the bills. He left without the bills. Linda did not pause more in the future after giving the coin part of someone's change. Having the customer leave without his bills is an example of ______________________.

(9) If an instruction precedes a behavior and increases the rate of the behavior, it is called a(n) ______________________.

(10) Jerome didn't do his share of cleaning, so every time that the apartment became dirty, Bob asked Jerome to help clean it. After he was asked, Jerome would do his share. As a result, Jerome's rate of cleaning increased. Bob's request for help is a(n) ______________________.

Define a reinforcer.

LESSON 8 **FORM B** **GRADE:** ____________

NAME: ______________________ **DATE:** ____________

(1) Joe tried tapping his TV set when the picture went out. This procedure restored the picture, but Joe forgets to tap his TV set when the picture goes out. A restored picture is an example of a(n) ______________________.

(2) The teacher firmly told Francie to start doing her homework. Immediately thereafter, Francie started doing her homework. The teacher's demand is an example of what? ______________________

(3) Any event that occurs after the beginning of a behavior and leads to an increase in the rate of the behavior is called a(n) ______________________.

(4) Four-year-old Tony almost never greeted his father at the door when his father got home from work at night. The father then started giving Tony a big kiss every time he greeted his father at the door. Within a week, Tony was greeting his father every night. What behavioral procedure was the father using? ______________________

(5) Suppose that every time people fail to do what you want them to do you tell them to do it. If this increases the rate at which they do what you want them to do, the arrangement would be called a(n) ______________________.

(6) Janice carefully typed her term paper for the first time. A week later she found that she had received an A for the paper. Thereafter, she frequently typed her term papers. The A is an example of what? ______________________

(7) Glover and Gary (1976) gave students one point for each different verb form that they used in describing possible functions of an object. The delivery of points increased their rate of using different verb forms. The points would be an example of a(n) ______________________.

(8) Marty complained of a headache, so his teacher let him lay his head on the desk. Marty doesn't complain about headaches any more. The teacher's permission to put his head down is an example of a(n) ______________________.

(9) Dana didn't kiss his girlfriend very often. One day she bit him just after a kiss. He kisses her quite often now, and she always bites him just after the kiss. Her bite is an example of a(n) ______________________.

(10) If you arrange to deliver an event following every instance of a behavior and the rate of the behavior increases, then you would refer to this procedure as ______________________.

Explain how a behavioral scientist would prove that an event is a reinforcer.

LESSON 8 **FORM C** **GRADE:** ____________

NAME: ______________________ **DATE:** ______________

(1) An event that seems unpleasant but increases the rate of a behavior that it follows would be called a(n) ______________________.

(2) When Sue was a tiny infant her father had a bright idea. Maybe it would increase her rate of smiling if he followed each adorable smile with a lullaby. It did. Sue's father was using what behavioral procedure? ______________________

(3) Suppose that a person is late to class and the teacher asks him or her to be on time in the future. If his or her rate of being on time increases, this would be an example of ______________________.

(4) If an event ______________________ a behavior and ______________________ the probability of that behavior, the event is called a reinforcer.

(5) May came home from school and told her parents that she had finally beat up the little boy who had been tormenting her every day. May's father took her out for a special ice cream treat for beating up the little boy. May has not beaten the horrible little boy since then. The ice cream treat is an example of a(n) ______________________.

(6) Glover and Gary (1976) delivered points to students after each different function that they listed for an object. If the rate of listing different functions increased, then delivering the points would be called ______________________.

(7) Larry commented that he liked long hair. His friends always agreed and frequently discussed how stupid other people's reactions to long hair were. Larry commented on the virtues of long hair more and more frequently. The event consisting of one of his friends saying "yeah, man, that's right" would be an example of a(n) ______________________.

(8) Verna spanked Tom every time he interrupted her. Tom seemed to interrupt even more than usual after she started spanking him. The event consisting of spanking Tom would be called a(n) ______________________.

(9) To prove that an event is a reinforcer, you would have to use a(n) ______________________ design.

(10) Kim complained of problems every once in a while. One day when Kim complained, his teacher, concerned that the problems might be interfering with school, had a long talk with him. After that, Kim complained more often about his problems and thus had more talks with the teacher. By talking with Kim after a complaint, the teacher was using what behavioral procedure? ______________________

Explain the difference between a "reinforcer" and a "reinforcement."

LESSON 9 **FORM A** **GRADE:** ____________

NAME: ______________________ **DATE:** ____________

(1) Dave always started pestering his mother for a snack just about the time she started cooking dinner. While this irritated her, she tried to be a good mother and explain why he couldn't have a snack at that time. She finally decided that this wasn't working and that she would be better off ignoring his requests. What procedure would she be using if she ignored his requests and he stopped them? ______________________

(2) When Sam was young, he often came home and started talking with his father about his day at school. His father usually listened and asked questions. Sam started talking with his father more often as a result. What behavioral procedure was Sam's father using? ______________________

(3) For five weeks, Professor Johnson told his students to type their weekly take-home exam and they did. He then forgot to tell them during the rest of the semester and all of them no longer typed their exams. By forgetting to tell them Professor Johnson inadvertently used what procedure? ______________________

(4) One day Harry stroked Tabby softly and the cat started to purr. Harry thereafter frequently stroked Tabby softly. Tabby's purr would be an example of a(n) ______________.

(5) Karen told John to stop using cocaine immediately. John never used cocaine again. John's change in behavior is an example of what behavioral concept? ______________

(6) Ann thought it would be cute to teach her son to swear. So every time that he swore she laughed and paid a lot of attention. Her son did not swear any more as a result. What behavioral procedure was Ann using? ______________________

(7) If you tell someone to stop a behavior and the behavior decreases, you are using what behavioral procedure? ______________________

(8) Pinkston and her colleagues (1973) instructed the preschool teacher to stop paying attention to Cain's aggressive behavior, which she did. Cain's aggressive behavior decreased. What behavioral procedure did the teacher use? ______________________

(9) Professor Adams disrupted faculty meetings with insane ideas. His colleagues argued vehemently with him. However, the chairman finally convinced them to simply ignore Adams. Soon, Adams wasn't disrupting meetings anymore. The faculty's ignoring Adams's insane ideas is an example of what? ______________________

(10) Jimmy's dad asked many questions when Jimmy complained about how bad life was. Later Dad stopped asking questions but Jimmy complained as much as before. What behavioral procedure was Dad using when he stopped asking questions? ______________
Define the term *extinction*.

LESSON 9 **FORM B** **GRADE:** ________

NAME: ____________________ **DATE:** ____________

(1) Extinction is defined as ______________________ the delivery of a reinforcer following a behavior, thereby producing a(n) ______________________ in the rate of that behavior.

(2) Angela didn't spend any of her free time with her classmates, so her fourth-grade teacher started complimenting her whenever she did spend time with them. Soon, Angela spent a lot of time working on class projects with the other children. One of the teacher's compliments would be an example of what? ______________________

(3) Mim asked Gary to help her remember to count calories. For a month he reminded her. Then he stopped reminding her and Mim's rate of counting calories decreased. What behavioral procedure did Gary inadvertently use to produce the decrease? ______________

(4) Harry used to go to the store whenever Fay asked. However, since he took up jogging, Harry won't go to the store when Fay asks. After ten weeks of asking with no results, Fay finally gave up asking. What behavioral procedure did Harry use to eliminate her requests?

____

(5) If Pinkston and her colleagues (1973) had told the preschool teacher to tell Cain to "stop being aggressive" and he had stopped, what behavioral procedure would the teacher have been using? ______________________

(6) Martha's son pinched her all the time and she invariably asked him not to do it or told him it wasn't nice. Eventually, Martha stopped paying any attention to the pinching and it stopped. What behavioral procedure was she using? ______________________

(7) Dollie wanted Jim to light her cigarettes for her, so she started kissing him whenever he did light her cigarette. Pretty soon he was lighting it all the time. What behavioral procedure was she using? ______________________

(8) Within six months of forming the Happiness Commune, each member had stopped paying attention to whether other members helped keep the house clean. The result was that the amount of cleaning behavior drastically decreased for each member. This is an example of what behavioral procedure? ______________________

(9) Ben teased Jan about her weight a lot and she usually protested. Jan decided that she would simply ignore all future teasings. She noticed that Ben's rate of teasing did not change. What behavioral procedure did Jan use? ______________________

(10) Dan wanted Karen to smile more so he worked up his nerve and said to her, "Karen, you have a beautiful smile; I sure would like it if you smiled more." To his delight, Karen smiled more. What behavioral procedure did he use to increase her rate of smiling? ______________

____

Explain why asking someone to stop doing something cannot be an example of extinction.

LESSON 9 FORM C GRADE: ______________

NAME: ______________________________ DATE: ________________

(1) Joyce started fixing her husband a fancy breakfast whenever he hung up his clothes. She noticed that he started hanging up his clothes most of the time after that. What behavioral procedure did Joyce use? ______________________________

(2) During the reversal condition, Pinkston and her colleagues (1973) instructed the preschool teachers to once again attend to Cain's aggressive behavior as they had done during baseline. Cain's aggressive behavior once again increased. An instance of the teachers' attention is an example of a(n) ______________________________ .

(3) Ben did a good job every week of vacuuming as long as the president asked him first. Ben's rate of vacuuming decreased dramatically when the president no longer asked him. The president's procedure is called ______________________________ .

(4) Bobby whispered in class until the teacher made an announcement about the whispering. After the announcement, Bobby stopped whispering. The teacher's announcement is an example of what behavioral concept? ______________________________

(5) Lora asked silly questions that caused the professor to get mad. He tried ignoring the questions and found that Lora kept asking silly questions. Ignoring her questions is an example of what behavioral procedure? ______________________________

(6) Mary interrupted Sally all the time, and her friends paid attention to her interruptions rather than Sally's conversation. Sally finally talked them into ignoring Mary, however, and Mary's rate of interruptions decreased. What behavioral concept does the group's ignoring of Mary's interruptions illustrate? ______________________________

(7) John could be a star swimmer if he would only practice more. The coach had talked with him, praised him when he did swim many laps, but still John did not practice enough. Finally, the coach told him in no uncertain terms to practice. John's rate of practice increased dramatically. The coach's talk is an example of what behavioral concept? __________________

(8) Suppose that you have been in the habit of telling people to perform behavior A and they do it. If you now stop telling them to do it and they stop doing it, what behavioral procedure are you using? ______________________________

(9) If you stop delivering Event A following a behavior and the rate of the behavior decreases, what behavioral procedure are you using? ______________________________

(10) Bull, a regular at the restaurant, was always calling for Ronald's service by yelling "Hey, boy, come here." This annoyed Ronald greatly so he finally decided not to serve Bull when he called him a boy. Pretty soon Bull stopped calling him "boy." What behavioral procedure did Ronald use? ______________________________

Explain why telling someone to stop doing something is not an example of extinction even if the person stops doing it.

LESSON 10 **FORM A** **GRADE:** ____________

NAME: ________________________ **DATE:** ______________

---

(1) By asking the sanitation workers to rate how well the trash was packaged before and after the new rules were enforced, Stokes and Fawcett (1977) were determining the ____________ ________________________ of the behavioral definitions implicit in the new rules.

(2) Gary's parents were a problem. They frequently ranted and raved about all the "hippies" running around the university. Gary and Lois decided to try to change this by ignoring all unfavorable comments about young people and by praising his parents for being so in touch with young people when they made favorable comments. His parents gradually started talking more nicely about young people. What behavioral procedure did Gary and Lois use? ____________________________________

(3) If one behavior is reinforced and all others are extinguished, this is termed ______________ ______________________ .

(4) Parents who find their son reading a novel will probably ask him questions about his reading. Parents who find their son reading a comic book will often ignore him altogether. If the son starts reading novels more often and comic books less often, what behavioral procedure would account for the change? ____________________________________

(5) Janice Johnson was a new social-welfare caseworker. Mrs. Brooks, one of her clients, became annoyed at Janice's habit of discussing her own children but never trying to find what welfare help Mrs. Brooks needed. So Mrs. Brooks started ignoring all discussions about children and paid attention only when her own welfare problems came up. If Janice started talking more about Mrs. Brooks's problems, then this is an example of ______________________ .

(6) Mel was new to the freedom group. At first he talked about his worries of a drug bust, how to dress so that the rest of the world accepts you, and so forth. But everyone ignored him. Soon he was talking about how everyone should be free to do his or her own thing, and everyone paid attention. This is an example of what behavioral procedure? ________________

(7) Gale's teacher watched her while she made a series of connected handwritten "l's." The teacher praised her when the loops were smooth and said nothing when they were rough or irregular. Gradually Gale learned to write smooth and beautiful "l's." What procedure did her teacher use? ____________________________________

(8) Good discussion leaders are remarkably successful in getting everyone into a group discussion. They generally encourage and praise anyone who speaks. Even shy people, if strongly encouraged and praised, will contribute their ideas more often. This increase in the rate of everyone's talking is the result of what behavioral procedure? ________________

(9) Mary was happy and bubbly when John took her out drinking to the Stables because they didn't know anyone there and ended up talking to each other a lot. However, she was very withdrawn when he took her out drinking to the Fort because they knew many people there. Naturally John gradually took her out more often to the Stables. What behavioral procedure did Mary use to change John's selection? ____________________________________

(10) One characteristic of differential reinforcement is that one behavior should be increased through the use of ____________________________________ .

Explain how you determine whether two responses are the same or different.

LESSON 10 **FORM B** **GRADE:** ____________

NAME: ______________________ **DATE:** ____________

---

(1) Mr. Howard taught a ninth-grade geography class. One boy, Ben, said very little. Mr. Howard decided that, rather than continue to put Ben on the spot by constantly asking him questions, he would compliment him when he said anything. If Ben's rate of talking increased, Mr. Howard would be using what behavioral procedure? ______________________________

(2) Stokes and Fawcett (1977) found that correct trash-packaging behaviors increased and incorrect ones decreased when only correctly packaged trash was collected. What behavioral procedure did they use? ______________________________

(3) When David continued reading even when he had forgotten a prior word, he found that he read much faster. When David frequently looked back at a previous word, he found that he read slower. Gradually he learned to continue reading, and to stop looking back. What behavioral procedure caused him to change his reading behavior? ____________________

(4) Gary found that, if he smiled when he was with Jane, she would pay a lot of attention to him. However, if he smiled when he was with Gloria, she would ignore him. Naturally, Gary started smiling a lot when he was around Jane but hardly at all when he was around Gloria. What behavioral procedure is at work changing his pattern of smiling? ____________________

(5) Billy found that he couldn't pound in a nail if he held the hammer near its head but that he could pound in the nail if he held the hammer by its handle. He quickly learned to hold it by its handle. What behavioral procedure is this an example of? ____________________

(6) Differential reinforcement involves the behavioral procedures of ____________________ ______________ and ______________________________ .

(7) Manuel smiled broadly and said "bueno" every time that Sara properly trilled the "r's" in "perro," the Spanish word for dog. He let improper trills just pass by without comment. Gradually Sara learned to make the correct trill. What behavioral procedure did Manuel use? ______________________________

(8) A baby may say "dada" to many adult males other than his father. The parents will probably ignore the misdirected "dada's" and pay attention to the "dada's" said to the father. What behavioral procedure is this an example of? ______________________________

(9) Bernie decided that it would be good for his girlfriend to jog more often so he told her that she had to do it. She did. What behavioral procedure did Bernie use to increase her rate of jogging? ______________________________

(10) Mr. Green, the football coach, made a point of praising all team-spirited behavior while ignoring behavior antithetical to a good team spirit. As a result, team-spirited behavior increased relative to antithetical behavior. What behavioral procedure was he using? ______________________________

What is the difference between "reinforcement" and "differential reinforcement"?

LESSON 10 **FORM C** **GRADE:** ____________

NAME: ________________________ **DATE:** ______________

(1) Lee often talked with John and Darrin during lunch. One day John and Darrin were having an important conversation when Lee sat down. The two of them continued having their discussion, so Lee moved to another table of friends. From then on John and Darrin always ignored Lee when he joined them. Eventually, Lee stopped sitting with them. What behavioral procedure accounts for Lee's changed behavior? ____________________

(2) Stokes and Fawcett (1977) studied the effect of collecting properly packaged trash and not collecting improperly packaged trash. Does the example involve two (or more) different behaviors? ____________________

(3) When John was 5 years old, he used jerky movements of his fingers to tune his radio and he could rarely get his favorite station. Sometimes his movements were less jerky by accident and he could then get the station. Gradually, he developed a smooth movement that let him tune in his favorite station quite easily. What behavioral procedure built into the way radio tuners work leads to smooth tuning movements? ____________________

(4) One characteristic of differential reinforcement is that all but one behavior should be decreased through the use of ____________________.

(5) Ben was an excellent ski instructor. He made a nice comment when you made your turn smoothly, but said nothing when you goofed it up. He didn't even laugh when you fell down. His students learned smooth turns quickly. What behavioral procedure did he use to teach smooth turning? ____________________

(6) Roger's parents reinforce him when he watches TV cartoons but ignore him when he watches educational programs. What behavioral concept describes the procedure that resulted in his watching of one but not the other type of program? ____________________

(7) Grannies often spoil a child even when the parents are careful not to. If a child learns to beg for candy from Granny but is careful to avoid doing so around her parents, what procedure is unwittingly being used by the adults? ____________________

(8) When people are learning to drive a car with a manual transmission, they often have trouble learning how to shift. One problem is that, if they take their foot off the accelerator too slowly when they start to shift, the engine races. On the other hand, if they take their foot off the accelerator too rapidly, the car will suddenly slow down. They must learn to let the accelerator off at just the right speed. The process of decreasing responses that are too slow or too fast while increasing responses that are the right speed is the result of what behavioral procedure?

____

(9) If a behavior is reinforced in one situation and extinguished in another situation, the behavioral procedure that is being used is called ____________________.

(10) John's coach, Ms. Davidson, permitted him to leave practice early on any day that he correctly performed a high dive. John's rate of correct high dives increased as a result. Time off from practice is an example of a(n) ____________________.

Why is being reinforced for reading about physics while being extinguished for reading about poverty problems not an example of differential reinforcement?

LESSON 11 **FORM A** **GRADE:** ________

NAME: ____________________ **DATE:** ____________

(1) Janice's parents taught her, through role playing, how to assertively turn down an invitation to go out to a movie. The father played the role of the boy inviting her and when she said "no thank you" in a polite but firm manner, they praised her. When she didn't do it quite right they just repeated the role-playing situation without comment. Janice quickly learned to be assertive. Janice's parents used what behavioral procedure to teach her the correct reaction?

____

(2) John's teacher helped him overcome being a loner. At first he paid attention to him only when he looked at other children, then only when he was near them, and finally only when he was playing with them. What procedure did the teacher use to modify John's loner behavior?

____

(3) Frank rarely opened a door for Marsha. She decided to kiss him every time that he did so. Pretty soon Frank was opening the door for Marsha all the time. What behavioral procedure did Marsha employ to get him to open doors? ____________________

(4) Sammy's mother praised him every time that he brought out the garbage and he did so regularly. When he was 12, she stopped praising him, feeling that he was old enough to accept responsibility. Sammy's rate of taking out the garbage rapidly decreased after that. What behavioral procedure did Sammy's mother inadvertently use to reduce his rate of taking out the garbage? ____________________

(5) The term *shaping* is used to describe a particular use of what behavioral procedure?

____

(6) Dean wanted to teach Jason to hit badminton shots away from his opponent (in this case, Dean), so he hit easy shots only when Jason had hit a shot at least one step away from him. Next he required Jason to hit it two steps away. These two criteria for reinforcement are called ____________________ to hitting the shots far away from Dean.

(7) By giving tickets to David only when he met a behavioral criterion related to using the equipment properly, and then changing that criterion until completely correct use developed, Renne and Creer (1976) were using what behavioral procedure? ____________________

(8) Yancey noticed that when he complimented Fran, she smiled and thanked him for his compliments. However, when he complimented Dan, Dan looked slightly embarrassed and ignored the compliment. Soon Yancey was frequently complimenting Fran but almost never complimenting Dan. What behavioral process is involved in changing Yancey's rate of complimenting his two friends? ____________________

(9) Tom smoked only 15 cigarettes yesterday and Vera praised his willpower mightily. Vera was sure that such praise would help Tom learn to stop smoking altogether. Stopping smoking would be called Vera's ____________________.

(10) Reinforcing one behavior and extinguishing all others and then changing to another behavior that more closely approximates the target and repeating the process is called ____________________.

Explain what an approximation is.

LESSON 11 **FORM B** **GRADE:** ____________

NAME: ______________________ **DATE:** ____________

(1) Mrs. Baker began the process of overcoming the tone-deafness of Toneless Tony by asking him to sing A flat, which she then played on the piano. She praised him when he came within a half tone of it and simply tried again if he did not. He took two lessons to teach. Mrs. Baker was using what behavioral procedure to teach Tony to sing withdin a half tone of A flat? ______________________

(2) A behavior that is similar to a target behavior would be called a(n) ______________________.

(3) Tad wanted to take up jogging. So during the first week, he bought himself a Super Sundae every time that he ran a mile in under 12 minutes. During the next week he bought himself a Super Sundae only when he ran the mile in under 11 minutes. He continued this each week until he could run the mile in under 6 minutes. What behavioral procedure did he use on himself to attain this goal? ______________________

(4) James wanted to teach his best friend to recognize to what music it was appropriate to do the Twirling Chicken. So he let her initiate the dancing each time and praised her when she danced to the right music and didn't say anything when she danced to the wrong music. Her ability to pick the right music increased rapidly. What behavioral procedure did James use to help her learn what was the correct music? ______________________

(5) Ralph Radical wanted Bob to be antiwar. At first, Ralph agreed with Bob whenever he said anything mildly antiwar. Then, Ralph agreed only when Bob made strong antiwar statements. This is an example of what behavioral process? ______________________

(6) Shaping begins with the selection of an ultimate goal called a(n) ______________________.

(7) Clarence's father told him to undertake more projects that involved the use of a hammer, so he did. What behavioral procedure was his father using to increase the rate of using a hammer? ______________________

(8) Renne and Creer (1976) attempted to teach the correct use of inhalation equipment to asthmatic children. The correct use of the equipment would be called the ______________________ of their experiment.

(9) Charlie Brown smiled at the little redheaded girl only when she sat within 5 feet of him at lunch, then only when she sat within 2 feet, and finally only when she sat next to him. Charlie Brown's goal of getting her to sit next to him is called the ______________________.

(10) John often smelled gamey because he usually forgot to put on his underarm deodorant. Barb decided to do something about it so for the next two months she praised John every time that he remembered to put his deodorant on. John gradually became less gamey. What behavioral procedure was Barb using? ______________________

Define shaping.

LESSON 11 **FORM C** **GRADE:** ____________

NAME: ________________________ **DATE:** ______________

(1) Renne and Creer (1976) gave David a ticket at first for looking at the dial 4 times out of 15 breaths; that would be called a(n) ______________________________ to their ultimate goal of looking at it for all 15 breaths.

(2) At first his teachers at New West Freedom School often talked with Kerr about his reading. Later they lost their enthusiasm and stopped talking with him. Kerr gradually stopped reading. What behavioral procedure were they using later? ________________________

(3) Dr. Franklin used a sawhorse-like portable railing for Bobby to lean on and learn to walk again. She moved this farther and farther away from Bobby until he stood on his own and actually walked. She first reinforced Bobby just for standing with his weight on the sawhorse, then reinforced him only when he leaned just a little, and finally reinforced him only when he stood on his own. She was using what behavioral procedure to change Bobby's behavior? ________________________

(4) For a situation to involve shaping, two conditions must be met: (a) a(n) ______________ ______________ must be specified; and (b) differential reinforcement must be applied to a series of ________________________ .

(5) Marie told Fred to stop swearing whenever a minor annoyance occurred. Fred's rate of swearing decreased as a result. What behavioral procedure did Marie use? ______________ ______________

(6) Bobby was trying to pronounce it correctly but the best he could say was "refrigelator." June, his mom, praised him for saying it so well. "Refrigelator" would be called a(n) ________ ______________ to June's target behavior of "refrigerator."

(7) Last week Mary started kissing Dave every time that he lit her cigarette in the hopes that he would light her cigarette more often. Dave didn't get the message, however, and still doesn't light her cigarette very often. What behavioral procedure did Mary use? ____________ ______________

(8) At first, Mary necked with John only after they had been discussing his problems. Later, Mary necked with John only after a fight. Finally, she necked with him only after a terrible, screaming fight. What behavioral process accounts for the increasing severity of John and Mary's fights? ________________________

(9) Dave's coach praised him only when he swam the 100-yard freestyle in under 50 seconds. Dave soon got so he could do it. What behavioral procedure was his coach using? _____ ________________________

(10) Bobby didn't start playing very much chess until after he started winning. Now he plays a lot. Winning is an example of what behavioral concept? ________________________

Explain the relationship between shaping and differential reinforcement.

LESSON 12 **FORM A** **GRADE:** ____________

NAME: ________________________ **DATE:** ______________

(1) Jerry's mother agreed to teach him how to sew. She paid attention to him only by pointing out the good aspects of his sewing skill while he was sewing. This attention was very important to Jerry. She could keep Jerry hard at work sewing by keeping the sessions brief. What principle of effective reinforcement, if any, did Jerry's mother neglect? ________________

(2) If a person has recently had a lot of a certain reinforcer, the person is ____________ ____________ with respect to that reinforcer.

(3) Willie did not vote for Honest Richard even though he felt sure that Honest Richard would make it possible for him to get a good job and even though he was absolutely sure that he would never get a good job otherwise. Considering that Willie did not have a good job, nor had he ever had one, what principle of effective reinforcement is absent so that the effectiveness of Richard's election promise of a good job for Willie is weakened? ________________ ________________

(4) Jane's brother wasn't a very warm person. She felt that he would be friendlier if he would just hug people a little bit. She decided on a strategy of praising him, first for standing close, then, when that was learned, for touching briefly, and, finally, for hugging. Hugging would be termed a(n) ________________________.

(5) Reinforcers should be delivered only when the desired behavior occurs. This is called the Principle of ________________________.

(6) John reinforced Marty's reading with M & M's. He gave Marty a reinforcer only when he had finished reading a sentence out loud, and he always gave it to Marty as soon as he had finished. After about 100 sentences, Marty didn't want to read anymore. Had John continued at that point, he would have violated what principle of effective reinforcement? ____________ ________________

(7) Reinforcers should be delivered as soon after the behavior has occurred as possible. This is called the Principle of ________________________.

(8) Kay decided to go out for basketball. She went to practice 6 days a week, usually putting in 3 hours of practice. The coach praised her play only when she played well and immediately after good plays. Even with that she didn't feel that she got praised too often. The coach restricted her praise to "good play," but never gave any other feed-back, pointers for improvement, indication of appreciation for efforts, or even a friendly comment. Kay quit after concluding that such praise just didn't make all that work worth doing. What principle of effective reinforcement did the coach neglect? ________________________ ________________

(9) Brigham and his colleagues (1972) delivered tokens to children immediately after they sat down for their handwriting lesson. The tokens could be traded for activities that they enjoyed but did not get to participate in too often. Delivering tokens immediately after sitting down, in order to reinforce the accuracy of writing, violates what principle of effective reinforcement, if any? ________________________

(10) Whenever Betty complained of being sick, Mrs. Upton allowed her to stay home from school. Mrs. Upton usually ignored other things that Betty talked about. Now Betty complains often about her illnesses but not about other problems. What behavioral procedure accounts for Betty's becoming a hypochondriac? ________________________

Name the four principles that govern the effectiveness of a reinforcer.

LESSON 12 **FORM B** **GRADE:** ____________

NAME: ______________________ **DATE:** ____________

---

(1) Mr. Mack was going to teach his infant son to be a terrific athlete. So, when his son was 6 months old, Mr. Mack designated the half hour after dinner as time to reward his son for sitting up by giving him a spoon of applesauce. His son didn't seem interested in the applesauce. A behavior analyst would guess that the applesauce did not work very well because the baby was already ______________________ on food (use technical term).

(2) The Principle of Contingency states that the reinforcer should be delivered ____________ ______________________ when the behavior occurs.

(3) The Spanish Club met for lunch each day. You were passed the ice cream if you asked for it in Spanish but not if you asked for it in English. Members soon learned the Spanish word for ice cream. What procedure was the club employing with respect to asking for ice cream in Spanish? ______________________

(4) Judy encouraged Tom to read by patting his head often while he was reading. Each pat lasted about a second and occurred only while he was reading. She spent very little time with him otherwise. Judy did not give too many pats to Tom. Tom soon stopped reading. What principle of effective reinforcement, if any, does Judy's procedure omit? ______________________

(5) Hall and his colleagues (1972) gave Jerry 25¢ at the end of the month for each time that he was observed wearing his braces (and only for wearing his braces). The money permitted him to buy things that he wanted, and he never seemed to have too much money. What principle of effective reinforcement, if any, did they violate? ______________________

(6) Mary and Ken played tic-tac-toe in class. Mary was apparently reinforced by the challenge of Ken's responses. He made his mark immediately after she made her mark. By the 20th game, they were tired of tic-tac-toe. What principle of effective reinforcement accounts for their getting tired of the game? ______________________

(7) Members of the Utopian Commune agreed to rely on expressions of love to maintain work behaviors in their community. These expressions of love were extremely important to every member of the group and no one ever got too many of them. If the members provided one another with these expressions immediately after both work and nonwork behaviors, what principle of effective reinforcement, if any, would be neglected? ______________________ ______________________

(8) Carey tutored Dave, the star football tackle, in poetry by having him compose short poems on a blackboard while she watched. She reserved her praise for the good aspects of his compositions and gave her praise as soon as he wrote a line. She kept the sessions short so he wouldn't tire of the tutoring. To her surprise, her praise was very important to him. What principles, if any, did she omit in her procedure? ______________________

(9) The Principle of Size states that you must be sure to give the person enough of the reinforcer to be ______________________.

(10) Jane's brother wasn't a very warm person. So she decided to praise him for standing close to people, then for touching them briefly on the arm, and finally for hugging them. His standing close to someone would be called a(n) ______________________ to the goal of having him hug people.

State the Principle of Deprivation.

LESSON 12 **FORM C** **GRADE:** ____________

NAME: ________________________ **DATE:** ______________

---

(1) Senor Jimenez taught 4-year-old Janice to say his name right by saying a syllable, HEE, and hugging her only when she said it right. He repeated this with the other syllables and finally hugged her only when she said the whole name right. What procedure did he use to teach her how to say his name? ______________________________

(2) Reinforcers should be selected according to whether the person has already (recently) had a lot of that reinforcer. This is known as the Principle of ______________________.

(3) Jane's brother wasn't a very warm person. So every time that he acted cold and distant, she would tell him to stand close and touch people. His rate of standing close and touching people increased after she started the procedure. What is the name of her procedure? ______________________

(4) Hal never used to invite Dana to parties very often. Finally, on occasions when Hal did extend an invitation, Dana would quickly offer to tutor Hal in whatever course he was having trouble in. These offers were terribly important to Hal because Dana was the only person who could explain the material well enough to enable Hal to pass the exams. And he had to pass the exams to retain his athletic scholarship. Dana was smart enough to never make his offer at other times. What principle of effective reinforcement, if any, did Dana neglect? ______________________

(5) Enough of the reinforcer must be delivered to be worthwhile. This is known as the Principle of ______________________________.

(6) He was every employee's dream—he praised your work no matter how well you did it. While he didn't load you down with praise, everyone liked it, and he gave it right after you finished a job. Still, it wasn't effective—no one improved the quality of his or her work. What principle of effective reinforcement, if any, is he neglecting? ______________________________

(7) Kevin lent his truck and his muscles to help Bob move. At first he carried boxes to the front door, where Bob took them and carried them inside and put them in the right room. Bob always thanked Kevin as soon as he brought a box to the door and no other time. Since Kevin was a loner, he hardly ever got any praise from people, but when he saw Bob drinking a beer without offering him any, he decided that getting thanks didn't justify all the hard work. What principle of effective reinforcement, if any, did Bob neglect? ______________________

(8) Sarah tried to help John overcome his shyness by talking with him about his behavior after they returned from social gatherings. During these conversations, she only praised him for the assertive acts that he had made during the event. John never got too much praise from Sarah during these conversations. Every instance of her praise was very important to him. What principle of effective reinforcement, if any, did Sarah neglect in providing help to John in this way? ______________________________

(9) Ayllon (1963) gave Doris towels only when she was in her room; she had hoarded them for nine years, so each one was important to her. By the time that she had been given 600 towels, she started removing them from her room. Ayllon used what principle of reinforcer effectiveness to *reduce* the reinforcing properties of towels for Doris? ______________________

(10) Mrs. Mack wanted to teach her infant son to be a terrific singer. So she gave him a spoonful of applesauce prior to the morning feeding for every pretty sound that he made. Her son soon warbled like a canary. A behavior analyst would say that the applesauce was effective because

the child was ________________________________ with respect to food at that time of day.

State the Principle of Immediacy.

LESSON 13 **FORM A** **GRADE:** ____________

NAME: ______________________ **DATE:** ____________

(1) Maria's parents put her on a chore system where she earned a portion of her allowance. The money was given to her right after she told them that she had done the chore. The pay was pretty good—for example, 10¢ for taking out the garbage, 25¢ for the dishes. Maria was always broke, so the money was welcome. But the parents hardly ever bothered to check the job after Maria told them it had been completed. As a result, it often wasn't done right and sometimes it wasn't done at all. If her parents asked you why the procedure wasn't working very well, you would probably tell them that they were weakening the effectiveness of their reinforcer by ignoring the Principle of ______________________.

(2) When someone is reinforced for every response, he or she is said to be on a(n) ______________________ schedule of reinforcement.

(3) Don's father used to have an endless interest in hearing about the latest chapter in his science-fiction books. Later his father listened to Don's account only after he had read an entire book. If you consider a response to be the reading of one chapter, and the books had 5, 19, and 11 chapters, what schedule of reinforcement was his father using later to reinforce reading of chapters? ______________________

(4) If a person is reinforced after different numbers of responses each time, he is on a(n) ______________________ schedule.

(5) Jake "gets off" after exactly 13 puffs on a joint. What schedule of reinforcement is Jake's puffing on? ______________________

(6) Staats and associates (1964) studied the rate of making reading acquisition responses of children when they were given a reinforcer after every response and when they were given a reinforcer after varying numbers of responses that averaged five. Name the schedule that produced the highest rate of responding. ______________________

(7) When Don came home late at night the door was always locked. So he would dig out his keys, insert the key in the lock and turn it to the left. The door never opened so he had to then turn the key to the right and it would open. What schedule of reinforcement was his key-turning behavior on? ______________________

(8) Frank wanted to increase the rate at which his infant daughter Alice imitated his behavior when he said "Can you do this?" So he gave her a bite of ice cream each time she imitated. She usually lost interest after about 15 imitations. If Frank asked you how he could increase the number of times that she imitated him while still using ice cream, you should suggest that he switch to a(n) ______________________ schedule of reinforcement.

(9) The ratio schedule that produces alternating periods of responding and resting is called a(n) ______________________.

(10) Johnny found that, if he nagged his mother long enough, she would eventually give him a cookie. Sometimes she gave him the cookie after 15 nags, other times after 5 nags, and so on. What schedule of reinforcement is Johnny's nagging behavior on? ______________________

Describe an advantage and a disadvantage of the ratio schedules.

LESSON 13 **FORM B** **GRADE:** ______________

NAME: ________________________ **DATE:** ______________

(1) Professor Irving often talks with students about what field to major in; she tries to interest them in Psychology. She finds that about one in ten on the average end up by becoming psych majors. If getting majors is a reinforcer for her, what schedule is her talking with students on? ______________________________

(2) Maria's parents put her on a well-administered chore system in which she earned an M & M right after completing each chore: washing dishes, mowing the lawn. They gave her the M & M only when they had verified that she did a good job on the chore. Maria never got M & M's otherwise (or any other kind of candy, for that matter). If her parents asked you why this procedure was not working very well, you might tell them that they were weakening the effectiveness of the M & M's by ignoring the Principle of ______________.

(3) Staats and associates (1964) delivered a reinforcer after varying numbers of reading acquisition responses that averaged 5. What is the name of the schedule that they were using? ______________________________

(4) If a person is reinforced for some responses but not for every response, he is said to be on a(n) ______________________________ schedule.

(5) Koegel and Rincover (1977) found that retarded children would imitate (at the request of an adult who had never reinforced them) for much longer when they had been trained on what schedule: continuous or fixed ratio? ______________________________

(6) In Professor Smith's course students could start on the next lesson only after they had correctly answered ten questions about the current lesson. If starting on the next lesson is a reinforcer, then having to make ten correct responses would define a(n) ______________ ______________ schedule of reinforcement.

(7) David was very obnoxious in class. His teacher used to tell him to stop, explain why what he was doing was inappropriate, and generally spend a lot of attention on him. She finally decided to totally ignore his obnoxious behavior. David kept right on doing it, however. What procedure did his teacher use? ______________________________

(8) What schedule of reinforcement is usually used with shaping? ______________________

(9) Ann worked in a special room on her algebra homework problems. Dr. Otterman could observe through a one-way mirror and tell when she had completed seven problems. He then went in and complimented her on her progress. What schedule is she on for working problems? ______________________________

(10) The schedule that produces the highest and most uniform rate of responding is called a(n) ______________________________.

Name and define two types of schedules that involve counting the number of responses.

LESSON 13 **FORM C** **GRADE:** ________

NAME: ____________________ **DATE:** ____________

(1) What schedule of reinforcement would you use in order to most increase the length of time that it takes a response to extinguish after reinforcement is stopped? ____________________

(2) If every 100th response is reinforced, the person may stop responding. This would be known as ____________________.

(3) Maria's parents put her on a well-designed chore system in which she earned a portion of her allowance, which was given to her right after correctly doing a chore. They gave her good money: 25¢ for putting dishes in the washer, 15¢ for feeding the animals, and so on. They always checked to make sure the job was well done. But Maria earned more money than she could spend by baby sitting. If her parents asked you why the procedure didn't work very well, you would probably tell them that they were weakening the money reinforcer by ignoring the Principle of ____________________.

(4) Staats and associates (1964) found that reading acquisition responses could be increased by delivering a marble after every response. What schedule of reinforcement were they using? ____________________

(5) Sarah sold Tupperware to Barbara but Barbara usually would not buy the newest item on the first try. Usually Sarah had to try many times (2, 3, 4 or 5 times), but Barbara always bought the new item eventually. What schedule is Sarah's selling behavior on? ____________________

(6) Rich agreed to paint the house as part of his chores if he could have a rest break after every 100 brush strokes. After he counted 100 strokes he got a drink of water and took a brief break. What schedule of reinforcement is his painting on? ____________________

(7) Maria's parents had put her on a well-designed chore system in which she earned a portion of her allowance for each chore: 5¢ for each time she took garbage out, 15¢ for feeding the cats, and so on. They kept a careful record of her chore behavior after making sure it had been done and then paid her at the end of the week. Maria spent the money on things she wanted and never seemed to have enough. If her parents asked you why this procedure was not working well, you might tell them that they are weakening the effectiveness of the money reinforcement by ignoring the Principle of ____________________.

(8) Angie seemed to have a hearing problem. She never answered a question the first time it was asked of her. She always said "What?" to the questioner and then would answer the second time it was asked. What is the name of the schedule that the questioner is on? ____________________

(9) Bob lived near the common phone in the dorm, so he had to answer it much of the time. Furthermore, most of the dorm members didn't bother to thank him for answering it. He found that, on the average, he got thanked only once in four times. What schedule was his phone answering on? ____________________

(10) A schedule of reinforcement in which the response is never reinforced is called ____________________.

Describe the rate and pattern of responding with a fixed-ratio schedule and a variable-ratio schedule; compare the rates for each schedule.

LESSON 14 **FORM A** **GRADE:** ____________

NAME: ________________________ **DATE:** ______________

---

(1) Ken gets credit for one unit of work every time he tightens 18 nuts on the frame of a washing machine. What schedule is he on for getting credit? ______________________________

(2) In most books, there are passages or scenes that are boring. However, most people just keep reading with the hope that a really exciting scene or passage will soon come along. Such a scene may occur on the average of only once in 20 pages, yet most people continue reading. Their reading behavior is on a(n) ____ schedule.

(3) Of the four intermittent schedules that you have studied, which one produces the highest sustained rate of responding? ____________________________________

(4) Chester works in a factory in which his supervisor comes by to check on him every 10 minutes. If it is reinforcing for him to be found working, what schedule is his working on?

____

(5) Gladys loved rock music. When she drove along in her car she listened intently when music was being played but stopped listening when the announcer started talking or playing a commercial or reading the news. Music as a stimulus would be called a(n) ___________ ________________________ for Gladys' listening behavior.

(6) Mawhinney and associates (1971) might have given tests in two ways: after every 3 weeks and after differing periods of time averaging 3 weeks. Which schedule would produce a more uniform rate of studying? ______________________________________ (Write the name of that schedule.)

(7) In which interval schedule do people maintain a uniform rate of responding? __________ ________________________

(8) Ron and Betty are only interested in the few scenes of the movie showing disco dancing. These came after 5, 25, 15, and 15 minutes. What schedule of reinforcement is their movie viewing on? ____________________________________

(9) If you think that an example involves an interval schedule, you should ask "If the person makes no response at all, will there eventually arrive a time at which _______________ ________________________ will produce the reinforcer?"

(10) Richard is a radar scanner whose job is to look for unidentified planes on his radar screen. He usually sees one on the average of every 4 hours. What schedule is his looking behavior on? ____________________________________

Name and define the two interval schedules.

LESSON 14 **FORM B** **GRADE:** ____________

NAME: ______________________ **DATE:** ____________

(1) In which interval schedule do people work at a gradually increasing rate as the time for the reinforcement approaches? ______________________

(2) Teachers frequently check on their students' work by walking around the room and looking to see whether or not they are working. The students are being reinforced for working on what schedule? ______________________

(3) Marty's teacher complimented him after he completed 6, 8, 6, and 4 problems. What type of schedule was he on? ______________________

(4) If you think that an example involves an interval schedule and the behavior is ongoing, ask "If the person does not emit the behavior for a time, will there eventually arrive a time when emitting it for a(n) ______________________ will produce the reinforcer?"

(5) A schedule in which the person is reinforced for the first response that occurs after a constant period of time is called a(n) ______________________ schedule.

(6) Sarah wanted her son Dan to become an intellectual. So she encouraged him to read books, and every time that he came and explained an interesting fact or theory to her, she gave him 25¢ right then and there. She gave him the quarter only if he explained his finding well. Dan saved the money to buy books with and seemed delighted with the amount. He never seemed to get enough quarters. What principle of effective reinforcement, if any, did Sarah fail to employ? ______________________

(7) Mawhinney and associates (1971) studied student study patterns when tested daily and when tested at 3-week intervals. If the professor stopped reinforcing studying, which of the schedules that he used would lead to more enduring studying behavior? ______________________ (Write the name of that schedule.)

(8) John stays "properly" dressed in his room expecting visitors (he is a bit pompous). He has a visitor on the average of once every 65 minutes. If he is reinforced by his visitors for being properly dressed, what schedule is he on? ______________________

(9) John's father gives him an extra dessert for every four straight times that he brings his own plate into the kitchen. What schedule is John on for bringing his plate into the kitchen? ______________________

(10) Darrell didn't like football but he sure liked the cheerleaders. So he tuned in at the beginning of half time. Exactly 5 minutes later the cheerleaders came on and did a routine. What schedule was Darrell's watching behavior on? ______________________

Describe the pattern of responding produced by each of the four schedules.

LESSON 14 FORM C GRADE: ____________

NAME: ______________________ DATE: ____________

(1) In most joke books, an average of only one in ten jokes is hilarious, and the rest are terrible. But most people will plow through all the jokes looking for the good ones. What schedule of reinforcement is a joke reader on? ______________________

(2) If you think that an example involves a ratio schedule, ask "If the person makes the response very rapidly, will the next reinforcer arrive ______________________?"

(3) The author of a behavior analysis textbook sits in his office hour after hour typing new examples. He is reinforced by finally finishing the 20th example for a lesson. If typing out one example is the response, what schedule of reinforcement is the author on? ______________________

(4) What two types of intermittent schedules produce a tendency for people to stop responding after reinforcement? ______________________

(5) Bernie's mother used to remind him to start his homework as soon as he got home from school. But she stopped doing it last month and Bernie almost never starts his homework right after school like he used to. What behavioral procedure did his mother use to produce this disastrous change in behavior? ______________________

(6) When Danny gets in the car to go on a trip (no matter how long), he immediately begins asking "Are we there yet?" Sometimes the trips last just to the corner market and other times to a nearby lake. Assuming that having one of his parents say "Yes, we are there" is a reinforcer, Danny is on what schedule of reinforcement for his questions? ______________________

(7) A schedule in which the person is reinforced for the first response that he or she makes after differing periods of time is called a(n) ______________________ schedule.

(8) If the author of a book were to put his or her climactic scenes too far apart in the book, the readers might quit reading even though they were still being reinforced occasionally. This would be an example of ______________________.

(9) Mawhinney and associates (1971) tested students at 3-week intervals. Their study behavior would be on what schedule of reinforcement? ______________________

(10) Gloria the peeper has to wait an average of half an hour to see a naked man. Sometimes it is only a few minutes between "sightings" and sometimes many hours. What type of schedule is her peeping on? ______________________

Explain why being reinforced every 10 minutes isn't necessarily a fixed-interval schedule.

LESSON 15 **FORM A** **GRADE:** ____________

NAME: ________________________ **DATE:** ______________

(1) If a response produces reinforcement after differing periods of time, we say that response is being reinforced according to a(n) ________________________ schedule (two words).

(2) Katherine got fed up with Gladys' lack of enthusiasm, so she had a long talk with Gladys one day and told her to act more enthusiastic. Gladys became a changed person, acting much more enthusiastic as a result. What behavioral procedure did Katherine use to increase Gladys' enthusiasm? ________________________

(3) Two observers counted the number of times that Fearsome Freddy hit another child. Observer One counted 15 hits, and Observer Two counted 20 hits. Compute the reliability. ____________ Is it adequate? ____________

(4) Karen was into target shooting with a .38 magnum. She found that from 50 feet she could hit a bullseye about once in ten tries, sometimes more, sometimes less. If hitting the bullseye is the reinforcer for shooting, what schedule is her shooting on? ________________

(5) John's teacher helped him overcome being a loner. At first she paid attention to him only when he looked at other children, then only when he was near them, and finally only when he was playing with them. What procedure did the teacher use to modify John's loner behavior? ________________________

(6) Professor King gave Margot, the star basketball player, the assignment of composing a poem to hand in every day of the semester. He read the poem and returned it with praise for the good aspects of it the next class period. He praised only the good features of the poems. He was careful not to provide too much praise. And he was grateful that his praise did seem to be very important to Margot. In spite of his careful procedure, Margot's poetry writing did not improve. What principle of effective reinforcement, if any, did he neglect? ____________ ____________

(7) The Barket Street baby-sitting club awards 10 points to any mother who takes care of another club member's child for an hour and charges 10 points to a mother whose child is cared for. Marge's rate of baby sitting for other club members increased after she joined the club and was awarded points. The points would be called a(n) ________________.

(8) Shaping involves the differential reinforcement of a series of responses that are successive approximations to a(n) ________________________ response.

(9) If a person's behavior is no longer reinforced, what schedule of reinforcement is it said to be on? ________________________

(10) Sallie tried to teach Harry how to throw a frisbee. She praised him right after every correct throw and only when he threw it well. Harry was very turned on by Sallie so her praise was really important to him. He never seemed to get enough of it. What principles of effective reinforcement, if any, did Sallie fail to employ? ________________________

LESSON 15 **FORM B** **GRADE:** ____________

NAME: ______________________ **DATE:** ____________

(1) Name the four principles that govern the effectiveness of a reinforcer. ____________ ____________, ____________, ____________ ____________, and ____________

(2) The gang always brought the premium beer when they went to the beach. One day they decided to do an experiment to see if anyone could tell the difference. They gave Flora a swig of the premium beer without showing it to her and then asked her to name it. If she said it was the premium beer they all cheered. Then they gave her a swig of the cheapo beer and if she said it was the premium beer they ignored her. They kept doing this to see if she could learn the difference. She got the correct answer the last 20 swigs but then fell down and slept for the rest of the day. What behavioral procedure was the gang using to teach her the difference?

____

(3) Backward Ben hated the idea that behavioral methods might improve the ease of learning. As he worked through this very book he rejoiced every time that he missed an answer—saying to himself "See, behaviorism isn't so hot after all!" But he found that, try as he might, he could only miss an average of one question in 89. What schedule of reinforcement is his question answering on? ____________

(4) If you were concerned about the problem of satiating someone by reinforcing them for every instance of behavior that they emit, what type of schedule would you use to reduce the problem? ____________ (do not name a specific schedule).

(5) You observe the rate at which Johnny nags his mother and the rate at which he teases his sister. You decide to use a multiple baseline across behaviors to examine the effect of extinction of these two behaviors. First you observe both behaviors prior to treatment for three days. Then you convince his mother to ignore nags and observe both behaviors for another three days. Finally, you convince his sister to ignore teasings and observe both behaviors for a final three days. Since Johnny is now disgustingly nice you drop the experiment. In looking at your data, you determine that the highest value of nagging was during baseline and that it occurred 19 times on one of those days. If you wished to draw a graph, the ordinate for both behaviors would increase by steps of ____________.

(6) Differential reinforcement involves two basic behavioral processes. They are ____________ ____________ and ____________.

(7) If you reinforce the first response that occurs after a fixed amount of time has passed, you are following a(n) ____________ schedule.

(8) Clarence had to write a five-page essay for his art history class every week. If a page is one response, what schedule of reinforcement is his essay-writing behavior on? ____________ ____________

(9) When shaping a new behavior both reinforcement and extinction are used in the procedure of differential reinforcement. What is the best schedule to use for the reinforcement part of differential reinforcement? ____________

(10) Johnny used to be very brave; but one day when he fell down and skinned his knee he cried. His mother immediately rushed over to him and held him and brought him inside for an ice cream treat to help him forget his pain. Johnny now cries a lot when he hurts himself. His mother always comforts him and gives him an ice cream treat. What behavioral procedure did his mother unintentionally use to increase Johnny's crying? ____________

LESSON 15 **FORM C** **GRADE:** ____________

NAME: ______________________ **DATE:** ____________

(1) Roy always looked through the newspaper for ads of food sales. He found that the sale occurred sometimes after a week, sometimes after five weeks, but that they averaged every two weeks. If finding a food sale reinforced his reading the ads, what schedule of reinforcement is his ad-reading behavior on? ______________________

(2) Interval recording is a method of observation in which a response is recorded if some part of a behavioral episode is observed within one of a series of ______________ intervals. Time sampling differs only in that the series of intervals are ______________ ______________.

(3) Jason Johnson aspired to become a great poet. But the trouble is that he couldn't sit still long enough to write very much poetry. So he set himself the goal of writing a 25-stanza poem each day. He started by writing a one-stanza poem, then a two-stanza poem, and so on until he had worked up to 25 stanzas. Writing a one-stanza poem would be called a(n) ______________ ______________ to the 25-stanza poem.

(4) What level of reliability is considered acceptable for a new behavioral definition? _____

(5) To square a complex graph you should first find the condition with the largest value of the ordinate and then proceed as with a simple graph. Thus you should divide the largest value of the ______________________ by the largest value of the ______________ ______________.

(6) Experimental designs are used to discover exactly why a behavior changed. They are used to rule out ______________________ explanations based on coincidence.

(7) Dan was concerned about his son's small vocabulary so he decided to promote crossword puzzles as a way to build vocabulary. He bought a book of crossword puzzles and paid his son $5 for finishing a complete puzzle. He paid for the puzzle as soon as it was completed. His son seemed always to need money to fix his old dragster and he seemed to feel that $5 was good pay for completing a puzzle. When Dan's son didn't seem to have an improved vocabulary after 25 puzzles, Dan got suspicious and checked the puzzle book to find that the answers were listed in the back. What principle of effective reinforcement did the presence of the answers negate? ______________________

(8) The elementary school teacher who grades students' tests as soon as they finish them is enhancing the effectiveness of her grade as a reinforcer by what principle? ______________ ______________

(9) Reliability is computed by the formula ______________________.

(10) If a person is required to make a high number of responses for each reinforcement, his responding may decrease because of what is called ______________________.

LESSON 16 **FORM A** **GRADE:** ____________

NAME: ______________________ **DATE:** ______________

(1) Johnny made many baby noises. However, when he said "dada," his parents paid a lot of attention to him. When he made other sounds, they ignored him. He came to say "dada" a lot. What behavioral process was at work? ______________________

(2) If a behavior occurs with increased probability in the presence of an S^D, then we say that the stimulus exerts ______________________ over the behavior.

(3) A discriminative stimulus is a stimulus that precedes a behavior and is present only if that behavior will be ______________________.

(4) Jeff swears a lot around the dorm but doesn't swear much at home. His dorm friends encourage swearing; his parents don't. Since Jeff swears more in the dorm than at home, what behavioral procedure is at work? ______________________

(5) When James called anyone "Ocoee" other than the beautiful brunette, he was ignored. When he called the beautiful brunette "Ocoee," she smiled at him and started a conversation. What behavioral procedure is his learning to call the right person "Ocoee" an example of? ______________________

(6) If the question "What is 2 + 2?" always gets Ward to say "4," then we say that the question exerts ______________________ over his behavior.

(7) Redd and Birnbrauer (1969) had Bill give a retarded child edibles for playing cooperatively with other children and had Grundy not reward the child for cooperative play. Bill would be called a(n) ______________________ for playing cooperatively while Grundy would be called a(n) ______________________.

(8) Staats and Butterfield (1965) showed Carlos a card with the word "inspect" on it; they gave him a token if he said "inspect" but nothing if he said any other word. They repeated this for about 700 new words. What behavioral procedure did they use? ______________________

(9) Burris's classmates helped him learn the meaning of "reinforcer" by asking him two questions: "If Rose asked for some candy and got it but didn't ask for any more in the future, what is the candy called?" and "If Rose asked for some candy and got it, and if she asked for more in the future, what is the candy called?" His classmates praised him if he said "reinforcer" in response to the second but not the first question. He soon came to answer the questions correctly. His behavior of answering "reinforcer" is called ______________________.

(10) The commune uses a green tag as a "welcome signal" for anyone who is welcoming visitors. If the occupant welcomes visitors only if the green tag is out, the green tag is a(n) ______________________ for visiting behavior.

Explain the difference between discrimination training and differential reinforcement.

LESSON 16 **FORM B** **GRADE:** ____________

NAME: ______________________ **DATE:** ______________

(1) Adolph asked a friend to help him learn German pronunciation. His friend praised him when he pronounced "der" so that the "e" had an "ay" sound to it and so that the "r" was held longer than normal to make the sound "dayrr." His friend ignored him when he pronounced the word so that the "e" had an "uh" sound as in "dur." What behavioral procedure gradually improved Adolph's pronunciation? ______________________________

(2) When a person is more likely to emit a particular behavior in the presence of the S^D than in the presence of the *S*-delta, we call the behavior ______________________________.

(3) Sheila was trying to become more assertive around men. When she was assertive with Bill, he responded favorably; when she was assertive with Ken, he ignored her. As a result Sheila became more assertive around Bill but not Ken. The increased probability of assertive behavior in the presence of Bill means that Bill has come to exert ____________ ____________ over her assertive behavior.

(4) When Charlie Brown smiled at the little redheaded girl, she ignored him. When he smiled at Lucy, she was very nice to him. If Charlie Brown was reinforced by "niceness," what type of stimulus is Lucy? ______________________________

(5) Reinforcing a behavior in the presence of one stimulus and extinguishing a different behavior in the presence of the same stimulus is called ______________________________.

(6) "What does 2 + 2 equal?" is called a(n) ______________________________ for the behavior "4."

(7) Reinforcing one behavior while extinguishing a second behavior in the presence of stimulus A and extinguishing the first behavior while reinforcing the second behavior in the presence of stimulus B is considered to be an example of what behavioral procedure?

____

(8) Redd and Birnbrauer (1969) studied the results of having one behavior analyst give a retarded child edibles when he played cooperatively with other children while a second behavior analyst did not. The child learned to play cooperatively when the first adult was present but not when the second adult was present. What behavioral procedure accounts for this result? ______________________________

(9) Jeff's dorm friends paid attention when he said "x@#!" but ignored him when he said "gosh" or "darn." Jeff gradually said only "x@#!" What behavioral procedure is at work? ____________

____

(10) Dickie's mother taught him to recognize the picture of her favorite candidate, Aaron Burr, by sometimes showing him a picture of Burr and sometimes of Jefferson and asking "Who is this?" She praised him when he answered correctly. Soon he answered "Burr" to the first picture but not the second. His answering behavior would be called ______________________________.

Explain the difference between a reinforcer and a discriminative stimulus.

LESSON 16 **FORM C** **GRADE:** ____________

NAME: ______________________ **DATE:** ______________

---

(1) Sammy had trouble learning how to pronounce 1492, so his teacher praised "fourteen ninety-two" and ignored responses like "forty nine two." What behavioral procedure is the teacher using to teach Sammy the correct pronunciation? ____________________

(2) Adolph had three flash cards with the German words "und," "der," and "kopf" written on their fronts and the translations written on their backs. Adolph would look at the fronts of the three cards and point to the one that he thought meant "the," and then he would turn the card over to see whether he was right. If being right is a reinforcer for Adolph, what behavioral procedure is at work here? ____________________

(3) Professor Tod always made positive comments about statements Gene made. Professor Rose rarely had a reaction. Gene talked a lot to Professor Tod and he talked only a little to Professor Rose. Professor Rose is what kind of stimulus? ____________________

(4) Donna used to be confused about what constituted a straight in poker. Her husband often asked her two questions: "What is 4, 5, 6, 7, and 8 called?" and "What is five hearts called?" He praised her when she said straight to the first question but not when she said straight to the second question. Gradually she came to say "straight" only when asked the first question. Her behavior of saying "straight" is called ____________________.

(5) Ted ignored Dick when he pronounced Aaron Burr's name as "Brrr" and praised him when he said "Bur." What behavioral process is this an example of? ____________________

(6) After much practice, Xavier had learned the square root of many numbers. If his teacher asked him "What is the square root of 81?" he promptly said "9." But he did not give 9 as the square root of any other number. The increased probability of saying "9" when asked the square root of 81 means that the question has come to exert ____________________ over that behavior.

(7) Jonah had three goldfish. He played a game with his friend Robert to see if Robert could name his goldfish. If he called the big goldfish "whale" Jonah praised him but ignored him if he called the goldfish "Tiny." If he called the small goldfish "Tiny" Jonah praised him but not if he called the small goldfish "whale." What behavioral procedure was Jonah using? ____________________

(8) A stimulus that occurs before a behavior and increases the rate of the behavior is called a(n) ____________________; a stimulus that occurs after a behavior and increases the rate of the behavior is called a(n) ____________________.

(9) If a stimulus that precedes a behavior is associated with extinction, it is called a(n) ____________________.

(10) Doug got a lot of attention if he was reading a mechanics book, but his father ignored him if he was reading anything else. Doug became an avid reader of mechanics books. What behavioral process accounts for Doug's reading habits? ____________________

Define stimulus control.

LESSON 17 **FORM A** **GRADE:** ______

NAME: ______________________ **DATE:** ____________

(1) Mr. Wyler worked long and hard to teach Fran to study most of the time that she was in third-grade spelling. However, this did not change her habit of goofing off all the time in other classes. Mr. Wyler suggested to Ms. Green that she also reinforce Fran only for studying in third-grade math. Pretty soon Fran was the champion studier in all of her classes. What procedure had her teachers used to bring about this remarkable change? ______________________

(2) Reinforcing a behavior in each of a series of situations, until the behavior generalizes to other members of that same stimulus class, is called ______________________.

(3) Professor Smart always got a big smile whenever she referred to the pretty brunette as "Kay" in class, but she didn't seem to recognize her outside of class. One day, however, as she was walking across campus she looked up, saw the pretty brunette, and said "Hi, Kay" and was rewarded by a giant smile. The occurrence of the naming behavior outside of class would be called ______________________.

(4) If a behavior is more likely to occur in the presence of the S^D than the *S*-delta it is called a(n) ______________________.

(5) The grouping of all situations in which Professor Smart might encounter Kay at the University—class, hallway, campus, student union, and so on—would be called a(n) ______________________.

(6) Bornstein and associates (1977) taught Jane to be assertive in response to being interrupted by another person. They then taught her to be assertive in several other types of situations. When they tested her assertiveness in three untrained situations, they found her to be quite assertive. What behavioral procedure did they use? ______________________

(7) Reinforcing a behavior in the presence of a particular stimulus and extinguishing it in the presence of other stimuli is called ______________________.

(8) James usually acted very businesslike around Mr. Smith because he seemed to appreciate it. James usually did not act businesslike around Mr. Clevis because he ignored such behavior and acted in a slower and more relaxed manner. In this situation, we would say that Mr. Smith exerted ______________________ over James' businesslike behavior.

(9) A set of related stimuli is called a(n) ______________________.

(10) Dr. Rutherford taught Karen a number of "nonshy" behaviors using role playing in his clinic. However, she never could get up nerve enough to employ them anywhere else. So Dr. Rutherford arranged to have another psychologist reinforce Karen for "nonshy" behavior also in a role-playing situation. Karen then acted in a nonshy way with her archeology instructor. The occurrence of nonshy behavior outside the role-playing situation would be an example of ______________________.

Define generalization.

LESSON 17 **FORM B** **GRADE:** ____________

NAME: ______________________ **DATE:** ______________

(1) Sally was a health-food nut. Whenever Ralph ate granola for breakfast she praised his diet. Pretty soon he usually ate granola. Then he started eating vegetables for dinner instead of TV dinners and she praised him. Pretty soon he was eating only health foods. What behavioral procedure did Sally use? ______________________________

(2) Miller and Weaver (1974) showed students a series of examples of extinction. If you regard each example as a stimulus, then the collection of all examples of extinction would be termed a(n) ______________________________ .

(3) Generalization is defined as the occurrence of a behavior in the presence of a(n) ______________________________ .

(4) Professor Brainbuster usually got a smile when he called the studious dude in the front row "Ted" but not if he called him "Dan." Likewise, he usually got a smile when he called the burly athlete in the back row "Dan" but not if he called him "Ted." What behavioral procedure are these guys unknowingly applying to the prof's behavior? ______________________

(5) If Danny is reinforced for calling the giant old tree in front of his house a "tree," he might see the giant oak down the street and call it a tree also. If he does, the occurrence of his labeling behavior is called ______________________________ .

(6) The Klines ignored anything little Sarah said if it included "I ain't" but attended to her if she said "I am not." Soon Sarah said "I am not" but no longer said "I ain't." What behavioral procedure did the Klines use to produce this behavioral change? ______________________

(7) The collection of all tall woody plants (called trees) would be an example of a(n) ______________________________ .

(8) Peggy never volunteered to answer a question in class. However, a question arose one day in one of her classes concerning her greatest love, classical art, and she got so excited she volunteered to answer the question before she had time to think. She was called on and praised for having the right answer. She volunteered often in that class in the future. Somewhat later, the same thing happened in another class and again she volunteered and had the right answer. After that she started to volunteer in all of her classes. Even though no one was intentionally arranging it, Peggy's behavior changed as a result of what procedure?

____

(9) The increased probability of a discriminated behavior that is produced by a stimulus is called ______________________________ .

(10) A novel stimulus is any stimulus in whose presence a behavior has not previously been ______________________________ .

Define generalization training.

LESSON 17 **FORM C** **GRADE:** ____________

NAME: ____________________ **DATE:** ____________

(1) The occurrence of a behavior in the presence of a novel stimulus is called ____________ ____________.

(2) Generalization training is a procedure in which a behavior is reinforced in each of a series of situations until it ____________ to other members of that same stimulus class.

(3) Davey looked at the big old elm and said "That's a tree, mom" to his surprised mother. She praised him for knowing it and he often told her that the elm was a tree. One day he said, "Hey mom, that is a tree too, isn't it?" and pointed to a giant oak. Again she made a big fuss over his knowledge. After several more trees, Davey started referring to all big woody plants as "trees." What behavioral procedure did his mother use? ____________

(4) A stimulus that precedes the behavior and is present only if the behavior will be reinforced is called a(n) ____________; a stimulus that precedes the behavior and is present only if the behavior will be extinguished is called a(n) ____________.

(5) Dr. Rutherford taught Karen a number of "nonshy" behaviors using role playing in his clinic. However, she never could get up enough nerve to employ them anywhere else. So Dr. Rutherford arranged to have another psychologist reinforce Karen for "nonshy" behavior also in a role-playing situation. Karen then started to act in nonshy ways at school, on her job, and even among strangers. What behavioral procedure did Dr. Rutherford employ to help Karen? ____________

(6) Professor Smart always got a big smile whenever she referred to the pretty brunette as "Kay" in class, but she didn't seem to recognize the brunette outside of class. One day, as she was crossing campus, she looked up, saw the brunette, and said "Hi Kay" and was rewarded with a giant smile. From then on she recognized Kay no matter where she saw her. What behavioral procedure did Kay use to teach Professor Smart to recognize her? ____________

(7) The collection of all people that you encounter during a day would be called a(n) ____________.

(8) Miller and Weaver (1974) reinforced students for correctly labeling the examples contained in this book. They then observed that the students could correctly label examples that they had not seen before. The occurrence of the students' labeling behavior in the presence of the new examples would be called ____________.

(9) Rex praised his daughter for saying "15" when asked "What does 8 + 7 equal?" but not when asked "What does 9 + 4 equal?" What procedure was Rex using? ____________

(10) Damien helped his little brother learn addition by showing him simple problems that were printed on a series of flash cards. Damien gave his brother a chocolate-covered peanut after showing him the card "3 + 9 = ?" if his brother said "12" but not if he said any other number. Damien used the same approach to answers to the other cards. What procedure did he use? ____________

Define stimulus class.

LESSON 18 **FORM A** **GRADE:** ____________

NAME: ______________________ **DATE:** ______________

(1) Terry was taught to add by a teacher who showed him two piles of blocks, with two and three blocks in each, and who asked the question "How much is 2 + 3?" As the training went on, the blocks were moved farther and farther from Terry. The blocks would be called a(n) ______________________ .

(2) The problems that taught Roger to look at a red ant and write "red" in response to the question "This is a ______________________ ant" were not the only kind of problems given to him. He was also shown a picture of a red mat. If the first time he saw the mat he answered "red" to the question "This is a ______________________ mat," the occurrence of his response would be an example of what behavioral process? ______________________

(3) Melba taught Hilda to read the word "dog" by making cards with the word "dog" printed across the head of a picture of a dog. She then made a series of cards with less and less of the dog sketched in. The gradual elimination of the picture is called ______________________ .

(4) Tom gets a ride home after school every day from Carol. The first day she didn't know the way so he told her which way to turn at "Five Corners"; next day he only said "here" at the turn and didn't tell her which way to turn; on following days he gave no instructions at all. Carol learned the way perfectly in 3 days. What behavioral procedure did Tom use? ______________________

(5) An added stimulus that increases the probability that a person will make the correct response in a discriminative situation is called a(n) ______________________ .

(6) Mr. Kline taught Roberta to label the floor as a rectangle by asking her "What shape is that? A rect____________?", then "What shape is that? a rrrr______________________?", and, finally, with no prompt. He then used the same procedure to teach her that the piece of paper was a rectangle. After several such examples, Roberta came to label an object with parallel sides, right angles, and length greater than width as a rectangle. What procedure did Mr. Kline use? ______________________

(7) Schaefer (1963) used the German word *ich* to replace the English "I" in several short stories by Poe. The context of redundant sentences was enough to serve as an effective prompt for proper translation. By placing the German word in many different sentences, students learned to always recognize that word even where the sentence was not an effective prompt. What behavioral procedure did Schaefer use to teach the meaning of *ich*? ______________________

(8) Programmed instruction requires an overt response, provides immediate ______________________ on the correctness of the response, and uses small steps.

(9) Programming is the temporary use of a prompt to teach a(n) ______________________ .

(10) Samantha was shunned by the other faculty members when she wore jeans in their presence, but her students loved such casual dress. Eventually, Samantha did not wear jeans if she was going to be around the faculty, but she did if she was going to be around students. What behavioral procedure influenced her when she wore jeans? ______________________

Define the procedure of fading.

LESSON 18 **FORM B** **GRADE:** ____________

NAME: ______________________ **DATE:** ____________

(1) In *Programmed Reading* the child is shown a picture of a girl in a bag and then required to fill in the blank "That is Ann in the ba___." Showing one or more letters contained in the correct answer is called a(n) ______________________.

(2) Mr. Hearthstone taught Greg to sing middle C by first playing the note loudly on the piano and asking Greg to copy it. The sound of the note played on the piano would be called a(n) ______________________.

(3) One way to teach children to print is to show them a letter and ask them to copy it. This method is made simpler if some light dashed lines are added to the page for them to draw over. These dashed lines can then be made fainter and fainter until they are no longer needed. What behavioral technique is being used if "P" versus "B" is taught this way? ______________________

(4) Janice took flying lessons from Barbara. The plane had dual controls so both of them could fly the plane at the same time. At first, Barbara steered the plane, and, since her steering caused Janice's steering mechanism to also move, Janice could feel the correct steering. Then Barb encouraged Janice to steer with them both moving the controls together. Gradually, Barb reduced her control until Janice was steering by herself! What behavioral procedure had Barb used? ______________________

(5) The temporary use of a prompt to establish a specific discrimination is called ______________________.

(6) The gradual elimination of a prompt is called ______________________.

(7) Ann pointed to the table and asked Shigura "What is this?" and then said the word "table" so he could hear it. She praised him when he also said the word "table." Gradually, she said the word more and more softly. Teaching Shigura to use the word "table" correctly utilized what behavioral procedure? ______________________

(8) A prompt is a(n) ______________________ that increases the probability of a person's making the correct response in a discriminative situation.

(9) Darlene praised her daughter for saying "crow" when shown a picture of the large black bird and ignored her for saying "crow" when shown the picture of the small black bird. What behavioral procedure was Darlene using? ______________________

(10) Bob showed Tom a big red ball and asked "What is this?" When Tom answered "ball," Bob gave him an edible treat; when Tom answered anything else, he ignored him. After many trials, Tom would always say "ball." But when asked to identify a little green ball he looked blank. So Tom held the little green ball up many times, asked what it was and gave Tom an edible treat when he said "ball." When Bob held up any kind of a ball after that, Tom always called it a ball. What behavioral procedure did Bob use to teach Tom the idea of "ball"? ______________________

Define the procedure of programming (not programmed instruction).

LESSON 18 **FORM C** **GRADE:** ______________

NAME: ______________________ **DATE:** ______________

(1) Moore and Goldiamond (1964) had the correct answer light up while the incorrect answers remained dark. They then gradually increased the brightness of the incorrect answers until they were as bright as the correct answer. What behavioral procedure were they using when they gradually made the correct and incorrect answers equally bright? ______________________

(2) Fading is the use of a prompt to establish a specific ______________________.

(3) A method for gradually changing a response is called ______________________; a method for gradually changing a stimulus is called ______________________.

(4) Darlene praised her daughter for saying "crow" when shown a picture of the large black bird and ignored her for saying "crow" when shown the picture of the small black bird. Darlene then gave the child hints for "bigness" when showing the picture of the crow. She gradually withdrew these hints. What behavioral procedure was Darlene using? ______________________

(5) Roger was shown a picture of a red ant and the words "This is a r___d ant" (he had been taught to fill in such a blank). Next he got a picture of a red ant and the words "This is a r___ ant." After each problem, Roger was given an M & M if he filled in the blank correctly and was ignored if he got it wrong. As the sequence developed, fewer of the letters in the word "red" were given to him. Those letters would be called a(n) ______________________.

(6) Sheila was ignored when she sat next to Marvin if he was listening to their new stereo with the headphones on, but she was given a lot of attention if she sat next to Marvin when he was listening to the stereo without headphones. Sheila came to sit next to Marvin only when he did not have the headphones on. What behavioral procedure influenced when she sat next to Marvin? ______________________

(7) Karol was shown pictures of many red objects: ants, balls, houses, fire engines. He was asked the questions "This is a ______________________ (ant, ball, and so on)" with each one. At first, the questions had one or more of the letters in "red" attached to the blank as a clue. But these were gradually eliminated. What behavioral procedure was being used to teach Karol to label red objects as "red"? ______________________

(8) Mr. Hearthstone taught Greg to sing middle C by first playing the note loudly on the piano and asking Greg to copy it, which he could easily do. Mr. Hearthstone then played the note more and more softly until Greg was singing the note without any reminder from the piano. What behavioral procedure did Mr. Hearthstone use? ______________________

(9) Suppose that Bev answered "ball" more often when a ball was shown to her and she was asked "What is this?" than she did when shown a rock and asked the same question. We would call her behavior of saying "ball" in this situation ______________________.

(10) The temporary use of a prompt to teach a generalization is called ______________.

Define a prompt.

LESSON 19 **FORM A** **GRADE:** ____________

NAME: ______________________ **DATE:** ______________

(1) Buzz explained to Carol how to grip the ball in order to throw a curve. She tried it and threw a perfect curve! What behavioral procedure did Buzz use? ____________________

(2) If a teacher provides a behavioral demonstration of what another person is supposed to do, the teacher's behavior is called the ____________________.

(3) When a teacher describes a behavior that he or she would like a learner to produce, this description would be called a(n) ____________________ (not an "instruction").

(4) If a learner produces a behavior that someone else describes orally, the learner's behavior would be an example of ____________________ behavior.

(5) Henry found that, if he used abbreviations in the rough copy of his book, his typist did not write the word out but simply copied the abbreviations. When Henry typed the full word, the typist also typed the full word. Since Henry wanted the full word typed out, he gradually stopped using abbreviations and started typing full words. The change in Henry's typing behavior is the result of what behavioral procedure? ____________________

(6) Shawn showed Sherril several shimmering seashells. "What are these? Are they several shimmering seashells?" Shawn praised Sherril for saying "They are several shimmering seashells." Next time that Shawn asked, he gave as a hint only the phrase "several shimmering sea . . ." Each successive time he dropped a word from the hint. Finally, Sherril could say the whole thing without any part of the hint. What behavioral procedure did Shawn use? ____________________

(7) Carol explained in detail to Buzz how to sew a buttonhole. He tried it and sewed a perfect hole the first time. What behavioral procedure did Carol use? ____________________

(8) Ada demonstrated the essential elements of fielding. These elements included getting her body in front of the ball, kneeling to one knee, keeping her eye on the ball, and so on. Then she hit some balls to the children and had them try to field them. When they fielded the ball correctly, she praised them. What method for changing behavior was Ada using? ____________________

(9) Professor Brainbuster defined *role* in a lecture as "the prescribed behavior for a given status." He then gave an oral quiz and graded his students on whether or not they repeated these words in defining *role*. The students' behavior was taught through what behavioral procedure? ____________________

(10) Ada had Gordie stand at the plate and call "strike" for only the good pitches. She praised him when he was right and ignored him when he was wrong. She hoped this method would teach him which pitches were worth swinging at. What method is she using to teach Gordie to call "strike" for the good pitches but not for the bad pitches? ____________________

Explain how to differentiate between instructional and imitative training.

LESSON 19 **FORM B** **GRADE:** ____________

NAME: ______________________ **DATE:** ____________

(1) Frank explained in detail how Felicia should sight the rifle on the target. His explanation would be referred to as a(n) ______________________ in the behavioral procedure of instructional training.

(2) An imitative stimulus is technically known as the ______________________ for the imitative behavior, because it is associated with reinforcement for that behavior.

(3) Ada hit several balls to Billy. If he kneeled with one knee on the ground when fielding a ball, she praised him and hit him another ball. If he bent down with his knees straight when fielding the ball, she immediately stopped hitting him balls for a while. Ada used what method to teach Billy to put one knee down when fielding? ______________________

(4) Marcia's roommate explained what clothing to buy and how to put on makeup in order to be "in style." Marcia did these things and found that she got asked for a lot more dates. Marcia's behavior changed as a result of what behavioral procedure? ______________________

(5) Sometimes a nontalker in a discussion class may learn to use an effective argument simply by listening to another person use it. The nontalker may, in the future, use that same line of argument and be reinforced. Changing the person's behavior in this way would be an example of ______________________ .

(6) Imitation training and instructional training will continue to work only if the person's imitative or instructed behavior is ______________________ .

(7) If a learner copies the behavior of another person, the learner's behavior is called ______________________ .

(8) Hollandsworth and colleagues (1978) demonstrated for Herbert how to ask questions designed to clarify interview questions. They then watched his ability to ask such questions in a simulated interview and reinforced correct performance. What behavioral procedure did they use to teach Herbert how to ask questions of the interviewer? ______________________

(9) Two ways that a person can learn from a lecture are by doing things that the lecturer tells him to do, which would be an example of ______________________ , and by copying arguments and information that are contained in the lecture, which would be an example of ______________________ .

(10) Dr. Feelgood taught Marcia to act assertively by setting up a series of role-playing situations that required her assertiveness. He provided feedback on her performance until she was acting quite assertively toward him. He then brought in an assistant, Felix, and had him present her with a number of situations requiring assertiveness. After his help, they found that Marcia had no trouble acting assertively with other people in other situations. What behavioral procedure did Dr. Feelgood and his assistant use to create this result? ______________________

Define imitative training, referring to its three parts.

LESSON 19 **FORM C** **GRADE:** ____________

NAME: ________________________ **DATE:** ______________

---

(1) If a person demonstrates to other people how to perform a behavior, watches them do it, and then reinforces successful performance, he or she is using what behavioral procedure?
____

(2) The use of verbal descriptions of behavior and reinforcement to teach a new behavior is called ____________________________________.

(3) John's father sawed the first board to show John how to use the power saw. He then watched John cut a board and praised him when he followed the father's example. This would be an example of what behavioral procedure? ____________________________________

(4) Ada patiently explained to Sam exactly where to look when he was pitching. She then had him throw several pitches while she was watching and praised him only when he did it right. What procedure for changing Sam's behavior did Ada use? ____________________

(5) Tom explained in detail how Frank should operate the chain saw, watched him try, and praised his performance. What behavioral procedure did Tom use? ____________________

(6) Cursive writing is often taught in school by showing children examples of the properly formed letters and words. The children are required to copy these letters over and over. The teacher praises good copies. This would be an example of what behavioral procedure?
____

(7) Mary showed Tommy two blocks and asked "How many are there? Two?" and praised him when he said "Two." She then repeated the question at various times during the day, each time saying "Two" softer and softer until Tommy answered "Two" without any help. Mary then showed Tommy two toys and repeated the procedure. When she showed him two spoons and asked him how many, he said "Two" without any hint. What behavioral procedure did Mary use? ____________________________________

(8) A verbal description by one person concerning what behavior another person should produce would technically be called a(n) ____________________________________ for that instructed behavior (because it is associated with reinforcement).

(9) Hollandsworth and his colleagues (1978) provided a verbal description to Herbert of how he should make clear responses to interview questions. They then observed his performance in a simulated interview session and reinforced correct responses. The behavior analysts were using what behavioral procedure to teach Herbert to make clear answers? __________
____

(10) Barb showed Kenny a picture of a tree and asked, "What is this?" When Kenny couldn't answer, she asked, "Is it a tree?" and he said "yes." She then got Kenny to say "tree." Several other times during the week she showed him the same picture and asked him, "What is this, a tree?" but saying "tree" more and more softly until he could identify the tree without her hint. Barb was using what behavioral procedure? ______________________________

Define instructional training, referring to its three parts.

LESSON 20 **FORM A** **GRADE:** ____________

NAME: ________________________ **DATE:** ______________

(1) Carey earned a point for every page of the SRA Reading Program that she finished. She could trade each point for one cookie. Carey's parents noted that she usually earned a few points early in the morning and then quit working for that day. The points probably lose their effectiveness as a conditioned reinforcer because Carey soon becomes ________________ ________________ with respect to the backup reinforcer of cookies.

(2) If a conditioned reinforcer remains associated with another reinforcer, the conditioned reinforcer's effectiveness will decrease when the person is ________________________ ________ with respect to the other reinforcer.

(3) His father wanted to teach Larry to always wear safety goggles when using the chain saw, but he didn't want to be nagged about it. So every time that Larry was about to use the chain saw, his father would watch him while wearing goggles, and he would praise Larry whenever Larry also wore them. Pretty soon Larry always wore them. His father then would just pick up and hold the goggles but not put them on, while praising Larry for wearing them. Finally, Larry's father didn't touch the goggles but just praised Larry for wearing them, which he always did. What behavioral procedure did Larry's father use to teach him to wear safety goggles? ____________________________________

(4) One day Mary let her hair fall freely rather than braiding it. When she happened to meet Kevin walking across campus, he stopped and talked with her for the first time ever. Later, when she went home for Thanksgiving break, she again decided to wear her hair loose. The occurrence of loose hair at home is an example of ______________________________.

(5) Any reinforcer that loses its effectiveness permanently through unpaired presentations is called a(n) ____________________________________ reinforcer.

(6) When towels were no longer paired with social attention by Aylion and Michael (1959), the towels lost their effectiveness as reinforcers. Thus, towels should be considered to be a(n) ____________________________________ reinforcer.

(7) A reinforcer associated with <u>many</u> other reinforcers is called a(n) ________________ ________________.

(8) Ms. Whalen walked through the room while the children were working on their math and graded their work right then and there. Each child was allowed to play outside for 10 minutes after he or she had completed ten problems correctly. She found that the rate of work in the class went up dramatically as a result of this approach. Playing outside would be classified as a(n) ____________________________________ with respect to the grade.

(9) Marlon's teachers gave him a button every time he picked up his toys after he was finished playing. Marlon could use the button to get a snack, a story, or a long walk. If these three events are reinforcers, the button would be called a(n) ____________________________.

(10) Bev learned to cube the number 5 by multiplying 5 × 5 to get 25 and then multiplying by another 5 to get the answer 125. Bev's two responses in this example constitute a(n) ____________________________________.

Define stimulus/response chain.

LESSON 20 **FORM B** **GRADE:** ____________

NAME: ______________________ **DATE:** ______________

(1) A stimulus/response chain is several related responses in which the results of one response serve as a(n) ______________________ for the next response.

(2) Whitman and Dussault (1976) helped James set up a point system in which he earned points by such behaviors as studying and attending class, and spent them on such activities as visiting his girlfriend and watching TV. Visiting his girlfriend and watching TV would be considered ______________________ reinforcers for the points.

(3) Willie's mother reinforced Willie for doing something thoughtful with a "thank you" and, later, an M & M. Later, Willie's mother started reinforcing him with only a "thank you." He started doing fewer thoughtful things until he eventually stopped altogether. This pattern indicates that "thank you" is what type of reinforcer? ______________

(4) If a person is given two math problems such as "2 + 2 = ?" and "4 + 3 = ?" his or her responses to the problems would not constitute a stimulus/response chain, because the response to one problem does not serve as a(n) ______________________ for the response to the second problem.

(5) Any event that loses its effectiveness only temporarily through satiation is called a(n) ______________________ reinforcer.

(6) One major advantage that conditioned reinforcers have over their backup, with respect to their effectiveness as reinforcers, is that conditioned reinforcers can easily be delivered according to the Principle of ______________________.

(7) One day when Fat Frank was once again teasing Slim Simpson, Simpson gave Frank a look that said "I'm going to hurt you very much if you do that again!" And Frank immediately started being very nice. A few days later, when Heavy Harry started teasing Simpson, Simpson once again produced that look. What is the name of the behavioral procedure that accounts for Simpson producing the look around Harry? ______________

(8) A generalized reinforcer is an event that is associated with ______________ ________ other reinforcers.

(9) Carol's teacher showed her a picture of a maple tree and asked "What is this? Is it a tree?" and gave her a token whenever she said "tree." On subsequent occasions, the teacher said "Is it a tree?" more and more softly until Carol could identify it as a tree without the hint. Then the teacher used the same procedure to teach Carol to identify an oak as a "tree." When she had succeeded, Carol suddenly could identify any tall, woody object as a tree. What behavioral procedure had the teacher used? ______________

(10) In Sociology 71, students had to pay credits if they wanted to come to class. In class they could see movies, listen to guest speakers, and participate in discussions. The credits would be classified as what kind of reinforcer? ______________________

Define conditioned reinforcer.

LESSON 20 **FORM C** **GRADE:** ____________

NAME: ______________________ **DATE:** ____________

(1) What type of reinforcer is most likely to always be an effective reinforcer? ____________ ____________

(2) When reciting "Mary had a little lamb," you would first say "Mary," and this response would serve as a discriminative stimulus for the second response, "had," and so on. Thus each word would serve as a(n) ______________________ for the next word, and the entire sequence would be called a(n) ______________________ (if there were some "final" reinforcement).

(3) Everyone at the behavioral research commune had to earn 100 points a week to be eligible to continue living there. In January, the commune changed that rule so that the members did not have to earn 100 points. They were now on their honor to earn 100 points a week simply to help keep the commune running. The commune soon learned that the members earned fewer and fewer points each week. These results suggest that points should be classified as what kind of reinforcer? ______________________

(4) A reinforcer that makes a conditioned reinforcer effective is called a(n) ____________ ____________.

(5) Members of the behavioral commune gave a ticket worth one point to anyone they saw complimenting another person. These points could be traded for theatre or sports-events tickets, a special dessert at dinner, or the loan of a typewriter or other house tools. The points in this situation would be called a(n) ______________________; the desserts and other privileges would be called a(n) ______________________ for the points.

(6) Getting the correct answer on a self-quiz may be a minor reinforcer for a student. However, if getting the correct answer on the self-quiz is associated with doing well on a class quiz, it may be a fairly strong reinforcer. What type of reinforcer is getting correct answers on the self-quiz if it is associated with a good grade on the class quiz? ____________ ____________

(7) Claire started using big words like "ephemeral" when she was around Dale because he praised her for having such a good vocabulary. But she rarely used big words around other guys until she met Kevin, who also praised her for a rare usage. After that she just used her complete vocabulary wherever she was. What behavioral procedure did Dale and Kevin combine to employ to change her behavior in this way? ______________________

(8) Every time that Jean made an approving statement to her teachers, Polirstok and Greer (1977) gave her a token. The tokens could be exchanged for music tapes, extra gym, lunch with a favorite teacher, or extra English credit. These tokens could be considered to be ______________________ reinforcers.

(9) Melody had been praised very strongly by her father for using the word "gregarious" for the first time one day. After that, Melody used the word in a conversation with her mother. What is the name for the behavioral process of using "gregarious" with her mother? ______________________

(10) A sequence of responses in which the results of one response serve as an S^D for the next response and in which the last response leads to a reinforcer is called a(n) ____________ ____________ (give full name).

Define generalized reinforcer.

LESSON 21 **FORM A** **GRADE:** ____________

NAME: ______________________ **DATE:** ______________

(1) A person will continue to follow instructions only if frequently ______________ for doing so.

(2) If a behavior occurs more frequently in the presence of the S^D than the S-delta, we say that the stimulus exerts ______________ over that behavior.

(3) We often think of people who bubble over with "fun" as having that trait ingrained in their personality. Yet a group could accidentally eliminate this behavior through the procedure called ______________.

(4) Flora taught her daughter Melody to read the word "cat" by printing the word on a card, asking her "What is this word?" and then showing her a picture of a cat. Each time she showed the picture of the cat for a briefer time until she stopped showing it at all. What behavioral procedure was Flora using? ______________

(5) The name for reinforcers that are paired with other events to make them effective conditioned reinforcers is ______________.

(6) Crazy Harry wanted to be able to identify Magic Mushrooms. He made up a card containing a drawing of an Amanita Muscaria with the words "Amanita Muscaria" underneath. He also made up cards containing pictures of other magic mushrooms. Whenever he came to the Amanita, he uncovered just a bit of the label until he could correctly name the mushroom. As time went on he uncovered less and less of the label until he could eventually identify it without looking at the label at all. He then repeated the process for several photographs of the mushroom until he could identify them without looking at any portion of the label. He found then that he could reliably identify the mushroom in the wild. His friends noticed that he got a bit crazier after that. What behavioral procedure did Harry use to teach himself to identify the Magic Mushroom? ______________

(7) In the process of teaching Marty to say "one," Danny would show Marty how to say "one" by saying it himself. Danny would then reinforce Marty if he correctly said "one." The method that Danny used to teach Marty to say "one" is called ______________.

(8) Primary reinforcers lose their effectiveness only temporarily through the process called ______________; conditioned reinforcers lose their effectiveness permanently through being ______________ from their back ups.

(9) Any time that Karen used a new word longer than three syllables her father immediately gave her a quarter and praised her improving vocabulary. Her father never did this unless Karen had used a new word. Karen certainly needed the money and seemed to think of it as a reasonable payoff for learning a new word. What principle of effective reinforcement, if any, did Karen's father fail to employ? ______________

(10) Everyone was given a "snerkel" each time he or she said something positive about the food. People could cash the snerkels in for a small amount of money or for privileges in the house (such as the use of games). What kind of reinforcer is the snerkel? ______________

LESSON 21 **FORM B** **GRADE:** ____________

NAME: ______________________ **DATE:** ______________

---

(1) Fred would neck with Gloria only in a drive-in theatre. Assuming that Gloria finds it reinforcing to neck with Fred, the drive-in would be called a(n) ______________________ for necking.

(2) Olivia explained to John in detail how to do a particular disco dance, even to drawing out little feet diagramming where John should move his feet. John tried it and Olivia provided feedback to him until he could do it perfectly. What behavioral procedure was Olivia using to teach the dance to John? ______________________

(3) Her parents never listened to Gladys during dinner, preferring to discuss the day's news instead. However, one day Gladys criticized the Republicans and her father acted very upset and had a long argument with her about politics. As a result, Gladys became an ardent critic of Republicans at home. Later, she criticized Republicans around some of her parents' friends and similarly got an argument and lots of attention. Gladys now criticizes Republicans whenever she is in the presence of conservative, business-oriented people. What behavioral procedure produced this behavioral change in Gladys? ______________________

(4) Mr. Howard pointed to a VW Beetle going by and asked little Alicia "What is that? Voom, voom." She said "car." Mr. Howard pointed to another Beetle later and said the "voom, voom" much more softly. He repeated this until she could identify a Beetle as a car without the addition of the "voom, voom." Mr. Howard then used the same approach on a Mustang. From then on Alicia could identify any passenger vehicle as a car. What behavioral procedure did Mr. Howard use? ______________________

(5) Generalization is defined as the occurrence of a behavior in the presence of a(n) ____________ ______________________.

(6) Generalization training involves reinforcing a behavior in the presence of each of a series of situations until generalization occurs to other members of that same ____________ ______________________.

(7) Replacing a baby's diaper consists of placing the child on her back, removing the old diaper, putting on and pinning a new diaper. This sequence of behaviors would be called a(n) ______________________.

(8) Sue frequently told Ken that she couldn't jog with him because she didn't know how to run. To help her learn how, Ken took her out on their lawn and jogged for her, showing her where on the foot to land, how to extend the legs, how to coordinate swinging the arms with the leg movements. Sue then tried and Ken provided feedback. In a few minutes, Sue was able to run almost as smoothly as Ken. What behavioral procedure did Ken employ to teach Sue how to jog? ______________________

(9) If the probability of a behavior decreases because an event that used to follow it has been stopped, what behavioral principle is being used? ______________________

(10) Discrimination training is a procedure in which a behavior is ______________________ ____________ in the presence of one stimulus and ______________________ in the presence of a second stimulus.

LESSON 21 **FORM C** **GRADE:** ____________

NAME: ______________________ **DATE:** ______________

(1) Katie showed her son a picture of a house for successively briefer times when trying to teach him to read the printed word "house." The picture would be called a(n) ______________ ______________ for assisting in establishing the response of reading the word.

(2) Mary's mother checked every 15 minutes to see if she was cleaning her room. If it was reinforcing for Mary to be found cleaning, what schedule was she on? ______________ ______________

(3) Fran tried to increase the amount of study time put in by her daughter Melanie, so she frequently asked Melanie whether she had been studying. If she had, then Fran immediately gave Melanie a special snack. Melanie loved the snacks; in fact she would do anything to get one. She never got too much of the snack. Trouble is that Melanie didn't study nearly as much as she told her mother that she did so her overall study time was not affected by being given the snack. What principle of effective reinforcement was Fran failing to employ? ________ ______________________

(4) If a reinforcer is paired with one back up reinforcer it is called a(n) ______________ ______________ reinforcer; if it is paired with many back up reinforcers it is called a(n) ______________________________ reinforcer.

(5) During World War Two, Colonel Peterson frequently showed an outline of a British Spitfire fighter plane to his Civilian Defense recruits and asked them what it was. To help them he made a spitting sound. Every time that she showed the outline after that she made a slightly softer spitting sound until everyone could identify the Spitfire with no clue. Later she showed them a picture of the Spitfire as it flew and asked them what it was, again adding the spitting sound. They soon learned to identify it. At that point they could identify a Spitfire whether it was flying overhead or depicted in pictures. What behavioral procedure had Col. Peterson used? ______________________________

(6) If Gloria peeps only when the light is on in Todd's room, then we would call her peeping a(n) ______________________________ behavior.

(7) Eli wanted to teach his friend to say "hi" when Eli said "Yassou," the Greek word for hi. So at first he said "Yassou" and waved at his friend. Gradually he delayed the wave until his friend was responding "hi" even before the wave. The wave used in addition to the greeting would be called a(n) ______________________________.

(8) Believe it or not, Davey didn't know how to organize his time properly to make the most of his studying. So his friends explained to him how to highlight important points, how to review them, how to work in an area without distractions, how to set aside a specific part of each day to study, and how to study when there were no current assignments. Davey tried their suggestions and found that they worked extremely well. In fact, he got all A's that semester, while, to his surprise, his friends got C's. What behavioral procedure did his friends use to teach him how to study effectively? ______________________________

(9) Barb and Carey loved to go window shopping. Barb had undertaken to teach Carey how to dress in the latest hip fashions. When Carey expressed the opinion that some garment looked really hip Barb would praise her taste. She did it immediately, but only if Carey were correct. Carey was always delighted when Barb told her she had good taste and never seemed to get too much praise of this sort. What principle, if any, did Barb overlook? ______________

Question 10 on the next page.

(10) Cutting a tree down with the chain saw required Tom to do the following: get the chain saw, check its fuel if necessary, open the choke, start it, and cut a wedge from the front of the tree and a straight cut in the back. Then the tree fell on his cabin and wrecked it. What is the name for this sequence of behaviors that Tom so carefully carried out? ____________________

LESSON 22 **FORM A** **GRADE:** ________

NAME: ________________ **DATE:** ________

(1) Three types of punishers are ________________, ________________, and ________________.

(2) Tom told his mother several times that disco dancing Saturday night was far more important to him than saving his soul Sunday morning. She simply ignored him each time that he said that. Pretty soon he stopped saying that. The reduction in his frequency of making that statement is the result of what behavioral procedure? ________________

(3) To be most effective, a punishing stimulus should be ________________ on the behavior that you want to decrease in frequency; it should follow the behavior ________________; the person should be relatively ________________ of the punisher; and the ________________ (or intensity) of the stimulus should be sufficiently large.

(4) Dericco, Brigham, and Garlington (1977) shocked Jane each time she puffed on a cigarette while engaged in a casual conversation. Her rate of smoking decreased. The shock is called a(n) ________________.

(5) Bob broke the rule about dinner complaints. When he was reminded that he had broken the rule, he broke it again. The more he was reminded, the more he broke it. The reminder was a(n) ________________ for Bob.

(6) A punisher is defined as an event that (1) ________________ a behavior and (2) ________________ the frequency of that behavior.

(7) On the few occasions that Marty swore, his mother told him "Stop that, I'm going to tell your father," and his father spanked him. Recently, however, she took pity on him and, while still telling Marty "Stop that, I'm going to tell your father," did not tell his father. Pretty soon Marty was swearing all the time. What kind of punisher is the mother's statement? ________________

(8) Professor Brainbuster ridiculed Annie Anarchist because she made what he considered to be trivial comments. As a result, Annie made even more comments. The increase in Annie's comments is a result of what behavioral procedure? ________________

(9) Bob broke the written rule about dinner complaints. Another member of the group reminded him that he had broken the rule. He never complained at dinner again. If you view the written rule about dinner complaints as a stimulus, what is its technical name? ________________

(10) Kevin repeatedly said racist things in the presence of members of his frat. One day he made a racist comment, and another member said "Kevin, please don't say that any more. It is disrespectful." Kevin never repeated that comment again. Kevin's racist comment was eliminated by what procedure? ________________

Define punisher.

LESSON 22 **FORM B** **GRADE:** ____________

NAME: ______________________ **DATE:** ____________

(1) When Ben used to insult his friends, they would argue with him about the insults. Now they no longer argue with him but just pretend that he didn't say anything. Ben's rate of insults has decreased dramatically. What behavioral procedure is at work here? ______________________

(2) Mary tried to teach her child to count by saying "No, that's wrong" whenever the child made a mistake. The child never repeated those mistakes. Mary's statement would be called a(n) ______________________.

(3) Frank ran a red light one day when he was in a hurry to get to class. A police officer caught him and gave him a ticket. Frank didn't go through a red light again after that. The red light would be called a(n) ______________________.

(4) Dericco, Brigham, and Garlington (1977) shocked Jane each time that she puffed on a cigarette while engaged in a casual conversation. Her rate of smoking decreased. Giving her a shock each time she puffed on a cigarette is an example of what behavioral procedure? ______________________

(5) *Punisher* and *reinforcer* both refer to events that ______________________ a behavior.

(6) Gloria hit Lenny every time that he attempted a soul kiss. His rate of attempting a soul kiss increased. What behavioral procedure did Gloria use to bring about this increased rate? ______________________

(7) A stimulus that occurs before the behavior and is associated with the punishment of that behavior would be called a(n) ______________________.

(8) Bob broke the rule about dinner complaints, but a reminder didn't work to stop his complaining. The group members decided to fine him 25¢ in addition to the reminder. This worked. The reminder now works all by itself for Bob. What kind of punisher is the reminder? ______________________

(9) Tom was spanked every time he teased his little sister. His rate of teasing increased as a result. Spanking would be called a(n) ______________________.

(10) If a person's behavior is decreased through punishment in one situation, any decrease in other situations would be called ______________________ and will not necessarily occur.

Name four principles that will increase the effectiveness of punishment.

LESSON 22 **FORM C** **GRADE:** ________

NAME: ____________________ **DATE:** ____________

(1) One day, Mrs. King spanked Marcie in front of the class right after she caught her teasing a friend. Marcie never teased a friend in class again. Her teasing decreased due to what behavioral procedure? ____________________

(2) Punishment and extinction both produce the result of ____________________ the frequency of a behavior.

(3) The procedure in which a punisher is administered for the occurrence of a particular behavior, and in which it reduces the rate of that behavior, is called ____________ ____________.

(4) Mary nagged her mother for snacks while dinner was being cooked. Mary's mother repeatedly said no, but Mary nagged even more. Mary's mother finally screamed "No!" at Mary, and Mary stopped nagging. One of mother's screams as a stimulus would be an example of what behavioral concept? ____________________

(5) Punisher A reduced the rate of the behavior as long as it was paired with Punisher B. But when it was no longer paired, its effectiveness gradually diminished. What type of punisher is Punisher A? ____________________

(6) Every time that Tom threw a ball in the house, Paula, his mother, spanked him. For some unknown reason, Tom threw the ball around inside the house even more after that. What behavioral procedure did Paula use to produce this change in Tom's ball throwing? ____________________

(7) Yvonne told everyone in her class that she didn't think that President Nixon should have got us out of Vietnam until the United States had won. Her classmates ignored her, knowing that she liked to get attention by taking controversial positions. They ignored this same statement every time that she made it; pretty soon she stopped saying it. What behavioral procedure had her class members used to reduce her rate of making that statement? ____________________

(8) Steve used to pester Carla for a date. However, Carla completely ignored his requests. Steve no longer pesters Carla for a date. What behavioral procedure did she use to decrease the rate of requests? ____________________

(9) An event that follows a behavior and reduces the future probability of that behavior is called a(n) ____________________.

(10) McNees and his associates (1976) posted stars identifying clothing that was most often stolen. Customers stole much less after the posting than before. If the customers stole less because they had in the past been punished in similar situations for stealing, then the star would technically be called a(n) ____________________.

Explain in behavioral terms why people use punishment so often.

LESSON 23 **FORM A** **GRADE:** ________

NAME: ____________________ **DATE:** ____________

(1) Pierce and Risley (1974) marked the number of minutes early that a recreation center would have to close each time a rule violation was observed. This reduced rule violations dramatically. If these numbers were no longer paired with the actual closing of the center, they would probably lose their effect. If they did, what type of punisher would they be? ____________________

(2) Frank's parents took away his erector set each time he played too roughly with it. If Frank's rate of rough play decreased, this would be an example of what behavioral procedure? ____________________

(3) Previously when Beth burped at the dinner table, her parents argued with her about it. Now they no longer argue with her, and her rate of burping has decreased. What behavioral procedure is involved? ____________________

(4) Tommy hit his little brother frequently and was always spanked. After a while, his mother decided to stop spanking Tommy. She was surprised to see that Tommy rarely hit his little brother after her change in behavior. What behavioral procedure accounts for the decrease in Tommy's hitting his brother? ____________________

(5) Tommy hit his little brother frequently. One day Tommy's mother just happened to see Tommy hitting him and immediately ran in and spanked Tommy. Tommy hit his brother again, and his mother spanked him. Tommy rarely hit his brother after that, but when he did, he got a spanking. Spanking in this case is an example of what behavioral procedure? ____________________

(6) Tommy hit his little brother frequently. One day Tommy's mother just happened to see Tommy hitting him and immediately ran in and spanked Tommy. Tommy hit his brother again, and his mother spanked him. Tommy hit his brother even more often after that and always got a spanking. The stimulus "spanking" in this case is an example of a(n) ____________________.

(7) When Larry pouted, Carol used to sympathize with him. Since she has decided to no longer sympathize with his pouting, his rate of pouting has decreased sharply. What procedure did Carol use? ____________________

(8) There are two types of punishment. In one, a behavior produces an event, and the rate of the behavior decreases; in the second, a behavior is followed by ____________ ____________ of an event, and the rate decreases.

(9) A <u>punisher</u> is any event (produced or withdrawn) that ____________________ a behavior and ____________________ the rate of the behavior.

(10) If an event is withdrawn following a behavior, and the rate of the behavior decreases, then the procedure is called ____________________.

Define time out, and explain why it is an example of punishment.

LESSON 23 **FORM B** **GRADE:** ____________

NAME: ______________________ **DATE:** ____________

(1) To decide whether a procedure is punishment or extinction, ask "Is the event normally in the person's environment ______________________ he emits the behavior, or is it normally in his environment ______________________ he emits the behavior?"

(2) If a stimulus signals that a reinforcer will be withdrawn when a particular behavior occurs, that signal would be called a(n) ______________________.

(3) Punishment can occur in two ways: a behavior can produce an event, and the rate of the behavior ______________________; or a behavior can lead to the ______________________ of an event, and the behavior decreases.

(4) If Pierce and Risley (1974) had ignored all rule-violating behavior and the rate of such behavior had decreased, what procedure would they have been using? ______________________

(5) Lora's parents made her stay inside each time she pinched her little brother. If she stopped pinching him, this would be an example of what behavioral procedure? ______________________

(6) Dave frequently made gross comments about the food, and his friends always acted outraged. His friends then decided to no longer act outraged when he complained. Dave stopped complaining. The decrease in Dave's complaining is the result of what behavioral procedure? ______________________

(7) Alice griped about the dorm food a lot. Every time she made such a comment, she was fined 25¢. She stopped making such comments quickly. The decrease in griping is the result of what behavioral procedure? ______________________

(8) Tommy hit his little brother frequently. His mother decided that she would send Tommy to his room whenever he hit his little brother. Tommy stopped hitting his little brother after this change in his mother's behavior. Sending Tommy to his room for hitting is an example of what behavioral procedure? ______________________

(9) Frank was always making anarchistic suggestions about how to run the perfect commune. Melody didn't agree and always explained to Frank exactly why she disagreed. Soon she had convinced Frank so well that Frank didn't make anarchistic suggestions anymore. Melody's act of disagreeing with Frank, as a stimulus, would technically be called a(n) ______________________.

(10) When Tommy first suggested violent actions to dramatize opposition to war, other antiwar people supported his ideas. However, now that they have stopped agreeing with his positions, he is making fewer and fewer violent proposals. The group used what procedure to reduce Tommy's violent proposals? ______________________

Define punishment by contingent withdrawal.

LESSON 23 **FORM C** **GRADE:** ______________

NAME: ______________________________ **DATE:** ________________

(1) The procedure in which the failure to make a response is followed by the delivery of an aversive event ______________________________ (should, shouldn't) be labeled "punishment."

(2) If an event is normally in a person's environment but is taken away whenever the person emits a particular behavior, and if the rate of that behavior decreases, this procedure would be an example of ______________________________ .

(3) The temporary loss of a privilege contingent on the occurrence of a particular behavior is a form of punishment by withdrawal called ______________________________ .

(4) Every time Ted pouted, his parents took away some of his play time by sending him to his room. Afterward, they discussed with him why they had sent him to his room. He pouted more often. What procedure did his parents use? ______________________________

(5) Pierce and Risley (1974) withdrew the privilege of playing in the recreation center when a rule was violated. The rule-violating behavior decreased dramatically. What behavioral procedure did they use? ______________________________

(6) Hedley started all sorts of stories about members of the group. They decided to suspend him for 24 hours whenever he told such a story. Hedley stopped telling such stories. The decrease in his storytelling is the result of what behavioral procedure? ______________________________

(7) The frat members no longer argued with Larry when he griped about the food. Soon he stopped making such comments. This is an example of what behavioral procedure? ______________________________

(8) Every once in a while, Marge would do a favor for John. If he said "Thank you," it seemed she never did that favor again. If he didn't say anything, she would do it again. "Thank you" is a(n) ______________________________ for Marge's doing-favors behavior.

(9) When Professor Odd made absurd statements to his friends, they would argue with him. Recently, they have stopped arguing with him, and his rate of making absurd statements has decreased. What behavioral procedure did they use? ______________________________

(10) One day Ken said something about engineering students that Bob didn't like, and Bob said "Why don't you shut up, you damned fool; you don't know anything about engineering!" Ken never again said anything about engineering students around Bob. The decrease in Ken's comments about engineering students is the result of what behavioral procedure? ______________________________

Explain how to distinguish between punishment by contingent withdrawal and extinction.

LESSON 24 **FORM A** **GRADE:** ____________

NAME: ______________________ **DATE:** ____________

(1) Larry used to argue a lot. But he finally realized that every time that he got into a really intense argument he lost a good friend. So he decided to stop arguing, and in fact never did again. What behavioral procedure did his social environment use to reduce his rate of arguing? ______________________

(2) Azrin and Powell (1969) developed a pill dispenser that sounded a buzzer at the prescribed time for taking a pill. The buzzer could be turned off only by dispensing a pill. The behavior of dispensing the pill would be an example of ______________________ behavior.

(3) If every third response is followed by the termination of a negative reinforcer, that behavior is on what schedule of intermittent reinforcement? ______________________

(4) The moment that Brad guessed that he might get a cold, he started taking a lot of vitamin C. As a result, he never got a cold. Taking vitamin C would be an example of a(n) ______________________ behavior.

(5) Terry used to come home late from school. But when his mother started scolding him for not being on time, he started coming home on time. Coming home on time would be an example of ______________________ behavior for Terry.

(6) If the termination of an event increases the rate of a behavior that the termination follows, the event is called a(n) ______________________ .

(7) Andy frequently forgot to bring any money along on his dates with Leslie. As a result she usually paid for the movie or drinks. Finally, Leslie explained that she couldn't afford to pay for all their dates. From then on Andy brought along money. What behavioral procedure did Leslie use to increase Andy's rate of bringing along money for their dates? ______________________

(8) Behavior analysts, unlike traditional psychologists, do <u>not</u> equate negative reinforcers and ______________________ .

(9) Penny just hated it when Kenny got fresh with her. So she would always haul off and slap the hell out of him when he did. Kenny no longer is fresh with Penny. What behavioral procedure did Penny use to stop Kenny from acting fresh? ______________________

(10) Anytime that Reg left any of his toys in any part of the house outside of his own room, his parents picked them up and kept them for a week before returning them. As a result, Reg stopped leaving his toys in the rest of the house. What behavioral procedure did his parents use to eliminate the behavior of leaving toys in the rest of the house? ______________________

Define escape and avoidance behavior.

LESSON 24 **FORM B** **GRADE:** ____________

NAME: ________________________ **DATE:** ______________

(1) When Lester showed up for a date with Felicia in his grubby clothes, she wouldn't let him put his arm around her in the movie—in fact, she wouldn't let him touch her at all. Lester stopped showing up for dates with Felicia in his grubbies. Felicia used what behavioral procedure to reduce his rate of showing up in his grubbies? ____________________________

(2) Bev didn't like doing any kind of dirty work at the sorority. On "work Saturdays" she would start working but after a little while she would remember a doctor's appointment that she had to leave for immediately. Leaving for a doctor's appointment would be an example of ____________________________________ behavior.

(3) Everyone at the police station was pretty sure that Paul knew more about the crime than he was admitting. Captain Thomas therefore kept questioning him until he finally "broke" and admitted what he knew. Captain Thomas immediately stopped the questioning. Paul admitted later under similar questioning knowing about a number of other crimes. Paul's "confessions" would be an example of ____________________________________ behavior.

(4) Epstein and Masek (1978) required their patients to pay a $1 fine if they failed to take their medication at the prescribed time. The patients' rate of taking their medication at the correct time increased as a result. The patients' behavior would be called a(n) ____________ ________________________ response.

(5) Positive reinforcers and negative reinforcers are both events that can be used to ____________________________________ the rate of a behavior.

(6) Larry was a conservationist freak. When he and Fran went for a hike, he would always remind her when she littered by saying something like "Hey, you dropped something." Pretty soon Fran stopped littering when on a hike with Larry. What behavioral procedure did Larry use to eliminate littering? ____________________________________

(7) If a behavior <u>terminates</u> a negative reinforcer, the behavior is called a(n) ______________ ______________________ behavior.

(8) Frank and Jerry used to whisper and giggle a lot in the movie theater. One day, the manager kicked them out of the theater for being noisy. They never made noise again in the theater. What behavioral procedure did the manager use to decrease their whispering and giggling?

____

(9) If a behavior <u>prevents</u> a negative reinforcer from occurring, it is called a(n) ____________ ______________________ behavior.

(10) Professor Brainbuster had an uncanny knack for guessing when Meredith had not read the assignment. He would inevitably call on her to answer a question about the material on those days. After having this happen a few times, Meredith always read the assignment. What behavioral procedure did the professor use to increase her frequency of reading the assignment? ____________________________________

Define a negative reinforcer, and distinguish it from a positive reinforcer.

LESSON 24 **FORM C** **GRADE:** ______________

NAME: ____________________ **DATE:** ______________

(1) Mrs. Norris had become annoyed by Carol's frequent failure to do her homework for her American history course. So she started making Carol do her homework during the outside recess period. Carol soon started doing her homework the night before so she wouldn't miss recess. Mrs. Norris used what behavioral procedure to increase Carol's frequency of doing her homework the night before? ______________________________

(2) Avoidance behavior is any behavior that ______________________________ the occurrence of a negative reinforcer.

(3) Escape behavior is behavior that ______________________________ a negative reinforcer.

(4) A negative reinforcer is any event that is ______________________________ by a behavior and that causes the rate of the behavior to increase.

(5) Epstein and Masek (1978) required their patients to pay a $1 fine if they failed to take their medication at the prescribed time. The patients' rate of taking their medication at the correct time increased as a result. The $1 fine would be called a(n) ____________ ______________ .

(6) Frank and Jerry used to whisper and giggle a lot in the movie theater. One day, the manager came in and asked them to follow him. He made them miss 5 minutes of the movie because they were bothering other customers. They never whispered and giggled again after that. What behavioral procedure did the manager use to reduce their noisemaking? ____________ ______________

(7) Karen hated to have work pile up on her to the extent that she had to rush to get her assignments done. As a result, when a term paper was assigned in a class early in the semester she immediately started to work on it a little each day even though it wasn't due until the end of the semester. Working on the term paper early in the semester would be an example of ______________________________ behavior.

(8) Melody didn't really start working hard on her studies until they piled up. Since she didn't like having work piled up, she would start to work practically day and night to get out from under the burden. Melody's rate of work when work had piled up would be an example of ______________________________ behavior.

(9) Mrs. Feingold didn't like it when her third graders goofed off by doing such things as sharpening their pencils more than once a day. Billy was the worst offender. At the beginning of the school year he would get up about every 15 minutes to sharpen a pencil (not to mention staring out of the window). Mrs. Feingold started saying to Billy "You are not using your time very wisely by sharpening your pencil so often, Billy." As a result, Billy learned to sharpen all of his pencils in the morning. What behavioral procedure did Mrs. Feingold use to reduce Billy's frequency of pencil sharpening? ______________________

(10) Barb earned points for doing her chores, studying, and being helpful around the house. Barb lost points for teasing her little brother. As a result, Barb soon stopped teasing her brother. What behavioral procedure was used to reduce her rate of teasing her brother? ______________________________

Explain what "punishing someone for not making the desired response" would be called by a behavior analyst and why.

LESSON 25 **FORM A** **GRADE:** ____________

NAME: ______________________ **DATE:** ______________

(1) Wendy agreed to encourage Carol to speak more loudly as a step toward helping her to become more assertive. At first Wendy praised Carol only if she could hear her; later only if she could hear her 5 feet away; and still later only if she could hear her from 10 feet away. Carol speaking loud enough to be heard from 5 feet away would be called a(n) ________ ____________________ to the ultimate goal.

(2) The question "What is the sum of 8 and 2?" is called a(n) ____________________ with respect to the response "4."

(3) Mr. Levin observed five groundskeepers to determine whether they were working. He first observed Ken for 30 seconds, then shifted to Diane for 30 seconds, and so on for the other three workers. He started over again every two and a half minutes. What method of observation is he using? ______________________________

(4) If a behavior is reduced in frequency by removing an event usually in the person's environment any time that the behavior occurs, the name of the procedure is ______________ ______________; if a behavior is reduced in frequency by stopping the delivery of an event that had followed the behavior in the past, the name of the procedure is __________ ______________.

(5) Judy was curious to find out how much of the time the President was smiling. So she watched several of his news conferences. She divided the conferences into a series of intervals 15 seconds long and recorded whether he was smiling or not during each interval. (He smiled 79% of the time!) What method of observation was she using? ______________ recording

(6) Jim broke the rule about dinner complaints, but a reminder didn't work to stop him complaining. The group decided to fine him $1.00 in addition to the reminder, which worked. What behavioral procedure did the group use? ______________________________

(7) Gail liked to go to the disco but Harvey almost never took her. She finally started nagging him like the hounds of hell until he would say "Alright, we'll go to the disco tonight." She uses this approach often now and therefore often goes to the disco with Harvey. What behavioral procedure did Gail use to increase her attendance at the disco? ______________

(8) Ben is observed to say positive things to people the following number of times per day: 8, 7, 14, 6, and 9. To make a graph of these data, you would label the ordinate with numbers that increase in steps of ______________________________.

(9) Bob observed Ruby's rate of smoking during three different periods: before the case shocked her, while the case shocked her, and after the case stopped shocking her. Bob used what type of design to study the effect of the shocks on Ruby's smoking? ______________

(10) Sally hated to carry out the garbage at night after dinner. So her father carried the garbage out for her if she studied for at least an hour after dinner. Since he has started doing that, Sally has done a lot more studying. Sally's study behavior would be an example of ______________ ______________ behavior.

LESSON 25 **FORM B** **GRADE:** ____________

NAME: ______________________ **DATE:** ______________

(1) Suppose that Dr. Brown developed a behavioral definition of generosity. He might then ask a number of non-behaviorists to rate the generosity of several individuals appearing in video-tape recordings. If he compared their ratings of generosity with the level of generosity according to his behavioral definition, he would be able to determine the ______________ ______________ of his definition.

(2) Customers in grocery stores are often given trading stamps as incentive to continue buying at a particular store. The trading stamps can later be exchanged for anything from a toaster to a vacation. What kind of reinforcers are trading stamps? ______________

(3) Jane kept track of her reading rate for two weeks for each homework assignment. She read about 150 words per minute and usually didn't finish her homework. Then she took a speed reading course. After finishing the course she observed her reading rate again for two weeks and found that it had increased to 700 words a minute. Her homework was much easier to finish as a result. What kind of design was she using to determine the effect of the course on her reading rate? ______________

(4) If Tommy learns to say "49" when asked "What is the square of seven?" but not when asked for the square of other numbers, we would say that the question "What is the square of seven?" has come to exert ______________ over his behavior of saying "49."

(5) Peter used to drink beer after beer immediately upon arriving home from work. His wife begged him for months to stop doing it, but to no avail. Finally, she decided to leave the house anytime that he drank so much beer and stay gone until the next day. Peter has stopped drinking beer. What behavioral procedure did his wife use to reduce beer drinking? ______________

(6) A behavior will take longer to extinguish if it has been on a(n) ______________ ______________ schedule of reinforcement. (Give most general label.)

(7) Consider a multiple baseline design in which two behaviors are observed for 6 days, then the first behavior has a treatment applied to it for six days and finally the treatment is also applied to the second behavior for six days. If the highest rate of the first behavior is 12 and the second is 18, what size steps should be used for the ordinate? ______________

(8) Wendy agreed to encourage Carol to speak more loudly as a step toward helping her to become more assertive. At first Wendy praised Carol only if she could hear her; later only if she could hear her from five feet; finally only if she could hear her from 10 feet away. Hearing her from 10 feet away would be an example of a(n) ______________.

(9) Mrs. Franklin taught Jimmy to label a large circular line as a "circle" by asking him "What is this, you know, a circle" and praising him when he said "circle." Next she gave as a hint only "you know, a cirk" leaving the "le" sound off. Finally, she gave no hint at all, and Jimmy could label the circle correctly. What behavioral procedure did Mrs. Franklin use? ______________ ______________

(10) Sue repeatedly said racist things in the presence of members of her group. One day she made a racist comment, and another member said "Sue, that is disrespectful of Black people." Sue never repeated that comment again. Sue's racist comment was eliminated by what procedure? ______________

LESSON 25 **FORM C** **GRADE:** ____________

NAME: ______________________ **DATE:** ____________

(1) The statement that "shyness is the behavior of avoiding eye contact, speaking so softly that the words cannot be heard, and failing to make one's wishes known" would be an example of a(n) ______________________.

(2) Howard's swearing bothered his friend, Barbara. So every time he swore she gave him a look designed to singe his eyebrows. Howard's rate of swearing remains unchanged. What behavioral procedure did Barbara use with respect to Howard's swearing? ______________________

(3) Ken was only interested in those parts of the movie that showed scenes of Hawaii where he had lived as a boy. These scenes came after 13, 31, 35, and 77 minutes of the movie. What schedule of reinforcement was his movie watching on? ______________________

(4) Two observers, who worked in the same office as Ruby, observed to see whether she was smoking during each 15-minute period of the day. What is the reliability of their observations? ____________ If this is not a new definition, is it acceptable? ____________

First:	S N S N S N N S N N
Second:	S N S N S N N N S N

(5) For the effective use of punishment or reinforcement, it is necessary to deliver them (or a promise) very soon after the behavior has occurred. This is known as the Principle of ______________________.

(6) If a book asks a child to read a word like "cat" but shows the child a picture of a cat as a hint, and then shows less and less of the cat in subsequent pages where the child must read the word, the picture of the cat would be called a(n) ______________________.

(7) Martin wore a wrist counter to count the number of times that he said something positive to someone. On any day that he counted at least 15 positive statements, he permitted himself to watch TV that night. The counts on the counter would be a(n) ____________ reinforcer; the TV would serve as a(n) ______________________ reinforcer for the counts.

(8) Flora wanted to teach her daughter to be an opera singer. When the daughter was two years old, Flora started devoting the half hour after dinner to singing lessons in which she used ice cream to reinforce singing. Her daughter didn't seem very interested in the ice cream. What principle of effective reinforcement, if any, had Flora neglected in choosing a time right after dinner? ______________________

(9) Claire likes to ride her snowmobile without any hat unless it is just too cold out. When it is too cold, she puts on a stocking cap. Putting on a cap is an example of ______________________ behavior.

(10) Ruby was using a special cigarette case that counted the number of times that she opened the case to take out a cigarette. Bob Behaviorist recorded the number of such openings for three weeks prior to helping Ruby stop smoking. This three-week period of measurement is called a(n) ______________________.